Dress at the Court of King Henry VIII

For Mike

Dress at the Court of King Henry VIII

The Wardrobe Book of the Wardrobe of the Robes prepared by James Worsley in December 1516, edited from Harley MS 2284, and his Inventory prepared on 17 January 1521, edited from Harley MS 4217, both in the British Library

Edited and with a Commentary by

Maria Hayward

MANEY
2007

ISBN 978-1-904350-70-5 (clothbound)
ISBN 978-1-905981-41-0 (paperbound)

Published by Maney Publishing, Suite 1C, Joseph's Well, Hanover Walk, Leeds LS3 1AB, UK
www.maney.co.uk

Maney Publishing is the trading name of W. S. Maney & Son Ltd

Printed and bound in the UK by The Charlesworth Group

Contents

Acknowledgements

A generous grant towards the cost of the illustrations and reproduction fees was awarded to me by the Barbara Whatmore Charitable Trust. Barbara Whatmore was very interested in and hugely supportive of the work of the Textile Conservation Centre (TCC) and she assisted Karen Finch in establishing the TCC up as a charitable trust. Further grants were received from the Peter Moores Foundation, the Mercers' Company and the Pasold Research Fund. Much of the research has been funded by Arts and Humanities Research Council (AHRC) and this book forms one of the publication milestones of the AHRC Research Centre for Textile Conservation and Textile Studies (2002–07). The Research Centre was based at the TCC and involved a partnership between the Universities of Southampton, Bradford and Manchester. Grateful thanks also go to the AHRC and to the Paul Mellon Centre for British Art for small awards in 2003 and to the British Academy for a small award in 2004.

I also owe a huge debt of gratitude to the staff of the British Library, the National Archive, Kew, the John Rylands Library special collections, the library at Winchester School of Art and the Hartley library, University of Southampton. I must also thank the Master, Fellows and Scholars of St John's College, Cambridge, for their permission to cite documents in their collection and Malcolm Underwood for allowing me access. Grateful thanks also go to colleagues at the Abbeg-Stiftung Foundation, Riggisberg, for allowing me to visit and study items in their collection.

Many people have contributed to this book in a variety of ways. I am most grateful to all my colleagues at the TCC, University of Southampton, for their help and encouragement. In particular, I would like to thank Nell Hoare, for her ongoing support, Dinah Eastop for her constant interest and guidance and Chris Bennett for her help with the text. I would also like to thank Julia Bennett, Mary Brooks and Andrea Poole. In addition I would like to acknowledge the help that I have received from the following, who were all very generous with their time and knowledge: the late Janet Arnold, Claude Blair, Jütta von Bloh, Jim Bolton, Alison Carter, Wendy Childs, Siân Cooksey, Karen Finch, Hazel Forsyth, Steve Gunn, John Hodgeson, Anna Jolly, Santina Levey, Lesley Miller, Shelagh Mitchell, Lisa Monnas, Linda Newington, Bettina Niecamp, Harriet North, Susan North, Karen Parker, Johannes Pietsch, Mary Rose, Ann Saunders, Regula Schorta, Trish Skinner, Kay Staniland, David Starkey, Anne Sutton, June Swann, Malcolm Underwood, Elspeth Veale, Karen Watts, Mary Westerman, Joelle Wickens, Chris Woolgar, Linda Woolley, Anna Wright and Robert Yorke.

I would especially like to thank Dinah Eastop, Caroline Johnston, Jane Malcolm-Davies, Susan North and Ann Saunders for generously reading and commenting on drafts of the text and transcript. Their insightful and perceptive comments were invaluable in revising the book. However, my largest debt is to Alasdair Hawkyard, without whom this book would have been much poorer. Any remaining errors are my own. I must thank Liz Rosindale and Linda Fisher of Maney for seeing this book through to publication. Finally, I wish to thank Mike and my family for their interest, support and encouragement.

Photographic Acknowledgements

I am most grateful to Mike Halliwell for preparing the images for this book to such a high standard. I would also like to thank Shelagh Mitchell for undertaking the initial picture research. The source of each image is acknowledged in its caption and the images are reproduced by kind permission of their owners as follows:

Figures 1.8, 4.3, 5.7, 6.1, 6.14, 7.7, 9.9, 9.10, 9.11, 10.5, 10.7, 11.5, 11.6, 11.8, 11.9, 12.7, 12.10, 12.11, 13.7, 15.8, 16.1, 16.8, 16.9, 17.1, 17.3, 18.2, 18.3, 19.1, 19.8, 20.7, 20.8; and Plates IB, IIIA, VIC, VIIB, VIIIC are reproduced by Gracious Permission of Her Majesty the Queen.

Figures 7.3, 20.4, 20.9 of the Medici burial clothes are reproduced from the Janet Arnold Collection by courtesy of her executors.

Figures 6.5, 9.6, 9.7, 20.1, 20.2 of the Medici burial clothes are reproduced with the permission of Mary Westerman for the Janet Arnold slide archive and the Galleria del Costume, Palazzo Pitti.

Abegg Stiftung, Bern 3.5, 6.2, 6.3, 6.4, 19.2, 19.3, 20.5, 20.6
Ashmolean Museum, Oxford 6.16, 16.7, 18.1, 19.11
The Duke of Bedford and the Trustees of the Bedford Estates Pl. IIIB
Bern Historical Musem 5.1, 5.2
Bibliothèque de Méjanes, Aix-en-Provence 5.8
Bibliothèque Nationale de France 1.2
The Blair Charitable Trust, Blair Castle, Perthshire 2.5
Bodleian Library, Oxford 12.5, 15.7
British Library 1.1, 4.2, 15.3
British Museum 6.18, 8.4, 9.4, 11.3, 13.1, 15.2, 15.5, 19.5, 19.9
The Duke of Buccleuch and Queensbury, KT 10.1, 12.9

Cambridge University Library 4.1
College of Arms, London 4.4, 13.2, 15.4, 19.10; Pl. VIIIB
Dean and Canons of Windsor Pls IVB, IVC
Department of Conservation and Technology, Courtauld Institute of Art 20.12, 20.14
The Devonshire Collection, Chatsworth 7.1
Fitzwilliam Museum, Cambridge 1.5, 4.5, 13.5, 14.2
Frick Collection, New York 12.6, 13.6
Galleria del Costume, Palazzo Pitti 6.5, 9.6, 9.7, 20.1, 20.2
Guildhall Library, City of London 3.1
Herzog-Anton-Ulrich Museums, Braunschweig 2.3
Isabella Gardner Museum, Boston 19.4
Kunsthistorisches Museum, Vienna Pl. VIB
Kupferstichkabinett, Staatliche Museen zu Berlin (Bildarchiv Preussischer Kulturbesitz) 8.5
Lambeth Palace Library 9.13
Magdalene College, University of Cambridge 5.4
Mauritshuis, The Hague 16.6; Pl. VIA
Mercers' Company 3.6
Metropolitan Museum of Art, New York 13.4
Musée du Louvre, Paris 2.4
Museo del Prado, Madrid 2.6
MuseoThyssen-Bornemisza, Madrid Pl. IC
Museum of the Condé region, Chantilly, France 13.3
Museum of London 6.6, 6.9, 6.15, 9.12, 11.1, 11.2, 16.3, 16.4, 16.5, 20.10, 20.11
National Archive, Kew 2.2, 3.2, 3.3, 4.6, 7.5, 7.6, 14.1 and the back cover
National Gallery, Ireland 15.1
National Gallery, London 9.1, 9.16, 12.8
National Gallery of Art, Washington 11.7
National Portrait Gallery, London Front cover: 1.3, 2.1, 5.5, 5.6, 6.8, 6.12, 7.2, 9.3, 9.8, 9.14, 9.15, 10.2, 10.6, 11.4, 12.1, 12.3, 12.4, 15.6, 16.2, 17.2; Pls IA, ID, IIIC, IIID, IVA, VB, VC, VIIA, VIIIA
National Trust 1.4, 7.4
New College, Oxford (Bridgeman Art Library) 12.2
Private Collection 8.1
Private Collection 20.3
Royal Albert Memorial Museum, Exeter 16.10
Royal Armouries, Leeds 1.6, 1.7, 6.10, 6.11, 11.10, 19.6, 19.7
St John's College, Oxford 10.3
Saint Louis Art Museum, Missouri 9.5
Staatliche Kunstsammlungen Dresden, Rüstkammer 6.2, 6.3, 6.4
Städelsches Kunstinstitut, Frankfurt am Main 1.9
Textile Conservation Centre, University of Southampton 4.5, 9.2, 13.5, 14.2
Trinity College, Cambridge Pl. VA
Vermögen und Bau Baden-Württemberg, Staatliche Schlösser und Gärten 6.7
Victoria and Albert Museum 3.4, 5.3, 6.13, 10.4, 16.17, 20.13
Wadham College, Oxford 9.2
Walker Art Gallery, Liverpool Pl. IIA
Waterford Museum of Treasures 16.11
Westminster Abbey Muniment Room 4.7, 8.2, 8.3
Worshipful Company of Barbers Pl. IIB

Abbreviations of Principal Works Cited

The following abbreviated forms have been used for manuscripts, book titles, journal articles and names of institutions cited more than once. Where a work has only been cited once, its full details are given in the endnotes. The place of publication of all books is London unless otherwise stated. This list takes the place of a bibliography. The principal primary sources, both manuscript and printed, have been annotated to provide additional detail on their significance to the text.

Alçega, *Pattern Book* Alçega, J., de., *Tailor's Pattern Book 1589*, introduction by J. L. Nevinson (Carlton, 1979). The earliest printed tailor's book, reproduced in facsimile.

Anderson, *Hispanic Costume* Anderson, R. M., *Hispanic Costume 1480–1530*, The Hispanic Society of America (New York, 1979).

Anglo, *Great Tournament Roll* Anglo, S. *The Great Tournament Roll of Westminster* (Oxford, 1968). A visual record of the tournament held to celebrate the birth of Henry's son in 1511.

Anglo, *Images* Anglo, S., *Images of Tudor Kingship* (1992).

Anglo, *Spectacle* Anglo, S., *Spectacle, Pageantry and Early Tudor Policy* (Oxford, 1969).

APC Dasent, J. R., et al., *Acts of the Privy Council of England*, 46 vols (1890–1964).

Arnold, *Patterns* Arnold, J., *Patterns of Fashion: the Cut and Construction of Clothes for Men and Women c. 1560–1620* (1985). Detailed analysis and patterns of examples of sixteenth-century dress.

Arnold, *Queen Elizabeth* Arnold, J., *Queen Elizabeth's Wardrobe Unlock'd* (Leeds, 1988).

Arnold and Westerman Bulgarella, 'Innovative' Arnold, J., and Westerman Bulgarella, M., 'An innovative method for mounting the sixteenth-century doublet and trunk-hose worn by Don Garzia de'Medici', *Costume*, 30 (1996), pp. 47–55.

Ashelford, *Visual History* Ashelford, J., *A Visual History of Costume: the Sixteenth Century* (1983).

Ashmole, *Garter* Ashmole, E., *The Institution, Laws and Ceremonies of the Most Noble Order of the Garter* (1672, 1971).

Astle, *Will* Astle, T., ed., *The Will of Henry VII* (1775).

Auerbach, *Tudor Artists* Auerbach, E., *Tudor Artists* (1954).

Bäumel and Swann, 'Die Schuhsammlung' Bäumel, J., and Swann, J., 'Die Schuhsammlung in der Dredener Rüstkammer: Ein Uberblick über die Geschichte und den Bestand', *Waffen-und Kostümkunde* (1996), pp. 3–34.

Benecke, *Maximilian* Benecke, G., *Maximilian I, 1459–1519: An Analytical Biography* (1982).

Bentley, *Excerpta Historica* Bentley, S., *Excerpta Historica* (1831). Transcripts of a useful selection of household accounts and other sources.

BHM Bern Historical Museum

BIHR *Bulletin of the Institute of Historical Research.*

Bindoff, *House of Commons* Bindoff, S. T., ed., *The House of Commons 1509–1556*, 3 vols (1982).

BJRL *Bulletin of John Rylands Library.*

BL British Library, London.

Additional — includes copies of Henry VII's accounts and one bundle of warrants from Henry VIII's great wardrobe.

Arundel — includes a set of chamber accounts.

Cotton — includes drawings of the king's tents.

Egerton — includes an inventory of the king's jewels.

Harley — includes James Worsley's wardrobe book and inventory and half of the 1547 inventory of Henry VIII's possessions.

Royal — includes a number of documents recording the king's jewels.

Stowe — includes the inventory of Catherine Howard's jewels.

Blair, '16th century' Blair, C., 'A 16th century reference to the making of a coat of mail', *The Arms and Armour Society*, 18.3 (2005), pp. 105–06.

Blair and Pyhrr, 'Wilton 'Montmorency' armor' Blair, C. and Pyhrr, S., 'The Wilton "Montmorency" armor: an Italian armor for Henry VIII', *The Metropolitan Museum Journal*, 38 (2003), pp. 95–144.

Blair, 'Maximilian' Blair, C., 'The Emperor Maximilian's gift of armour to King Henry VIII and the silvered engraved armour at the Tower of London', *Archaeologia*, 99 (1965), pp. 1–52.

BM British Museum.

Bod Lib The Bodleian Library.

Douce MS 363

English History b 192/1

Rawlinson MS D 775, 77c, 777

Boulton, *Knights of the Crown* Boulton, D'A. J. D., *The Knights of the Crown: The Monarchical Orders of Knighthood in Later Medieval Europe 1325–1520* (Woodbridge, 1989).

Brewer, *Death of Kings* Brewer, C., *The Death of Kings* (2000).

Brockliss, 'Concluding remarks' Brockliss, L. W. B., 'Concluding remarks: the anatomy of the minister-favourite', in

J. H. Elliott and L. W. B. Brockliss, eds, *The World of the Favourite* (New Haven and London, 1999), pp. 279–309.

Brooke and Crombie, *Henry VIII* Brooke, X., and Crombie, D., *Henry VIII Revealed: Holbein's Portrait and its Legacy* (Liverpool, 2003).

Brown, *Four Years* Brown, R., ed., *Four Years at the Court of Henry VIII*, 2 vols (1854).

Bruce, *Making Henry* Bruce, M. L., *The Making of Henry VIII* (1977).

Buck, *Clothes* Buck, A., *Clothes and the Child: a Handbook of Children's Dress in England 1500–1900* (Carlton, 1996).

Burke, 'Presenting' Burke, P., 'Presenting and re-presenting Charles V', in H. Soly, ed., *Charles V 1500–1558 and his Time* (Antwerp, 1999), pp. 393–477.

Burnham, *Cut* Burnham, D. K., *Cut my Cote* (Toronto, 1973).

Caley, 'Extract' Caley, J., 'Extract from a MS in the Augmentation Office: Wardrobe account of Henry VIII', *Archaeologia*, 9 (1789), pp. 243–52.

Campbell, *Art of Majesty* Campbell, T., *The Art of Majesty: Henry VIII's Tapestry Collection* (New Haven and London, forthcoming).

Campbell, *Materials* Campbell, W., ed., *Materials for a History of the Reign of Henry VII*, 2 vols (1873–77). Transcripts of a useful selection of household accounts and other sources.

Capwell, 'Italian arming doublet' Capwell, T. E., 'A depiction of an Italian arming doublet, c.1435–45', *Waffen-und Kostümkunde* (2002), pp. 177–95.

Carmi-Parsons, 'Family' Carmi-Parsons, J., 'Family, sex and power: the rhythms of medieval queenship', in J. Carmi-Parsons, ed., *Medieval Queenship* (Stroud, 1994), pp. 1–12.

Carter, 'Mary Tudor's wardrobe' Carter, A., 'Mary Tudor's wardrobe, *Costume*, 18 (1984), pp. 9–28.

Castiglione, *Courtier* Castiglione, B., *The Book of the Courtier*, ed. G. Bull (Harmondsworth (1967).

Cavendish, *Life of Wolsey* Cavendish, G., *The Life and Death of Cardinal Wolsey*, ed. R. Sylvester, EETS, 243 (1959). Almost contemporary biography of Cardinal Wolsey.

Chapman, *Sisters* Chapman, H. W., *The Sisters of Henry VIII* (1969).

Chrimes, *Henry VII* Chrimes, S. B., *Henry VII* (1972, 1981).

Clark, *Medieval Horse* Clark, J., ed., *The Medieval Horse and its Equipment c.1150–c.1450* (1995).

Collection of Inventories *A Collection of Inventories and Other Records in the Royal Wardrobe and Jewelhouse and of the Artillery and Munitions in Some of the Royal Castles* (Edinburgh, 1815).

CoA College of Arms, London.
MS M6, M13.
MS M1bis, M6bis, M13bis, M16bis.
MS I 7, I 14.
MS Z.d.11 The 1539 New Year's gift roll.
Latin MS 239 Catherine of Aragon's wardrobe book for 1519–20.

Collins, *Jewels and Plate* Collins, A. J., ed., *Jewels and Plate of Queen Elizabeth I: The Inventory of 1574* (1955).

Colvin, *HKW* Colvin, H. M., *The History of the King's Works*, 6 vols (1982).

CPR *Calendar of Patent Rolls, 1485–94* (1956), *1494–1509* (1963).

Crawford, 'King's burden' Crawford, A., 'The King's burden', in R. Griffiths, ed., *Patronage, the Crown and the Provinces in Later Medieval England* (Gloucester, 1981), pp. 33–56.

Crawford, *Letters* Crawford, A., ed., *Letters of the Queens of England 1100–1547* (Stroud, 1994).

Crowfoot, Pritchard and Staniland, *Textiles and Clothing* Crowfoot, E., Pritchard, F., and Staniland, K., *Medieval Finds from Excavations in London: 4 Textiles and Clothing c. 1150–c. 1450* (1992).

CSP Edward VI Knighton, C. S., ed., *Calendar of State Paers, Domestic, Edward VI* (1992).

CSP Milan Allen, B., ed., *Calendar of State Papers, Milan, 1385–1618* (1912).

CSP Scotland Bain, J., et al., *Calendar of State Papers Relating to Scotland and Mary, Queen of Scots* (1898–1952).

CSP Spanish Bergenroth, G. A., et al., *Calendar of State Papers, Spanish* (1862–64).

CSP Venetian Brown, R., ed., *Calendar of State Papers, Venetian*, 9 vols (1864–98).

Cumming, 'Great vanity' Cumming, V., '"Great vanity and excesse in Apparell": Some clothing and furs of Tudor and Stuart royalty', in A. MacGregor, ed., *The Late King's Goods: Collections, Possessions and Patronage of Charles I in the Light of the Commonwealth Sale Inventories* (London and Oxford, 1989), pp. 322–50.

Cummins, *Hound and Hawk* Cummins, J., *The Hound and The Hawk: The Art of Medieval Hunting* (1988).

Cunnington, *Handbook* Cunnington, C. W. and P., *Handbook of English Costume in the Sixteenth Century* (1954).

Cyrus-Zetterström and Ekstrand, *Royal Silks* Cyrus-Zetterström, U. and Ekstrand, G., *Royal Silks* (Stockholm, 2004).

Davies and Saunders, *Merchant Taylors* Davies, M. and Saunders, A., *The History of the Merchant Taylors' Company* (Leeds, 2004).

Dillon, 'Arms and armour' Dillon, H. A., 'Arms and armour at Westminster, the Tower and Greenwich, 1547', *Archaeologia*, 51.1 (1888), pp. 219–80.

Doran, *Elizabeth* Doran, S., ed., *Elizabeth: The Exhibition at the National Maritime Museum* (2003).

Dunlevy, *Dress in Ireland* Dunlevy, M., *Dress in Ireland* (1989).

EETS Early English Text Society.

Egan and Pritchard, *Dress Accessories* Egan, G. and Pritchard, F., *Medieval Finds from Excavations in London: 3 Dress Accessories* (1991).

Eichberger, *Women* Eichberger, D., ed., *Women of Distinction: Margaret of York, Margaret of Austria* (Mechelen, 2005).

Evans, *Dress* Evans, J., *Dress in Medieval France* (Oxford, 1952).

Evans, *Jewellery* Evans, J., *A History of Jewellery 1100–1870 AD* (1970).

Feuillerat, *Revels* Feuillerat, A., ed., *Documents Relating to the Revels at Court in the Time of King Edward VI and Queen Mary* (Louvain, 1914, reprinted 1963).

Flury-Lemberg, *Textile Conservation* Flury-Lemberg, M., *Textile Conservation and Research* (Bern, 1988).

Foister, *Holbein* Foister, S., *Holbein and England* (New Haven and London, 2004).

Fraser, *Six Wives* Fraser, A., *The Six Wives of Henry VIII* (1992).

FSL Folger Shakespeare Library, Washington.

Furnivall, *Boke* Furnivall, F. J., ed., *The Boke of Nurture* (1867).

Glanville, *Silver* Glanville, P., *Silver in Tudor and Early Stuart England* (1990).

GM Guildford Muniment Room.

Gordon, *Wilton Diptych* Gordon, D., ed., *Making and Meaning: The Wilton Diptych* (1993).

Gunn, *Charles Brandon* Gunn, S. J., *Charles Brandon, Duke of Suffolk c. 1484–1545* (Oxford, 1988).

Hall, *Chronicle* Hall, E., *The Union of the Two Noble and Illustre Families of Lancaster and York* (1809). This is the chief narrative source for Henry VIII's reign and includes many descriptions of the clothes worn by the king, his household and court.

Harris, *Stafford* Harris, B. J., *Edward Stafford, Third Duke of Buckingham, 1478–1521* (Stanford, 1986).

Harvey, *Men* Harvey, J., *Men in Black* (1995).

Harvey, *Elizabeth of York* Harvey, N. L., *Elizabeth of York: the Mother of Henry VIII* (New York, 1973).

Harvey and Mortimer, *Funeral Effigies* Harvey, A., and Mortimer, R., *The Funeral Effigies of Westminster Abbey* (Woodbridge, 1994).

Hayward, *1542 Inventory* Hayward, M. A., *The 1542 Inventory of Whitehall: the Palace and its Keeper* (2004).

Hayward, 'Gifts' Hayward, M. A., 'Gift giving at the court of Henry VIII: the 1539 New Year's gift roll in context', *Antiquaries Journal*, 85 (2005), pp. 125–75.

Hayward, 'Luxury' Hayward, M. A., 'Luxury or magnificence? Dress at the court of Henry VIII', *Costume*, 30 (1996), pp. 37–46.

Hayward, 'Packing' Hayward, M. A., 'The packing and transportation of the goods of Henry VIII, with particular reference to the 1547 inventory', *Costume*, 31 (1997), pp. 8–15.

Hayward, 'Repositories' Hayward, M. A., 'Repositories of splendour: Henry VIII's wardrobes of the Robes and Beds', *Textile History*, 29 (1998), pp. 134–56.

Hayward, 'Sign' Hayward, M. A., '"The sign of some degree"?: The financial, social and sartorial significance of male headwear at the courts of Henry VIII and Edward VI', *Costume*, 36 (2002), pp. 1–17.

Hearn, *Dynasties* Hearn, K., ed., *Dynasties: Painting in Tudor and Jacobean England 1530–1630* (1995).

'Henry VIII's jewel book' Trollope, E., ed., 'King Henry VIII's jewel book', *The Associated Architectural Societies*, 17.2 (1883–84), pp. 155–229.

Hinton, *Gold and Gilt* Hinton, D., *Gold and Gilt, Pots and Pins* (Oxford, 2005).

HMC Historical Manuscripts Commission.

HO *A Collection of Ordinances and Regulations for the Government of the Royal Household*, published by the Society of Antiquaries (1790). A very useful collection of household ordinances.

Hunniser, *Period Costume* Hunniser, J., *Period Costume for Stage and Screen: Patterns for Women's Dress 1500–1800* (California, 1991).

Hutton, *Rise* Hutton, R., *The Rise and Fall of Merry England: The Ritual Year 1400–1700* (Oxford, 1996).

Ives, *Anne Boleyn* Ives, E. W., *Anne Boleyn* (Oxford, 1986).

James, *Kateryn Parr* James, S., *Kateryn Parr: the Making of a Queen* (Aldershot, 1999).

Jardine, *Worldly Goods* Jardine, L., *Worldly Goods* (1996).

Jones and Underwood, *The King's Mother* Jones, M. K., and Underwood, M. G., *The King's Mother: Lady Margaret Beaufort Countess of Richmond and Derby* (Cambridge, 1992).

JRL John Rylands Library, Manchester.

Kantorowicz, *King's Two Bodies* Kantorowicz, E. H., *The King's Two Bodies: a Study in Medieval Political Theory* (1957, 1981).

Kipling, *Receyt* Kipling, G., ed., *The Receyt of the Ladie Kateryne*, EETS, 296 (Oxford, 1990). Useful primary source describing the arrival of Catherine of Aragon and her marriage to Prince Arthur.

Kipling, *Triumph* Kipling, G., *The Triumph of Honour: Burgundian Origins of the Elizabethan Renaissance* (Leiden, 1977).

Knecht, *Rise and Fall* Knecht, R. J., *The Rise and Fall of Renaissance France* (1996).

Jerdan, *Rutland Papers* Jerdan, W., ed., *The Rutland Papers*, Camden Society (1842).

La Toison d'Or *La Toison d'Or: Cinq Siècles d'Art et d'Histoire* (Bruges, 1962).

Laynesmith, *Last Medieval Queens* Laynesmith, J. L., *The Last Medieval Queens: English Queenship 1445–1503* (Oxford, 2004).

Leland, *Collectanea* Lelland, J., *De Rebus Britannicis Collectanea*, ed. T. Hearne, 4 vols (1774). Includes a number of useful sources.

Linthicum, *Costume* Linthicum, M. C., *Costume in the Drama of Shakespeare and His Contemporaries* (New York, 1936).

Lisle Letters Byrne, M. St Clare, ed., *The Lisle Letters*, 6 vols (Chicago, 1981). Full transcripts of and commentary on the letters to and from Lord and Lady Lisle.

Lloyd and Thurley, Images Lloyd, C. and Thurley, S., *Henry VIII: Images of a Tudor King* (Oxford, 1990).

Loades, *Chronicles* Loades, D., *Chronicles of the Tudor Kings* (1990). Extracts from a number of Tudor texts with modern spelling.

Loades, *Tudor Court* Loades, D., *The Tudor Court* (New Jersey, 1987).

Lockyer, *Habsburg and Bourbon* Lockyer, R., *Habsburg and Bourbon Europe 1470–1720* (1974).

LP Brewer, J. S., Gairdner, J., and Brodie, R. H., eds, *Letters and Papers, Foreign and Domestic, of the Reign of Henry VIII, 1509–1547*, 21 vols and addenda (1862–1932). This is the most important calendar of the extant documents from Henry VIII's reign.

LP Hen VII Gairdner, J., *Letters and Papers of Richard III and Henry VII*, 2 vols (1861–63).

LRS London Record Society.

LTS London Topographical Society.

Lurie, *Language* Lurie, A., The *Language of Clothes* (1981).

Martienssen, *Katherine Parr* Martienssen, A., *Queen Katherine Parr* (1975).

Martin, 'Sir John Daunce' Sir John Martin, C. T., 'Sir John Daunce's accounts of money received from the Trasurer of the King's Chamber', *Archaeologia*, 47 (1883), pp. 295–336.

Mertes, *English Noble Household* Mertes, K., *The English Noble Household 1250–1600: Good Governance and Politic Rule* (Oxford, 1988).

Mikhaila and Malcolm-Davies, *Tudor Tailor* Mikhaila, N., and Malcolm-Davies, J., *The Tudor Tailor: Reconstructing Sixteenth Century Dress* (2006).

Millar, *Catalogue* Millar, O., ed., 'Abraham van der Doort's Catalogue of the Collections of Charles I', *Walpole Society*, 37 (1960).

Millar, *Holbein* Millar, O., *Holbein and the Court of Henry VIII*, The Queen's Gallery (1978).

MMA Metropolitan Museum of Art, New York.

MoL Museum of London.

Monnas, *Merchants* Monnas, L., *Merchants, Princes and Painters: Silk Fabrics in Italian and Northern Painting 1300–1550* (New Haven and London, forthcoming).

Murphy, *Bastard Prince* Murphy, B. A., *Bastard Prince: Henry VIII's Lost Son* (Thrupp, 2001).

Myers, *Black Book* Myers, A. R., ed., *The Household of Edward IV: The Black Book and The Ordinance of 1478* (Manchester, 1959).

Nevinson, 'Portraits' Nevinson, J. L., 'Portraits of Gentleman Pensioners before 1625', *Walpole Society*, 34 (1958), pp. 1–13.

Nevinson, 'Sixteenth century doublet' Nevinson, J. L., 'A sixteenth century doublet', *Documenta Textilia: Festschrift für Sigrid Müller-Christensen Herausgegeben von Mechthild Flury-Lemberg und Karen Stolleis* (Munich, 1981), pp. 371–77.

NG National Gallery, London.

Nichols, *Chronicle of Calais* Nichols, J. G., ed., *Chronicle of Calais*, Camden Society, OS 35 (1846).

Nichols, *Epistles* Nichols, F. M., ed., *The Epistles of Erasmus*, 2 vols (1904).

Nichols, 'Inventories' Nichols, J. G., ed., 'Inventories of the wardrobes and plate of Henry Fitzroy, duke of Richmond and the wardrobe stuff at Baynard's Castle of Katherine of Aragon, princess Dowager', *Camden Miscellany*, 3 (1855).

Nichols, *Literary Remains* Nichols, J. G., ed., *The Literary Remains of King Edward VI*, 2 vols (1857).

Norris, *Costume* Norris, H., *Costume and Fashion: III.i The Tudors 1485–1547* (1938).

NPG National Portrait Gallery, London.

NS New Series.

NUL Nottingham University Library Manuscripts Department.

OED Oxford English Dictionary.

Orsi Landini and Niccoli, *Moda a Firenze* Orsi Landini, R., and Niccoli, B., *Moda a Firenze 1540–1580: Lo stile di Eleonora di Toledo e la sua influenza* (Florence, 2005).

Ortiz, *Resplendence* Ortiz, A. D., et al., *Resplendence of the Spanish Monarchy: Renaissance Tapestries and Armor from the Patrimonial Nacional* (New York, 1991).

Pollard, *Henry VIII* Pollard, A. F., *Henry VIII* (1905).

Pollard, *Henry VII* Pollard, A. F., ed., *The Reign of Henry VII from Contemporary Sources*, 3 vols (1913–14).

PPC Nicholas, N. H., ed., *Proceedings and Ordinances of the Privy Council of England, 1368–1542*, 7 vols (1834–37).

PPE Nicolas, N. H., ed., *The Privy Purse Expenses of Henry VIII* (1827). Transcript of Henry VIII's privy purse accounts.

PPE Elizabeth Nicolas, N. H., ed., *Privy Purse Expenses of Elizabeth of York: Wardrobe Accounts of Edward IV* (1830).

PPE Princess Mary Madden, F., *Privy Purse Expenses of the Princess Mary 1536–44* (1831).

Pronay and Cox, *Crowland Chronicle* Pronay, N. and Cox, J., eds, *The Crowland Chronicle Continuations* (1986).

Pyhrr et al., *The Armoured Horse* Pyhrr, S. W., et al., *The Armored horse in Europe 1480–1620* (New Haven and London, 2005).

RA Royal Armouries, Leeds.

Rangström, *Lions* Rangström, L., et al., *Lions of Fashion: Male Fashion of the 16th 17th 18th Centuries/Modelejon Manligt Mode 1500-tal, 1600-tal, 1700-tal* (Stockholm, 2002).

RC Royal Collection.

Reese, *Master* Reese, M. M., *The Royal Office of the Master of the Horse* (1976).

Richardson, *Mary Tudor* Richardson, W. C., *Mary Tudor: The White Queen* (1970).

Ridley, *Love Letters* Ridley, J., ed., The *Love Letters of Henry VIII* (1988).

RL Royal Library, Windsor.

Roberts, *Holbein* Roberts, J., *Holbein and the Court of Henry VIII* (Edinburgh, 1993).

Rodríguez-Salgado, *Armada* Rodríguez-Salgado, M. J., *Armada, 1588–1988* (1988).

Rogers and Ward, *Süleyman* Rogers, J. M., and Ward, R. M., *Süleyman the Magnificent* (1988).

Ross, *Edward IV* Ross, C., *Edward IV* (1974).

Rot Parl Strachey, J., et al., *Rotuli Parliamentorum*, 1278–1504, 6 vols (1767–77).

Rowlands, *Age of Dürer* Rowlands, J., *The Age of Dürer and Holbein: German Drawings 1440–1550* (1988).

Rowlands, *Holbein* Rowlands, J., *Holbein: The Paintings of Hans Holbein the Younger* (Oxford, 1985).

Rowlands and Starkey, 'Old tradition' Rowlands, J. and Starkey, D. R., 'An old tradition reasserted: Holbein's portrait of Queen Anne Boleyn', *Burlington Magazine*, 125 (1983), pp. 83–92.

Russell, *Field of Cloth of Gold* Russell, J. G., *The Field of Cloth of Gold: Men and Manners in 1520* (1969).

Rutt, *Hand Knitting* Rutt, R., *A History of Hand Knitting* (1987).

Scarisbrick, *Henry VIII* Scarisbrick, J., *Henry VIII* (1981).

Scarisbrick, *Jewellery* Scarisbrick, D., *Jewellery in Britain 1066–1837: A Documentary, Social, Literary and Artistic Survey* (Norwich, 1994).

Scarisbrick, *Tudor* Scarisbrick, D., *Tudor and Jacobean Jewellery* (1995).

Scott, *Visual History* Scott, M., *A Visual History of Costume: The Fourteenth and Fifteenth Centuries* (1986).

SJC St John's College, Cambridge.

Skelton, *Magnificence* Skelton, J., *Magnificence*, ed. P. Neuss (Manchester, 1980).

Snodin and Howard, *Ornament* Snodin, M., and Howard, M., *Ornament: a Social History Since 1450* (New Haven and London, 1996).

Snodin and Styles, *Design* Snodin, M., and Styles, J., *Design and the Decorative Arts: Tudor and Stuart Britain 1500–1714* (2004).

SoA Society of Antiquaries.

Somers-Cocks, *Princely Magnificence* Somers-Cocks, A., ed., *Princely Magnificence: Court Jewels of the Renaissance 1500–1630* (1980).

Spufford, *Great Reclothing* Spufford, M., *The Great Reclothing of Rural England: Petty Chapmen and Their Wares in the Seventeenth Century* (1984).

SP Bergenroth, G. A., et al., *State Papers of King Henry the Eighth*, 11 vols (1830–52).

SR Luders, A., et al., *Statutes of the Realm*, 10 vols (1810–28).

Stangl and Lang, *Mönche und Scholaren* Stangl, A., and Lang, F. T., *Mönche und Scholaren: Funde aus 900 Jahren Kloster Alpirsbach 1095–1995* (Karlsruhe, 1995).

Staniland, 'Getting there' Staniland, K., 'Getting there, got it: archaeological textiles and tailoring in London, 1330–1580', in D. Gaimster and P. Stamper, eds, *The Age of Transition: the Archaeology of English Culture 1400–1600*, Society for Medieval Archaeology Monograph 15 (1997), pp. 239–49.

Staniland, 'Royal entry' Staniland, K., 'Royal entry into the world', in D. Williams, ed., *England in the Fifteenth Century* (Woodbridge, 1987), pp. 297–313.

Starkey, *English Court* Starkey, D. R., ed., *The English Court from the Wars of the Roses to the Civil War* (London and New York, 1987).

Starkey, *European Court* Starkey, D. R., ed., *Henry VIII: a European Court in England* (1991).

Starkey, *Inventory* Starkey, D. R., ed., *The Inventory of King Henry VIII* (1998). Full transcript of the 1547 inventory taken after Henry VIII's death.

Starkey, 'Old blue gown' Starkey, D. R., 'Henry VI's old blue gown: the English court under the Lancastrians and Yorkists', *The Court Historian*, 4.1 (1999), pp. 1–28.

Starkey, 'Representation' Starkey, 'Representation through intimacy: a study in the symbolism of monarchy and court office in early modern England', in I. Lewis, ed., *Symbols and Sentiments: Cross-Cultural Studies in Symbolism* (1977), pp. 187–224.

Starkey, *Six Wives* Starkey, D. R., *Six Wives: The Queens of Henry VIII* (2003).

Stow, *Annales* Stow, J., *The Annales or Generall Chronicle of England* (1615).

Stow, *Survey* Stow, J., *A Survey of London Written in the Year 1598*, with an introduction by A. Fraser (Stroud, 1994).

Streitberger, *Court Revels* Streitberger, W. R., *Court Revels 1485–1559* (Toronto, Buffalo and London, 1994).

Strickland, *Queens of England* Strickland, A., *Lives of the Queens of England*, II (Chicago, New York and San Francisco, 1851).

Strickland, *Queens of Scotland* Strickland, A., *Lives of the Queens of Scotland and English Princesses Connected with Regal Succession of Great Britain* (New York, 1859).

Strong, *Holbein* Strong, R., *Holbein and Henry VIII* (1967).

Strong, *Portraits* Strong, R., *Tudor and Jacobean Portraits: National Portrait Gallery*, 2 vols (1967).

Strong, *Splendour at Court* Strong, R., *Splendour at Court: Renaissance Spectacle and Illusion* (1973).

Strype, *Memorials* Strype, J., *Ecclesiastical Memorials* (Oxford, 1822).

Sutton, 'Coronation robes' Sutton, A. F., 'The coronation robes of Richard III and Anne Neville', *Costume*, 13 (1979), pp. 8–16.

Sutton, 'Lovekyn' Sutton, A. F., 'George Lovekyn, tailor to three kings of England, 1470–1504', *Costume*, 15 (1981), pp. 1–12.

Sutton, *Mercers* Sutton, A. F., *The Mercery of London: Trade, Goods and People, 1130–1578* (Aldershot, 2005).

Sutton, *Reburial* Sutton, A. F., Visser-Fuchs, L., and Hammond, P. W., *The Reburial of Richard Duke of York 21–30 July 1476*, The Richard III Society (1996).

Sutton and Hammond, *Coronation* Sutton, A. F., and Hammond, P. W., eds, *The Coronation of Richard III: the Extant Documents* (Gloucester and New York, 1983).

Symonds and Preece, *Needlework* Symonds, M., and Preece, L., *Needlework Through the Ages* (1928).

Tarrant, *Development* Tarrant, N., *The Development of Costume* (Edinburgh, 1996).

Thomas and Thornley, *Great Chronicle* Thomas, A. H., and Thornley, I. D., eds, *The Great Chronicle of London* (1938).

Thurley, *Royal Palaces* Thurley, S., *The Royal Palaces of Tudor England: Architecture and Court Life 1460–1547* (New Haven and London, 1993).

Thurstfield, *Medieval Tailor* Thurstfield, S., *The Medieval Tailor's Assistant* (Bedford, 2001).

TNA The National Archives (formerly The Public Record Office, Kew). This is the chief repository for records relating to Henry VIII's wardrobe, court and household.

- E36: Exchequer: Treasury of Receipt: Miscellaneous Books.
- E101: Exchequer: King's Remembrancer: Accounts, Various.
- E154: Exchequer: King's Remembrancer: Inventories of goods and chattels.
- E315: Court of Augmentations and Predecessors and Successors: Miscellaneous Books.
- E403: Exchequer of Receipt: Issue Rolls and Registers.
- E404: Exchequer of Receipt: Warrants for Issue.
- LC2: Lord Chamberlain's Department: Records of Special Events.
- LC5: Lord Chamberlain's Department: Miscellaneous Records.
- LC9: Lord Chamberlain's Department: Accounts and Miscellanea.
- OBS: Obsolete Lists, Indices and Miscellaneous Summaries and Reports Associated with The National Archive's Holdings.
- SP1: State Papers, Domestic, Henry VIII.
- SP10: State Papers, Domestic, Edward VI.

Tout, *Chapters* Tout, T. F., *Chapters in the Administrative History of Medieval England*, IV (Manchester, 1928).

VAM Victoria and Albert Museum.

Veale, *Fur Trade* Veale, E. M., *The English Fur Trade in the Later Middle Ages*, LRS (1966, 2003).

WAM Westminster Abbey Muniments.

Weir, *Six Wives* Weir, A., *The Six Wives of Henry VIII* (1991).

Wilcox, *Bags* Wilcox, C., *Bags* (1999).

Williams, *Documents* Williams, C. H., ed., *English Historical Documents, 1455–1558*, V (1967).

Woolgar, *Great Household* Woolgar, C. M., *The Great Medieval Household in Late Medieval England* (New Haven and London, 1999).

Wriothesley, *Chronicle* Wriothesley, *A Chronicle of England*, Camden Society, NS, 11 (1875).

Young, *Tournaments* Young, A., *Tudor and Jacobean Tournaments* (1987).

Introduction

THIS BOOK is modelled on Janet Arnold's *Queen Elizabeth's Wardrobe Unlock'd* (Leeds, 1988) in terms of its structure, format, approach and its close focus on the dress of one royal individual: hence the discussions of Henry's physique, portraiture, personal wardrobe, jewellery, regalia and ceremonial robes. In addition to chapters on the great wardrobe, the king's artificers and wardrobe of the robes, the book includes full transcripts of James Worsley's wardrobe book commissioned in December 1516 and his inventory compiled in January 1521.[1] Along with the inventory of the wardrobe of the robes taken after the king's death in January 1547, the 14 extant volumes of great wardrobe accounts and various bundles of warrants, this wardrobe book and inventory represent the only other substantial record of the king's clothes in English archives.[2]

However, in a number of small ways this book differs from Janet's model. In part, this reflects the difference in the available evidence between the first and second halves of the sixteenth century, and in part it acknowledges that a monarch needs to be considered in the context of their court and household.[3] For this reason, Henry VIII has been compared with his father, Henry VII, to provide historical context, and with the other rulers of Europe who were his social equals, in order to assess how they used clothes to define their royal image. The contents of this book also reflect developments in historiography such as the rise in interest in the structure and composition of early modern courts.[4] Court ceremonial was linked to the annual cycle, while the pattern of coronations and funerals dictated royal dress and behaviour, just as strongly as personal inclination. For these occasions, royal dress was often intended to be seen in the context of the textiles used to furnish the rooms the king appeared in and, consequently, these furnishings have been referred to where relevant. Equally, the Henrician court was European in outlook, while demonstrating moments of marked insularity.[5] All of these features created a magnificent court with Henry VIII at the centre. Finally, the book is chiefly concerned with the study of male dress, as there was a male monarch, an essentially all male household and a strongly masculine court. However, this male bias is tempered by the chapters on the dress of Henry's wives, their households and his children. Finally, there is increasing interest in the cut, construction and recreation of Tudor dress.[6] In part, this was instigated by Janet Arnold who took patterns from extant garments and documented how they were made.[7] This was the inspiration for the final chapter which presents some of the evidence on cut, construction and decorative techniques that can be drawn from the written sources.

Some themes were not included in this book because they have been covered elsewhere. Consequently, there is not a chapter on the materials used by the king's artificers because many facets of this topic have been addressed by a range of scholars, including Lisa Monnas on Italian silks, Anne Sutton on mercery and Elspeth Veale on fur.[8] In contrast, the material on Henry VIII's suppliers poses other challenges, including the volume of primary data and secondary sources. It is also a topic that would draw this book too far away from its original inspiration.[9] The difficulties of working with the range of written and visual primary sources available to a historian of the mid Tudor period have been discussed elsewhere, so removing the need for a specific chapter on sources.[10] However, the great wardrobe accounts, the chief source for this book, are discussed in detail. Shorter discussions on other key groups of sources appear in the relevant chapters. In addition, the list of Abbreviations of the Principal Works Cited (pp. xi–xv) has been annotated to highlight the most important manuscript and printed primary sources.

Sixteenth-century textiles and dress have a specialist vocabulary, as does the court and the royal household. Consequently, this book is aimed at the readers with an interest in, and knowledge, of the period. However, the text is also intended to be accessible to readers with a more general knowledge and some additional information has been provided to assist them with the technical terms and other more period-specific detail. All dates are old style, with the year taken to begin on 1 January. For a discussion of measurements, dating and regnal years, see the Transcription Notes (pp. 367–68), while definitions of textile and dress terms are given in the Glossary (pp. 433–35). All lengths, prices and weights have been given in the original form. Metric conversions have been supplied for lengths and weights.

Some data has been presented in the form of tables. In most cases the material has been arranged alphabetically. However, where the tables refer to items of clothing, these have been grouped by type, such as outer garments, doublets and hose, associated items, accessories, headwear and footwear, and then listed alphabetically within these groupings.

Quotations taken from primary sources retain the original spelling. Where the meaning is potentially ambiguous, an explanation has been provided in square brackets. A large number of quotations have been used in this book, to provide the reader with direct access to the original sources, but in some instances the quotations are placed in the notes to ensure the flow of the main text. A number of quotations come from four primary sources. First, there are James Worsley's wardrobe book and inventory which are transcribed at the end of this book and their reference numbers are cited as follows: the entry number prefaced with A in square brackets refers to BL MS Harley 2284, for example [A421] and the entry number prefaced with B in square brackets refers to BL MS Harley 4217, for example [B23]. The third is the 1542 inventory of the palace of Whitehall and the entry number is given in square brackets, for example [211]. Finally, the entries from the 1547 inventory, taken shortly after Henry's death, are given in parentheses, for example (9987).

Notes

1 BL Harley MSS 2284 and 4217.

2 BL Harley MS 1419, ff. 398r–415v; Starkey, *Inventory* (14177–590). The 1542 inventory of the palace of Whitehall includes a short entry for the king's clothes kept there, along with a much longer listing of clothes that had belonged to Jane Seymour; TNA E315/160, ff. 1r–2r, 94r–98v; Hayward, *1542 Inventory* [1–28], [2095–259].

3 Janet Arnold did discuss the key groups of women in Elizabeth's service (the maids of honour and the ladies and gentlewomen of the bed chamber and privy chamber) but only in the context of gifts given to the queen. For a discussion of the Tudor court, see Starkey, *English Court*, and Loades, *Tudor Court*.

4 For example, A. G. Dickens, ed., *The Court of Europe: Politics, Patronage and Royalty 1400–1800* (1977); J. Adamson, ed., *The Princely Courts of Europe 1500–1750* (1999); The Society for Court Studies was established in 1996.

5 Including Starkey, *European Court*, and G. Richardson, *Renaissance Monarchy: The Reigns of Henry VIII, Francis I and Charles V* (2002).

6 Including J. Hunniset, *Period Costume for Stage and Screen: Patterns for Women's Dress 1500–1800* (California, 1991), Thurstfield, *Medieval Tailor* and Mikhaila and Malcolm-Davies, *Tudor Tailor*.

7 Arnold, *Patterns*. A few of her patterns and replicas were included in Arnold, *Queen Elizabeth*.

8 For example, Monnas, *Merchants*, Sutton, *Mercers* and Veale, *Fur Trade*.

9 The London Record Society is keen to publish a selection of the great wardrobe accounts with a full analysis of the suppliers, set in the wider context of the London mercantile community. The latter will draw on recent scholarship such as Sutton, *Mercers*, and Davies and Saunders, *Merchant Taylors*.

10 For example, J. Arnold, *A Handbook of Costume* (1973), Lloyd and Thurley, *Images*, and Ashelford, *Visual History*.

I

Henry VIII: The Man and his Image

HOUSEHOLD ORDINANCES, narrative sources and books of accounts make clear the social, political and religious role of textiles and dress in creating a suitable context for early modern royalty.[1] This role was often articulated in terms of the need for royal magnificence, and it was expressed through court ceremonial. The ways in which textiles were used in these ceremonies find many parallels in the royal and princely courts across Europe, and England was no exception. Luxury textiles were expensive and highly prized. Giangiorgio Trissino's observations after visiting the *studiolo* and *grotta* of Isabella d'Este, marchioness of Mantua, vividly illustrate this point. Trissino stated that 'her true liberality can be understood by the splendour of her dress, the magnificent décor of the house, and by the beautiful — one might almost say, divine — fabrics with which the whole is adorned'.[2] While such splendour was to be expected in Italy, a major producer of luxury silk textiles at this period, England was another matter. Some Italian visitors to England were pleasantly surprised by what they found, suggesting that their expectations had not been very high. The papal nuncio, Francesco Chieregato, wrote to Isabella d'Este, describing the jousts held by Henry VIII at Greenwich in July 1515:

> In short, the wealth and civilization of the world are here; and those who call the English barbarians appear to me to render themselves such. I here perceive very elegant manners, extreme decorum, and very great politeness; and amongst other things there is this most invincible King, whose acquirements and qualities are so many and excellent that I consider him to excel all who ever wore a crown.[3]

Henry VIII dominated his court and so it is fitting that this book should begin by looking at the man in terms of his physical build, his personality and how these changed over time. A number of contemporary descriptions have been quoted at length to provide a sense of the king and to emphasise the qualities admired or reproved by those who met him. These quotations also provide context for the portraits of the king painted by Hans Holbein the Younger and the other artists of the Tudor court.

Henry VIII's physical form

A sense of Henry VIII's appearance can be derived from the descriptions of his physique, most of which date to the first 25 years of his 37-year reign. In terms of stature and colouring, Henry inherited the looks of his maternal grandfather, Edward IV, who Sir Thomas More described as 'Princely to behold ... of visage lovely, of body mighty, strong and clean made'.[4] These physical traits were readily apparent in Henry even before his accession to the throne.[5]

As an adult, Henry was tall and statuesque. His armour made in 1515 indicates that he was at least 6 ft 1 in. (1.84 m) in height, and that he was broad-shouldered in an age when broad shoulders were symbolic of male strength.[6] This physical trait was further emphasised by the cut of gowns and doublets at this period which stressed the shoulders and drew the viewer's attention away from the waist. The king was not alone in having an impressive build: John Fisher, bishop of Rochester, was equally tall.[7] Henry also shared his striking stature with his uncle Arthur Plantagenet, Lord Lisle. Late in 1533 Lisle asked the king for a suit of 'hosting harness' or field armour. On 20 January 1534 Sir Francis Bryan wrote to Lisle, noting that 'at his Grace's next repair to Greenwich ... he will look one out for you himself'.[8] The implication was that Henry would select one of his own armours for Lisle, indicating that they were a similar size.[9]

Filled with the spirit of optimism brought about by the accession of a new, young king, Lord Mountjoy described Henry in 1509 as having no wish for 'gold or gems or precious metals, but virtue, glory, immortality'.[10] Henry's enlightened outlook was ascribed to his humanist education and his circle of friends which included Sir Henry Guildford and Sir Thomas More (Fig. 1.1).[11] Henry had a wide range of intellectual interests and he often chose More as his companion, taking him:

1.1 *Henry VIII reading in his bedchamber in Henry VIII's Psalter, c. 1540. The king wears a red, fur trimmed gown over a cloth of gold doublet and tawny hose. By permission of the British Library, Royal MS 2A XVI, f. 3*

> into his private room, and there some time in matters of astronomy, geometry, divinity and such other faculties, and some time in his worldly affairs, to sit and confer with him, and other whiles would he in the night have him up into the leads there to consider with him the diversities, courses, motions and operations of the stars and planets.[12]

Henry also excelled in music, tennis, dressage and the full range of martial skills which he honed through hunting, making him a fully rounded Renaissance prince. Hall's description of Henry's activities on his summer progress in 1511 makes this very plain.[13] The king spent his time:

> in shooting, singing, dancing, wrestling, casting of the bar, playing at the recorders, flute and virginals, and in setting of songs, making of ballads and [he] did set two godly Masses, every of them of five parts, which are sung oftentimes in his chapel and afterwards in divers places. And when he came to Woking, there were kept both jousts and tourneys. The rest of his time was spent playing in hunting, hawking and shooting.[14]

John Taylor, clerk of Parliament, recalled seeing the king on 8 July 1513 practising archery in a garden with the yeomen of the guard. Henry 'cleft the mark in the middle and surpassed them all, as he surpasses them in stature and personal graces'.[15] Henry continued to be complimented on his sporting prowess late into the 1520s. In 1529 Erasmus observed that Henry 'had such natural dexterity, that is the ordinary accomplishments of riding and throwing the dart he outstripped everyone'.[16]

Many of the descriptions emphasised the quality of Henry's clothes and so provided ample justification for the money spent on his wardrobe. He was recognised as 'the best dressed sovereign in the world: his robes are the richest and more superb that can be imagined: and he puts on new clothes every Holyday'.[17] Henry's use of his wardrobe to create a sense of magnificence was conveyed very powerfully when Pasqualigo, who accompanied the Venetian ambassador Sebastian Giustinian, described the king on St George's day 1515. It is the detailed observations made by Giustinian that makes this description so telling about how Henry sought to create a particular visual impression with his clothes:

> he wore a cap of crimson velvet, in the French fashion, and the brim was looped up all round with lacets and gold enamelled aigletes. His doublet was in the Swiss fashion, striped alternately with white and crimson satin, and his hose scarlet, and all slashed from the knees upwards . . . round his neck he had a gold collar, from which there hung a rough-cut diamond, the size of the largest walnut . . . and to this was suspended a most beautiful and very large round pearl. His mantle was of purple velvet lined with white satin, the sleeves open with a train verily more than four Venetian yards in length. This mantle was girt in front like a gown, with a thick gold cord, from which there hung large garlands entirely of gold, like those suspended from a cardinal's hat; over this mantle was a very handsome gold collar, with a pendant St. George entirely of diamonds . . . Beneath the mantle he had a pouch of cloth of gold, which covered a dagger.[18]

Contemporary notions favoured blond or sandy hair, pale skin and blue eyes, so Henry was regarded as being very good-looking in his youth. At the age of 24 he was said to be 'the handsomest potentate I ever set eyes on . . . his complexion [is] very fair and bright, with auburn hair combed straight and short, in the French fashion, and a round face so very beautiful that it would become a pretty woman'.[19] Sebastian Giustinian, the Venetian ambassador, writing on 10 September 1519, echoed these sentiments when he described Henry (aged 29) in the following terms: 'he is much handsomer than any other sovereign in Christendom; a great deal handsomer than the King of France; very fair, his whole frame admirably proportioned.'[20] Being used to praise of this kind meant that the king took criticism badly. At the time of Anne Boleyn's trial, Lady Rochford testified that Anne had been critical of the king's poetry and his virility. Such comments were newsworthy, and Eustace Chapuys recorded that 'She was also charged, and her brother likewise, with having laughed at the king and his dress'.[21]

By the late 1530s Henry's health began to decline and, with it, his physique. In the autumn of 1538 George Constantine observed to the dean of Westbury that 'it grieveth me at heart to see his Grace halt so much upon his sore leg'.[22] Once age saw the decline of his physical skills, courtiers resorted to classical comparisons to flatter the king. In 1540 Sir Thomas Chaloner described Henry to Charles V as the equal of Hercules, Pollux, Castor, Hector and Hippolitus.[23] However, in December of that year, Marillac, the French ambassador, informed Francis I that the 'King has taken a new rule of living; to rise between 5 and 6 a.m., hearing mass at 7 a.m., and then ride until dinner time, which is 10 a.m.'.[24] This regime did not have lasting benefits. In February 1541 Henry had to postpone a visit to Dover because he suffered from 'a slight tertian fever . . . one of his legs, formerly opened and kept open to maintain his health, suddenly closed, to his great alarm, for, five or six years ago, in like case, he thought to have died'.[25] Although he recovered, Henry took to walking with a staff, and staffs became an integral part of his appearance. On 18 May 1542 when Lady Northumberland petitioned the king about her poverty, Robert Swift observed in a letter to the earl of Shrewsbury that Henry 'bowed down upon his staff unto her'.[26]

The French ambassador Castillion described Henry VIII as 'a wonderful man and has wonderful people about him, but he is an old fox'.[27] In later life, he was troubled with poor sight, just as his paternal grandmother had been. Amongst his personal possessions in 1547 there were 'a glasse to reade with set in wodde with a handell' (3195) and 'a Spectacle case of golde engraven with the Armes of England with twoo spectacles' (2088).[28] Equally, by 1542 he was 'already very stout and daily growing heavier, he seems very old and grey ... three of the biggest men to be found could get inside his doublet'[29] (Fig 1.2). The impact of his increased size on his appearance was pronounced. In part, the emphasis that male dress placed on the shoulders, and the bulky image created by wearing layered clothing, turned Henry's increasing size into a virtue, ensuring that he presented an even more impressive and imposing figure at court.[30] In part, the king's own bulk ensured the substantial male silhouette was copied at court.

1.2 *Henry VIII in later life, by Cornelius Matsys,* c. *1545. The ageing king wears the high-necked doublet typical of the 1540s under a gown with a fur collar. Bibliothèque Nationale de France*

Late in 1546, letters sent by courtiers and ambassadors highlight the king's poor health. In December 1546 the privy council informed Nicholas Wotton the king had a fever 'upon some grief upon his leg' but now he was 'well rid of it'.[31] The imperial ambassador, Van der Delft, was less optimistic when he wrote to Mary of Hungary on 24 December, noting that 'the King is so unwell that, considering his age and corpulence, he may not survive another attack such as he recently had at Windsor'.[32] On 10 January 1547 the French ambassadors wrote to Francis I with news that the king's health was a little better but that they had 'great reason to conjecture that, whatever his health, it can only be bad and will not last long'.[33] Henry's physical decline was also charted in Goodwin's *Annales of England* and the *Life of Herbert of Cherbury*.[34] Amidst all of this speculation, Henry died on 28 January 1547, aged 55, in the 38th year of his reign.

The king's painted image

Unlike his daughter Elizabeth, Henry VIII did not pass any legislation seeking to control the production or dissemination of his image. Even so, Henry undoubtedly intended his portraits to be magnificent and awe-inspiring. Holbein's dynastic mural in the privy chamber at Whitehall, which depicted Henry with Jane Seymour and his parents, was described as leaving those that saw it 'abashed and annihilated'.[35] Even so, access to this image was strictly limited because relatively few people gained entrance to the privy chamber and not all of those that did succumbed to its spell. However, the printing press ensured that Henry VIII's portrait was disseminated widely. This could be in the form of single woodcuts such as the illustration of the king's coronation in Stephen Hawes' pamphlet *c.* 1510 (Fig. 4.1) or pages in books, including Holbein's frontispiece for the Coverdale Bible produced in 1535.[36]

Henry VIII's portrait was developed and disseminated in a very different way to that of his rival, Francis I.[37] Jean Clouet created an informal, half-length portrait of Francis I that was used both for portraits and official documents. In contrast, although Holbein developed a distinctive image that came to typify Henry's portraiture, it did not replace the formal portraits of the king found in government documents and on the Great Seal. In official documents the king was depicted crowned, seated and dressed in his robes of estate.[38] The same was true of the royal seal which presented two very traditional images of kingship, the dual roles of law giver and warrior. In 1525 letters patents were issued to Cardinal Wolsey authorising him to have a new great seal engraved 'on the one side, where the King's figure is graven sitting in majesty in a chair, crowned with a crown imperial' and on the other 'the King's figure is graven on horseback holding a sword in his hand, a rose is to be graven under the sword and under the horse a greyhound running'.[39] By Edward VI's reign, the style of the king's portraits on the coinage were considered very carefully, with the king's dress playing an important part in creating the image that was presented to the populace. On

25 September 1551, the council wrote to Sir Edmund Peckham, high treasurer of the mints, stating that Edward VI 'prefers the patterns of the 12*d* and 6*d* with Roman numerals, with the parliament robe and the collar of the order . . . The king and we think his face should be shown in three-quarters . . . We send a pattern, noted by his hand'.[40]

While Henry VIII's likeness could be disseminated in various forms, his portraiture is most pertinent for a study of his clothes. The development of Henry's portrait during his reign focuses around a fairly small group of seven images or patterns which were copied during his lifetime and after his death.[41] These have been classified as follows: type one (*c.* 1520), three portraits probably produced by French artists (Pl. IA); type two (*c.* 1527), a group of portraits, again by foreign artists;[42] type three (*c.* 1535), including a portrait attributed to Joos van Cleve depicting Henry holding a scroll with an inscription form St Mark (Pl. IB); type four (*c.* 1536), the Thyssen-Bornemisza portrait (Pl. IC);[43] type five (1537), the Whitehall cartoon with the king looking to the front (Fig. 6.8); type six (*c.* 1535–47), the late non-Holbein pattern, possibly the work of an Anglo-Flemish workshop (Figs. 1.3 and 6.12); and type seven (*c.* 1542), the final pattern, Henry in a cassock or coat holding a staff, with the exemplary portrait in the collection at Castle Howard and a good copy in the National Portrait Gallery (Pl. ID).[44]

1.3 *Henry VIII, unknown artist,* c. *1535–40. The king's wide, low-necked doublet is worn with a shirt with a small, upright collar edged with a frill. National Portrait Gallery, London (NPG 3638)*

There are only two full-scale images of Henry VIII definitely painted by Holbein: the portrait in the Thyssen-Bornemicza collection and the Whitehall cartoon, also known as the Chatsworth cartoon. Holbein achieved the creation of the king's distinctive image, exemplified by the Whitehall cartoon, by lengthening the king's legs below the knee, so making him appear even more imposing.[45] There are many versions of Henry VIII's later portraits but the largest group are of portrait type five, which was modelled on the Whitehall cartoon. These include full-length versions such as the portraits at the Walker Art Gallery, Liverpool (Pl. IIA) or Chatsworth, and three-quarter-length pictures including those in the Galleria Corsini, Rome and at Blickling Hall, Norfolk (Fig. 1.4). The full-length pictures fall into two groups, depending on whether his gown is trimmed with white fur or dark fur. Most of his portraits present a three-quarter or frontal image, the latter style being echoed in the three miniatures produced of the king by Lucas Horenbout and painted *c.* 1535 (Fig. 1.5).[46]

Between 1542 and 1547 Henry VIII acquired several paintings including 'a Table with the picture of the whole stature of the kinges Majestie in a gowne like crymsen satten furred withe Luernes' (10718). While it is tempting to suggest that this is a version of the full-length image of the Walker Art Gallery type, it is impossible to make a positive identification. This was not the only portrait of the king listed in the 1547 inventory of his picture collection, which included two portraits of Henry (10612, 10665), in which he was described as 'being yonge'. He also owned a double portrait of himself with Jane Seymour described as 'a table like a booke with the

1.4 *Henry VIII, by Hans Holbein. Blickling Hall, The Lothian Collection. The National Trust/NTPL John Hammond*

1.5 *Miniature of Henry VIII, by Lucas Horenbout, 1525–27. In this portrait the low neckline of the shirt echoes that of the doublet, as was fashionable in the 1520s. PD.19-1949, Fitzwilliam Museum, Cambridge*

picture of Kynge Henry theight and quene Jane' (10613).[47] There were also several miniatures in the jewel house, including 'a Tablet of golde hauing on thone side the kinges Picture peynted' (2661) and 'a Harte of golde enameled with the kinges picture in it' (2925). While most of the descriptions are frustratingly vague, it is evident that several portraits of the king have been lost, including 'the phisnamy of kinge henrie theight . . . like an antique' (16717) and an unfinished portrait (11672) kept in the new library at Whitehall.

Paintings or 'tables with pictures' had a relatively small financial value in the first half of the sixteenth century and consequently their descriptions in the inventories of the period were often very brief. This can make identifying sitters, artists or extant pictures difficult.[48] Taking Henry VIII's own collection of 152 pictures that was housed at Whitehall in 1542, 59, or just over a third, were portraits. In most instances (52 portraits) the sitter was identified by name, with no further details given about their dress or the composition. Two notable examples were the portraits of 'the Frenche king having a doublet of crymsen colour / And a gowne garnisshid with knottes made like peerle' [671] and 'the Frenche Queine Elienora in Spanysh aray and a Cappe on her hed / and an oringe in her hande' [672]. Of the remaining seven portraits where the sitter was not identified by name or title, descriptions of the clothing or distinctive accessories were provided, so making it possible for the palace keeper to identify these images.[49] As all of the images of Henry VIII and his family were identified by name, hardly any additional information about their clothing was recorded. The development in the way pictures were described by the seventeenth century is indicated by the description of Holbein's portrait of Henry (now in the Thyssen collection) in Charles I's picture inventory: 'the picture of King Henrie the 8th in his youth In a guilden dublett, with a glove on his right hand. In a reed and guilded frame. A Whitehall piece. 1 ft o ½ in by 8 ½ in.'[50]

The clothes depicted in the king's portraits reflect Henry's belief in his own magnificence, but they do not reflect fully the diversity of the king's wardrobe in terms of colour or type of garment.[51] This is compounded by the parallels between the king's clothes in the Thyssen portrait, the Whitehall cartoon and the six versions of the king's full-length portrait derived from the cartoon: the Walker Art Gallery, Liverpool; the Egremont collection, Petworth House; the Devonshire collection, Chatsworth House; Trinity College, Cambridge; the duke and duchess of Rutland, Belvoir castle and Parham house.[52] The latter depict Henry VIII dressed in a red velvet gown embroidered with bands of couched rabask work, trimmed and lined with fur, either dark sable or pale lynx, worn over a high-necked doublet and a low-cut jerkin of cloth of silver, the skirts of which covered the upperstocks of his hose, but parted to reveal his codpiece, and flat slashed shoes. Gowns, doublets and hose of the types depicted in the king's portraits can be traced in the great wardrobe accounts and warrants. It is possible that the officers of the wardrobe of the robes lent items to Holbein, but there is no direct evidence of this. Equally, it is likely that Holbein produced heavily annotated drawings of the king recording details of his clothes and jewellery, just as he did for his other sitters, such as William Parr, first marquess of Northampton (Fig. 17.1).[53]

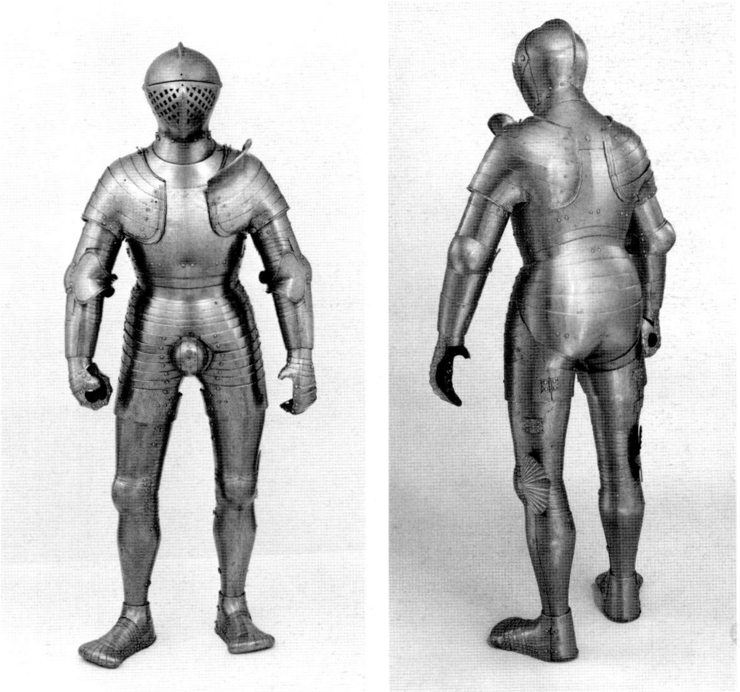

1.6 and 1.7 *Henry VIII's foot combat armour, front and rear views, Greenwich, c. 1520. The armour clearly reveals Henry's slim, athletic figure as a young man. The Royal Armouries, Leeds. © The Board of Trustees of the Armouries*

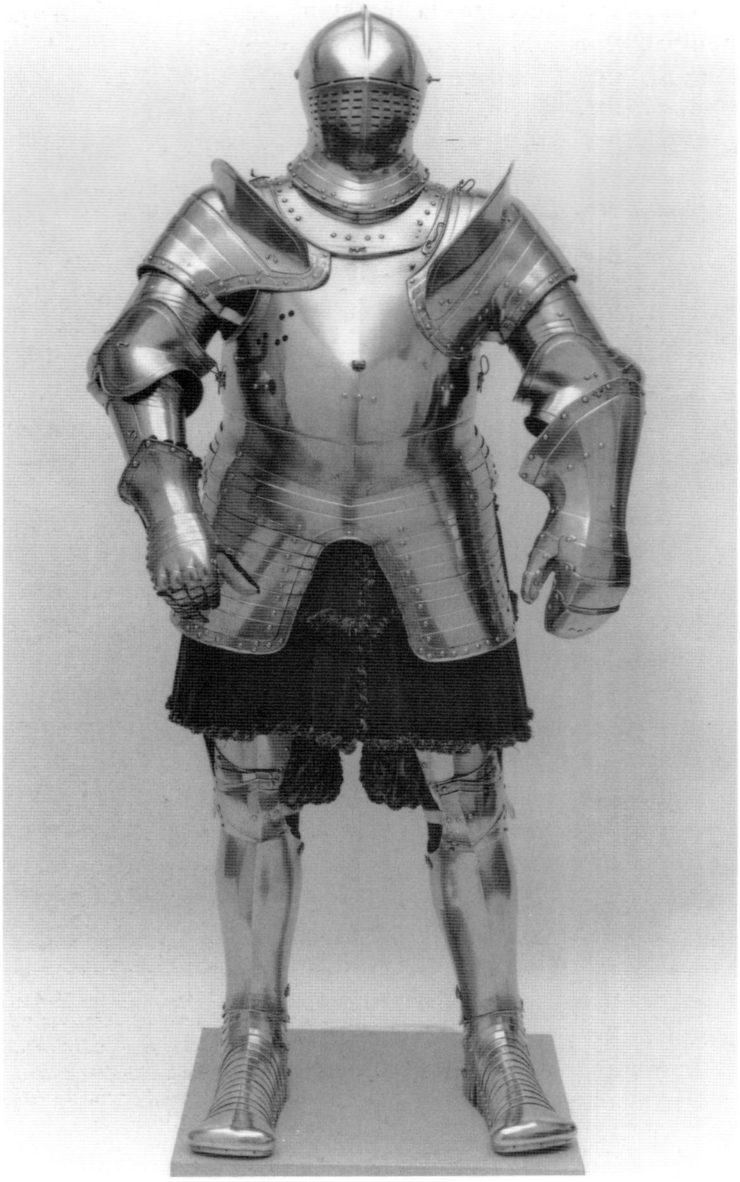

1.8 *Henry VIII's armour, front view, Greenwich, c. 1540. The change in Henry VIII's body shape is all too evident in this suit of armour. RCIN 72834. The Royal Collection © 2004, Her Majesty the Queen Elizabeth II*

1.9 *Simon George, by Hans Holbein the Younger, c. 1540. The understated but ornate self-coloured couched embroidery on George's gown is very evident on his left shoulder, while the blackwork on his shirt collar indicates that this style of embroidery was popular by c. 1540. Inv. no. 1065. Städelsches Kunstinstitut, Frankfurt am Main*

Charting change in the king's appearance

Tailored clothes reflect the size and shape of the wearer and how that shape changes during a lifetime. Although the king's clothes have not survived, the written sources describe the changes and these changes are made visible by objects and visual sources. It is possible to set the contemporary descriptions of the king's changing vital statistics in context by measuring his suits of armour. Armour was designed to be a very good fit and as such it accurately reflects the shape of his body — only the codpiece was allowed to be exaggerated in its size, stressing the king's virility.[54] Consequently, these armours provide a record of his height and his youthful body at the start of his reign and then how his shape matured.[55] The silver and engraved parade armour *c.* 1515 decorated by Paul van Vreland records the king's height. It also provides a clear indication of the king's slim build as a young man (Figs 1.6 and 1.7).

Taking one measurement, it is possible to trace his increasing waistline: 35½ in. (0.9 m) in 1515 (the silver engraved armour), 37¾ in. (0.95 m) in 1520 (the Greenwich armour), 41¾ in. (1.06 m) in 1527 (the Genouilhac armour), increasing to 52½ in. (1.33 m) in 1539–40 (the Windsor armour), equating to a probable waist measurement of 49 in. (1.2 m).[56] Not only does the sequence of Henry's armours provide direct evidence of Henry's expanding body, individual armours provide evidence of alterations in order to accommodate these changes. The cuirass of the Tower armour, dating from 1540, was extended by 2¼ in. (5.7 cm), while the cuirass of the Windsor suit was enlarged by 2⅛ in. (5.3 cm). The cuisses of the Windsor suit were also cut back to accommodate the king's growing thighs (Fig. 1.8).[57]

Although the king's armour can provide a lot of evidence about the king, it is necessary to look at his portraits to see that his hair was cut in a bob for the first half of his reign and then cropped close to his head. The latter reflected the influence of continental styles in England. In 1529 Charles V had his hair cut short in the Italian style shortly before travelling to Italy, and those attending on him were quick to emulate him at the imperial court. Jan Cornelisz Vermeyen had painted Charles with this shorter haircut by *c.* 1530.[58] Stow recorded that in 1535 Henry 'caused his own [hair] to bee polled'.[59] After 1536 Henry was depicted with very short hair, as were other members of the court. This trend can be traced in a number of Holbein's portraits, including the preparatory sketch of Simon George and the resulting portrait (Fig. 1.9).

Henry had a short, trimmed beard for most of the time between 1519 and 1535. On 10 September 1519 Giustinian reported that on hearing that Francis I had a beard 'he allowed his to grow, and as it was reddish, he then got a beard which looks like gold'.[60] Stow recorded that Henry and Francis agreed not to shave their beards until they met in person.[61] However, Sir Thomas Boleyn informed Wolsey on 16 November 1519 that people in France knew that Henry shaved his beard because of pressure from Catherine of Aragon.[62] Catherine's actions were seen as evidence of her supporting Spanish interests, but Boleyn managed to smooth matters and the French king's mother declared that 'Th[eir love] is nat in the berdes but in the harts'. On 10 November 1531 Lodovico Falier described Henry to the senate, stating that 'His face is angelic rather than handsome; his head imperial and bald [cropped], and he wears a beard, contrary to English custom'.[63] In 1535, Stow's *Annals* recorded that 'from henceforth his beard [was] to be notted and no more shaven' and this is supported by the portraits of the king dating from the 1540s.[64]

The importance of the royal image is reflected in the number of mirrors that Henry owned. In part, this was because mirrors were novel and so highly prized. Mirrors also brought the owner much greater scope for self-scrutiny and personal grooming. On 20 February 1540 Melanchthon wrote to Henry to recommend Michael of Leipzig as being 'a very excellent maker of mirrors'.[65] Whether the king took Michael into his service is uncertain, but by 1547 Henry owned a number of mirrors, including 'a small glasse sett in Siluer gilte' (2328) and 'a faire greate Lookinge steele glasse sette in crymysen veluette richelye enbrowdred with damaske pirles with knottes of blewe' (10789). These mirrors would have ensured that the king was well aware of how he was ageing. At his accession he had been described as being not 'a person of this world, but one who descended from heaven'.[66] However, Henry described his own body in less poetic terms in his will: 'And for my body which when the soul is departed, shall then remain but as a cadaver, and so return to the vile matter it was made of, were it not for the crown and dignity which God hath called us unto.'[67]

Notes

1 Sets of regulations, known as household ordinances, were drawn up to ensure that the royal household was run efficiently and economically, while still reflecting the king's magnificence. The most important of these were the Black Book of Edward IV, *c.* 1471–72, which heavily influenced the ordinances drawn up under the Tudors, the Eltham Ordinances drawn up by Thomas Wolsey in 1526 and the revisions to the latter compiled by Thomas Cromwell in 1539; see Myers, *Black Book*, pp. 13–34.

2 Jardine, *Worldly Goods*, p. 413.

3 *CSP Venetian, 1509–19*, p. 918.

4 *Lisle Letters*, I, p. 13. The letters exchanged between Lord and Lady Lisle, who were resident in Calais, and John Husee, their factor in London, are possibly the best set of extant Tudor business letters. Lisle was implicated in the Botolph Conspiracy. His papers were confiscated, he was placed in the Tower and he died there on 3 March 1542.

5 On 5 October 1507 de Puebla, the Spanish ambassador, wrote to Ferdinand of Aragon and he stated that 'There is no finer youth in the world than the Prince of Wales. He is already taller than his father, and his limbs are of a gigantic size'; Pollard, *Henry VII*, I, pp. 298–99.

6 Fraser, *Six Wives*, p. 54; to put this in context the average height of people in medieval London was 5 ft 7½ in. (1.72 m) for men and 5 ft 3 in. (1.60 m) for women. In the Tudor and Stuart periods, the average male height remained the same, with women decreasing to 5 ft 2¼ in. (1.58 m); A. Werner, *London Bodies: the Changing Shape of Londoners from Prehistoric Times to the Present Day* (1998), p. 108.

7 Fisher was described as being 'tall and comly, exceeding the common and middle sort of men: for he was to the quantitie of 6 foote in height'; Strong, *Portraits*, I, p. 120.

8 *Lisle Letters*, I, p. 15; for this and the related correspondence, see ibid., II, pp. 108, 114, 168, 171, 183–84.

9 On 6 May 1534 Husee wrote to Lord Lisle, noting 'that this day I received by the King's commandment an osting harness, complete for your lordship'; ibid., II, p. 184.

10 Pollard, *Henry VIII*, p. 41.

11 According to Erasmus, 'You would say that Henry was a universal genius. He has never neglected his studies; and whenever he has leisure from his political occupations, he reads, or disputes — of which he is very fond — with remarkable courtesy and unruffled temper', ibid., p. 98.

12 W. Roper, *The Life of Sir Thomas More*, EETS (1935), p. 11.

13 Edward Hall's *Chronicle, The Union of the Two Noble and Illustre Families of York and Lancaster* was printed in 1548 by Richard Grafton. Hall was a stalwart supporter of the Tudors. He was MP for Wenlock in 1529, autumn reader at Grey's Inn and a common-sergeant in 1533 and an under-sheriff of London on 2 June 1535. Hall's will was proved on 25 May 1547 and it is likely that he died in April of the same year; see A. E. Pollard, 'Edward Hall's will and Chronicle', *BIHR*, 9 (1932), pp. 171–77. At the time of his death Hall had completed the *Chronicle* up to 1532, with the rest of Henry VIII's reign being completed posthumously. The level of detail found in Hall's *Chronicle* indicates that he had access to household accounts and other documents, especially Gibson's revels accounts; see S. Anglo, 'Financial and heraldic records of the English tournament', *Journal of the Society of Archivists*, 2 (1962), pp. 184–85; Anglo, *Tournament Roll*, p. 49.

14 Hall, *Chronicle*, p. 515.

15 *LP* I.ii, 2391.

16 Dillon, 'Arms and armour', p. 239.

17 *CSP Venetian, 1509–19*, 1287.

18 Brown, *Four Years*, I, p. 85.

19 *LP* II.i, 395.

20 *CSP Venetian, 1509–19*, p. 559; *LP* III, 402.

21 Ives, *Boleyn*, pp. 238, 398.

22 *LP* XIV.ii, 400.

23 'Even Hercules of old could hardly have bent the yew bow so well with the sinewy strength of his arms . . . and in wrestling, Pollux would have been no match for him in striving for the wreath of oak leaves. Whenever he sought to turn the powerful neck of a warhorse, controlling it with cunning voice and hand, you would think he was Castor himself; and if he put on his shining armour, his splendid helmet with nodding crest and his gilded breastplate he would excel even Trojan Hector. When he hunted deer through the woods with nets and a pack of hounds, not even Hippolitus . . . could have surpassed him in glory'; Bruce, *Making Henry*, p. 194. In 1540 Melanchthon wrote to Henry, beginning his letter by comparing Henry to Alexander, Ptolemy, Philadelphus, Augustus and Mark Anthony; *LP* XV, 231.

24 *LP* XVI, 311.

25 *LP* XVI, 589. In a letter written on the same day to Montmorency, Marillac was blunter, attributing the problem to the king being 'very stout and marvellously excessive in eating and drinking'; *LP* XVI, 590.

26 *LP* XVII, 331.

27 A. Weir, *Henry VIII: King and Court* (2001), p. 438.

28 The quantity of pairs listed in the 1547 inventory tallies with the painting by Jacob Cornelisz (1470–1533) called *Woman Selling Spectacles*, indicating that glasses were being made in bulk rather than being specially commissioned; see W. Winkler, ed., *A Spectacle of Spectacles* (Leipzig, 1988), pp. 18–20. The spectacles fitted onto the nose and could be held in place with ties.

29 Norris, *Costume*, p. 255.

30 The king's reduced mobility was catered for with a pair of invalid chairs 'for the kinges maiestie to sitt in / to be caried to and fro in his gallaries & Chambers' kept at Whitehall [3676] and a chair for use 'in the kinges howse whichh goeth vp and downe' [3680].
31 *SP*, XI, 394 (*LP* XXI.ii, 619).
32 *LP* XXI.ii, 606.
33 *LP* XXI.ii, 684.
34 'Henry, long since grown corpulent, was . . . of late lame by reason of a violent ulcer in his leg, the inflammation whereof cast him into a lingering fever which, little by little, decayed his spirits. He at length began to feel the inevitable necessity of death' and 'Our King, having laboured under the burden of extreme fat and [an] unwieldy body, and together being afflicted with a sore leg, took . . . his death bed' respectively; Brewer, *Death of Kings*, p. 113.
35 Thurley, *Royal Palaces*, p. 209.
36 Sion College Library, no. 17 (now part of the Lambeth Palace collections); illustrated in Lloyd and Thurley, *Images*, p. 34.
37 Foister, *Holbein*, pp. 192–93.
38 For a detailed analysis of how Henry VIII's portrait on formal documentation evolved, see Auerbach, *Tudor Artists*, pp. 25–37, 59–72.
39 *LP* IV.i, 1859.
40 *CSPD Edward VI*, 546.
41 For a very detailed analysis of the portrait types see Strong, *Portraits*, I, pp. 158–59.
42 See The Weiss Gallery, *Tudor and Stuart Portraits 1530–1660*, no. 2: a portrait of Henry *c.* 1520–30, of the English School, in which he wears a doublet of cloth of gold with a low, round neckline and slashed sleeves, under a fur-trimmed gown.
43 The Thyssen portrait is very small, measuring just 28 cm by 20 cm.
44 While Strong has attributed the Castle Howard version of this portrait to Lucas Horenbout, Rowlands, rejects this view; see Rowlands, *Holbein*, p. 146.
45 Rowlands, *Holbein*, p. 226.
46 Two versions are at Windsor, forming part of the Royal Collection, while the other is at the Fitzwilliam Museum, Cambridge; see R. Strong, *Artists of the Tudor Court: the Portrait Miniature Rediscovered 1520–1620* (1983), pp. 34–37.
47 In addition there was an overtly religious image of 'the king his highnes standing vpon a Mitre with iij Crownes having a Serpent with vij heddes going owte of it / having a Sworde in his hand wherin is written *Verbum dei*' [726].
48 Even an artist of Holbein's calibre painted only a few portraits of the king, with the bulk of his sitters being drawn from the English nobility and foreigners in England, including the merchants of the Hanseatic League; Foister, *Holbein*, pp. 175–262.
49 The seven portraits are nos. 741, 747, 769, 771, 774, 776 and 798. The descriptions could be quite detailed: for example, 'a woman in a French whode / and a Gowne like clothe of golde the slevis turnydvp with white and powdred with blac' [798].
50 Millar, *Catalogue*, p. 29.
51 Hayward, 'Fashion', pp. 169–71.
52 Illustrated in Brooke and Crombie, *Henry VIII*, pp. 74–75; Monnas, *Merchants* (forthcoming).
53 Monnas, *Merchants* (forthcoming); see S. Foister, 'The production and reproduction of Holbein's portraits', in Hearn, *Dynasties*, p. 22; also Foister, *Holbein*, pp. 54–58.
54 However, in 1536 Chapuys reported that 'according to the account given of him by the concubine, he has neither vigour nor virtue'; *CSP Spanish*, V.ii, 55 (*LP* XII, 901).
55 C. Blair, 'New light on four Almain armourers: 1', *The Connoisseur*, 144 (1959), p. 20; C. Blair, 'New light on four Almain armours: 2', *The Connoisseur*, 144 (1959), p. 244.
56 Blair and Pyhrr, 'Wilton "Montmorency" armor', p. 137. In 1535 John Dudley, master of the armoury, referred to some of the king's armour 'which was meet for his Grace three years past'; TNA SP1/95, f. 197 (*LP* IX, 187).
57 Blair, 'New light 2', p. 244; Scarisbrick, *Henry VIII*, p. 486.
58 Musée Royaux des Beaux-Arts de Belgique, Brussels.
59 Norris, *Costume*, p. 312.
60 *CSP Venetian, 1509–19*, p. 559.
61 Norris, *Costume*, p. 312.
62 *LP* III.i, 514.
63 *CSP Venetian, 1527–33*, p. 293.
64 Norris, *Tudor Costume*, p. 312.
65 *LP* XV, 231.
66 *CSP Venetian, 1509–19*, 336.
67 Pollard, *Henry VIII*, p. 340.

II

Henry VIII: European Prince and King of England

Hans Holbein's large group portrait *Henry VIII and the Barber Surgeons* presents the king dressed in red. His fur-lined cloth of gold robes of estate and the closed imperial crown emphasise his place at the pinnacle of English society and are beyond compare in England. The visual message was reinforced by the inscription which reads 'To Henry the eight the best and greatest King of England . . . Defender of the Faith, and next to Christ, supreme Head of the Church of England and Ireland' (Pl. IIb). The words and image combine to assert Henry VIII's personal magnificence. However, for Henry VIII to be seen in context, he must be compared with his peers, his fellow monarchs and princes of Christendom. This was certainly how Henry VIII saw himself. His growing collection of portraits at Whitehall included the Holy Roman emperor (10584), the kings of France, Spain, Scotland and Denmark (10639, 10584, 10702, 15366), the prince of Orange (10723), the archduke of Austria (15409), the dukes of Savoy, Bourbon and Saxony (10698, 10654, 10595), a former pope (15379) and the sultan of the Ottoman Empire (10728). Henry VIII was marking the rise of a new royal house in Europe. Henry VIII also displayed portraits of the English royal line from Henry V (10617) to Richard III (10650), so emphasising the house of Tudor as the rightful successors to the throne.

Drawing strongly on evidence from letters, which is expanded by reference to inventories, accounts and portraits, this chapter begins by reviewing what magnificence meant to a sixteenth-century king.[1] Henry VIII and many of the other rulers in Europe consciously used their clothes to reinforce their nationality, status and authority.[2] Therefore, this chapter places Henry VIII in his social and political context by comparing him to his fellow monarchs and rulers in Europe.

Magnificence and the role of royal dress

Magnificence is a difficult word to define because it encompasses a range of meanings and ideas.[3] It stems from the Aristotelian concept or virtue meaning 'liberality of expenditure combined with good taste'.[4] However, magnificence can also convey ideas of sovereign bounty or munificence, glory, greatness of reputation, sumptuous surroundings, grandeur or an imposing appearance. Consequently it was also used as a title, as with Lorenzo or Süleyman the Magnificent, and the Venetian ambassador referred to Henry VIII as 'Lord Magnifico'.[5] In spite of, or possibly because of, the gradations of meaning, the idea of magnificence as an essential royal trait recurred in contemporary writings ranging from household ordinances to drama.

Magnificence developed as a political and social concept at the Burgundian court, and it was promoted in the early sixteenth century in Fillastre's work *Toison d'Or*. It was regarded as the most important of the Burgundian virtues. As such, magnificence was a *vertu generalle* and justice was dependent on magnificence.[6] Henry VII used the idea of magnificence to promote the validity and legitimacy of the Tudors, just as Edward IV had done to promote the house of York. Edward IV's Black Book described the court of the biblical king Solomon, which was very magnificent, as 'the exemplar of householding' because:

> The trouth of Salamon is worthines was more than his fame did expresse; semyng also to her the euery master officer in his sober demenyng, his honestee, his riche araye, and all theyr mnerly cerimoniez don in that court, that eche of hem myzt be lykenyd to a king of her cuntree.[7]

When Holbein chose to depict Henry VIII as Solomon, the image must have been intended to bring this idea to mind (Pl. IIIa).[8] Such an image linked magnificence to a certain style of rule. It also linked magnificence to the use of specific objects and the rich swathes of cloth in this picture help to emphasise Solomon's wealth. Even so, there was always the danger of magnificence appearing as wasteful extravagance, which was just as open to criticism as parsimony was. Consequently, polemicists like Sir John Fortescue believed that magnificence was an essential facet of kingship. He identified the objects that typified royal grandeur in his book *The Governance of England*:

> riche clothes, riche furres, other than be wonned to fall vndre theyerely charges off his warderober, rich stones . . . and other juels and ornamentes conuenyent to his estate roiall . . . bie also horses off grete price, trappers, and do other such nobell and grete costes, as bi sitith is roiall mageste.[9]

Fortescue's text stresses the role of appropriate clothing and furnishings in asserting the monarch's rightful place at the head of English society. This view was epitomised by Henry VIII's sumptuary legislation which defined the king and his immediate family by their right to wear purple and cloth of gold.[10] While the dress of the king could create distance between the monarch and his subjects, it could also create proximity on specific occasions, so emphasising the king's role as *primus inter pares*, first amongst equals. This idea was demonstrated through the clothing Henry VIII provided for the revels and jousts, the livery he shared with the other Garter knights or as he processed to parliament.

According to Hall, Henry VIII's coronation banquet was 'greater than any Caesar had known', and on occasion Henry did take Julius Caesar as a role model. Other classical exemplars that caught the king's imagination included Hercules, and he dressed as this classical hero at his meeting with Francis I at Guisnes in 1520.[11] On this occasion Henry wanted to present himself as a *rex magnificus* in the true chivalric tradition that Hercules epitomised. Such an event allowed Henry to demonstrate his princely virtues or *virtus* of honour and justice because there was a strong link between magnificence and magnanimity, magnanimity and justice.

John Skelton's play *Magnificence* was written between 1515 and 1523. As the central character, Magnificence was compelled to face fortitude, one of the cardinal virtues, and adversity. Fairly early on in the play, Magnificence states that:

> For doubtless I perceive my magnificence
> Without measure lightly may fade
> Of too much liberty under the offence.[12]

It is telling that several references were made to the Merchant Taylors' company of London, making the obvious link between tailors, clothes and a sumptuous appearance. Although Skelton implies that the tailors had a rather over-inflated opinion of their skills:

> What, will ye waste wind and prate thus in vain?
> Ye have eaten sauce, I trow, at the Tailors' Hall.[13]

However, the play has been seen as criticising Henry VIII's false magnificence in comparison with his father's true magnificence which had a strict moral underpinning.[14]

Why was dress such a good vehicle for the expression of royal magnificence? In great part, it was the rarity of these expensive and sumptuous garments because no one else had access to such garments on such a scale. While a few members of the nobility, like Edward Stafford, duke of Buckingham, could rival the king's wardrobe, not even he could sustain a comparable level of expenditure without complaint.[15] Only slightly further down the social scale, access to silk clothing was limited to a very small group.[16]

Clothes have several other traits that make them ideal vehicles for royal magnificence. They can be transitional, marking the move from childhood to adulthood, from informal to formal or from one activity to the next. They can be ephemeral, as in the case of the revels clothing that was designed to create a temporary impression. They can be changeable, creating a particular image for one occasion or to convey a certain impression, and then worn in different combinations to create a new style. The evolving nature of dress in this period can be considered on two other levels. First, there were fashionable or small changes in details of garments, decoration, colour or cloth type which took place on an annual basis. Second, there were changes which can be charted over a longer time period that can be seen in the change in the range of garments worn. These long-term trends have been styled *tracht* changes.[17] The ability to replace and renew your wardrobe to reflect both sets of trends was the mark of the very wealthy.

Asserting royal authority through dress

When two sixteenth-century monarchs met on peaceful terms it was important that they were accorded the same level of honour and etiquette. Henry VIII's reign saw several occasions where he met with Francis I and Charles V, and each was orchestrated to ensure dignity was preserved. On Thursday, 8 June 1520, Henry VIII and Francis I met each other for the first time and their meeting was carefully choreographed to ensure that they were both mounted or on foot at the same time.[18] This sense of equality was further emphasised by wearing identical clothes, as Henry VIII and Charles V did when they rode from Greenwich to London on 6 June 1522. En route they changed into coats of cloth of gold embroidered with silver 'bothe of one suite'.[19] They appeared together two days later on Whit Sunday and again they emphasised their unity by dressing alike: 'themperor and the kyng with great honor both apparelled in cloth of siluer reysed, gounes and cotes and all their apparell white except their bonettes.'[20] Equally, Henry VIII and Francis I both wore white and cloth of silver when they met in the autumn of 1532.[21] Fictional representations of meetings between Francis and Henry, such as that depicted in the lower border of the Treaty to Withhold Consent to a General Council while the Pope Remains a Prisoner dated 18 August 1527, presented the same story.[22] Both men wore gowns of cloth of gold over long-skirted doublets with a black bonnet and closed imperial crown. Francis's gown was lined with ermine, Henry's with sable and, while there were differences in the colour of their doublet, hose and jerkins, these differences were minimal. The overall impression was of equality.

Henry VIII also met with the emperor Maximilian I during the 1513 campaign, but this was on slightly different terms to his meetings with Francis and Charles. On one level aximilian outranked Henry because an emperor outranks a king, yet on a more pragmatic level, Maximilian was being retained by Henry, he wore his livery and he was in receipt of wages. This complex relationship was expressed in the following terms when Maximilian met Henry and he was lodged in a tent of cloth of gold like the king: 'as no Emperor had ever been soldier to a king, so no soldier before was ever lodged in such a tent.'[23] Their ambiguous relationship continued after the 1513 campaign, as did Maximilian's use of clothing as an expression of deference. On 18 January 1516 Sir Robert Wingfield wrote to Wolsey concerning his interview with the emperor. Wingfield noted that Maximilian was very pleased to have

Henry's support and on hearing the news 'he put off his bonnet thrice'.[24]

Matters were very different when Francis I was captured by imperial troops at the battle of Pavia in 1525. Francis was held captive in Madrid, while awaiting ransom. When Charles came to visit Francis, he took off his hat but retained the little red bonnet he wore underneath, to convey a mixed message of courtesy while retaining the upper hand.[25] Similarly, the finality of the English victory over the Scots at Flodden in September 1513 was expressed succinctly by Catherine of Aragon in terms of access to and control over the clothes of the dead king James IV. Catherine wrote to Henry from Woburn en route to the shrine of Our Lady of Walsingham to give thanks for the victory. She stated proudly that 'your Grace shall see how I keep my promise, sending you for your banners a King's coat'.[26]

Creating a sense of Englishness through dress

Castiglione's central character in his book *The Courtier* commented on the regional variations to be observed in styles of dress, noting that 'some dress after the French style, others like the Spaniards and others again like the Germans; and there are those also who dress after the manner of Turks . . . It would, therefore, be rewarding to know, given all this confusion, what way is best'.[27] He went on to state that 'the French tend to be . . . overdressed and the Germans . . . their clothes are skimped', while true elegance was embodied by the Italians.[28] Perhaps not surprisingly, English dress did not feature on Castiglione's list. However, references to English attitudes towards, and styles of, dress can be found in other sources such as the books of costume plates that started to be produced in central Europe by the mid sixteenth century.[29] These books illustrated the styles of dress that characterised the different European countries and the accompanying text often made a link between dress, social standing and morality.

The English had a strong sense of their own national identity which was often expressed by comparing themselves favourably with others. They had a reputation for ostentation in their dress which was exaggerated when Henry VIII met Francis I at the Field of Cloth of Gold in 1520. The size of the livery collars and other chains worn by the English attracted scathing comments from the Venetian ambassador.[30] These collars denoted knighthood, certain posts in the royal household or at court and membership of the king's council. However, in terms of dress, the basic garments were held in common throughout north-western Europe. Even so, there were subtle variations in details such as necklines, colour preference and styles of decoration that created the distinctive nature of dress at the different European courts. Equally, contemporaries were aware of characteristic styles of dress worn in other countries and the features which allow identification. And there was an interest in styles of dress derived from other countries.[31]

The English climate inevitably played a part in influencing what was worn and when. On 4 June 1529 Cardinal Campeggio, papal legate to the Tudor court, wrote to Jacobo Salviati, bishop of Verona and secretary to Clement VII, to inform him about events relating to Henry's search for an annulment. However, as a postscript he noted that, 'Here we are still wearing our winter clothing, and use fire as if it were January. Never did I witness more inconstant weather'.[32] Some years earlier, the Venetian ambassador had observed in 1513 that 'In England it is always windy, and however warm the weather the natives invariably wear furs'.[33] The vagaries of the English weather were emphasised by Bartholomew Ticcioni. He ended his letter to Margaret of Savoy, asking the emperor to send him some money because 'the weather is much hotter than he should have expected, and he can no longer wear with honour his winter clothes'. He also requested some silk for his clothing.[34] This need for a range of clothes to reflect seasonal changes is very evident in Henry VIII's wardrobe of the robes.[35]

Henry VIII had typical English colouring: pale skin, pale eyes and fair or sandy hair. This colouring appears to have influenced what colours of cloth the English bought and, consequently, what cloth was imported. Stephen Vaughan acknowledged that there were distinctive national tastes for certain colours when Sir William Paget commissioned him to buy some white damask in Brussels. After searching for some time, Vaughan reported that all he could find were 'suche slubberyd cullours as I wold be shamyd to send yow'.[36] Two days later Vaughan wrote to Paget again, stating that he:

> cannot get good white damask. All the good silks are sent into England. The Court here is nothing so gallant of women as our Court in England. Here are no dames that will wear whites. They be but counterfeits to our dames, so that whites, yellows, reds, blues and such fresh colours go from hence straight into England.[37]

The English fondness for bright, clear colours described by Vaughan was not restricted to women. Henry's wardrobe warrants regularly included orders for doublets, hose and gowns in these 'fresh colours', including yellow, white, orange and carnation.

While bright colours were popular, so was good black cloth. The portraits of Holbein, Bronzino and Titian all indicate the frequency with which their sitters opted to be painted dressed in black.[38] Good or true black was expensive and it made an excellent foil for jewellery. As such it was favoured by rulers including René of Anjou and Philip the Good, as well as finding favour at the Spanish court.[39] Although neither Henry VII nor his son were painted wearing black, it also played a very significant part in their wardrobes, both as young men and when they got older. In this the Tudor kings were echoing well established trends. Black was elegant and when embellished with ornate self-coloured embroidery, guards, slashing and passementerie it was far from understated.

French styles of dress were influential at the English court. In a letter dated 17 November 1497, Andreas Franciscius described England and the English. He noted that 'They dress in the French fashion, except that their suits are more full, and, accordingly, more out of shape'.[40] This comment emphasises the role of France as the arbiter of fashion in northern Europe, while hinting that the English could not, or did not, always follow their lead. Consequently, news from France was always of interest. On 14 December 1514 Silvestro de' Gigli, bishop of Worcester, described the meeting of Francis I and the pope at Bologna. He noted 'silk and gold and new fashions in which the French are very clever' which he attributed to 'French vanity'. As might be expected, Francis was dressed in cloth of gold for the meeting. However, Francis was accompanied by 300 archers 'who looked like bargemen, with dirty faces, with greasy and bald coats'. Their lack of gold livery collars caught Silvestro's attention, as did the fact that 'they showed no diminution . . . of their innate haughtiness'.[41] Even so, the French influence at the English court was pervasive.[42]

By 1547 Henry had garments in a range of foreign styles in his wardrobe, including items in the French, Spanish, Italian and Turkish mode, as well as French and Milan bonnets. By adopting garments from other countries, Henry VIII could express a sense of his cosmopolitan taste, make overtures of friendship or make an alliance explicit. It is evident that these continental, slightly exotic styles, appealed to the king. As indicated above, there is also the question of how accurately foreign styles were copied and how far accuracy mattered. In addition to borrowing the style of a complete garment, it was also possible to adopt and adapt styles of ornament such as slashing. Consequently, the defining features of English dress in the mid Tudor period cannot be easily codified after so long, but the factors that were important can be drawn out of contemporary thought (Fig. 2.1). These include a fondness for both bright colours and black, low-cut necklines for women, a bulky, layered appearance for men, fur for warmth and status, some use of slashing but not in such an extreme form as found elsewhere in Europe, resulting in a style that was distinctive but not unduly elegant.

2.1 *Thomas Wentworth, first baron, 1549, attributed to John Bettes. Wentworth's substantial image, created by the fur-lined black gown worn over his doublet, is very much in the English style. National Portrait Gallery, London (NPG 1851)*

Henry VIII in a European context

At the start of his *Chronicle* of Henry VIII's reign, Hall summed up the state of play in Europe:

> Now after the death of this noble prince [Henry VII], Henry the VIII, sonne to Kyng Henry the VII beganne his reigne the xxii daie of April, in the yere of our Lorde 1509 and in the xviii yere of his bodily age: Maximian then beeyng Emperoore and Lewes the xii reignyng in Fraunce. And Fernando beeyng the kyng of Arragon and Castell, and kyng Iames the fourthe then rulyng ouer the Scottes.[43]

The emphasis placed on Henry's fellow monarchs put Henry in his social and political context. Although England was on the periphery of the Continent physically in 1509, she was closely bound into Europe by trade, political affinity and religious allegiance. English kings before and after Henry consciously sought interaction with their European neighbours and links were made and maintained through marriage, alliances, the sending and receiving of ambassadors and trade. A new king presented an opportunity for reframing or reinforcing traditional allegiances. On 8 May 1509 the Venetian Sanuto described Henry VIII's accession in more partisan terms when he stated that 'This King . . . is liberal and handsome, the friend of Venice and the enemy of France'.[44] This comment indicates the shifting pattern of alliances and the tenuous friendships which shaped the balance of power in Europe. England was undeniably a minor player when compared to France and Spain, but English monarchs could still influence the balance of power, even if only fleetingly.[45]

In an age of personal monarchy, the physical appearance and youth of the monarch played an important part in determining and reinforcing the royal image. When Henry VIII came to the throne he was a young king aged 17, set in the context of an ageing European monarchy: Louis XII of France (47), Ferdinand of Aragon (47), Maximilian I of the Holy Roman Empire (50). By 1516 this situation had changed. Henry was now 25 and his immediate rivals were Francis I of France, aged 22, and Charles I, king of Spain, aged 16 (soon to be the emperor, Charles V). This resulted in a spirit of rivalry expressed through feats of arms and armed conflict. In August 1519 Henry wrote to Pope Leo X, noting that if God granted

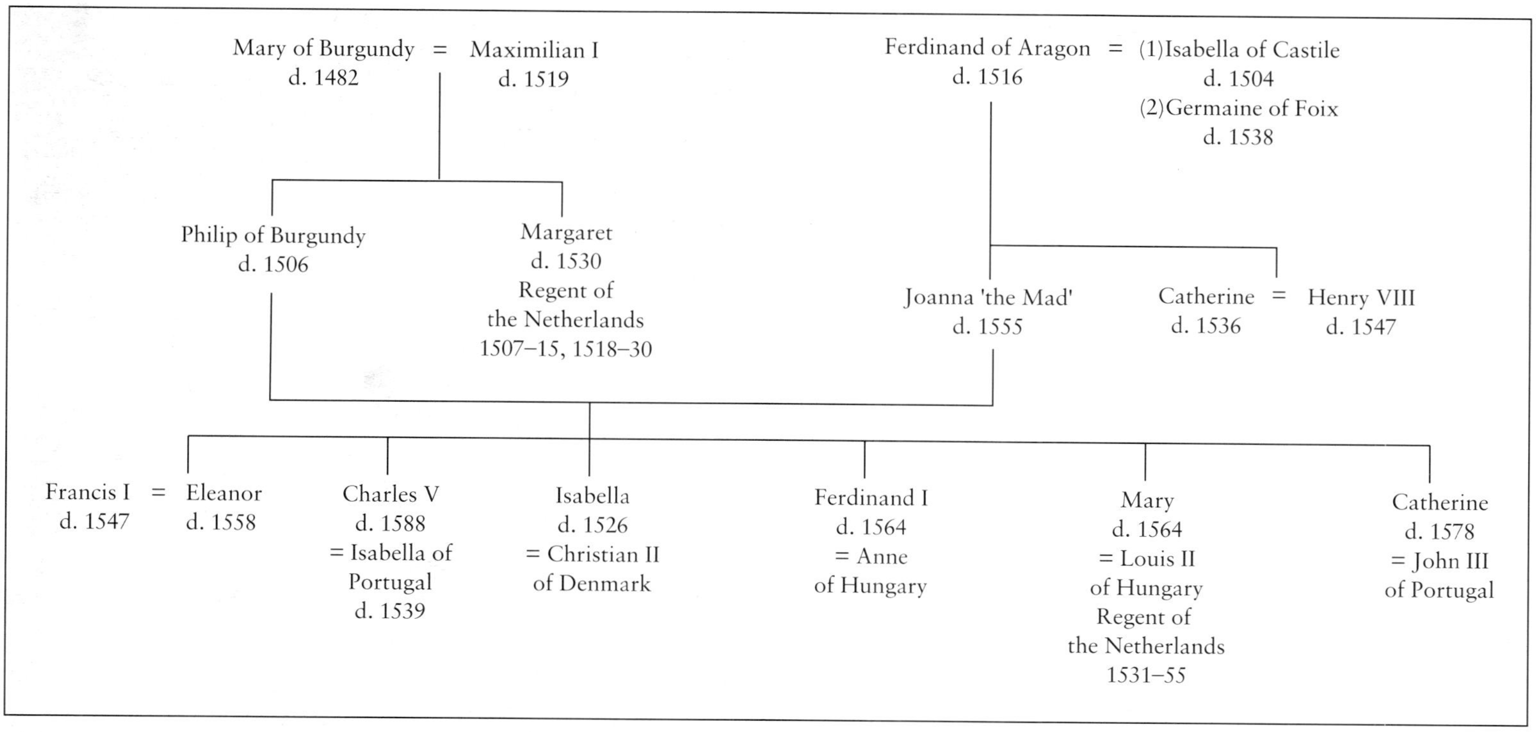

Family tree 1 The rulers of Europe in the mid-Tudor period

him a son before the expedition against the Turks departed, he would lead the army in person.[46]

Henry VIII described England as a little country in the corner of Europe.[47] However, small boundaries could be compensated for by large claims and impressive titles. On 15 January 1535 Henry VIII declared in his privy chamber in the presence of Sir Thomas Audley, lord chancellor, Thomas, duke of Norfolk and treasurer of England, Thomas, earl of Wiltshire, keeper of the privy seal, and Thomas Cromwell, chief secretary and others that from this point he should be styled 'Henricus Octavus, Dei gratia Angliae et Franciae Rex, Fidei Defensor et Dominus Hiberniae et in Terra Supremum Caput Anglicanae Ecclesiae'.[48]

For the first two decades of his reign, Henry VIII presented himself as a Renaissance prince through his use of court culture, through access to the English order of chivalry and through the use of his fashionable wardrobe. As part of his wish to be *primus inter pares* with Francis I and Charles V, he sought a papal title in recognition of his religious orthodoxy, on a par with the titles of the *Most Christian King* and the *Most Catholic King*, given to the kings of France and Spain. In 1521 Henry's efforts were rewarded with the title of *Defender of the Faith*. However, the late 1520s saw a shift in Henry's position within Europe from a highly orthodox stance to one which challenged and then rejected papal authority. Henry's Break with Rome was brought about by a series of Acts of Parliament including the Submission of the Clergy (1532), the Act in Restraint of Appeals (1533) and the Act of Supremacy (1534). After this point Henry had to project an image of strong kingship that could resist challenges from external Catholic powers and internal opposition to religious change. His retention of many traditional facets of the royal liturgical wardrobe helped to emphasise the elements of continuity in his reign.[49]

Henry VIII's interaction with the three leading European powers

The papacy and the Holy Roman Empire were at the heart of European politics in the early sixteenth century, but the Ottoman Empire was fast making its presence felt in the subtly shifting balance of power. On 18 June 1525 Hieronymous Niger reported how the pope rode from the Vatican to St John Lateran on 30 April on a Turkish horse. The horse could be seen to represent the newly formed treaty against the Turks between the pope, the emperor elect, the king of England, Archduke Ferdinand and the duke of Milan, but 'it is commonly believed to be against France'.[50] Not surprisingly the leaders of these three powers were represented in the English royal collection because they all impinged on Henry's kingship to differing degrees. Henry owned a tapestry depicting 'the Busshoppe of Rome and Themperor' (13523) and stained clothes with 'the picture of Charles themperor' (10722) and 'the picture of Solymaname the torque beinge his whole stature' (10728). Although Henry had been a loyal supporter of the papacy at his accession, the situation had changed drastically by 1547. By then, Henry displayed examples of markedly anti-papal imagery in the form of 'a table of the busshopp of Rome and the foure euaungelistes casting stones apon him' (12321) which can be identified as Girolamo da Treviso's *Four Evangelists stoning the Pope*.

THE PAPACY

By the sixteenth century the papacy was well established as an ecclesiastical and secular power.[51] According to the *Great Chronicle* the pope presented a cap and sword to a new monarch as an indication of papal support for their monarchy: 'The effect and cause of the sond of the said capp & sword by auctorite whereof the kyng was admytted by the pope and his hool counsayll protectour and deffendour of ye Church of Cryst.'[52] Leo X granted a sword and cap to Henry VIII, which was presented to him on 21 May 1514.[53] Leonard Spinelly, of the pope's chamber, was met when he landed on 19 May and accompanied to London where he deposited the cap and sword on the high altar of St Paul's. On 21 May, Henry, accompanied by the nobility, the ambassadors of Spain, Venice, Saxony and Friesland and the captive duke of Longueville, and William Browne, lord mayor of London, went to St Paul's. They processed, preceded by the pope's sword and the king's own sword. Then 'The cap was put on the King's head, and the sword girt about him by the Archbishop of Canterbury, after the order of the book'.[54] Afterwards, the king held a dinner for the ambassadors and a Venetian observer noted that the Spanish ambassador did not stay because he was 'ashamed of the peace made by his King with France'.[55] James Worsley's inventory taken in 1521 included entries for a sword and cap, which must be those presented to the king in 1514: 'a Riche swerde that was sent the king from the popes holynes the hafte & shethe of siluer & gilt with a longe gyrdell of cloth of gold with bokelles pendauntes and studdes of siluer and gilt' [B335] and 'a Cappe of mayntenaunce of russet veluete with the holy goste enbrauderd with perles and a longe gyrdell of gold of damaske faste to the same' [B336].

The pope also sent golden roses. In April 1510 Julius II wrote to William Warham to inform him that he was sending Henry a golden rose, which he had blessed and anointed with crism 'et odorifero musco aspersam'. Warham had to present the rose to the king at a special mass, the details of which were outlined in the letter.[56] Henry rewarded Dr Fisher 'that brought an halowed Rose from the popes holynes' on 8 July with £100.[57] By 1521 two golden roses were listed in the royal jewel house:

> Re^d from the popes holynes in a^o ij^do h viij . . . a Rose of gold w^t ix braunches standing upon iij acornes & a corse safor in the toppe
> Re^d from the popes holynes by doctor hanyball a Rose of gold w^t ix braunches standing upon iij lyons fete and a corse saphre in the toppe.[58]

Equally, the papacy could confer titles on kings in acknowledgement of their piety and support for the Catholic church. Henry VIII was keen to acquire such a title and on 25 August 1521 Wolsey informed Richard Pace that he was to present Henry's book, *Assertio Septem Sacramentorum*, to the pope 'covered with cloth of gold, subscribed by the king's hand; wherein the King's grace hath devised, inserted in the said book by the King's own hand'.[59] Several months later Pope Leo X conferred the title *Fidei Defensor* upon Henry VIII on 11 October. According to Lorenzo Campeggio the book was an 'aureus libellus', while John Clerk recorded that the pope had read it with enthusiasm.[60] Although Leo X died on 2 December, Henry's new title was celebrated in February 1522.[61] By 1542 six copies of the king's book were listed under the abbreviated title of *Assertio Regis* in the library at Whitehall (2420–25).

The political role of the pope was very significant, both in terms of internal politics within Italy, as in the case of the election of Giovanni de'Medici as Leo X in March 1513, and the potential for patronage for his family and Medici clients, and in terms of European politics. Consequently, each papal election provoked much interest in Europe and Wolsey's candidature was promoted at the elections in 1521 and 1523.[62] Both Henry and Charles V supported Wolsey's aspiration to be the second English pope.

In 1523 Giulio de'Medici was elected and he took the name Clement VII. This papal election was to affect Henry on many levels. On 30 November Cardinal Gonzaga wrote to the king, apologising for not sending him any hawks and explaining that he had been prevented by the death of Adrian VI and the need to go to Rome.[63] More significantly, Rome was sacked by imperial troops in 1527 and this had profound consequences for Henry when he sought an annulment from Charles V's aunt, Catherine of Aragon (Fig. 2.2). On Sunday 29 June 1533 Clement VII celebrated mass, attended by the ambassadors of Ferrara, Milan, Venice and England who bore the water for the pope's hands. On Wednesday 9 July the excommunication of Henry VIII was requested as a consequence of his marriage to Anne Boleyn. On Friday 11 July Henry's excommunication was announced, unless he repudiated Anne and took Catherine of Aragon back by October of that year.[64]

Papal influence extended into England prior to the Break with Rome in several ways. The most visible reminder was the presence of an English cardinal in the person of Thomas Wolsey. However, more importantly, when Henry appealed to Rome for the annulment of his marriage to Catherine of Aragon in 1529, Clement VII sent Cardinal Campeggio to preside over the hearing. Campeggio tried to persuade Catherine of Aragon to enter a convent as Louis XII's wife had done, and 'who still lived in greatest honour and reputation with God'.[65] When all else failed, Campeggio adjourned the legatine court and Charles Brandon stated that 'there was never a legate nor cardinal that did good in England'.[66] Brandon would not be the last to express this view.

THE HOLY ROMAN EMPIRE

Events in the Holy Roman Empire had a direct impact on Henry VIII in several respects. At the time of Henry's accession, Maximilian I of Austria (1459–1519) was Holy Roman Emperor. He had been elected as emperor in 1493 aged 34, although he had held the title of King of the Romans since 1486. He married twice and had three legitimate children: Philip the Fair (1478–1506), Margaret (1480–1530) and Franz (1481), 12 illegitimate children and six grandchildren, including the future Charles V and Ferdinand I. While Maximilian was emperor, there were four major secular powers in Europe: France, Spain, the Empire and England. Consequently,

Pl. Ia *Henry VIII, unknown artist,* c. 1520. *National Portrait Gallery, London (NPG 4690)*

Pl. Ib *Henry VIII, by Joos van Cleve,* c. 1535, *RCIN 403368, LC16. The Royal Collection © 2004, Her Majesty the Queen Elizabeth II*

Pl. Ic *Henry VIII by Hans Holbein the Younger,* c. 1536, *cat. no. 191. © Museo Thyssen-Bornemisza, Madrid*

Pl. Id *Henry VIII, unknown artist,* c. 1542. *National Portrait Gallery, London (NPG 163)*

Pl. IIa *Henry VIII, by Hans Holbein the Younger,* c. 1536, *(WAG 1350). National Museums of Liverpool (The Walker)*

Pl. IIb *Henry VIII and the Barber Surgeons, by Hans Holbein the Younger,* c. 1540. *By courtesy of The Worshipful Company of Barbers*

Pl. IIIA *Charles Brandon and Mary Tudor, attributed to Jan van Mabuse, Woburn Abbey. By kind permission of His Grace the Duke of Bedford and the Trustees of the Bedford Estates*

Pl. IIIB *Miniature of Solomon and the Queen of Sheba by Hans Holbein the Younger, c. 1535. The Royal Collection © 2006, Her Majesty the Queen Elizabeth II*

Pl. IIIC *Henry VII attributed to Michael Sittow, 1505. National Portrait Gallery, London (NPG 416)*

Pl. IIID *Elizabeth of York, unknown artist, 1500-03. National Portrait Gallery, London (NPG 291)*

Pl. IVA *Prince Arthur, Anglo Flemish School, c. 1500. Private collection; on loan to the National Portrait Gallery, London (NPG L221)*

Pl. IVB *Henry VIII at prayer, from the Black Book of the Garter (MS DOC 162a). Reproduced by permission of the Dean and Canons of Windsor*

Pl. IVC *Garter knights in procession, from the Black Book of the Garter (MS DOC 163). Reproduced by permission of the Dean and Canons of Windsor*

Pl. VA *Henry VIII processing to parliament, 1512. The Coronation Roll, Trinity College, Cambridge*

Pl. VB *Catherine of Aragon, unknown artist,* c. *1530. National Portrait Gallery, London (NPG 163)*

Pl. VC *Anne Boleyn, unknown artist,* c. *1530. National Portrait Gallery, London (NPG 668)*

Pl. VIA *Jane Seymour, by Hans Holbein the Younger, c. 1536. The Hague, 278. Royal Picture Gallery, Mauritshuis, The Hague*

Pl. VIB *Jane Seymour, by Hans Holbein the Younger, c. 1536. Vienna, GG 881. Kunsthistorisches Museum, Wien*

Pl. VIC *Detail of Henry VIII with Prince Edward and Jane Seymour, from* The Family of Henry VIII, *unknown artist, c. 1545. RCIN 405796 OM 43. The Royal Collection © 2004, Her Majesty the Queen Elizabeth II*

Pl. VIIA *Mary Tudor, attributed to Master John, 1544. National Portrait Gallery, London (NPG 428)*

Pl. VIIB *Detail of Henry VIII arriving at Guisnes riding in procession with Wolsey, from* The Field of the Cloth of Gold, *unknown artist, c. 1545. RCIN 405794 OM 25. The Royal Collection © 2004, Her Majesty the Queen Elizabeth II*

Pl. VIIIa *Henry Howard, earl of Surrey, by William Scrots,* c. *1545. National Portrait Gallery, London (NPG 5291)*

Pl. VIIIb *Detail showing Henry VIII on board ship from* The Embarkation of Henry VIII at Dover, *unknown artist. RCIN 405793, OM 24. The Royal Collection © 2004, Her Majesty the Queen Elizabeth II*

Pl. VIIIc *Henry VIII jousting before Catherine of Aragon. The Westminster Tournament Roll, The College of Arms*

2.2 *Detail from the Treaty to Withhold Consent to a General Council while the Pope Remains a Prisoner, 18 August 1527. The figures in clerical dress represent the Catholic church in captivity to the emperor after imperial troops had sacked Rome. The National Archive E30/1114*

foreign policy and trade were governed by a shifting pattern of alliances and treaties.

Maximilian was described in 1513 as being 'of middle height, with open and manly countenance; pallid complexion; has a snub nose and grey beard. Is affable, frugal, an enemy to pomp. His attendants are dressed in black silk or woollen'.[67] While on this occasion Maximilian's household was in mourning for his wife, towards the end of his life Maximilian sought to save money by reducing his expenditure on the livery issued to his household.[68] Maximilian was frequently short of money and he was described as 'the man of few pence'. Pope Julius II went further and dismissed him as 'light and inconstant, always begging for other men's money which he wastes in chamois-hunting'.[69]

From 1514 Maximilian travelled with his coffin and he died five years later on 12 January 1519. His death raised the question of who would succeed him. In 1513 Maximilian had offered to secure Henry's election as his successor. Henry declined, as he did in 1516 and 1517. However, in 1519 Henry put his name forward as the third candidate, standing alongside Charles V and Francis I.[70] His motivation was undoubtedly the same as that of Francis I: the prestige of holding such an office and to prevent Charles V being elected.[71] Henry and Francis prudently withdrew so Charles was elected unopposed, leaving only three secular powers in Europe. England was now in the advantageous position of holding the balance of power. Equally, some political theorists believed that England was an empire in its own right. In 1517 Cuthbert Tunstall told Henry that 'the crown of England is an Empire of itself much better than now the Empire of Rome'.[72]

Calls for religious reform from within the Holy Roman Empire, most notably by Martin Luther, were to have a marked effect in England. While Luther's beliefs were to transform Europe, his appearance belied this. In April 1521 Luther was described as being 'of middle height, emaciated from care and study so that you can almost count his bones through his skin . . . He is affable and friendly, in no sense dour or arrogant'.[73] Although Henry VIII did not share Luther's religious beliefs, he was quick to see how the political implications of Luther's ideas could resolve his marital problems. Luther was aware of Henry's actions and when Henry's first marriage was annulled he noted that 'Junker Heintz will be God and do whatever he lusts'.[74]

While the Empire was made up of a number of princely states and cities, the region was associated with a distinctive style of dress. Slashing was the distinguishing feature of

German dress and garments decorated with slashing were often described as being in the 'Almain' style. Even so, slashing is usually cited as developing as a consequence of the Swiss victory over Charles the Bold, duke of Burgundy, at the Battle of Grandson in 1476. However, there is portrait evidence to suggest that slashing developed on women's sleeves in Italy in the late 1480s.[75] The style continued in Europe and on 8 August 1540 Sir Henry Wotton wrote to Henry from Brussels describing the military exploits of the duke of Cleves, adding that it 'must needs be a good sight, to see a lantzknecht, his cap full of feathers, his doublet and hosen cut and jagged, his sword by his side, an arcabowse in his neck'.[76] Examples of male dress decorated with slashing were illustrated in the costume book of Matthäus Schwarz, a citizen of Augsburg from 1496–1564 who kept a pictorial record of his own clothes (Fig. 2.3).[77] The introduction of slashing to the English court has been linked to the marriage of Henry's younger sister Mary to Louis XII of France. While this is hard to prove, a number of garments made in the 'Almain style' featured in Henry's accounts and inventories, especially in the 1510s and 1520s. However, by the 1540s the king no longer favoured this style of decoration.

THE OTTOMAN EMPIRE

When Catherine of Aragon stated that 'The King of France is the greatest Turk', she was implying that Francis I was not to be trusted because of his tacit alliance with Süleyman the Magnificent.[78] Under the leadership of Süleyman the Magnificent (1494–1566), the Ottoman Turks rose to be a very significant power in Europe. Süleyman was born on 6 November 1494 at Trebizond and he became sultan in 1520. Through his military campaigns in mainland Europe and the Mediterranean and as an ally to the French and the Lutheran princes in opposition to Charles V, he played a key role in European

2.3 *Das Schwarzsche Trachtenbuch, inv. no. 1769. Published with the kind permission of the Herzog-Anton-Ulrich Museums, Braunschweig, Kunstmuseum des Landes Niedersachsensen*

politics until the treaty of Chateau-Cambrésis in 1559. On 24 September 1526 Campeggio, the papal legate, wrote to Henry stating that 'All Christendom is in danger from the Turk, now that the king of Hungary has been defeated and slain'.[79]

The impact of Süleyman's sultanate was felt at Henry's court in several ways. The threat of war was an underlying theme, as indicated when the duke of Norfolk wrote to Cromwell 16 April 1538, 'I am sorry Christendom is likely to suffer by the Turk this summer, but am pleased that we are like to sit without business and that the King's back friends [i.e. those who watch the king's back] have more need of His Majesty than he of them'.[80] However, the Turks also represented the exotic and arabesque ('rabask' work) and Moresque designs derived from Islamic sources were popular at the Tudor court. Henry's doublet in the Thyssen portrait was couched with arabesque designs (Pl. Ic). Equally Turkish styles of dress, or what the English perceived to be Turkish styles, pervaded both fashionable dress and the costumes produced for the revels in the 1540s. Henry owned a number of gowns in the Turkish style, including 'A Turquey gowne of Crimsen veluett of a newe making Embraudered with Venice golde and silver like vnto Clowdes lined with Crimsen Taphata faced with Crimsen satten' (14194). Cawarden's store of revels clothes included

> viij Cootes for Turkes of Clothe of golde with workes Videlicet purple blacke and grene garded vpon paliwise with <blewe> Sarcennet longe sleues of clothe of golde And blewe satten thunder sleues of redd & white / Sarcennet Lozengewise viij hedde peces to the same Turkes fashion blewe redd and yellowe Sarcennette. (8627)

Süleyman earned his epithet through his sumptuous court and his military achievements. While Henry VIII excluded himself from English sumptuary law, Süleyman's magnificent appearance was achieved by ignoring the Muslim sumptuary laws or *hadith* that stated that men were not to wear silk. Süleyman and his predecessor had access to Italian silks as well as to very high quality Ottoman silks, as indicated by a reference in a 1505 Bayazid Treasury inventory to 'a gown of black Italian pile on pile velvet with roses, lined or trimmed with cotton and with sable furs'.[81] In 1544 Jerome Maurand witnessed an audience with Süleyman who was dressed in a cream satin caftan and a turban with a bonnet of red velvet decorated with a brooch with a ruby the size of a walnut.[82] A cream satin caftan in the Topkapi Saray, decorated with impressed lines and similar to the garment described above, has been tentatively identified as having belonged to Süleyman.[83]

The principal male garment of the Turkish court was the caftan which placed the emphasis on the quality of the fabric rather than the complexity of cut and construction. The caftan was usually full length but it could be made shorter for riding, hunting or fighting. The upper body was fairly fitted to the waist and then the skirts flared out. The sleeves could be either long or short; those with short sleeves often had matching full-length sleeves that were attached with buttons. Buttons running down the front from the neck to the waist were the usual method of fastening and they often looped into decorative frogging. Caftans could be quilted or fur-lined for warmth in the winter or just lined with cotton for summer wear.[84] By the 1540s Henry VIII started to order cassocks which echoed elements of the caftan's cut.

As in western male dress, the visual impact was created by wearing several layers often of contrasting colours. The commander of the Ottoman fleet in 1533 was described as wearing 'a gown of yellow satin and over that one of damask with great flowers in gold thread. Over that he had one in scarlet'.[85]

Unlike European monarchs, the Ottoman sultans did not wear a crown as a symbol of their authority, favouring a jewelled turban instead. However, Süleyman was quite prepared to adopt western symbols of authority to stress his intention to conquer Europe. In March 1532 Marino Sanuto was shown a crowned helmet that had been commissioned from Venetian goldsmiths by Ibrahim Pasha, grand vizier to Süleyman. The jewel covered helmet cost 144,400 ducats and it was decorated with four crowns. Süleyman wore the crowned helmet as he rode in procession outside the walls of Vienna in May of that year when his troops were camped outside the city.[86] On auspicious or dangerous occasions Süleyman could wear a linen or cotton talismanic shirt decorated with prayers and verses from the Koran. In 1539 Hürrem Sultan sent a talismanic shirt to Süleyman while he was on campaign, urging him to wear it because 'it had sacred names woven in it and would turn aside bullets'.[87] While Henry's shirts did not have such talismanic properties, they did acquire a degree of importance by being worn next to the king's skin and so in direct contact with royalty.[88]

Royal wardrobes and royal style: analysis of four case-studies

Sumptuous clothes could help establish and then maintain a successful monarch's reputation for magnificence and strong rule, but clothes could not disguise weak government or poor political acumen. A brief analysis of the way in which four of Henry's contemporaries used their wardrobes puts Henry's own use of clothes into context. These four individuals typified the following approaches: a flamboyant use of clothes, the creation of a specific identity, a lack of interest in clothes for their own sake and the use of clothes to distract attention from weak or ineffective rule. Henry shared his approach to clothes with Francis I. For them, their clothes were integral to the creation and maintenance of a magnificent royal image.

ELEGANT CONSPICUOUS CONSUMPTION OF CLOTHES: FRANCIS I

Unlike Henry VIII, Francis I was not the son of a king. He was born at Cognac on 12 September 1494. His father was Charles, count of Angoulême, from a junior branch of the Valois, and his mother Louise of Savoy was the daughter of the count of Bresse. As such he was the cousin of Charles VIII.

After the death of Anne of Brittany's short-lived son in 1512, Francis was styled as the dauphin.[89] A combination of a natural love of clothes and a need to assert himself as the rightful heir may well explain how Francis used his wardrobe to define his rule.

At the time of his accession Francis was 20. He was crowned on 25 January 1515 in Reims cathedral and after he went on pilgrimage to the priory of Corbeny to visit the shrine of Saint-Marcoul.[90] On 8 February 1515 Charles Brandon wrote to Wolsey, asking for money because 'I am fain to buy new array, for the King will have us at his coronation, and . . . to bring him at his entry, the which will not be done at little charge'.[91] Francis made very effective use of the liturgical and ceremonial year to project certain, often contrasting, images of his kingship: humility, magnificence, wealth and informality. In April 1516 Lord Mountjoy wrote to Henry describing how Francis had gone in procession at Lyons, which was generally believed to have been 'to pray for the victory against the Emperor' and on that day 'the King went barefoot and wore a gown of silver tinsel'.[92] When Francis granted a public audience in Paris to the English ambassadors on 17 December 1518, he 'was dressed in a robe of cloth of silver, figured with beautiful flowers, the lining being of Spanish heron's feathers. His doublet was of very costly cloth of gold. He wore no crown; only his usual cloth cap'.[93] As these and other sources make clear, Francis favoured white cloth of gold and silver for formal occasions.

Francis and Henry shared the same build and the same attitude to their kingship. In 1520 Edward Hall described Francis as a 'goodly prince, stately of countenaunce, mery of chere, broune coloured, great iyes, high nosed, bigge lipped, faire brested and shoulders, small legges, and long fete'.[94] When courtiers sought agreement between England and France, they often made comparisons between Henry and Francis. In February 1542 Paget wrote to Henry telling him how the admiral of France had 'entertained the writer by saying how like their masters were, not only in personage, but also in wisdom and affection, delighting both in hunting, in hawking, in building, in apparel, in stones, in jewels, and of like affection one to another' (Fig. 2.4).[95] Francis's love of clothes was summed up by Marino Cavalli, the Venetian ambassador to France, in 1546: 'His dress . . . is full of braids and trimmings, rich in precious stones and ornaments; even his doublets are woven with gold thread; his shirt is of fine quality and comes out through the doublet's opening in accordance in French fashion.'[96]

For all its splendour on specific occasions, the French court had a degree of informality and a measure of easy access to the king and the king's apartments not known in England. Members of Francis's household wore their hats in his presence. Equally, the king could appear before ambassadors and other important dignitaries informally dressed. On 3 February 1517 Sir Robert Wingfield wrote to Henry, noting how Francis had 'left to give audience to the Archbishop of Paris, which he did, booted and spurred and returned the same afternoon'.[97] When Clarenceux herald was sent to France in April 1520 to proclaim the challenge for the jousts, Francis I met him on his arrival even though he was 'coifed and in his nightgown'.[98]

2.4 *Equestrian portrait of Francis I, by Jean Clouet, Musée du Louvre. Francis I wears a red textile base or skirt over his armour in this equestrian portrait, and the base is the same colour as the horse harness and trappings. Photo: RMN*

Francis I's first wife, Claude, was the eldest daughter of Louis XII. She died aged 24, having had seven children in eight years, five of whom lived beyond infancy. However, only two, Henry and Marguerite, outlived their parents.[99] His second wife was Eleanor of Austria, queen of Portugal, and the widowed sister of Charles V. This marriage was linked to the Peace of Cambrai in 1529, the treaty which gave Francis I his freedom. Eleanor often chose to wear Spanish dress to emphasise her family ties to her French husband. Over 12 years later a meeting between Francis and Charles was arranged in January 1540, and Bonner reported to Cromwell that 'Francis would have declared more mirth abroad than he could perceive in him. He had on a scarlet cloak and looked pale'.[100]

FOLLOWING FRENCH FASHION: JAMES V

The relationship between England and Scotland was complex and exacerbated by their close proximity.[101] Scotland was a small country, a fifth of the size of England, and consequently royal income from its landed estates was modest. Under James III, royal income was approximately £5,000 per annum, a tenth of English royal revenues. Although James IV and V were to double royal income, rising inflation and debasement undermined the benefits of this. Government centred on the monarchy but a strong government was limited by the frequent minorities and marked regional independence.[102] Even so, Scotland had good economic and political links with France, the Netherlands and Scandinavia, and the court was heavily influenced by Renaissance culture.

When James IV signed the Treaty of Perpetual Peace with Henry VII in 1502, he agreed to marry Margaret Tudor. Consequently, James IV was Henry VIII's brother-in-law, and his son, James V, was Henry's nephew. In spite of a planned meeting in 1541, uncle and nephew never met because James did not attend. The Scottish defeat at Flodden on 9 September 1513 resulted in the death of James IV and the accession of James V aged 18 months. His mother shared the regency with the young king's uncle, John, duke of Albany, who had spent a lot of time in France. Albany's aspirations to power during the minority of James V caused anxiety in several quarters. Jean de Planis wrote to Wolsey in October 1515, observing that for the opening of the Scottish parliament Albany had walked in state with the sword, the sceptre and his ducal coronet carried before him.[103] Margaret's role as regent during the early minority of her son James V was equally charged: although she was widow of one Scots king and mother of another, she was also English and a Tudor.[104]

Gifts of clothing to James V and his court became part of the struggle between Henry VIII and Francis I over who could exert influence in Scotland. A report sent to Henry dated 20 January 1524 noted 'the Scots have pensions out of France and velvets and silks from the King's wardrobe'.[105] When Henry sent Lord William Howard to Scotland as his ambassador in October 1534, the king's instructions stated that Howard should 'practise with the lord Treasurer to get the measure of the king of Scot's person, and cause garments to be made for him of such stuff as he shall carry with him for the purpose by such a tailor and brouderer as he shall carry with him for the intent and present them to the King with the horses assigned to him'.[106] The fact that this approach worked indicates that James had inherited his mother's fondness for clothes. Indeed, when he travelled to France to marry Madeleine, daughter of Francis I, he took the opportunity to go shopping. The Parisians noted that James could be seen 'with a servant or two running up and down the streets of Paris buying every trifle himself and every carter pointing at him and saying "yonder goes la roy de Ecosse"'.[107] In the same way, clothes of a particular style could be worn as an expression of allegiance with a specific country. In 1525 Henry held a triumph to celebrate the capture of Francis I and a mass was heard at St Paul's cathedral. However, not everyone at the English court saw reason to celebrate: 'The bishop of Scotland was muche marked this day, for whensoever he came to the Court before this time his apparell was sumptuous, his whodde was euer veluet or crimosyn Satyn: but after the takyng of the French kyng he wore onely blacke Chamlet, by whiche token men iudged his Frenche harte.'[108]

Scotland's link with France was cemented by marriage. James V made his formal entry into Paris on New Year's eve 1536 wearing a hat costing ten crowns and 'ane cott of sad cramasy velvott . . . reschit all oer with gold cuttit out on plain clayth of gold freinyeit with gold and all cuttit out knit with horns and lined with red taffate'.[109] The couple were married on New Year's day and the bride wore 'a precious close crown of gold upon her head, and under it a coif of gold set with

2.5 *James V of Scotland and Mary of Guise, by unknown artist. SNPG O NO 41. Blair Charitable Trust, Blair Castle, Perthshire, Scotland*

stones very precious with other sumptuous apparel according to her degree'.[110] However, Madeleine died six months later in July 1537, and the following year James took a second French bride, Mary of Guise (Fig. 2.5). Mary brought her trousseau from France, along with a French tailor, and she continued to order clothes from France after her marriage.[111] James's preference for a French bride, French dress and French allies signalled his wish to assert his own identity, free from his uncle's influence.

GROWING DISINTEREST: CHARLES V

According to Charles V (1500–56), he spoke 'Spanish to God, Italian to women, French to men, and German to my horse'.[112] Charles V, king of Spain and Holy Roman Emperor, was born in Ghent, the son of Philip the Fair (1478–1506) and Joanna the Mad (1479–1555). With the death of his grandfather Ferdinand of Aragon on 23 January 1516, Charles became the joint ruler of Spain with his mother, and he made his official entry into Valladolid in November 1517. A report sent to Henry from Saragossa on 30 June 1518 described how 'the King with the company ... dressed in cloth of gold a la Moresca' took part in jousts and games of canes on St John's day. The festivities continued on St Peter's day but 'because of the cost of the preceding day the King ordered that none should wear better than sarcenett'.[113] Charles was elected as Holy Roman Emperor in 1519 and crowned in 1520. After this he travelled to Spain. At this point his dress combined Spanish elements with strands from European fashion.[114] At the age of 20 he was described by the papal legate as 'gifted with good sense and prudence far beyond his years; and indeed he has, I believe, much more in his head than appears in his face'.[115]

The creation and maintenance of Charles V's imperial image drew on a number of elements including portraits, tapestries, armour, architecture, speeches, official letters, printed texts and woodcuts.[116] Equally, when he chose, Charles could dress as magnificently as Henry or Francis. Early in February 1521 Spinelly wrote to Wolsey from Worms to tell him about the meeting there between the emperor who was 'arrayed with a rich gown of cloth of gold furred with sables'.[117] His personal livery colours were yellow, white and red, and this was often expressed for his own wardrobe as cloth of gold, cloth of silver and an appropriate red fabric. In the full-length portrait of Charles by Titian (Fig. 2.6) he is believed to be wearing the clothes of white, cloth of gold and sable that he wore for his coronation, although without the iron crown of the Holy Roman Emperor. However, unlike Henry VIII, Charles was described as being 'rather simple in his clothing' in everyday life.[118] On 24 February 1522 Wingfield and Spinelly informed Wolsey that 'Yesterday the Emperor and his brother, with a party of twenty, all arrayed in cloth without any manner of silk or cloth of gold, played at the jeu de cannes'.[119]

As his reign progressed, Charles increasingly favoured understated clothes, even for more formal occasions. On 15 March 1525 Sampson wrote to Wolsey from Madrid, informing him of how Charles V had responded to the news of his victory at Pavia, which he heard about on his 25th birthday. He went to hear mass and on the next day went in procession to the chapel of Our Lady 'in a cape of black frieze'. Afterwards the emperor stated, 'Now shall we go to have a solemn mass, giving thanks to God; and I would that we should make it much more solemn with good inward devotion than with any manner of outward pomp'.[120] Later, when 'advised to wear some fresh raiment, to show his joy', Charles refused. In 1536 Charles's choice of violet velvet for his entry into Rome met with a less than enthusiastic response, while in 1540 the French felt his black Italian cloak and a coat and cap of black cloth were inappropriate to his imperial rank for his entry into Paris.[121]

2.6 *Charles V and a hound, by Titian. Museo del Prado, cat. no. 409*

MASKING FAILURE: CHRISTIAN II

Events in Denmark and Sweden in the early 1520s highlighted the consequences of weak royal rule. Denmark, like England, was on the periphery of early modern Europe, but the challenge to Christian II's authority would have been a salutary lesson for other European monarchs. Christian II had been king of Denmark from 1513. While he appreciated the views of Erasmus, he also saw the appeal of the ideas promoted by Luther. However, he was married to one of Charles V's sisters, so he was obliged to support the Catholic church. Having lost Sweden in 1521, Christian surrendered the Danish throne in 1522.[122] The elector of Schleswig-Holstein took his place as Frederick I and Christian fled from Denmark with his queen in March 1523. By May they were in the Netherlands. On 4 June William Knight wrote to Wolsey, informing him that Christian would be in Calais shortly.[123] On 15 June 1523 the exiled king of Denmark, his wife and their three children landed at Dover.

However, Hall did not approve of their clothing, noting on their arrival that the Danish king, queen and their retinue were 'poore and euil appareled'.[124] Even so, two weeks later Henry VIII and Christian II confirmed the Anglo-Danish treaty made by their fathers.[125] Henry also paid all of Christian's expenses while he was in England.[126] Christian's ongoing need for financial support caused Margaret of Austria to write to Charles V on 18 October 1524. She had learnt that their allowance was 500 florins a month and the queen was allowed 2,000 florins a year for clothes. However, they currently spent over 800 florins a month, even though Margaret's maître d'hôtel, Sonastre, had tried to establish some order in their household.[127] The separate allowance for clothes emphasises just how important image was in maintaining the perception that Christian and his wife were the rightful rulers of Denmark as they travelled in Renaissance Europe.

In contrast, Gustavus Vasa, who had challenged Christian II of Denmark's right to rule over Sweden in 1521, used dress to establish a distinct identity for his new ruling house. Following two years as lord protector (1521–23), Gustavus was crowned king of Sweden after his election by the nobility. The re-establishment of the Swedish monarchy resulted in the development of a new court and administrative structure. Physically, Gustavus was about 5 ft 9 in. (1.8 m) tall with short fair hair cut in a fringe and a hand-trimmed beard, a small straight nose and slim legs, and Per Brahe described him as wearing 'manly and powerful kingly apparel'.[128]

His court was modelled on the German-speaking courts of the Holy Roman Empire. His clothes were predominantly in the German style and his tailor, George Ballinger, was German. He favoured *pluderhosen* worn with the *braquette* or codpiece and a matching doublet. *Pluderhosen* were knee-length breeches or hose which were made from a number of panes, often heavily decorated with slashing. Gustavus was painted by an unknown artist *c.* 1557, dressed in a short back gown worn over a black doublet and long hose in the Almain style, all heavily embroidered with gold thread worked in fashionable Moorish designs of the types that can be seen in Henry VIII's portraits.[129] As in England, French fashions were also influential. Gustavus favoured the short gown or chammer, and after 1542 the *manthar* or French coat was a new introduction into Sweden. This development may have been linked to the embassy that Gustavus sent to Francis I. Gustavus defended his decision to wear clothes cut in foreign styles and made in bright colours by saying that he must follow the example of other rulers because 'we Swedes are no more goats or swine than they are'.[130]

Notes

1 In the sixteenth century letters became increasingly important as a means of communication about business, politics and people's private lives; see D. R. Starkey, *Rivals in Power: Lives and Letters of the Great Tudor Dynasties* (1990). Consequently, the evidence recorded in letters, both in terms of factual detail and private opinion, is invaluable. However, the personal nature of some letters does raise questions about the subjectivity of the writer and that two writers with inevitably record different details when describing the same event. On 3 May 1515, Peter Pasqualigo wrote a letter describing the May day celebrations when the queen rode out 'richly attired in the Spanish fashion'. Nicholas Sagudino described Catherine at the same event as being 'richly attired with 25 damsels mounted on white palfreys, their dresses slashed with gold lama' (*LP* II.i, 411 and 410). This pair of letters raises a further point: the role of the editor and translator in conveying the spirit and the terminology of letters not originally written in English.

2 For a discussion of how Henry used his tapestry collection, see Campbell, *Art of Majesty*.

3 This chapter develops the ideas put forward in Hayward, 'Luxury', pp. 37–46.

4 See the *Shorter OED*; also Skelton, *Magnificence*, p. 25.

5 Brown, *Four Years*, I, p. 90.

6 Kipling, *Triumph*, pp. 61, 163.

7 Myers, *Black Book*, p. 81.

8 RL 12188; Rowlands, *Holbein*, p. 150; Foister, *Holbein*, pp. 152–54.

9 C. Plummer, ed., *Sir John Fortescue on The Governance of England* (Oxford, 1885), p. 125. A similar point of view was presented in the *Secretum Secretorum*: 'It sitteth to his dignite honourably to be clothed, and ever in faire garnementis and robes passing other in fairnesse. And he shold were dere, rich and straunge ornamentes. Fittyng also it is for a kyng to have a prerogative in his arraie above all others, wherby his dignite is worshiped and made faire, his pouste [power] or might not hurt, and due reverence to hym at all tyme yeve'; M. A. Manzalaoui, *Secretum Secretorum: Nine English Versions* (1977), pp. 36–37.

10 F. E. Baldwin, *Sumptuary Legislation and Personal Regulation in England* (Baltimore, 1926); Hayward, 'Luxury', pp. 37–46.

11 He was 'apparelled like Hercules in a shirt of siluer of damaske written in letters of purple ye border enfemes et infauntes cy petit assurance'; Hall, *Chronicle*, p. 619.

12 Skelton, *Magnificence*, p. 80.

13 Ibid., pp. 151–52.

14 Gordon Kipling cites Maynard's group portrait of *The Family of Henry VII with St George and the Dragon* as evidence of Henry VII's spiritual magnificence (Fig. 5.7); *Triumph*, pp. 29–30, 65.

15 *LP* III.i, 728; Harris, *Stafford*, p. 172. Stafford's accounts for the year ending September 1520 (which included the Field of Cloth of Gold and Charles V's visit to Canterbury) show that he has spent £4,200 on clothes; ibid., p. 102.

16 In 1462, Francesco Sassetti, the director of the Medici bank, had 37 items in his wardrobe which were worth 485 florins, but none were made from silk; J. Bridgeman, '"Pagare le pompe": Why Quattrocento sumptuary laws did not work', in L. Panizza, ed., *Women in Italian Renaissance Culture* (Oxford, 2000), p. 217.
17 F. Redlich, 'A needed distinction in fashion study', *Business History Review*, 37 (1963), pp. 3–4; N. Harte, 'State control of dress and social change in pre-industrial England', in D. C. Coleman and A. H. John, eds, *Trade, Government and Economy in Pre-Industrial England* (1976), p. 141.
18 Hall, *Chronicle*, p. 610.
19 *LP* III.ii, 2309.
20 Hall, *Chronicle*, p. 640.
21 On 31 October Carlo Capello noted that 'the Frenche Kyng caused two gownes to be made of white velvet, pricked with gold of damaske, and the capes and vestes were of frettes of whipped gold of damaske very riche; whiche two gounes he sent to the Kyng of Englande, praying hym to chose the one, and to weare it for his sake, whiche gladly tooke it, an so that Tewesdaie, the twoo Kynges were both in one suite'; *CSP Venetian, 1527–33*, 823.
22 TNA E30/1114 (*LP* IV.ii, 3356.3).
23 Nevinson, 'Portraits', p. 3. Hall noted that 'Themperour as the kynges soldoure ware a Crosse of sayncte George with a Rose . . . brought to a tente of cloth of gold and blewe veluet, and all blewe veluet was embroidered with HK of fyne golde'; *Chronicle*, p. 549. A narrative painting called *The Meeting of Henry VIII and the Emperor Maximilian, c.* 1545, by a Flemish artist is one of four narrative paintings owned by Henry (RC, inv. no. 20). It depicts Henry VIII and Maximilian as equals.
24 *LP* II.i, 1413.
25 Anderson, *Hispanic Costume*, p. 43.
26 *LP* I.ii, 2268.
27 Castiglione, *Courtier*, p. 134.
28 Ibid., p. 135.
29 U. Ilg, 'The cultural significance of costume books in sixteenth-century Europe', in C. Richardson, ed., *Clothing Culture 1350–1650* (Aldershot, 2004), pp. 49–62.
30 *CSP Venetian, 1520–26*, 67.
31 A. Ribeiro, 'On Englishness in dress', in C. Breward, B. Conekin and C. Cox, eds, *The Englishness of English Dress* (Oxford and New York, 2002), pp. 17–18.
32 *LP* IV.iii, 5636.
33 *CSP Venetian, 1509–19*, 219.
34 *LP* II.i, 1863.
35 See below, p. 97.
36 *LP* XIX.ii, 745.
37 *LP* XIX.ii, 751.
38 A. Hollander, *Fabric of Vision: Dress and Drapery in Painting* (2002), p. 127, where she notes the 'symbolic importance and psychological effect' of the use of black in dress and in art.
39 J. Huizinga, *The Waning of the Middle Ages* (1924), p. 249.
40 C. H. Williams, ed., *English Historical Documents, 1485–1558* (1967), p. 190.
41 *LP* II.i, 1281.
42 As one observer noted, the English courtiers were 'all French in eating, drinking and apparel, yea, in French vices and bragges, so that all the estates of England were by them laughed at, the ladies and gentlemen were dispraised, so that nothing by them was praised but it were after the French turne'; Hall, *Chronicle*, p. 597.
43 Ibid., p. 505.
44 Pollard, *Henry VII*, I, p. 331.
45 Francis Bacon observed in his essay *Of empire* written in 1597 that 'During that triumvirate of kings, King Henry VIII of England, Francois I, King of France and Charles V, Emperor, there was such watch kept, that none of the three could win a palm of ground, but the other two would straight away balance it'; Seward, *Prince*, p. 78.
46 *LP* III.i, 432.
47 Starkey, *European Court*, p. 13.
48 'Henry VIII, by the grace of God, king of England and France, Defender of the Faith and Lord of Ireland and Supreme Head of the Church of England on earth . . .'; *LP* VIII, 52.
49 See below, pp. 129–33.
50 *LP* IV.i, 1430.
51 H. D. Fernandez, 'The patrimony of St Peter: the papal court at Rome c.1450–1700', in J. Adamson, ed., *The Princely Courts of Europe* (1999), p. 142.
52 Thomas and Thornley, *Great Chronicle*, p. 274.
53 *LP* I.ii, 2527.
54 *LP* I.ii, 2929.
55 *LP* I.ii, 2930; also *LP* I.ii, 3003. Henry VIII rewarded Spinelly with a benefice worth £200 per annum.
56 *LP* I.i, 418.
57 TNA E36/215, p. 68. Henry reciprocated in May 1512, sending the pope a gift of 12 white caps; *CSP Venetian, 1509–19*, 168.
58 'Henry VIII's jewel book', p. 162. The second rose was delivered by Dr Thomas Hanibal, master of the rolls.
59 *LP* III.ii, 1510.
60 *LP* III.ii, 1592, 1574.
61 Hall, *Chronicle*, p. 174.
62 Scarisbrick, *Henry VIII*, pp. 107–10.
63 *LP* III.ii, 3579. He added that he could 'not send the hawks this year on account of the cold but will send them next year'.
64 *LP* VI, app. 3.
65 *LP* IV.ii, 4858.
66 *LP* IV.iii, 5780.
67 *LP* I.ii, 2391.
68 The norm consisted of winter and summer sets of clothes, slippers for indoor wear every three months and a pair of outdoor shoes every four weeks; Benecke, *Maximilian*, p. 124.
69 Seward, *Prince*, p. 64. His second wife, Bianca Maria, was frequently short of money. In her earliest surviving letter to Maximilian dated 26 March 1497, she informed her husband that she had had to pawn her underwear and household linen; Benecke, *Maximilian*, p. 95; also pp. 96, 103.
70 Scarisbrick, *Henry VIII*, pp. 97–105.
71 Knecht, *Rise and Fall*, pp. 105–07.
72 *LP* II.ii, 2911.
73 Lockyer, *Habsburg and Bourbon*, pp. 199–20. Leo X issued a bull, *Exsurge Domine*, in June 1520 denouncing Luther and his beliefs, which began 'Arise O Lord! And judge Thy cause. A wild boar has invaded Thy vineyard'; ibid., p. 119.
74 *LP* XVI, pp. 50–51.
75 Anderson, *Hispanic Costume*, p. 29.
76 *LP* XVIII.ii, 20.
77 Herzog-Anton-Ulrich-Museum, Braunschweig. See G. Mentges, 'Fashion, time and the consumption of a Renaissance man in Germany: the costume book of Matthäus Schwarz of Augsburg, 1496–1564', in B. Burman and C. Turbin, eds, *Material Strategies: Dress and Gender in Historical Perspective* (Oxford, 2003), pp. 12–32.
78 G. Mattingley, *Catherine of Aragon* (1942), p. 179.
79 *LP* IV.ii, 2515.
80 *LP* XIII.i, 784.
81 Rogers and Ward, *Süleyman*, p. 164.
82 Ibid., p. 27.
83 Ibid., p. 174.
84 Ibid., pp. 165–66.
85 Ibid., p. 166.
86 Jardine, *Worldly Goods*, pp. 379–80.
87 Rogers and Ward, *Süleyman*, p. 175.
88 Starkey, 'Representation', pp. 204–07.
89 Francis was made a captain of a 100 lancers and he was admitted to the council; Knecht, *Rise and Fall*, p. 68.
90 Ibid., p. 96.
91 *LP* II.i, 134.
92 *LP* II.i, 1837.
93 The English ambassadors were also suitably splendid: the lord chamberlain wore a gown of crimson satin, lined with sables, bishop wore his rochet, Lord St John wore a gown of black satin, while the captain of Guisnes wore cloth of gold and sables; *LP* II.ii, 4661.
94 Hall, *Chronicle*, p. 610.
95 *LP* XVII, 128.
96 R. J. Knecht, *French Renaissance Monarch: Francis I and Henry II* (London and New York, 1984), p. 94.
97 *LP* II.ii, 2866.
98 *LP* III.i, 748.
99 Ives, *Anne Boleyn*, p. 40.
100 *LP* XV, 115.
101 As Hall noted, in 1513 Henry and the council 'forgat not the olde Prankes of the Scottes, which is euer to inuade England when the kyng is out'; *Chronicle*, p. 555.
102 J. Wormald, *Court, Kirk and Community: Scotland 1470–1625* (1981), pp. 10–13.
103 *LP* II.i, 1098.
104 Mary wrote many letters to her brother. In 1523, in spite of her noting that 'all things is kept from me as far as the duke may', she went on to write, 'Now I will advertise you . . . he hath eight-and-twenty cannons'; L. O. Fraudenburg, 'Troubled times: Margaret Tudor and the Historians', in S. Mapstone and J. Wood, eds, *The Rose and the Thistle: Essays on the Culture of Late Medieval and Renaissance Scotland* (East Linton, 1998), p. 51.
105 *LP* IV.i, 43.
106 *LP* VII, 1350.
107 *LP* XI, 916.

108 Hall, *Chronicle*, p. 693.
109 *LP* XII.i, 12; Strickland, *Queens of Scotland*, I, p. 272. For a description of the wedding, see *LP* XI, 1395.
110 *LP* XII.i, 12.
111 R. K. Marshall, *Costume in Scottish Portraits, 1560–1830* (1986), p. 30.
112 Martienssen, *Katherine Parr*, p. 178.
113 *LP* II.ii, 4277.
114 For the definitive study of Spanish dress, see B. Carmen, *Instrumentaria española en tiempos de Carlos V* (Madrid, 1962).
115 C. Hare, *A Great Emperor, Charles V, 1519–1558* (1917), p. 63. Philip Melanchthon observed that 'more glorious and marvellous than all his successes was the Emperor's control of his temper. Never a word or an action was the least overbearing'; ibid., p. 120. In middle age he was described by the Venetian ambassador as being 'of moderate height and has a grave look. His forehead is broad, his eyes blue, with a look of energy, his nose aquiline and a little bent, his lower jaw long and projecting so that his teeth do not meet and one cannot hear the ends of his words distinctly'; Lockyer, *Habsburg and Bourbon*, p. 215.
116 Burke, 'Presenting', pp. 394–403.
117 *LP* III.i, 1155.
118 Burke, 'Presenting', p. 409.
119 *LP* III.ii, 2067.
120 *LP* IV.i, 1189.
121 The French felt that 'His Majesty ought to have dressed in the style appropriate to his rank and fame'; Burke, 'Presenting', p. 409.
122 Wingfield wrote to Wolsey in September informing him that 'the Easterlings handle the king of Denmark roughly, and his own people have killed the governor . . . whereby appeareth that ill life and ill governance cometh often to ill end'; *LP* III.ii, 2558.
123 *LP* III.ii, 3075.
124 Hall, *Chronicle*, pp. 657–58.
125 *LP* III.ii, 3142.
126 Nicholas Hurleton, clerk of the green cloth, received four receipts dated 2, 13 and 29 June and 29 July (three for £100 and one for £42) from Sir John Dauntsey; *LP* III.ii, 3208.
127 *LP* IV.i, 747.
128 Rangstrom, *Lions*, p. 292.
129 Inv. no. Grh 467, National Museum, Stockholm; illustrated in ibid., pp. 26–27, 295. In 1548 Gustavus's wardrobe contained 40 doublets, 25 outer garments, 65 pairs of breeches, 56 items of headwear, 13 pairs of shoes and a large selection of accessories; ibid., p. 291.
130 Ibid., p. 291.

III

Creating Magnificence: The Role of the Great Wardrobe

Clothing has been studied as an example of a semiotic system, in which clothes speak to both the wearer and the viewer.[1] However, there is another language of clothes, the technical terminology used to describe the fabric types, colours and details of cut and construction. In the mid Tudor period, this specialist vocabulary was the regular working tool of the clerks who kept the great wardrobe's accounts, the merchants who supplied the cloth and the tailors who converted cloth into clothes. However, their familiarity with both the materials and the clothes meant that details were often omitted from written records. For the modern reader, lack of familiarity with the handwriting and these technical terms in English or Latin, the latter often heavily abbreviated, can make the language of clothes of the late fifteenth and early sixteenth centuries difficult to understand.[2]

The records of the great wardrobe are central to this research, although the clothes described within them are sadly lacking. This chapter evaluates the role of the great wardrobe as a repository of skills and goods. As both a building and a department of the royal household, it was central to the production of clothes for the king and his household and to the consumption of the large stocks of high quality silks and linen held there. The keeper, the yeoman tailor, the clerk and the porter were essential to the effective operation of the wardrobe and the creation of the warrants and volumes of accounts that recorded its business. The scale of the business handled and the quantity of money spent there by the king's officers reflects the cost of Henry VIII's magnificent appearance.[3]

The great wardrobe: its function, premises and staff

By the late fifteenth century the great wardrobe was established as a fixed institution that was attached to the royal household. Its peripatetic days following the king's household were long gone.[4] Even so, the role of the great wardrobe remained unchanged. The fourteenth-century wardrobe had five key functions: acquiring raw materials, converting the fabric and fur into clothes, storing of raw materials, distributing the completed garments and accounting for the money received and spent by the keeper.[5] This list accurately describes the role of the early and mid Tudor keepers of the great wardrobe such as Sir Robert Lytton and Sir Andrew Windsor.

The great wardrobe was located within the former home of Sir John Beauchamp and it consisted of a main building with shops, houses and a range of tenements. When Beauchamp died in 1360, the property was acquired by Edward III and the great wardrobe had moved in by October 1361. According to John Stow, Beauchamp's:

> executors sold the house to King Edward III, unto whom the parson of St Andrew's complaining that the said Beauchampe had pulled down divers houses, in their place to build the same house, where through he was hindered of his accustomed tithes, paid by the tenants of old time, granted him forty shillings by year out of that house for ever.[6]

The wardrobe buildings are identifiable on the Agas map of 1561–70 (Fig. 3.1).[7] They were located within the ward of Baynard's castle and the parish of St Andrew's by the castle. The plot fronted onto Carter lane, to the north, St Andrew's to the south, Puddle Dock hill to the west and Addle hill to the east.[8] When the great wardrobe was inventoried after the king's death in 1547 (14591–980), the principal rooms consisted of the parlour, the king's chamber, the closet and the privy wardrobe. The entries for the workrooms were equally brief and they were minimally furnished as the following indicates: 'The entrie: Ladders j (14668); The Skynnerie: Cheastes ij (14669), Tables j (14670), Trestelles ij (14671); The Taillorie: Greate Cheastes j (14672); The Countinghous: Cheastes withe ij Lockes j (14673), Chariottes j (14674), Coferstanderdes j (14675).'[9]

The great wardrobe consisted of a number of buildings, including workshops.[10] It rented out some of its property to

The porter's chief role was 'to keep the door' or control access to the wardrobe because the fabrics stored there were expensive and it was important to ensure that only approved personnel could come and go at will. As indicated by the career of Richard Gibson, the office of porter was often held in conjunction with another office such as that of yeoman tailor.[52] Gibson held these posts during Henry VII's reign: on 22 January 1501 he was appointed as yeoman tailor and on 22 May 1504 as porter.[53] On 13 June 1509 he was reappointed by Henry VIII and the wording of the grant suggests that he was not the first to combine these offices.[54] In November 1534, Ralph Worsley, a relative of Henry VIII's yeoman of the robes, was made porter after Gibson's death, with wages of 4*d* a day and livery.[55] By 1543 the office had changed hands again. In that year John Patrick, who was described as 'porter of the Kynges Wardropp in Lundon', was laid to rest in St Andrew by the Wardrobe.[56]

The queen's wardrobe

The chief difficulty with studying the queen's wardrobe during Henry VIII's reign is the lack of documentary evidence. Hints about its organisation and staffing have to be gleaned from what limited records there are. While some material survives from Catherine of Aragon's wardrobe, much of it is fragmentary and undated.[57] In contrast, there are several sets of accounts for Catherine Parr, making it possible to piece together how the queen's wardrobe functioned. The queen's wardrobe was smaller and much less formally structured than the great wardrobe. This is not surprising as there were periods without a queen consort. Consequently, much of the responsibility for buying cloth devolved to the yeoman of the queen's robes. He also received cloth periodically from the great wardrobe and the king's wardrobe of the robes. Most of the cloth used for liveries was bought as required, with some of it being channelled through the wardrobe of the robes.

Baynard's castle was built by Henry VII in 1500–01.[58] It fronted onto the river and Thames street and it was situated between Blackfriars and Paul's wharf. It acted as a repository for the queen's goods, as well as being the formal base for her wardrobe of the robes and for stocks of cloth. Catherine Parr's accounts include an entry for Mr Fritton riding from Oking to London 'for certeyn the Quenes Graces furde gownes from Baynardes' in October 1544 and a sumpterman received 2*s* 8*d* in the following month 'for his ch[arges going] with the sumpter horse from Ok[ing for certain] gowns for the Queen's [Grace from Ba]ynardes Castell'.[59] Henry VIII granted the castle to all of his wives apart from Jane Seymour and it acted as their London residence. Baynard's castle was granted briefly to the duke of Richmond and it passed to Catherine Parr's brother, William Herbert, in 1546.[60] Baynard's castle fronted onto the Thames and was not far from the great wardrobe.[61] Even so, the accounts of Mark Milliner make it clear that he delivered items directly to the officers of the queen's robes as they travelled with Catherine Parr.[62] Items were regularly delivered to Whitehall, Greenwich, Ampthill, Oatlands, Guildford, Windsor and Hampton Court.

Catherine Parr's accounts show that she was served by the same core group of artificers as the king — a tailor, skinner, embroiderer, goldsmith, saddler — but without the keeper and other wardrobe officials. The accounts for 1543–44 and 1544–45 have been summarised in Table 3.1, listing the chief artificers and suppliers and showing the scale of their business with the queen.[63] While the accounts for 1544–45 are fragmentary, they support the pattern of business seen in 1543–44. They also indicate that Catherine Parr did not settle her debts promptly, a habit reflected in the bundle of unpaid bills found amongst her papers after her death (1752–66). Catherine Parr's accounts also show that the expenditure relating to the queen's clothes and livery for her household was managed by her chancellor, her receiver general and most importantly, her treasurer, Wymond Carew. In the year 1544–45, he made a payment of £50 against a bill for £102 18*s* 10*d* presented by Richard Benam, saddler, and he settled in full Peter Richard's account for spangles costing £24 12*s* 10½*d*.[64]

Catherine spent heavily on her wardrobe and the livery for her household, as her household accounts for 1543–44 demonstrate. At the end of the account is an entry for the queen's silk woman, Mistress Vaughan, who had supplied silk goods worth £336 10*s* 3*d* to the following: £186 12*s* 5*d* to the wardrobe, £128 13*s* 6*d* to the stable, 16*s* to the tailor, 62*s* 8½*d* to the coffer maker, 65*s* 3½*d* to the embroiderer and £14 4*d* for other items and in reward.[65] It is hard to compare Catherine's overall expenditure on her wardrobe with that of her husband because Henry VIII's accounts do not survive for 1543–44 or 1544–45. However, his expenditure in 1542–43 was £7,263 13*s* 6½*d*, essentially double that of his wife.

The queen's wardrobe must have accounted for its expenditure in a similar way to the great wardrobe because in May 1544 a payment of 40*s* was made by the queen to the clerk of the wardrobe for paper, pens, ink and three or four ledgers 'as allowed at the audit'.[66] This formed part of a pattern of accounting. In the same month Walter Bucher received £5 10*s* from Wymond Carew for paper and ink 'as accustomed'.[67]

Great wardrobe documentation: warrants and accounts

Warrants ordering clothes from the great wardrobe were dated and addressed to the keeper.[68] These warrants listed the garments the recipient was to receive, the types, colour and costs of the fabrics to be used and whether any fur, headwear or footwear were to be provided. They were usually written in English on vellum or paper, signed by the king and sealed (Fig. 3.2). However, in the final years of Henry VIII's reign, documents were signed by the stamp rather than by the king, and subscribed by a member of the household: in October 1545 a warrant for 'watche lyveries to the yeomen waighter' in the Tower was subscribed by the comptroller of the household.[69] The king's own warrants were treated in the same way, as indicated by a warrant dated January 1546 for 'certain stuff and workmanship delivered for your Majesty's apparel', subscribed by Richard Cecil, the yeoman of the robes.[70]

Table 3.1: *Expenditure within Catherine Parr's wardrobe in 1543–44 and 1544–45*

Artificers	1543–44	1544–45
Tailor	John Scut £143 1*s* 1*d*	John Scut: for the queen £17 16*s* 11*d*; for others £10 17*s* 4*d*
Skinner	Catherine, wife of Thomas Addington, late queen's skinner £241 8*s* 8*d*	For the queen £8 3*s*
Embroiderer	Guillaume Brellant £422 8*s* 4*d*	An old debt £160; the queen's apparel £40 9*s*; for others £12 15*s*; badges £29 13*s* 4*d*; work for the stable £19 8*d*
Silk women	Mistress Shakerley £56 4*s* 7*d*	
	Mistress Vaughan £336 10*s* 3*d*	Things delivered for the queen £74 11*s* 2*d*; for other persons £10 17*s* 11½*d*; for the stable £72 15*s* 4*d*; an old debt £35
Goldsmith	Peter Richardson £867 14*s* 10*d*	Peter Richardson £13 12*s* 6½*d*
Milliner	~	Mark Milliner £26 3*s* 4*d*
Saddlers	William Hobson, groom saddler £23 3*s* 3*d*	William Hobson, the queen's saddler £19 12*s* 4*d*
	Richard Baynam, yeoman saddler £201 18*s* 10*d*	The yeoman saddler: an old debt £61 18*s* 10*d*; for the queen £104 4*s* 10*d*
	Edward Steward £111 16*s*	
Mercers	William Lock £546 4½*d* Simon Loo £26 1*s* 8*d*	Silk for the queen £164 10*s* 6½*d*; silk for others £48 15*s* 9*d*; other cloth £45 10*s* 8½*d*; stuff supplied to the stable £15 14*s*; an old debt £146 4½*d*
Drapers	~	Hewetson cloth for the queen's sumpters £10 13*s*
		George Hysus woolen cloth for certain persons £12 5*s*
Shoemaker	Godfrey Lowley £42 2*s* 7*d*	Shoes slippers and buskins for the queen £15 9*s* 7*d*
		For others 45*s* 3*d*
Hosier	Robert Hardy £20 11*s* 2*d*	~
Wardrobe of the robes	provision of stuff for the queens use £90 2*s* 4½*d*; livery for the queens servants £85 14*s* 6*d*; the maundy £21 19*s* 11½*d*	~
New Year's gifts	£201 12*s* 4*d*	£465 10*s* 4½*d*
Cloth for the queen's barge	£18	~
Necessaries bought for the wardrobe	£25 15*s* 3*d*	~
Total	£3,980 15*s* 9½*d*	£1,615 6*s* 2*d*

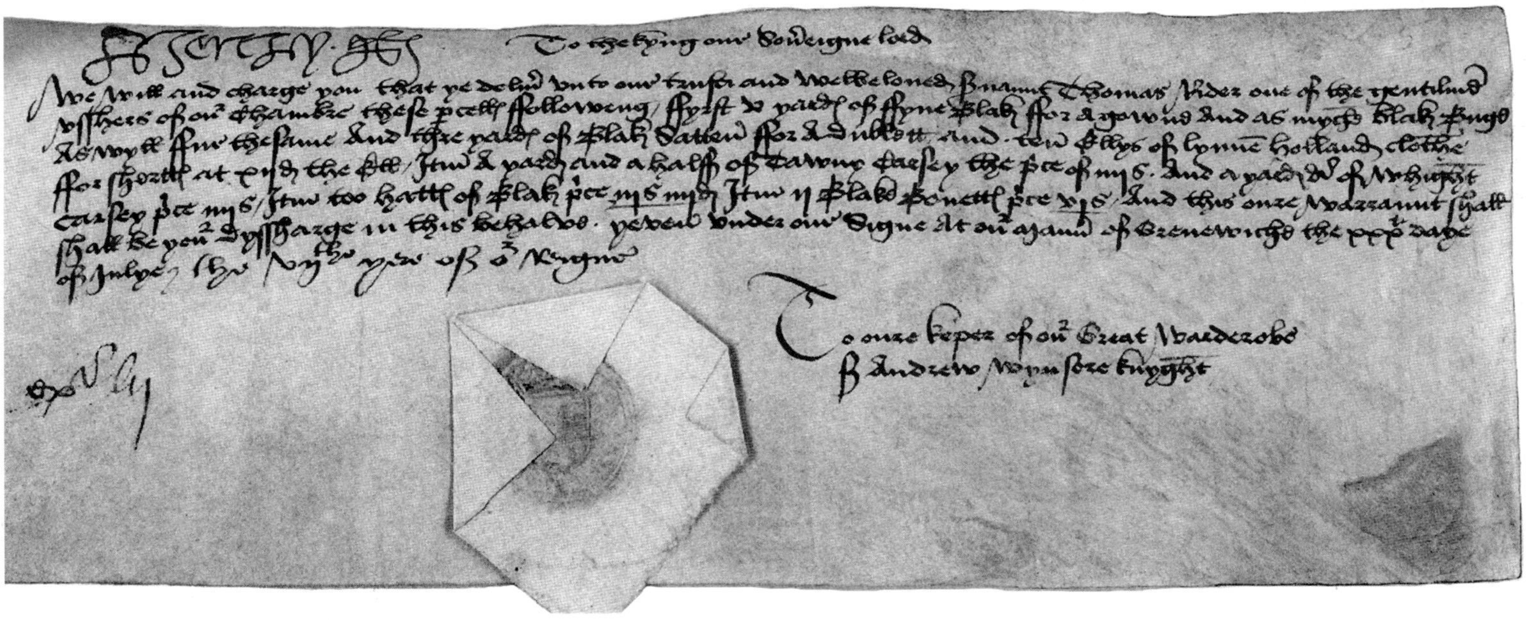

3.2 *A warrant subsidiary to the account of the great wardrobe. The National Archive, Kew, E101/418/5*

Henry R To the kyng our Souereigne lord

We will and charge that ye deyuer vnto our trusti and welbeloued seruaunt Thomas Rider one of the gentilmen vsshers of our Chambre these parcelles Followeng / Fyrst v yerdes of Fyne Blak For a gowne And as myche blak Buge As wyll Fur the same And thre yards of Blak Satten For A dublett and ten Ellys of lynnen Holland clothe For shertes at xij*d* the Ell / Item A yard and a half of Tawny Carsey the price of iiij*s* And a yard di of whight carsey price iiij*s* / Item too hattes of Blak price iij*s* iiij*d* Item ij Blak Bonettes price vj*s* And this oure Warraunt shall be your dyssharge in this behalve yeven vnder our Signe At our Mannor of Grenewiche the xxx^{ti} daye of Julye the vij^{the} yere of our Reigne.

To oure keper of our Great Warderobe
Sir Andrew Wynsore knyght

Warrants were issued regularly for the king's robes, his wardrobe of the beds, the chapel, the stable, the king's children and events such as the maundy celebrations, Candlemas and the festivities of order of the Garter. Livery was provided to several groups within the royal household including the footmen, the henchmen, the musicians, the officers of the hunts and the yeomen of the guard. Individuals also received livery, many of whom only feature once or twice in the surviving documentation. However, individuals who regularly received a grant of clothing could be given a warrant dormant which meant that on a given date each year they would be provided with an issue of clothing.

It is evident from a comment on a warrant issued to Thomas Westby, clerk of the closet, dated 22 May 1532 that warrants sometimes got lost. The warrant noted that 7 yards (6.4 m) of scarlet broad cloth for a gown and hood were 'to be taken of our gift owt of our grete wardroppe wherof we dyd signe vnto hym a bill the last yere which he affermeth to be lost'.[71] There was also a possibility of misinterpreting written orders for clothes, as indicated in the letter from John Husee to Lady Lisle on 23 February 1538: 'And where your ladyship writ that there was fault found because Mistress Frances' sleeves were not turned up with tinsel, and that her kirtle was not silver, I followed your ladyship's bill of proportion in it, for if your ladyship had written so to have had it should not a 'lacked.'[72]

In general the warrants instigate the making of clothes or furnishings, so the warrant predates when the items were made. However, on occasion, it is evident that items were included on warrants after they had been made. This is most noticeable with the king's warrants, once he ordered his clothes on a six-monthly basis.[73] While this method of ordering allowed the tailors to plan their work, it did not provide any freedom to add in items that were needed at short notice. Two examples of this are the red mourning robes ordered for the king after Jane Seymour's death in October 1537, but listed on a warrant dated 8 March 1538 and the coat of mail and brigandine ordered for the king for the invasion of France which began in May 1544 but listed on a warrant dated 26 February 1545.[74]

The great wardrobe operated on an accounting year that ran from Michaelmas to Michaelmas rather than following the regnal year. The annual accounts consolidated all of the information recorded in the warrants and so provide an overview of who received what and when. The format of the accounts changed during the reign of Henry VII.[75] Prior to his reign, the accounts first listed the sources of the great wardrobe's income, then recorded the quantities of cloth bought and from whom, starting with drapery and then listing the furs, mercery and miscellaneous items; then listed the wages of the tailors and skinners employed by the keeper and finally recorded the general expenses of and repairs to the wardrobe and its associated buildings. However, during Henry VII's reign details were recorded under the name of the recipient, listing the supplier, the goods and the person who would make up the item if appropriate. The annual accounts were compiled so that they could be audited in order to produce an accurate assessment the expenditure. Indeed, the accounts have been described as 'narrow in scope and specific in purpose' because these were financial documents produced by accountants who were chiefly concerned with making accurate records of expenditure.[76]

The great wardrobe produced two types of annual accounts. Both were written in secretary hand, the official business hand used by royal clerks, and almost all of them were written in Latin.[77] First, there were summary accounts which consisted of 12 to 18 sheets of paper, and 16 of these survive from the possible 37 years of Henry VIII's reign, written in Latin.[78] These accounts recorded the money received by the keeper, the total spent and the difference between the two. There are also two extracts from the pell accounts which record how much money came to the great wardrobe from this source.[79] Second, there are the particular accounts (Fig. 3.3). These formed much larger volumes than the summary accounts. They were usually written on parchment and 15 survive from the possible 37 years.[80] The accounts included all the warrants issued and so provide information on the garments made, the makers, the suppliers of the cloth, furs and accessories, details about colour, yardage and the cost.

The accounts include good copies that were produced at the end of each year as part of the auditing process and rough

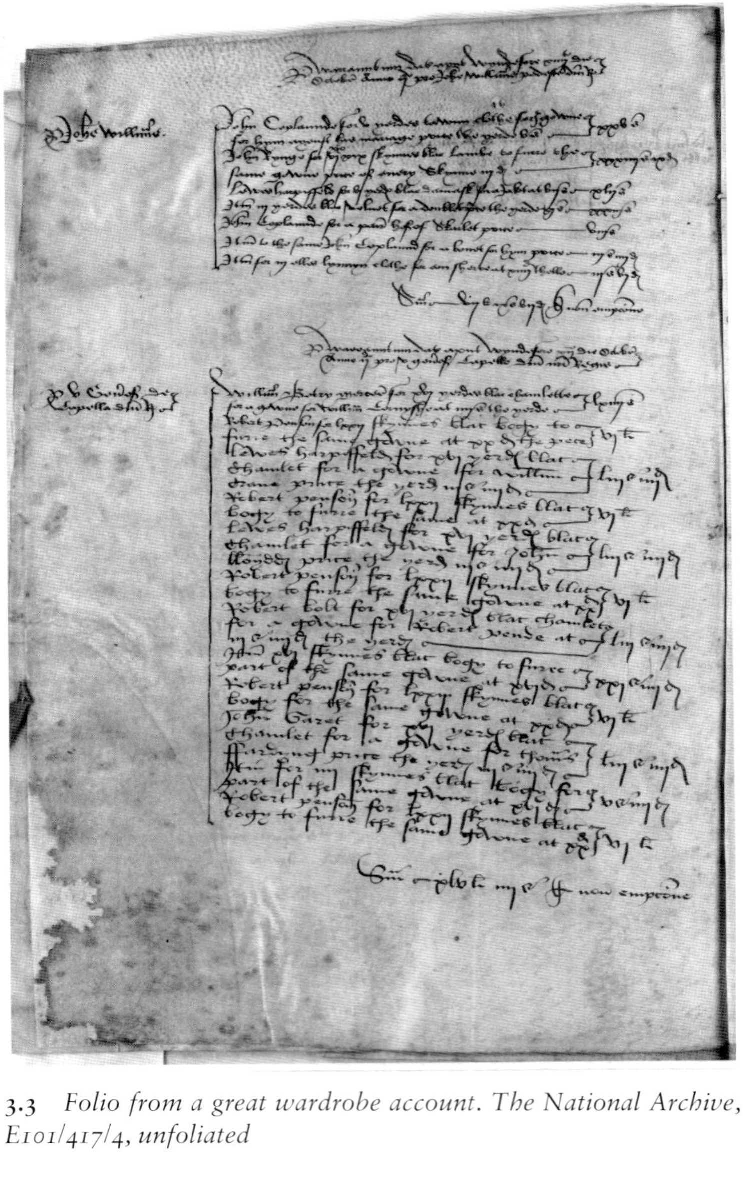

3.3 *Folio from a great wardrobe account. The National Archive, E101/417/4, unfoliated*

copies that the keeper would have kept during each working year. The latter include some of the accounts submitted by the craftsmen working for the great wardrobe. A few warrants have gone into private hands, especially collectors of autographs of historical figures.[81] Although quite a substantial amount of documentation survives for the great wardrobe from the reigns of Henry VII and Henry VIII, very few of the accounts have been published.[82]

The account books have a standard format, starting with the receipts from the exchequer, followed by the amount of cloth remaining on account, a list of the warrants and a record of the total payments made upon the warrants, details of material delivered for summer and winter livery to the lord treasurer, the barons and other officers of the exchequer and the officers of the wardrobe, fees paid to the rector of St Andrew's, Baynard's castle, the keeper, the clerk, the yeoman tailor and the porter, expenditure on paper, parchment and wax, and finally a list of cloth remaining.

Evidence of clothing provision found in other royal accounts

Not all of the king's clothes or the liveries provided for the royal household were ordered through the great wardrobe. The king's privy purse accounts, the chamber accounts, the accounts of the lord chamberlain and of the revels all include orders for clothing. While these accounts provide the date, a description of the item purchased, often the name of the supplier and the price paid, the entries can be frustrating if they only provide a general description of the items or list multiple items but just record the total price paid.

There are four sets of royal privy purse accounts: those of Elizabeth of York, Henry VIII, Princess Mary and Edward VI.[83] As the name suggests, these accounts recorded private payments on items for the account holder or for those they favoured. Some livery was paid for via the king's privy purse, which was administered by the groom of the stool. In 1530, 40*s* was given to John Wood, keeper of the goshawks, for his fellows and himself to buy their liveries.[84] The king also paid for the clothing provided for Thomas Smith, a page of the chamber, who went to Calais with him in 1532.[85] In 1537 a list of payments made by Sir Thomas Heneage, groom of the stool, covered all those who were 'at your Majesty's wages, exhibition and finding'. The remit was wide-ranging and included £40 per annum for Lady Margaret Douglas, for her clothes and those of her attendants, Cokkes, a footman with the late princess dowager (Catherine of Aragon), 4*d* a day, and two coats a year for James 'late of the bottle with Queen Anne [Boleyn]', 40*s* and 22*s* 6*d* for a coat, along with coats for 15 falconers, six archers, four players at interludes and Owen Flod, crow keeper.[86]

Other clothing was funded by the chamber. This included livery provided for groups as in the case of livery of broadcloth delivered to Sir John Dudley for the armourers on a number occasions including 15 April 1538 or for individuals including £10 a year in January 1539 to Piero le Doux, the king's cook for his livery.[87] A few items were even funded by the court of augmentations, as in the case of the livery provided on 20 July 1541 for Thomas Tyrrel and Jason Johnson, royal messengers.[88]

Some payments also went through Thomas Cromwell's hands as indicated in his papers. In the autumn of 1532 he received warrants dated 3 October ordering him to provide 21 red camlet coats guarded with velvet for the minstrels, and another with the same date for the delivery of coats costing 15*s* to John Reed, Thomas Freer, Anthony Fever and Nevill Derby.[89] In March 1533 he made payments to Avery, yeoman of the crossbows, for livery coats, and to Richard Gresham and William Botry for silks and velvets.[90] However, an undated document which the editors of *Letters and Papers* ascribe to *c.* 1533 but which must date closer to 1530 indicates that even at this stage in his career he had a key role in overseeing the livery of the king's household. Henry Norris, groom of the stool, sent a letter to him stating that 'the King commands that you shall apparel all of his minstrels in red camlet, with H and K embroidered after the old sort'.[91]

The price of magnificence: the budget for the great wardrobe

The chief sources of the great wardrobe's income were the exchequer, the chamber, the sale of unused cloth and rent collected from the properties owned by the wardrobe (Table 3.2). This funding could be supplied either by assignment or by prest. The draft declaration of the account for the year spanning the end of Henry VII's reign and the start of his son's reign (1508–09), recorded that silks held in stock were sold to John Fligh, Hugh Denys and William Smith,[92] while the account for 1510–11 listed the wardrobe as having 15 tenants.[93]

Henry VII observed in his will that the expenses of his household and wardrobe 'have continually had for the bering of the charges of the same, so large and sure assignments, that we trust there is little or nothing owing in behalf'.[94] Even so, Henry VII's household accounts and other papers reveal that balancing the income and expenditure of the great wardrobe was a recurring problem. The keeper frequently needed additional funds to balance his accounts. On 26 June 1498 Sir Robert Lytton received £904 15*s* 6*d* for the debts of the wardrobe over two years.[95] Further payments of £71 3*s* 6½*d* and £159 7*d* were made to him on 11 June 1502 and 30 May 1503 respectively.[96] In both cases, the practice of submitting accounts for two-year periods allowed the king to address the overspend before the final account was submitted. However, in some instances back payments were very late indeed. On 5 July 1505, £2,015 19*s* 11*d* was paid 'for the provision of our wardrobe in the first year of our reign'.[97]

In view of the premium placed on the royal wardrobe and the appearance of the household by the Tudor kings, it is not surprising that the cost of royal magnificence was high.

velvets'. A delivery of black velvet by William Lock on 13 April 1537 indicates that the book was in use immediately after Sir Anthony Denny's formal appointment as keeper.[135] There is a second, also undated, 44-page manuscript titled 'James Rufforthe hys booke for pellettes and Silkes' which records a much fuller list of silks including tissues, cloth of gold, cloth of silver and tinsel.[136] A number of the entries were annotated with a cross or short written notes recording cloth leaving the store such as 'm^{d} xxxv^{ui} peces and Rem^{ts} gon sins the first note taken'.[137]

Deliveries continued to be made to the silk store after Henry's death in January 1547. By this time the store was in the care of James Rufforth and it was housed in the secret wardrobe. In 1549 a range of silks were supplied by the Venetian merchant Dominico Erizo (16184–97, 16223–33, 16258–61, 16312–16).[138] They included 40 yards (36.6 m) of 'clothe of siluer purple with workes' (16228) and 18 yards (16.5 m) of 'Black vellat raysed with siluer'.

Suppliers to the great wardrobe

London was the centre for English trade and it was the main source of luxury goods supplied to the Tudor court. The court was served by a network of English merchants supplemented by a group of alien merchants, chiefly from Italy and the Hanse. The Londoners were keen to ensure that their position was safeguarded against unlicensed traders of the type that accompanied the French ambassadors in 1518. The ambassadors, led by Bonnivet and the bishop of Paris, had come to negotiate a marriage treaty and the surrender of Tournai, and they, along with much of their entourage, were housed at the merchant taylors' hall. According to Hall their retinue included:

> a great numbre of rascals & pedlers, & Iuellers, and [they] brought ouer hattes and cappes and diuerse merchaundise vncustomed, all vnder the coloure of the trussery of the Ambassadours . . . When these lordes were in their lodgynges, then the French harder men opened their wares & made the Taylers hal lyke to the paunde of a parte' 'many an Englishman grudged, but it auailed not.[139]

While the Londoners did not welcome these rival traders, the king was anxious to encourage European merchants with high-quality wares to come to England. Between July and December 1546, Henry VIII granted licences to five Italian, French and Flemish jewellers, allowing them to bring 'all manner of jewels, pearls and precious stones . . . of skins and sable furs . . . clothes and new gentleness of fashion . . . as he or they shall think best for the pleasure of us [and] our dearest wife, the Queen . . . '.[140]

A lot of cloth changed hands at the European cloth markets and the volume of trade there was always of interest to the king. On 7 August 1538 William Lock wrote to Henry VIII from Antwerp, reporting that cloth sales at the market had been very good.[141] Even so, there were sometimes problems of availability, especially of the more luxurious fabrics. John Husee explained to Lady Lisle in a series of letters that he could not get the type of cloth of gold that she wanted in London. On 22 May he noted that 'There will be no cloth of gold like the other. Mr Locck's is all plain', while on 26 May he informed her that 'There is no cloth of gold to be had such as you wish. Unless you will have plain cloth of gold, you must provide it from Antwerp or elsewhere'.[142] As this example demonstrates, the full range of types and colours of cloth was rarely available all year round in any large European city. On 31 July 1546, Stephen Vaughan sent 17¼ ells (11.9 m) of black velvet and 16 ells (11.1 m) of black damask at 13*s* and 6*s* the ell to Lord Cobham, and in his letter he wrote, 'I marvel that you buy silk here, where is neither so good choice as in London, nor is it so good cheap the money considered'.[143]

The great wardrobe accounts provide a very good indication of who was supplying the king and his court with cloth. However, they do not provide a complete picture. A number of sales were made directly to the king and to the wardrobe of the robes.[144] Worsley's inventory includes a number of entries recording the purchase of silks and how this cloth was then allocated to the king's tailor and hosier. The group of suppliers who traded directly with the wardrobe was much smaller and was dominated by the Italian merchants such as Anthony Bonvisi, Peter Francis de Bardi, Anthony Carsidony and Nicholas Venasses. The key English suppliers were William Botry, Richard Gresham and William Lock. Another way of looking at the Italian merchants trading in London is to consult their business papers which are particularly rich for the London house of the company of Peter Francis de Bardi and Giovanni Cavalcanti for the period 1521 to 1531.[145] These include two principal accounts, three letter books and a register of the cloth they sold.

Taking one English merchant supplying the wardrobe, Sir Richard Gresham, mercer of London, was licensed on 5 April 1516 to export cloth and other English merchandise not belonging to the staple of Calais and to import silk and gold cloths, woad, alum and wine.[146] He was listed as a supplier to the great wardrobe in the extant accounts for 1510–11, 1521–22, 1523–25 and 1526–27. However, his business with the wardrobe was modest in terms of the quantity of cloth and the range of goods: linen and sarsenet in 1510–11, lockram and velvet in 1521–22 and velvet only in 1523–25 and 1526–27. In contrast Gresham was recorded in Worsley's inventory as supplying the wardrobe of the robes with more silk fabrics, namely camlet [B718–20, 734], damask [B687, 695], satin [B638–39, 643–44, 657–61, 673] and velvet [B540–41, 567–70, 573, 583]. These silks had to be shipped to England and it was always possible for the cargo to be lost or damaged during transit. On 4 February 1542 he was paid £1,116 6*s* 6*d* for velvets, damasks and satins bought from him by the king.[147] On 31 October 1545 Wriothesley wrote to Paget, noting that Gresham had a new delivery of silks: 'he has brought home certain silks of which many be wet; and offers to sell them to the King but is content to bear the loss. They are velvets, satins, damasks and sarsenets.'[148] Thomas Gresham (*c.* 1518–79) was Sir Richard's second son.[149] He was not listed in any of the extant great wardrobe accounts and was listed just once in the 1547 inventory as having bought a 'fayer greate table Dyamounte ring' for Edward VI from Erasmus Skeetz (3687).[150] However, his portrait of 1544 demonstrates the elegant black clothes favoured by the merchants associated with the royal court (Fig. 3.6).

3.6 *Sir Thomas Gresham aged 26, unknown artist, Flemish School, 1544. Gresham's doublet and gown are heavily embroidered in black silk, so creating a sense of understated wealth and taste. MCPC Catalogue no. 043. By courtesy of the Mercers' Company*

An absence of objects made by the great wardrobe

The great wardrobe accounts record the details of hundreds of items of clothing from Henry VIII's reign, yet extant clothing from the mid Tudor period is the least well represented group of source material for this research. What garments do survive are frequently in very poor condition or fragmentary, so making their conservation and interpretation challenging, or they have been altered or repaired, so changing their original appearance.[151] However, garments in poor condition can often reveal a lot about construction methods, the materials used for interlinings and stiffenings that would be concealed in new garments. The simple truth is that there are no known surviving garments from Henry VIII's wardrobe. While something might be found in the future, currently a hawking glove in the Ashmolean is the closest it is possible to come to clothing worn by the king.[152]

English royal dress was not collected in the way it was in Swedish Royal Armouries or the ducal wardrobe at Dresden, so there is no comparable collection of clothing associated with the Tudor monarchs. Most items of English royal dress were recycled but some pieces, possibly with sentimental value, were retained. An old gown 'of purpull veluete syngle that was king Henry the vijth' was listed in his son's wardrobe book of 1516 [B78], as were the garter and parliament robes of prince Arthur [B13–18]. The same garter robes were listed in 1547 inventory (14177–78). This practice was not restricted to Henry VIII. Elizabeth I's wardrobe of the robes inventory dated to 1600 included a selection of Edward VI's clothes: his robes of the order of St Michael, one kirtle for the Garter, a kirtle and hood for parliament, three gowns, three frocks, two coats, two riding coats, a jerkin, three doublets with hose, a selection of buckles, aglets and buttons and a dagger.[153] A selection of Mary's clothes were also present, including five French gowns, a gown, a loose gown, seven kirtles, five French kirtles and two foreparts.

In November and December 1623 an inventory was taken at Denmark house on the Strand of the objects in the charge of Richard Brown.[154] His charge included a selection of Henry VIII's clothes that were listed after Anne of Denmark's coronation robes. These were predominantly outer garments, consisting of two robes for the order of St Michael, three short gowns, four cloaks, ten coats, a nightgown and a cassock. Finally, there were 'two chests with sleeues and peeces of garments the chests being almost full of them but utterly unusefull and of noe value', 'seauenteene Borders of gould wrought upon Holland like enbr[audered] which were king Henry his bands' and 'A Grene veluet coffer with king Henry his Shirts in the same'.[155] It is possible that these clothes were a relic of when Denmark house had been the home of the duke of Somerset, Edward VI's first protector, because Somerset had acquired some of the late king's possessions.[156] Almost all of these items were still at Denmark House in 1649 and they were sold in the Commonwealth sale.[157] At this point Henry VIII's wardrobe ceased to exist.

Notes

1 Lurie, *Language of Clothes*.
2 For a discussion of this problem in relation to dress terminology in the fourteenth and fifteenth centuries, see Scott, *Visual History*, p. 18.
3 For the artificers who worked there, see below, pp. 317–29.
4 Tout, *Chapters*, IV, pp. 349–437; K. Staniland, 'Clothing provision and the Great Wardrobe in the mid-thirteenth century', *Textile History*, 22.2 (1991), pp. 239–52.
5 Tout, *Chapters*, IV, pp. 412–13.

IV

The Cycle of Royal Life: Coronations to Funerals

HENRY VIII's life was punctuated by a series of births, marriages and deaths that shaped both his destiny and that of the country. The format of these events — encompassing christenings, marriages, churchings, coronations and funerals — was controlled by tradition and the specific details were often described in household ordinances and the accounts produced by the royal heralds. Special clothing was provided for the royal protagonists, while bulk orders of livery were supplied to their household for coronations and funerals. In this cycle, a funeral can be seen as the starting point because a royal death initiated the new reign and ended the old. However, this chapter begins with the ritual marking the start of a new reign, the coronation, and moves through the reign towards death and a funeral.

Royal magnificence on these occasions was emphasised with dress, jewellery and associated textiles, while spectacle was used to support contemporary ideas of the sanctity of kingship. Sir Francis Bacon expressed this by comparing princes 'to heavenly bodies, which cause good or evil times, and which have much veneration but no rest'.[1] Specific clothes were associated with the different ceremonies, their style and materials dictated by tradition. Much of the evidence for what was worn and by whom comes from four main sources: the accounts of the lord chamberlain who oversaw coronations and funerals, the accounts of the great wardrobe, official accounts prepared by the heralds and comments from independent observers. Each of these highly significant events is considered in generic terms and Henry VIII's participation is discussed. Henry's experience of these ceremonies is then compared with that of the other members of the house of Tudor. This makes it possible to assess how far these occasions were dictated by precedent and how far they were tailored to suit specific agendas.

Coronations

The coronation marked the relationship between the visible, material aspects and the invisible, immaterial aspects of early modern kingship.[2] Elizabeth I put this duality into words when she described herself a few days after the death of her sister Mary: 'I am but one bodye naturallye considered though by hys [God's] permission a bodye politique to governe.'[3] The liturgy, through the conference of the sacrament of coronation, provided the means by which this transformation occurred, while the robes and regalia symbolised the process.

English coronations were held on a Sunday. They were the culmination of a three-day cycle of events starting with the monarch's arrival at the Tower of London for a series of rituals there, his procession through London to Westminster and the coronation itself. The anointing and crowning were followed by a banquet in Westminster hall and a tournament held in the Westminster palace yard. The king's champion's chief royal duty was performed at the coronation. The king's champion was a hereditary post which rested since 1377 in the hands of the Dymoke family of Scrivelsby, Lincolnshire. In June 1509 Sir Robert Dymoke issued the traditional challenge at Henry's coronation, just as he had previously at the coronations of Richard III and Henry VII:

> The seconde course beyng serued: in at the haule doore entered a knight, armed at all poyntes, his bases rich tissue embroidered, a great plume & a sumptuous of Oistriche fethers on his helmet, sittyng on a great courser, trapped in tissue and embroidered with tharmes of England and of Fraunce, and an herauld of armes before hym.[4]

All Tudor coronations were celebrated in Westminster abbey. However, the possibility of crowning Catherine Howard at York in 1541 as the culmination of the progress to the north was considered. The timing of a queen's coronation was often linked to her being pregnant or having had a child.

On 26 January 1540 Sir William Eure wrote to Cromwell, informing him that 'the queen of Scots, now with child, is to be crowned on Sunday 1 February'.[5] On 10 April that year the French ambassador wrote to Francis stating that Catherine Howard was thought to be pregnant and that 'if it be found to be true, [the King would] have her crowned at Whitsuntide. Already all the embroiderers that can be got are employed making furniture and tapestry, the copes and ornaments taken from the churches not being spared'.[6]

Excommunication was a very serious matter for any individual threatened with it, especially an anointed monarch. Pope Julius II excommunicated James IV of Scotland but the pope's death in February 1513 prevented him expelling James from the faithful. The task of excommunicating him fell to Leo X, as one of the first acts of his pontificate. Consequently, after recovering James's body at Flodden, Henry VIII sought papal approval for holding a funeral ceremony in St Paul's cathedral. Permission was withheld on the grounds that James was an excommunicate and Henry acknowledged that 'it is due punishment for one who hath perjurously broken his league'.[7] Henry VIII was threatened with excommunication twice, in July 1533 and in August 1535, and he would have been well aware of the consequences.[8]

The regalia

As Sir John Eliot noted in *The Boke Named the Governor*, the regalia was the most potent symbol of Tudor kingship. The coronation provided the context in which the monarch received the regalia 'in an open and stately place before all their subjectes' so ensuring 'perpetuall reverence, whiche is fountayne of obedience'.[9] The crown was the most significant item of Tudor regalia because Henry VII adopted the closed, arched imperial crown, surmounted with a cross. This form replaced the open crown traditionally worn by English kings, so reinforcing the idea of the *imperium*, or empire, of English kings.[10] The description of the crown's border in 1547 gives a good indication of the quantity and quality of gemstones used: 'The border garnished with vj Ballaces v saphires fyve pointed Dyamountes Twentie Rubies Nyneteene perles and one of the crosses of the same Crowne garnished with a greate Saphire an Emerade crased iiij ballaces and nyne perles nott all of one sorte and three Saphires' (1). The points of the crown consisted of alternating crosses and fleur-de-lis, some of which were embellished with enamelled figures including 'an Image of our ladie and her child' and 'an Image of a king'. The king's crown was worn with 'a Capp of purple vellat lyned with blacke satten' (1). The rest of the regalia consisted of a pair of gold bracelets set with ballaces and pearls (2), a sceptre with a dove on the top (3), a gold rod (4) and an orb (5). A list of jewels from 1528 also included a reference to 'a ruby ring the King was sacred with'.[11]

The regalia of the queen consort was smaller and lighter than that provided for the king, in recognition of the weaker female form and of the queen consort being inferior to the king. The consort had less regalia and, unlike the king, the queen did not have an orb.[12] Most important was the difference in the quality of the stones used, as indicated by the description of the queen's crown: 'the bordour [was] set with vj Saphures not all of a fynes the less Saphures vj Balacys not fyne iiij small balacys of litle value xxiiij bigge pearlis not fyne and viij small perlis.'[13] The queen's crown was also worn with 'a Cappe . . . of purple vellat with a roll in it' (6). However, references to the queen wearing a circlet instead of a crown appear in several of the narrative accounts. Catherine of Aragon's circlet was listed in the 1521 inventory as 'a Cerclet of golde newe made for the Quene at the Coronacion sett with a fayre Emerade iiij fayre Saphures iiij Rosis of Diamoundys iiij balacys all set in Rosis and xiiij perlis like of a sorte'.[14] This circlet was still part of the queen's regalia in 1547 (8), along with a sceptre with a dove on the knop (7).

Edward VI, being a minor, needed a smaller, lighter crown and one was made for him 'against his coronacion'. The gemstones and pearls were taken from caps and collars that had belonged to his father. The crown had a:

> nether Border sett with ix pointed diamountes and ix Settes of peerles and v peerles in every sett being vppon the same border certeyne Borders of Antiques of golde sett with viij rocke Rubies and xx peerles with foure borders which make the Crown Imperiall sett with iiij Emerades iiij Rubies and iiij diamountes with lxxj peerles and with a Lardge Ballace in the toppe percede sett with a litell crosse of golde in the toppe of the Ballace enameled. (3279)

After making it, Everard Everdes, the king's goldsmith, had 36 of the 81 garnishing pearls, 39 of the 100 small garnishing pearls and four of the 24 pearls of unspecified type left over (3680–82). In addition, a second new piece of regalia was commissioned for the duke of Somerset, acknowledging his role as Protector. He had a coronet with six 'Trafelles of gold every one having foure peerles and a small pointed diamounde', three 'Saphires sett In Collettes of golde' and three 'small Ballaces vnsett' (3683–85).

The Tudor regalia was destroyed during the Commonwealth because, without a monarchy, there was no need to preserve it. In France, Francis I established the idea of the inalienability of the French regalia and crown jewels. This was possibly as a consequence of Mary Tudor removing the celebrated diamond, called the Mirror of Naples from France after the death of Louis XII.[15] This ruling was evident after the death of the dauphin, when Mary Stuart returned the diamond and pendant pearl that Francis I had bought for her at a cost of 65,000 ducats.[16]

Coronation robes

Eliot identified a second reason for public coronations: 'we be men and nay aungels, wherefore we knowe nothinge but by outwarde significations.' He added that 'reporte is nat so commune a token as apparayle'.[17] Eliot's comment emphasises the part played by the monarch's robes in the coronation. These were the first set of formal robes made for a new monarch at the start of their reign. A queen regnant wore a sequence of robes very similar to those made for a king with just minor concessions made for female modesty at the time of anointing. In contrast, the robes for a queen consort reflected her subsidiary role by there being fewer sets of garments and their being less magnificent.

Distinct sets of robes were required for the specific days of the coronation and at set times on the day of the coronation itself. The style of these robes was laid down in the *Liber Regalis* which was drawn up in Richard II's reign and formed the basis of the *Little Devise*. Worsley's wardrobe book included an entry for the king's 'Coronacion Robes of purpull Veluete' which were valued at £200 and consisted of 'a kyrtell furred with menever', 'a Taberd furred with menever', 'a hode furred with menever & a Cappe of estate' and 'a Mantell furred with Ermynes' [B1–4]. The public nature of the coronation ensured that the robes were made of the very best quality materials. This is evident in a letter sent by Magdalene of France, the first wife of James V, as she prepared for her coronation in Scotland: 'Tell the King ... that I commend myself very humbly to his good grace ... and remind him of the pearls he promised me. Send me also the paternosters to accompany my robe, for it has none ... I pray you to let the martin with which my robe is to be furred be beautiful.'[18]

The first coronation portraits to survive from the Tudor period are those of Elizabeth I.[19] However, the picture of Richard II in majesty painted *c.* 1395 shows the young king wearing his coronation mantle of crimson velvet lined with ermine, with a cape of ermine.[20] Although now lost, the building accounts for Whitehall record that painters were paid for 'drawing and setting owte with colours the coronacion of our seide soverigne lorde'.[21] Henry VIII commissioned these murals celebrating his coronation for the low gallery at Whitehall.

During the fifteenth century, English queens were provided with white robes, symbolising purity, as they travelled from the Tower to Westminster. For example, Margaret of Anjou wore 'white damask poudred with gold, riche perles and precious stones'.[22] In a similar vein, Anne Neville, Richard III's queen, wore a mantle and kirtle made from 27 yards (24.6 m) of white cloth of gold furred with miniver and ermine with a mantle lace of Venice gold and white silk.[23] A drawing of Anne wearing these robes has been preserved in the English version of the Rous Roll.[24] Queen consorts continued to wear white under the house of Tudor. Henry VII's ordinances laid down the procedures for a queen's coronation as follows: 'and as for her array for her body, shee must bee in her sircote of white damaske, or white cloth of gould, with a mantle of the same poudred with ermines ... shee must bee bare harded and bare visaged till she come to Westminster, that all men may see her.'[25]

The wearing of royal robes was a sign of the right to rule. Thus their misappropriation was irrefutable evidence of aspiration to royalty. The complaints brought against the duke of Albany in March 1516 included the charge that he would not allow Queen Margaret to have custody of her son and that he 'wears himself the robe royal and the cap of maintenance, has the sceptre carried before him, acts in all points like a king, and appropriates the revenues of the Crown, so that it is much to be expected that he will destroy the young King, now that her son, the young Duke, is dead, most probably through his means'.[26] Albany's assumption of royal dress and income were seen as clear signifiers of an intention to usurp royal power.

THE JOINT CORONATION OF HENRY VIII AND CATHERINE OF ARAGON

The coronations of the monarch and their consort could be separate events or they could have a double coronation as Henry VIII and Catherine of Aragon did (Fig. 4.1), which echoed that of Richard III and Anne Neville on 6 July 1483. Joint coronations were unusual and so Henry's decision to have a double coronation marked him out from the other Tudors. Henry and Catherine's coronation began on Friday 22 June 1509 and for his vigil he wore a doublet of cloth of gold of damask satin under a long gown of purple velvet furred with powdered ermine and open at the sides. On Saturday 23 June they processed from the Tower to Westminster. The coronation itself took place on Sunday 24 June, Midsummer's day, when the couple walked from the palace of Westminster to Westminster abbey. Like his father before him, Henry VIII was provided with the traditional set of coronation clothes. The descriptions record not only the materials and construction of these garments but also indicate their significance:

4.1 *Woodcut depicting the coronation of Henry VIII and Catherine of Aragon, from the pamphlet 'A Joyfull Medytacyon ... of the coronacyon of our moost naturall soveragne lorde' by Stephen Hawes,* c. *1510. Both are dressed in the traditional coronation robes, and Catherine of Aragon's hair hangs down loose over her shoulders, as required by the household ordinances. Cambridge University Library, Sel. 5.55. By permission of the Syndics of Cambridge University Library*

ij Shirtes wherof one shall be of lawne the other of Crymesyn Tartaryn they bothe largely open behynde and before & ouer the Shulders & the boughtes of the Armes and laced with Anlettes of Siluer and gilte And with laces Agglett with siluer & gilt.
a large breche to the myd thigh pynched together before and behynde.
a breche belte of veluet to gather the same togider.
a payr hosyn of Crymesyn Satyn vampesshed.
a Coote of Crymesyn Satyn largely openyd as the Shertes ben to the which Cote his hosen shall be laced with Ryban of Silke.
a Sircote cloth of crymysyn Satyn furred with menyver pure Wherof the handes Coller and the Spayrs shall be garnysshed with ryban of golde.
a hoode of Astate furred with menever pure purfilled with Ermyns.
A grete mantell of Crymysyn Satyn furred with pure menyver And a grete lace of Silke with ij Tasselles also of Crymysyn.
a litill hatt or Cap of astate of Crymysyn Satyn ermyned & garnysshed with Ryban of gold.
a payr of lynnen Gloves to be put uppon the kinges handes aftir he is anoynted.
a Tabard of white Tartaryn after the Shape of a dalmatyk to be putt uppon the kinges Coote when he is anoynted.
A Coyff to be put vppon the kinges hed whiche the kyng shall were viij dayes after.
A payr of Sabatons.
A Cap of blacke veluet for the fillyng of the Crowne And an other of blak Satyn for to sitte strayte uppon his hed under that.
the kinges Roobes of purpyll veluet.
the kinges Robes ageynst the parliament of Crymesyn veluet.[27]

Catherine of Aragon was provided with less clothing than her husband, but the garments she did receive mirrored his colour and materials. For her entry into the Tower and for the coronation procession when she was borne to Westminster, she wore:

a kirtill and a mantell with a Treyne of white cloth of Golde, the kirtill furred with menever pure and the mantell with Ermyns powdred with a mantellace of White Silke & Golde with botones and Tasselles of the same And Ryban of gold of venyce for the same mantell And the seid kirtill garnysshed with lxx Aunelettes of Siluer & gilte.[28]

For succeeding stages of the coronation itself she had two sets of velvet robes, the first of purple and the second of crimson, which were very similar to those provided for the previous day.[29] According to Hall, Catherine's litter was 'borne on twoo White Palfries the Litter couered and richely appareled, the Palfries Trapped in White clothe of gold, her persone appareled in white Satyn Embrodered, her heire hangyng doune to her backe, of a very great length, bewtefull and goodly to behold, and on her hedde a Coronall, set with many riche orient stones'.[30] *The Great Chronicle* recorded that she was dressed 'In a Rych mantell of cloth of Tyssu, In her here wyth a cerculet of sylke gold & perle abouth hir hede . . . hir mantell & furre of powderid ermyns withyn the same'.[31] In addition, like her husband she had 'A payr of Sabatons couered in crimesyn cloth of Golde lyned with Crymseyn Satyn garnysshed with Ryban of venyce golde'.[32] Canopies were traditionally carried over queens of England as they made their way to be crowned. In 1509 *The Great Chronicle* noted that there was a sudden heavy shower of rain as Catherine of Aragon passed a tavern called the Cardinal's Hat and her canopy was not 'sufficient to deffend hyr ffrom wetyng of hir mantell'.[33]

Two groups within the king's household did not receive the standard red livery. They were the henchmen and the footmen. Their role in the coronation procession required something more impressive. Henry was accompanied by nine henchmen provided with two sets of clothing and a courser with saddles and trappers covered with crimson velvet and fringed with green and white silk.[34] For their first set of clothing the henchmen wore gowns of white cloth of gold and doublets of crimson satin, and for their change of attire they were given gowns of crimson velvet lined with white sarsenet and doublets of green satin.[35] The king's footmen were provided with doublets of green satin and jackets of white cloth of gold.[36] This provision echoes the style of his father's coronation but varied in the details. Henry VII had seven henchmen, who were also provided with two gowns: first 'partie gownes of Cloth of gold white and grene' and then gowns of crimson velvet 'wrought with Goldsmythe worke'.[37] His four footmen received the same, but jackets rather than gowns.[38]

Lady Margaret delighted in her grandson's coronation. To ensure that she could see him in his finery, she paid 2*s* 10*d* 'for the hyre of the howse in the Chepesyde where my lades and the princesse of Castell stode whan ye kyng and the Quene came frome the Toure to Westminster to be crowned'.[39] In addition, her household accounts show that she attired herself and her women in new, tawny-coloured clothes made from a variety of types of cloth. One of her servants, Robert Fremingham, received 4*s* 8*d* for his costs going from Greenwich to London three times to buy the silk.[40] He bought 41 yards (37.5 m) of tawny satin and 25 yards (22.8 m) tawny damask from William Lock, 32½ yards (29.7 m) of tawny satin from Richard Clifford, 29½ yards (26.9 m) of tawny damask, 20½ yards (18.7 m) of tawny velvet, 24 yards (21.9 m) of black velvet and five pieces of tawny camlet from Lewis Harpesfield and four plain bonnets of black velvet from Mistress Stanhope.[41] Robert Hilton's view of the wardrobe at Hatfield shows how the cloth was distributed: seven gowns of tawny satin for her gentlewomen taking between 12 and 13½ yards (10.9 m–12.3 m) of cloth, a gown of tawny velvet for Mistress Parker and gowns of tawny damask for the other six, while her three chamberers, Jane Walter, Margaret Stukeley and Perot Doren, each received gowns of tawny camlet.[42] In contrast, her chief male officers were dressed in russet: Master Parker and Master Zouche had gowns of russet damask, while Master Stanhope had a gown of russet satin.[43]

Textiles were also used to decorate the ceremonial route and to drape the coronation church. The great wardrobe accounts noted that 'the kynges pulpytte at Westmynster Church oughte to arayed Steyers Reyles and all with Red Worsted'. In addition, red worsted was used to drape 'the Sieges Royall in the same as in the myddes thereof to be arrayed with cloth of Golde and with Quysshyns of the same'. Finally, 'asmoche Raycloth be purveyed fore as shall serue vnder foote from the marble chayre in Westmynster halle into the pulpytt in Westmynster church goyng out of the grete Gate of the palaice and entring at the weste dore of the church and at the west dore of the Quere'.[44] Tapestries also played a significant role at Tudor coronations.[45]

The ambassadors from Aragon and Castile, who attended the joust after the coronation, were impressed because they 'had neuer seen the kyng in harneys'. Hall, the chronicler, recorded that 'ye Spanish Ambassadours desyred to haue some of the badges or deuises which were on the kynges trapper: his grace therof knowing, commaunded Euery of them to take therof what it pleased them, who in effect toke all or the more parte: for in the beginning they thought that they had bene counterfeit, and not golde'.[46] An indication of the cost of the coronation can be gleaned from the king's book of payments. John Shirley, the cofferer, received £1,000 on 24 May 'on a warrant signed towards the expenses of the king's coronation', while Henry Smith was given £100 on 3 June.[47] On 8 July Andrew Windsor received £3,000 towards the great wardrobe's expenses for the coronation and on 26 August he was allocated a further £2,322.[48]

INDIVIDUAL CORONATIONS: HENRY VII AND EDWARD VI

Not surprisingly, Henry VII's coronation followed the pattern of his Yorkist predecessors, so reinforcing the legitimacy of his claim to the throne.[49] Indeed the 'litle devise of the coronacion of ... Prince Henrie the vijth' was copied from that drawn up for Richard III.[50] So on 27 October Henry dined with Thomas Bourchier, archbishop of Canterbury at Lambeth palace, and then he processed to the Tower of London. He stayed there overnight and created new knights of the Bath. An entry for 87 ells (59.6 m) of Flemish cloth 'for the Bathe at westminster' costing 54*s* 10½*d* provide a hint of the provision made for these ceremonial baths.[51] The following day Henry VII walked, bare-headed, under a canopy from the Tower to Westminster hall, dressed in a purple velvet robe edged with ermine. Henry VII was anointed and crowned on Sunday 30 October 1485 at Westminster abbey. The tournament planned for the next Sunday was postponed until 13 November.[52]

Henry VII's coronation robes were made by his tailor, George Lovekyn. They consisted of a 'longe mantelle with a trayne of crimson satin furred with menever' with a matching hood, kirtle and cap of estate, a similar long mantle of purple velvet with a train furred with powdered ermine, with a matching hood, kirtle, sircote and cap of estate and the king's parliament robes made from crimson velvet, also with a hood, kirtle and tabard.[53] Lovekyn made a number of other items for Henry VII, his henchmen and his footmen, with the bill for his labour coming to £15 4*s* 4*d*. Earlier in the same set of accounts there is a list of payments for materials which helps to fill out the brief descriptions given in Lovekyn's list. These included 43¾ yards (40 m) of crimson velvet required 'for the parliament Robe' costing £67, along with three buttons for the mantlelace (8*s*) and a mantlelace of crimson silk (3*s* 8*d*). In addition to the formal robes, Henry VII received a range of other garments that played a traditional role in the coronation. For these Lovekyn required 6 yards (5.4 m) of crimson satin for a dalmatic for the king (£4), 3 yards (2.7 m) of cloth of gold 'for capes off estate and a skabard of a swerde' (£6), ¾ yard (0.68 m) of cloth of gold for the king's sabatons (30*s*) lined with the same quantity of crimson satin, 3 yards (2.7 m) of crimson sarsenet 'for a Sherte for the king', a piece of sipers for another shirt, ¾ yard (0.68 m) of holland for a pair of gloves for the king and an ell (0.67 m) of the same for a coif.[54]

Sir Robert Willoughby, joint steward of the household, spent £1,506 18*s* 10¾*d* on preparations for the coronation.[55] Provision was also made within the great wardrobe as indicated by the account of the keeper, Alvered Corneburgh. For the period 22 August 1485 to 2 February 1486 Alvered made payments of approximately £1,300.[56] In August 1487 Henry paid £39 4*s* 1*d* for 'robes for our chancellor and chancellery against our coronation'.[57]

In contrast to his grandfather, the accounts for Edward VI's coronation provide the most complete record of the clothes worn by a Tudor king on being crowned. Edward VI succeeded his father on 21 January 1547 and he was crowned a month later on 20 February (Shrove Sunday). On the proceeding day, Edward had processed through London dressed in white velvet and cloth of silver under a crimson canopy. The accounts record that the clothes were very traditional but also indicate that they were subtly different from those provided for his father:

> In primis A riche gowne of cloth of golde and all ouer Imbrodered with damaske with a square cape furred with Sable.
> Item a gyrkyn of whit welvit wrought with venis Syluer garnished with precios stones as Rubyes dymondes and Treuloves of perles.
> Item a doblet of whit welvit according to the Same Imbrodered venis Silver garnisshed with Like precios stones and pareles.
> Item a whit welvit cape garnished with Lyke precios stones and pereles.
> Item a payre of Buskins of whit welvit.
> Item his horse capparison of Crimson Saten Imbrodered with parles of damaske golde.[58]

This list of clothes compares well with the account of the young king's procession through London:

> The kynges Royall Majestie walking a lytell before his canopy, because the people might the better see his grace, his highness being richly apparelled with a riche gowne of cloth of silver all over embrodered with damaske golde, with a girkyn of white velvett, wrought with Venyce silver, garnished with precious stones, as rubies and diamonds, with true-loves of pearles, a doblet of white velvet according to the same, with like precious stones, and perles, and a pere of buskenes of white velvet. His horse caparison [was] of crymoysyn sattyn, imbrodered with perles and damaske gold.[59]

On the Sunday, Edward came by boat to the privy stairs at Westminster where the stairs were lined by the gentleman pensions who were 'apparelled all in Red Damaske, with their Pole Axes in their Hands, and the Guard in their rich Coates, likewise with their Holbardes, standing on either Side by all the Way when his Grace should pass'.[60] He was then taken to the room where the court of augmentations met, where he put on his ceremonial robes:

> A Robe of Crimson velvet with a long Trayne, furred with powdered Ermynes throughout. A Surcoat of the same, furred with Mynver pure, the Coller, Skirts and Sleevehands garnished with Ribbons of Gold, with Two Taberds, Four fingers broad, with a Hood, likewise powdred, which were called his Parliament Robes, wearing on his Head a Capp of Blue Velvuett.[61]

Edward prostrated himself before the high altar in the abbey and then he was 'unarraied and unclothed by his Great Chamberlaine' and 'apparelled in a Coate of Crimson Satten, open and buttoned before and behind, on the Shoulders and the Elbowes, with a Coyfe of Gold on his head'.[62] After the anointing, his shirt was laced up, a linen coif was place on his head and a pair of linen gloves was placed on his hands. He was dressed in 'a Robe of crymsyn Saten with a Longe trayne furred with poudered ermyns' and 'a Syrcote of the same furred with mynvur puere with ij Taberdes of the Same eged with pouderyd ermyns iiij fyngeers brode'. This was accompanied by 'a hode of crymsyn Saten furred with powdered ermins as face as yt was tourned downe around a boute his neke'. He was then crowned.[63] The young king made a final change of clothes, dressing in 'other Royall Apparel, as a Surcote of Purple Velvet furred with Ermynes, etc a rich Cronne was also sett upon his Head'.[64] More specifically, the 'Royal Apparel' consisted of:

A robe of purple velvet with a Longe trayne furred through out with poudered Ermyns And also on his showlders and a Lytill beneth with Lyke ermyns [and] a Syrcot of the same veluet furred with mynever pure with ij tabardes set on the Same furred with Lyke ermines with a hood of the same also furred with ermyns so farre as yt was turnide downe abowt the necke.

Finally, four caps and a hat of maintenance were made for Edward's coronation at a cost of £15 18*s* 4*d*.[65] Three were made from purple velvet and lined with crimson satin, while one cap and the hat were made from crimson satin. The hat was decorated with 'a greate bawle of damaske golde', while each of the caps was ornamented with 'a great rose of gold raised'.

MARY I AND ELIZABETH I

Both of Henry VIII's daughters were crowned as queens in their own right. Mary I ordered a set of cloth of gold coronation robes or robes of estate for her coronation in 1553.[66] The cloth of gold was woven with Tudor roses and fleur-de-lis. Elizabeth I was crowned on 14 January 1559, and in a spirit of frugality rather than sisterly love Elizabeth recycled her sister's coronation robes. She wore the same mantle and kirtle but had the bodice of the kirtle remade to give it a more fashionable V-shaped waistline.[67] The robes consisted of 'one Mantle of Clothe of golde tissued with golde and silver furred with powdered Armyons with a Mantle lace of silke and golde with buttons and Tassells to the same [and] one kirtle of the same tissue the traine and skirts furred with powdered Armyons the rest lined with Sarceonet with a paire of bodies and sleeves to the same'.[68]

The first extant Tudor coronation portraits come from Elizabeth's reign. The two versions seem to derive from an image contemporary with the coronation. The earlier of the two is a miniature of Elizabeth in her coronation robes, painted *c.* 1559–70s, by an artist from the English school. Even though a miniature, the artist attained a high level of detail on her clothing, possibly indicating that he had access to the robes.[69] The half-length portrait of Elizabeth in her coronation robes dates from *c.* 1600.[70] In addition there is a sketch of Elizabeth's coronation procession drawn in *c.* 1560–70 which depicts Elizabeth being carried in a litter that 'was trimmed down to the ground with gold brocade'.[71]

QUEEN CONSORTS

Elizabeth of York

Elizabeth was crowned on St Catherine's day, Sunday 25 November 1486. It is very likely that the choice of date — the feast of a major intercessory female saint — was intentional on the part of Henry VII.[72] The timing was also significant because Elizabeth was crowned barely two months after the birth of their first child, Henry's son and heir. The ceremony was suited to Elizabeth's status but the separate coronation was intended to indicate that Henry's claim to the throne was valid in its own right rather than being dependent upon his wife.

As she travelled to the Tower by barge on the Friday, Elizabeth was entertained by a series of aquatic pageants, a feature that was repeated for Anne Boleyn's coronation.[73] The representatives of the livery companies met Elizabeth in barges that had been 'freshely furnyshed with Baners and Stremers of Silk richely besene — the Armes and Bagges of ther Crafts'.[74] Elizabeth's arrival by river was a departure from usual practice of the queen making her entry into the City on horseback and riding to the Tower. The next day she was carried in a litter from the Tower to Westminster. Her master of the horse, Sir Roger Cotton, was given £40 to buy eight coursers in Flanders for the chair or litter to serve the queen at her coronation.[75] Elizabeth was accompanied by the king's mother, Lady Margaret Beaufort, rather than her own mother or her sisters. This and the change in style of her arrival may have been intended to indicate that Elizabeth's coronation was a break with the Yorkist traditions and as such was a means of establishing the new royal house.

For her coronation, Elizabeth of York, like other English queens, was provided with several sets of robes. So 'on the Morne, the Day of the Coronation, she was appareled in a Kirtill and a Mantell of Purple Velvett furred with Ermyns with a Lace afor the Mantell. On her Hair [she wore] a Serklett of Golde richely garnyshede with Perle and precious Stonys'.[76] This compares well with the section in Henry VII's ordinances which described the robes worn by a queen on the morning of her coronation: 'and in the morne [she is] to be arrayed with kirtle, sircote and mantle of plaine purple velvet . . . and the estate that beareth the trayne to have her sircote, and mantle of plain purple velvett like as the Queene, saving not of soe deepe a colour.'[77]

The emphasis placed on subtle gradations of colour indicates contemporary appreciation of such distinctions. Later that day, Elizabeth was:

rially apparelde, having about her a Kyrtill of whithe Cloth of Golde of Damaske, and a Mantell of the same Suete furrede with Ermyns, fastened byfor her Breast with a great Lace curiously wrought of Golde and Silk, and riche Knoppes of Golde at the Ende tasselled; her faire yelow Hair hanging downe pleyne byhynd her Bak, with a Calle of Pipes over it. She had a Serklet of Golde richely garnyshed with precious Stonys uppon her Hede.[78]

Fragmentary accounts survive for Elizabeth's coronation. These include payments of 13*s* 4*d* to Griffiths White, spurrier, 42*s* 7*d* to John Massy, tawyer, 24*s* to John Bromhall, joiner, for staves for her canopy, £65 10*s* 2*d* to John Ring, skinner, £17 to Roger Barlow for worsted, £4 1*s* 9*d* to Robert Drayton, for fur, 65*s* 4*d* to Thomas Ludury, lorimer, for bits, £54 12*s* 9*d* to William Rothwell, mercer, for scarlet and £97 8*s* 4*d* Walter Povey, tailor, for scarlet and ray.[79] While this list provides many insights into the range of craftsmen involved in preparing for Elizabeth's coronation, it cannot be the full list of materials because, for example, there is no cloth of gold. A separate bill recorded that £65 10*s* 2*d* was also paid to Ring, for ermine, miniver pure and powderings of him bought for furring 'of dyvers of ye quenes robes ayenst her coronacion'.[80] The other extant payments for the queen's coronation included scarlet and the furring of the henchmen's gowns.

At the coronation banquet, the duke of Bedford's clothes and horse trapper were embroidered with dragons and red roses, both symbols of Henry VII's heritage.[81] Henry VII attended his wife's coronation and remained for the banquet afterwards but, in order to ensure that she was the focus, he was screened from view on a 'goodley stage covered and well besene with Clothes of Arras and wele latyzede'.[82] Even so, the king was 'as a comely and roiall Prince, apparailled accordingly'.[83] Jousts were held to celebrate her coronation and on 5 October 1487 Sir Richard Guildford received 100 marks towards their cost.[84]

Anne Boleyn

At the time of her coronation, Anne was six months pregnant. According to Archbishop Cranmer her coronation was held after the marriage 'which took place about St Paul's day [25 January] last' because 'the condition thereof doth well appear, by reason she is now somewhat big with child'.[85] Chapuys reported how Anne and her father had disagreed about her dress. Anne added a length of fabric to the skirt of her gown. Her father desired her to remove it in order to emphasise her condition.

On 28 April 1533 Henry VIII appointed Lady Cobham to attend upon Anne at her coronation. Lady Cobham had to provide her own mount but she was assured of harness for her horse by the master of the queen's horse and of her robes by the keeper of the great wardrobe.[86] At the same time orders were drawn up detailing what need to be prepared for Anne. These included a kirtle and mantle of cloth of gold furred with ermine with a lace of silk and gold with tassels, to be worn with a gold circlet garnished with precious stones for the day of the procession through London. She was to wear a kirtle and mantle of purple velvet furred with ermine for the day of the coronation with a lace. Livery was to be given according to the precedents of the great wardrobe.[87]

When on 19 May Anne Boleyn travelled from Greenwich to the Tower by barge, her journey was 'enlived by barges with musicians, a dragon and terrible monsters and wylde men castyng fyer, and makyng hideous noyses'.[88] She remained at the Tower until the end of the month.[89] Her coronation, unlike that of her husband, was accompanied by a series of pageants in London held on Saturday 31 May, at the king's request for his 'moste deare and welbeloued wyfe Quene Anne'.[90] The City companies not only paid for the pageants, they added to the spectacle by their attendance. 'The mayor, aldermen and crafts of London are to do their service as accustomed, and the streets between the Tower and Westminster are to be garnished with tapestry, arras and silk, and the banners, standards and pennons of the crafts to be ready to garnish the barges and stand where the wardens be of each occupation.'[91] Anne rode from the Tower to Westminster. She was followed by 'fower chariotts, with ladies . . . rytchlie behanged and also divers other ladies and gentlewomen riding on horsebacke all in gounes made of crymson velvet'.[92]

A warrant for a litter for Queen Anne Boleyn (but almost certainly not the one used for the coronation) allowed 32½ yards (29.7 m) of crimson velvet at 13*s* 4*d* the yard (0.91 m), lined with 19 yards (17.3 m) of crimson damask, 46*s* 8*d* for making the litter and 33*s* 4*d* for painting it.[93] One description of the procession through London described her riding in 'an open litter of white cloth of gold, drawn by two palfries in white damask'.[94]

Anne was anointed and crowned by Archbishop Cranmer with the crown of St Edward the Confessor on Whit Sunday (1 June).[95] Observers noted that 'she wore a surcote and mantle of white cloth of tissue, the latter furred with ermine. Her hair hanging down, but on her head was a coif with a circlet of rich stones'.[96] She was accompanied by the leading ladies of the court with 'the olde Dutches of Norfolke bearing upp her traine in a robe of scarlett with a cronett of golde on her bonett . . . and after her tenne ladies following in robes of scarlett furred with ermins and rounde cronettes of gold on their heads; and next after theim all the Queenes maides in gounes of scarlett edged with white lettushe furre'.[97]

The sketch depicting the coronation banquet is unflattering of Anne. However, it does indicate her place at the centre of attention, a position reinforced by the fact that 'the King and divers ambassadors looked on from a little closet out of the cloister of St Stephen's' for the banquet.[98] It gives only a fleeting impression of her dress (Fig. 4.2). However, after the coronation banquet she 'withdrew her selfe with a fewe ladyes . . . to her chamber; and there shifted her [changed her clothes], and after went into her barge secretely to the king'.[99]

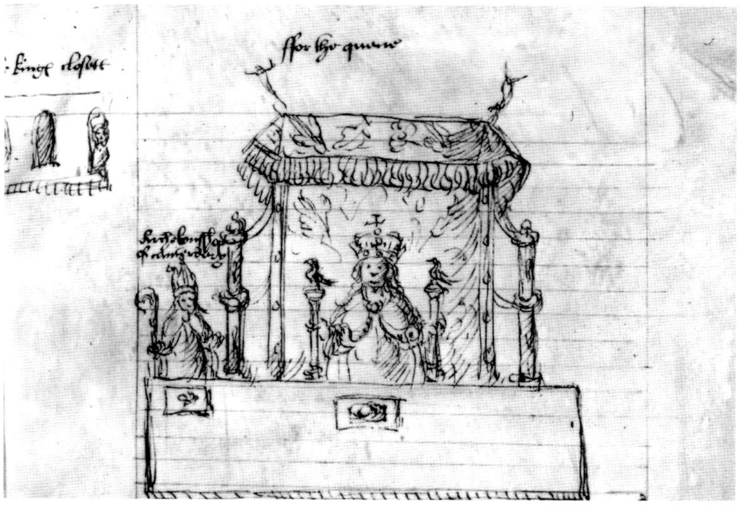

4.2 *Part of a seating plan showing Anne Boleyn at her coronation banquet, unknown artist, 1533. Anne Boleyn is depicted sitting in state under a cloth of estate wearing her regalia. By permission of the British Library, MS Harley 41, f. 12r*

Anne dressed in the French fashion for her coronation, as a sign of her support for France. This was reinforced by 12 members of the household of the new French ambassador, Jean de Dinteville, leading her coronation procession. They were dressed in blue velvet with blue and yellow sleeves, while their horse trappers were of blue sarsenet decorated with white crosses. Francis I allowed de Dinteville 500 gold *écus* (£100) to cover the cost.[100] Nevertheless, her coronation medal issued a year after the event depicted Anne wearing an English gable head-dress and her bodice having a square neckline filled in with a partlet with a round neckline and no collar, tight-fitting upper sleeves.[101] Undoubtedly, the choice of the English hood was intentional, and the aim was to present her as an English woman with English taste.

Of the nobility present at her coronation, the duke of Suffolk acted as high steward and he wore a doublet and hose covered with pearls and rode a horse with a crimson velvet trapper. Lord William Howard was dressed all in crimson and he rode a horse with a purple velvet trapper with the white Howard lion embroidered on it and slashed to reveal the white satin lining.[102] As lord chancellor, Sir Thomas More was allowed £20 to buy a new gown enabling him to appear dressed in a style suited to his office.[103]

Although Anne scrupulously adhered to the traditional coronation clothes, her efforts to catch the public eye and favour were not as successful as she might have wished. Many disapproved of the king's divorce from Catherine of Aragon. Of Anne's gown, it was said to be 'covered with tongues pierced with nails, to show the treatment which those who speak against her might expect'. By the same token 'The letters H. A. were painted in several places, for Henry and Anne, but were laughed at by many'.[104]

Henry's other queens

Only two of Henry VIII's queens were crowned. However, this was not what the king had planned. Following Jane Seymour's proclamation as queen at Greenwich on 4 June 1536, there was a celebratory procession 'with a great traine of ladies following after her'.[105] A coronation for her was planned for the autumn of that year but it was postponed on account of plague.[106] According to Paget and Rich, the king 'perceiving how the plague had reigned in Westminster, and in the Abbey itself, he stood in a suspense whether it were best to put off the time of the queen's coronation. "Wherefore" he quoth "It were good that all my council be assembled here to determine upon every thing touching the same coronation"'.[107] According to Husee, the likely date was 29 October, the Sunday before All Hallows.[108] This was a view that he shared with Henry, Lord Mounteagle.[109] On 18 September 1536 Chancellor Audley asked Cromwell 'if the Coronation go forward at Hallowmass'.[110] At this point, £320 had been spent on the coronation but it was postponed.[111] It is most likely that Henry would have rearranged Jane's coronation shortly after Edward's birth had she lived.

There is some evidence that Henry VIII considered crowning Catherine Howard at York in 1541 on his progress to meet with his nephew James V of Scotland. On 16 September 1541 Henry entered York where he was lodged at the King's manor. According to Marillac he had sent from London 'his richest tapestry, plate and dress, both for himself and his archers, pages and gentlemen, with marvellous provisions of victuals from all parts. This seems to betoken some extraordinary triumph, like an interview of Kings or a coronation of his Queen'.[112]

Betrothals/Marriage by proxy

A feature of diplomacy in the late fifteenth and early sixteenth centuries was international peace treaties providing for marriages between the children of the various parties. In February 1527 Sir Gregory Casale and Sir John Russell, the English ambassadors in Spain, informed Wolsey that they had promoted the suit of the duke of Richmond for the hand of Catherine de Medici 'upon our own mind'.[113] Betrothals and the matrimonial rite could be carried out *per verba de praesenti* (one with immediate effect) or *per verba de futura* (one with future effect). Betrothals enabled monarchs to contract marriages for their children even when very young.

The practice of contracting betrothals played a crucial role in determining the succession and in developing foreign policy. In January 1527 noted that Henry VIII offered Mary's hand in marriage to Francis I in return for a pension, the county of Guisnes and an annuity of salt. As part of the negotiations, the king sent his picture along with that of Mary to Francis I.[114] In contrast, in October 1528 Cardinal Campeggio noted that Mary was heir to the throne. However, he observed that 'they have thought of marrying the princess, by dispensation from His Holiness, to the king's natural son, if it can be done. At first I myself had thought of this as a means of establishing the succession, but I do not believe that this design would suffice to satisfy the king's desires'. Such a marriage would have been incestuous but there is evidence to suggest that Henry VIII considered it.[115] On 9 December 1539, Philip, Count Palatine, made an offer for Mary's hand in marriage and enquired as to the size of her dowry. The count was required to disclaim the throne unless Henry died without a male heir.[116] Such proxy marriages could always be repudiated.

Selecting a spouse, either personally or for offspring, required the exchange of portraits, visits by ambassadors and the presentation of gifts, usually in the form of jewellery. A gold ring with the letter M set with black diamonds and dating from the second half of the fifteenth century has traditionally been identified as the engagement ring of Mary of Burgundy, daughter of Charles the Bold. She married Maximilian in 1477. A second ring, also with the letter M, is thought to be the ring worn by Mary of Hungary on her wedding day.[117] Even though what is known about betrothals is often limited, they adhered to standard procedures and verbal forms. However, betrothals did not necessarily result in marriage, so the expenditure on clothing, jewellery, feasting and jousting represented a calculated risk.

HENRY VIII'S BETROTHALS

Henry VIII was betrothed twice, under very different circumstances. First, he was betrothed to Catherine of Aragon, his brother's widow, and then nearly 40 years later he was betrothed to Anne of Cleves. Following the premature death of Prince Arthur in April 1502, a papal dispensation enabling Catherine of Aragon to marry Arthur's younger brother Henry was required. In October 1502 Robert Sherborne, dean of St Paul's, delivered the bull granting the dispensation. The duke of Estrada wrote to Catherine's mother, observing that 'The King wishing to make the marriage very solemn, will communicate the bulls to the principal personages of the kingdom, who usually assemble in Westminster on the Day of All Saints'.[118] On 25 June 1503 Catherine and Henry were betrothed 'at the Bishop of Salisbury's place in Fleet Street', three days before Henry's twelfth birthday.[119] Henry said, 'I am rejoiced ... to contract matrimony with thee Catherine and take thee for my wife and spouse and all other for thee forsake during my and thine lives natural'.[120] However, Henry repudiated their betrothal on 27 June 1505, the day before his 14th birthday, in the presence of the bishop of Winchester. Henry declared that 'I do not intend in any way to approve, validate or ratify that pretended contract by anything that I have said or may say, or have done or may do'.[121] In comparison, the details of Henry's second proxy marriage are minimal. In 1539 Sir Anthony Browne, master of the horse, was sent to celebrate the marriage on the king's behalf with Anne of Cleves. Browne was dressed in white satin as befitted a bridegroom.[122]

PRINCE ARTHUR TO CATHERINE OF ARAGON

The marriage of Arthur and Catherine of Aragon was formally agreed by treaty in July 1497. Two years later, on 19 May 1499, the young couple were formally betrothed at Bewdley, Herefordshire. The Spanish ambassador represented Catherine at the 'nuptial ceremony *per verba de praesenti* between the said Prince and Princess of Wales' which was presided over by the bishop of Coventry and Lichfield.[123] The ceremony was formal:

> After the power had been read, the Prince of Wales took, with his right hand, the right hand of Doctor de Puebla; and Richard Peel [Pole], Lord Chamberlain of the Prince and Knight of the Garter, held the hands of both in his hands. In this position, the Prince declared that he accepted De Puebla In the name and as the proxy of the Princess Katherine, and the Princess Katherine as his lawful and undoubted wife.[124]

MARGARET TUDOR TO JAMES IV OF SCOTLAND

Negotiations for Margaret's marriage with James IV of Scotland began in 1498 when she was only nine. Lady Margaret Beaufort and Queen Elizabeth of York pressed for a delay because 'they fear the King of Scots would not wait, but injure her, and endanger her health'.[125] Concern was based on Lady Margaret's own experience: she married at 12 and she was only a year older when she had her first and only child.[126] Possibly as a consequence of these doubts, Henry VII considered other potential sons-in-law. On 17 November 1498 Raimondo de Soncino noted that Henry VII was 'more inclined towards the eldest son of Denmark, who is fourteen years old'.[127]

The betrothal took place on St Paul's day (25 January), 1502, within Queen Elizabeth of York's apartments at Richmond palace. 'Furst the king the qwene with ther noble Childern except the prince hard the high masse.'[128] The bishop of Rochester preached the sermon and James IV was represented at the ceremony by the archbishop of Glasgow, the earl of Bothwell and 'the elect of Murrey'. After the mass the party moved from the chapel to the queen's great chamber and it was there that Margaret made her pledge: 'I Margaret the furst begoten doughter of the right Excellent Right Hie and myghty prince and princesse Henry be the grace of god king of Ingland and Elizabeth qwene of the same wittandly and of deliberate mynde hauyng xij yeres complete in Age in the Moneth of Nouembre last bepast contracts matrimone.'[129]

No descriptions survive of what Margaret wore. The heralds present noted that 'The lord bothmle [Bothwell] sent to the officers of armes the gowne of cloth of gold that he ware when he was Fyanced in the name of his souuerayne lord and a C crownes'. The gown was accepted but the money was sent back.[130] Henry VII presented plate to the archbishop of Glasgow, a gold cup, 1,000 crowns of gold and 'a goodly bagge of Crymson veluet wele garnyshed' to the elect of Murrey, 'A purse with jC crownis of gold and a gown of fine satyn' to the king of arms of Scotland and 'to diuerse vthires gentill men ... gownys of veluet'.[131] After this, 'the trumpettes standing on the ledis at the chambre ende blew up And the lowde Noise of mynstrelles pleid in the best and most Joiful manner' and then 'the qwene toke her doughter the qwene of scottes be the hand and dyned both at oon messe Coueréd'.[132]

The marriage was celebrated with a tournament at which 'The duc of Bokyngham Richely besoon his horsse furst trapped with a Riche demy trapper embrawderd with castelles after chaunged his horsse and an other Richer trapper of blew and Crimson weluet with garters and other his bagis of nedel warke'.[133] This was followed by a banquet and 'Incontinent after the Pryses were given, there was in the Hall a goodly Pageant, curiously wrought with Fenestrallis, having many Lights brenning in the same in Manner of a Lantron out of which sorted divers Sortes of Morisks. Also very goodly Disguising of Six Gentlemen and Six Gentlewomen, which danced divers Dances'.[134] Several payments made to John Atkinson and John English who had organised the pageants at Prince Arthur's wedding to Catherine of Aragon suggest that they had a hand in the entertainments at the betrothal.[135]

MARY TUDOR TO CHARLES, PRINCE OF CASTILE

The *Chronicle of Calais* recorded that 'the lordes on bothe partyes concluded the marriage betwixt the duke of Burgoyne and the lady Mary dowghtar to kynge Henry the Seventhe, where on seynt Thomas day the Apostle was great triumphe made in Calles'.[136] However, Margaret of Savoy did not confirm the treaty until 1 October 1508. On Sunday 17 December 1508, Mary aged 12, was betrothed to Charles of Austria, prince of Castile, and married by proxy, at Richmond palace. A description of the revels held to celebrate the marriage was published in English and Latin by Pynson.[137] Charles's place in the ceremony was taken by Sieur de Berghes, the emperor's chamberlain and a leading noble of Brabant. He gave Mary a gold ring which was placed on her middle finger. Charles was made a knight of the Garter, *in absentia*, and he sent his bride a gift of a ring decorated with a K (for Charles in its Latin form, *Karolus*) made from diamonds surrounded by diamonds and pearls. The ring was engraved *Maria optimam partem elegit que non auferetur ab ea* (Mary has chosen the best part, which will not be taken away from her).[138] In spite of these fine words, Mary was just one of ten women that Charles undertook to marry before he actually married Isabel of Portugal. Other gifts of jewellery sent to Mary came from Margaret of Austria (a balas ruby set with pearls) and the emperor, Maximilian (a brooch with a large diamond and a ruby set with pearls).[139] A jewel known as *le riche fleur-de-lys* and valued at 50,000 crowns was given to Henry VII as a gift by the Flemish ambassadors.[140]

The preparations for the marriage of Mary to Charles in 1508 included the selection of the jewellery that she was to wear on her wedding day:

a coronelle for her hedde, of golde and stone
a goodlie devise for her necke, set with stone and perle
a goodlie gurdille of goolde, of as goodly facion as may be devised
ij braselettes of golde, set with stone and perle.[141]

She was also to have 'a faire coffer of Iverye to lay in her jewels'. Ladies were appointed to give attendance on her and 'to have charge to devise for the apparel of her person on the advice of the Lady Mistress'.[142] A list of clothing to be provided for Mary was also drawn up under headings including garments 'in the English facion' and 'in the facion of Milan'.[143]

The arrangements for the marriage lapsed on the final sickness and death of Henry VII. In February 1514 the marriage between Mary and Charles was mooted, once again, and Henry VIII was anxious that Mary should be dressed 'in the fashion of those parts'.[144] In order to ensure this, Henry contacted Margaret of Savoy 'praying her to devise for the making thereof after such manner as shall be please her, all things being queenly and honourable'. Dr Knight acted as the king's envoy during these preparations, and he noted that he had 'received a book containing the apparel of my Lady's chambers and stables and an account of her plate, but not of her apparel, and that he was expressly commanded to keep the said book secret till the King's pleasure was further known'. However, on 3 April 1514 Knight wrote to Wolsey signalling that there was a problem and noting that 'Those about the Prince of Castile would gladly hinder his marriage with the Lady Mary, saying he is a child, and she is a woman full grown'. The wedding did not take place. 'So thus the kynge of Englande reteyned styll hys syster and all the preparacion that he had done for her conueyaunce, whyche was verye costely.'[145] On 30 July 1514 Mary renounced her marriage with Charles and negotiations began for her marriage to Louis XII of France.

MARY TUDOR TO LOUIS XII OF FRANCE

Fourteen days after the renunciation of her marriage to Charles, Mary, then aged 18, was betrothed to Louis XII of France, aged 52. The impetus behind the marriage was Louis's wish to have peace with England. A minute written by Bishop Fox and dating from May 1514, which predates the formal renunciation of Mary's marriage to Charles by several months, recorded the agreement by the king of France to accept jewellery and furnishings to the value of 200,000 crowns, as Mary's dowry.[146]

The betrothal ceremony took place on 13 August 1514 at Greenwich palace. Archbishop William Warham officiated, with the duke of Longueville representing Louis.[147] The duke gave Mary a gold ring which she placed on the fourth finger of her right hand. The clothes worn by Mary and Catherine of Aragon (as English princess and English queen consort) were very similar, denoting the friendship and now complimentary status of the two women.[148] An eye-witness described the consummation of the marriage by proxy in a letter dated five days later: 'The bride undressed and went to bed in the presence of many witnesses. The marquess of Rothelin, in his doublet, with a pair of red hose, but with one leg naked from the middle of the thigh downwards, went into the bed, and touched the Princess with his naked leg. The marriage was then declared consummated.'[149] After this Mary got dressed again in a gown of cloth of gold and purple satin worn with an ash-coloured kirtle and then went to hear mass. Mary and Catherine also wore caps of cloth of gold 'covering the ears in the Venetian fashion'.

On the following day the duke of Longueville was released and amongst the parting gifts Henry gave the duke the gown that he had worn at his sister's wedding which was valued at 300 ducats. Before her departure, Mary attended a banquet where she wore cloth of gold and the diamond known as the Mirror of Naples given to her by Louis. Catherine accompanied Mary on her journey to Dover later that year.

PRINCESS MARY TO FRANCIS, THE DAUPHIN

On 28 February 1518 the Venetian ambassador informed the doge that he had been presented to the two-year-old Princess Mary. He noted that the 'greatest marks of honour [were] being paid her, universally, more than to the Queen herself'.[150] Royal marriages were often linked to the needs of foreign policy and the proposed alliance of the princess Mary to the dauphin was a direct consequence of the Universal Peace which was celebrated in 1518. The treaty had initially focused upon the return of Tournai to France upon receipt by Henry of a large sum of money. However, the birth of a son to Francis I on 28 February 1518 led to articles of marriage between the dauphin and Princess Mary drawn up and sealed by 9 July, with the ceremony taking place in the queen's great chamber at Greenwich on 5 October.[151]

After the betrothal the king went to the high altar of the chapel at Greenwich and swore his oath to the treaty. Mary stood in front of her mother and she was 'dressed in cloth of gold, with a cap of black velvet on her head, adorned with many jewels'.[152] The ambassador noted that Wolsey 'placed on her finger a small ring but in which was set a large diamond'. He went on to record that 'the whole of the choir being decorated with cloth of gold, and all the court in such rich array that I never saw the like'. A public celebration was held at St Paul's, and in October 1518 Sir Edward Belknap was paid for making 'of an hall place in the body of Powles Church for the marriage of the Princess'.[153] Henry presented gifts to the French ambassadors including 'a rich robe of cloth of gold, lined with cloth of silver, made for the King's own use' to the Lord Admiral and clothes worth 500 crowns to each of the gentlemen in waiting from the French king.[154] On 6 June 1520 the treaty made at the Field of Cloth of Gold was ratified, confirming the marriage of Mary to the dauphin, including sums of money to be paid to England and the need for an arrangement with Scotland, to be made by Wolsey and the duchess of Angoulême.[155]

PRINCESS MARY AND CHARLES V

The marriage treaty was signed at Windsor in 1522: Henry VIII's daughter Mary was then six and Charles V, the emperor, was in his early 20s. Wolsey wrote to Tunstal and Wingfield on 3 April 1525, stating, 'I send you herewith an emerald, which my Lady Princess sendeth to the emperor. You at the delivery of the same, shall say "that her grace hath devised this token for a better knowledge to be had whether his majesty doth keep constant and continent to her, as with God's grace she will to him"'.[156] The choice of an emerald was significant because the stone was believed to fade if the wearer was unfaithful. The ring was delivered to the emperor on 24 May 'which he put on his little finger, and said that he would wear for her sake'.[157] However, later that year he married Isabel of Portugal.

The negotiations for this marriage revealed how Charles was bound to Henry VIII in respect of the marriage to Mary: a loan and indemnity to be repaid to Henry amounting to 130,000 ducats a year and other loans he had made in anticipation of receiving her dowry of 1,000,000 ducats. In contrast Isabel's dowry consisted of 900,000 *doubles d'or Castillaines*, each equal to 365 *maravedis*, of which 160,732 were for her dowry and 151,319 was a loan to the emperor during the revolt in Castile. The money was to be paid in instalments over four years, with the first payment in each of the first two years to be made in jewels.[158] On 16 June the English ambassadors to the emperor wrote to Henry that Charles was anxious for his approval of the Portuguese marriage. They sought to mollify the king by adding that 'since ye may have with much thank my lady Princess in your hand, which is a pearl worth the keeping'.[159]

PRINCE EDWARD AND MARY, QUEEN OF SCOTS

On 10 March 1543 the privy council noted that negotiations were in hand for the marriage of Mary queen of Scots to Henry VIII's son, Prince Edward 'the goodliest child in the world'.[160] Ten days later the English ambassador to Scotland, Sir Ralph Sadler, reported a conversation with Sir George Douglas in the aftermath of the English victory at Solway Moss: '"Well" quoth I, "Mr Douglas, the king's majesty hath had large offers, as ye know, both for the government of the realm, and to have the child [Mary Stuart] brought into his hands, with also the strongholds, according to your promises".'[161] As a consequence of Henry's 'rough wooing', Edward was betrothed to Mary on 1 July 1543. The marriage treaty made provision for Mary to be assigned dower lands in England with an annual value of £2,000 upon consummation of the marriage, rising to £4,000 in the event of the prince's death.[162] Mary's infancy was stressed in a letter from Sadler to the council when he referred to her being 'a little troubled with the breeding of teeth'.[163]

Marriage

Erasmus's essay on marriage was read by Lord Mountjoy. On being asked his opinion of it, Mountjoy told Erasmus that 'I like it so much that I have made up my mind to marry'.[164] However, finding a suitable partner was not always straightforward. Many of the royal and noble families were closely interconnected, so raising the question of consanguinity. This could be addressed by the grant of a papal dispensation, but this became a central issue when Henry questioned the validity of his marriage to his older brother's widow, Catherine of Aragon. Ultimately, Henry sought to have his marriage annulled, and he promoted a range of arguments to support his claim. These included asking the pope to sanction his bigamous marriage to Anne Boleyn.[165] Other impediments to marriage included one of the individuals having a precontract with someone else, as in the case of Anne of Cleves being promised to the duke of Lorraine.

A royal marriage did not need to be a public occasion. The household ordinances stated that 'it must be knowne whether the King will marrie openly or priviely'.[166] Marriage to a king gave a woman her status as a queen consort. It was a rite of passage and in turn it provided an opportunity for the king to reaffirm his position as the rightful monarch. Consequently, marriage was a confirmation of legitimacy and the right to rule. For a queen consort, marriage was the ceremonial start of her new regal life, ideally followed by coronation, childbirth and death. For the queen, marriage was a route to pregnancy and motherhood.

The role of the queen consort was to provide legitimate children to secure the royal line and to create further alliances through marriage. However, no children were born after 1537 to Henry or indeed any Tudor monarch. The last Tudor marriage took place in July 1554 when Henry's daughter Queen Mary married Philip in Winchester cathedral. Marriage was seen as being the right path for a woman, especially a queen regnant. This is evident from Elizabeth I's response to the Speaker of the House of Commons on 28 January 1563 after they had petitioned her that she should marry: 'The weight, and greatnes of this Matter might cause in me being a woman wanting both witt and memory some feare to speake, and bashfulness besides, a thing appropriate to my Sex.'[167]

Wedding clothes for the bride and the groom were very important. The bride's wedding clothes usually formed a significant part of her trousseau and the cost of this trousseau reflected both on her and her male relatives. On 8 June 1468, Edward IV agreed the payment of £2,450 *6s 8d* for his sister Margaret of York's trousseau, her household goods and livery for her retinue.[168] During the fifteenth century, white became increasingly common as the colour for the bride's wedding clothes. When Margaret married Charles the Bold in 1468 she wore white silk, and in 1477 Charles's daughter Maria wore white silk damask embroidered with gold with a short ermine-lined cloak when she married the future Maximilian I in 1477.[169] White was associated with virginity, and more particularly with the Virgin Mary, and distinct parallels can be drawn between the clothes worn by queens for their marriage and coronation, and the representations of the Virgin at her Assumption. White cloth of gold/silver was expensive and often difficult to obtain, which further enhanced its appeal.

It was less common for the groom to wear white before the mid sixteenth century. When Elector Maurice of Saxony married Agnes of Hesse in 1543, he wore 'black velvet stockings and doublet embroidered with silver lacework with gold zindel underneath' with 'a black floral-patterned velvet coat with edging of silver lace-work and with silver ribbons on the sleeves'.[170] However, five years later his brother Augustus was dressed in white silver brocade woven with a design of pomegranates which he wore with a pair of knitted white silk stockings.

In contrast, James IV of Scotland provided the pretender Perkin Warbeck with a 'spousing' gown of white damask at the time of his marriage to Catherine Gordon, daughter of the earl of Huntley in 1498.[171] The double portrait of James V and Magdalene of France, perhaps depicting them in their wedding clothes, shows him wearing a white satin doublet and hose with a short blue velvet gown furred with sable, while she wore a white damask gown embroidered with gold.[172] For his second marriage to Mary of Lorraine, James V wore 'ane hat thrummit with gold' decorated with 'hostage federis' and 'ane Image with ane rubie to the King's Grace's bonnet'. He was dressed in a 'coat of Venice satin, rich with silver'.[173] They had a joint portrait painted at the time of their marriage and they were dressed in a similar style and colour (Fig. 2.5).

Only one of Henry VIII's children married. The gown worn by Mary at her wedding has been tentatively identified as 'one frenche gowne of riche golde tissue with a border of purple satten allover enbrodered with purles of damaske golde and pearle lined with purple Taphata <lackinge sondrie> with small pearle taken of[f]'.[174] If the suggestion is correct, it is telling that she not only kept this gown but that it was listed amongst the 'Gownes late Queene Maries' in the 1600 inventory of her sister Elizabeth's wardrobe of the robes. As the description indicates, pearls were very popular in the early sixteenth century and they were often worn at royal weddings. Extensive use of pearls was made to decorate the wedding dress of the princess Mary of the Netherlands who married Louis of Hungary in 1521.[175]

However, not all royal marriages attracted a lot of attention. Henry VIII's marriages were private affairs, with few present, and their dates and times hard to fix. When on 24 November 1533 his illegitimate son, the duke of Richmond, married Lady Mary Howard, the imperial ambassador noted that 'there is no other news except the duke of Richmond is to be married tomorrow to the duke of Norfolk's daughter'.[176] His next dispatch is lost, but he never mentioned it again. The little information extant about the French queen's marriage to the duke of Suffolk on 13 May 1515 (their second ceremony in just over two months) may reflect national and international outrage at the union (Pl. IIIA).

HENRY VIII

Henry married six times (Fig. 4.3). Each time he selected his own wife, indeed in the case of his first, he may have gone against his father's wishes. The ceremonies declined in lavishness as his reign progressed with the exception of his marriage to Anne of Cleves. He married two brides from abroad and four English women. On their landing in England, foreign brides were customarily received by noblemen selected by the monarch for the task. Anne of Cleves was received in this manner, but there was no need for such a reception for Catherine of Aragon, who had lived in England since 1501. Henry's first and last brides were widows, neither of whom had children from their previous marriages.

It was quite common in the sixteenth century for one or both partners in a marriage to have been married before and have children from that relationship. All of Henry's wives, bar Catherine of Aragon, had to consider Henry's children from earlier marriages. Equally, the dower lands passed from one queen to the next, along with the jewellery and the chapel goods. The latter is very clearly demonstrated in the 1542 inventory of Whitehall palace by the entry for the chapel stuff of the late Catherine Howard and its subsequent delivery to

4.3 *Miniature of Henry VIII by Lucas Horenbout, c. 1525, RCIN 420640 GR 2. The clothes worn by the king are very similar to those in Figure 1.5. The Royal Collection © 2004, Her Majesty the Queen Elizabeth II*

Catherine Parr.[177] The role of a queen was to provide a son and heir quickly, to be a fair landowner, to remain free of debt and to eschew English politics.[178]

Catherine of Aragon

Catherine and Henry were not betrothed at the time of Henry VII's death on 21 April 1509. But within eight days of his accession, Henry sent Bishop Fox, of Winchester, to the Spanish ambassador to expedite their marriage. Fox explained to the ambassador that 'You must remember now the king is king and not prince. One must speak in a different way in this matter than when he was prince ... Until now things were discussed with his father and now one must treat with him who is king'.[179] Henry presented matters differently to Margaret, the regent of the Netherlands, on 27 June 1509. His letter, sent three days after his coronation and 16 days after his marriage, explained that the marriage was his father's final wish: 'he, being then on his death bed ... gave us express command that he should take in marriage the Lady Catherine ... which we would not, neither in this nor a thousand other things whatsoever they be, disobey or infringe.'[180] They married in the oratory of the friary church at Greenwich: she wore white and had her hair loose, both symbolic of her virginity.

Anne Boleyn

Henry married Anne Boleyn secretly before sunrise on 25 January 1533. On 9 February 1533, Eustace Chapuys told Charles V that 'The other day the Lady told a priest who wishes to enter her service that he must wait a little until she had celebrated her marriage with the King. She keeps the Queen's jewels and there is nothing said about returning them'.[181] On 22 February Chapuy reported the rumour that Thomas Cranmer 'married the King to the Lady, in the presence of the father, mother, brother and two of her favourites and one of his priests'.[182] Later he mentioned how 'On St Matthias' Day [24 February] the Lady received the King at dinner in her chamber richly ornamented with tapestry and the most beautiful sideboard of gold that was ever seen'. The king was heard to comment that Anne had a 'grand dote and a rich marriage'.[183] Subsequently, Chapuys stated that 'On Saturday, Easter Eve, dame Anne went to mass in Royal state, loaded with jewels, clothed in a robe of cloth of gold of frieze ... she had in her suite 60 young ladies and was brought to church, and brought back with the solemnities, or even more, which were used to the Queen'.[184]

On 28 May Cranmer, who notwithstanding Chapuy's report had not officiated at the marriage, recognised it. Its informality is indicated in the records of the heralds under the heading 'for the largeese for the sayd officers':

> That ys to wytte l li for the moost honorable and ioyous marriage and l li for the qeynes excellent coronation as euer hath been due at suche like tymes
> Memorandum that the sayd officers dooth remyt vnto the moost honorable bontefulnesse of the kinges highness the l li for the moost honorable marriage forbycause they were not present.[185]

Jane Seymour

On 18 March 1536 Chapuys informed the emperor's minister Granville that 'The new amours of this king with the young lady [Jane Seymour] of whom I have before written still go on, to the intense rage of the Concubine [Anne Boleyn]'.[186] Two months later on 20 May he noted that 'Mrs Semel [Jane Seymour] came secretly by river this morning to the king's lodging and that the promise and betrothal was made by 9 o'clock. The king means to keep it secret till Whitsuntide, but everyone begins already to murmur suspicion'.[187] Henry married Jane on 30 May 1536 (that is, 11 days after Anne's execution). Husee wrote to Lady Lisle on 31 May, noting that 'The king was married yesterday in the Queen's closet at York place'.[188] According to Sir John Russell in a letter he wrote to Lord Lisle, 'the king hath come out of hell into heaven, for the gentleness of this, and the cursedness and unhappiness of the other'.[189] Russell also observed after attending Henry's marriage to Jane 'that the richer she [Jane] was in apparel, the fairer and goodly lady she was and appeared; and the other [Anne] he said was the contrary, for the richer she was apparelled, the worse she looked'.[190]

It has been suggested that Henry wore white for the wedding.[191]

Anne of Cleves

The king's second foreign marriage was planned in some detail. The French ambassador wrote to Francis I to inform him that 'On the 5th of November [1539], the king told his lords that he expected the arrival of his spouse in about twenty days, and that he proposed to go to Canterbury to receive her'. Anne was welcomed all along her route to England, starting at Antwerp where 'many English merchants met her grace four miles without the town in fifty velvet coats and chains of gold'.[192]

The king's clothes for the days preceding the ceremony, which coincided with Anne's arrival in the country, and the day of the wedding itself were recorded by Hall.[193] For their formal meeting two days later at Shooter's hill on 3 January, Henry VIII was 'mounted on a goodly courser, trapped in rich cloth of gold traversed lattice wise square, all over embroidered with flat gold of damask, pearled on every side of the embroidery, the buckles and pendants were all of fine gold'. This level of opulence was exceeded in the king's attire, which Hall described in detail:

> His persone was apparelled in a coate of purple velvet, somewhat made lyke a frocke, all over enbrodered with flat gold of damaske with small lace mixed betwene of the same gold, and other laces of the same so goyng trauerse wyse, so that the ground lytle appered:about whyche garment was a rych garde very curiously enbrodered, the sleves and brest were cut lyned with cloth of golde, and tyed together with great buttons of Diamonds, Rubyes, and Orient Perle, his swoorde and swoorde gyrdle adorned with stones and especiall Emerodes, his night cappe garnished with stone, but his bonet was so ryche of Iuels that few men could value them. Besyde all this he ware in baudricke wyse a collar of such Balystes and Perle that few men ever saw the lyke.[194]

For the wedding on 6 January, the king appeared at eight o'clock in the morning, 'his Grace beyng apparelled in a gowne of cloth of gold, raised with great flowers of syluer, furred with blacke Jenettes his coat Crymosyn sattyn all to cutte and embrodered & tied with great Diamondes, & a ryche Coller about his necke'.[195] He had changed his clothes within an hour, when 'the kyng with a goune of ryche Tyssue lyned with Crymosyn Veluet embroidered, came to his closet'.[196]

Anne dressed in her native fashions when she arrived in England, for the days preceding the ceremony and on her wedding day. On 3 January she 'issued out of her tent beyng apparelled in a ryche gowne of clothe of golde reised, made rounde without any trayne after the Dutche fassyon, and on her head a kall, and ouer that a round bonet or cappe set full of Orient perle of a very proper fassyon, and about her necke she had a partelet set full of riche stone which glystered all the felde'. The clothes worn by her attendants echoed Anne's: 'After her fashion, her ladies and gentlewomen were apparelled very rich and costly with chains of divers fashions.'[197] On her wedding day, Anne 'was apparelled in a gowne of ryche cloth of gold set full of large flowers of great & Orient Perle, made after the Dutche fassion rownde, her here hangyng downe, whych was fayre, yelowe and long. On her hed a Coronall of gold replenished with a great stone and set about full of braunches of Rosemary, about her necke and middle, Iuelles of great valew & extimacion', which she wore all day, but she changed after dinner. She then wore 'a gowne lyke a mannes gowne, of Tyssue with longe sleues gyrte to her, furred with ryche Sables, her narrowe sleeues were very costly, but on her head she had a cap as she ware on the saturdai before with a cornet of laune, which cap was so ryche of Perle and Stone, that it was iudged to be of great valew'.[198]

Henry and Anne were married privately on 6 January 1540 in the queen's closet at Greenwich. Later 'she went publicly in procession'.[199] On the following Sunday Anne's wardrobe had undergone a change. At the jousts held to celebrate the marriage, Hall noted that 'On whiche daie she was appareiled after the Englishe fassion, with a Frenche whode, whiche so set furth her beautie and good visage, that euery creature reioysed to behold her'.[200]

On 4 July 1540, when Henry was seeking to justify the annulment of his marriage to Anne, he noted that 'there is but one imp of his body'.[201] According to Lord Russell, the king asked him 'if he thought her the woman so fair and of such beauty as report had been made of her; to which he answered that he took her not for fair but to be of a brown complexion'.[202] Sir Anthony Browne revealed that after the king had seen Anne on New Year's day he 'deferred sending the presents that he had prepared for her, viz., a partlet furred sables and sable skins for her neck, with a muffler furred and a cap, but sent them in the morning by Sir Anthony Denny with a cold message'.[203]

Catherine Howard

On 12 July 1540 Joan Bulmer told Catherine Howard that people were aware that Henry VIII planned to annul his marriage to Anne of Cleves and that 'it is thought that the King will set Katherine Howard in the same honour'.[204] Joan sought a post in Catherine's household, adding, 'for I trost the quyne of Bretane wyll not forget her secretary'. Henry married Catherine on 8 August at Hampton Court.[205] A week later the French ambassador noted that the king had been hunting, but now had a larger court which 'verified what hitherto when as in doubt touching the Queen who has succeeded the sister of the duke of Cleves; for this morning prayers were made in the churches for the King, the Queen and Prince Edward'.[206] Early in 1541 the ambassador observed that on 19 March Henry had gone from 'Westminster to Greenwich by water, accompanied by the mayor and crafts masters of London, with the solemnity and triumph at the first passage of new queens; for she who is queen at present had not yet passed under the Bridge'.[207]

Catherine, Lady Latimer (née Parr)

Following Catherine Howard's execution, Francis I's ambassador noted that 'the common voice is that this King will not be long without a wife, for the great desire he has to have further issue'.[208] At first sight Lady Latimer must have seemed an unpromising choice, as she had not had any children by her previous marriages. This point was made clear in a letter by Chapuys who had 'heard in a good quarter that the said lady [Anne of Cleves] would like to be in her shirt, so to speak, with her mother, having especially taken great despair at the King's espousal of this last wife, who is not so nearly so beautiful as she, besides that there is no hope of issue, seeing that she had none with her two former husbands'.[209] On 10 July 1543 Cranmer issued a marriage licence for Henry's final marriage, authorising the king '(who had deigned to take the Lady Katherine, late wife of Lord Latimer, deceased) to have the marriage solemnised in any church, chapel or oratory without the issue of banns'.[210] They were married two days later. The ceremony was celebrated in an upper oratory called 'the Quynes Pryevey closet' at Hampton Court.[211] Unlike Henry's marriages to Anne Boleyn, Jane Seymour and Catherine Howard, the ceremony was not a private one. Those present included Sir Anthony Denny, the ladies Mary, Elizabeth and Margaret Douglas, Catherine, duchess of Suffolk, Anne, countess of Hertford, Joan, Lady Douglas and Anne Herbert. It is not known what Henry or Catherine wore. An observer recalled 'the putting on of the wedding ring'. He also recorded their vows: 'Then, releasing and again clasping hands, the lady Katharine likewise said "I, Katharine, take thee Henry to be my wedded husband, to have and to hold from this day forward . . . to be bonayr and buxome in bed and at board, till death us depart"'. Chapuys described the wedding as taking place 'privately and without ceremony'.[212]

ESTABLISHING THE DYNASTY: HENRY VII AND ELIZABETH OF YORK

Elizabeth of York was in Yorkshire at the time of Henry Tudor's landing in 1485 and his victory at Bosworth. Although their marriage had been promoted by Lady Margaret Beaufort, it was not a certainty.[213] Nevertheless, they were married on 18 January 1486 after receiving a dispensation from the bishop of Imola, the papal legate. Imola's dispensation was confirmed in a bull dated 27 March 1486 issued by Pope Innocent VIII. There are no extant detailed descriptions of the wedding beyond the brief references made by Bernard André.[214] However, amongst the plate delivered to the king at the New Year in 1486 there was an entry 'for the quenes weddyng ryng' at a price of 23*s* 4½*d*.[215] On 28 February 1486 Piers Curteys, gentleman usher of the chamber, received £95 3*s* 6½*d* for stuff bought for the king's use against Christmas and his marriage.[216]

PRINCE ARTHUR AND CATHERINE OF ARAGON

Catherine's entry into London on 11 November 1501, on her arrival from Spain, was marked by a series of pageants which included references to the provision of children and heirs to the throne. These were appropriate for a royal entry preceding a marriage.[217] Catherine's wedding clothes had been made for her before her departure from Spain, and their luxury and singularity was the subject of comment:

> And aftir theim rode the Princes upon a great mule richely trapped aftir the manour of Spayne, the Duke of Yorke on her right hande and the Legate of Rome on her left hande. She was in riche apparell on her body aftir the manour of her contre, and upon her hed a litill hatte of a praty brede with a lase of golde at this hatt to steye hit, her heere hanging down abowt her shoulders, which is faire aburne, and in maner of a coyfe betwene her hede and her hatt of a carnacion colour, and that was fastenyd from the myddis of her hed upwardes so as men might weell se all her heere from the myddill parte of her hed downward.[218]

Elizabeth of York's privy purse accounts refer to the preparations made for Arthur. These include a payment of £47 made on 24 November 1502 to John van Delf and Alexander Hove, goldsmiths, in full payment of stuff made for the prince's wedding.[219] Equally, Henry VII ordered a jacket of crimson cloth of gold 'wrought in the stool' for him which may well have formed part of his wedding clothes.[220] Arthur came to the city four days before the wedding and lodged with the bishop of Salisbury. On the night before the wedding, he slept in the wardrobe and on the day he entered St Paul's at the south door 'and the princes houshold seruantes to geue there attendaunce and convey hym to the hault place'.[221] Henry VII also ordered 100 jackets with bases and sleeves for the yeomen of the guard that were made from green and white cloth, as opposed to satin or damask, and so were described as being 'of the second sort'.[222] Green and white were the Tudor livery colours.[223]

The author of *The Great Chronicle* recorded that 'my lord prince and my foresaid lady pryncesse beyng both clad in whyte satyn, maryed'. Catherine's gown had a train which 'my lady Cecyle systir unto the Quenys Grace' bore.[224] A more detailed account recorded that:

> The garmentes of the Lord Prince and Princes bothe were of whight saten, but for the straunge dyversitie of rayement of the countreth of Hispayne to be discryvyn: she were that tyme and daye of her maryage uppon her hed a coyf of whight silk with a bordre of goold, perle, and precious ston, beyng of an unche and an half of brede, the which covered the great parte of hir visage and also a quantite of her body toward her wast and myddill; her gown very large, bothe the slevys and also the body with many plightes, moch litche unto menys clothyng; and aftir the same fourme the remenant of the ladies of Hispayne were arayed; and beneth her wastes certayn rownde hopys beryng owte ther gownes from ther bodies aftir their countray maner.[225]

The notes drawn up in advance of the wedding included the following requirement:

> Item affor the careclothe. Item it shalbe of white Bawdeken and prouided by my lord Chambrelain and by hym delyuerd to the princes Chamberlain And the Spice and wynes to be prouided by my lord Stuard and deliuerd to the princes Chambrelain and his officers thy to haue thordering of the same. And that the Carecloth be holden by iij lordes to be assigned by my lord Chambrelain.[226]

As part of the preparations Henry VII ordered a new cloth of estate 'of rich cloth of gold tissue with portcullises, roses and Ss, lined with buckram, with fringe of gold and silk . . . the valances lined with crimson damask'.[227] Horses and all of their accoutrements were also provided for the wedding, including:

> a Riche Litter [to] be redy to receyue and convey the said princesse to the west door of the churche of paules.
> thre hensmen in side sadelles and harnesse all of oon sute be arredied by the maistre of the quenes horse to folowe next to the said princesse litter.
> a faire palfrey with a pillion richely arreyed and ledde in hand for the said princesse doo folowe next vnto the said hensmen.
> xj palfroys in oon sute be ordeyned for uche ladies attending vpon the said princese as shal folowe next vnto the said pillion.
> v Chares diuersely apparailled fir the ladie and gentilwomen be redy the same tyme at the said Tower wherof oon of the chief must be richely apparailled and garnysshed for the said princesse.[228]

The festivities following the marriage included dancing. To demonstrate their accomplishments, 'the Lady Princes and oon of hir ladies with her in apparell aftir the Spanyssh guyse cam doun there dauncyng othir two baas daunces'.[229] Then Arthur's younger brother Henry and his sister Margaret graced the dancefloor and stole the show: 'Thirde and last cam doun the Duke of York, havyng with him the Lady Margaret his sister on his hond, and dauncyd two baas, daunces. And aftirward he, perceyvyng himself to be accombred with his clothis, sodenly cast of his gowne and dauncyd in his jaket.'[230] A joust completed the celebrations and the duke of Buckingham took a leading role in this. The colour of his tent stressed his loyalty to the house of Tudor, while the livery worn by his servants stressed his own identity: 'the Duke of Bokyngham [was] in his pavylion of silke, whight and grene, beyng iiij square with propir turrettes and pynacles of curyous werk, set full of red rosys of the Kinges bagges, the which pavylyon was borne and upholdid and also conveyed with right many of his servantes on foote in jakettes of silke, blak and red.'[231]

MARGARET TUDOR AND JAMES IV OF SCOTLAND

For Margaret's journey to Scotland in 1503, she 'was richly drest, mounted upon a faire Palfrey'.[232] She heard mass in York, 'Then cam the Quene richly arrayed in a Gowne of Cloth of Gold, a ryche Coller of precyouses Stones and a Gyrdle wrought of fin Gold haunting gon to the Yerth'.[233] For one of their meetings, James IV 'was arrayed of a Jakette of blak Velvett borded of the Selfe, and the Lists of the said Bordeur wer of Cramsyn Veluyt, fourred with whytt'.[234]

The marriage took place on 3 August 1503. The chief warrant for her wedding clothing dated the previous June cost £60 19*s* 9½*d*, but this figure did not include the cost of much of the fabric.[235] As Margaret was still in mourning for her mother, the first part of the warrant provided her with a black satin gown, with a black satin purfil and lined with the same and a matching kirtle and pair of sleeves, a nightgown with sleeves and a purfil of black velvet, hoods and frontlets of black velvet, black sarsenet for a frontlet for riding and a tippet. The black was alleviated with a tawny damask kirtle bordered with crimson velvet and pairs of sleeves made from green and tinselled green satin, crimson, green and tawny sarsenet.

On 7 August Margaret wore 'a ryche Gonne of Cloth of gold with a purfill of black velvet and a rich Coller of Perle and Stone', and on 13 August she attended church 'arayed in a Gonne of Porple fygured Velvett, brothed of Thred of Gold fourred with rmynes, a grett Rebras beneath, and had on a ryche Coller of Pyerrery and a ryche Gyrdelle'.[236]

In addition, her trousseau included five special gowns that were all lined or trimmed with fur: black satin with hanging sleeves lined with ermine, with powdering for the collar, vents and sleeves; tawny cloth of gold tissue furred with powdered ermine and another of cloth of gold with raised work and lined with the same; purple velvet lined with shanks and with a broad purfil of pampilion; purple velvet on velvet with a wide purfil of powdered ermine with powdering for the collar, vents and sleeves and a gown of crimson satin bordered with cloth of gold furred with black budge and shanks. She had a nightgown of black velvet, a short gown of black velvet, a gown of cloth of gold with raised work and lined with the same and a gown of purple cloth of gold, along with seven other gowns of velvet, camlet and satin. These could be worn with kirtles of cloth of gold of dornix, green satin, black satin and tawny damask.

Margaret's coronation as queen of Scotland preceded her marriage to James later the same day. She was 'cronned with a varey ryche Cronne of Gold garnished with Pierrery and Perles'. Their clothes were sumptuous and alike in many of the details. James wore:

> a Gonne of Whit Damaske, figured with Gold and lynned with Sarsenet. He had on a Jakette with Slyffs of Cramsyn Satyn, the Lifts of Blak Velvett, under that sam a Doublet of Cloth of Gold, and a Payre of Scarlette Hosys. Hys Shurt brodered with Thred of Gold, hys Bonnet Blak, with a ryche Balay, and hys Swerd about hym . . . The Qwene was arayed in a rich Robbe, lyke Hymselfe, bordered of Cramsyn velvet, and lyned of the self. Sche had a varey riche Coller of Gold, of Pyerrery and Perlces, round her Necke, and the Cronne apon hyr Hed: Her Hayre hangyng. Betwyx the said Cronne and the Hayres was a varey riche Coyffe hangyng downe byhynd the whole length of the Body.[237]

As custom dictated, she 'deliverd hyr Robbe of Maryage to the Officers of Scotlaund', and the heralds claimed it. 'But on the morow she gaffe them the Somme of xl Nobles for largesse, and they brought ageyn the said Robbe into the warderobe of the sayd Qwene, as she desyred in hyr Recompensing.'[238]

For her journey, Henry VII issued her with 'Thre Fotemen wer allwayes ny hyr varey honestley appoynted; and had in their Jaketts browdered Portecollys'.[239] These footmen were provided with livery that was identical to that issued to the footmen with Prince Henry: doublets of tawny and black velvet, gowns of tawny medley and caps, hats, shirts, hose, leather points and double-soled shoes. On the following day they received their more formal livery which they would wear as they accompanied the princess to Scotland: doublets of black velvet, green satin and green damask, jackets of white cloth of gold and black velvet paned, jackets of black velvet with embroidered crowned portcullises, glaudekins of tawny cloth.[240] The costs of the two sets of livery were £11 9*s* 3½*d* and £20 9*s* 6*d*. One of their specific duties was to accompany her litter which was 'convayed by two Fotemen arrayed as the others, one varey riche Lyttre borne by two faire Coursers varey nobly drest. In the wich Litere the sayd Qwene was borne in the Intryng of the goode Townes or other ways to her good Pleysur'.[241]

MARY TUDOR AND LOUIS XII OF FRANCE

The clothes that Mary wore for her marriage were carefully orchestrated in advance by her brother and her husband. In September 1514 Louis XII wrote to Wolsey about his forthcoming marriage and in particular about the clothes being made for Mary, noting that Marigny and Jehan Perreal of Paris were to have oversight of her clothes 'à la mode de France'.[242] Louis's concern highlights contemporary ideas about the elegance of the French style. It was important for Mary to be appropriately dressed so that she cut a figure in her husband's court. A number of warrants, receipts and inventories survive, providing details of the trousseau that Henry VIII gave to his sister. On 1 October 1514 a list was drawn up of the clothes and plate delivered to Mary.[243] In the following week a series of bills recorded the receipt of payment for goods for her trousseau.[244] On 12 October three inventories of the goods provided for the queen of France were compiled: the plate for her chapel, buffet and kitchen, the furniture for the chapel and her clothes, hangings and stable stuff.[245] The inventory of Mary's gowns included garments in the French fashion, the Milanese fashion and the English fashion.[246]

Two inventories of Mary's trousseau survive. The first had headings for apparel devised for the French queen, gowns of the French fashion, after the Milan fashion, after the English fashion, as well as reference to livery provided for her footmen in three qualities.[247] The other document written in French lists robes and petticoats of the English fashion, robes, bonnets and 'esquillettes' of the Milanese fashion, manteaux, hoods and 'scabelles' delivered at Abbeville on 12 October 1514, their receipt being acknowledged by Thomas Bohier, A. de Beaune and Henry Bohier.[248] Another inventory listed the chapel stuff, clothing, linen and tapestries belonging to Mary and delivered there earlier to Louis XII by Sir Andrew Windsor.[249]

For their first meeting at Abbeville Mary and Louis both wore crimson and cloth of gold. French custom required the clothes of the king and queen to be of the same colour and fabric when they appeared in public together.[250] However, for her formal entry into Abbeville Mary wore a gown of white gold brocade of the English style with a new style of frontlet on her head. Having emphasised her lineage during her entry into the town, Mary wore a gown of French style of cloth of gold trimmed with ermine for her wedding on 9 October, the feast of St Denis, in the great hall of the Hôtel de la Gruthuse. By adopting French dress, she demonstrated her new allegiance to her husband and his country.

Members of the English delegation accompanying Mary to France described the wedding, and more importantly the gifts of jewellery given to her by Louis. On the Monday she received 'a marvellous great pointed diamond with a ruby almost two inches long, without foil'. A ruby followed on the Tuesday, and on the Wednesday a great diamond and a tablet with a great round pearl.[251] Following the marriage she was crowned queen of France on 5 November with the crown of Jean de Navarre at St Denis. Although her clothing was not mentioned, it was noted that 'the Dolphyn all the season held the croune ouer her hed, because it was of greate waight to her greuance'.[252] Mary formally entered Paris on 6 November, because an uncrowned queen of France could not enter the city. She was met by the Paris city guard and she was carried 'in a chayre couerd about in white cloth of golde . . . on her hed a coronal all of greate perles, her necke and brest full of Jueles'.[253] A series of pageants were positioned along the ceremonial route from Porte St Denis to the palace. The pageants were devised by Pierre Gringore to celebrate the occasion, which was recorded in a manuscript illustrated with seven miniatures.[254] In a letter to Wolsey, the earl of Worcester described how Louis 'hath a marvellous mind to content and please the queen . . . and is devising new collars and goodly gear for her . . . He showed me the goodliest and the richest sight of jewels that ever I saw . . . And another coffer also there was that was full of goodly girdles, collars, chains, bracelets, beads of gold and other divers goodly jewels'.[255]

After the death of her husband on 31 December 1514, Mary was required to wear the white mourning of French queens, as 'une Reine Blanche'. She wore white during the month that she passed in solitude at the Hotel de Cluny, next to the Convent de Cluny and then she wore black. Some who saw Mary wearing the black velvet hood and white gown found them very becoming, including the Venetian ambassador who described her as 'the most beautiful and attractive woman ever beheld'.[256] Sir Robert Wingfield wrote to Henry on 14 January, advising that 'if the Queen of France be with child, she be kept from danger. If she be a maid as I verily think she is to obtain possession of her person'.[257]

Henry spent considerably on his sister's trousseau. An undated bill or account of John Ring, skinner, recorded his charges for furring gowns for the French queen that amounted to £84 19*s* 6½*d*.[258] The gowns of white cloth of gold of tissue were furred with ermine, yellow cloth of gold after baudekin furred with ermine, crimson cloth of gold of damask furred with mink, yellow tilsent damask gold furred with pampilion, purple cloth of gold of tissue furred with sable, black velvet furred and decorated on the collar and cuffs of powdered ermine and another six gowns. Further garments were ordered by a warrant dated 3 December 1513.[259] Edward Bensted also paid £221 6*s* 8*d* towards the costs of her marriage to embroiderers, silk women and tailors, one of whom was French.[260] Henry had not settled all the outstanding bills by the time she was widowed. Not surprisingly, Sir Charles Brandon took care to receive the widowed French queen 'with her dower apointed, and all her apparel, iuels and husholdes stuffe deliuered'.[261]

Christenings

On account of the high infant mortality rate and to safeguard their souls, children were christened soon after birth. Parents rarely attended. English royal christenings required the silver font kept at Canterbury to be brought to London. On 19 December 1518 a payment of £4 was made to the prior of Christchurch Canterbury for carrying and re-carrying the font to Canterbury.[262] The household ordinances stipulated how a royal child should be christened.[263] They stated that 'a Dutches to beare the child, and a Dutches to beare the crisome on her shoulder; on a kercheife of fine ermines; and if it bee a Prince, an Earle to beare his trayne; and if it bee a Princesse, a Countesse to beare her trayne'.[264] The infant was to be 'borne in a rich mantle of cloth of gould furred with ermins; a traine thereon borne upp'.[265] As confirmation was carried out at the same time as the christening, two sets of godparents were required, and the ordinances also stipulated the role of the parents, the godparents and what should be done with the gifts.

The account of the christening of Princess Bridget, the seventh daughter and youngest child of Edward IV and Elizabeth Woodville, who was born on 10 November 1480, echoes the household ordinances. Bridget was christened on St Martin's day, the day after her birth, and the record noted that 'The Lorde Matrauers ... Hauinge A Towell aboute his necke' and 'My lady Matrauers dyd bere A Ryche Crysom Pynned Ouer her lefte breste'.[266]

In anticipation of the birth of a son Henry issued a warrant to the great wardrobe on 12 March 1510. The warrant ordered red say to cover the steps of the font which was to be delivered to Ralph Jennet and William Cheyney, yeomen of the wardrobe of the beds. Linen was supplied for the base of the font, with 2 ells (1.3 m) of sipers or linen for a strainer, 4 ells (2.6 m) to cover the font and 6 ells (3.9 m) of good linen cloth for 'aprons and napkins for the four gentlemen and the sergeant of our vestry, according to the old use and custom in that case heretofore used' along with lior, ribbon, gilt nails and hooks.[267] The child was to be wrapped in a bearing cloth as indicated by a delivery made to the king's nursery of 8 yards (7.3 m) of purple velvet for a 'beryng payne' with a long train on 29 September 1510.[268]

HENRY VII'S CHILDREN

There is very little evidence relating to the christenings of Henry VII's children. Prince Arthur was christened at Winchester cathedral and pride of place in the procession belonged to 'my Lady Cicily the quenes Eldist Sister bering the Prynce wraped in a mantell of crymesyn clothe of golde furred with Ermyn with A trayne which was borne by my Lady the Marquesse of [. . .] and Sir John Cheyney supported the myddill of the same'.[269] Unusually, Elizabeth of York was present 'in the churche abyding the comyng of the Prynce', and she witnessed her son being put in the font, 'as the officers of Armes put on their cotes and all the torcheis were light . . . from thence the Prynce was had to his traverse'.[270] Nicholas Kingston, gentleman usher of the chamber, was paid £18 12*s* 'for the christening of our first born son' on 1 October 1486.[271] This included £5 11*s* for making a font, 44*s* for railing the church with iron and timber, seven pieces of say for draping the font and erecting a gallery from the queen's lodging to the prince's lodging. A warrant dated nearly five years later on 1 September 1491 recorded the payment of £6 3*s* 4*d* for stuff delivered to Benjamin Digby, yeoman of the queen's beds for the christenings of Margaret and Henry: 8 ells (5.2 m) of cloth to go around the font, nine pieces of lawn, six within the font and three covering the font, four pieces of sipers, two for the edge of the font and two 'for seling of the window where my lord Henry was chaunged', dressing the font for the two christenings and lior to hang the cloth of estate.[272]

HENRY VIII'S CHILDREN

In comparison to his own christening, the evidence is more detailed for the christenings of four of Henry VIII's children: Henry, Mary, Elizabeth and Edward.

Prince Henry, the king's shortlived first son, was held at Richmond on Sunday 5 January 1511, four days after his birth.[273] He was christened at the friary church, which was hung with arras in the body of the church and on the south side.[274] The French king gave the prince a salt weighing 51 oz and a cup of 48½ oz of fine gold, £10 to the midwife and a chain worth £30 to the Lady Mistress.

On 8 January 1511 Catherine of Aragon told Margaret of Savoy about the birth and christening: 'Catherine mande à Marguerite qu'il lui est né un fils le premier jour de l'an; qu'il a été baptise et a eu pour marraine ladite Marguerite, representie par la Comtesse de Surrey.'[275] The French, papal, Spanish and Venetian ambassadors attended the christening, and the Frenchman followed 'the advice of Winchester and the Great Chamberlain' who had advised him that 'it would be well to present a chain of 200 crowns to the Prince's nurse'.[276]

Princess Mary was born 18 February 1516 at four in the morning at Greenwich, and she was christened two days later at the church of the Grey Friars. As was traditional, the church 'was hung with cloth of needlework garnished with precious stones and pearls'.[277] Mary was carried by the countess of Surrey, with the duke of Norfolk at the head and the duke of Suffolk at her feet.[278] The heralds recorded that 'from the churche dore to the coorte gate stode the garde in theyr best cootes & other of theym of the kynges seruauntes to the number of ijC & xv & euery of them holdyng a torche'.[279]

On Princess Elizabeth's birth, Catherine of Aragon refused to send Anne Boleyn the christening robe that she had brought from Spain, stating, 'God forbid that I should ever be so badly advised as to give help, assistance, or favour, directly or indirectly in a case so horrible as this'.[280] At her christening, the dowager duchess of Norfolk carried Elizabeth who was dressed 'in a mantle of purple velvet, with a long train furred with ermine' into the Grey Friars' church at Greenwich.[281] On 15 September 1533 Chapuys informed Charles V that 'The daughter of the lady has been named Elizabeth, not Mary. The christening has been like her mother's coronation, very cold and disagreeable both to the Court and to the city, and there has been no thought of bonfires and rejoicings usual in such cases'.[282]

Prince Edward was the last of Henry's children. After Edward's birth John Husee wrote to Lord Lisle, saying, 'I pray Jesu send his Grace long to prosper and live, and the King's Higness many more sons'.[283] He was baptised on 15 October 1537 in the chapel royal at Hampton Court, three days after his birth. The young prince was taken from the queen's apartments by the marchioness of Exeter, the duke of Norfolk and the duke of Suffolk (Fig. 4.4).[284] Edward was dressed in a white gown with a long train, which was carried by William Fitzalan, eleventh earl of Arundel and Lord William Howard.[285] After the christening Edward was brought to his mother's chamber 'in the presence of the kyng and the quene

4.4 *The baptism of Edward VI. The prince was carried to his christening by his godparents under a cloth of estate. MS M.6, ff. 77v–78r. The College of Arms*

there had the blessyng of them bothe all myghty godes owr Ladyes and sens George'.[286] The inclusion of the king's daughters in the ceremony allowed Henry to emphasise the dynastic security of his family.

Twenty-four trumpeters were present and 'the sergeauntes of the trumpettes with all the company of that office [were] to be redy with their trumpette to stande & to sounde as they shalbe appoynted by the Lord chamberleyn'.[287] After his christening, Edward was proclaimed as duke of Cornwall.[288] The christening marked a significant point in the rise of the Seymour family. As a consequence, two of Jane's brothers were honoured: Edward being made earl of Hertford and Thomas knighted on 18 October.

The preparations necessary for a royal christening can be seen from a warrant dated 16 October 1539, the day after the prince's christening. The warrant recorded that Ralph Warren provided ray cloth for the base of the font, William Hewetson supplied 18 pieces of red English say of the largest size, while John Baven sold 12 pieces of red ribbon and 12,000 gilt nails for the christening. In addition, six men were paid at a rate of 12*d* a day for four days' work, along with three horses and food for them, with the total coming to £31 11*s* 8*d*.[289]

OTHER ROYAL CHRISTENINGS

The form of royal christenings was used for the children of the king's close relatives. Lady Frances, so named in honour of Francis I, was the daughter of Mary Tudor (the 'French queen') and the duke of Suffolk. She was born on Thursday 17 July and christened on the following Saturday, when 'The font was hanged with a rich canopy powdered with roses half red and half white with the sun shining and fleur-de-lys of gold and the French Queen's arms in four places in the same canopy, all of needlework'.[290] The level of pageantry and formality reflected Mary's status as the queen dowager of France and the king's sister. This was also reflected in the choice of godparents: the Queen Catherine and Princess Mary stood as the child's godmothers, *in absentia*: 'In the said chancel were, as deputies, for the Queen and Princess, Lady Boleyn and Lady Elizabeth Grey.'[291]

Churchings

A queen's churching was symbolic of her purification after the birth of her child and it marked her return to court life. The length of time between birth and churching depended on the health of the mother or the gender of the baby. Eleanor of Castile (Edward I's queen) lay in for 40 days for a son and just 30 for a daughter.[292] Elizabeth of York was ill after the birth of Prince Arthur, at Winchester: 'After that the Quene was purified and hole of an Agu that she had.'[293] Elizabeth also paid for a religious foundation in the form of a chapel dedicated to the Virgin Mary in Winchester in thanksgiving to God for her safe delivery.[294] Holy water was believed to be efficacious in helping the mother recover, as indicated by Sir John Wallop in a letter dated 18 December 1536:

> Against my lady's lying in I have sent her two bottles of water which I brought from Avignon, meet for that purpose, especially when she comes near churching time for she shall be so much the more readier by five or six days if she shall use the virtue of the same, which is restraintive and draweth together like a purse . . . Furthermore when a woman's breasts be long it raiseth them higher and rounder.[295]

Churching served as a thanksgiving for a safe delivery. It also provided an opportunity to re-enact the churching of the Virgin Mary as celebrated on Candlemas. As for all women, the ceremony for the queen's churching took place at the door to the chapel or closet. She would be greeted by the priest with the words, 'Enter the temple of God, adore the Son of the Holy Virgin Mary who has given you the blessing of motherhood'.[296]

In previous centuries, the queen wore new clothes for her churching. The clothes ordered for Edward III's queen for her churching, after the birth of her first son at Woodstock, consisted of three suits of clothes, one of red velvet, one of red and gold 'diaspinus' and one of purple velvet trimmed with miniver and gold squirrels. These garments were more impressive than the clothes that had been ordered for Philippa's coronation, in recognition of the significance of the birth of the heir to the throne.[297] Unfortunately, there are no references to special clothes being ordered for the churching of any of Henry VIII's wives, and no descriptions of the ceremonies have come to light. However, the churching of Edward IV's queen, Elizabeth Woodville, after the birth of their first child in February 1466 is known to have been magnificent.

The procession included heralds and pursuivants, and the queen 'went to church in stately order, accompanied by many priests bearing relics and by many scholars singing and carrying lights . . . Above her was a canopy. Behind her were her mother and maidens and ladies to the number of sixty'.[298]

After the birth of Prince Henry in 1511, Hall noted that 'before the Quenes churchinge, the kyng rode to Walsingham. The Quene beyng Churched or purified, the kyng and she remoued from Rychemonde'.[299] Churching was rarely described in much detail. For example, Henry's sister Margaret, queen of Scots, after her delivery at Harbottle castle, wrote to the duke of Albany, head of the council in Scotland, to inform him that 'by the grace of Almighty God I am nowe delivered and have a cristen sowle, being a yong lady'.[300] Lord Dacre decided to move her from Harbottle on 16 November, where her presence was 'uneasefull and costelye by occasion of farre cariage of everything', and take her to Morpeth 'after her grace have sought the churche and be purified'.[301] Sadly, Jane Seymour did not survive long enough after Prince Edward had been delivered to be churched. She died within 12 days of his birth, having received extreme unction.

Preparation for death: Henry VII

On 20 November 1504 Henry VII settled £10 a year on the University of Cambridge in return for a service to be held at the church of St Mary the Great in Cambridge for him. Henry VII's provision for a requiem service was 'for the good and prosperous estate' of Henry VII 'during his lif . . . and after the deceas of the said kyng . . . then and from thensforth as long as the world shall endure to hold and kepe the said Anniversarie yerely'. It further stipulated that the 'Chancellor, Maisters and Scolers of the said Universite of Cambridge and their Successours shall yerely for ever . . . provide ordeigne and have at every suche Annversarie an herse to be sette in the myddes of the same churche before the high Crucifixe . . . covered and apparelled with the best and moost honourable stuffe to the said Universite belongyng for the same'.[302]

The first service was held on 11 February 1505. This marked the anniversary of the death of Elizabeth of York. The university's accounts recorded a payment in February 1505 of 3*s* 4*d* to 'Joanni Spencer pro vehactione palli funeralis rege' and another payment of 20d 'pro cera ad exequias domini regis'.[303] This pattern continued until 1509 when the service was held on 11 February and again on 21 April after Henry VII's death. Henry VIII gave an offering of 6*s* 8*d* at the 'masse of Requiem for his fader late king Henry the vijth' in 1511.[304]

A hearse and a hearse cloth were required to be present during the service. The hearse cloth was listed in an inventory of 1513 that recorded 'alle the Jewelles that longyth to the Universitie lyinge in ye Universite chapell vestary' and it was described as 'a palle of clothe of Tyssewe'.[305] It survives and it measures 431 cm by 310 cm (Fig. 4.5).[306] The cloth was made from black cloth of gold with a woven pomegranate design and red velvet which formed a central cross. The cross was made from a half loom width of cut pile silk velvet.[307] The Tudor coat of arms, supported by a dragon and a greyhound, was placed in the centre of the cloth, with eighteen alternating badges of roses and portcullises (two of the roses are now missing) stitched on the velvet cross. The crimson velvet has a black warp, a yellow weft and a crimson silk pile warp.[308]

The hearse cloth was made from four widths of cloth of gold stitched together with an additional half loom width added to each long side.[309] The cloth of gold has a silk warp and weft with a pile warp and binding warp. The metal threads consist of a silver gilt metal strip wrapped round a yellow silk core (gold on a silver/copper alloy) and the hearse cloth has examples of single, double and triple wrapped filaments on silk cores. All of the metal threads are S wound, with the exception of the double and triple threads. The core fibres were silk and they were all pale yellow or white in colour.[310]

While there are no references to where the Cambridge hearse cloth was made, it was very similar in design and materials to a pair of cloths ordered on 8 February 1505. Stephen Jasper, the king's tailor, made a pall of white cloth of gold tissue with a cross of crimson velvet and a pall of black

4.5 *The hearse cloth of Henry VII, c. 1504–05. Fitzwilliam Museum, Cambridge. Photo: © The Textile Conservation Centre, University of Southampton*

cloth of gold tissue with a cross of crimson velvet. Both were lined with buckram and additional buckram was provided for laying between the palls for freighting. They was embellished with 36 roses and portcullises worked on crimson satin. The labour and a small amount of the materials cost £4 9*s* 9*d*.[311] On the same day a suit of vestments was ordered, consisting of vestments for priest, deacon and subdeacon with apparel of green cloth of gold baudekin and five altar cloths of baudekin of diverse colours for the friars at Richmond which were decorated with two crucifixes flanked by Mary and John, three portcullises with crowns imperial embroidered at the feet of the crosses, three crosses, two portcullises and two roses with crowns imperial and five portcullises and eight roses.[312] The implication is that these textiles were intended to be used to celebrate a similar service to that at Cambridge, but in the chapel at Richmond.

The most obvious sign of Henry VII's preparations for death is the chantry chapel he built at Westminster abbey which was initially intended for the reburial of Henry VI, who Henry VII sought to have canonised as a Lancastrian royal saint (Fig. 4.6).[313] As late as 1530 two inventories of Henry's jewels included entries for 'a silver gilt box containing the ring wherin Henry VI espoused his queen'.[314] The ring was not listed in the 1547 inventory, or possibly was described in different terms. However, the chapel came to house the double tomb of Henry VII and Elizabeth of York.[315]

On 10 August 1528 Archbishop Warham was granted a license to alienate land to the annual value of £20 to the use of the prior and convent of Christchurch, Canterbury, for the support of one or two secular chaplains to pray for Henry VIII and Catherine of Aragon and the souls of Henry VII and Elizabeth of York.[316] The services continued from 1510 to 1548, when they were banned by Edward VI. They were revived by Mary but ceased after 1558.

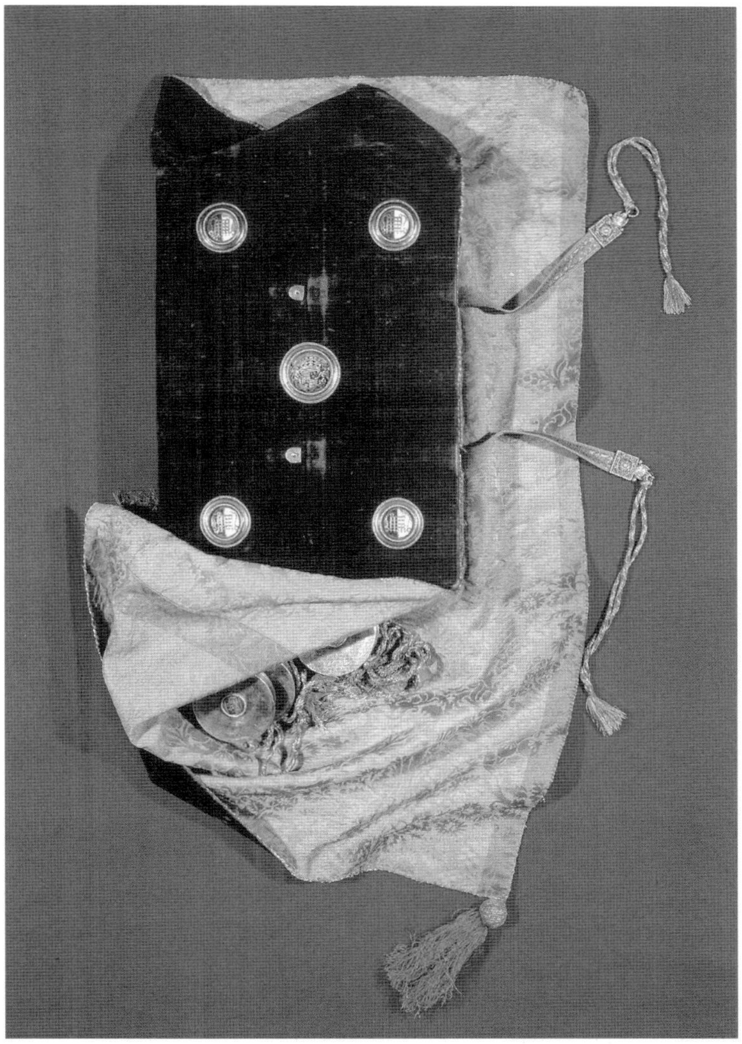

4.6 *Overall image of the interior of the cover of the founding indenture of Henry VII's chantry chapel, Westminster abbey, 1504, showing the velvet chemise binding with a silk damask lining and tassel. The National Archive, E33/1*

Obsequies: the living remembering the dead

Obsequies formed part of the routine observations for the dead. They were held on the seventh and 30th day after death and the first year's anniversary. In November 1502 Elizabeth of York made an offering of 5*s* 'at the obyt of the Kinges Fader holden at Westminster'.[317] Within court circles, funeral rites or ceremonies were observed for foreign royalty and they followed a similar format to royal funerals but on a smaller scale. Consequently, black livery was issued to a group of mourners, a hearse and banners were provided and a chief mourner was appointed. The details of a number of foreign obsequies observed during Henry VIII's reign appear in the lord chamberlain's accounts: Louis XII, king of France in 1515; Ferdinand V, king of Aragon on 28 February 1516; Maximilian I, Holy Roman Emperor, on 11 February 1519; Louise of Angoulême, lady regent of France, on 27 October 1531 and Isobel, wife of Charles V, on 6 June in 1539. After Henry VIII's death early in 1547, the Protector Somerset honoured Francis I, king of France, with an obsequy on 20 June 1547.[318] All the obsequies were held at St Paul's, with the single exception of those for Louise of Angoulême, performed at Waltham abbey. A bill of receipt dated 13 February 1515 by Sir Andrew Windsor for £91 11*s* 8*d* survives for the obsequies of Louis XII from Sir John Dauntsey.[319] The cost was relatively modest in comparison to other royal obsequies including Louise of Angoulême (£180 11*s* 6*d*), Isobel of Portugal (£342 1*d*) and Francis I (£649 18*s* 4*d*).

The king was rarely the chief mourner at these occasions. His absence enabled a member of the nobility to represent him. At the obsequies for Louis XII, the duke of Norfolk was the chief mourner and he received 10 yards (9.1 m) of black cloth for his gown, slope and mantle. He was accompanied by the lord Steward, the lord Chamberlain, the marquess of Dorset, the earl of Devonshire and Lords Mounteagle and Herbert, all of whom received 6 yards (5.4 m) for a gown and hood. Garter king of arms also received 6 yards (5.4 m) for a gown and hood, while Norrey king of arms, Somerset and Carlisle received 4½ yards (4.1 m) each for gowns and hoods. A majesty cloth was made from 16¾ yards (15.3 m) of black sarsenet with four valances trimmed with 3 lb 6 oz (1.53 kg) of black silk fringe and with the celure lined with green buckram. Thirteen and a half pieces of black cloth were hired to hang the choir of St Pauls from the high altar to the choir door on both sides, to provide a cloth before the high altar, to cover the inner and outer bars about the hearse and to place upon the ground within the outer bars and to cover the furniture and the cushions where the mourners were. After the service, refreshments were provided: two hippocras bags, 1 lb 3 oz (0.53 kg) of cinnamon, 10 oz (0.28 kg) of ginger, 11 lb (0.31 kg) of sugar, ½ oz (0.014 kg) of grain, 1 oz (0.028 kg) of nutmeg, 1 oz (0.028 kg) of cloves, 4 gallons (18.16 b) of wine and 20 lb (9.07 kg) of comfets.[320]

The duke of Norfolk was also the chief mourner at the obsequies of Ferdinand and Maximilian, but he was accompanied by different members of the nobility on each occasion: the duke of Suffolk, the marquess of Dorset, the earls of Surrey, Shrewsbury, Devonshire, Worcester, the imperial ambassador, Lord St John, Sir John Peche, Sir Andrew Windsor for Ferdinand, and Dorset, the earl of Kent, the Lord Darcy, Lord Fitzwater, Lord Cobham, Sir Thomas Lovell, Sir Henry Marney, Sir Andrew Windsor, Sir John Cutte, Robert Knollys for Maximilian. In addition, at the latter, offerings of 6*s* 8*d* were provided for Wolsey, the chancellor of England, and 'to my lord legate of Rome, a crown each [worth 4*s* 4*d*] to the three ambassadors and 5*s* for "my lord Norfolk"'.[321]

European observers took note of the solemnity of the obsequies held in London for royal dignities. On 25 February 1519 Sebastiano Giustinian told the doge about the 'very sumptuous obsequies have been celebrated here for the Emperor. His demise is held in small account'.[322] Similarly, on 8 June 1539 Thomas Boys wrote to Lord Lisle, noting that on this day:

> the goodliest solemnities were done for the Empress at Paul's and in every church in London. All Paul's was hung with black cloth with the arms of the Emperor and the Empress, and there was made in the church a goodly rich hearse with the arms of the Empire. My lord Chauncellor represented the King; the dukes of Norfolk and Suffolk, with nine earls were mourners; and there were ten bishops with their mitres.[323]

The hearses provided for funerals in England were traditional in their form, as was the case with the hearse at the funeral of Abbot John Islip in Westminster abbey 1532 (Fig. 4.7).[324] In contrast, royal funerals in Europe incorporated elements of Renaissance design. The obsequies held for Ferdinand of Aragon in Brussels in March 1516 included a triumphal car drawn by four white horses with gilded unicorns' horns. They were draped with the badges of the countries that he had conquered and inscribed 'Ferdinando Regi, Betico, Parthenopaeo, Cantabrico, Africano, Indico, Catholico Invicto'.[325] The funeral effigy was dressed in armour and held a sword, while Ferdinand's crown was born on a cushion on a white horse following behind. On the second day his achievements were represented by 14 horses draped with the insignia of his kingdoms and 14 standard bearers carrying flags of the same arms. This imagery was magnified in the pageant car drawn in Charles V's obsequies held in Brussels in 1558.[326] The car was decorated with the pillars of Hercules, his motto *Plus oultre*, with Faith holding the cross seated on a stone labelled *Christus* and the flags of all the countries that Charles had ruled over.

4.7 *Miniature of the funeral of John Islip, abbot of Westminster, 1532, showing the mourners around his hearse. Abbot Islip's mortuary roll, Westminster Abbey Muniment Room. By courtesy of the Dean and Chapter*

Funerals and burial

More than any other ceremony in the early modern period, royal funerals emphasised the dual nature of kingship.[327] The provisions associated with death in Tudor England were more varied than for the other occasions discussed in this chapter. They included funerals, prayers and obits for the dead and obsequies for foreign royalty. The funerals of kings, their queens consort and their children were all of the same type: they were public and they were controlled by the heralds.[328] The cost and the scale of royal funerals reflected the status of the dynasty: Prince Arthur's funeral in 1502 cost about £600 and Elizabeth of York's in 1503 over £3,000. Even the funerals of short-lived royal offspring were expensive. In October 1495 John Shaa received payments of 1,000 marks (£333 6*s* 8*d*) and £318 9*s* 7*d* for 'the burial of our daughter Elizabeth'.[329]

The household ordinances provide a full account of how the king's body should be dressed for burial:

> Furst his body [should be] washyd and clensyd after sporgyng.
>
> Thanne the bodie bawmed yff it may be gete wrapped in lawn or Raynes.
>
> Then hosen shert and shone with rede leder and doo oon them hys surrecote cloth . . . hys cape of astate on hys hede layd apon a feyr borde on a clothe of gold richely hys hondys on hys bely with a septure ther in on hys face a kerchyff and soo shewd on to hys lordes and gentills by the space of ij dayes and more yff the wedder will suffice.
>
> Than take hym away and bowell hym wrappe hym in Raynes well trameled in Roppis of silke / thanne in tarteron trameled / and thenne in veluet and soo in clothe of gold will trameled thanne lede hym and coffre hym / and yf ye carry hym maake an ymage like hym clothyd in a surcote with a mantell of astate the lassess goodly lyng on the body hys septure in hys hond / and a crown on hys hede / and soo cary hym in a chare opyn . . .
>
> Item before the fore hors of the chare his owne herould in hys cote armour and thenne a lorde or a knyght for his body Rydyng with the kynges corse present that is to sey on a courser trappet withe his armes his harneys vpon hys bassenet or salet crowned a shyld and a spere till he

come to the place of his enterryng and at masse the same be offred be some natable prince.[330]

The funeral effigy was used to represent the change in the nature of the monarch's body, from the visible physical form to the invisible spiritual form. It also stressed the continuity of the monarchy, with the effigy dressed in royal robes and wearing regalia. The figure was carved to resemble the king and represent him as the body lay in state.[331]

The role of the poor mourners was distinct and prescribed in the early Tudor funerals. These poor men carried torches and said prayers for the soul of the deceased because the prayers of the poor were believed to be the most efficacious in speeding the passage of the soul through Purgatory. By the time of Elizabeth I's funeral in 1603, the Church of England had rejected the doctrine of Purgatory, and the gentleman pensioners from the royal household took the place formerly occupied by poor men in her funeral procession.[332]

As with coronations, a set of traditional perquisites were given at royal funerals. According to a marginal note on the 1547 inventory, a cloth of estate made of blue velvet fringed with purple silk and without any arms taken from the wardrobe at Greenwich 'did serue at the buriall of king henry the viij[th] at whiche tyme it was a fee to the gromes of the pryvey chambre and so takin by theym' (9296).

Royal funerals signified the end of a reign and the start of another. They also marked the dissolution of a household and the appointment of another, with new possibilities for patronage and promotion. After the chief officers of Henry VII's household had broken their staffs of office and dropped the pieces into the grave:

All the heraudes did [take] of theire cotearmours and did hange them uppon the Rayles of the herse: cryinge lamentably in French 'The Noble kynge Henry the Seaventh is deade'. And as soone as they had so done, everie heraud putt on his cotearmour againe and cryed with a loude voyce 'Vive Le noble Roy Henry le VIIIme' whichh is to say in englyshe tonge 'God send the noble Kynge Henry the eight longe life'.[333]

HENRY VIII

In 1517 Henry VIII declared a wish to be buried at Windsor 'when the most high God called him out of the world'. In January he contracted the Florentine sculptor, Pietro Torrigiano, then living in the precinct of Westminster abbey, to make a tomb of white marble and black touchstone for himself and his wife, one quarter larger than that Torrigiano was making for the king's parents.[334] The tomb was to be completed in four years at a cost of £2,000 under the direction of Cardinal Wolsey. Nothing came of this. In 1529 Henry confiscated the components of a tomb started for Wolsey. This had not been finished by the time of the king's death in 1547.

The chronicler Hall wrote 'in the monethe of January, he yielded hys spirite to almightie God, and departed thys worlde, and lyeth buryed at Wyndsore'.[335] His corpse needed to be prepared and:

commandment was given to the apothecaries, chirgeons, wax-chandlers and others, to do their duties in spurging, cleansing, boweling, cering, embalming, furnishing, and dressing with spices the said corps; and also for wrapping the same in cerecloth of many folds over the fine cloth of rains and velvet, surely bound and trammel'd with cords of silk: which was done and executed of them accordingly, as to the dignity of such a mighty prince it appertaineth.[336]

In his will Henry stated that he wished to be buried in the Garter chapel, 'midway between the stalls and the high altar, in a tomb now almost finished in which he will also have the bones of his wife, Queen Jane'.[337] In addition, he wanted 13 poor men, who were to be called poor knights, to be given 12*d* a day and to receive a long white robe each year. Quarterly obits would be held at which £10 would be distributed in alms.

Henry's body initially lay in state in the privy chamber at Whitehall for five days:

Then was the Corps in the Chest had into the midst of his privy Chamber and set upon tressels with a rich pall of Cloath of gold and a Cross thereon, with all manner of lights thereto requisite, having divine service about him with Masses, obsequies and prayers, and continually watche being made by his Chapelrys Ordinary and Gentlemen of his Privy Chamber to the number of 30 persons.[338]

St James's palace was put at the disposal of Catherine Parr as the queen dowager. The great chamber, along with a presence chamber, the queen's own chamber and a closet were provided with black hangings, foot carpets and cupboard cloths.[339]

The preparations for Henry VIII's burial on 14 February 1547 brought his household together in its final service for its late master. Two weeks earlier, the duke of Somerset and the other executors had appointed five men 'to have the speciall charge of all thinges necessarie for thenterrement'.[340] Shortly afterwards, a list of orders was prepared to ensure the smooth passage of the funeral cortege as it progressed from London to Windsor, reminiscent of those produced for the Field of Cloth of Gold.[341] The great wardrobe was heavily involved supplying mourning livery for the household and black hangings for the king's apartments, as well as banners and decorations for the hearse.[342] The chapel royal provided the services and the music, while the altar of Whitehall palace chapel was 'adorned with al manner of plate and jewels of the revestry . . . And the high altar very richly adorned with plate and jewels and other ornaments'.[343]

Henry VIII's effigy was described in the following terms:

the picture was made veray like unto the Kinges Majesties person, both in stature favowre forme and apparell, the which was laid a long uppon the Cophyn with twoo greate Cussyns under his head. The Crowne Emperiall of Englande of goulde sett with precious stones, and under that a night cappe of blak satten sett full of stone and golde, was uppon his heade. His shurte as it apperid abought the coller and handes seem to be of fynne goldsmithes worke. The picture was apparrellid with robes of crymsyn velvet furred with mynifer powdred with armyns, the colore of the Garter with the George abought his nekk, a crymsyne satten dublett embroydered with gold, twoo bracelleetts of golde abought his wrests sett with stone and perle a fayre armering sworde by his side, the septure in his right hande and the balle in the lefte hande a payer of new gloves, with many rings sett with rych stones on his fyngers.[344]

The accounts of Henry's funeral included payments for a pair of sabatons made of incarnate cloth of gold 'with works' which were lined with crimson satin and a pair of shoes made of crimson velvet. Both the shoes and the sabatons were made by Henry Johnson, Henry's cordwainer, at 3*s* the pair.[345]

Henry's courser, 'the whiche the Master of the Horse leades in his hande to the Buryall', was caparisoned in a trapper of purple cloth of gold, with the reins and stirrup leathers

The princess dowager: Catherine of Aragon

Catherine of Aragon had been ill for some time before her death at Kimbolton on 7 January 1536. The news was most welcome at court and, according to Hall, 'Quene Anna ware yelowe for the mournyng' on the Sunday after Catherine's death.[384] However, Chapuys stated that it was the king who 'was clad all over in yellow, from top to toe, except the white feather he had in his bonnet'.[385] Her death provided Henry with the final opportunity to emphasise her status as the princess dowager of Wales.[386]

Catherine was buried in Peterborough cathedral on 24 January 1536, with the level of ceremony that Henry deemed appropriate to her rank as princess dowager and the widow of his late brother. By selecting the Benedictine abbey of Peterborough (situated in the Fenland, far from the capital and court), Henry ignored Catherine's request to be buried within a convent of the Observant Friars (preferably at Greenwich or Richmond, which might have embarrassed him). He also decided against having a hearse set up in St Paul's cathedral. When Ralph Sadler queried this, reminding the king that he had provided a hearse for his sister Mary, Henry answered that this was because Mary had been a queen.[387] An indignant Chapuys informed Charles V that 'They do not mean to bury her as Queen'.[388] The heraldry on the banners provided by the Painter-Stainers' company for the funeral depicted the arms of Spain and Wales, but not England:

for iiij large Banners with Images bettyn with fyne golde in hoyle havynge in skottchyns of Armes in euery banner one of the trynetye one of oure lady one of sanct george And one of sancte kateryne — each ¾ yard by ½ yard on blue double sarsenet fringed with silk £10 13*s* 4*d*

for iiij banner rollis on[e] kynge Henry the vijth with his mariage on[e] of kynge fernande hir father with his mariage on[e] of prince arthur And hir selfe and on[e] of hir armes alone betten with fyne golde in oyle on[e] double sarsenet with silk fringe £8

x bannerrolls of dessentes one of the kyng on[e] of the emperoure on[e] of Spayne on[e] of price arthur on[e] of richemond and somerset on[e] of lancaster and Spayne one of portyngale and lancaster on[e] of castile on[e] of aragon and on[e] of granada £15.[389]

Henry disingenuously tried to persuade Chapuys that the funeral was appropriate. He offered him black livery for himself and his servants. However, Chapuys declined the mourning cloth 'which the king wishes to give me, and would gladly by this means bind me to be present at the interment, which the king greatly desires but . . . I will not go since they do not mean to bury her as Queen'.[390] He boycotted the interment on that score. There had never been any likelihood of the French ambassador or his retinue attending, and Henry never contemplated offering them black livery.[391]

A range of funerary textiles were produced for Catherine of Aragon's funeral. However, unlike with the funerals of Elizabeth of York and Jane Seymour, where the hearse clothes and clothes of estate were either made specially within the great wardrobe or taken from one of the royal wardrobes of the beds, Catherine's were made by the Painter-Stainers, including 'a large magestye clothe of blacke sarsnet lynede with bokeram conteynyng vj yerdis in lengyth and vj yerdis in bredith wroght with a large dome the iiij evangelistes & iiij large skochins of armes with crownalls bettyn golde' costing £12, and 'xx yerdis of valance of blacke sarsnet doble wrytyn with lettres of golde And with Serten armes and bages' costing £3 6*s* 8*d*. They also provided 'a magestye clothe of blake tuke for the hearse at Sawtry [abbey in Huntingdonshire] with the 4 evangelists and 4 coats of arms', '12½ yards of valances of tuke with letters of gold and arms and badges' and '16 yards rachments for the hearse written with letters of gold on black tuke'.[392]

Catherine did have a funeral effigy and the king appointed the mourners.[393] The chief mourner was Lady Eleanor Brandon, and Catherine, duchess of Suffolk, was the second mourner.[394] Several of the king's letters informing people of their appointment as mourners at Catherine's funeral have survived, including one sent to Lady Bedingfield on 10 January. As her role was to accompany the body from Kimbolton to Peterborough, she needed to be at Kimbolton by 25 January. Confident that Lady Bedingfield would not dare decline, Henry sent sufficient black cloth with the letter for her, two gentlewomen, two gentlemen and eight women. This suggests that Lady Bedingfield had to organise and pay for the cloth to be made up in appropriate garments. A habiliment of linen for her head and face was also promised.[395] However, not all the king's letters received a positive response. John St John requested that his wife should be excused from this duty on two grounds. First, she 'has been lately sick of breeding young bones and not yet well recovered', and second, as he was in Catherine's service he had 'all such horses and servants with me, as my said poor wife should be furnished with'.[396]

An anonymous account of the burial gives a good indication of how long it took for the mourning apparel to be made for Catherine's ladies: 'On the Wednesday after the robes of the Queens 10 ladies were completed, who had not till then made any mourning, except with kerchiefs on their heads and old robes.'[397] The full extent of the mourning issued to female mourners can be assessed from several extant lists of the noble female mourners which are headed by her daughter, Princess Mary.[398] They were provided with items supplied by the queen's silk woman, and Mary received the most: three fine mantles, three fine double barbs, three frontlets, three pasts, three rolls and 15 ells (9.5 m) of very fine holland for 12 kerchers.[399] At the other end of the list were ten women who were drawn from Catherine's household: Mistress Twyford, Mistress Laurence, Mistress Darrell, Mistress Brown, Mistress Fynes, Mistress Mary, Dorothy Wheeler, Margery Atwell, Elizabeth Atwell and Dorothy Doltes.[400]

Execution and private burial: Anne Boleyn and Catherine Howard

Two of the king's wives were executed: Anne Boleyn and Catherine Howard. They were buried with little ceremony. A list of dispersements for August 1536 by John Gostwick mentions four payments that throw light on Anne's imprisonment and execution. Gostwick paid the lieutenant of the Tower £100 'for a composition for such jewels and apparel as the late Queen had in the Tower'; the bill for food and drink provided for Anne amounted to £25 4*s* 6*d*; Anne had been allowed £20 'to give in alms before her death' and the executioner from Calais received £23 6*s* 8*d* in reward and clothing.[401] The bodies of Anne Boleyn and Catherine Howard were buried in the chapel of St Peter *ad Vincula*, within the walls of the Tower of London and close to the place of their execution.

Anne had been accompanied to her execution by four ladies in waiting, one of whom carried her head to the chapel, while the other three helped to move her body. Anne's clothes were removed then as perquisites for the Tower officers, and her body was placed in an elm box made to hold bow-staves.[402] She was buried close to the four men who were implicated in her fall and had been executed the day before. Less detail is known about the burial of Catherine Howard. She was executed on Monday 13 February 1542. Catherine's 'body was then covered with a black cloak and her ladies took it away'.[403]

Surviving the king: Anne of Cleves and Catherine Parr

Two of Henry's wives survived him: Anne of Cleves and Catherine Parr. Catherine Parr died on 5 September 1548, six days after giving birth to a daughter, and she was buried at Sudeley Castle, Gloucestershire. She had a fairly simple funeral at which Lady Jane Grey was the chief mourner, and the funeral sermon was preached by Catherine's almoner, Miles Coverdale. When her coffin was opened in 1782, witnesses noted that her body was dressed in rich clothes and wrapped in 'cerecloth [that] consisted of many folds of coarse linen, dipped in wax, tar, and perhaps some gums: over this was wrapt a sheet of lead fitting exactly close to the body'.[404]

Anne of Cleves survived until 16 July 1557, dying in Chelsea and being buried in Westminster abbey on 3 August. Under Mary I, she had conformed with her stepdaughter's Catholicism. Her conformity was reflected in the choice of banners made for her funeral. These included:

a great banner of her arms on sarsenet 40*s*
4 banners of saints on sarsenet £6
16 baneroles wrought on sarsenet with gold and silver 15*s*
2 dozen scutchions on buckram in fine gold 48*s*
5 dozen on buckram in parte gold 100*s*
6 dozen on paper royal 38*s*
9 dozen on paper royal in colours 90*s*.[405]

Mary would have approved the selection, even if she had not actually made it herself and she met the costs of her stepmother's funeral.

THE KING'S SISTERS: MARY AND MARGARET TUDOR

The king's sisters received very different funerals. The younger sister Mary was to die first. She died on 25 June 1533. For 25 days her coffin lay in state in the chapel at Westhorpe. Her coffin was covered with a cloth of blue velvet. Her effigy was dressed in the robes of the queen of France. She was buried at Bury St Edmund's abbey on 21 July. At the Dissolution her coffin was moved from the abbey church to the parish church in the town. Henry also ordered a funeral service with a hearse for her in Westminster abbey on 10 and 11 July. Henry covered the charges of the heralds and pursuivants for ten days' attendance in Suffolk as well as the cost of the black cloth, banners and pall produced in the great wardrobe. However, it is not possible to tell how much her husband, the duke of Suffolk, spent because his accounts do not survive.[406] The elder, Margaret, died on 18 October 1541. She was buried at Perth in Scotland at her son James V's expense. Henry heard the news as his summer progress to the north drew to a close. His failure to mark his sister's death with a service at Westminster probably tells us nothing about his feelings towards Margaret, but it could reflect his displeasure at the king of Scot's failure to keep their rendezvous at York. James did not behave well with regards to his mother's estate. Although, 'She asked that lady Margaret Douglas, her daughter, might have her goods', the Scot's king sought to withhold them from his half-sister.[407]

ROYAL CHILDREN

Infants

Several of Henry VIII's siblings died in infancy and were accorded funerals. His own shortlived son and namesake was similarly mourned in 1511. However, on other occasions Catherine of Aragon and Anne Boleyn gave birth prematurely, and the records make no mention of any formal funeral. The evidence is equally scant for funerals being provided for the young children of the house of York. No documents exist for the funerals of Edward IV's children who died young, Margaret in 1472, George in 1479 and Edward in 1484, nor for Richard III's son.[408]

Princess Elizabeth, the second daughter of Henry VII and Elizabeth of York, died in 1495. Her funeral was arranged by Cardinal Morton, Lord Daubenny, Lord Dynham, Sir John Ryssley, Sir John Litton, and John Shaa.[409] Her body was accompanied from Eltham by 40 poor men in black gowns and hoods to Westminster, where another 60 awaited the arrival of the cortege. She was buried in the abbey and 'the graue is on the Right syde of the aultre and before saint edwardes shryn the fete towchyng ner to the fundacion of the shryn'.[410] The hearse was accompanied by a number of scutchions, bannerols, lozenges and pencils:

In primis the peynter lx and xij large schochyns of gold betyn on papir Roiall lozenge wise price the piece xij*d*
Item vj Smalle schochyns of gold for the hers viij*d*
Item xxx lozenges of gold betyn on bokeram for the draught hors and the chare and a lytyll oon for the fore hers hede xx*d*
Item a C lozenges of couleur iij*d*
Item viij banerolls of the kynges armes to garnyshe the hors xiij*s* iiij*d*
Item xxiiij pyncell for the garnyshyng of the same vj*d*.

In addition, 'ther wer iiij great banners had owt of the kynges garderobbe'.[411]

Henry VIII's younger brother Edmund, duke of Somerset, was born on 20 February 1499 and died a little over a year later on 19 June 1500 at Hatfield, a house belonging to the bishop of Ely. Three days later his body was 'brought and conveyed honourably through fflete strete with many noble personages, the Duke of Bokyngham beyng the Chief

370 *LP* XII.ii, 977.
371 *LP* XII.ii, 972.
372 *LP* XII.ii, 1012.
373 CoA MS M6 ff. 1–3.; Wriothesley, *Chronicle*, I, pp. 70–71.
374 CoA MS M6, ff. 1v, 2v, 5v.
375 Strickland, *Queens of England*, II, p. 172.
376 CoA MS M6, f. 7r.
377 Ibid., f. 8v.
378 Ibid., f. 10v.
379 Nichols, *Literary Remains*, I, p. xxv.
380 Hall, *Chronicle*, p. 825.
381 Jones and Underwood, *The King's Mother*, pp. 236–37.
382 SJC D91.4, pp. 5, 13.
383 SJC D4.7, p. 38; this figure is strikingly close to the estimate made of her funeral costs in January 1509 (£1,033), when it was feared that she was dying; see Jones and Underwood, *The King's Mother*, p. 237.
384 Hall, *Chronicle*, p. 818.
385 *CSP Spanish*, 1536–38, pp. 19, 28 (*LP* X, 141, 199).
386 Shortly after her death Sir Edmund Bedingfield wrote to Cromwell to inform him that 'the bowelling and cering is already done in the best manner'; *LP* X, 41.
387 *LP* X, 76.
388 *LP* X, 141.
389 CoA MS M6bis, f. 114v.
390 *LP* X, 141.
391 *LP* X, 76.
392 CoA MS M6bis, ff. 114v–115r.
393 Her effigy was to be 'a cast or puffed Ymage of a princesse apparailled in her Robes of Estate with a Coronall upon her hed . . . with Rings Golves and Juells upon her handes'; see W. Illingworth, 'Copy of an original minute of council for preparations for the ceremonial of the funeral of Queen Catherine the divorced wife of King Henry the Eighth', *Archaeologia*, 16 (1809), p. 24.
394 Fraser, *Six Wives*, p. 231; *LP* X, 282.
395 *LP* X, 65.
396 *LP* X, 57.
397 *LP* X, 284.
398 CoA MS I14, ff. 77r–80r.
399 CoA MS M6bis, ff. 48v–51r.
400 CoA MS M6bis, ff. 50v–51r.
401 *LP* XI, 381.
402 *LP* XI, 381.
403 *LP* XVII, 124.
404 T. Nash, 'Observations on the time of death and place of burial of Queen Katherine Parr', *Archaeologia*, 9 (1789), pp. 1–15.
405 CoA MS I 14, f. 117r.
406 Richardson, *Mary Tudor*, p. 263.
407 *LP* XVI, 1307.
408 A. F. Sutton and L. Visser-Fuchs, 'The royal burials of the house of York at Windsor', *The Ricardian*, 11 (1998), pp. 366–67.
409 CoA MS I14, f. 15v.
410 Ibid., f. 17v.
411 Ibid., f. 18r.
412 Pollard, *Henry VII*, I, p. 216.
413 TNA LC 2/1, ff. 4r–v, 6r.
414 Bentley, *Excerpta Historica*, p. 124.
415 *CSP Spanish*, II, p. 24.
416 Hall, *Chronicle*, p. 519.
417 *LP* I.i, 707.
418 TNA E36/215, pp. 105, 109.
419 *CSP Spanish*, *1509–25*, pp. 270–73.
420 *CSP Venetian*, *1509–19*, 1103.
421 Uncertainty over pregnancy was also common; see *LP* VII, 1193.
422 Crawford, *Letters*, p. 156.
423 Paul, *Catherine of Aragon and her Friends*, p. 15.
424 Pollard, *Henry VII*, I, p. 223.
425 Chapuys recorded that 'I have just this moment heard that the Duke of Richmond died this morning, which is not a bad thing for the interests of the Princess' (*LP* XI, 148); Murphy, *Bastard Prince*, pp. 176–77.
426 Ibid., p. 176.
427 *LP* XI, 221.
428 *Lisle Letters*, IV, 939 (*LP* XII.i, 947).

V

Henry VII: Establishing the House of Tudor

Henry VII was a usurper and the founder of a new royal house. He needed to present himself and his family as the legitimate rulers of England. Both he and his household drew on the royal style established by the Lancastrian and Yorkist courts and on Burgundian ideas of magnificence. Central to the success of his government were his personality, his personal image and his court. Henry VII was parsimonious. In contrast, his son Henry VIII, and his granddaughters, Mary I and Elizabeth I, were often tempted into extravagance, whether they could afford it or not. All four indulged in clothing and jewellery. However, while Henry VII was careful with his money, he was politically shrewd and he had experienced life on a shoestring at several European courts. He was well aware of the need to dress according to his station.[1]

Henry VII's reign, which lasted from 1485 to 1509, straddles the cusp between the fifteenth and sixteenth centuries. Consequently, it tends to suffer at the hands of traditionally organised studies on dress history which focus on specific centuries.[2] Henry VII is often included in books on the sixteenth century, so grouping him with the other Tudor monarchs, even though the style of dress worn by the king and his subjects had much more in common with the fifteenth century. Equally, the range of colours and types of cloth and the quantities of clothes owned by individuals has very little in common with dress by the middle of the sixteenth century or even by the 1530s. As a consequence, Henry VII tends to look dowdy in comparison with his children and grandchildren. Therefore it is more logical to compare him with his immediate predecessors, Edward IV and Richard III. Although only a small number of great wardrobe accounts survive for Edward IV's and Richard III's reigns, they provide enough evidence to get a sense of their clothes.

Male dress in the late fifteenth century

The late fifteenth century was typified by a return to a simpler style of male clothing than that seen in the preceding decades. Emphasis was placed once again on the true shape of the human body, with clothes tailored to the natural shoulder and waist lines. More subtle, dark, strong colours and darker furs were used, and new effects were created by layered clothing. This simplified style has been described as 'attenuated minimalism'.[3] This simplification reflected quite a marked change in style in male dress in the 1480s. The gown was the principal garment and, while it retained its simple cut, it began to get fuller. The gown also developed a roll collar or lapels that could be faced with fur. Because the gown covered the doublet and hose, there is limited visual evidence as to what these looked like, and the accounts suggest that they were fairly understated because they were not the focal point of the outfit. The gown was usually worn with a brimless wool cap and square-toed shoes. Men generally wore their hair long, at least to shoulder length, and they were usually clean shaven.[4]

There are very few examples of male dress from this period, and those that do survive have been altered, so making their original cut and construction hard to distinguish. In 1476 the Swiss ransacked the tents and baggage of Charles the Bold, duke of Burgundy, at the battles of Grandson and Nancy. Amongst the Burgundian Booty, there were several items of male dress.[5]

These included a man's semicircular cape made from red cloth of gold with a large pomegranate design with roses in asymmetric waves (Fig. 5.1).[6] The design has a very long repeat: it is 2.8 m long and 0.57 m wide. The fabric had been arranged so that the pattern would be seen best from the back, suggesting that the original use of the material had been as a cope. The red velvet elements of the design consist of three heights of cut and uncut pile and the areas of single height cut pile are scattered with uncut loops of gold thread in two heights.[7] The velvet is thought to be Italian and to date from *c.* 1430.[8] The booty also included a man's coat in red satin, fitted in the upper body and with no collar (Fig. 5.2).[9] It has long sleeves, which are very full in the head, while the lower section is more fitted. The coat's skirts are full and would have come to the wearer's mid-thigh. It is made from fifteenth-century satin, which was probably made up after 1476. Traditionally, it has been suggested that the silk was taken from the Burgundians by the Swiss at the Battle of Grandson. The satin is a 10-end warp satin with a displacement of three woven in widths of 0.6 m. The coat is lined with a dark grey linen woven in a 2/1 twill that was piece-dyed and waxed.[10] However, it was altered to make it conform with the styles that were fashionable in the 1530s.[11]

5.1 *Mid to late fifteenth-century man's cloth of gold cloak. Bern Historisches Museum, BHM 23*

5.2 *Late fifteenth-century man's red satin coat, with sixteenth-century alterations. Bern Historisches Museum, BHM 20a*

The Yorkist courts

Only one great wardrobe account survives from the reign of Edward IV (1461–83). Even so, it is possible to get a sense of how much he was spending on textiles and dress from other sources. In the period from April 1461 to September 1462, George Darrell, the keeper of the great wardrobe, spent £4,784 2*s* 10½*d* on clothes and cloth. This exceeded the allocation for the great wardrobe by £1,481 11*s* 5¾*d*, but it did include Edward's coronation.[12] Between September 1462 to April 1465, Edward spent an average of £2,000 a year on his wardrobe and that of his household.

Edward IV's sister Margaret of York had married Charles, has duke of Burgundy, in 1468. Her wedding party included John Paston III, who was very impressed by the Burgundian court. Interest in European styles of clothing would have been reinforced when Edward IV spent a period in exile in Bruges at the Burgundian court from 1470–71. There is a list of the clothes produced for Edward IV by George Lovekyn between 1470–72.[13] This included a jacket of cloth of gold lined with satin valued at £13 6*s* 8*d*, 14 yards (12.8 m) of black damask for a gown trimmed with velvet and a robe of gilt tawny satin lined with velvet priced £32 6*s* 8*d*.[14]

Edward IV's extant great wardrobe account runs from 18 April to 29 September 1480. It records the clothing and shoes ordered for the king under eight warrants (Table 5.1).[15] While these items represent a very small sample of the clothes ordered for him, it reveals that he had a considerably smaller range of garments than Henry VII. The clothes delivered to Edward IV's wardrobe of the robes included a long gown

Table 5.1: *Clothing ordered for Edward IV in the 1480 account*

Date of warrant	Items ordered
11 May 1480	1 long gown, 1 doublet, 3 demi-gowns, 4 tippets
2 June 1480	Shoes
19 July 1480	1 demi-gown, 1 jacket
24 July 1480	1 demi-gown, 4 doublets, 2 long gown, 24 shirts, 2 pairs of hose, 4 pairs of socks; shoes and boots
6 August 1480	1 doublet, 2 long gowns
17 August 1480	6 bonnets, 1 demi-gown, 1 gown, 2 hats, 2 tippets
Undated	1 base of a jacket, 8 bonnets, 2 doublets, 4 hats, 3 loose gowns, 3 pairs of hose, 1 stomacher, 1 straight gown
Undated	1 cloak, 4 pairs of hose, 2 tippets; shoes and boots

made of blue cloth of gold upon a satin ground lined with green satin, a black satin doublet, a demi-gown of black velvet lined with purple satin and a demi-gown of green velvet lined with black damask. While the warrants recorded the colour and type of linings provided for the garments there is little indication of the interlinings or the decoration employed. The linings were often of contrasting colours. There are also some references to the provision of ribbons and laces, some of which was used to make points and girdles. The range of colours and fabrics used was also quite limited (Table 5.2).

The figures in Table 5.3 represent the quantities of cloth bought during the year and cloth remaining in the wardrobe at the end of the accounting year. The quantities of high quality red and scarlet woollen cloth indicate that wool was still an important part of élite dress at this period. The small amount of tartaryn represents the last vestiges of a cloth that had been popular in previous centuries. Velvet was predominant over satin and damask, a trait that persisted at the Tudor court. The relatively small amount of cloth of gold and silver was intended for the king and his immediate family.

Table 5.2: *Analysis of the colour and fabric type of the clothes ordered for Edward IV in 1480*

Colour	Number of items	Fabric	Number of items
Black	24 (54.4%)	Camlet	1 (2.3%)
Blue	2 (4.6%)	Cloth of gold	5 (11.3%)
Crimson	2 (4.6%)	Damask	2 (4.6%)
Green	7 (15.9%)	Puke	4 (9%)
Purple	4 (9%)	Satin	11 (25)
Tawny	1 (2.3%)	Unspecified	2 (4.6%)
Unspecified	2 (4.6%)	Velvet	19 (43.2%)
White	2 (4.6%)		

Table 5.3: *Silk, woollen cloth and fine linens recorded in the 1480 account*[16]

Type	Quantity
Baudekyns of silk	7 pieces
Camlets	1,092 ¼ yards (998.7 m)
Cloth	Scarlet 209 ½ yards (191.6 m); Cloth in grain 28 ½ yards (26.1 m); Cloth of divers colours 170⅜ yards (155.8 m); White cloth 43 ¾ yards (40 m) = 452⅛ yards (413.4m)
Cloth of gold	270 ¾ yards (247.6 m)
Cloth of silver	17⅞ yards (16.3 m)
Damask of silk	198⅜ yards (181.4 m)
Linen	Lawn — 5 pieces; Holland 2,369 ½ ells (1,634.9 m); Flemish cloth 2 ells (1.4 m); Brussels cloth 707 ¾ ells (488.4 m) (at the rate of 120 ells to the 100) = 5 pieces and 3,079 ¼ ells (2124.7 m)
Sarsenet	Changeable and other colours 795 ¾ yards (727.6 m)
Satin of silk	633⅜ yards (597.2)
Tartaryn	5⅞ yards (5.4)
Velvet	Single 1,312 ½ yards (1200.2 m); Double 149⅝ yards (136.8 m) = 1,462⅛ yards (1,336.9 m)
Total	12 pieces; 4,928 ½ yards (4,506.6 m); 3,079 ¼ ells (2,124.7 m) (at the rate of 120 ells to the 100)

A portrait of Edward IV by an artist from the Anglo-Flemish school depicts him wearing a black doublet, black bonnet and a sumptuous gown of black cloth of gold with a large pomegranate design.[17] According to the *Crowland Chronicle*, at Christmas 1482 the king appeared:

> clad in a great variety of the costliest clothes, very different in style from what used to be seen hitherto in our time. The sleeves of the robes hung full in the fashion of the monastic frock and the insides were lined with such sumptuous fur that, when turned back over the shoulders they displayed the prince (who always stood out because of her elegant figure) like a new and incomparable spectacle set before the onlookers.[18]

This supports the view of Gabriel Tetzel, who believed Edward IV's court to be 'the most splendid Court that could be found in all Christendom'.[19] Such splendour came at a price, and the estimated annual expenditure of Edward IV's household varied between £10,000 and £12,000 a year.[20] He also spent heavily on jewellery. A bill dated 5 September 1478 included some quite modest items: a flower of gold garnished with a fleur-de-lis of diamond costing £6 and four rings of gold garnished with four rubies at 10*s* each.[21] Edward IV dressed his sons in a style befitting their rank. He gave his son 'the right highe and mighty Prince Richard Duke of York', two gowns on a warrant dated 2 June 1480: one of black satin lined with purple velvet and another of green satin lined with black sarsenet.[22]

There is not much evidence about the clothes worn by Richard III during his short reign (1483–85). Beyond his coronation robes, details of just five of his gowns are known. The most spectacular was a gown made from cloth given to him by his wife Anne, of purple cloth of gold patterned with roses and garters. The other four were all made of crimson cloth of gold and were lined with satin, damask or velvet, all in green.[23] However, the implication of these rich clothes is that Richard, like his brother, also used his wardrobe to emphasis his right to rule and to assert his kingship.

Henry VII

Henry Tudor was the only son of Edmund Tudor, earl of Richmond, the half-brother of King Henry VI, by Lady Margaret Beaufort. He was born, several months after his father's death, at Pembroke castle on 28 January 1457. On his mother's remarriage, he was entrusted to his uncle, Jasper Tudor, earl of Pembroke. In 1461 Edward IV seized Pembroke castle. Bedford went into exile, while Henry entered the household of Sir William Herbert who was granted Bedford's confiscated lands.[24] On the murder of Henry VI in May 1471, Henry Tudor became the heir of the house of Lancaster.

On 2 June 1471 Henry went into exile for 13 years in Brittany. The Breton Chambre des Comptes includes a reference to Henry in the wardrobe accounts of Duke Francis II from May or June 1472. The accounts recorded the delivery:

> to my lord of Richmond, [of] a long robe by gift of my said lord [the duke] seven ells of fine [?] black velour, costing 4 royals an ell, £35, for lining the upper arms, half a third of black, costing 23*d*; and for the lining four ells of changeable taffeta at 2 royals an ell, costing £10, and the making of each, sum, £45 13*s* 4*d*. To him for a short robe

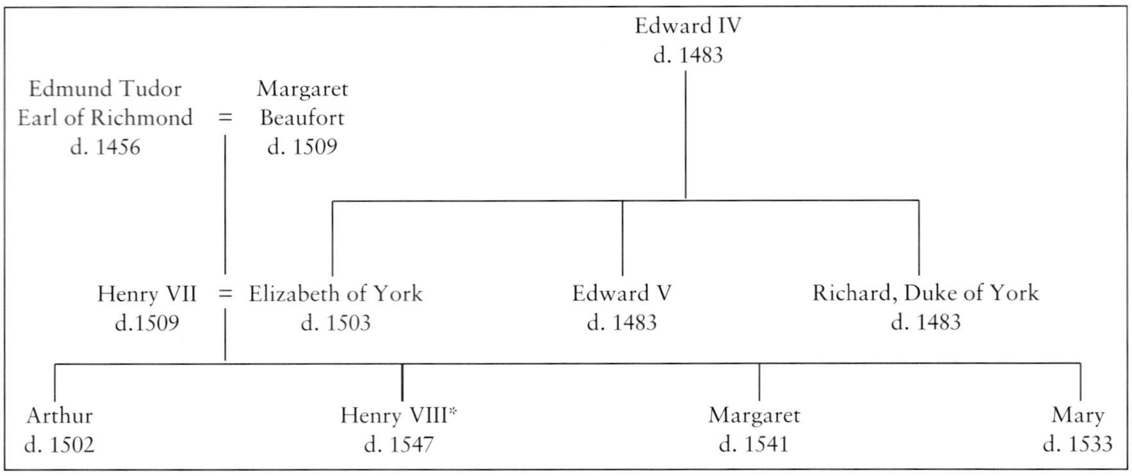

Family tree 2 The family of Henry VII

[pourpoint], an ell and a half of black damask at £4 an ell, and padding, 1 écu, [total] £7 2*s* 10*d*.[25]

Following his attainder by Richard III early in 1484 he fled to France dressed as a servant. A year later, supported by Charles XII of France, he sailed from Harfleur on 1 August and on 7 August landed at Milford Haven. He met and defeated Richard III at the Battle of Bosworth on the 22nd and was crowned king on 30 October.

A sketch survives of Henry as a young man with shoulder-length hair and wearing a felt cap with a turned-up brim with a single brooch. He wears a doublet with a round neck and no collar, with an embroidered band of decoration around the neck and a centre-front opening worn with a gown, but there is essentially no detail of the gown's construction. While the clothes are of the period, the sketch was drawn, or rather copied, by Jacques Le Bourcq de Valenciennes, Hainault Herald, in the mid sixteenth century, thus raising doubts as to the accuracy of both the likeness and the clothes.[26]

Henry VII's appearance was described by Polydore Vergil:

> His body was slender but well built and strong; his height above average. His appearance was remarkably attractive and his face was cheerful, especially when speaking; his eyes were small and blue, his teeth few, poor and blackish; his hair thin and white; his complexion sallow. His spirit was distinguished, wise and prudent; his mind was brave and resolute and never, even at moments of the greatest danger, deserted him. He had a most pertinacious memory.[27]

In 1498 the Spanish envoy, Pedro de Ayala, explained to Ferdinand and Isabella 'one of the reasons why he leads a good life is that he has been brought up abroad. He would like to govern England in the French fashion, but he cannot . . . The king has the greatest desire to employ foreigners in his service. He cannot do so; for the envy of the English is diabolical, and, I think, without equal'.[28] Possibly one of the reasons that he continued to employ the Parisian George Lovekyn as his tailor was because Lovekyn provided him clothes in the French style.

In fulfilment of a long-standing arrangement negotiated by his mother, Henry VII married Elizabeth of York on 18 January 1486, their first son Arthur being born on 19 September. Elizabeth was crowned two months later on 25 November 1487. Two years later Princess Margaret was born on 29 November 1489 and their second son followed in 1491 when Prince Henry was born. Others were to follow and in April 1497 Lady Margaret stated 'Blessed be god the kyng the quene and alle oure swet chyldren be yn good hele'.[29] In 1504 Hernan duque de Estrada recorded Henry VII's devotion to Prince Henry, adding that 'certainly there could be no better school in the world that the society of such a father as Henry VII. He is so wise and attentive in everything; nothing escapes his attention'.[30]

Andrea Trevisano, the Venetian ambassador to the doge described his meeting with Henry VII in September 1497. It was a time of heightened sensibilities at court because it coincided with Perkin Warbeck's invasion. The ambassador wore crimson damask, while 'His Majesty wore a violet coloured gown, lined with cloth of gold, and a collar of many jewels, and on his cap was a large diamond and a most beautiful pearl'. He also met Elizabeth of York who was 'dressed in cloth of gold'.[31] To reinforce the sense of dynastic potential of the Tudors, Trevisano was also introduced to Lady Margaret Beaufort and Prince Arthur.

While the Yorkist pretender Perkin Warbeck was at the court of Margaret of York in the Netherlands, Margaret had provided him with a guard dressed in the blue and murrey livery of the house of York.[32] He had all the trappings of the prince that he pretended to be. On his attempt to raise England against Henry VII, 'He put aside he habit in which he had disguised himself in this place, and clothing himself in gold, he set out with some of the king's men'.[33] On 25 November 1498, shortly after his imprisonment, Henry gave Warbeck one set of clothing. Warbeck received a doublet of black damask, two linen shirts and two pairs of kersey hose costing 29*s* 3*d*.[34] This gift of livery visually subjugated Warbeck to Henry VII's authority by making him a member of the royal household.

About the same time, Henry VII paid £7 13*s* 4*d* to Robert Southwell for horses, saddles and other necessaries for bringing Warbeck's wife, Lady Catherine Gordon, a cousin of James IV, to London.[35] She was placed in the service of Elizabeth of York, and later of Catherine of Aragon.[36] Henry VII provided Lady Catherine with clothing in a warrant dated 10 October 1498, including a black velvet gown furred with mink, a black cloth gown furred with lettice and a plain bonnet of black velvet.[37] She also received clothes from two further warrants dated 12 November 1502 and 16 April 1503.[38]

Henry VII managed his displays of authority with care. For his meeting with the ambassadors after his defeat of the Cornish rebels at Blackheath in 1497, he sought to stress his royal status: it was noted that 'The King was well arrayed with a very costly jewelled collar'.[39] However, when he made his formal entry into London he adopted a different approach: 'He did not enter the city with any triumph, whereas on the former occasion when he returned it was his wont to come with pomp, neither did he choose any of the resident ambassadors to go out to meet him, saying that he had not gained a worthy victory.'[40]

The opulence of Henry VII's court

In the winter of 1496–97 the Venetian ambassador stressed the continuity in form between the court of Henry VII and those of his predecessors by noting that he 'does not change any of the ancient usages of England at his court, keeping a sumptuous table'.[41] Although Henry VII has been accused of avarice, he knew when to be extravagant, unlike his heir, for whom extravagance was habitual.[42] This is graphically demonstrated by the Stonyhurst vestments purchased by Henry VII for his chantry in Westminster abbey.[43] A set of 29 copes and chasubles was ordered, but only a single cope, a chasuble and a chalice veil have survived. The extant cope reveals that the cloth of gold was woven to shape with Henry's badges of the Tudor rose on scrolling stems linking three crowned Beaufort portcullis (Fig. 5.3). The vestments were made by Anthony Corsi of Florence and the Bonvisi of Lucca, while the orphries were embroidered under the direction of Robinet and Morse.

Edward IV acquired a lot of jewellery and plate. In his slightly longer reign, Henry VII bought considerable more. Between 1491 and 1509 it has been estimated that he spent £200,000 on jewels and plate.[44] There are no extant inventories from Henry VII's jewel house or his wardrobe of the robes and beds taken either during his lifetime or posthumously. However, it has been inferred that 735 of the 887 entries in the 1521 jewel house inventory had belonged to Henry VII.[45] It is possible to trace the items marked with the HE monogram for Henry and Elizabeth of York within the inventories of Henry VIII, and these initials are chiefly found on two groups of objects: furnishings and plate.

The turnover in the jewel house was rapid. The half-century that elapsed between the inventories of 1521 and 1574 saw the disappearance of 11 out of every 12 of the items listed in 1521.[46] In 1521 there were 22 pieces of plate with the HE monogram.[47] By 1532, when another inventory was taken on the death of the keeper, Robert Amadas, the number had fallen to 14.[48] This figure had halved to just seven in 1547.[49] While this is a very small sample, it highlights the trend of recycling precious metals, either as coinage during a shortage of specie, or being reworked when pieces became outmoded or damaged. The only piece of jewelled plate marked with HE in 1521 that remained in the jewel house in 1547 was a holy water stock decorated with five small point diamonds, 13 small rubies, one coarse emerald and 19 pearls [31].[50] More personal items marked HE appear in two lists of Henry VIII's jewels, dating from the middle of his reign: 35 long buttons, a ring, two gold tooth picks, a gold dial with HE on one side and a portcullis on the reverse and a round, silver-gilt hand warmer.[51]

Analysis of Henry VII's purchase of tapestry reveals how his taste had been influenced by his exile on the Continent.[52] In 1485 he bought a set of tapestries depicting *The Story of Troy* from the Greniers in 1485. Henry also owned a set depicting *Esther and Ahasuerus* which he may have chosen on account of the analogy with his own marriage. Henry VII was equally careful to use pageantry to create magnificence at his court. This display required objects such as 'an arminge Swourde whiche was kinge henrie the vijth his swourde with pomell parcel guilte oure ladie of Bolloigne on thone side set in golde and the Crosse of Saincte George on thother side with a Chape of golde' (14442). It also required the co-ordination of events at court. On 9 December 1485 Richard Guildford, master of the armoury, received £50 2*s* 2*d* for jousts at Westminster.[53] In the following year Richard Pudsey was paid £10 for items for a disguising held on Twelfth Night.[54] On 15 February 1494 Walter Alwyn was paid £14 13*s* 4*d* for full payment for the disguising at Christmas.[55]

Richmond palace, 'Rich Mount', was the focal point for much royal display. Henry VII developed the palace after the loss of Sheen on 30 December 1497. He used the finished building for the first time for the wedding celebrations of Arthur and Catherine of Aragon when it was described as an 'earthly and second paradise of our reign of our region of England, and . . . of all the great part and circuit of the world, the lantern spectacle and beauteous exemplar of all lodgings'.[56]

The order of the Garter figured prominently in the ritual of Henry VII's court. Of his robes for the European orders, there is no record. However, the letter acknowledging his receipt of the order of the Golden Fleece is dated 16 October 1491.[57] On 24 November 1502 he ordered garter livery for Maximilian, king of the Romans. The black velvet mantle was lined with white satin. It was embroidered with a garter of damask gold and fastened with a lace of Venice gold and Damascene buttons. It cost £28 7*s* 5*d*.[58] Maximilian's garter has survived (Fig. 7.4). In March 1487 Henry VII presented to the lords and knights of the order 'our livery for this present year of such suit of cloth, fur and multitude of garters as to their estate hath been used and accustomed'.[59] Two years later the king provided Garter robes 'of sanguine cloth in grain, damask, garter with letters and rolls of junkes' for Elizabeth of York, whose gown was furred with wombs of miniver pure, Lady Margaret Beaufort, whose robes were furred with miniver pure, and to the other members of the order.[60] In 1499–1500 his garter robes consisted of 6½ yards (5.9 m) of blue cloth for a gown and a hood lined with 18½ yards (16.9 m) of white damask and embellished with 240 garters with letters of gold and a roll for the hood, costing £18 6*d*.[61] On 29 April 1503 Elizabeth of York paid 100*s* to Friar Hercules for gold and his making a lace and buttons for the king's garter mantle.[62]

5.3 *The Stonyhurst cope, of velvet cloth of gold brocaded with loops of silver and silver-gilt woven to shape, c. 1495–1505, on loan to the Victoria and Albert Museum. © V&A Images, Victoria and Albert Museum, London*

The part played by the nobility in enhancing the splendour of the royal court was significant. In 1500 when Henry VII met Archduke Philip at Calais, the duke of Buckingham was dressed 'in soo large and so riche a gowne of clothe of golde [and] his courser richly trapped and the trapper enramplished with littel prety belles of silver and gilt, of a very goodly fascyon' (Fig. 5.4).[63] The earl of Northumberland wore 'a large and a riche gowne of clothe of golde; the erlle of Suffolke in an other garment of clothe of golde, and a hatte of silke garnysshed with a cheyne of gold, and the goodliest plumashes off whit austriche feders that ever I saw'.[64] At the marriage of Arthur and Catherine of Aragon in 1501 Buckingham wore a gown 'wrought of nedyll work and sett upon cloth of tyssu furrid with sablys' and valued at £1,500.[65] He was also the chief challenger at the jousts held to celebrate the wedding, where he appeared 'in a chappell hangid or curteynyd abowth whyth white and grene satyn palid, brawderid Right goodly upon every side and ende whith iiij grete Rede Rosis, and the coveryng thereof payntid with azure, and set at every corner whyth a gilt pynnakyll'.[66]

A warrant dated 27 June 1502 included an entry for 2 yards (1.8 m) of black velvet for bordering a gown of crimson velvet 'which we have given to a painter'. This perhaps is evidence that the king was providing his clothing for a painter producing a portrait.[67] A garment of this type was certainly more luxurious than anything Henry VII was giving as livery. In the portrait painted by Michael Sittow in 1505 (Pl. IIIc), Henry VII was depicted wearing a richer gown of red cloth of gold with sleeves edged (and possibly lined) with white fur, a tippet of dark brown fur, worn over a black doublet and a cap of black felt with a deep turned up brim but no decoration. Interestingly, his only jewellery was the collar of the Golden Fleece.[68] In the terracotta bust by Pietro Torrigiano, *c.* 1509, he wears a doublet fastened down the centre front with a very small stand collar.[69] Two years after his death, Torrigiano was commissioned to cast full-size effigies for the tombs of Henry VII (Fig. 5.5), Elizabeth of York and Lady Margaret Beaufort which he had completed by the time of his return to Florence in 1522.[70] Henry VII is shown dressed in a long gown, worn with a fur tippet and felt cap.

Henry VII's wardrobe

Four sets of great wardrobe accounts survive out of a possible 24 volumes from Henry VII's reign. These accounts indicate how regularly the king ordered clothing and other items for himself and of how much he spent (Table 5.4). The accounts date from 1498–99, 1502–03, 1504–05 and 1505–06, that is the second half of his reign. They inevitably provide a view of Henry VII as an older, established monarch. In addition there are 54 warrants from ten accounting years headed 'for our use' ordering clothes, shoes, lengths of cloth and furnishings for his use that have survived as a suppliment to the accounts.

5.4 *Edward Stafford, third duke of Buckingham, unknown artist. Master and Fellows, Magdalene College, Cambridge*

5.5 *Henry VII by Torrigiano, 1512–18. National Portrait Gallery, London (NPG 290)*

Table 5.4: *Overview of the number and value of the king's warrants in the extant great wardrobe accounts*

Date	Date of warrants	Cost
1498–99	14 warrants: 29 October, 6 November, 12 December 1498, 28 January, 26 February, 2 March, 3 & 13 April, 14, 15, 24 & 26 May, 4 & 21 June 1499	£362 9*s* 7½*d*
1502–03	12 warrants: 6 November (2), 24 December 1502, 4 January, 15 &16 March, 4 April, 31 May, 2, 21 & 27 June, 20 July 1503	£333 7*s* 10½*d* [plus 20 July]
1504–05	9 warrants: 2 & 27 November, 11& 24 December 1504, 5 January, 8 & 20 February, 26 March 1505 [check against hard copy]	£88 10*s* 2*d*
1505–06	16 warrants: 6, 12 & 21 May, 9 June, 8 & 21 July, 31 November, 6 & 18 December 1505, 15 January, [. . .], 28 March, 8 April, 18 June, 29 July, [. . .] 1506	£285 6*s* 4*d*

Of these 11 which are undated or the date is only partially legible, two come from the accounting year 1492–93, 12 from 1493–94, one from 1494–95, one from 1496–97, three from 1497–98, two from 1498–99, 14 from 1501–02, 10 from 1502–03, one from 1505–06 and eight from 1508–09.

While the warrants enhance the chronological overview of the reign when compared with the account books, they shed no light on what the king was wearing before 1492, and even after that year the data is limited. The large clusters of warrants from 1493–94 and 1501–02 probably provide a fair reflection of the total number of warrants issued, while for the other years the much smaller number of warrants can only hint at the garments the king was ordering.

On 30 August 1485, eight days after his victory at Bosworth, clothing was delivered to Henry VII. The order was very opulent: a long gown of rich cloth of gold priced at £6 2*s* the yard and lined with black satin, two short gowns of purple cloth of gold, also lined with black satin, doublets of black and crimson satin, linen for shirts and a long gown of tawny velvet lined with violet satin.[71] The total value of the delivery came to £336 18*s* 4*d*, and it included horse harness, as well as clothes for the henchmen. On 30 January 1486 Nicholas Barley, skinner, received £181 14*s* 8*d* for furs for the king and for furring clothes. His charges covered furring a gown of purple velvet with ermine, two pairs of boots with martens, a gown of black velvet with sables, a gown of cloth of gold with pinked ermine, a gown of purple velvet with ermine and a gown of cloth of gold furred with ermine for the queen.[72] On 28 February 1486 a payment of £95 3*s* 6½*d* was made to Peter Curteys, gentleman usher of the chamber, for stuff bought for the king's use against Christmas and 'our marriage'.[73]

On 8 September 1486, Anthony Gyle, 'our cordwainer', received £15 for stuff delivered for the king's use.[74] Several months later on 17 February 1487, John Fligh, yeoman of the robes, paid for 5 yards (4.5 m) of black satin two doublets, linen and buckram for lining for the king.[75] Six days later Fligh, paid for 2 yards (1.8 m) of crimson satin to cover a pair of brigandines.[76]

In May 1490 Marone Stroes, a Florentine, got £225 6*s* 8*d* for silk and silk goods sold by him: 13¼ yards (12.1 m) of

Chroniques de Hainault, 1447–50. Philip the Good stood in the centre of the scene dressed all in black. He was flanked by his colourfully dressed courtiers, while his chancellor, Nicholas Rollin, echoed the duke's style and was clothed in black.[106] Black was an expensive colour to achieve, thus good quality garments in black were beyond the purses of all but the rich and powerful. Even so, Henry VII did not wear black to the exclusion of all else. He also ordered a number of items in tawny and a lesser number in crimson, purple and plain cloth of gold. Occasionally he also had items made in russet. Tawny was prevalent throughout English society and also at the court of James IV of Scotland.[107] Two other colours were reserved for specific activities: blue for Garter robes and violet for his maundy robes.

Surface decoration, even if considered in the broadest sense of the term, was uncommon. Indeed, very little use was made of embroidery, guards or slashing. The most common form of decoration was an applied border around the hem of a cloak, which was either self-coloured or in a striking contrast, such as a cloak made from scarlet in grain, bordered and partially lined with black velvet and the remainder lined with black satin.[108] Fur was also used with restraint and the repertoire was limited. Budge was most prevalent, with some sable and lamb. The budge was mostly black, but Henry VII did make more use of white budge and lamb more than his son would. Even so, on occasion he did purchase sable, as indicated by a payment to John Fligh, yeoman of the robes, of £3 10*s* for tawing ten timbers of sables and 20*s* for five skins.[109] Small quantities of miniver, lettice and calibre were also purchased, which were used almost exclusively on the gowns and kirtles ordered for the king's wife and daughters.

The male wardrobe consisted of a fairly limited range of garments: the glaudekin, gown, demi-gown, doublet (usually with a tippet), jacket, cloak, tippet, riding gown, hose and stomacher. Even so, there had been a significant increase in the variety of garments available between the reigns of Edward IV and Henry VII. This proliferation of styles provided more choice for the discerning male. The long gown, of which the glaudekin was a variant, was the garment most commonly ordered by Henry VII and also worn by his sons and most of the men in his household. The doublets favoured by the king in later years often had a collar made from a contrasting fabric and were usually worn with a tippet and a stomacher, the latter frequently being lined with scarlet. In contrast, there are very few references to hose and very little detail was recorded about those that are mentioned. This may reflect that hose were quite plain and understated because they were generally covered by the long gown. In contrast, Henry VIII's hose were more visible and consequently more significant in the king's overall appearance.

Henry VII also received a regular delivery of black satin bags, with black bag rings, presumably worn looped over his belt or girdle. These girdles could be quite ornate, as in the case of the fragmentary silk velvet belt of Sigismondo Pandolfo Malatesta (d.1468). There are ten fragments of the girdle varying in length and 4 cm in width. They are tablet woven with stripes of velvet and gold loops and 1 cm long fringes along each selvedge.[110] Purses or bags continued to be popular as fashion accessories into the sixteenth century, but the introduction of the pocket into men's clothing during Henry VIII's reign in the 1530s led to their supersession.

The quantity of apparel owned by individuals escalated under the Tudors. Why this escalation occurred is hard to explain. Even so, certain observations can be made. Henry VIII's wardrobe contained a much wider variety of luxury cloths than his father's, in a bigger range of colours and with far more surface decoration and fur. The number of different types of garments and varieties of each type of garment also increased. By the middle of his reign, Henry VIII spent far more on his clothes than his father had — his spending on himself increased from approximately £300–400 a year to £1,500 for a single six-month period and on his wardrobe as a whole from about £1,500 to more than £3,000.

Elizabeth of York

Elizabeth was the eldest daughter of Edward IV and Elizabeth Woodville, being born on 11 February 1465. Elizabeth was blonde and pretty. In 1476, when affianced to the dauphin of France, she wore clothes in the French style.[111] At Christmas 1484 'far too much attention was given to dancing and gaiety and vain changes of apparel presented to Queen Anne and the lady Elizabeth . . . who were alike in complexion and figure'.[112] This association with Anne reflects an attempt by Richard III to present a united family front after the political upheavals of the previous 18 months.[113] As part of his bid for the throne, Richard III had declared her illegitimate. Not withstanding this impediment and her consanguinity to Henry VII, the pair married on 18 January 1486 in advance of a papal dispensation issued on 2 March 1486.

In comparison to the increasing variety of garment types available to men (see Tables 5.1 and 5.5), late fifteenth-century female dress consisted of a very limited range of garments, and there was remarkably little change in their overall form or profile until the end of the first decade of the following century. The gown had a fitted bodice, flattening the wearer's bosom and a square neckline. Sleeves often had large cuffs, while the skirt was often cut with a train that could be looped up to reveal the kirtle. The waistline was at the natural level, with a girdle worn around the hips. A hood covered their hair.[114]

The evidence relating to Elizabeth of York's wardrobe is meagre. In a later copy of a half-length portrait by an unknown artist dating from *c.* 1500–03 she is shown wearing a crimson gown, probably made of velvet, with a fitted bodice with a square neck and long, fitted sleeves with fur cuffs. With this she wore the English gable headdress (Pl. IIID).[115] Charles I's picture inventory listed a now missing portrait of her 'in a black dressing adorn'd with gould and pearls in a goulden habbitt with white ermin'.[116] Her portrait was also included in the dynastic image that Holbein created for the privy chamber at Whitehall. The general appearance of the painting is known from a seventeenth-century reproduction by Remigius van Leemput (1607–75).[117] The picture provides a full-length image of Elizabeth in a gown of tawny cloth of gold with a deep border of miniver around the hem, tight-fitting sleeves with turned-back cuffs of the same fur. The bodice is tight-fitting with a square neckline, and it is also trimmed with miniver and partially in-filled with a linen partlet. On her head she is wearing an English gable headdress with long lappets hanging down over her shoulders, and the main, black velvet section of the hood hanging down her back. She was also depicted in the transept window of Great Malvern priory church and the royal window at Canterbury.[118] The gilt bronze effigy on her tomb cast by Torrigiano shows her in a simplified form of the gown and gable headdress.[119]

It is constructive to compare the portraits of Elizabeth of York with two images from the late fifteenth century. In the devotional triptych painted for Sir John Donne by Hans Memlinc *c.* 1477, Lady Donne wears a gown similar in style to that of Elizabeth, with an ermine collar and ermine trimming the hem on her gown in the Flemish style, but this decorative technique was also to be found in England.[120] In a portrait of Margaret of Austria painted by a Netherlandish artist *c.* 1493–95, Margaret wears a gown of cloth of gold with a neck that is almost square but with a slight downward turn at the corners, with a simple headdress of a type that developed into the French hood in the sixteenth century. Of some interest is that Elizabeth of York is never depicted wearing the sideless surcote, which had very deep armholes, heavily flared skirt resting on the hips that was worn by queens until the sixteenth century. It could be fur lined or fur trimmed as in the case of the surcote worn by Queen Margaret in the Hugo van der Goes altarpiece showing James III of Scotland adoring the trinity.[121]

There are very few references to Elizabeth in the great wardrobe documents. When provision was made for her by Henry VII it was generally not for her personally but for her wardrobe of the beds or ceremonial provision, such as velvet for her taper and her palm. This practice continued under Henry VIII. An entry in the accounts for the Michaelmas term 1485 records several items of clothing for the queen, including 10 yards (9.1 m) of crimson velvet and 6 yards (5.5 m) of russet damask costing £20 4*s*.[122] At the same time she received a fur lining for a gown made from 64 timbers of ermine skins, costing £54 2*s*, which was supplied by Gerard Venmer and Hildebrand Vain, while Richard Storey, the queen's skinner, received £31 14*s* for setting in powderings and furring a gown for the queen.

Shortly after Richard Smith received £11 5*s* 6*d* for black damask and crimson satin bought for the queen.[123] Henry did order the occasional small gift for 'our dearest wife', such as 9½ yards (8.6 m) of crimson satin for a kirtle in September 1497 and a pair of fur-lined night boots in an undated warrant.[124] The wardrobe accounts for 1486 also include a few items provided by Henry VII 'for her own use'.[125] A range of mercery was delivered to John Fligh by Thomas Fuller in February 1486 included 10 yards (9.1 m) of black velvet costing £8 and 12 yards (10.9 m) of purple velvet costing £12 12*s* for two gowns for Elizabeth.[126] A payment was made to Richard Smith, yeoman of the queen's wardrobe, for £11 5*s* 6*d* for silks, and £20 to John Yotton, her secretary, to pay her creditors.[127] The king's privy purse records that £20 was delivered to the queen for a gown in July 1501.[128] In the following year, the king bought furs for the queen costing £20.[129]

Further insights into her wardrobe can be gleaned from Elizabeth's privy purse accounts, which included purchases of clothes for herself, her children and some members of her household. Elizabeth made regular purchases of new garments as well as paying for repairs to her clothes and for moving her clothes from one house to another. Her gowns were often made of black velvet, although there are references to some of crimson satin. The accounts usually do not record many details, but there is a hint that the queen favoured gowns with wide sleeves, because Robert Ragdale lined a gown of black velvet with wide sleeves with black sarsenet for her.[130] She also wore wool gowns, and to keep them presentable she had them reshorn. Elizabeth of York had gowns made specifically for riding. Robert Johnson made such a gown from 13 yards (11.8 m) of black satin, with an edging and cuffs of black velvet, a lining of black buckram and sarsenet for the vents.[131]

Her gowns were usually decorated with a deep border of fabric, usually in a contrasting weave or colour. On 2 May 1502 Elizabeth bought black tinsel satin for the edge of a black velvet gown costing 45*s* 10*d* and black satin to edge a gown of crimson velvet for 11*s*.[132] They could also have a purfil, as in the case of a gown of russet velvet with a purfil of cloth of gold of damask and a gown of purple velvet with a purfil of cloth of gold.[133] Parallels for these styles of decoration can be found in the wardrobe of Charlotte of Savoy which included a gown described as 'à grant queue', the rest with collars and trimmed at the hem with a deep band of fur (the depth determined by the length of the skins if they were used set upright).[134] For outside wear Elizabeth had a new cloak in June 1502 of black damask, lined with black sarsenet and edged with black velvet.[135] All of the fabric was supplied by Henry Bryan of London and the cloak cost 3*s* 4*d* to make.

The gowns were worn with a kirtle. Elizabeth's accounts include a number of references for new kirtles, including 12*d* for lining and hemming a kirtle of black satin in February 1503.[136] The queen received a limited range of underwear, including scarlet petticoats costing 8*d* each and linen petticoats costing 12*d* which were provided by Robert Ragdale.[137] Anne Saye supplied three smocks on 2 August 1502 priced at 3*s* 4*d* in total, while Thomas Humberston made six pairs of socks and Richard Justice provided white fustian for socks.[138]

Elizabeth also made smaller purchases from a variety of suppliers. These included laces, ribbon and lengths of sarsenet for girdles costing 40*s* bought on 3 October from Mistress Bourne at Langley, and 6 yards (5.5 m) of sarsenet for two tippets from Ellis Hilton costing 12*s*. The range of footwear Elizabeth ordered was similar to that provided for Lady Margaret Beaufort: 12 pairs of single-soled shoes with laten buckles (12*s*), six pairs of double-soled shoes with laten buckles (6*s*), two pairs of buskins (8*s*) and two pairs of buskins (8*s*).[139] Her preferred supplier for headwear was Mistress Lock. Elizabeth sent Edmund Calverd from Richmond to London to Mistress Lock for a bonnet on 25 May 1502, while she provided 'frontlets, bonnets and other stuff' on 31 January 1503.[140] Elizabeth's privy purse accounts provide little evidence of specific pieces of jewellery bought by her, but there are a number of payments to the two pages of the chamber who were responsible for looking after her jewels.[141] However, it is quite possible that she owned more ornate pieces like the 'collere of rubies set with threis of perle' that belonging to Margaret of Denmark, wife of James III.[142]

Elizabeth of York died on 11 February 1503, shortly after giving birth. When Henry VII heard of her death he 'privily departed to a solitary place, and would no man should resort unto him'.[143]

Lady Margaret Beaufort

Lady Margaret Beaufort was the mother of Henry VII and grandmother of Henry VIII.[144] Born on 31 May 1443, the daughter of John Beaufort, duke of Somerset and Margaret Beauchamp, she married three times: to Edmund Tudor, half-brother of Henry VI, in *c.* 1456, to Sir Henry Stafford, the second son of Humphrey, duke of Buckingham, in 1458, and to Thomas, Lord Stanley, in 1472. Her only child, Henry VII, was born in 1457. In 1499 she took a vow of chastity and established a separate household at Collyweston, while her husband continued to live at Lathom.

A small group of images exist of Lady Margaret Beaufort (Fig. 5.6). Her style of dress is the same throughout: she was dressed in a black gown with a white linen gable headdress with a tippet worn over a coif, a wimple covering her neck and chin and a pleated barb which reached from her chin down onto her chest. This style of dress was semi-religious in its connotations and it served to enhance her reputation for piety and as a stalwart supporter of her son. Indeed it served a similar function to the style of dress adopted by Margaret of Austria in the late 1510s.[145] The effigy by Pietro Torrigiano on her tomb at Westminster abbey was made 'according to a patron drawen in a cloth' commissioned from Maynnart Wewyck, a Dutch painter, by her executors. All of the surviving portraits of Lady Margaret were painted after her death, but some seem to derive from a portrait painted during her lifetime about 1500.[146] Another image, probably also created before her death in 1509, was owned by Henry VIII: 'a Table with the picture of the Duches of Richmounte and Darbie sittinge vppon her knees' (15406). Several versions of this are known.[147]

At her death she owned plate and great jewels worth £4,213 4*s* 3½*d*; small jewels valued at £250 3¼*d*; chapel stuff assessed at £1,193 18*s* 2*d*; the wardrobe of the beds valued at £982 14*s* 1½*d*; the wardrobe of the robes coming to a more modest £126 19*s* 7*d*; silk and napery worth £158 3*s* 4½*d*; palfreys and chairs coming to £100 and £3,595 8*s* 9½*d* in ready money.[148] Quantities of her goods were sold and the probate costs of her will amounted to £80 which was paid to the archbishop of Canterbury.[149] An allowance of £81 8*s* 3½*d* was made 'for stuff appraised at a higher sum than it can be sold for and for stuff lost'. Her bequests were to her immediate family: 'certein plate of gold Iuelles and other stuff' worth £490 5*s* for Henry VIII, £202 10*s* for Catherine of Aragon, £25 2*s* 6*d* for Margaret, queen of Scots, and £82 8*s* 4*d* for Princess Mary.

5.6 *Lady Margaret Beaufort, unknown artist. National Portrait Gallery, London (NPG 551)*

Unlike Elizabeth of York, a number of the accounts for Lady Margaret's household have survived. While there are gaps, they provide a glimpse of her personal wardrobe and the provision that she made for her household (Table 5.6). The accounts are detailed and especially valuable because the clerk made an annual summary of her expenditure. While he was not consistent in the headings that he used, the figures provide an overview of her levels of expenditure on items such as cloth, fur and metal thread.

There is little about Lady Margaret's clothing in the accounts for 1498–99. Those for 1505 record that she bought 2¾ yards (2.5 m) of dark tawny for a nightgown and 24 white lamb skins costing 2*s* 6*d* to line her night slop.[150] She had a gown of black damask furred with 50 pinks and no less than 300 fine pinks, and a bonnet of ermine with 200 powderings.[151] Smaller items included furring, a pair of sleeves for a gown costing 4*d*, a kirtle and pair of sleeves costing 14*d*, a kirtle with grey poots costing 8*d* and lining the pleats of her mantle with cotton.[152] Her purchases in 1507 included 14*s* 10½*d* for 1¾ yards (1.6 m) of scarlet for a petticoat.[153] Her petticoats were furred with three skins of black lamb costing 6*s*. She also ordered a new gown of black cloth trimmed with black velvet and lined with black buckram. In the following year, her orders included 20 yards (18.2 m) of black velvet for gowns for her at 10*s* 4*d* the yard, costing £10 6*s* 8*d*, and 6,000 pins costing 3*s*.[154]

Table 5.6: *Summary of Lady Margaret Beaufort's expenditure on dress and textiles from her household accounts*

Date	Summary details recorded in the account books
1498–99	Cloth of gold, silks, furs, woollen cloth & other necessaries £258 17*s* 5½*d*; goldsmiths work and jewels £43 3*s* 4*d*; gold wire and embroiderer's work £23 9*s*; dives stuff bought £102 11*s*; saddles with necessaries to them belonging £25 21*d*
1502–03	Certain pieces of woollen cloth bought for poor folk £24 4*s*; furs £4 26*s* 8½*d*; cloth of gold £9 18*s*; diverse silks bought as velvet, damask, satin, camlet, sarsenet and others £39 10*s* 1*d*
1503–04	Certain pieces of wool and divers pieces of frieze bought for poor folk £13 8*s* 10½*d*; certain pieces of linen and canvas £20 14*s* 9*d*; gold and gold wire and working silk and ribbon £47 5*s* 4½*d*; certain silks including satin, damask £110 2*s* 4*d*; velvets £41 16*s* 5*d*; fustian and buckram £10 3*s* 3*d*; certain other necessaries £8 17*s* 1½*d*; furs for my lady £6 14*s* 2*d*
1504–05	Certain pieces of woollen cloth and divers pieces of frieze and cotton for the poor £59 9*s* 7*d*; certain pieces of linen cloth £17 17*s*; silks, as velvets damasks, satins, sarsenet £32 11*s* 6*d*; cambric £6 8*s* 4*d*; cottons, canvas and buckram £14 10*s* 11*d*; cloth of gold £90 1*s*; certain raw silk for my lady £5 3*s* 10*d*; gold wire and damask gold 73*s* 2½*d*; pieces of diaper £3 15*s* 11*d*; furs £9 9*s*
1505–06	Certain stuff bought for my lady's almsmen, women and children £6 16*s* 9*d*; divers silks bought as damask, satin, camlet, sarsenet £66 13*s* 11*d*; other stuff and necessaries bought for £15 5½*d*; sipers 9*s* 4*d*; furs and the wages of certain skinners £14 14*s* 7*d*; gold wire, silver wire, silks, fringes, ribbon £21 3*s* 1½*d*; worsted, fustians and buckrams £6 8*s* 2*d*; woollen cloth and frieze £29 15*s* 8¾*d*; diaper and linen £24 15*s* ¼*d*; canvas £7 16*s* 11*d*; packthread and other thread of divers colours 12*s* 4*d*
1506–07	Stuff bought for her alms men, women and children 10*s* 9½*d*; certain stuff bought and other apparel for my lady's maundy £8 18*s* 7*d*; velvet, satins and damasks £82 10*s* 2*d*; other stuff bought £8 14*s* 10*d*; other stuff including pearls £7 14*s* 8*d*; plate and jewels £38 8*s* ½*d*; furs £7 15*s* 1*d*; working silks 45*s* 3½*d*; working metal thread £16 10*s*; linen cloth £11 4½*d*; woollen cloth £10 3*s* ½*d*; worsted £6 3*s* 4*d*; kersey 38*s*; cloth of gold £112 7*s* 6*d*
1507–08	My lady's maundy £10 11*s* 8*d*; cottons and friezes of diverse colours for poor folk and the store of the wardrobe £14 11*s* 6*d*; furs as lamb and budge 44*s*; stuff bought as certain woollen cloth, girdles, ribbons £17 0*s* 7½*d*; thread, needles £2 8*s* 2*d*; linen £20 7*s* ½*d*; linen and diaper bought of Hammond Nicholson hardwareman £92 18*s* 4*d*; other cloth 27*s* 6 ½*d*; velvet £41 5*s*; satin £37 10*s*; sarsenet 6*s*; certain gilt gold, round gold, flat gold, silver wire £30 12*s* 6*d*; raw silk £12 4*s* 8*d*
1508–09	Frieze and cottons, bonnets bought from Robert Hilton for my lady's almsmen and poor folk £23 13*s*; woollen cloth bought for the wardrobe £5; linen and canvas £3 13*s* ½*d*; certain furs £11 10*s* 7*d*; black velvet, black satin, russet damask £113 12*s* 2½*d*; working gold, gold of Venice, silver wire, raw silk £38 16*s* 4*d*
1509	Divers velvets, satins, damasks, sarsenet £136 4*s* 11*d*; certain bonnets, frontlets £3 11*s* 4*d*; Robert Hilton for provision of stuff £68 10*s* 3*d*

In addition, there are several inventories of Lady Margaret's household goods, including her wardrobe of the robes at Collyweston at time of her death in 1509. It provides a remarkable insight into the size, composition and value of the wardrobe of one of the leading women in the country. She owned 20 gowns, all black, seven of which were valued at £39 5*s* 8*d*, three petticoats, six mantles plus one hood and tippet and one cloak. Along with some furs, a selection of lengths of cloth of gold and other silks, her wardrobe of the robes was valued at £126 19*d* 7*s*.[155] In addition, in 'my lady's chamber' there were further lengths of silk and linen, along with two tippets of crimson and one 'old broken gown'.

The 1509 inventory reveals that Lady Margaret favoured two styles of gown: a gown with a train which could either be half or full length which usually took 11 yards (10 m) of fabric, and the round gown which did not have a train, thereby requiring less cloth, merely 8 yards (7.3 m). Whichever style, most of her gowns were edged with fur, often of a contrasting colour. The accounts of her cofferer record regular purchases of fur made on her behalf. Like Elizabeth of York, she owned a riding gown. The black velvet gown had an 'oute edge lynede with blake bokeram', possibly as a concession to its use while riding.[156] Her three petticoats were all scarlet. One was plain but the other two were furred with either black or white lamb. All of her mantles bar one were made from black cloth. The one exception was 'a mantill of Tawny clothe single cont ij yerdes'.[157] In March 1509, John Nicholas received 8*s* 2*d* for 50 pinks, 12 skins of leather, 2 lb (0.9 kg) of white thread, the hire of a workman for a day and a night furring Lady Margaret's gown of satin, and for his own board wages for a fortnight.[158] The quantity of black clothing is remarkable. It indicates a number of things: her wealth, her maturity and her piety. It may also have been a response to the deaths of Prince Arthur and Elizabeth of York and her possible association with the mourning ordinances of 1503.[159]

The accounts also provide information about Lady Margaret's use of accessories. She made regular purchases of sipers, as indicated in a payment to Mistress Stanhope of 7*s* 2*d* for sipers and pins in 1505.[160] In 1506 a silk girdle bought for her from Haymond Glass, hardwareman, cost 20*d*.[161] A range of footwear also appears in the accounts. Maydwell, a shoemaker in Stamford, provided a pair of slippers and a pair of shoes, as well as 'setting' or shaping a pair of buskins for Margaret.[162] In August 1504 Robert Hilton submitted a bill for making a pair of buskins of orange leather for 'my lady' costing 6*d*.[163] The bill also included a pair of shoes made from the same leather, two pairs of slippers and two pairs of shoes. Amongst a group of items listed under the heading 'Small trash' there were two pairs of gloves edged with powdered ermine and a pair of knitted gloves.[164] Lady Margaret's delight in gloves can be seen in a letter she wrote to on 25 April 1497 to the earl of Ormond on his return from an embassy to Burgundy: 'I heartily thank you that you list so soon remember me with my gloves which were right good save that they were too much for my hand. I think the ladies in that part be great ladies all, and according to their great estate have great personages.'[165]

There is also evidence of Lady Margaret's personal jewels. In July 1504 Lady Margaret paid £20 to Sir Hugh Ashton for jewels bought in France.[166] From her household accounts for 1506 there were payments to John Mondy, goldsmith, for four rings of gold wire for 27*s*, setting of four rubies and making the four rings for 16*s* and enamelling the chain, buckle and pendant of a girdle, 9*s* 6*d*.[167] She paid 13*s* for a flower with a diamond, 12*s* 4*d* for a flower with a ruby and 20*s* for making them.[168] Jewels of this type were popular throughout the fifteenth century, as indicated by a surviving example of a white enamelled brooch in the shape of a rose with a tourmaline set in the centre.[169] On 28 January 1509 John Vauntrix received 28*s* for a brooch of gold having three personages and 8*s* for the fashioning, and 29*s* for a gold brooch with Our Lady of Pity and 8*s* for the fashioning.[170] Short sight in later life seems to have been a family failing inherited by her son and grandson. In 1507 John Veryght, goldsmith, was paid 23*s* 4*d* for making a pair of spectacles of gold.[171] By 1509 she owned 'oon greate Case with spetakilles'.[172] At her death a number of her personal jewels were in the custody of Mistress Fowler, including several which made a punning reference to her name, such as 'oon pomaunder of golde fasshynede to a peare with a wrethe of white & rede & a margarett in thende'.[173] She also had five great pearls and 'oon pece of the holy cross sett in golde with peerless and preciouse stones'.[174]

Lady Margaret was one of the last ladies of the Garter, that is she was a member of the Garter in her own right, not as the wife of a Garter knight. At the time of her death, she owned 'a olde scarlet gowne with garters having a longe trayn'.[175] Like others, she adorned her household and chapel fittings with garters: she had 'ij bunches of Garters for vestments' priced at 8*s* 4*d*.[176] Her possession of parliament robes is not listed in her wardrobe book, but these can be inferred from the 'Stringes for parliament Robys'.

A very few references to Lady Margaret occur in her son's great wardrobe accounts. These are linked mainly to religious ceremonies, as with Elizabeth of York, and her inclusion at such occasions at this level, including the Candlemas celebrations in 1497 indicates her authority at Henry VII's court.[177] She also took part in maundy ceremonies of her own. The sum of 12*s* was spent on 3 yards (2.7 m) of tawny cloth for 'my lady's maundy gown' in 1502.[178] In 1506 her maundy gown, made of tawny cloth, cost 14*s*.[179] In addition, 68*s* 3*d* was distributed between 63 poor folk, 84 pairs of women's hose (32*s* 8*d*), 73 caps (35*s* 6*d*) and 63 pairs of shoes (17*s* 8*d*).[180]

Robert Hilton was a key supplier of cloth for Lady Margaret and her household. He provided cloth on three occasions in 1504.[181] However, other purchases were made in London, as indicated by the payment of 3*s* 2*d* made to Sir Thomas Cheston for the carriage of a chest full of silks from London to Cheston and then on to Hatfield. On another occasion 10*d* was paid to Richard Addeton for 'time and botehire' in London to provide velvet.[182] Some of her cloth came from further afield. In 1508 Thomas of Boston supplied several lengths of silk, and he also received a payment of 6*s* 8*d* for transporting silk bought for her in Calais.[183]

The implication of a number of the entries is that Hilton may also have been Lady Margaret's tailor. If he was, he did not enjoy an undivided monopoly as other tailors are mentioned in the accounts. In 1505 an unnamed tailor received a payment of 20*d* 'for sewing my ladys gere for iiij dayes' and another 12*d* for helping to make Mistress Perot's gowns, kirtles and petticoats.[184] In 1508 Robert Long was paid 4*s* 3*d* for riding from Hatfield to London and back with two horses over three days 'to get mistress Benet silk woman to my lady's grace with the expenses for her and her servant'.[185]

The view of Lady Margaret's wardrobe at Hatfield taken by Hilton provides a clear indication of the amount of cloth that she had in store and how it was distributed. Her stock consisted of 70¼ yards (64.2 m) of black velvet, 66 yards (60.3 m) of black satin, 88½ yards (80.9 m) of tawny satin, 16½ yards (15 m) of black damask, 4¾ yards (4.3 m) of tinselled satin, 68¼ yards (62.4 m) of black sarsenet, 20½ yards (18.7 m) of tawny velvet, 80½ yards (73.6 m) of tawny damask, 35½ yards (32.4 m) of russet damask, 12¼ yards (11.2 m) of russet satin, 3 yards (2.7 m) of yellow satin, 2 yards (1.8 m) of white damask, 57 yards (52.1 m) of tawny camlet, 18 yards (16.4 m) of black camlet and nine rolls of buckram.[186] The distribution of the cloth was carefully recorded. During 1508–09:

> 3 yards of black satin to Master Treasurer for his new year's gift, one doublet for Master Parker taking 3 yards, one doublet for master Zouche taking 3 yards, a coat for Master Parker, whereof the other half is tinselled satin needing 4½ yards, a doublet for Master Parker, whereof the other half is tinselled satin taking 1½ yards, stomachers for my lady requiring 1 yard, one edge, collar and cuffs for a gown of black velvet needing 1¾ yards, a pair of sleeves for a kirtle taking ¾ yards, the overbodies and sleeves of a gown for my lady furred with ermine needing 2 yards, two gowns for my lady using 22 yards, half a doublet for master parker, the other half being tawny satin needing 1½ yards and a 'covering my lady's cophin' using 5¾ yards coming to 49¾ yards of satin.[187]

Ever prudent, Lady Margaret gave some of her clothes away as was customary as gifts, while in other cases the fabric was recycled. When Hilton compiled his view of the wardrobe at Hatfield he noted under the heading 'Black velvet', 'to mistress Mabell Clifford one gown lined with black damask given unto her by my ladies grace', while another black velvet gown had been used to edge the gowns of three of her ladies and to provide the body and sleeves of a gown for Mistress Clifford.[188]

Henry VII's children

The aspirations of the Tudors and the fragility of these hopes are summed up in Elizabeth of York's words of comfort to Henry VII on learning of the death of Arthur. She reminded him that 'his mother had never no more children but him only, and that God by his Grace had ever preserved him, and brought him where he was. Over that, howe that God had left him yet a fayre Prince, two fayre Princesses and that God is where he was, and we are both young ynoughe'.[189] The idea of the continuity of the house of Tudor was reinforced by the creation of family images, an idea copied by Henry VIII. The strongest image is presented in the altarpiece of Henry VII, Elizabeth of York and their seven children with St George and the Dragon *c.* 1505–09. It is conceivable that this altarpiece was intended for St George's chapel, Windsor (Fig. 5.7). A reduced version of this image forms the central motif of the illumination on the ordinances of the Confraternity of the Immaculate Conception of London, 1503. The king and queen kneel at an altar together with their children, looking upwards towards Joachim and Anne at the Golden Gate.[190] Both these groups depicted the members of Henry VII's family, living and

5.7 *The Family of Henry VII with St George and the Dragon, unknown artist of the Flemish School, c. 1505–09. RCIN 401228 OM 19 WC 2054. The Royal Collection © 2004, Her Majesty the Queen Elizabeth II*

dead. A depiction of a smaller family group of Henry VII, Elizabeth of York, Prince Arthur along with the donors Sir Reginald Bray, Sir Thomas Lovell and Sir John Savage survives in the stained glass window at Great Malvern.[191] Later Henry VIII included the long-dead Jane Seymour in pictures of himself with his three children.

Henry VII and Elizabeth of York had seven children, three sons and four daughters, three of whom did not survive infancy. For much of the reign, John Fligh, Henry VII's yeoman of the robes, undertook the delivery of the clothes ordered by the king for his children. When they were very young, provision for the new infants also included furnishings for the royal nursery and livery for the women in attendance there. Provision was made for the birth of Arthur in Winchester in 1486 and establishing the royal nursery.[192] On 8 June 1487, a payment of £46 was made to Lady Elizabeth Darcy as lady mistress and the others attending Arthur.[193] Early in 1488 Henry VII also provided livery for the women attendant on his son: Lady Elizabeth Darcy, the lady mistress, Catherine Gibbs, the nurse, Elizabeth Wood, gentlewoman, and two unnamed gentlewomen rockers each received 3 broad yards (2.7 m) of velvet for a gown.[194] Later in the year, the nursery staff were paid as follows: the lady mistress 40 marks, the nurse £20, Elizabeth Wood £6 13*s* 4*d*, Amy Boteler and Emelyn Hobbes £3 6*s* 8*d* and Alison Biwimble 53*s* 4*d*.[195] In July 1489 the prince's nurse received £15 for her wages for three-quarters of a year.[196] In May 1490 Alice Davy was paid as nurse to Princess Margaret.[197] Much later, on 3 July 1515 Henry VIII gave his childhood nurse, Anne Luke, an annuity of £20.[198]

As the king's children grew up, the range of tasks undertaken by some of the women working in the nursery changed, but a few individuals remained in post. On 15 March 1498, the half-year wages of the women attendant upon Henry, Margaret and Mary were paid at a rate of 33*s* 4*d* each to Jane Coling, Frideswyde Putnam, Margery Gower, Jane Care, Alice Skidmore and Alice Biwimble.[199] In the following year, Anne Crown, mistress of the nursery, received on 19 February 3 yards (2.7 m) murrey in grain, with the same to Joanne Case, and 15 yards (13.7 m) tawny cloth for five gowns for gentlewomen of the nursery costing £7 5*s*.[200] In 1496–97 Elizabeth Denton was mistress of the nursery and she received 3 broad yards (2.7 m) in grain for a gown, as did Anne Skeron, nurse to the lady Mary and Jane Coling, Frideswyde Putnam, Margery Gower, Joanne Case, Alice Skidmore and Alice Biwimble.[201] The only reference to provision for 'our dearest 'creation of duke unto the right high and excellent prince my lord Henry'.[232] On the first day of the jousts, the challengers wore green and white, the Tudor livery colours, while on the second day the challengers wore blue and murrey, Henry's colours as duke.

Following Henry's installation as a knight of the Garter on 19 May 1495, Sir Charles Somerset was given £13 *6s 8d* for offerings and expenses.[233] Later that year, on 27 October, Henry VII paid £7 *10s* for 'diverse yards of silke bought for my Lorde of York and my Lady Margarete'.[234] By a warrant dated 1496–97 he was provided with a gown of black camlet furred with black budge, a coat of black satin and a petticoat of scarlet. An old fur of budge was repaired so that it could go back into a gown.[235] On 4 December his father also ordered a crimson velvet gown furred with black budge for him, possibly to be worn at Christmas.[236]

On 1 April 1498 John Fligh was paid *4s 4d* for a tippet of sarsenet for Prince Henry.[237] In the following month Henry was given a riding gown of green velvet lined with black satin, a doublet of crimson satin and a pair of tawny buskins.[238] At the end of the year a set of formal robes were made for him consisting of a long crimson velvet gown furred with ermine with 2,800 powderings, a black velvet gown furred with sable, crimson velvet bonnets, scarlet petticoats and a doublet of tawny satin.[239] Like his elder brother's Garter livery for 1499, his consisted of a blue cloth gown and a matching hood, but Henry's only had 160 garters.[240] Later in the year he received 7 yards (6.4 m) of black velvet for a glaudekin lined with tawny damask, 3½ yards (3.2 m) of black velvet for a coat, 1¾ yards (1.6 m) of black satin for a jacket and 1½ ells (1.1 m) of sarsenet to repair the lining of a gown.[241]

Table 5.7: *Overview of the orders of clothes for Prince Henry in the extant great wardrobe accounts and loose warrants*

Date	Date of warrants	Cost
Temp Henry VII	4 December 1497(the duke of York), 8 August 1498 (the king's children)	Values not given
Temp Henry VII	10 August [. . .] — the king's children	Values not given
1497–98	[. . .], 13 April (the king's children), 3 May (the duke of York), 21 July (the king's children), 7 September 1497 (the king's children on the king's warrant)	Values not given
1498–99	6 & 16 November 1498, 6 February (the king's children), 11 April (the duke of York), 8 August 1499 (the king's children)	£134 *8s 6½d*
1501–03	10 November (2) 1501, 12 & 14 February, 25 August, 24 November 1502, 11 March, 12 June 1503	Values not given
1502–03	24 November 1502, 12 March, 12 June, 25 August 1503	£61 *3s 10½d*
1504–05	1 February 1505 (2)	£16 *13s 5d*
1505–06	4 July, 12 December 1505, 26 January, 15 August 1506 (2)	£118 *7s ½d*
1508–09	7 October 1508	Values not given

Henry was brought up with his sisters and younger brother. In 1499 Erasmus described meeting at Greenwich the royal children:

> In the midst stood Prince Henry, now nine years old, and having already something of royalty in his demeanour in which there was a certain dignity combined with singular courtesy. On his right was Margaret, about eleven years of age, afterwards married to James, King of Scots; and on his left played Mary, a child of four. Edmund was an infant in arms.[242]

In November 1501 Henry played a key role at his brother's wedding. For the occasion he was attired sumptuously.[243] He had two long gowns, three glaudekins, a riding gown, one gown, three jackets, four doublets, eight pairs of hose, three tippets, five bonnets, as well as boot, shoes and spurs. One of the long gowns was of tawny cloth of gold of tissue furred with ermine, with a glaudekin of purple velvet furred with jennets and another of crimson velvet upon velvet hatched with gold and furred with budge. His horses were appropriately caparisoned. Henry received a saddle for his courser and a saddle and harness covered with crimson velvet embroidered with gold for his hoby. There was also a purple velvet saddle and harness.[244] Henry was allowed livery for four footmen and two minstrels, in blue and yellow. (These were the colours given to Mary on becoming princess of Wales.[245]) His lute player, Giles Duwes, got 16 yards (14.3 m) of good black camlet for a gown 'for the solemnization of the marriage of our dearest son'.[246] Two of his household officers, Sir Thomas Brandon and Sir John Druby, received 150 yards (137.2 m) of tawny cloth and the same of blue cloth, costing *3s 4d* the yard 'for gowns for 100 persons appointed to attend upon our dearest and rightly beloved son the duke of York as Marshal of England at the marriage of our dearest son the prince'.

On 14 February 1502 Henry received a fashionable cloak of crimson in grain bordered with black velvet and 12 pairs of knit hose.[247] Following his elder brother's death in the following April he succeeded to the dukedom. For his formal investiture, his father ordered 15½ yards (14.1 m) of white damask to line a gown and hood of crimson velvet for his son and for himself a mantle made from 20 yards (18.2 m) of blue velvet and lined with 19½ yards (17.8 m) of white damask and 21¼ yards (19.4 m) of white satin to line a gown and hood of crimson velvet.[248] In August he had a doublet and jacket of black and black budge to perform a gown of black velvet furred with budge, and in November a jacket of crimson and black velvet.[249] Henry VII ordered a doublet of white cloth of gold for 'the prince' on his own warrant dated 24 December.[250] The following year saw his creation as prince of Wales and earl of Chester on 18 February 1503.

Henry went into mourning on the death of his mother in February 1503.[251] His mourning consisted of a long gown of black cloth furred with black budge, with a matching hood and tippet, a riding gown of black cloth, also furred with budge and a cloak of black cloth lined with black satin bordered with black velvet. The order also included two black satin doublets and a sleeveless jacket of black velvet lined with sarsenet. In addition he received 12 pairs of hose, 12 pairs of gloves and shoes, two tippets of black sarsenet and a horse house or trapper of blue velvet 'for his nag'. He received a further order of mourning dated 12 June 1503 with another long gown just with a tippet of black cloth, a doublet of black satin and new black linings being put into a jerkin of black velvet and a riding gown of black cloth.[252]

On 14 January 1504 Henry Wyatt, master of the jewel house, prepared an indenture recording the jewellery issued to Ralph Pudsey for Henry's use.[253] The indenture was periodically amended and by January 1509 had 47 entries. The most expensive, a cross set with five table cut diamonds, was valued at £13 6*s* 8*d*. A list of Henry VIII's jewels dating from 1528 listed 'divers brooches and aglets, which were the King's when his Grace was prince' and an inventory from two years later included a garter from his youth.[254] The fact that he kept them suggests that Henry may have felt a sentimental attachment to pieces from his childhood, that is if he had not forgotten about their existence.

Lady Margaret Beaufort lavished presents on her grandson. In March 1506 she bought him a horse costing £6 13*s* 4*d*.[255] She also gave him a new saddle and harness which was made by one Palmer at a cost of 10*d*. The harness was made of stoolwork 'bordered about with black velvet' costing 10*s*, with nine gilt buckles and pendants on the saddle and six gilt flowers on the harness.[256] She bought him another saddle for his first public appearance jousting in June 1507, and in 1508 she sent him a gift after he had been 'running at the ring'.[257]

On 1 February 1505 comes the first real hint of Henry's abiding passion for sport. The warrant issued then included a black satin arming doublet with a matching partlet and waist girdle. The doublet and the sleeves, apparently made separately, were lined with linen and canvas. The order also included two dozen white and green silk points, a pair of arming spurs and a pair of arming shoes.[258] The rest of the warrant tempered sumptuous items with prudent reworking of garments: making a jacket of tinselled satin lined with black sarsenet, a jerkin of crimson velvet hatched lined with black satin, a jacket and gown of crimson velvet furred with black budge and bordered with cloth of gold worked in the stool, and mending a long gown of purple velvet and making two jackets from an old glaudekin.

In December 1505 Henry VII ordered a range of new clothes and accessories for his son including hose and shoes. A number of existing items were furred: a glaudekin of crimson velvet with jennets, a riding gown of purple velvet with libards, a glaudekin of purple velvet with black budge, a jacket of crimson velvet without sleeves with black budge and two jackets of black velvet with black budge.[259] This order could well have been connected with the unexpected arrival in England of Archduke Philip and his wife Joanna. A further warrant issued on 26 January 1506 included some sumptuous garments, a doublet of cloth of gold, scarlet hose, a doublet of russet satin and a black velvet riding gown, which were appropriate to the reception of Philip and Joanna. On 9 February 1506 Henry VII made Ferdinand a knight of the Garter. The king paid for a mantle and hood of crimson velvet, lined with white satin, for Ferdinand of Castile.[260] Ferdinand reciprocated by making Prince Henry a knight of the Golden Fleece. In August 1506 a warrant included a black velvet nightgown furred with martens, a black velvet jerkin furred with black budge and a black satin doublet.[261]

It looks as though Henry VII used clothing as a means to promote Prince Henry, as his heir apparent and the future king. The final surviving warrant from Henry VII's reign, ordering clothing for the prince dates from October 1508. It includes a glaudekin of crimson velvet furred with black budge, a jacket of purple tilsent of the new making without sleeves furred with ermine and a jacket of yellow cloth of gold after camlet making with a base furred with black coney.[262]

PRINCESS MARY

Princess Mary was born in the spring of 1496. The earliest warrant for her, dating from 6 November 1498, was for black satin for a kirtle, crimson velvet for a gown edged with mink and furred with calibre, black velvet for a gown furred with 27 ermine backs for the edge of the gown and with miniver pure.[263] On 8 August 1499, she received a range of items, including gowns of purple tinsel satin and blue velvet and kirtles of tawny, crimson and green.[264] For the marriage of Prince Arthur, Mary had two new dresses, one of russet velvet, the other of crimson velvet, to be worn with a green satin kirtle and matching sleeves. In contrast, her older sister received gowns made from cloth of gold.[265] She received just two items from her mother: a gown of black satin and a kirtle on 14 June as well as some clothes from the great wardrobe later in November.[266] The delivery from the great wardrobe included a black velvet gown with sleeves furred with mink, a black satin kirtle lined with black cloth and linen for the upper bodies and crimson velvet to decorate the hem, scarlet for a petticoat, linen for smocks, rails, kerchers, 1,000 pins and sipers.

Four months after her mother's death in 1503, under a warrant dated 26 June, Mary received a range of clothes: black cloth for two gowns edged with black velvet, black cloth for another gown and miniver and ermine for furring the gown, two kirtles of black satin and black damask bordered with black velvet, a black worsted kirtle, a bonnet of powdered ermine, linen for three smocks, three biggins, kerchers and rails.[267] Under the next warrant over a year later, Mary got a sumptuous gown of cloth of gold furred with miniver pure and ermine. Powderings were provided for furring the collar, cuffs and purfil of the gown and a fur of poots for the upper bodies and sleeves. Grey furs for the collar, cuffs and purfil of another gown were also supplied.

After 1504 she received clothes on warrants issued roughly every six months and while black was a recurrent theme it was usually tempered with pale fur or trimmed with another colour. On 16 June 1505 she was given a gown of black tilsent with an edge of crimson velvet, a gown of black velvet with an edge of cloth of gold and lined with black sarsenet and making a kirtle of green satin.[268] In the following January she received mink skins for the collar, cuffs and purfil and edge of a gown of black tinsel and black velvet for the upper body of the gown and a fur of shanks for the purfil.[269] That summer, she was given black sarsenet for lining and performing a gown, crimson velvet for the collar, cuffs of the gown, black cotton to line

171 SJC D91.19, p. 9.
172 SJC D91.11, p. 1.
173 SJC D91.10, p. 1. The white represented Elizabeth of York, the red Henry VII, and the flower was a reference to herself.
174 SJC D91.15, f. 56r.
175 SJC D91.2, p. 3.
176 SJC D91.11, p. 1.
177 TNA E101/413/11, no. 52. William Grey, yeoman of the chaundry, received a yard (0.91 m) of purple velvet to bind the tapers of Henry VII, Elizabeth of York and Lady Margaret.
178 SJC D91.20, p. 16.
179 SJC D91.21, p. 101.
180 Ibid., pp. 107, 109.
181 SJC D91.20, pp. 150, 167, 181.
182 SJC D91.21, p. 22.
183 SJC D91.19, p. 108.
184 SJC D91.21, p. 32.
185 SJC D91.19, p. 72.
186 SJC D91.4, pp. 3–15.
187 Ibid., p. 5.
188 Ibid., p. 3.
189 Chrimes, *Henry VII*, p. 303.
190 Christ Church Oxford, MS 179, f. 1r; illustrated in Laynesmith, *Last Medieval Queens*, pl. 8.
191 Chrimes, *Henry VII*, pp. 333, 335–37.
192 Campbell, *Materials*, II, pp. 176–77.
193 TNA E404/79, 211.
194 TNA E101/412/20, no. 10.
195 TNA E404/79, 39.
196 TNA E404/80, 643/260.
197 Ibid., 487.
198 *LP* II.i, 658 and 659.
199 TNA E404/82, not numbered.
200 TNA E36/209, f. 20v.
201 TNA E101/414/8, no. 27.
202 TNA E101/415/7, no. 144.
203 TNA E101/413/11, no. 31.
204 TNA E101/412/15, no. 18; E101/414/8, no. 32.
205 TNA E36/209, f. 14v, E101/415/7, no. 56 and E101/415/10, ff. 6r–v, 19v–21v.
206 Private collection; illustrated in Hearn, *Dynasties*, no. 1, p. 36.
207 *CSP Spanish, 1485–1509*, p. 11.
208 TNA E101/412/20, no. 22.
209 Ibid., no. 13.
210 Ibid., no. 25.
211 Bentley, *Excerpta Historica*, p. 88.
212 TNA E404/81, no. 14.
213 Starkey, *Six Wives*, p. 76.
214 *CSP Milan*, I, p. 539.
215 Thomas and Thornley, *Great Chronicle*, p. 288.
216 *LP Henry VII*, p. 113.
217 *LP* IV.iii, 5773.13.
218 SJC D91.20, p. 21.
219 TNA E101/415/10. She also shared two warrants with Mary during this period with a total value of £15 5*s* 10*d*.
220 *LP Hen VII*, I, p. 395; Chapman, *Sisters*, p. 24.
221 TNA E101/415/7, no. 51.
222 *PPE Elizabeth*, p. 34.
223 Ibid., p. 93.
224 Ibid., p. 20.
225 Ibid., p. 89.
226 Anglo, *Images*, p. 92.
227 Bibliothèques de Méjanes; Starkey, *European Court*, p. 37; Bruce, *Making Henry*, p. 240.
228 Bentley, *Excerpta Historica*, p. 95.
229 TNA E404/81, not numbered.
220 Bentley, *Excerpta Historica*, p. 99.
231 Loades, *Chronicles*, p. 60.
232 *LP Henry VII*, I, p. 388; Bruce, *Making Henry*, p. 44. Heron's Chamber accounts recorded two payments of £66 13*s* 4*d* in October 1494.
233 Bentley, *Excerpta Historica*, p. 103.
234 Ibid., p. 105.
235 TNA E101/413/11, no. 11.
236 TNA E101/412/15, no. 16.
237 Bentley, *Excerpta Historica*, p. 116.
238 TNA E404/82, not numbered.
239 TNA E36/209, f. 8v. In the same month he received four pairs of knitted closed hose and two pairs of long hose; ibid., f. 12v.
240 Ibid., f. 19v. His range of footwear can be gauged from a warrant dated 6 February 1499: 16 pairs of double-soled shoes, a pair of high pinsons, a pair of low pinsons, a pair of slippers and a pair of night boteau.
241 TNA E101/412/15, no. 18.
242 Nichols, *Epistles*, pp. 201–02.
243 TNA E101/415/7, no. 52.
244 Ibid., no. 39.
245 Ibid., no. 50.
246 Ibid., no. 67.
247 Ibid., no. 37.
248 Ibid., no. 29.
249 Ibid., nos 94 and 157.
250 Ibid., no. 150.
251 Ibid., no. 141.
252 Ibid., no. 113.
253 TNA E101/415/11; F. Palgrave, *The Ancient Kalendars and Inventories of the Treasury of his Majesty's Exchequer*, III (1836), pp. 393–99.
254 *LP* IV.ii, 5114; *LP* IV.iii, 6789.
255 SJC D91.21, p. 155.
256 Ibid., p. 103. This compares well with a saddle and harness in the 'Almain' fashion that was ordered for Henry in February 1505 by his father. It was covered with black velvet, had ten gilded buckles and pendants and it cost £5 15*s* 4*d*; TNA LC 9/50, f. 231r.
257 SJC D91.19, pp. 34, 93.
258 TNA LC 9/50, f. 230r.
259 TNA E101/416/3, f. 15r.
260 Ibid., f. 20r. The satin and making cost £9 3*s*.
261 Ibid., ff. 28v–29r.
262 TNA E101/416/7, not numbered.
263 TNA E36/209, ff. 9r–v.
264 Ibid., f. 28r.
265 TNA E101/415/7, no. 51.
266 *PPE Elizabeth*, p. 22; TNA E101/415/10, f. 6v.
267 Ibid., f. 26v. She also received two partlets of black satin, a bonnet and a frontlet of black velvet.
268 TNA E101/416/3, f. 10v.
269 Ibid., ff. 16v–17r.
270 TNA E101/416/7, not numbered.
271 See above, pp. 67–68.
272 TNA E101/412/15, no. 18.
273 TNA E36/209, f. 27v.
274 *CSP Spanish*, I, p. 375.
275 BL Cotton MS Vespesian, c. XII, f. 207; quoted in Crawford, *Letters*, p. 166.
276 BL Egerton MS 616, f. 17; quoted in Crawford, *Letters*, p. 168.

VI

Henry VIII's Wardrobe Unlock'd

James Worsley's inventory recorded four items given to Henry VIII by Francis I in 1520:

a gowne of purpull veluete lyned with white tissewe . . . Cx li, a Cloke of tissewe lyned with purpull cloth of gold of damaske . . . Cxl li, a shamer of cloth of tissewe lyned with cloth of gold of dammaske welted with white cloth of tissewe . . . C iiijxx li and a Frocke of blacke veluete & cloth of gold tissewe lyned with purpull sarcenet . . . set with xxiiij payr of aglettes of gold xl li besides the goldsmiths werke [B68-71].

These garments demonstrate the quality and value of the king's wardrobe, the ways in which clothes formed part of the pattern of royal gift exchange and how examples of French fashionable dress, such as the chammer, came into the king's possession. The king's wardrobe was continually evolving and Henry VIII was able to order any style of clothing from his tailor that was available, and he did so on such a regular basis that his clothing reflected seasonal or annual changes in colour and fabric as well as changing nuances in style.

The ways in which the king used his wardrobe were dictated by the requirements of the annual cycle, such as the days for wearing purple, crimson, mourning, and the Garter livery and the ritual cycle of royal lives, starting with coronation and ending with a funeral. However, at other times the king had more freedom over what he wore and the value of his clothing can be seen in other terms: financial, sartorial, residual — all of which are linked to the concept of the culture of appearance and the hierarchy of appearances.[1] Status was implied by wearing a wider variety of clothes or more layers of clothing and by having special clothes for specific occasions. The size of an individual's wardrobe is revealing about their disposable income. In most instances they will have multiple examples of the same type of garment. Consequently, the lack of variety of garments will mean that acquisition will always peak regardless of the size of the disposable income. However, the regularity of Henry's purging of his wardrobe meant that there was always an incentive to buy more.

In his report on England on 10 September 1519 Sebastiano Guistinian noted that Henry spent '16,000 ducats for the wardrobe, for he was the best dressed sovereign in the world'.[2] Continually wearing new clothes is impressive, and the rapidity of the changes is noticed by those familiar with the wearer. Display of this sort is most impressive in an urban environment or the sort of close-knit context typified by the royal household.[3] Such an urban context was also likely to ensure that exotic items entered the king's wardrobe as in the case of 'a garment of white lynnen clothe of Indian making enbrawdered with white Silke' (11589).

Henry VIII's wardrobe: male dress in the first half of the sixteenth century

The first half of the sixteenth century saw the continued proliferation of garment types for men, marking the shift from the limited wardrobe of the late fifteenth century to diversity both in the range of different garments and variants of type of garment (Table 6.1). Both trends were very evident in Henry VIII's wardrobe, as was an increasing emphasis on decoration which became more elaborate as time progressed. Jewellery together with a growing range of accessories contributed to the magnificent appearance of the king. Yet male dress was also emphatically masculine with the bulky profile, the emphasis on the shoulders and the codpiece. Castiglione's courtier knew about the social significance of clothes and Henry VIII betrayed an awareness of this in his selection and use of clothes.

Evidence of Henry's wardrobe can be derived from a variety of sources. The 14 extant great wardrobe accounts are analysed here (Table 6.2). In addition, there are warrants from several years where no accounts survive. This information has been evaluated below but not included in the tables because it is not possible to tell if any of the warrants have been lost. Two inventories are also considered: James Worsley's inventory dating from 1516–21 and the 1547 inventory. With the latter, it is often not possible to tell exactly which items were acquired in 1546–47 and which had been there longer. All of these sources combine to provide a sense of

6.4 *Side view. Staatliche Kunstsammlungen Dresden, Rüstkammer, Inv. no. I 1. Photo: Abegg-Stiftung, CH-3132 Riggisberg (Christoph von Viràg)*

embraudered with vencie gold and Cordauntes of the same and fringed / with a narrow frindge of veanice golde the Cape and ventes lined with like stuffe and embraudered the rest Lined with blacke satten' (9918).

Spanish gowns, just like Spanish cloaks, feature in Henry VIII's wardrobe in the last few years of his life. A depiction of an ambassador sent to the court of Charles V wearing a Spanish gown *c.* 1519 appears in the autobiography of Sigmund von Herberstein written in 1560.[10] Examples were listed in the 1547 inventory including 'a spanishe gowne of purple Damaske lined with purple Taphata faced with purple satten with xlij paire of aglettes of golde' (14207) and 'A shorte spanyshe gowne of Crimsen Satten garded with iij weltes of Crimsen veluett formed downe with venice golde with ij borders embraudered with venice gold furred with Sqirrelles and faced with Sables' (14206). Other exotic styles drawing on foreign inspiration included the Turkey or Turkish gown: 'A Turquey gowne of Tawnye veluett of newe making Enbraudered with A brode garde and ij small gardes of venice golde and Tawney Silke lyned withe Tawney Taphata and faced withe Tawny Satten' (14196).

The evolving cut of the doublet can be seen in Henry's portraits. The low, round neckline of the 1500s and 1510s developed into a high neckline with a standing collar by the 1540s. In 1541 a number of the king's doublets were described as having a collar, often of a contrasting colour, as in the case of 'a dublet of white satten pulled out and lined with white sarsenet embroidered and frogged with damask and venys siluer with a coler of golde'.[11] The crimson satin doublet made for Don Garzia de'Medici, has a round stand collar, the upper edge of which is trimmed with snips of *c.* ¼ in. (6 mm) deep. There are two buttons on the collar, 11 on the centre-front and two on each sleeve at the wrist.[12]

The doublet was fairly fitted to the body, with a natural waistline and long skirts as indicated when Henry VIII summoned Pasqualigo to Greenwich on May day 1515. 'The king was dressed for hunting and he asked, "The King of France, is he as tall as I am?" I told him there was but little difference. He continued, "Is he as stout?" I said he was not; and he then inquired, "What sort of leg has he?" I replied "Spare". Whereupon he opened the front of his doublet, and placing his hand on his thigh, said: "Look here and I also have a good calf to my leg".'[13] Doublets could have integral or detachable sleeves and they usually fastened with buttons or ties.[14] Doublets were often made with matching hose and they could be worn under a jerkin and over a waistcoat or petticoat.

There were 134 doublets listed in Worsley's wardrobe book made from 29 types of fabric with 25 of velvet, 23 of tilsent and 17 of satin. Only a few specific construction details were recorded by him: a high collar [B225], a placard and foresleeves [A256] and wide sleeves [A84]. The king's doublets were often very richly decorated: for example, 'a doublet of purpull syluer tynsell maylyd the foreslevys and placard garnysshed with fyvtie and thre dyamundys set in gold and with roullys of perle to the same doublet euery Roulle havyng thre perles set in gold, a hundryth and twelve / the brest being botonyd with twelfe botons of gold blake Inamyled.'[15] As with the king's hose, during the 1520s, some of his doublets were made in the 'almain' style such as 'an almayn doblet of tylsent with oken Levis lyned with blake sarcenet tufted with fyne lynen cloth' [B260].

Hose were an integral part of any male outfit and they were often made to match the doublet that they were worn with (Fig. 6.5). The terminology used to describe hose was evolving in this period, and it does not appear to have been used in a consistent manner. Dress history books often distinguish the component parts as follows: the upperstocks or breeches, the netherstocks or stockings and the codpiece. References to netherstocks do appear in warrants and inventories as in the following example from the 1547 inventory: '6 paier of nether stockes for hose of yellowe Taphita with viij paier of nether stockes withowt fete of redde Bawdkin' (8642). However, entries in the accounts and wardrobe books were often less precise. The word hose was often used to describe the complete garment but it could also denote either the upperstocks or netherstocks. Equally, the word stocks was often not qualified with the term 'nether' or 'upper', but it was used in such a way as to indicate that the writer was referring to the upper stocks — this is indicated by several factors including the amount of fabric being used (usually 1¼ yards (1.1 m)), the context ('stocks for two pairs of leather hose'), the quality

6.5 *Doublet and hose of Don Garzia de' Medici, 1562, reproduced with the permission of Mary Westerman for the Janet Arnold slide archive, Galleria del Costume, Palazzo Pitti*

6.6 *Codpiece, 1540–60, made from layers of brown twill woven wool cloth, found at Worship Street, London. C547. Museum of London*

of the fabric being supplied, usually cloth of gold, cloth of silver, satin and velvet, and that a matching doublet was also ordered.

References to codpieces are lacking. The reason for this omission is that the codpiece was considered an integral part of the upperstocks and as such did not need particular reference. Portraits emphasise the changing profile of the codpiece throughout Henry's reign, indicating that the codpiece was often heavily padded and ornately decorated. Extant codpieces in the collections of the Museum of London indicate that the simple codpieces were made from layers of fabric stitched together (Fig. 6.6) and that they could be secured to the main section of the upperstocks in a number of ways, usually using laces or points.[16] The codpieces with the hose of Augustus, Elector of Saxony, and Don Garzia de'Medici have a more complex construction and method of attachment.[17] While the codpiece on fashionable hose was chiefly intended for show and more practically, it covered the front opening of the hose, on armour and military dress the codpiece performed a much more practical role. In 1547 the king's armouries listed 'two half breches with Codpeces of stele' (8358) and 369 'Kodpeces of stele' (8424).

The upperstocks or breeches changed in shape and style during Henry's reign, and several distinctive types can be found in his accounts and wardrobe books. Worsley's wardrobe book indicates that Henry had 79 pairs of hose and the upperstocks were made from 22 fabrics and four pairs of 'Almain' hose. In addition, the entries for hose made by William Croughton or Hosier in Worsley's wardrobe book indicate that he was provided with cloth to make 39 pairs of hose, for stocking 30 pairs of hose and for welting eight pairs of hose. He was chiefly working with cloth of gold, tilsent, tissue and velvet. The upperstocks of the hose were often made to match a doublet and as doublets became increasingly ornate so did the hose: 'a payer of proper stocks of hosen of crymsen satten embraderyd with threds of venys gold lined with crymesen sarsenet'[18] and 'one paire of crimesen golde tincell [hose] with Borders of Damaske golde embrawderid with passemaine fringid' (14266).

The most distinctive style of upperstocks worn by the king was known as 'Almain' hose, that is, hose in the German style. This was a highly distinctive style that was popular with the king for the period between 1521 and 1538. While the accounts identify 'Almain' hose, they do not always highlight the specific characteristics of the style. The accounts for 1523–25 included two pairs of hose, one pair of purple cloth stocked with purple cloth of gold tissue and welted with cloth of silver and black tinsel and one pair of white cloth in the 'Almain' fashion, stocked and embroidered with white black and purple satin, lined with linen and flannel.[19] However, slashing was a key element of the design as indicated in the entry for a pair of hose of white cloth, the upperstocks slashed, made in the 'Almain' style.[20] By the time the 1547 inventory was compiled, no pairs were described as being in the 'Almain' fashion.

Three pairs of hose of this type, or *pluderhose*, can be seen in the chapel dedicated to the Sture family in Uppsala cathedral. These hose consisted of panes of velvet, with an inner lining of silk, all gathered into a cuff at or just above the knee. The hose of Svante Sture had black velvet panes lined with a grey-green taffeta and both fabrics were used to make the codpiece. The velvet was lined with red-brown fustian and the hose had a pocket. Nils Sture's hose had panes, knee bands and a codpiece of black velvet which were lined with black worsted. In a similar style, Erik Sture's hose had panes of black velvet and a codpiece of black velvet and brown taffeta. The same taffeta, possibly originally plum-coloured, was also used as the lining. The lengths of the breeches were 60 cm, 60 cm and 68 cm respectively.[21]

According to the antiquarian John Stow, Henry VIII wore netherhose cut from 'ell broad taffety' unless 'by great chance there came a pair of Spanish silk stockings from Spain'.[22] A warrant from 1510–11 included entries for 2¼ yards (2 m) of woollen cloth to make two pairs of hose and 3½ yards (3.2 m) of woollen cloth to make another three pairs of hose.[23] Henry VIII also had linen hose. On a warrant dated 6 January 1539 Croughton was paid 40*s* for 12 pairs of linen hose and 13*s* 4*d* for four pairs of quilted linen hose.[24] Knitted silk hose made on the Continent were highly prized and, as Stow hinted, they found their way into Henry's possession especially in the 1540s. On the warrant dated 27 March 1543 Croughton was paid 10*s* for lining with linen ten pairs of knitted hose and working with 'oilet holes' and 20*s* for 'dyinge 12 par knytt hoose in le skarlett lined with lined and with oilet holes'.[25] The warrant also showed a payment 30*s* for three pairs of hose bought from Milan, lined with white cloth and linen and with eyelet holes and ties around the knee with ribbon. In 1547 the 'kinges owne warderobe howse' at Whitehall contained 'xij paier of hooses of blacke silke knitte' (9926). Knitted wool hose were made in England, and in 1519 hose knitted in Nottinghamshire cost 5*d* a pair.[26] On 20 December 1532, 7*s* 6*d* was 'paid to parker of the Robes for a payer of nyte hosen for the king'.[27] These types of hose were held up with garters and the king's wardrobe warrants contain regular entries for garter ribbon.

In contrast, Eric XIV of Sweden (1533–77) favoured hand-knitted silk or chamois leather hose. An inventory of his clothes taken in 1566 listed 27 pairs of silk hose or stockings including ten pairs of red, eight of black, four of violet, as well as pairs in pink, yellow, brown and ash grey. His hose made of chamois leather were equally brightly coloured and the red pairs were slashed to reveal a gold and green lining. Eric also had 15 pairs of hose cut from cloth, but the choice of colours remained consistent: black, grey, violet, red and pink.[28]

There are several extant examples of netherstocks including a pair of linen netherstocks found at Alpirsbach, without feet but with a codpiece. The hose measure 102 cm in length and 78 cm around the waist (Fig. 6.7).[29] There are also pairs of leather or chamois leather netherhose such as the chamois leather hose from Svante Sture's pluderhose. These measure 102 cm at the waist and 50 cm in length, while those worn by his brother Erik were 68 cm long. They were lined with undyed fustian.[30]

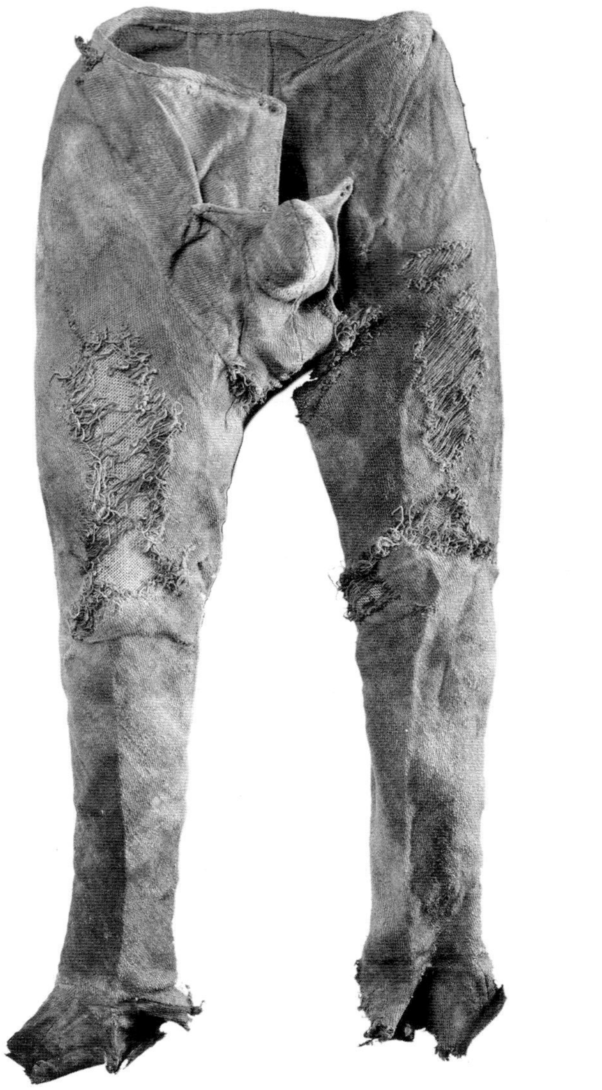

6.7 *Pair of linen hose,* c. *1490–1529, Kloster Alpirsbach (K-12-8-23). © Vermögen und Bau Baden-Württemberg, Staatliche Schlösser und Gärten. Photo: Adi Bachinger, Karlsruhe*

The mercenary's uniform believed to have been made for Andreas Wild von Wynigen and preserved in Berne Historical Museum consists of a doublet, hose and beret. The attribution of the garments cannot be supported and it is most likely that they are a sixteenth-century copy, possibly made by von Wynigen's grandson.[31] The netherstocks are made of yellow fulled wool and have brown soles to the integral feet, while the upperstocks are also of yellow fulled wool lined with linen, which has been slashed. Puffs of yellow silk have been pulled through the slashes. As usual, the upperstocks have a codpiece.[32] There is another pair of red and cream striped hose with shoes made in one, in the collection at Ambras in the Tyrol. It is quite possible that some of Henry VIII's arming hose were made in this style, although it is unlikely that they were distinguished from normal hose in the accounts.[33]

The grave of Don Garzia de'Medici, the 11th child of Cosimo I and Eleanor di Toledo, who died in 1562, provides a good example of trunk hose (Fig. 6.5).[34] The hose were made of panes of crimson velvet lined with crimson satin and interlined with linen, decoration in the form of couched lines of metal-wrapped thread, for each leg there are 13 panes, nine single panes at the front and back and around the hip and five cut as a group for the inside leg/crotch area. The hose have a slashed, padded, velvet codpiece, lined and bound with crimson satin and two eyelet holes. The yellow silk knitted hose or upperstocks of Elector Augustus of Saxony, *c.* 1552–55, are slashed and the yellow taffeta interlining has been pulled through the slashes and this technique has also been applied to the codpiece. Eyelet holes are worked in the waistband and some of the matching yellow ties are still present.[35]

Slops were baggy or loose-fitting breeches or hose which do not feature often in Henry VIII's wardrobe. On 22 November 1532 6*s* 8*d* was paid out of the privy purse 'to Cicyll for a pyer of sloppes for the kinges grace'.[36] In the account for 1535–36 there was a pair of hose, 'upperstocked with purple velvet, made like slops, embroidered and tied above the knee with a cord of silk and gold, lined with purple sarsenet and white cloth'.[37] Slops appear in the last three extant Henrician accounts: 1537–38, 1538–39 and 1543–45. On the warrant dated 27 March 1544 one pair of slops of black satin lined with black velvet buttoned up the leg with buttons of black silk and drawn at the knee with black silk lace possibly worn with the 12 knee bands, five lined with taffeta and one lined with scarlet were ordered at the same time.[38] Prince Edward also started to wear slops at around this time. His warrants for 1544 and 1545 included new pairs of slops and older pairs that were being translated.[39] By 1547 there was just one pair of slops 'of blacke vellut enbrodrid with A Passamaine of golde and Silver' (14353) in the king's wardrobe, along with three pairs made of linen for the king to bath in (11525). However, a single reference in a warrant dated 2 November 1510 suggests that the term could be used to describe a different type of garment. A payment of 13*s* 4*d* was made for a yard of blue velvet for the sleeves and collar of 'a slop of cloth of gold of damask'.[40]

Variety in the male wardrobe: the glaudekin, gabardine, cloak, frock, coat, cassock and nightgown

Throughout his reign Henry had access to a variety of outer garments including the glaudekin, the cassock, the frock and the nightgown. These garments presented a range of different styles and forms, some of which were fashionable throughout the reign, while others dropped out of use being replaced by new garments. In addition some garment types such as the coat developed a range of distinctive variants. Worsley's wardrobe books identified 'Almain' coats, arming coats, demi-coats, riding coats and short coats in addition to coats.

The glaudekin was a long gown which had been fashionable at the court of Henry VII (Fig. 6.8). Henry VIII wore glaudekins in his youth and they continued to be made for him until 1510–11.[41] These glaudekins were made from 15 yards (13.7 m) of black velvet and similar quantities of purple velvet, furred with sable. John Ring supplied 50 skins of black bogy for performing the fur in an existing glaudekin of crimson velvet. Six glaudekins listed in Worsley's wardrobe book include examples made from cloth of gold damask [A404], cloth of gold upon satin [A406], cloth of silver [A405] and 'a Glaudkyn of Russet tylsent lyned with Russet veluete' [A89]. The choice of fabrics suggests that the glaudekin was

6.8 *Whitehall cartoon of Henry VII and Henry VIII by Hans Holbein the Younger, 1537. National Portrait Gallery, London (NPG 4027)*

a formal garment that quickly became outdated. Even so, according to the March 1538 warrant, a glaudekin of red velvet without sleeves edged with the same velvet and lined with black satin was ordered as part of a group of mourning clothes ordered for the king. It was almost immediately converted into a cloak with sleeves.[42]

A gabardine was a long coat with wide sleeves. It was fashionable in the first half of the sixteenth century, and the king appears to have worn gabardines only until about 1518.[43] After that date its place was taken in Henry VIII's wardrobe by the frock. In 1511 8 yards (7.3 m) of scarlet were bought to make two gabardines for the king, one of which was left unlined while the other was lined with 4 yards (3.7 m) of black satin.[44] A warrant dated 26 April 1517 included a gabardine of russet cloth bordered with white velvet. No gabardines were listed in Worsley's wardrobe books or the king's wardrobe in 1547.

The cloak was less common as an outer garment in the earlier part of Henry's reign than the gown. That said, with the exception of 1510–11, cloaks were included in each subsequent, extant account. In the 1510s and 1520s, the numbers were small — usually two or three a year — but by the 1530s the average order included six cloaks. In the 1518–19, 14½ yards (13.2 m) of right crimson satin costing £13 1s were bought to line a cloak of crimson velvet.[45] Worsley's inventory contained several cloaks made from a variety of materials including 'a cloke of wolvis Skynnes lyned with blak Satten with twoo Bukkelles and pendauntes of golde geven to the kinges grace by my lorde Sandys' [B137], 'a cloke of violett frisado garded with purpull veluet the cape tyed with vj flatte Agglettes of golde' [B138] and 'a Spaynisshe cloke of Blak Frisado with a Border of Goldesmythis worke geven by the Quenes grace to the king' [B139]. There were also double cloaks as indicated by the provision of 'xviij yerdes di of blacke cloth of gold dammaske for a dobill cloke' [A699].

However, from the 1540s onwards the cloak became increasingly popular. Worn over the doublet, it was predominantly a short, knee-length garment, circular or semicircular in shape.[46] A specific type of short, circular cloak was referred to as the Spanish cloak, and during this period it was very much in fashion at court. Henry VIII had a number of short cloaks, including some in the Spanish style and others in the Turkish style, as in the case of 'Turkey cloaks ribband with nettes of silver and, between the knittynges or the meshes, flowers of golde'.[47] The 1547 inventory included some very sumptuous cloaks made from a broad range of materials: 'A Cloke of elkes Skinnes lined with blacke Satten with x buttons of golde' (14296) and 'A Cloke of Sables lined with blacke Caphae Damaske wrought with roses with 10 rounde Buttons set with litle sparkes of counerfet Rubies and Saphiers' (14294). Cloaks were often provided with special cloak bags that could be highly decorated, as in the case of 'a Cloke bagge of blacke vellut all ouer embrawdrid with venice gold' (14564).

There are several examples of sixteenth-century cloaks. First, there is the damask short cloak made for Don Garzia de'Medici, 1562. It has a double guard down both fronts and around the lower edge, as well as sleeves (Figs 20.1 and 20.2).[48] Second, there are two slightly later examples, both with stand collars, in the collection of the Victoria and Albert Museum. The first is a French satin cape, the collar, front edges and the hem of which are embroidered with couched metal thread. In addition, the collar and front guards have appliqué worked in a strapwork design. The other cloak is a Spanish cape, similar in cut to the other cape, and it is made from embossed velvet, with a silk fringe applied around the hem. It also has guards of embroidery applied down the front edges and around the hem.[49]

A frock was a loose outer garment, similar to a coat. Like the coat it was often highly decorative in form. Twenty-seven frocks were listed in Worsley's wardrobe book and another 13 were ordered for the king, along with eight matching sets of frocks and doublets and one frock with a mantle made from 25 yards (22.8 m) of black velvet [A1067]. They could vary in length as indicated by 'a shorte Frocke of crimosyn cloth of gold of tissewe lyned with sarcenet' [B42]. Frocks first appeared in Henry's great wardrobe accounts in 1523–25, and they continued to be made for the king on a regular basis thereafter. In April 1541 Henry gave away 'a froke of purple gold chamlett facyd with luserns and layed on this passementes of purple sylkes and threds of gold'.[50] The frock often had quite full skirts and sleeves as the following entry from the 1547 inventory indicates: 'A Frocke of grene bawdkin with damaske wourke the bodies lyned with grene vellut the bases Sleves with grene Satten tied with xxxvij paire of Aglettes of golde' (14322).

The coat was a loose-fitting outer garment with sleeves. New coats were ordered for Henry in every extant set of accounts. Eleven were ordered in 1516–17 and another 14 in 1517–18, but only a single example in 1523–25, 1527–28 and 1531–32. Worsley's wardrobe book listed 30 coats (excluding the specialist examples such as Almain coats) with velvet being the most commonly used fabric (13 examples) in addition to velvet tissue [B170] or velvet pirled and cloth of silver tilsent [A209]. More exotic examples included a coat of wolf skin [B143]. New coats ordered for the king could either be made as separate items [A382], ensuite with a hood [A957] or with a doublet [A957]. Short coats were made throughout the reign, while the evidence for demi-coats is more mixed. Although only one demi-coat was ordered in the king's warrants (for 1516–17), a coat of this type was listed in the 1547 inventory: 'a Demie Coote of purple Satten with sleves all over embrodrid with venice golde lined with purple vellut' (14280). Coats were equally common in the 1547 inventory including examples made from leather (14275), satin (14274) and velvet (14277).

In 1540 Edward Hall described a coat worn by Henry VIII as a 'coate of purple velvet, somewhat made lyke a frocke, all over enbrodered with flat gold of damaske with small lace mixed betwene of the same gold'.[51] Equally, the similarities between the cut of the coat and the cassock were emphasised in several items delivered to Whitehall from Sudeley in May 1549: 'oon Coote of crimsen velvet alouer embraudred with veanice golde The same is but a Cassocke' (17648).

Coats were often very richly decorated using a range of techniques, as in the case of 'a Coote of purple vellat allover

embraudered with veanice golde and a Border of embraudery of veanice golde the same being cutt and pulled owte with golde sarcennet and Lined with purple vellat and purple satte' (9922). The coat was made in a variety of specific types. They could have pronounced skirts which incorporated a number of pleats that then became the focus for decoration: 'a Cote of crimsen vellat embrawdered with golde and freng vppon euery pleyte with damaske and venice Siluer' (11249). Some coats were made with long sleeves which had horizontal openings above the elbow, through which the arms could pass through. Examples can be seen in the portraits of the duke of Norfolk and Sir John Godsalve, and Henry VII wears the sleeves fully of his glaudekin in the Whitehall cartoon.[52]

The cassock was a loose-fitting jacket made with wide sleeves. It varied from being knee-length at the start of Henry's reign to mid-thigh-length by the 1540s.[53] Four cassocks, two of crimson tissue, one of crimson cloth of gold with works and one of purple tinsel, all edged with crimson velvet, lined with crimson satin and equipped with eight satin pockets were ordered for the king on a warrant dated 26 February 1545.[54] Another four cassocks, two of purple tissue, two of purple tinsel, all edged with purple velvet, lined with purple satin were also mentioned, along with making and translating three cassocks, two of purple velvet and one of crimson velvet embroidered, new lined with purple satin. Ten cassocks were listed in 1547, three of which also had matching bases. They were made of very good quality fabrics, including three made from gold tinsel and one from silver tinsel and predominantly purple or red or shade of red in colour. For example, 'a Cassacke of incarnate flat silver tissued with golde and silver edged with incarnate vellut lined with crimsen Satten' (14351). References in the 1547 inventory also indicate that long gowns with straight sleeves were made in the style of the cassock: 'a long Cassock gowne with streight sleves of Crimsen vellet rewed with golde welted with Crimsen veluett and Lyned with Taphata' (14222).

Scrutiny of Holbein's drawings and portraits reveal that a number of his male sitters chose to be painted dressed informally, whereas his female sitters chose otherwise.[55] A small number of nightgowns were listed in Worsley's wardrobe book. Beyond their being of velvet, the entries are uninformative: some were lined with fur as in the case of 'a night gowne of russet veluete furred with sabullus' [B100], while others were unlined, possibly for summer: 'a night gowne of russet veluete single' [B80]. The amount of cloth provided by Worsley to the king's tailors to make a nightgown varied slightly between 12¼ (11.2 m) and 13 yards (11.8 m) [A1168, A958]. The examples from the 1543–45 accounts were all black and made from damask. They were also more ornate than the earlier examples: a nightgown of black damask with two borders and an edge of black velvet furred with budge, a nightgown of black damask with three velvet guards purfelid and a nightgown of black damask, guarded with a broad guard and two narrow, with fringe, the skirts lined with buckram.[56] There is an example of a man's loose gown or nightgown dating from 1600–10 at Hardwick Hall made from mulberry coloured satin with tabbed wings at the sleeve heads.[57]

Alternatives to the doublet: jackets and jerkins, chammers and shamews

Jerkins and jackets were worn over the doublet. While they were often sleeveless, this was not always the case. The terms sometimes appear to have been used interchangeably, but actually they were used to identify two different styles. It is evident from the orders placed with the great wardrobe that jackets were far more common and popular than jerkins, with jackets being made in every year bar one but jerkins only featuring in three accounts. A warrant from the first year of the reign included a jacket of embroidery 'with scales' that was furred with black budge.[58]

Only two new jackets were made separately in Worsley's book for the king, but they also appeared as orders for matching items: a jacket and demi-coat of velvet [A1020], 26 jackets with matching doublets in a range of fabrics including cloth of gold baudkyn [A484], cloth of silver damask [A418], tilsent [A682] and velvet [A993], jackets and partlets [A1289], jackets with demi-sleeve and doublets [A502]. These were in addition to the 100 jackets (excluding four quartered jackets) listed in Worsley's book: for example, 'A Jaquet with di slevis of purple blak and white Satten enbrawdered with lettres' [B321]. Twenty-eight of the jackets were made from velvet, while the rest were made from 27 different fabrics or fabric combinations.

In a wardrobe list of 1541 'a jaquet of carnacion cloth of golde embrodryd with iij small gardes of carnacion vellat gold and lined with crymsen satten'.[59] Strangely, no jackets were listed in the inventory taken after the king's death in 1547. However, seven jerkins were listed there (14332–38). These were made in a variety of colours of velvet: black (1), purple (3), russet (1), crimson (1) and tawny (1) and they were all embroidered. For example, 'one Jerkin of tawnie vellut with wide sleves of tawnie Satten all over embrawdrid with venice gold and tawnie silke with a paire of hoose of tawnie satten of like embrawderie' (14336). The jerkins were all furnished with sleeves (three with wide sleeves, two with straight sleeves and two with sleeves of an unspecified type) and they all had hose. The sleeves were usually made of a different type of material to the main body of the garment but of the same colour. Where this was the case, the hose were made of the same material as the sleeves.

Jerkins were occasionally made from leather, as in the case of a brown leather jerkin made for a young man or adolescent, *c.* 1555–65, with a stand collar and moulded pewter buttons (Fig. 6.9). The leather was decorated with punched heart- and star-shaped motifs arranged in bands delineated with scored lines.[60] A more sophisticated and later example of a leather jerkin can be seen in the Stibert Museum, Florence. Dating from *c.* 1595–1610, the jerkin is embroidered with yellow silk and silver metal thread. It is lightly padded over the chest and stomach, with a stand, roll collar and fastens with buttons and by lacing through worked eyelet holes. Worked eyelet holes inside the armholes were intended for securing separate sleeves.[61]

6.9 *Dark brown leather jerkin for a young man, decorated with vertical and diagonal scored bands and diamond-, star- and heart-shaped pinking. Tower of London, C65, Museum of London*

In 1518 the chronicler Hall referred to the chammer as 'a new fassion garment . . . which is in effect a goune, cut in the middle'.[62] He was commenting on the chammers worn by the members of Admiral Bonnivet's retinue when he came on embassy to England — the implication is it was of French origin. The chammer was a type of jerkin constructed from a lattice of strips of fabric or passementerie. A contrasting fabric was often placed behind the strips to highlight the effect. Worsley's wardrobe book and inventory lists 19 chammers that were made from a range of fabrics including velvet upon velvet, satin, tilsent damask gold and cloth of gold damask raised with silver. These included 'a shamer of Russet cloth of gold tissewe furred with sabullus valet Clxxij li' [B23], 'a shamer of cloth of golde tissewe furred with luzardes Cxlviij li' [B24] and 'a shamer of cloth of golde of dammaske Reysed with siluer furred with sabullus valet Cxl li' [B25]. The inventory descriptions were often quite brief, however some appear to have had sleeves, as in the case of:

> a Shamer of purple veluet furred with luzardys weltid with the same the vpper slevis and forslevys sett with xlvj Trayfullis of pearlis Sett in gold and oon euery trayfoile v pearlis and xvj other Trayfullis of pearlis Sett in gold and in euery trayfull iij pearlys and on diamounde in the middys of euery trayfull one Pearle lacking byfore they came into the warderobe [B131].

Others had high collars [A135–36]. Chammers were in vogue for only a short period. They appear in the wardrobe accounts for 1521–22, 1526–27 and 1527–28. None were listed in the 1547 inventory.

The shamew (or shemew) is said to have originated in the 1530s. It was a loose garment like a coat that was worn open at the front.[63] An order for shamews in the great wardrobe account for 1526–27 enables us to date their appearance a decade earlier. The shamews ordered establish that these garments were at least partially fitted, with skirts. Three shamews were made for the king: one of black satin welted with six welts of black velvet, three in the middle of the base and three in the skirts lined with frieze and satin, one of black velvet with six double borders of black satin lined with frieze and furred with sable and one of black velvet embroidered with six Milan stitches, three in the middle of the bases and three in the skirts, furred with black budge.[64] The last example also had sleeves because buckram was provided for stiffening them. Each shamew cost 13*s* 4*d* to make. On the same warrant the king ordered a shamew for Francis Weston to be made of black velvet with two borders of the same velvet which cost 6*s* 8*d* to make. In addition to these three examples, one shamew was listed in the 1547 inventory as being stored in 'tholde juelhous at Westminster': 'a Cote or Shamewe of purple clothe of golde with workes furred with sables garded with purple vellat and enbrawdered with golde' (11247). The wording of this entry emphasises the similarities between the shamew and the coat.

Accessories: partlets, placards, stomachers, petticoats and tippets

The partlet was worn with a low-cut doublet, jerkin or coat to cover the neck and chest. It could have a collar and detachable sleeves, and was often very ornate. Henry VIII ordered partlets regularly up to the middle of his reign and then less frequently after that. Partlets could be made in a range of sizes, to suit the type and style of the garment they were worn with. Worsley's inventory included 'a lytell partelet of tawny saten lyned with sarcenet' [B153], while William Hilton was given 'iij yerdes quarter of grene veluete for a longe partelet' [A1062]. Worsley's inventory also recorded 'a Riding Cote of blake saten with ij cutt borders of blake veluete & ij in the myddes with <a> russet partelet of blake veluete lyned with blake sarcenet' [B273] and 'a shorte Cote of blake saten with iiij borders of blake veluete cutte with a russet partlet of blake veluete lyned with sarcenet' [B275].

A list of items belonging to the wardrobe of the robes during the time of John Parker's yeomanry included ten highly ornate partlets:

> ij partlettes of black velvett inbrowderyd, ij partlettes of white velvett inbrowtheryd, a partlett of crimsen velvett inbrowderyd, a partlett of Grene velvett inbrowderyd, a partlett orenge colour velvett inbrowderyd, a partlett of white lether perfumyd with ij borgonyon gardes of white velvett inbrowderyd, a partlett of blacke velvett furde with bogge, a partlett of blake satten furede with conye.[65]

Partlets, like stomachers, were often ordered in bulk. A warrant dated 1539 included six velvet partlets, three black, one green, one crimson and one white. They were all embroidered with gold and silver, lined with satin and sarsenet and had buttons of Venice gold.[66] By 1547 there were four partlets in the king's wardrobe of the robes that were all made from velvet and lined with satin, all embroidered with Venice gold, all described as being made 'withowte Sleves' (14339), meaning a matching pair of sleeves. In addition, there were 'Twoo partelettes of white threade' (11585) kept with the king's shirts.

A placard could be worn with a doublet, a coat or a gown, if it had a low-cut front, for warmth. Placards were only listed in one of the king's great wardrobe accounts, that for 1517–18, when two were made for his use: one of black velvet furred with ermine to be worn with a coat and the other of crimson satin for a doublet of crimson satin lined with crimson sarsenet and embroidered.[67] As these entries indicate, a placard was often made ensuite with the garment with which it was intended to be worn, such as 'a doblet of white saten with placard & foreslyues of white cloth of siluer and russet tynsell paned & welted with the same lyned with white sarcenet' [B290]. Worsley's wardrobe book listed eight doublets with matching placards of this type.[68] A group of the king's clothes delivered to Thomas Alvard in November 1534 included four doublets with foresleeves and placards of cloth of silver, purple silver tissue, purple and crimson velvet.[69] However, placards did not feature in the king's wardrobe in the 1540s when he started to wear coats and doublets with high necklines.

Stomachers for men were worn with doublets and covered the chest. They were ordered throughout the king's reign and often in large numbers: 50 in 1516–17 and 92 in 1543–45. Worsley's wardrobe book reveals that Hilton made 18 for the king in the 11-month period from 1 July 1517.[70] They were all made from satin, the fabric of choice, in a range of colours including crimson, purple, white, green, russet, black and yellow. John de Paris made none in the period immediately following. In 1539 Malt made eight stomachers of black and white satin lined with scarlet and eight stomachers of purple and crimson satin lined with scarlet.[71] Even so, just one stomacher was listed in the king's wardrobe in 1547: 'A stomacher of grene clothe of Golde' (14553). As with the placard and the partlet, the stomacher fell into disfavour with the king in the 1540s.

The male petticoat or waistcoat was a waist-length garment worn under the doublet. It was usually sleeveless but not exclusively, and it was often quilted for warmth. It was worn in two ways. As part of formal dress, it would not be worn without a doublet. As part of informal wear, it could be worn with just a shirt or nightshirt.[72] On such occasions, if it was worn, the hose were attached to the petticoat rather than to the doublet.

Scrutiny of the orders for clothes made by Henry VIII suggests that he did not buy any petticoats earlier that 1533–34, but later he ordered them with regularity. These petticoats were usually made from double or triple layers of cambric that were quilted together. However, the inclusion of '3 petycottes of white taffeta 2 old one new' and '1 old petycote of linen cloth quylted' in an inventory dating from Parker's time as yeoman of the robes (*c.* 1526–36) indicates that Henry had owned and worn petticoats in the 1520s.[73] This is verified by an account for the wardrobe of the robes for 1521–22 allowing 3 yards (2.7 m) of black sarsenet for lining three petticoats of black satin which cost 13*s*.[74]

Although fancy fur tippets formed part of the fashionable female wardrobe, they did find favour with Henry VIII. He had three tippets of sable and five other neck tippets of unspecified material, one of which was lined with sable.[75]

Clothing for bathing

At both Whitehall and Hampton Court the king enjoyed a luxurious bath house.[76] The 1542 inventory of Whitehall records a list of 'Sondrye Lynen seruing for the king his grace in his Bayne' which show how the king was dressed when he used his bath house. The entries describe a set of items mostly made of plain white linen holland: six coifs, 13 kerchers, six double rails, six double stomachers, three pairs of slops, six aprons, four handkerchiefs, three of them fringed with Venice gold and red and white silk, with the fourth edged with a cordaunt of white silk, 25 rubbers and 12 handkerchiefs of plain cambric [570–78].

Sporting dress

Many of the coats made for the king reflected his enthusiasm for sport: riding coats, hunting coats, stalking coats, tennis coats and hawking coats. Of these, the riding coat was the most heavily used and new coats were made for him in each of the extant sets of accounts. His hunting coats were often green but not always and, unusually for the king's wardrobe, they were quite often made from woollen cloth such as kendal, rather than silk. The riding cloak was far less common, with the king ordering just three examples in 1517–18. The brief entries in the accounts make it quite difficult to tell how these coats (and cloaks) differed from those made for the king for general daywear in terms of cut. It is possible that the cut was fairly standard and the differentiation came in terms of colour and cloth type.

Henry spent a lot of time in the saddle, either as a means of transport or for pleasure. In 1520 Richard Pace noted that 'The King rises daily, except on holy days, at 4 or 5 o'clock, and hunts till 9 or 10 at night. He spares no pains to convert the sport of hunting into a martyrdom'.[77] Little had changed by 1526 when Hall noted that 'all this Sommer the kyng tooke his pastime in huntyng'.[78] However, the Eltham Ordinances recorded that 'Whensoever the King's grace hath gone further in walkeing, hunting, hauking and other disportes, the most part of the noblemen and gentlemen of the court used to passé with his grace, by reason whereof the court hath been left disgarnished but also the King's said disports lett, hindred, and impeached'.[79] As he grew older, Henry took more interest in falconry. Early in January 1543 Henry VIII wrote to Albert, two boys called William and Ralph. The women employed included the wife of William Armourer, who was one of the king's footmen, and the wife of one Barnard. The bulk of the work was undertaken by Mrs Armourer. The payments made to her reveal the cost of the materials as well as the scale of her trade. On 29 October 1530 she was paid £6 18*s* for 23 ells (15.8 m) of cambric for six shirts for the king at 6*s* the ell and 36*s* for making the shirts, at 6*s* each. She supplied 6 yards (5.4 m) of ribbon costing 2*s*, which may have been to trim the shirts, or possibly the six coifs priced at 18*s*.[109] She also supplied two shirts each for Mark Smeaton and the two Williams at a price of 6*s* 8*d* each, but this figure may include the price of the cloth as well as the making, and four shirts for Ralph at 3*s* 4*d* each. On 31 March 1531 Mrs Barnard was paid 53*s* 4*d* for making two shirts for the king, and in the following year on 27 September she received the same sum for making eight shirts for the king.[110] On 10 January 1531 the wife of Robert Philip, who lived at Greenwich, received 2*s* 6*d* for making two linen bags to keep the king's shirts in, and on 14 February a further 5*s* 4*d* for two bags sent to York Place.[111] None of these women were described as seamstresses, although this is what they were. Indeed the post of the king's seamstress was not created until the accession of the Stuart kings.[112]

While many slept in their shirts, some could afford night shirts. According to William Thomas, a groom of the privy chamber with Prince Arthur, he regularly attended his master at Ludlow after marriage and 'made [him] ready to bed and . . . conducted him clad in his night gown unto the Princess's bedchamber door often and sundry times'.[113] Night shirts were given to the king as New Year's gifts, as indicated by the gift roll from 1526 which included two night shirts, one white and one wrought with black and white silk.[114] The king seems to have worn his night shirts until they became unfit for further use: at his death he had 'xxiij night Shirtes of sondrye sortes verey meane and worne' (11604). Night shirts were not for public wear. They were intimate apparel. Lord Seymour used to go into the bedchamber of the Princess Elizabeth while she was living with Catherine Parr and him at Chelsea. He visited her early in the morning dressed in his night shirt and slippers which Catherine Ashley, her lady in waiting, thought 'an unseemly sight to see a man so little dressed in a maiden's chamber'.[115]

The miniature of the duke of Richmond attributed to Lucas Horenbout (Fig. 11.5) depicts him wearing a white linen night shirt and a linen night cap embroidered with black work. It is likely that this miniature was painted between 1534–35 and its informality has been taken to indicate that the portrait was painted during a period of illness. But if one accepts on stylistic grounds a date of 1534–35 for its composition, thus not long after his marriage in November 1533 and its consummation, its eroticism is more readily explicable. The painting entitled *Edward VI and the Pope: A Protestant Allegory* shows Henry VIII propped up in bed wearing a night shirt and night cap worked with gold thread. The king possessed a range of night caps made from a variety of fabrics, including 'a night Cappe of blacke veluet partely embrawdered' (9565) and 'a night cappe of crymsen satten allover enbrawdered' (9568).

Handkerchiefs made from linen were becoming increasingly common fashion accessories kept in purses or pockets. They were often given as gifts. In 1540 the prince's nurse gave Henry a New Year's gift of 'a dossen hankerchers garnished with gold'.[116] They were often highly decorated, as in the case of 'three dossen handkerchers edged with golde and Silver' (12492).

Headwear

The antiquarian John Stow observed how towards the end of his life Henry VIII 'wore a round flat cap of scarlet or of velvet, with a broach or jewel, and a feather'.[117] In actuality, many of the king's bonnets were far more ornate. More typical was the 'bonnet of blake velvet garnysshyd with eight grett balessys set in gold and syxtene flowers of gold with four perlys in euery flower and a grett owche of gold with a gret balasse and other small dyamundes set in hyt also garnysshyd with fyve perlys and oon grett perle hangyng at hyt'.[118] A list of jewels delivered to Henry Norris at Eltham on 18 January 1526 included 23 hats and bonnets of different types: single- and double-turfed bonnets, caps, Milan bonnets, hats and night caps.[119] They were predominantly made from black velvet and heavily decorated with gold buttons, aglets, rolls and brooches. The subject matter of a number of the brooches was religious including a brooch of St Michael set with diamonds with a white rose on one side and a red rose on the other and another of St James of Paris work. Others had classical designs like Hercules and 'a broach of ziphus'. Regular gifts and purchases of bonnets meant that the coffer delivered to Whitehall from Greenwich in 1547 was full of caps: 46 caps and bonnets, a night cap and a woman's hat of black satin.[120] There were also three cap cases of black leather containing 18 caps.[121]

A number of hat badges surviving from this period corroborate the range of subjects mentioned in written sources. Portraits were quite common as indicated by a hat badge with an enamelled portrait of Charles V *c.* 1520.[122] Biblical scenes were also popular, as in the case of a hat badge 57 mm in diameter with an enamelled scene depicting Christ talking to the woman of Samaria at the well.[123] An embossed and chased gold cap badge in the collection of the Victoria and Albert Museum, *c.* 1536–40, is decorated with a male bust in classical style.[124] It has been suggested that an enamelled gold hat badge or 'jewel' of St George and the dragon, with a kneeling princess, was presented to Henry VIII by the Emperor Maximilian. However, while the badge is possibly of south German manufacture, Maximilian died in 1519, that is some two decades before the hat badge was made (Fig. 6.14).[125]

A range of styles of bonnets and caps were available, but those most frequently worn by the king were made from black velvet and had a narrow brim or turf which was the most common place for decoration. However, other short-lived fashions can be detected, as in the case of the use of thrums (additional pile, made from wool or silk) in the 1530s as a means of decorating hats. In 1539 Edmund Harman, the king's barber, gave Henry a 'crimson hat thrommed with a band of pirled gold and four tarsols' as a New Year's gift.[126]

6.14 *Hat badge said to have belonged to Henry VIII, Flemish or German, c. 1540. RCIN 442208. The Royal Collection © 2004, Her Majesty the Queen Elizabeth II*

An example of a red silk thrummed hat that has been attributed to Henry, but actually datable to 1590–1610, provides a good idea of the surface texture and appearance of thrummed hats from the early sixteenth century.[127]

The fancy caps and bonnets worn during the mid Tudor period were often provided with special cases to protect them when not worn. On 8 May 1535 John Husee wrote to Lord Lisle to inform him, 'I have sent you by this bearer, Harry Drywry . . . ij caps with under-caps, one of velvet another of satin, locked in a new cap-case wherof he hath the key'.[128] In February 1538 Husee wrote to Lady Lisle to tell her, 'by Swift I sent a cap with a white feather in a cap-case for Mr Basset'.[129] Henry had 'A Case coverid with grene vellut garnisshed with fringes of golde and silver havinge within the same diuerse Romes to laie Cappes in' (16025).

As part of their informal wear, men wore a range of headwear including night caps and cauls. Cauls could be worn alone or under a bonnet and could be plain, for example of 'blacke Silke' (2610) or decorative 'wrought of gold and Silke' (2609). The list of jewels in the keeping of Sir William Compton in 1519 included coifs of silk and gold, set with pearls.[130] Sir Nicholas Carew was painted, about 1528, wearing a pleated caul of cloth of gold under a Milan bonnet rather than his helmet, even though he chose to be depicted in his tournament armour (Fig. 12.9).

Footwear

The Milanese ambassador observed that Henry 'wants to have his feet in a thousand shoes'.[131] While this remark was an exaggeration, it rested on fact. Henry bought a lot of shoes. As Table 6.3 indicates, he had access to a wide range of footwear made with English and Spanish leather or velvet or satin uppers and with specialist types for riding, the tournament and even a pair for playing football costing 4*s*.[132]

Although the king bought quite large numbers of shoes with leather uppers, he generally wore shoes with velvet uppers (Fig. 6.15).[133] The rate of acquisition recorded in the accounts suggests that he may have worn a pair for as short a time as a week before discarding them. While black velvet shoes were ordered on a regular basis, coloured shoes were not uncommon. Twenty-one pairs of shoes (seven pairs of white, purple and crimson velvet shoes) were listed as 'remaynyng within the lesse standard of the kynges with the warderop of Robes' during Parker's period of office.[134] Henry also bought slippers which were usually made with textile uppers and would have been flat, and made to slip on, for indoor or informal wear. In 1527 Henry hurt his foot playing tennis and had to wear slippers at the evening entertainment, and the rest of the court followed suit.[135]

Boots, to cover the foot and leg, were worn for riding and for military dress. Henry had boots made on a regular basis, including special boots for winter. In July 1518 Budaeus wrote to Thomas Linacre, thanking him for his letter and explaining the delay in his reply by noting that he 'had just drawn on his boots to ride'.[136] Long boots could be worn with boot hose to protect the netherstocks. Boots were essentially for informal or practical wear, so it is not surprising that in the one full-length image of Henry VIII he was painted wearing shoes. In contrast, military dress was an accepted style of dress for a portrait of Philip II painted by Antonio Mor *c.* 1557.[137]

Henry VIII also made regular purchases of buskins. Buskins were a type of soft, short boot that covered the calves. They could be made from a range of materials including leather and velvet, and they could be highly decorative, as in the case of 'a payr of spanisshe buskyns enbrauderd with Roses & portcules' [B394]. A number of the king's buskins were furred for extra warmth in winter. Thomas Addington was paid 53*s* 4*d* in March 1544 for furring 16 pairs of buskins and a pair of boots with white lamb and black coney.[138] Towards the end of his life, Henry also ordered night buskins.

No shoes appear in the inventory compiled after his death. The reason for this apparent omission is possibly that in the last months of his life he found it uncomfortable to wear shoes. Modifications were made to his footwear as he got older. Shortly before his final illness, Richard Cecil signed a warrant for a yard and a half (1.37 m) of black velvet 'to make two pair of large slippers newly devised' for the king costing 21*s* on 14 January 1547.[139]

The collection in Dresden includes several examples of male footwear from the mid sixteenth century which throw light on Henry VIII's footwear. The first is a very rare single arming or tournament shoe made of leather with an eared sole which was raised at the waist in order to allow it to fit in stirrup.[140] The upper is cut quite high and laces at the side. The shoe is covered with black velvet, which is stitched to the forepart. Both the shoe and the velvet are lined with white

6.17 *The Calthorpe purse. T.246-1927. © V&A Images, Victoria and Albert Museum, London*

with 1,250 stitches to the square inch.[148] The purse was possibly made for the marriage of Sir Henry Parker to Elizabeth Calthorpe, who was a second cousin to Anne Boleyn.

Examples of leather and textile purses and pouches have been recovered from excavations in London, including one leather purse bound with silk.[149] The relatively poor survival rate for leather purses is probably because the leather was alum tawed, a type of leather which does not survive in damp conditions. Purses with metal frames were unusual before the fifteenth century, but there is one fourteenth-century example of a brass purse frame with swivel suspension loops. These purses could close with a drawstring set into a casing, threaded through small slashes in the body of the purse (a technique more usual on leather than textile) or rings, or the pouch could be stitched to a metal frame with a top fastening.

Many of the purses in Henry VIII's possession were small and were intended to hold money. They could be quite ornate, as in the case of 'a lytle purse of crimson Satten allover embraudered with a roose HR & garnished with peerle' (12494) and 'A litle Pursse of Spanishe woorke and a Girdell with three Tasselles of Silke' (14386), or quite plain, as in the case of 'three litle pouches the Ringes of alcumyne' (2559). Specialist pouches were made to hold specific groups of small items, such as hawking equipment. Henry owned a number of these, including 'a Hawking Pouche of chaungeable silke' (2606), 'twoo Double hawking bagges with ringes Siluer gilte enameled blacke' (2364) and 'vij hawkinge bagges wherof one velvet crimson one crimson Satten one white velvet striped with golde and iiij of bustyan' (11159). Pouches could also be used to store small precious items. A group of jewels in the custody of Sir William Compton in 1519 were kept in a number of bags and purses, including a bag embroidered with two peacocks and a Spanish purse with gold tassels.[150]

One further example of purses with specialised functions is the burse. When Henry went to war in France in 1544 he took with him a new great seal in 'a bag of crimson velvet curiously embroidered'.[151] This burse might be the 'Bagge of crimsen vellat with a kinges armes embraudered conteyneng in it a greate Seale of silver' (3412), listed amongst the king's possessions in 1547. It would have resembled the crimson silk velvet burse made for the great seal dating from 1560–1600.[152] It is decorated with the English royal arms worked in gold and silver thread, using a combination of raised and couched work.

Swords and daggers

The portrait of the earl of Surrey, unfinished by William Scrots at the time of his execution, presents him wearing his sword on his left hip and his dagger on the right. The same arrangement is visible in the Hampton Court portrait of an unknown man in red of about the same date (Fig. 6.1). Henry Fitzalan, Lord Maltravers, *c.* 1555, was also painted wearing a sword, the hilt of which was visible on his left. None of Henry's portraits depict him with a sword, but Holbein's cartoon for the Whitehall mural, *c.* 1537, and the group of full-length portraits based on it, depict the king with a dagger hanging from his sash and his left hand resting just above the hilt.[153] This suggests that when just a dagger was worn, it took the sword's place on the left hip.

Daggers and swords provided another vehicle for the craftsmen at court to demonstrate their skills, as is indicated by Holbein's design for a parade dagger (Fig. 6.18).[154] A comparable dagger 'of gold garnished with stones and pearls, the gargant garnished with stones and pearls and the layre', formed part of the security for the loan that the Fuggers made to Henry in 1545.[155] A list of 'the swords for the king lacking' dated 1536 included 'A sword that my lord Bewchamp gave the king, a bastard sword, an arming sword, a blue sword [and] a tuck'. Some were very ornate, as in the case of 'five woodknives, one with a gilt pommel, engraven with antique imagery and another with a pommel like a leopard's head'.[156] Swords and daggers were usually provided with velvet-covered scabbards with a chape and they were worn hanging

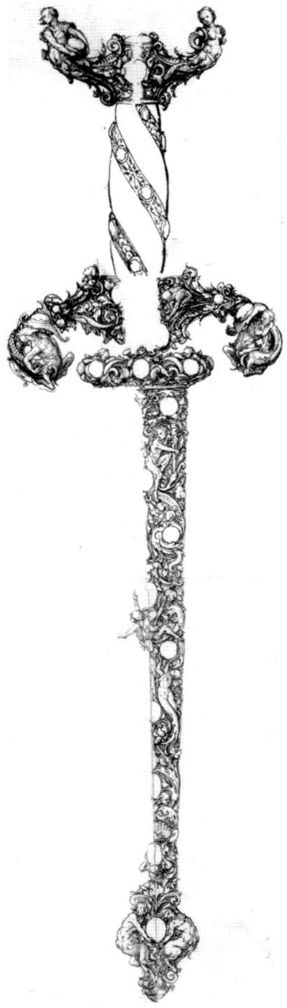

6.18 *Design for a parade dagger, by Hans Holbein the Younger, 1874-8-8-33. Reproduced by courtesy of the Trustees of the British Museum*

from velvet-covered girdles.[157] The girdles had a number of specialist metal fittings. These sword fittings could consist of a horizontal bar with three rivet holes and three rings on the lower edge which would have been attached to the sword belt and a pendant mount for the sling.[158] The king's swords and daggers were kept within the wardrobe of the robes and by 1547 the selection of weapons kept there was impressive (Table 6.4).

Other weapons owned by the king included handguns. In September 1538 William Hunt was appointed as keeper of the king's handguns and demi-hawks in the Tower of London with 10*d* a day.[160] Over six years later Alan Bawdson was appointed as the king's handgun maker with wages and livery of £12 a year.[161] Although handguns were not carried as fashionable accessories, the wardrobe of the robes had 'a goun to were lyke a dagger'. This may have been a novelty item, but it highlights the king's interest in such things and that the dagger was still the weapon of choice for the fashionable prince or nobleman.

Walking staffs

An inventory of items owned by the king taken while Parker was yeoman (*c.* 1528–37) included four staves:

Table 6.4: *Edged weapons in the wardrobe of the Robes in 1547*[159]

Type of weapon	Quantity
Blades (*swords, knives or daggers from the Levant or in that style*)	
– Turkey	2
Daggers	
– daggers	25
– poniards (*daggers with narrow blades*)	1
– Scottish daggers	2
Holmes (*sheath knives or swords*)	2
Knives	
– short	8
– stalking	1
– Turkey	1
– wood knives (*short hunting knives or swords*)	9
– wood knives, long	3
Skeins (*a knife or dagger*)	
– skeins	18
– skeins, short	9
Swords	
– almain	1
– arming (*used in battle or for the tournament*)	15
– back (*with a single-edged blade*)	2
– bastard (*of intermediate size between an arming and a two-handed sword*)	2
– bearing (*for carrying in processions, point up*)	4
– falchions (*broad sword with a convex or curved cutting edge*)	9
– Flemish	1
– French	5
– hangers (*short swords*)	1
– hangers, short	4
– rapiers	15
– Spanish	1
– two-edged	4
– two-handed	2
– tucks (*with a tapering blade of rectangular or diamond section*)	4
– tucks, long	1
– unspecified	4
– Venice	1

ij staves of cane garnissched with sylver and gylt at the hand end and a pykes in the end of yerne
a staffe of Vnicorne horne garnisched with sylver & gylt in the hand & a pyke in the end of yerne
a staff coveryd with blake satten garnissched in the hand with sylver & gylt and a pyke of yerne in the end.[162]

Following his tournament accident in January 1536 when for several days his death had been expected, Henry experienced difficulty walking. This problem worsened over the years. He also started to stoop. Walking staffs helped remedy both these problems.

He wished to disguise his infirmity and advancing years. By 1547 he had five walking staffs and four canes in his wardrobe of the robes. Many were highly decorative and they had a number of tools inserted into the top of them, such as the cane 'garnisshed with golde with a parfume of golde in the toppe and vndre that A Diall of Golde vndre that a kniffe with a thafte of Golde A paire of Twitches and a paire of Compasses of Golde' (14357). To meet any immediate need further examples were kept in the studies at Whitehall and in his removing coffers for use while moving from one royal house to another. His dependence on a staff became generally known in and out of court. Indeed, a staff was seen as adding to his gravitas. In one of the last portraits of him, now at Castle Howard, the king appears grasping a staff (Pl. ID).

The king's jewellery

Jewellery was a sign of status.[163] As an expression of personal magnificence, it provided another vehicle for the conspicuous display of wealth. Henry VIII used it to advantage. One of the features of his reign is the quantity and range of jewellery owned and worn by him which surpassed any previous English king: 'His fingers were one mass of jewelled rings and around his neck he wore a gold collar from which hung a diamond as big as a walnut.'[164] His clothing was also heavily bejewelled.[165] The style of the jewellery employed was intended to enhance his clothing. Fitted clothes with low necklines emphasised jewellery such as necklaces and collars worn round the neck, while jewels with personal significance could be concealed under clothes or by garments with high necklines.[166] Jewellery had other functions: it could be exchanged as gifts, used as security for loans and act as a repository for precious raw materials that could be recycled.

Henry liked jewels and owned a significant quantity. He was always susceptible to buying more. This is evident from the number of purchases of jewellery recorded in the chamber and privy purse accounts. A list of payments in May 1529 included a £22 10*s* to an unnamed jeweller in June 1528 for 'two pairs of beads like Turkeseys with gaudies and small bedestones of gold'. In the following December, Peter Romains received £198 for jewels on 17 December, Guillim Otene 641 crowns and Alvard Plumer 201 crowns for a variety of jewels.[167] A year later, Sir Francis Bryan was reimbursed £22 10*s* for a pearl that the king bought from a Frenchman in the retinue of the papal ambassador.[168]

Henry actively encouraged foreign merchants dealing in jewels to come to England. He granted these men special licences. For example, in April 1524, Nicoluccio Ninacciesi and John Lengram received licences to import jewels, provided that 'the king shall have the first choice'.[169] While presenting your wares in person was the most likely way to secure a sale, other methods were also employed. In 1546 Stephen Vaughan, Henry's agent in Antwerp, sent Secretary Paget a water colour of an 'owche' that was for sale and being offered to the king. Vaughan felt that 'the time is unmeet to pester the King with jewels, who already has more than most of the Princes in Christendom and therefore, although I told him (John Carolo) that I would send the pattern to the king, I send it only to you'.[170] The water colour depicts a pendant with a central table-cut diamond held by a satyr and a nymph and set in a scrollwork border with a pendant pearl. When all else failed a timely gift might work, as indicated by Chamberlain's letter to Paget dated 18 December 1545, in which he observed that 'when Borone the myllener could not agree with the King about the price of certain jewels, he gave them and hath had in licences double the value'.[171]

Most of the king's jewels were kept in the removing coffers or a series of coffers at the Tower or one of the leading royal houses. In 1528 a list was drawn up of the king's jewels 'in certain boxes and coffers' and during 1532–33 'a booke of iewelles delyuered by the kinges hyghnes at sondrie tymes unto Master Crumwell master and treasourer of hys iewelles in the xxiiij yere of hys most gracious regne'.[172] However, the pieces particularly liked by Henry were retained by the groom of the stool. A selection of the king's personal jewels were delivered to Henry Norris, the most important of which were nine carcans, including 'a Carkayne of hartes and a hande ar euery ende holding a device of a goodly balasse garnisshed with fyve perlis and iij diamontes and oon faire hanging perle'.[173] However, it is evident that sometimes some of these items were left at a particular royal house. On 21 September 1532 Henry Norris sent the king at Hampton Court the seven carcans, including the one described above and a gold chain, from Greenwich.[174]

The later Middle Ages saw the increased availability of a broader range of gem stones and advances in stone cutting from the of mirror or table cutting in the fourteenth century and a shift from the use of enamel to gem stones. New fashions in jewellery spread from Italy to northern Europe. Highly innovative designs were also supplied by artists such as Hans Holbein (Fig. 19.9).[175] Figurative jewellery depicting religious and classical figures was prized and cameos became increasingly popular. Alessandro de Medici sent his cameo portrait, which had been cut by Domenico del Polo, to Francis I. Francis I then retained an Italian cameo cutter in his service, and from 1515 that post was held by Matteo del Nassano.[176] Henry also employed a cameo cutter, Richard Astyll, and several cameos depicting Henry alone or with his son may be Astyll's work.[177] Equally, jewels decorated with or in the form of initials were very popular. In 1515 Henry gave his sister Mary a double A brooch to be reset as an M.[178] Holbein's portrait of Jane Seymour depicted her wearing an IHS pendant: 'a Ihesus furnysshed with xxxij Dyamountes and three perles pendaunt' (2636) (Pls VIA and VIB).[179] In his small panel portrait the king (Pl. IC) wears a long gold chain made up from twisted links alternating with Hs and hanging from it is a round pendant.

The regalia apart, the most striking items of jewellery owned by Henry consisted of the ornate jewelled collars of the type depicted in the portrait of the king in the Galleria Nazionale, Rome. His collar was made up of alternating links of large red stones, possibly rubies and pairs of large rubies (Fig. 1.4). One of the king's collars was described by Edward Hall in 1539: 'he ware in baudricke wyse a coller of such Balystes and Perle that few men euer saw the lyke.'[180] These collars were a symbol of kingship and Henry's contemporaries also had them. Francis I owned a collar of 11 large diamonds, pointed and table-cut, alternating with friar's knots of pearls.[181] The collars were invariably worn in combination with a number of other pieces, which could form part of a set or parure, jewels that were designed to be worn together.[182]

Not surprisingly, more inventories of the king's jewels survive than for his clothes. Typical of these lists is one of the king's jewels then in the keeping of Sir William Compton, compiled on 6 October 1519. It is headed by a baldrick of gold with nine balases placed between angels and 36 pearls weighing 99 oz (2.8 kg) and a gold chain made gable fashion weighing 122 oz (3.4 kg).[183] The value of his jewellery was primarily in the metal and the gem stones used, and good records of their whereabouts were essential. However, much of Henry's jewellery was remade to keep abreast of current fashion and to provide the king with variety. If the materials were durable, the settings were often transient. On 18 January 1526 a group of jewels were delivered to Robert Amadas at Eltham for repair and modification. The list consisted of a baldrick weighing 98¾ oz (2.7 kg), three collars weighing 88 oz (2.5 kg), 55½ oz (1.6 kg) and 48⅜ oz (1.4 kg) respectively, a girdle of 63½ oz (1.8 kg) and a chain of 124½ oz (3.5 kg).[184] In February 1535 Ralph Sadler and Stephen Vaughan listed the precious stones, pearls and gold recently delivered by the king to Cornelius Hayes, the royal goldsmith.[185] This included 29 balaces, 54 sapphires, four engraved carnelians, 11 jacinths, nine rubies with a total weight of 5 oz less 3½ demi-weight (0.14 kg); 60 great pearls and 440 small and great pearls of another sort.

The use of jewels on the king's clothes

A significant number of the king's garments, especially those made for special occasions, were heavily decorated with jewels and metal thread embroidery. The level of embellishment is indicated in a list of nine items delivered on 16 November 1534 to Thomas Alvard, the first keeper of Whitehall. The first entry was for a gown of purple damask, guarded with purple velvet and embroidered with gold cord and fringe. In addition 'he shall receyve set in botons of gold six score and ten dyamoundes and apon the gard abought all the said gown and on the slevys of flowers of perle set in gold in euery flower four perles syx score and elevyn flowers'.[186] Gem stones could be incorporated into buttons and flowers as above or a range of other fancy shapes as the following entries from the 1547 inventory indicate:

> Cxxx trueloves of golde euerie of theym having iiij perles takin frome garmentes of the king that dead is' (2164).
> lxx peescoddes of perles in euerie peescodde iij peerles takin likewise frome garmentes (2166).

These ornaments, made in large quantities, were placed on the sleeves, guards and body of the garments. However, they were essentially ephemeral decoration. Henry must have celebrated Shrove Tuesday 1546 wearing specially decorated clothes because there is an entry in the 1547 inventory which records 'lxij knottes of perles in euerie knott iij perles lacking one whiche was loste frome the kinges bodie on shrove tewesday last takin likewise frome the garmentes' (2165). While these materials were durable, there was no intention to keep the pieces in their settings for long or on the same garment. The underlying wish was for change and novelty. It was easy to meet this wish as labour was cheap in comparison to the materials which the king provided to his goldsmiths and jewellers. This process of consistent recycling was promoted by the ever-fashion-conscious monarch. One of the striking features of the 1542 inventory of Whitehall is the relative paucity of items of dress listed there. Of these, many lacked their jewels which had been removed and sent to the king. For example:

> oone Gowne of purple Satten furred with Pampilion / the Sleves and border set with oone hundred and thertye diamondes set oone Gowne of purple Satten furred in golde and a hundred thertye and oone Clusters of Peerle Like wise set in golde / and in every cluster is foure great Peerles [1].
> RM: Extra all the diamondes and pearles with the gold . . . and deliuered to the kinges Majesties owne handes vj^{ti} Augustii Anno xxxviij^{vo}

The gem stones were often set into collets or box-shaped settings in order to attach them to clothing: 'x Dyamountes sett in collettes of golde' (2113), 'a garnet in a Collet of siluer gilt' (2801) and 'a great Saphire sett in a Collet of Leade cutt in squares' (3677). They were stored either stitched to cloth as in the case of 'twoo yelowe Clothes having sewed vppon them Ciiij^{xx}j Diamountes of sondrie sortes sett in collettes of gold and lv Rubies of sondrie sortes sett likewise in <collettes of> golde all which were takin frome garmentes' (2169) or wrapped in 'a pece of white Sarcenette conteignenge certein lose seede perles' (3443).

This use of jewels to embellish male clothing reached a peak in the first half of the sixteenth century. It is shown to good effect in Holbein's panel portrait of Henry (Pl. Ic): 12 rubies set in gold are arranged in three rows of four on the front of his doublet, and there are another four rubies on his sleeve, in addition to the gold ornaments on his gown, one of which is visible on his right shoulder. In the second half of the century, while embroidery remained a significant means of decoration, gem stones were worn set in jewellery. As the century progressed, jewels placed directly on clothing shifted to the female wardrobe, as typified by the clothes of Elizabeth I and Catherine de Medici.[187]

Material choices: textiles fit for a king

The marginalia on the 1542 inventory besides the listings for the silk store at Whitehall reveal the quantities of cloth issued between 1542 and the king's death five years later. Table 6.5 lists the cloth supplied to Henry VIII and, while some of the fabric may have been used for furnishings rather than clothing or clothing for favoured members of the privy chamber, it is clear that he personally received a large range of types of silk and in a broad range of colours. It can be calculated that he got 7,404 yards (6,770 m) of silk over five years or about 1,500 yards (1,371.6 m) a year.

The extant accounts reveal evidence of how fabrics were selected for Henry VIII and how his tailor created a wardrobe of suitable magnificence. The fabrics chosen were expensive, purchased in large quantities and in a wide variety of colours. They were velvet, satin, damask and textiles with metal thread including cloth of gold and silver, tissue and tinsel. The clerks who compiled the wardrobe book on behalf of Worsley were very cognisant of many subtle variations in the types of cloth of gold and silver, both in terms of weave and the type of metal thread. Worsley's wardrobe book recorded a total

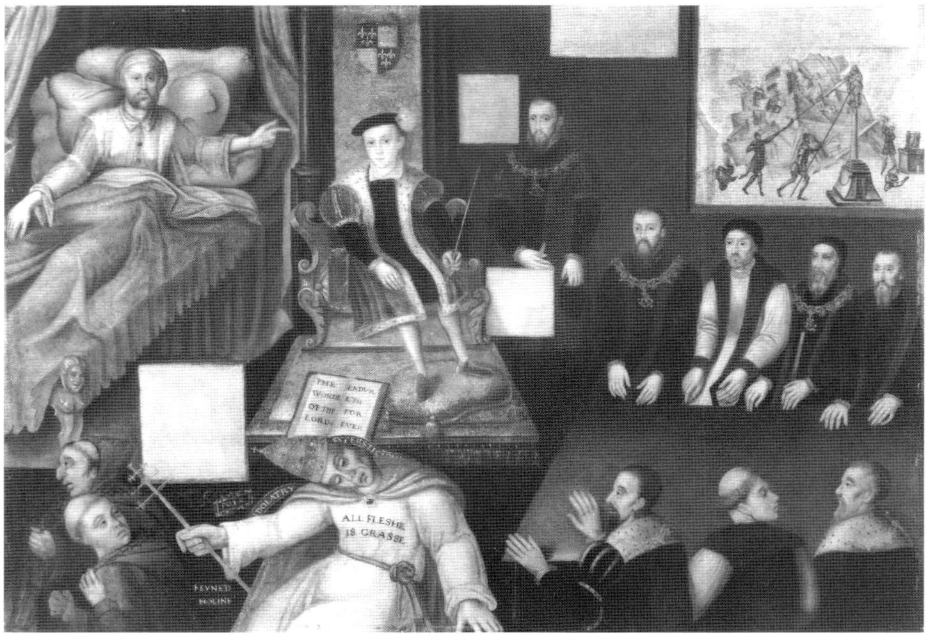

7.1 *Henry VIII's boxwood rosary, consisting of a cross, ten Ave beads and a Pater Noster, © The Devonshire Collection, Chatsworth. Reproduced by permission of the Chatsworth Settlement Trustees*

7.2 *Edward VI and the Pope, unknown artist, c. 1548–49. National Portrait Gallery, London (NPG 4165)*

fixed [he] went to Greenwich, and met the King as he was issuing forth to go to mass'.[6] Afterwards, he might dine in public (Fig. 13.1) and then meet with the privy council.

An individual's Sunday best could be worn on other special days. On 16 November 1501, two days after the marriage of Prince Arthur and Catherine of Aragon, Henry VII heard mass at St Paul's cathedral, 'accompanyed wyth many noblys and Gentylmen yn Rigth sumptuous apparayll & chaungid from the Soneday apparayll, yood unto the palays & there dynyd'.[7] Many Sundays had additional significance in the liturgical calendar as in the case of Trinity Sunday which fell on the Sunday after Pentecost. The household ordinances noted that 'Trinity Sonday is the churche holyday of the kinges howse and that day the king goeth a procession and every sergeant officer in the howse carieth a banner at procession'.[8]

Easter Sunday was held in especially high regard. On Easter Saturday the king was present for the hallowing of the font and he had his best sword carried before him as he went in procession. The king processed again on Easter Sunday and then 'a carpet must be redy for the king and quene to crepe to the crosse'. The carpet was then removed and the courtiers crept to the cross.[9] The significance of celebrating Easter wearing your best clothes is illustrated in 1538 when the Princess Mary asked whether she should wear mourning for Jane Seymour or not. When given permission to wear what she liked, Mary pressed Cromwell to obtain her father's approval for her to wear 'her whiten taffaty edged with velvet, which used to be to his own liking, whenever he saw her grace, and suiteth to this joyful feast of our Lord's holy rising from the dead'.[10]

Days of estate, crown-wearing days and days for wearing purple and scarlet

Court ritual focused around the high feast days of the liturgical year.[11] Observing these festivals correctly was a defining part of medieval kingship. On Candlemas (2 February) 1540 the French ambassador recorded how Henry had dismissed him 'until after dinner and [he] went to hear his two masses as he does every feast day'.[12] In turn, the king's role in these events was defined by specific clothes and accessories in order to create a sense of tradition and ritual. The type and colour of the robes worn by the king on the different occasions were outlined in ordinances such as the *Ryalle Book*, which recorded the ceremonial at the English court.[13] Henry VII's ordinances noted that 'The King goeing in procession in a day of estate in his robes royall ... the Chamberlaine bearinge the King's trayne'.[14] On New Year's day 1488 Henry VII wore 'a riche Gowne' under his robes.[15] More specifically, the household ordinances stated that on the feast of the Circumcision or New Year's day which was a day of estate, 'the King ought to weare his kirtle, his circote, and his pane of armes and if his pane bee 5 ermins deepe, a Duke's ought to bee but fouer, and an Earle's three: and the King to have on his head that day his hatt of estate, his sworde borne before him'.[16] The other days of estate were Candlemas (2 February), the Assumption (15 August), the Nativity of St John the Baptist (24 August) and Holy Rood day (14 September) when the king wore a cap of estate and partial robes.[17]

Crown wearing was also associated with the major religious festivals. These events were intended to evoke the memory of the monarch's coronation and the legitimacy of his rule, and in order to do so publicly the king wore his crown and robes of estate. Richard III's crown-wearing ceremonies were witnessed and described by the author of the *Crowland Chronicle*: 'after the Christmas festival had been solemnly held in the palace of Westminster, the king appeared on Epiphany wearing his crown ... as though at his original coronation.'[18] In the fifteenth century the crown-wearing days were Christmas day, the two feasts of St Edward the Confessor (5 January and 13 October), Epiphany (6 January), Easter, Whitsun, All Saints (1 November), and the anniversary of the monarch's coronation.[19] The household ordinances stated that on Twelfth night, which was a crown-wearing day:

> the King ought to goe crowned and in his robes royall, kirtle, sircote, his furred hudd about his necke, and his mantle with a long trayne and his lace before him, and his ermines upon his armes, of gould sett ful of riche stones with balaces, saphires, rubies, emeralds, and pearles; this ought to be hallowed and noe temporall man to touch it but onely the King; and an esquire of the body to bring it in a faire kerchieffe, and the King to putt them on himselfe.[20]

In 1488 on Twelfth night eve 'the King [Henry VII] went to the Evensong in his Surcoot outward, with Tabert Sleves, the Cappe of Astate on his Hede and the Hode aboute his Showlders, in Doctors wise. And that Nyght there was no Lorde in Roobes, saving the King'.[21] On the following day all the nobility wore their robes of estate and the king and queen wore their crowns. The spectacle of such occasions is reinforced by a payment made in January for setting up and taking down a scaffold for people to stand upon 'for the syght of the kynges bankyt vpon the xijth daye at nyght' at Greenwich.[22]

The feast of the Epiphany marked the Adoration of the Three Kings or Magi. Since the reign of Edward III, English kings had emulated the magi by making offerings of frankincense, gold and myrrh to the high altar, and Henry VII and Henry VIII continued this practice.[23] The household ordinances dictated that 'a propre pece of yellow sarsenet to enclose therin v nolbes of goulde' should be delivered to the gentleman usher, 'the Thus aforenamed in redde sarsenet and the myrre in white sarsenet eche of them to the michelnes other the quantetie of a tennis Ball or of a pairs ball and bound with a thredd of Sylk'.[24] Epiphany was also the anniversary of the baptism of Christ by John the Baptist. As such it was a significant day and other events could be celebrated on this auspicious day. In January 1540 the French ambassador told the constable of France that 'Tomorrow, Twelfth Day, this duke of Bavaria is to be made a knight of the Order of England'.[25]

According to Henry VII's ordinances there were four major feasts of the year when 'the King should weare eyther purple or redd velvett'.[26] These were Christmas day, Easter, Whitsunday and All Saints. The question as to the colour worn raises two points. First, there is the issue of whether purple meant a specific colour or a sense of royalty and splendour. Second, it suggests that royalty could be expressed by purple and red equally, and they were potentially interchangeable. On Christmas eve 1487, Henry VII 'went to the Masse of the Vygill in a riche Gowne of Purple Velwett furred with Sables'.[27] Some years later, Henry VII planned to celebrate Christmas at Westminster, but the festivities were tempered because of an outbreak of measles, and so 'The King in all this Fest wer noo Robes of Astate, but oder Gownes of riche Clothis of Gold, and in especiall, Gownes whiche was wrought by the Ladyes in the Stoolle an richely furred with Sabuls'.[28]

In general, on these days the king wore robes but no crown. Worsley's wardrobe book included a number of sets of purple clothes, including 'a Gowne of purpull tylsent furred with Ermyns a Jaquet a doblet & a payr of hose of purpull velwete enbrawderd & cutte upon white cloth of siluer with aglettes of golde' [A11] and 'a mantell of purpull tylent lyned with purpull saten' [A30]. Henry VIII was depicted dressed in red and kneeling at prayer in his closet in the *Liber Niger* of the order of the Garter. With a blue traverse behind him and a cloth of gold altar frontal before him, the king knelt on a cloth of gold cushion, dressed in a crimson fur-trimmed gown, wearing a black bonnet (Pl. IVB).

Processions involving the king formed a significant part of court ritual. They took place on Christmas day, Candlemas, Palm Sunday, Easter, Whitsunday, Trinity Sunday, Corpus Christi, the Assumption of Our Lady and All Saints. The king walked under a cloth of estate or canopy, accompanied by the leading members of the household and the nobility.[29] Up until 1540 when Corpus Christi was removed from the religious cycle, it was the principal feast of the Catholic church.[30] The significance of the feast can be seen from a payment made to Richard Justice, page of the robes to Elizabeth of York, on 23 July 1502. Justice was paid 8*d* a day for two days' travel to go from Richmond to London and back 'for a gowne of cloth of gold furred with pawmpilyon ayenst Corpus Xpi day', and 12*d* for his boat hire.[31] Although there is no record of what they wore, Henry VIII and Jane Seymour celebrated Corpus Christi with a procession to Westminster abbey on 15 June 1536. On such occasions, the host was carried under a canopy and the king's vestry included 'one Canapie of Crimsen vellet enbrodered with Ihesus for the Sacrament' (8967).[32]

The palace where Henry VIII chose to celebrate these major feasts was often highly significant.[33] It emphasises that as the reign progressed the king was increasingly based at Whitehall and at the other royal palaces close to the city such as Greenwich and Hampton Court. He chose to celebrate the majority of the major feast days at Greenwich (29%), although Whitehall (13%), Windsor (6%), Hampton Court (5%) and Richmond (3%) all played their part.[34] His proximity to the city meant that Henry could use or commandeer city pageantry. The king and his advisors also used the city and the Tower as venues for demonstrations of royal authority.

Provision made by the great wardrobe for Candlemas, Palm Sunday and Maundy Thursday

Each year the great wardrobe could make special provision for the king on three feast days: Candlemas, Palm Sunday and Maundy Thursday. The relative significance of these occasions can be gauged by comparing the cost and regularity of

Table 7.1: *The cost of Candlemas, Palm Sunday and Maundy Thursday under Henry VII and Henry VIII*

Year	The Taper on Candlemas	Palm Sunday	The Maundy
1498–99	~	9s 6d	£39 14s 0d
1502–03	~	~	£43 11s 6½d
1504–05	~	~	£44 18s 9d
1505–06	~	~	£47 15s 2d
1510–11	~	7s	£38 3s 3d
1516–17	14s	~	£54 9s 5d
1517–18	14s 7d	~	£59 2s
1521–22	4s	14s 3d	£68 14s 3d
1523–25	4s	~	£72 17s 10½d
1526–27	4s	~	£68 12s 5d
1527–28	4s	12s 6d	£69 18s 11½d
1530–31	6s 8d	48s 8d	£71 13s 1d
1531–32	7s 4d	~	£74 14s 6d
1533–34	~	53 4d	£79 8s 10d
1535–36	13s 4d	~	£84 3s 5d
1537–38	7s 2d	28s	£94 10s 4d
1538–39	7s	~	£108 11s 7d
1543–45	7s	~	£143 13s 7½d

the warrants issued to the great wardrobe (Table 7.1). Of these, the cost of the velvet used to wrap the candles of the king and his family on Candlemas and Palm Sunday and any associated items were small, never exceeding 53*s* 4*d*. These warrants were also the least consistently issued, although it is possible that in some or all of the years where the warrants are missing, the velvet was supplied by the wardrobe of the robes. In contrast the cost of the maundy provision was never less than £38 3*s* 3*d* and it increased annually, rising as high as £143 13*s* 7½*d* by the last extant set of Henry VIII's accounts.[35] While the provision for the king's robe remained the same and the price kept stable, the growing cost reflected the annual increase in the number of poor men given clothing.

Candlemas (2 February) marked the end of winter.[36] More importantly, the mass of the purification, popularly known as Candlemas, fell 40 days after Christmas. The service celebrated the Purification of the Virgin Mary after the birth of Christ, although as Mary was free from original sin such a ceremony was technically unnecessary. However, according to Simeon, the feast served to acknowledge Christ as the Messiah, who was the 'light to lighten the Gentiles'.[37] The ceremony also had a parallel with the churching of women after they had given birth. More specifically in this context, the churching of a queen was consciously compared with the purification of the queen of heaven.[38] Central to the mass was the presence of candles. The congregation placed tapers and candles before the high altar, where they were blessed, sprinkled with holy water and sensed with incense.

Even though it was quintessentially a female feast, the significance of the Virgin Mary to the liturgy meant that it was a significant day for reinforcing the position of the monarchy. Henry VII celebrated Candlemas 1490 by processing from the chapel at Greenwich to Westminster 'whiche hallis and alsoo the king chambres wer that day as Richely beseen and hanged as ever I saw them'.[39] Henry VIII's taper would have been carried by his lord chamberlain, who walked at his right hand as they entered the Chapel Royal.[40] As the household ordinances stated, 'Item on Candlemasse day, the Chamberlaine, or a Baron or Earle, may beare the King's raperie, goeing on the King's right hand, against the steward goeing in procession'.[41] The great wardrobe made an annual provision of silk velvet to wrap the tapers of the king and queen. On 28 January 1511 purple velvet was supplied to John Kettleby, sergeant of the chandlery, to garnish the taper of the king an the queen and crimson velvet for the king's 'son the prince' and the princess of Castile.[42] The distinction made by the provision of purple and crimson velvet, denoted the precedence of the king and his queen over other members of the royal family. It was also a day when the king was formally dressed. On Candlemas 1490 it was noted that 'The King was that Day in a riche Gowne of Purple, pirled with Gold, fured with Sables'.[43]

The king came down into the chapel from his closet 'and the carpet and cushion layd and spredd . . . the kinge kneleth . . . the said erle knele at the king right hand; and when the king hathe kissed the patent of the challis the erle shall kysse the taper and then delyver it unto the kinges handes and there the kings shall offer it'.[44] If the king celebrated Candlemas at Windsor, then he was required to hear mass in the Garter chapel accompanied by any Garter knights who were at court, dressed in their robes.[45]

On Palm Sunday the priest blessed the palms or branches brought by the congregation in remembrance of the palms spread before Christ on the entry into Jerusalem.[46] The blessing of palms was widespread, but the full service was generally restricted to cathedrals, urban parishes and the royal chapel. A warrant for the chapel royal dated 12 March 1532 ordered a yard of 'right purple velvet' for garnishing the king's palm and a yard of 'right crimson' velvet to garnish the palms of the queen and the princess Mary.[47] Henry VIII observed this practice to the end of his reign, as indicated by 'a warrant for velvet for your Majesty's Palme' being granted at the suit of the sergeant of the vestry in May 1546.[48] Having processed, the ordinances stated that 'as the king cometh by the crosse in the hall he leavith his palme there'.[49]

In addition, the gentlemen ushers were required to approach three or four of the knights at court 'to be ready to beare the canapie over the sacrament, the which the kinge almoner ought to beare that daie in procession if he be present that daie in courte'.[50] As on other important days when the king came down into the chapel, the gentlemen ushers were required to place a carpet and cushion for the king to kneel on.

Maundy Thursday, sometimes called Sheer Thursday, commemorated the Last Supper, where Christ washed the feet of his disciples.[51] Maundy Thursday was an occasion for crown wearing and it was a day of mourning. As such, blue was an appropriate colour for the monarch to wear. According to the *Great Chronicle* Henry VI wore 'a long blew goune of velvet' on Maundy Thursday 1471.[52] The chronicler went on to observe that this was 'as thouwth he hadd noo moo to change with' so making the occasion 'moe lyker a play than the shewyng of a prynce to wynne mennys hertys'. Notwithstanding these comments Henry VI was dressed appropriately for Maundy Thursday.[53] Violet was also associated with mourning, and Stow noted in his *Survey of London* that in '1485. The 1st of Henry VII, the mayor, aldermen, sheriffs and commonality, all clothed in violet, as in a mourning colour, met the king at Shoreditch, and conveyed him to Paul's Church, where he offered his banners'.[54] In 1503 Henry VII wore blue for his Maundy Thursday observances. This was the year that Elizabeth of York died and he wore the colour of royal mourning as a touching final tribute to his queen.

A sword was borne before the king on his way to mass on Maundy Thursday. At three o'clock in the afternoon the king and queen went to the chapel again, this time without a sword or mace, and there, attended by the bishop and dean or subdean, he washed the altars. While this was happening, the vice-chamberlain or a squire for the body held the king's cap. Afterwards the king returned to his closet and the queen to hers. 'After that is done the king goeth into his closet or into the wardrobe of the Robes and there he makith redy. And so cometh downe into the hall and the Chappell synging before hym.'[55]

In spite of their veneration for Henry VI, neither Henry VII nor Henry VIII wore blue on Maundy Thursday — 1503 was exceptional. The two Tudor kings preferred a gown made from 4½ yards (4.1 m) of violet wool, dyed in grain, and trimmed with marten fur. A new gown was made for the king each year, suggesting that the gown was given away after the ceremony. The king distributed gowns of russet wool with hoods and a pair of shoes to one poor man for each year of his life. In addition, the almoner was required to 'make his grace redie with his towel and apron' to wash the feet of the poor, while the ushers were 'to be abowt the king with perfumes'.[56]

In 1532 the goods needed for the royal maundy were ordered on two warrants dated 12 March. The first authorised the delivery of cloth, hooks and velvet to Richard Green, sergeant of the vestry. This included a length of purple velvet used to wrap the king's palm and 'for the washing of the altars on Maundy Thursday'.[57] This provision appeared in other years.[58] The second ordered the king's maundy.[59] The annual warrants also provide details about the travel arrangements made to deliver the maundy textiles to the king. One from 1543 included provision for carriage from London to St James's palace.[60]

The provision for Henry VIII's maundy ceremonies was consistent in every year bar one. The king's personal warrant dated 6 January 1539 included three items to be made for Thomas Cromwell, lord privy seal, 'for the king's maundy'. Cromwell was provided with a jacket of black velvet embroidered with cord and furred with squirrels and sables, a doublet of black satin, embroidered and fringed and the vents lined with the same satin and a cloak of marble coloured cloth (his own livery colour) guarded with russet velvet, the vents and collar lined with satin and fastened with silk buttons.[61] This special provision is an indication of Cromwell's political supremacy at this time.

The Tudor queens consort also distributed maundy.[62] Elizabeth of York's maundy ceremonies were modelled closely on those of her husband, the chief difference being that she distributed clothing and money to poor women. On 24 March 1502 Richard Pain, the queen's almoner, provided 114*s* 1*d* as money for 37 poor women for her maundy. Richard Smith received a late payment of £15 13*s* 4*d* for their clothing on 1 December 1502, and a month later Rult, the queen's almoner, was paid 15*s* 2*d* for 37 pairs of shoes.[63] At the same time Elizabeth gave lengths of cloth to the nurse 'to the prince brother to the queen', Edward V, and the sister of Sir Roger Cotton.

Catherine of Aragon's accounts provide further details.[64] In March 1520 the queen held her maundy ceremony at Greenwich, and 12*d* was spent on carriage of cloth and other items from London. Like the king, she wore a gown made from 3¼ yards (2.9 m) of violet cloth in grain. However, unlike the king's robe which was furred with martens, Catherine's robe was lined with 13 timbers and 10 skins of 'fine grey lossee skins' costing £5 14*s* 7*d*, with the furring cost a further 13*s* 4*d*. She was also provided with a linen apron and towel (4*s*) and the same for her almoner (2*s* 8*d*).[65] Cloth gowns and smocks were provided for 35 poor women at a cost of £16 9*s* 5*d*.[66]

After the Dunstable judgment permitting Henry VIII's separation from her, Catherine, no longer deemed queen, was not allowed to distribute maundy. Yet she tried to. In 1534 Chapuys remarked to the emperor that 'Your majesty may imagine the severity used towards the Queen in other things, when on Holy Thursday she was not allowed to hold her Maundy to the poor according to custom and orders have been given not to allow poor people to come near her, because the Lady says that the alms she has been accustomed to give have attracted the love of the people'.[67] A year later two of her staff informed Cromwell on 22 March that 'we have just learnt that the Princess Dowager intends to keep a Maundy, in spite of the King's order of last year to the contrary. She says she will keep it secretly in her chamber, and wishes to know if she may go to the parish church, where we think she will try to keep it if prevented from doing so privately'.[68] On consultation, Henry agreed to Catherine's observing a maundy, but stipulated that she could do so, not as a queen, but 'as the King's grandame did, and many houses of religion do now'.[69]

The evidence for Catherine Parr's maundy celebrations gives a good indication of the range of goods required. In April 1544 her almoner purchased one covered tub 2*s* 8*d*, three other tubs 6*s*, one closed basket 16*d*, two other baskets 2*s*, four bowls 4*s*, two half tubs 2*s*, boat hire 12*d* and flowers for the maundy 3*s* 4*d*.[70] Catherine Parr continued to observe her maundy after Henry's death. Her accounts running from March 1547 record a payment to 'Mistress Bartholomew for linen for the queen's last Maundy' costing £8 11*d* along with 36 purses costing 18*d* with 3*s* in each purse, coming to a total of £5 9*s* 6*d*.[71]

Days of mourning

The services held on certain days in the liturgical year, such as Ash Wednesday, Good Friday, All Saints' day (1 November) and All Souls' day (2 November), commemorated the dead. On these days the king wore blue, while the rest of the court wore black or they wore sombre colours, and the king's chamber or chapel was furnished with blue.[72] At the time of his coronation Henry VII was provided with 'xj yerdes of

jewels and cloth and clothing given away from Elizabeth I's wardrobe of the robes between 1561 and 1585.[105]

Perfuming the king, his clothes and his rooms

Perfumes were used to fragrance the king's body, clothes and napery as well as to scent his apartments.[106] The Black Book recorded that the officers of the robes played a key part in this process and that they were supplied with perfumes by the king's apothecary so 'that the kinges robes, dublettes, sheets and shertes be fumyd by all the yere'.[107] Scenting the body was achieved either by applying perfume directly to the skin, wearing a perfume-filled pomander or taking a scented bath. While Tudor women could have a pomander hanging from their girdle (Fig. 8.4), men also carried them.[108] The pomander could combine perfume with medicinal qualities. Cavendish described how Wolsey held in his hand 'a very fayer Orrynge, whereof the mete or substaunce with in was taken owt and fylled uppe agayn with the part of a Sponge, wherin was vynegar and other confeccions agaynst the pestylente Ayers'.[109] In contrast, contemporary etiquette books such as John Russell's *Boke of Nurture* describe how the bath tub should be draped with linen sheets 'euery shete full of flowers & herbis'. After washing, the bather was rinsed with rose water.[110] Henry had a bath house at the palace of Whitehall and special linen garments to wear while bathing.[111]

8.4 *Early sixteenth-century English gold pomander or musk ball decorated with pearls. 54.124, reproduced by courtesy of the Trustees of the British Museum*

The royal gardeners supplied some of fragrant plants used to perfume the king's clothes and napery. However, they could not meet all the needs of the court. Millicent Aylesbury, widow, supplied six dozen bags of white fustian weighing 14 lb (6.3 kg) filled with sweet powder for the king's sheets at 3*s* 4*d* the lb, and a bushel of dried rose petals with lavender to the king's removing wardrobe of the beds in November 1546.[112] Edward VI's privy purse accounts for 1550–51 indicate that such purchases were not usual and that the robes also used some perfumes of a better quality: ten dozen bags made from 10 yards (9.1 m) of taffeta at 3*s* 4*d* the yard containing 160 oz (4.5 kg) of fine powder made from 'ambergrese muske and swett at xvj*d* the oz', four great bags of sarsenet filled with rose leaves and sweet powder (20*s*), 12 dozen fustian bags filled with sweet powder (60*s*) and three bushels of dried rose leaves and lavender (15*s*), coming to £17 7*s* 8*d* in total.[113] Apothecaries traded in perfumes as well as medicines, as indicated by Catherine Parr's accounts. The bill of her apothecary, Thomas Alsop, came to £54 7*s* 5*d*. Of this, £7 14*s* 2*d* was spent on rose water, damask water and other stilled waters, while 'perfumes and all things belonging to the same' cost £3 11*s* 7*d*.[114] The 1547 inventory listed several perfumes including ambergris (2452), box (1930), cinnamon (3256, 9606) and balm or balsam (2407), along with 'a paper Declaring thuse thereof' (2404).

Clothes and accessories could also be scented. Perfumed gloves were fashionable at this period, and Henry had several pairs in his possession, including 'two paire of swete gloves garneshed with peerle damaske golde and veanice golde lyned with Satten the one white thother crymsen' (3430). While small pomanders were worn hanging from a girdle, perfume pans were used to scent whole rooms or suits of chambers.[115] A coffer belonging to Lady Margaret Beaufort contained three pomanders and 'a box with fumys' which had been amended to read 'fumygacon' in another hand.[116]

Rooms were also heavily scented, as Catherine Parr's accounts made clear. In July 1543 she paid for 'fine perfumes' for her chambers at Hampton Court, Guildford and Oking.[117] In the following months perfumes were bought for each house she removed to including Hanworth, the More, Grafton, Woodstock and Langley.[118] The scale on which perfumes were used at the Henrician court can be gauged from the purchases made for the king's revels in the autumn of 1527. Ellis, a painter, supplied 'Swete waters Swete powders parfumys' which included 42 gallons of sweet waters for the conduit costing £10 10*s*, a ½ lb (0.2 kg) of sweet powders to put amongst the king's napery priced at 6*s* 8*d* and perfumes to put under the pageant for 6*s* 8*d*.[119]

The physical context: buildings for storage and rooms for dressing

The office of the robes had a removing wardrobe which travelled with the king, and standing wardrobes at the Tower, the palace of Westminster until the fire in 1512, at Greenwich until the mid 1530s and at Whitehall after then. A sense of the scale of the wardrobe buildings and their location can be gleaned from the building accounts. For example, in January 1533 the accounts for the Tower refer to work being carried out in 'the tower in the king's garden next to the wardrobe of the robes' giving a hint as to the wardrobe's location. Other references include the provision of planks laid over the top of the window made in the new wardrobe, 'a new frame now made a wardrobe for the king' measuring 10 by 24 feet (3.1 by 7.3 m) by carpenters, bricklayers underpinning the 'wardrobe with robes', plasters plastering two new gable ends in the wardrobe, repairs made to the stonework and the joiners were paid for making new coffers.[120] The wardrobe of the robes also had space allocated for their use at the other principal houses where the removing wardrobe would store their chests while the king was in residence. In the building accounts for June and July 1534, Robert Hobbes, keeper of the More, paid *6d* for the repair of the master key to the door of the rooms used by the robes.[121]

The rooms occupied by the wardrobe of the robes needed to be dry and would have had a fire place to allow the officers to air the clothes and to warm them in winter. On 1 March 1517, James Worsley received £6 for 'new making' the hearths of two chimneys in the standing wardrobe of the robes in the Tower.[122] Equally, regular maintenance was necessary to keep the roofs in a good state of repair. In February and March 1536, carpenters at Windsor castle nailed down boards on the leads of the king's wardrobes and repaired the gutters, while in May to June repairs were made to the two locks and a new key was supplied for the robes, costing *4d*.[123] The wardrobe needed good security in order to prevent theft, as the king's clothes were very valuable. The key lines of defence were locks for the doors and bars for the windows. In April and May 1533, Richard Cecil was paid *2s 6d* for a large double-hoop stock lock with a hollow key for the wardrobe of the robes at Greenwich.[124] In the autumn of the following year, 116 'sodett' bars measuring 197 feet (60.5 m) in length were supplied for the new windows of the wardrobe of the robes and beds at a cost of *8s 2d*.[125]

Plenty of suitable flat storage for large, heavy garments was provided in wooden presses. On 18 October 1493 Henry VII issued orders 'to have our wardrobes of the Robes in our palois of Westminster to be transposed and made in such place there and under suche forme as oure trusty servaunt John Fligh . . . shall shewe unto you' with 'all things necessary to be provided for the robes' and 'for the pressing of theym accordingly to be made at our costs'.[126] The wardrobe of the robes was supplied with linen sheets to line the presses. In April 1511 the king's warrant included 20 ells (13.7 m) of linen cloth for a press sheet costing *20s* and it cost *16d* to make. The officers were also provided with 3 lb (1.3 kg) of oris at a price of *6s*.[127]

The 1526 Eltham Ordinances also make it clear that the officers of the wardrobe helped the king to get dressed each morning by bringing the clothes selected for that day to the door of the privy chamber:

> It is also ordered that the king's doublet, hosen, shoes, or any other garment which his pleasure shall be to weare from day to day, the gowne onely excepted, shall be honestly and cleanly brought by the yeoman of the wardrobe of the robes, or in his absence by some other of the same office, to the king's privy chamber dorre, without entring into the same; where one of the said groomes shall receive the said garments and apparelle, bringing and delivering the same to one of the six gentlemen, to be ministered unto the king's person, as shall stand with his pleasure.[128]

While the Eltham Ordinances state that the wardrobe officers did not help the king dress, with the transfer of the wardrobe staff into the privy chamber they would have dressed the king as part of their daily duties.

The development of the privy lodging at Whitehall resulted in increasing specialisation of the rooms and included the provision of a special dressing room or 'raying chamber' for the king and queen. The accounts for June to July 1531 included the provision of a new plate lock, varnished, along with staples, screws and vices for a door entering the king's library out of his dressing chamber costing *3s 4d*.[129] In the following January a payment of *13s 4d* indicates that the king's dressing room was decorated in a classical style. There was a bust over the chimney with a painted and gilded 'garland about the head'.[130] Several years later, in November to December 1535, a new key costing *6d* was bought for the queen's raying chamber door at Greenwich.[131]

The importance attached to the king's clothes and the clothes of his representatives is indicated by the provision of temporary places for them to change their clothes. When Henry VIII and Charles V met at Canterbury in 1520 'There were pytched ij Tentes a little with out the Cittie for the kyng and the emperor to chaunge them as they cam from dovor'.[132] However, it was not always possible to plan ahead. When Wolsey knew Francis I was riding to meet him, he 'was compelled to allyght in an old Chappell and there newly apparelled hyme in to more Richer apparell / And than mounted vppon a newe Mewle very richely trapped with a foote clothe & trapper of Crymmesyn veluett vppon veluett pirled with gold and ffrynged abought with a depe frynge of gold very costly'.[133]

The royal laundry

By the early sixteenth century, the significance of white, clean linen for shirts and smocks was well appreciated.[134] In 1480 the account of the washing done by Alice Shapster for Edward IV gives an indication of how much linen he owned. Her bill listed her charges for the 'for making and wasshing of xxiiij sherts and xxiiij stomachers, v dosen handcouverchieffes'.[135] In 1542 a system was formalised for the king's laundress washing Henry VIII's table linen. She was issued with four table clothes, 28 long and 28 short breakfast clothes, 28 hand towels and 144 napkins, and she was expected to clean a quarter of the linen every week.[136]

The household list for 1543 named John Whitskale as the yeoman of the laundry with a staff of four under him.[137] For Henry VIII's funeral, the officers of the laundry received black livery. Whitskale received 7 yards (6.4 m), while William

Tuke and Thome Timpley, grooms, and William Barled and John Messingre, pages, all received 4 yards (3.6 m).[138] While the yeoman and other officers of the king's laundry were male, the launderer was often female. However, this was not always the case, for example on 7 October 1509, 30*s* was paid to the queen's launderer upon his bill.[139] Even so, Henry VIII favoured female laundresses and Anne or Agnes Harris or Harrison is the best known.[140] Anne was named in the household ordinances of 1539 and her role was described in detail, including her allowance of two standards for the napery, sweet powder and carts to transport the laundry.[141] She received an annual salary of £10 but no allowance for wood, soap or 'any other thing'. This increased by £6 13*s* 4*d* on 22 March 1544, with 66*s* 8*d* 'for well serving the king' and £20 from 1 April.[142] Her post brought her other financial rewards as well. For example, on 12 July 1546 Anne was granted the Vine Garden and Mill Bank within the sanctuary of Westminster abbey.[143]

Anne washed the king's linen but not that of the boys of the privy chamber who were clothed at his expense. Four payments were made to an unnamed launderer from the king's privy purse and these all related to the laundry of 'the children of the kinges pryvat chambre', namely Mark Smeton, 'bothe the guilliams' and a child called Ralph: in September 1530 for 48*s* 4*d*, February 1531 for 14*s* 4*d*, September 1531 for 16*s* 8*d* and July 1532 for 20*s*.[144]

The Black Book specified that if there was a queen, then she should have a female laundress who was expected to be discrete.[145] Agnes Dean was appointed as laundress to Elizabeth of York and she received £3 6*s* 8*d* per annum, with 4*d* a day to cover the costs of her horse, when she accompanied the queen on her travels. In September and November 1502 Agnes received 33*s* 4*d* for a hundred days' travel expenses.[146] Shortly after Princess Mary's birth in 1516, Avys Wood was appointed as her laundress.[147] However, by 1521–22 Beatrice ap Rhys was her laundress with wages of £3 10*d*, rising to 16*s* 8*d* a quarter.[148] Beatrice's husband was a yeoman of the chamber in Mary's household, while her children received patronage from the princess.[149]

Although the king and the leading members of the nobility and ecclesiastical élite had their own launderers, when travelling they often had their washing done locally. This could be a small undertaking as in 1503, when Miles Worsley recorded a payment of 3*s* was made 'to a launder for wasshyng of my laddys clothes at Richmound'.[150] Or it could be a more long-term arrangement. When Wolsey visited in Calais in 1521 the accounts of his steward Robert Carter included a payment to Jacobyn Laak, a Calais local, for washing nine shirts on seven occasions between 24 September and 20 November at 1*d* each, coming to a total cost of 5*s* 3*d*. Laak also washed nine pairs of woollen hose at 3*d* a pair, costing 20*d*. Other payments made to Laak included 3*s* for washing six dozen of Wolsey's shirts, 'hedkerchyves pillowberes and other small clothes' and 12*d* for washing his shaving cloths.[151]

Knowledge of the appropriate cleaning techniques for clothes and accessories was important.[152] The Black Book noted that the staff of the laundry should be skilled in order to 'safly to kepe and tenderly to wasshe and preserue diligentlye the stuff for htekinges proper persone of the warderobis of beddes and robez'.[153] Accidents did occur, as indicated by a reference to eight pairs of 'new shetes for lordes' at Oatlands that were 'of iij bredethes and thre elles longe . . . be shrunk di quarter the pece' (12671). It is most likely that knowledge of appropriate cleaning techniques was passed on by word of mouth, as in the case of a letter sent at some point in the winter of 1539 by Antoinette de Saveuses to Lady Lisle. Antoinette referred to a pair of gloves that she had sent to Anne Basset, noting that 'When they are dirty one should wash them in cold water and white Spanish lye'.[154] Later in the century, published texts were available, as in the case of *A Profitable Book declaring approoved remedies to take out spottes and staines in silkes, velvets, linnen and woollon clothes*, published in London in 1583 by Leonard Mascall.[155] Unpublished manuscripts such as the Nuremberg *Kunstbuch* record fifteenth- and sixteenth-century recipes used by the nuns of the convent of St Catherine's, Nuremberg.[156]

Women were depicted washing clothes in tubs and laying cloth out to dry in a German copy of the text *Splendor Solis*

8.5 *A contemporary illustration showing various stages in the process of washing, drying and bleaching linen, from* Splendor Solis, *School of Nuremberg, c. 1531–32, MS 78 D 3, f. 31r. © Bildarchiv Preussischer Kulturbesitz, Kupferstichkabinett, Staatliche Museen zu Berlin (Joerg P. Anders)*

dating from the 1530s (Fig. 8.5).[157] In 1541 Raffe Alwood supplied 13 new metal hoops to the palace of Whitehall which were set onto 'wassshing tubes occupied within the gallery to wasshe the kynges clothes in'.[158] Some of the finishing techniques for the linen items cleaned in the laundry required specialist equipment such as a linen smoother or calendar. While such items are not specifically referred to in the household ordinances, they have been found in archaeological contexts and so could have been in use within the royal household.[159] It is evident from the items bought from Christian Bell in September 1543 that the queen's launderer undertook more tasks than just washing and bleaching. Bell provided a chafer to starch with (2*s*), an ash bag (12*d*), a sleek stone (8*d*) and a pewter basin to starch in (12*d*).[160] The same is true of Princess Mary. In July 1544 Mary's accounts included a payment of 8*d* for 'ij lb of starche for mistress launder'.[161]

Notes

1 See above, p. xviii.
2 *LP* IV.ii, 4449.
3 D. R. Starkey, 'The King's Privy Chamber, 1485–1547' (unpublished PhD thesis, Cambridge, 1973), pp. 268–72; and Hayward, 'Repositories', pp. 134–56.
4 See below, p. 248.
5 *CPR 1485–94*, p. 58.
6 *CPR 1494–1509*, p. 348. On 22 March 1504 Fligh was succeeded by Robert Hasilrigge, groom of the robes.
7 *CPR 1485–94*, p. 257. This post was granted to William Edwards, page of the robes; *CPR 1494–1509*, p. 368.
8 *CPR 1485–94*, p. 334.
9 *CPR 1494–1509*, p. 111.
10 Ibid., p. 351; also see Bindoff, *House of Commons*, III, pp. 335–36.
11 *LP* I.i, 94.94 and 193.
12 BL MS Stowe 146, f. 97r (*LP* I.ii, 2344).
13 TNA E101/418/5, no. 30 (*LP* I.ii, 3530).
14 *LP* II.i, 622.
15 *LP* III.i, 716.20.
16 *LP* IV.i, 1939.
17 TNA E101/417/6, f. 89 (*LP* I.i, 894).
18 TNA SP1/229, f. 104 (*LP* I.i, 1549).
19 *LP* III.i, 102.7 and 716.20.
20 *LP* III.i, 854.14.
21 *LP* III.ii, 2016.8.
22 *LP* V, p. 303.
23 *LP* IV.i, 1939.
24 *LP* IV.iii, 6243.
25 *LP* VI, 1195.7; *LP* XII.ii, 617.2.
26 Bindoff, *House of Commons*, II, pp. 27–29; Hayward, *1542 Inventory*, pp. 55–80; and N. P. Sil, 'Sir Anthony Denny: a Tudor servant in office', *Renaissance and Reformation*, 8 (1984), pp. 190–201.
27 *LP* X, 226.33–35.
28 *LP* XIII.ii, 734.10.
29 Bindoff, *House of Commons*, I, p. 603.
30 *LP* III.ii, 1451.15.
31 *LP* III.ii, 2074.5.
32 *LP* IV.ii, 4687.27.
33 *LP* XIV.ii, 781.
34 *LP* XIX.i, 1035.117.
35 *LP* XXI.i, 1442.
36 At the time of Edward VI's coronation, the officers of the robes were Robert Robotsham, yeoman, Walter Abraye, groom, Hugh Walley, page and Anthony Walker, clerk; TNA LC2/3.i, p. 97. Red livery was also given to Henry VIII's officers: Richard Cecil, yeoman, Thomas Sternold, groom, John Rowland, page; LC2/3.ii, p. 7.
37 Cecil and Sternold were left 100 marks, while Rowland was left £50. These sums were revised to £20; *LP* XXI.ii, 634.
38 Seven men held the office of clerk of the robes. The timing suggests that several of them only held the post for a short period: Laurence Gower (27 February 1511, *LP* I.i, 707); John Porth (1 June 1511, *LP* I.i, 804.1); John Plofield (April 1529, *LP* V, p. 311); John Briggs (April 1530, *LP* V, p. 318); James Joskyn (5 September 1537, *LP* XII.ii, 796.6); Nicholas Bristow (10 January 1541, *LP* XVI, 503) and Edmund Pigeon (June 1544, *LP* XIX.i, 812.97).
39 *LP* I.i, 804.
40 *LP* II.ii, p. 1473.
41 *LP* II.ii, p. 1474.
42 *LP* II.ii, p. 1478.
43 *LP* III.ii, pp. 1538–39.
44 *LP* III.ii, p. 1544.
45 *LP* V, p. 311.
46 *LP* XIII.2, 1280.
47 *LP* XII.ii, 796.6.
48 TNA LC9/51, ff. 17v and 164r.
49 TNA E101/421/16, unfoliated.
50 TNA E36/456, f. 19v.
51 TNA E101/423/10, ff. 25v–26r.
52 *PPE Elizabeth*, pp. 7, 35.
53 In 1536 this post was held by Henry Cryche; TNA SP1/103, f. 324r (*LP* X, 913).
54 *CPR 1485–94*, p. 99.
55 Ibid., p. 308. This grant replaced one dated 20 June 1485.
56 *PPE Elizabeth*, p. 7.
57 Hayward, 'Repositories', p. 136.
58 Ibid., p. 136.
59 *LP* IV.i, 2002.27; *LP* V, p. 313.
60 *LP* XII.ii, 617.2.
61 BL MS Royal 7C XVI, ff. 25r, 26r, 29r (*LP* XII.ii, 973).
62 TNA E101/422/15, unfoliated.
63 Ibid. They were paid £3 6*s* 8*d*, 50*s*, 50*s* and 33*s* 4*d* respectively.
64 TNA E315/161, f. 65r.
65 TNA E101/417/4, unfoliated.
66 See below, pp. 319–20.
67 BL MS Royal 7C.XVI, f. 58r.
68 *LP* XXI.ii, 199.103.
69 *Lisle Letters*, II, 484 (*LP* IX, 857).
70 TNA E101/423/10, f. 13r.
71 Furnivall, *Boke*, p. 64, lines 939–46.
72 TNA E101/417/4, unfoliated.
73 The wardrobe at the Tower in 1547 had a number of examples, including 11 hangings of crimson cloth of gold 'having xxxix yards of olde redde cotton to folde theym with for freating' (8986).
74 TNA E101/423/12, unfoliated.
75 TNA E101/423/10, f. 26r.
76 TNA E101/421/3, unfoliated; E36/455, f. 18r.
77 TNA E101/423/10, f. 25v.
78 TNA E101/417/4, unfoliated.
79 Hayward, 'Packing', pp. 8–12.
80 SJC D91.5, pp. 19–20.
81 TNA E101/425/4.
82 Leland, *Collectanea*, IV, p. 196.
83 *PPE Elizabeth*, pp. 17, 33, 68.
84 TNA E315/161, f. 60v.
85 Ibid., f. 145r.
86 BL MS Stowe 554, f. 42 (*LP* XVII, 880).
87 Myers, *Black Book*, p. 118.
88 TNA E101/423/10, f. 26r.
89 TNA E36/456, f. 28r.
90 TNA E36/455, f. 37v.
91 Nichols, *Chronicle of Calais*, pp. 57–58.
92 TNA E36/456, f. 19v.
93 BL MS Stowe 146, ff. 92r–v (*LP* I.ii, 2179).
94 TNA SP1/5, ff. 94v, 99v, 103v, 107r (*LP* I.ii, 2404).
95 Thurley, *Royal Palaces*, pp. 70–73.
96 Bentley, *Excerpta Historica*, p. 130.
97 *LP* XIII.i, 1278.
98 *LP* XIII.ii, 1191.1.
99 BL MS Harley 4217.

100 TNA SP1/133, ff. 234r–235v (*LP* XIII.i, 1278).
101 *LP* XIII.ii, 1191.
102 TNA E315/160; Hayward, *1542 Inventory of Whitehall*.
103 BL MS Harley 1419; Starkey, *Inventory*.
104 BL MS Harley 2284, front cover.
105 J. Arnold, *Lost from Her Majesties Back*, Costume Society Extra Series, 7 (1980).
106 See Hayward, 'Repositories', pp. 144–46; and K. Johansen, 'Perfumed garments, their preservation and presentation: "the good smell of old clothes"', in *Preprints of the ICOM CC 12th Triennial Meeting Lyon 29 August–3 September 1999*, 2 (Lyons, 1999), pp. 637–42.
107 Myers, *Black Book*, p. 118.
108 Scarisbrick, *Jewellery*, pp. 145–46.
109 Cavendish, *Life of Wolsey*, p. 23.
110 Furnivall, *Boke*, pp. 66–67, lines 977, 985.
111 See above, p. 107.
112 TNA SP1/245, f. 141r (*LP* App. I.ii, 1778).
113 TNA E101/426/8, m. 1v. Although the accounts refer to rose leaves, rose petals seem more likely.
114 TNA E315/161, f. 33r.
115 Some of the perfume pans listed in 1547 were large and very ornate: 'one perfume Panne of siluer and gilte embossed with Signes and plannettes and engraven with sundry Scriptures the toppe conteyneng a Mappe of a Country with two perfume panes in it of siluer white poiz iiij^xx xij oz' (1983).
116 SJC D91.11, p. 2.
117 TNA E315/161, f. 22v.
118 Ibid., ff. 23v–31v.
119 TNA E36/227, f. 55v.
120 *LP* VI, 5.
121 Bod Lib MS Rawlinson D.776, f. 226v.
122 TNA E36/215, p. 502.
123 Ibid., ff. 67r–v, 74v.
124 Bod Lib MS Rawlinson D.775, f. 66v.
125 Bod Lib MS Rawlinson D. 777, f. 169v.
126 TNA E404/81, not numbered.
127 TNA E101/417/4, unfoliated.
128 *HO*, p. 156.
129 TNA E36/251, p. 106.
130 TNA E36/252, p. 589.
131 NUL Ne01, unfoliated.
132 BL Additional MS 71,009, f. 33r.
133 Cavendish, *Life of Wolsey*, p. 52.
134 Thurley, *Royal Palaces*, p. 75.
135 Nicolas, *Edward the Fourth*, p. 122.
136 *HO*, p. 215; Hayward, *1542 Inventory*, p. 29.
137 *LP* XVIII.ii, 530.
138 TNA LC2/2, f. 30v.
139 TNA E36/215, p. 29.
140 *LP* XXI.i, 969.2.
141 *HO*, p. 215.
142 Ibid., pp. 215–16.
143 *LP* XXI.ii, 774, f. 232v.
144 *PPE*, pp. 75, 112, 165, 234.
145 Myers, *Black Book*, p. 197.
146 *PPE Elizabeth*, pp. 46, 64.
147 *LP* II.ii, p. 1473.
148 *LP* III.i, 1114; *PPE Mary*, p. 207.
149 Ibid., p. 245. Beatrice also supplied the Lady Mary with eggs and chickens; ibid., pp. 127, 132.
150 SJC D91.20, p. 88.
151 BL MS Harley 620, ff. 6v–7r.
152 M. A. Hayward, 'The Possessions of Henry VIII: A Study of Inventories' (unpublished PhD thesis, University of London, 1998), pp. 165–66.
153 Myers, *Black Book*, p. 196.
154 *Lisle Letters*, V, 1588.
155 A. Sim, *The Tudor Housewife* (Thrupp, 1996), pp. 55, 59.
156 For a transcript, translation and analysis of the *Kunstbuch*, see D. Leed, '"Ye shall have it cleane": Textile cleaning techniques in Renaissance Europe', in R. Netherton and G. R. Owen-Crocker, eds, *Medieval Clothing and Textiles*, 2 (Woodbridge, 2006), pp. 101–20.
157 MS 78 D 3, f. 75r, Kupferstichkabinett, Berlin.
158 Bod Lib MS English History b. 192/1, f. 2r.
159 Crowfoot, Pritchard and Staniland, *Textiles and Clothing*, p. 81.
160 TNA E315/161, f. 110r.
161 *PPE Princess Mary*, p. 160.

IX

Female Fashions at Henry VIII's Court

I am but a woman, with all the imperfections natural to the weakness of my sex; therefore in all matters of doubt and difficulty I must refer myself to your Majesty's better judgement, as to my lord and head.[1]

These words, spoken by Queen Catherine Parr as she sought to save herself from the accusations of heresy made against her by Bishop Gardiner and his supporters in the summer of 1546, exemplify the perceived place of women in Tudor society. This was a place that regardless of their own social standing was defined as being subservient to men: their father, their husband, their brother or their king. However, this is not to say that the female élite did not have an equally well defined sense of their own status which was expressed by their network of clients, their patronage both artistic and political and their dress. Henry's six wives were all queen consorts, as were both of his sisters, Margaret and Mary, while his daughters, Mary and Elizabeth, both succeeded as queens regnant, and his niece, Lady Margaret Douglas, is believed to have aspired to the throne.

Choosing a queen

Henry VIII's arrogant attitude towards his potential brides provoked Francis I to comment disapprovingly 'that it is impossible to bring ladies of noble blood to market as horses were trotted out at a fair'.[2] The king of France was not alone in voicing doubts about Henry. According to George Constantine, the duchess of Milan would not marry the king because 'she sayeth that the King's Majesty was in so little space rid of the Queens, that she dare not trust his Council though she durst trust his Majesty; for her Council suspecteth that her great-aunt was poisoned, that the second was innocently put to death, and the third lost for lack of keeping her in childbed'.[3] Even so, notwithstanding his marital upheavals, Henry VIII was married for 35 years, that is all but three years of his reign. The qualities that made a woman acceptable as a royal bride varied, but could include their nationality, virginity, royal lineage and physical attraction. According to Jacques Ferrard, men of different nationality had different opinions on what made a woman attractive: 'The Italian desires to have her thick, well set, and plump: the German prefers one that is strong: the Spaniard loves a wench that is lean: and the French, one that is soft, delicate and tender.'[4] The choice of a royal bride usually rested on considerations other than her physical attributes, although in the case of Henry VIII's fourth bride his repulsion for Anne of Cleves was an underlying impediment to the success of the marriage. The king commented to Sir Anthony Denny that Anne's looks were not what he had been led to believe, and that she had 'breasts so slack and other parts of body in such sort that [he] somewhat suspected her virginity'.[5]

The selection of a royal bride was a complex process which involved the exchange of portraits, letters and jewellery, visits by ambassadors and personal encounters. After the death of Elizabeth of York, Henry VII considered remarriage. He sent Francis Marsin, James Braybrooke and John Stile to see the recently widowed Joan, queen of Naples. Ever prudent, Henry provided his envoys with a list of points that he wanted answering, including what languages she spoke, her age and appearance, 'the favour of her visage', the length of her neck and the size of her breasts.[6] At the same time, he also considered Germaine de Foix, niece of Louis XII, Margaret of Savoy, the widowed daughter of Maximilian I and Joanna of Castile, the widow of Archduke Philip.

Barely was Jane Seymour buried in her grave when the king set himself the task of finding her replacement. Late in 1537 John Hutton was enlisted to help Henry and he started by drawing up a list of eligible women. From Brussels he informed Cromwell that 'I have not much experience among ladies, and therefore this commission to me is hard'.[7] Potential candidates included the daughter of the lord of Breidrood who was 14 and 'of goodly stature, virtuous, sad and womanly', and the widow of the late earl of Egmond who was 'over 40 but does not look it'. He observed that the duke of Cleves 'has a daughter, but there is no great praise either of her personage or her beauty'.[8] However, on 9 December 1537 the widowed duchess of Milan arrived and Hutton noted that she was 16 and 'very tall — taller than the Regent, of competent beauty, play so much as she was wont to and by her troth it was a good lady Newffvyll'.[30]

Obedience to her husband was emphasised in Jane Seymour's choice of motto, which was 'bound to obey and serve'. Henry VIII described Jane as being 'in every inclination, of that loving inclination, and reverend conformity, that she can in all things well content, satisfy and quiet herself with that thing which we shall think expedient and determine'.[31] Catherine Parr took as her motto 'To be useful in all I do'. When Thomas Wriothesley raised with the duchess of Milan the rumour that she did not wish to marry the king, she replied: 'As for my inclination what should I say? You know that I am at the Emperor's commandment.'[32]

The question of a queen consort's magisterial authority and the implications of her coronation were raised in times of crisis. One such expression of this was when the queen consort undertook regencies and was temporarily granted the full range of the king's powers. Both Catherine of Aragon and Catherine Parr were made regent on Henry's departures abroad in 1513 and 1544.[33] When on 7 July 1544 Catherine Parr was appointed regent, the privy council recorded that 'The queen's Highness shall be regent in his grace's absence; and that his grace's progress shall pass and bear test in her name, as in like cases heretofore hath been accustomed'.[34] During her regency of three months, she authorised documents with 'one ring of golde being sometyme Quene Katherynes Signet' (3218).

While fecundity was valued in a queen, barrenness was not. At least one Anglo-Saxon king, Edward the Confessor, had set aside his wife Edith, on account of her childlessness.[35] Catherine of Aragon's dilemma was that her sons died, leaving only a daughter, Mary. Anne Boleyn faced the same problem. The other equally dangerous side of female sexuality was represented by the possibility of an adulterous queen. To ensure a legitimate succession, the Treason Act prohibited any illicit sexual liaisons outside a queen's marriage. Doubts as to Anne Boleyn's fidelity in 1536 led to her downfall, and Catherine Howard's failure in 1541 to end her promiscuous relationship with Francis Culpepper led to her destruction.

Finally, Henry's wives were very conscious of the dignity that should be accorded to their status. This was manifested in many ways, including having the appropriate clothes and furnishings and the correct style. Controlling access to clothing and household trappings was managed relatively simply. Even so, the struggle between Catherine of Aragon and Anne Boleyn over access to the queen's barge and the queen's wardrobe proved to be acrimonious. Controlling how a person styled themselves or was addressed by others was much more difficult. This is evident from the problems that Henry VIII encountered when he sought to demote Catherine of Aragon and his two daughters, Mary and Elizabeth. On 12 May 1529 Campeggio explained how the English hoped to placate the emperor after the dissolution of Catherine's marriage, noting that 'they propose, in the first place, to content the Queen, leaving her the rank which she now holds, and all that she chooses to demand, except the King's person'.[36] However, when an individual chose to co-operate, it was much simpler. When Anne of Cleves accepted the annulment of her marriage, she voluntarily renounced her title and signed her letter 'Anna, daughter of Cleves'.[37]

The court as a centre of female fashionable dress

Henry VIII's court acted as a focal point for the dissemination of ideas about female fashionable dress in mid Tudor England. This was on account of the strong female element at court centring on the succession of queens and the women of their households, his daughters, his niece and, periodically, his sisters. The separate households of these women also provided points for discussion about what was fashionable.

The clothes worn by English women, or rather their hoods, were seen as inelegant in comparison with the styles worn in Europe. In part this was because England was located on the periphery of Europe. It was reinforced by the fact that women travelled less than men and thus they were not personally exposed to new fashions. What was specifically English about the clothes worn in England has been discussed in Chapter II.[38] Yet foreign styles were watched with great interest and copied. English inventories, accounts and letters abound with references to items being 'Almain', Venetian and French in style.

If Henry VIII's court was a focus for ideas, this raises the question of how these were disseminated. The vehicles for these ideas include fashion dolls, letters, conversation, portraits, foreign tailors, garments and patterns. The trousseau brought by a foreign bride could have an effect on what was perceived as desirable at her husband's court. The range of items that might be included can be gauged from the inventory of the trousseau of the French princess, Isabelle, second wife of Richard II.[39] Isabelle married Richard by proxy in Paris in March 1396 and met him for the first time eight months later.[40] How influential the clothes included in the trousseau might be, could be linked to the age of the bride, how popular the marriage was and how long the bride's retinue remained in the country. Isabelle was a child bride and her clothes had less of an impact on court dress than those of her predecessor, Anne of Bohemia.[41] While Catherine of Aragon is often said to have introduced the farthingale to England in 1501 when she arrived in Spanish dress to marry Arthur, it did was not generally adopted until the mid 1540s. The trousseau also allowed the father of the bride to demonstrate his wealth and generosity. When Princess Magdalene of France married James V of Scotland, her father Francis I provided her trousseau. He also 'caused her to pass his wardrobe with her gentlewomen and ladies, and take her stickis of claith of gold, velvet, and satins, damask, taffitis, and other silks, as many as she pleased, to make abulziements to clothe her and her Maries'.[42]

Patterns could be produced by unpicking garments. They were also exchanged between individuals and between countries. On 13 April 1513 Princess Mary thanked Margaret of Savoy for 'some patterns of costume of the ladies of her court', adding that she hoped 'to introduce the same fashion for her herself'.[43] While patterns provided factual information about cut and construction, employing foreign tailors was the surest way to introduce continental designs and clothing to England. Both Henry VII and his son employed a French tailor, as well as other European embroiders, hosiers and suppliers.

The idea of using dolls dressed in new styles to promote new styles originated in the fifteenth and sixteenth centuries. Two entries in the 1542 inventory of Whitehall suggest that fashion dolls were known at Henry's court. Jane Seymour's possessions included 'oone great babie lyeng in a boxe of wodde having a Gowne of white cloth of Silver / and a kyrtle of grene vellat / the Gowne tyed with smale Aglettes of golde with a smale peir of beades of golde and a smale Cheyne and color abowte the necke of golde' [2247] and 'two litle babies in a boxe of wodde / oone of them having a Gowne of crymsen Satten / and thother a Gowne of white vellat' [2248]. While precise details of the clothes worn by the dolls are not given, there were parallels between the dress of the first doll and Jane Seymour's gowns, in particular the aglets on the sleeves.

A slightly later example of a fashion doll survives in the Swedish royal collection.[44] The doll, called Pandora, who dates from the 1590s, is thought to have been made by or for Katarina (1584–1638) or Maria Eliasabet (1596–1618), the daughters of Karl IX. From the 1690s, there is a pair of dolls known as Lord and Lady Clapham.[45] They have garments for both formal and informal dress. In the case of Lady Clapham, her formal attire comprised of a mantua and matching petticoat made from white Chinese silk worn over boned stays and a quilted petticoat. For private, informal wear she had a nightgown with a matching petticoat of patterned Chinese silk.

However, it is worth noting that other types of doll were in circulation. Some were play things for children. Others were toys for adults. An example of the latter is the 'bambino with a damask dress embroidered with pearls' included in 1466 in the dowry of Nannina de'Medici, younger sister of Lorenzo de'Medici. Fifteen dolls are listed in the inventory taken of Catherine de'Medici's goods after her death in 1589. While it is possible that they were fashion dolls, with one 'dressed in the clothing of a lady', most were dressed in black and two were described as being 'in bereavement clothing'.[46] Dolls could also act as a focus for devotion and often represented male children, particularly the Christ child. For example, in 1486 the dowry of Antonia Rinieri contained 'a child dressed in fine linen in the image of Our Lord', while in 1515 Francesca Strozzi's dowry included a 'Messire Lord God, fully dressed with pearls'.[47] Extant examples of such dolls include an early fifteenth-century crib with a Christ Child from Liège and a late fifteenth century cradle from the Netherlands.[48] Images of female saints also appeared in this type of context as indicated by the presence of 'one saint of Margaret, with a dress of gold brocade, with gold lace and pearls and gold buttons on top' in the possessions of Christine Pantheon in 1493.

At court, there was always the chance of seeing people from other countries wearing unfamiliar or new fashions. On 17 September 1546 the regency council in the capital wrote to its colleagues attendant on Henry on campaign in France, that 'the Emperor's ambassador sent to invite us, the Chancellor, Great Master and Bishop of Winchester to dinner on Sunday next to meet the French ambassador's wife who is lately arrived to see their fashion'.[49] Three days later the council reported that the French ambassador's wife was 'a right proper woman, and for her apparel was well trimmed. The Emperor's ambassador's wife on the other hand, is of the meanest, but seemeth also very honest, and that she lacketh in beauty she helpeth with gay gear'.[50]

A factor, a man of business, could act for members of the nobility unable to maintain a permanent presence in London. These men served a dual role, providing information from London as well as access to services and commodities unobtainable in the localities. The best example of a factor in the mid Tudor period is John Hussey who acted for Lady Lisle, second wife of the king's illegitimate relative, Viscount Lisle, the deputy of Calais. While in Calais, Lady Lisle looked to the English court via John Hussey for information on what to wear and what to buy. On 18 July 1534 Hussey told her that:

> Yesternight . . . I delivered Mr Scut your letter with the xij yards of satin, who will make it after the best and most used fashion that now is, large and long, with double placards . . . and when the fur cometh, to see it trimmed after the best manner. And touching the cloth of silver, he saith it is scarce by reason that few weareth it and none but great personages, which maketh the it ghesoner [scarce] and dearer.[51]

Such observations and advice on dress formed a significant part of his correspondence with his employer and he was anxious to reassure her that her clothes were the latest court fashion. On 2 April 1537 he wrote, 'Madam, touching your nightgown and your waistcoats [they] are even in every point made as my Lady Beauchamp's; and it is the very fashion that the Queen and all the ladies doth wear, and so were the caps . . . Divers of the ladies hath their nightgowns embroidered, some with gold and some with silk'.[52] The series of letters also demonstrates that the most effective means of disseminating ideas about what was fashionable and desirable and what was not was the exchange of ideas either by discussion in person or via letters.

The form and function of female clothes

The mid Tudor period saw few changes in female fashion. A small number of garments formed the core of a woman's wardrobe and these underwent gradual change. The clothes worn at the beginning of the period by Elizabeth of York and at the end by Catherine Parr saw a move from a natural shoulder line to off the shoulder, a shift from a fitted bodice to a triangular form of the bodice and from sleeves which fitted the arms to large oversleeves. Indeed, sleeves became a very important area for display. The shape of skirts became more defined as the use of the farthingale became more common. By the 1540s a number of elements were drawn from male clothing, most notably in the style of the bodice of gowns/kirtles and the form of bonnets. When similar trends were seen again towards the end of the sixteenth century, Philip Stubbes was adversely critical.[53] Many of the small changes in style that did take place turned upon the use of gloves, hats and jewellery, in other words, accessories. Equally, the period saw a proliferation in the ornamentation of clothes and the beginnings of the fondness for ornament derived from nature seen in the embroidered borders on shirts and smocks and flowers in the form of jewels.

People at the time appreciated how clothes accentuated some parts of a woman's body. Henry VII's envoys said of the clothes of Joan of Naples: 'the said queen's breasts are somewhat large and full, inasmuch as they were trussed somewhat high, in the manner of the country, which caused her grace to seem much plumper and her neck to look shorter.'[54] The fashion was for tight-fitting clothes, or rather clothes that fitted a woman's upper body and arms. The effect of these clothes was to flatten and push up the chest, either to follow or alter the natural waistline which was drawn down into a point below the natural waistline. This overt display of a woman's breasts was a source of disapproval by the church.

Female clothes could also have an allegorical meaning. A good example of this can be seen in the poem by Olivier de la Marche *c.* 1493–94 called *Le Parement et triumphe de dames*. In this, the poet described the 23 items of jewellery and clothing that a lady put on as she got dressed. The list ranged from her slippers to her mirror. The poet ascribed a special meaning to each garment worn by his ideal woman, including her 'chemise d'honnestete', the kirtle or 'cotte de chastete', and her gown of cloth of gold lined with ermine.[55] Unlike many contemporary texts that linked clothes with voluptuousness and sinfulness, la Marche made a link between beautiful clothes and good behaviour by reference to biblical and classical examples.

Undergarments: smocks, shifts, bodies, farthingales and petticoats

Women's undergarments are often concerned with shaping, defining and protecting the body. In 1550 the fashionable shape of an English woman was described by Robert Crowley in the following terms: 'Her mydle braced in, as smal as a wande . . . A bumbe lyke a barrell, with whoopes at the skyrte.'[56] Even though there is no evidence of knickers or drawers being ordered for Henry VIII's female relatives, this does not mean that they were not provided with other forms of underwear.[57] In the mid Tudor period high quality female body garments (chiefly the smock or shift and the rail) were made almost exclusively from bleached white linen.[58] These garments worn close to the body had two main functions, to protect the skin from abrasion by the outer layers of clothing such as the bodies, the gown and the farthingale, and to prevent the clothes being soiled by sweat and grease exuded by the wearer's skin. Smocks figure in inventories and their entries there provide a sense of the variety and the level of decoration. The royal wardrobe in 1535 included three 'smokis of fine holland', two of which were 'wrought aboute the collers with gold and the thirde wrought aboute the coller and handis with silke'.[59] The smock or shift depicted in Holbein's drawing of Anne Boleyn (Fig. 9.11), has two thread ties to secure the stand collar which was decorated with embroidery. The 1547 inventory included an entry for 'one wastesmocke wrought with Siluer' (11389) and for 'iij Irishe smockes wrought with golde and silke' (10419).

The basic shape of these garments was dictated by the use of loom width linen fabric but, unlike shirts, they were given additional width by the insertion of gores. The linen was cut into a series of rectangles and triangles.[60] Triangular gussets were used to create ease at the underarm, while very fine pleating or gathers were used to ease extra fabric into the neckline. Shifts and smock were usually ordered in bulk from the great wardrobe, so it is not easy to tell how much fabric was required to make one. A warrant dated 27 September 1532 for Princess Mary included holland for smocks costing £4 12*s* 6*d* and cambric for rails costing £5 10*s*.[61] Another warrant dated 25 March 1533 included two dozen lawn partlets costing 40*s*, 34 ells (23.4 m) of holland for frocks and kerchieves priced at £5 13*s* 4*d* and 20 ells (13.8 m) of cambric for rails and necessaries costing £5 6*s* 8*d*.[62] On 8 April 1537 30 ells (20.7 m) of holland were supplied for smocks and rails for Mary costing £5, and 26 ells (17.9 m) cambric for kerchiefs and sleeves costing £8 13*s* 4*d*.[63]

Unsurprisingly, paintings provide little evidence about undergarments. What evidence exists is generally restricted to the collars, necklines and cuffs of smock and chemises. Even though little was visible, what could be seen allowed for the display of fine embroidery on clean, white linen underwear. Where the gowns had low, square-cut necklines, this was echoed in the necklines of the shifts worn with them. Catherine of Aragon's smock in Plate VB (*c.* 1530) has a small, delicate embroidered edging at the neckline. The neckline of Anne Boleyn's chemise in Plate VC (*c.* 1533–36) is edged with a simple yet striking triangular pattern working in black embroidery. This style continued in Jane Seymour's smock of 1536 (Pl. VIA) which was decorated at the neck with a very small geometric dot pattern but with very deep heavily embroidered cuffs. This style is also seen in the portrait of Princess Elizabeth *c.* 1546–47 (Fig. 11.6) where she has a very small blackwork edging on the neckline of the smock and deep frilled cuffs that hang down over her wrists. This visual evidence can be put in context by reference to the shift of Mary of Hungary, which was made of fine linen, with embroidery at the low, round neckline. A heavily embroidered example of a mid sixteenth-century linen shift is decorated with stylised bunches of flowers worked in a dull red silk thread using cross stitch and back stitch.[64]

Not all smocks were embroidered with blackwork. The smock in the portrait of Catherine Parr, *c.* 1545, shows white work embroidery on a new style of neckline with a turn back collar and with deep, pleated cuffs. Shifts worn with gowns of this style had the same type of collar. The Wadham shift, although slightly later in date, has this type of collar (Fig. 9.2). This shift is made from a fine, plain weave bleached linen. The overall length measures 123.5 cm and the outer sleeve length is 51 cm. The cut and construction date the shift to *c.* 1590–1620 and it has been attributed to Dorothy Wadham, founder of

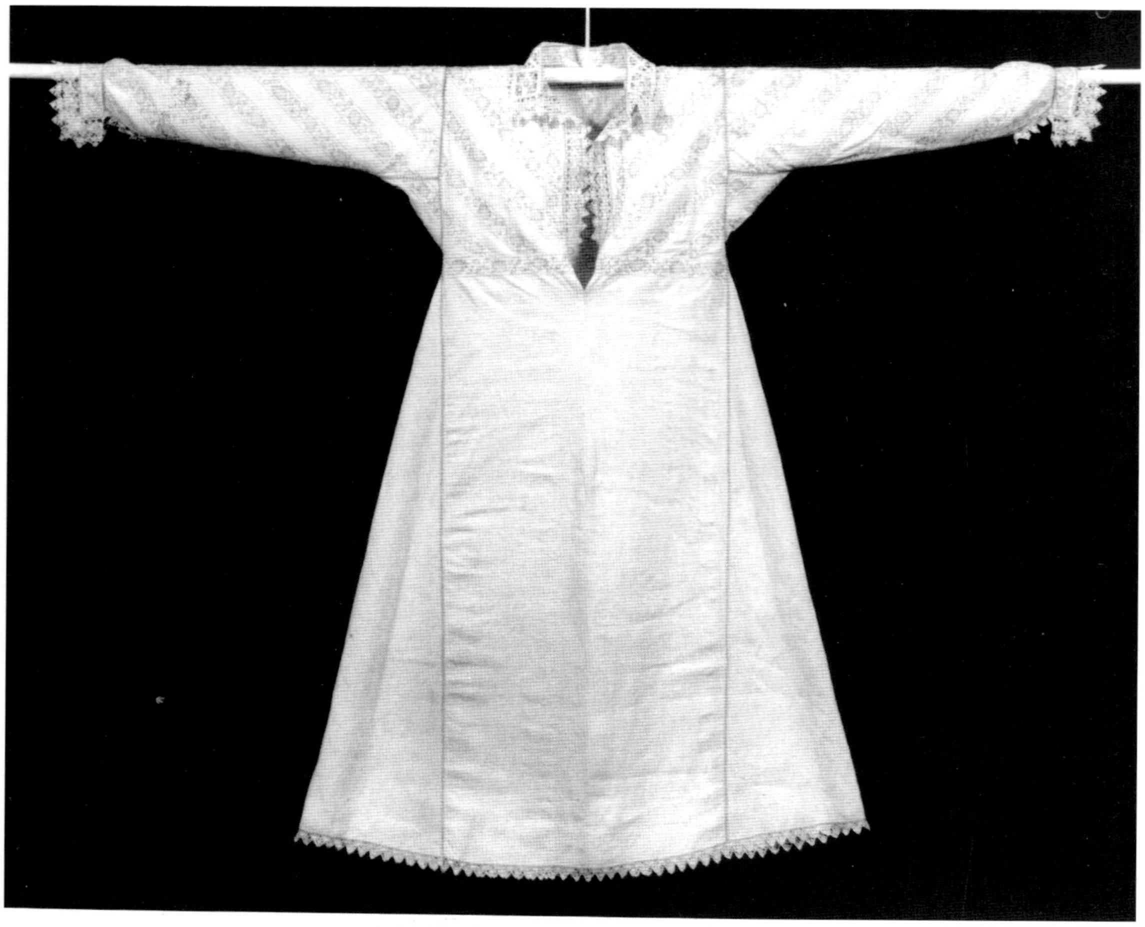

9.2 *The Wadham shift, by permission of the Warden and Fellows of Wadham College, Oxford. Photo © The Textile Conservation Centre, University of Southampton*

Wadham College, Oxford.[65] The shift is a T-shaped garment with long sleeves ending in tight cuffs and a neck band. The bodice and cuffs are embroidered in red silk, now faded to pink, using stem and speckling stitches that are worked in a leaf and berry pattern. The seams are open worked, using a knotted buttonhole stitch. The collar, cuffs and front opening are edged with bobbin lace worked from a linen thread finished with a vandyked edging.[66]

Many women during the Tudor period slept in their shifts. Thus there was no need for special nightwear. One exception is the night rail, a short cape or shawl that could come down as far as the waist and could be worn over the shift. However, no references appear to these in the accounts of Henry VIII's wives or daughters.

To give their chests definition, women wore bodies or a pair of bodies. Bodies were designed to flatten the chest and push the bust up, while providing little or no definition below the breasts. No examples of boned or stiffened bodies were mentioned in the extant great wardrobe accounts, but there are entries for upper bodying kirtles. However, the upper bodies do not appear to have been stiffened with bents or baleen. For example a warrant for Princess Mary dating from 8 April 1536 included 4 yards (3.6 m) of black satin for the 'upper bodies' for four kirtles costing 36*s* but there were no payments for stiffening materials.[67]

The nature of underpinnings is quite difficult to distinguish.[68] There is no visual evidence from the sixteenth century until at its very end, the portrait of Elizabeth Wriothesley, countess of Southampton, *c.* 1600. She is at her toilet and informally dressed in her pink silk bodies and an embroidered petticoat. Surviving examples, which all date to slightly later than the period under consideration, indicate that they could fasten down the front or the back, either with hooks or by lacing, and they could have tassets to ease the fit around the waist. A pair of red velvet bodies was found on the body of Eleanor of Toledo in her tomb at Florence. This pair, *c.* 1562, fastened with 18 sets of hooks and eyes, evenly spaced down the centre front. There is no evidence of any stiffening material, but the bodies are incomplete and the original linen lining has degraded. The front of the bodies curves down while being cut straight across at the back.[69] A pair of pale cream or ivory silk bodies worn by Pfalzgräfin Dorothea Sabina von Neuburg, who died aged 22 in 1598, would have laced down the centre back, with six tabbed skirts or tassets at the back, with a busk at the centre front and stiffening provided by narrow strips of baleen or bents inserted into 26 stitched channels on either side.[70]

The farthingale provided a method of supporting the skirt of the gown or kirtle, so giving it additional shape and definition. As such it provided a means of displaying the expensive fabric if it was heavily patterned or embroidered. The farthingale was first worn in Spain *c.* 1460s, but in a slightly different form because at that time women put the hoops of willow or osier on the outside of their skirts. Women wearing skirts of this type were depicted on a choir stall in Seville cathedral dating from the 1470s and a water colour of Spanish ladies *c.* 1540.[71] However, while this style was short-lived, the farthingale became a very distinctive feature of Spanish female dress which gave women's gowns a rigid bell shape.[72]

Catherine of Aragon is credited with introducing the farthingale to England when she arrived in 1501. In the absence of full-length portraits of women before the 1540s, it is not easy to chart its adoption. According to Edward Hall, on 7 March 1519 the female masquers wore black velvet gowns 'with hoopes from the wast douneward'.[73] The earliest known reference to farthingales in the great wardrobe accounts dates from 1545, when one was provided for Princess Elizabeth: 'vij virg. Satten de bruges crimsen pro una verdingale.'[74] Mary's own accounts for 1546 include an entry 'for making a vardingalle of crimsyn satin' costing 5*s*, and a yard and a half of 'brode clothe To the dowlles' costing 5*s*.[75] In the summer of 1548, Elizabeth Cavendish, better known to history as Bess of Hardwick, paid 4*s* 4*d* for 'a nertyngall' for her stepdaughter Ann, aged nine.[76] In 1553 Princess Mary's wardrobe accounts included 'two rounde Varthingallis of crymsen Satten edged with crymsen Vellat', 'a single verthingall' and a 'haulf a farthingall of crymsen Satten'.[77]

A pattern for a silk farthingale was included in Juan de Alçega's *Pattern Book* and, following the general premise of his book, there are clear instructions on how to cut the fabric rather than full making instructions. Alçega noted that 'the farthingale is 1½ ells [1.1 m] long, and a little more than 13 hand-spans wide, which seems to me to be sufficient for this farthingale'.[78] The visual effect created by the farthingale can be seen in the full-length portrait of Catherine Parr (Fig. 9.3), the smooth, conical shape of her skirt was achieved by wearing a Spanish farthingale. The three-quarter-length portrait of Princess Elizabeth, *c.* 1546 (Fig. 11.6) depicts the same triangular profile of her skirt and forepart.

During 1536–37 Jane Seymour paid for ¾ yard (0.68 m) of crimson velvet for the 'upperbodies' of a petticoat of scarlet which cost 9*s*.[79] This suggests a rather similar style of construction to that of a kirtle. She also ordered 1⅝ yards (1.4 m) of fine scarlet for a petticoat costing 35*s* 9*d*, and 1½ yards (1.3 m) of red cloth for a petticoat for her fool costing 7*s* 6*d*.[80] A decade later Catherine Parr ordered several petticoats for herself made from 1½ yards (1.3 m) of fine scarlet costing 33*s* 9*d*.[81] These orders highlight that a fairly standard quantity of cloth was required to make petticoats, as well as indicating the preference for scarlet petticoats.

9.3 *Catherine Parr, wearing a French gown, attributed to Master John, 1545. National Portrait Gallery, London (NPG 4451)*

Principal garments: the gown and the kirtle

While the accounts are precise about payments for gowns and kirtles, these garments are hard to distinguish in visual representations. If the gown was worn with a kirtle, it was always the outer garment. It could have a waist seam or be cut in one from the shoulder. The skirt was usually quite full and from *c.* 1500–30 it could have a train. After that date, a train was less common. Portraits indicate that necklines were invariably square-cut at the front, but with a V-shaped back which could be either shallow or could reach down to the waistline. Bodice shaping of this type was depicted in Holbein's drawing of a woman, *c.* 1528 (Fig. 9.4), showing both three-quarter front and back views of a woman, possibly a preparatory sketch for his portrait of Lady Guildford (Fig. 9.5). The neckline got wider in the 1530s and 1540s, so it is almost off the shoulders, as is the case in the full-length portrait of Catherine Parr. Equally, the square-cut neckline developed a downwards curve.

For much of the period, the bodice was shaped and stiffened to create a smooth profile. Consequently, the bodice flattened the breasts and pushed them up. However, in the 1540s a second type of bodice, more masculine in style, developed. This style can be seen in the portrait of a woman

9.4 *Costume study showing the front and back view of a woman wearing English dress and an English hood, c. 1527, by Hans Holbein the Younger. 1895-9-15-991. Reproduced by courtesy of the Trustees of the British Museum, London*

9.5 *Mary, Lady Guildford by Hans Holbein the Younger, 1527. Lady Guildford is dressed in a very similar style to the woman in the costume study, and it has been suggested that the drawings were preparatory sketches for this portrait. The Saint Louis Art Museum, Missouri, Museum Purchase*

of the Cromwell family (previously identified as Catherine Howard), by Holbein (Fig. 9.14), a miniature by him of Mrs Small (formerly known as Mrs Pemberton) *c.* 1540, and the portrait of Catherine Parr attributed to William Scrots (Fig. 10.6).[82] In all three instances the bodice had a V-neck with a stand roll collar, sometimes referred to now as a Medici collar. The bodice fastened up the centre front and the shaping of the bodice was much softer than in previous decades. Although Alçega included patterns for silk doublets for women in his pattern book, none of the bodices are specifically described as a doublet in the great wardrobe accounts.[83]

The number of gowns surviving from the sixteenth century is small. Most of these were once buried with the bodies of their owners. The wedding dress of Mary of Hungary, which dates from 1525, is made from a figured silk, with a square neckline and tight-fitting sleeves with flared cuffs.[84] This can be compared with the white satin gown of Eleanor of Toledo, wife of Cosimo I de'Medici (Figs 9.6 and 9.7).[85] This was a square-necked bodice embodying Italian and Spanish fashions, and a short train. It was worn over a crimson velvet bodice. There is a second gown thought to have belonged to Eleanor, which does not come from a burial context, made from red velvet, and the skirts of both gowns have the same cut and construction.[86]

A gown required a significant amount of cloth, especially if it was lined. A gown ordered for Catherine of Aragon took 20¼ yards (18.5 m) of black velvet that was bought from William Botry for £11 2*s* 9*d*. This quantity of cloth made the gown and lined the sleeves, forequarters and vents.[87] The descriptions of Jane Seymour's gowns are all quite simple, as in the case of 'a gowne of Russett Capha turned with russett vellat' (11223). The yardage required for making gowns and associated items are indicated in a letter from John Husee to Lady Lisle dated 25 April 1539. First, he notes that 'I send by the bearer, Cockes, your gown of taffeta, wherein is the placard, and as much taffeta as will make two placards more'. He then states that 'I have delivered Mrs Katherine 12 yards [10.9 m] of white damask, two and a half yards [2.2 m] of carnation velvet, a roll of buckram and half a yard [0.45 m] of velvet for a partlet'.[88]

Gowns were produced in a range of distinctive national styles. There are a few references to such gowns in the individual accounts for Henry VIII's queens. While the national characteristics of these costumes might have been exaggerated

9.6 *Overall view of Eleanor of Toledo's gown, 1562, after conservation. The shape of the skirt and the slight train are very evident from this picture. Reproduced with the permission of Mary Westerman for the Janet Arnold slide archive, Galleria del Costume, Palazzo Pitti*

9.7 *Detail of the bodice of Eleanor of Toledo's gown, 1562, after conservation. Reproduced with the permission of Mary Westerman for the Janet Arnold slide archive, Galleria del Costume, Palazzo Pitti*

for dramatic effect, the entries serve to emphasise the features of some of the different types: 'twoo Italion gownes with Ruffe sleues of Crymsen Tilsent Damaske golde garded barrewise with yellowe Tilsent Ragged and Lyned with crymsen gold sarcennet' (8660) and possibly 'Almain' styles: 'ij garments for frowes of white Siluer Sarcennet the sleues paned vpon with clothe of golde the color garded with Clothe of golde Two Frockes vnder the same withowt sleues of blacke Tilsent Twoo partelettes of Crymsen Satten Rewed with Syluer garded with grene vellet' (8661). The Dutch or round gown was described as being 'made round without any trayne'.[89] French gowns are mentioned in the accounts for 1546.[90] Several examples also appear in the revels listing of 1547.

The kirtle underwent significant changes during our period. In the late fifteenth century the kirtle was a dress with a tight-fitting bodice and skirt and with either integral or separate sleeves that could be worn on its own or under a gown. The skirt of the kirtle could have a train. By the middle of the sixteenth century the kirtle generally consisted of just a skirt. However, the entries in the accounts indicate that the kirtles worn by the women at the English court had bodices or upper bodies and often had sleeves. A warrant for Princess Mary dating from 8 April 1536 included 14 yards (12.8 m) of black velvet for two kirtles with sleeves of the same velvet costing £13 6*s*, and 14 yards (12.8 m) of black satin for two kirtles with sleeves of the same satin costing £6 6*s*. John Scut was paid 66*s* 8*d* for making and lining the four kirtles.[91] As only the front part of the kirtle was visible under the gown, it could be replaced by a forepart, a decorative panel that could be mounted on a petticoat. The kirtle, like the gown, could be given shape and structure by wearing a farthingale under it.

A good sense of the construction and quantity of cloth involved in making a kirtle can be gauged by looking at the accounts. A kirtle made for Catherine of Aragon during 1519–20 consisted of the following: for the upper bodying of a kirtle of black velvet ⅝ yard (0.56 m) of black satin (5*s* 3½*d*), for the hem of the kirtle, ¼ yard (0.23 m) of crimson velvet (3*s* 4*d*), and to make the upper parts of a pair of sleeves of black velvet ⅝ of a yard (0.56 m) of black satin (3*s*).[92] A simpler example of 'a kirtle for the queen' was made from 7¾ yards (7 m) of black satin bought from William Botry costing £3 5*s* 10½*d*, and a pair of sleeves for the queen from 1 yard (0.91 m) of black satin costing 8s.[93] These garments were similar in terms of the provision of materials to the kirtles made earlier for Elizabeth of York.

Some of the kirtles owned by Jane Seymour in 1536–37 were quite simple and undecorated, such as 'one kirtle of white vellat' (11264), while others were more ornate, including 'one kirtle of Carnacion clothe of golde raysed with Siluer Tysue' (11269) with what appear to be matching sleeves but that are listed separately (11325). On occasion, Jane's kirtles could be far more opulent. William Ibgrave, embroiderer, received a large quantity of pearls 'for the hinder part of the queen's kirtle': 140 pearls of the bigger sort, 400 pearls of the second sort and 1,562 of the small sort.[94] By the 1540s the kirtle often still had matching sleeves, but they had become much more of a vehicle for surface decoration. Examples listed in the 1547 inventory include a 'kertle compleate of crimsen satten alover embraudered with veanice golde and small peerless with a paier of Sleves to the same' (9929) and 'oon kertle of crimsen satten raised with newe making vellat and golde and striped with golde' (9940).

Unlike the gown, the kirtle does not tend to appear listed in the great wardrobe accounts as being made in styles adopted or adapted from other countries. The accounts suggest that as Henry VIII's reign progressed the kirtle became more highly decorated and it was a vehicle for display amongst the female élite at court. It seems not to have been worn for informal wear.

Items worn in association with the gown and kirtle: foreparts, sleeves, furs and tippets, stomachers, placards, partlets and neckerchiefs

The gown and kirtle were rarely worn alone. They were invariably seen in conjunction with other accessories. The forepart (a type of apron that was usually made of an expensive fabric and that was often decorated) worn with a gown or kirtle that was open at the front usually revealing a V-shaped panel. Previously, it was believed that the forepart only became fashionable from the mid 1540s.[95] However, Jane Seymour at her death in October 1537 owned one: 'one fore parte of a kirtle of Crymsen Satten enbrawdered with venice gold' (11275). In the following decades it became popular. In 1547 there were 20 foreparts of kirtles most of which had matching sleeves (9927–28, 9930–39, 9941–44), in the secret guardrobe in the long gallery at Whitehall, including 'one foreparte of a kertle of greane vellat allover embraudered with Cordiauntes of veanice golde with three paier of sleaues to the same', two kirtles (9929, 9940) and a further 20 pairs of sleeves (9945–63). These may have belonged to Catherine Howard, or more likely to Catherine Parr, whose clothes when brought from Sudeley lacked any kirtles or gowns. These foreparts were highly ornate and extremely sumptuous in terms of fabrics used and colour: nine of velvet, six of cloth of gold and five of satin; six of plain cloth of gold, five green, four purple and also crimson and one of yellow. In addition, 14 were described as embroidered all over, while five were overlaid with passamayne and one was woven with metal thread.

The shape of the forepart changed as that of the farthingale changed. Two examples of foreparts made later in the sixteenth century demonstrate this. The first, dating from *c.* 1575–85, is made from green silk velvet decorated with couched gold thread and ornamented with guards of dark cream silk worked with polychrome embroidery. The forepart was quite narrow in profile, indicating that it was intended to be worn over a cone-shaped Spanish farthingale. The second forepart dates from *c.* 1580–95 and is made from ivory satin worked with a stamped and embroidered design. The forepart was originally made to be worn with a Spanish farthingale, but it was extended so that it could be worn with the much wider French farthingale.[96]

Sleeves formed a very important part of the female wardrobe. They could be either integral with the gown and the kirtle or made separately and attached with points, lacing or possibly with pins. At the start of Henry VIII's reign, both Catherine of Aragon and Mary Tudor had some gowns made for them with wide sleeves. The style of English women's sleeves was described by a Venetian visitor in 1527.[97] There were several distinct styles of sleeve that could basically be subdivided into single sleeves and over- and undersleeves. Single sleeves could either be fairly fitted down the whole length, they could get wider at the end or they could be very full ending in a tight cuff. Sleeves of this third type can be seen in the portrait of a woman from the Cromwell family, *c.* 1540–41. They were often heavily decorated with lengths of passementerie, pairs of aglets and gemstones. The sleeves belonging to Jane Seymour included 'one payer of Sleves of blacke golde tissue teyed with tenne payer of aglettes of golde' (11311). This was one of a number of pairs that were tied with aglets along the lower seam, although none were attributed to being a specific style.

The other combination consisted of oversleeves and undersleeves, which could be interchangeable to create a range of different effects. The oversleeves were usually very large with deep turned-back cuffs or bell-shaped ends. They could be made of fur, as in the portrait of the countess of Salisbury (Fig. 9.8) or fur lined, as in the full-length portrait of Catherine Parr. The undersleeves or foresleeves could be left open fully or partially open along the lower seam and if this was the case they could be tied with aglets. Undersleeves could be made from pleated linen or more expensive silk fabrics. A pair of foresleeves appeared amongst the clothes ordered by Catherine Parr. They were made from 1 yard (0.91 m) of black lukes velvet for a pair of forestocks costing 15*s*.[98]

Different styles of sleeves became fashionable by the 1540s. Catherine Parr owned an impressive variety. Spanish sleeves were particularly popular. Princess Mary's accounts for 1546 included a payment of 10*s* for the translation of a pair of French sleeves into Venice sleeves of black velvet guarded with pastment of gold and great wreaths of Venice gold.[99]

hauing an edge of perle lackibg dyuers perles' (2847). The biliment, or habiliment as it was often referred to, consisted of two parts: the upper biliment and the nether biliment. On 30 November 1530 Christopher Milliner was paid *£6 19s 1d* out of the privy purse for 'edges of golde weyng ij unces and iij quarters and iij*s*'.[162]

The double portrait of the duke and duchess of Suffolk painted in 1515 is one of the earliest representations of the French hood worn by an English sitter (Pl. IIIA). The duchess was the widow of King Louis XII of France and accordingly she was often called the French queen. As the portrait makes clear, the hood did not cover the front of the wearer's hair, which was usually combed with a centre parting. In March 1520 Catherine of Aragon provided a French hood for her daughter Mary at a price of 11*s* which included the cost of 1 yard (0.91 m) of black velvet.[163] These two examples disprove the suggestion that Anne Boleyn introduced the French hood to England. On 25 March 1534 Ralph Warren supplied 3 yards (2.7 m) of black velvet for three French hoods for Mary, costing 57*s*, and John Scut was paid 18*s* for making the hoods.

On 7 July 1535 Leonard Smith informed Lady Lisle that he had 'bought a French hood, with all habiliments thereunto belonging of as rich and good sort as I could get in London'.[164] In September 1537 she wrote to Sir William le Gras asking him to send her more crespins and hats 'of the kind that the ladies of France use to wear, for the ladies here in the habiliments follow the mode of France', adding that she specifically wanted 'a half dozen of ladies' bonnets, three of them trimmed with velvet, and the other three trimmed with silk . . . and one that shall be finely trimmed with gold'.[165] In the following decade Catherine Parr was ordering ⅝ of a yard (0.56 m) of black lukes velvet for a French hood for costing 9*s* 4½*d* that was lined with ¼ of a yard (0.22 m) of black satin at 22½*d*.[166] A good example of a French hood of this type can be seen in the portrait of a member of the Cromwell family (Fig. 9.14) and in a portrait of Catherine Parr (Fig. 9.15).

French hoods were usually quite heavily decorated. Jane Seymour's wardrobe included 'oone French whode of blac Vellat' [2219] as well as 'oone billiament of blac vellat garnisshed with goldsmithes worke' [2220] and one of white satin [2221]. Catherine Howard's jewels included an 'upper habiliment of goldsmith's work enamelled and garnished with vij fair diamonds, vij fair rubies and vij fair pearls', and an upper habiliment decorated with eight diamonds and seven rubies given to her by the king at the New Year in 1540.[167] The bongrace could be worn with a French hood or separately. It provided protection for the forehead and the back of the neck.

9.13 *Catherine Parr, unknown artist. Lambeth Palace Library*

9.14 *Lady of the Cromwell family, formerly known as 'Catherine Howard', after Hans Holbein the Younger, 1540–41. National Portrait Gallery, London (NPG 1119)*

9.15 *Catherine Parr, unknown artist, collection unknown. Photo: National Portrait Gallery, London*

9.16 *Lady with a Squirrel and a Starling, thought to be Anne Lovell, by Hans Holbein the Younger. Anne Lovell is dressed in the style of a woman of middling rank and she wears and very fashionable lettice hood. © National Gallery, London (NG 6540)*

During 1536–37 William Lock supplied ⅝ of a yard (0.56 m) of black taffeta for 'a bonegrace' costing 5*s* for Jane Seymour.[168]

Close-fitting white fur bonnets often had a gable front and came down over the ears. The portrait evidence, Holbein's portrait of Alice Lovell (Fig. 9.16) and his drawing of Margaret Giggs, both from about 1528, and the portrait of Margaret Pole, countess of Salisbury *c.* 1535, suggests that these bonnets had an internal frame but were not decorated with a jewelled edge or border.[169] This type of bonnet was often made of a white fur known as lettice. Lady Lisle actively sought one. On 22 November 1533 Leonard Smith told Lady Lisle that he had 'spoken for a lettice bonnet for Mrs Frances, which will cost xiij*s* iiij*d*. As the skinner saith, you shall have it within vj days'.[170] On 23 January 1534 he informed her that he had 'delivered a lettice bonnet to Hugh Colton for my lord's daughter, which cost x*s* and iiij*d* for the box. If it be not fit for her my bargain is it shall be changed or amended'.[171] Some of these fur bonnets or caps were worn for night or informal wear, as in the case of a night bonnet of ermine ordered for Princess Mary in September 1532.[172]

The cap or bonnet was an accessory borrowed from male dress, the black velvet bonnet with the halo brim decorated with gold aglets, buttons and feathers. It was usually worn flat on the head rather than at an angle. Catherine Parr *c.* 1545 wore hers over a linen undercap edged with pearls. The descriptions of her caps, some of which were listed amongst her things brought from Sudeley in 1549, were similar to those made for her husband: 'a Cappe of blacke vellat garneshed with a brouche of gold having therin a Table Diamounte and xxj pair of aglattes and xiiij small buttons of golde' (3592).

During 1536–37 Christopher Milliner made a hat of black taffeta garnished with black silk and gold costing 30*s* for Jane Seymour, as well as a hat of green taffeta garnished with green silk and gold for the same price. The list of her clothes stored after her death at Whitehall included two very ornate velvet hats: 'one hatte of purple vellat enbrawdred with pirles of damaske golde garnished with smale perles and smale stones of sundrie sortes and frengid with golde' (11369) and 'one hatte of sadd crymsen vellat enbrawdred with lace of golde and tasselles to the same hatt with a case of crymsen vellat' (11370).

Women's hose or stockings were usually made from a woven woollen cloth, but by the mid sixteenth century they could also be knitted. In May 1502 Elizabeth of York paid 13*d* for 'ij yerdes of white fustian for sokkes for the Quene', while

10.1 *Miniature of Catherine of Aragon. By kind permission of the duke of Buccleuch & Queensbury, KT*

10.2 *Miniature of Catherine of Aragon by Lucas Horenbout, c. 1525–27. National Portrait Gallery, London (NPG 4682)*

and 'a nother couerying . . . of blewe veluet lined with purple chaungeable sarsenet' also with fronts and appraised at £8 3*s* 4*d* in total.[7]

The earliest evidence of Catherine's wardrobe once she was queen comes from the occasional references to the clothes ordered by Henry for her on his own warrants. On 5 November 1509 Henry ordered a gown for Catherine of purple velvet on velvet pirled with gold with a purfill of ermine. A further four ermine skins were supplied to fur the vents, along with 200 powderings.[8] In the following month, he gave Catherine a stomacher made from ¾ of a yard (0.68 m) of green satin.[9] Shortly after on 17 January 1510 Henry had a gown of russet tilsent furred with sable made for his wife.[10] More spectacular still was the gown with wide sleeves he ordered for Catherine in February 1510, which was made from crimson cloth of gold. The gown was furred with ermine, for which 15½ timbers and 12 wombs of ermine were supplied.[11] Stomachers appear to have been popular with husband and wife, and on 2 November 1510 Henry requested ½ yard (0.45 m) of green satin for a stomacher costing 4*s* and ½ yard (0.45 m) of green satin for another costing 6*s*.[12] In the following year Catherine received, on the king's warrant dated 14 April 1511, 21¾ yards (19.8 m) of russet velvet costing £10 8*s* 6*d*.[13]

Clothes were also made for the queen at the king's expense and recorded in Worsley's wardrobe book. Worsley recorded deliveries of 45 lengths of cloth to Catherine on 20 occasions between 31 December 1516 and 19 May 1520. These lengths of cloth were made up into kirtles, stomachers and gowns, and they were usually of cloth of gold, cloth of silver, tilsent, tissue, velvet or satin. A sense of the sumptuous quality of the fabric is evident. On 7 November 1519 Henry ordered 'iij yerdes of riche cloth of gold tissewe dammaske gold reised with pyrles damaske siluer for to lyne a gowne for the quenes grace' [A497] and 'xiij yerdes of cloth of siluer tissewe reysed with damaske gold for a gowne for ye quene' [A498]. The largest delivery made on 27 April 1519 consisted of seven kirtle lengths and two pieces of tissue for lining gowns. Henry also provided some items probably for wear at the Field of Cloth of Gold: on 14 May 1520 ½ yard (0.45 m) of crimson tissue pirled with gold for a stomacher [A691], and five days later two lengths, probably for gowns, 16⅝ yards (15.1 m) of black tilsent with Catherine wheels [A884] and 11 yards (10 m) of black tilsent damask gold [A885].

While these wardrobe entries and warrants provide details about the quality and colour of cloth used and the type and number of garments, they do not give much detail of the style. In contrast, her wardrobe books include a little more detail and there are a number of orders for gowns with Spanish sleeves. A gown of this type required 13 yards (11.8 m) of white satin £5 16*s*, along with 6 yards (5.4 m) of cloth of gold of damask (£16) for bordering the same and for lining the sleeves, while the gown was fully lined with black sarsenet.[14] Catherine was very proud of her Spanish background and chose to express this by wearing clothes in the Spanish style on key days in the liturgical and ceremonial year. On May day 1515 an ambassador observed that 'we accompanied the most serene Queen, who was richly dressed in the Spanish fashion' and 'in the meanwhile we visited the Queen, and there, in

Table 10.1: *Analysis of Catherine of Aragon's wardrobe in March 1520 by colour*

Colour	Gowns	Kirtles	Nightgowns	Partlets	Petticoats	Sleeves
Black	8	5	~	2	~	4
Blue	1	~	~	~	~	~
Crimson	2	1	~	~	~	1
Gold	~	1	~	~	~	~
Purple	3	2	~	~	~	~
Russet	2	1	~	~	~	~
Scarlet	~	~	~	~	2	~
Tawny	2	2	1	~	~	1
Unspecified	1	1	~	~	~	1
Violet in grain	1	~	~	~	~	~
White	~	1	~	~	~	1
Yellow	1	~	~	~	~	~
	21	14	1	2	2	8

Table 10.2: *Analysis of Catherine of Aragon's wardrobe in March 1520 by fabric type*

Fabric	Gowns	Kirtles	Nightgowns	Partlets	Petticoats	Sleeves
Cloth	1	~	~	~	2	~
Damask	~	1	~	~	~	~
Damask gold	1	4	~	~	~	~
French black	1	~	~	~	~	~
Sarsenet	1	~	~	~	~	~
Satin	4	2	1	2	~	3
Tinsel	1	3	~	~	~	~
Tissue	3	2	~	~	~	2
Velvet	9	2	~	~	~	3
	21	14	1	2	2	8

public, I addressed her in good Spanish, which pleased her more than I can tell you; and she commenced talking with me about Spanish affairs, and about her mother'.[15] Even at the time of her death, her wardrobe still included 'seevyn paire slippars of the Spanysshe fasshion, corkid and garnysshid withe golde'.[16]

Catherine's wardrobe accounts reveal that the colour black was predominant in her wardrobe, followed by purple and crimson (Table 10.1), while her choice of fabrics, velvet, satin and tilsent, echoes that of her husband (Table 10.2). Her accounts also show that Henry sent her a number of items that were described as being 'of the king's gift'. These were three pairs of satin sleeves, one of which was pleated (at 12*d* a pair), three kirtles of satin (at 3*s* 4*d* each) and four gowns, three of velvet and one of damask cloth of gold (at 5*s* each). The list recorded a number of garments that were made for Catherine, with the implication that the king provided the cloth and then paid for the making done by the queen's tailor. This interpretation accords with the list of lengths of cloth given to Catherine for specific garments recorded in Worsley's wardrobe book from 1516–20. A very fragmentary volume of Catherine's wardrobe of the robes datable to about this time provides further confirmation:

> a gown of purple satin with goldsmithswork of the king's gift, for lining the same 4½ yards of black sarsenet and for lining the upperpart of the sleeves, one yard of yellow sarsenet
> for lining a gown of green tinsel with wide sleeves lined with green velvet of the king's gift, 4½ yards of black sarsenet.[17]

The bill presented on 4 March 1520 by Richard Hanchet, the queen's skinner, came to £24 7*d* for the provision of the necessary skins and for furring five gowns for the queen, including her maundy gown and a pair of French sleeves for a gown of black velvet. Hanchet also furred a selection of gowns for members of the queen's household, including chammers for her French pages and a coat furred with white lamb for her fool.[18]

On her meeting with the emperor in May 1520 at Canterbury, Catherine complimented him by asserting their family ties by wearing cloth of gold and pearls.[19] When in June 1527 Henry told her of his doubts about the validity of their marriage, she refused to give up her role as his wife and queen. As part of her defiance she dressed yet more richly than usual, appeared in public and to observe her estate.[20] Catherine's household accounts at this time were kept by Griffin Richards, her receiver general, and they have survived for the six years following. Her accounting year ran from 16 March and her expenditure on clothes fluctuated between £759 and £877 except during 1526–27 when it rose to £1,152 (Table 10.3).[21] The sustained level of expenditure indicates that she persisted as though nothing had changed.

Catherine's wardrobe emphasised her very traditional perception of her position as queen. She chose rich dark colours and expensive fabrics. Her religious piety is shown by her wearing the habit of St Francis under her robes. In private she wore plain clothes as a sign of humility.[22]

Three years after the annulment of her marriage, Catherine died on 7 January 1536. After her death, Sir Edmund Bedingfield wrote to Cromwell to inform him that 'To the best of our power we have commanded the safe custody of the gates so that nothing can issue. The persons who have

Table 10.3: *Catherine of Aragon's household expenditure 1524–30*

Accounting year	Robes	Beds	Laundry	Total
1524–25	£866 0s 1½*d*	£55 8*s* ½*d*	£3 5*s* 10*d*	£4,440 12*s* 8*d*
1525–26	£877 10s 3½*d*	£11 15*s* 7*d*	£4 6*s* 6*d*	£4,677 8*s* 11*d*
1526–27	£1,152 12*s* 1½*d*	£56 15*s* 2*d*	£3 11*s* 4*d*	£4,830 6*s* 1½*d*
1527–28	£768 8*s* 10¾*d*	£14 4*s* 3*d*	£2 19*s* 10*d*	£4,135 3*s* 1½*d*
1528–29*	~	~	65s 8d	~
1529–30	£759 2*s* 10¾*d*	£5 13*s* 11*d*	£3 7*s* 5*d*	[. . .] 9*d*

* The account is badly damaged

custo[dy of her] jewels, plate and apparel have given us a just and plain declaration, containing much more than [we could] see or know before'.[23] On 22 January Richard Rich advised Cromwell that 'The gentlewomen claim divers apparel as given them by the lady Dowager, and the officers divers stuff as their fees. It would not be honourable to take the things given in her lifetime'.[24]

Anne Boleyn

As an adolescent Anne Boleyn spent approximately 15 months at the court of Margaret of Austria, in the Netherlands, where she learnt the French language and French manners. She told her father that she was 'all the keener to persevere in speaking French well'.[25] She then went to join the household of Mary Tudor as queen of France, and on Mary's return to England she stayed on to serve Queen Claude of France. She was recalled home late in 1521 and entered the household of Catherine of Aragon.[26]

George Cavendish praised her at court on account of 'her excellent grace and behaviour'.[27] Another observer noted that 'albeit in beauty she was to many inferior, but for behaviour, manners, attire and tongue she excelled them all, for she had been brought up in France'.[28] Lancelot de Carles described her as 'beautiful and with an elegant figure', and he paid Anne a particular compliment when he noted that 'no one would ever have taken her to be English by her manners, but a native-born Frenchwoman'.[29] John Barlow described Anne as 'very eloquent and gracious and reasonably good looking', while he thought Elizabeth Blount was 'more beautiful'.[30] In September 1531 Simon Grynée described her as 'young, good-looking, of a rather dark complexion'.[31] The Venetian diarist Sanuto described her in 1532 as being 'not one of the handsomest women in the world; she is of middling stature, swarthy complexion, long neck, wide mouth, bosom not much raised, . . . eyes which are black and beautiful, hair black, wonderful long hair'.[32] She clearly was very attractive to Henry. He wrote to her, 'wishing myself (specially of an evening) in my sweetheart's arms, whose pretty ducks I trust shortly to kiss'.[33]

Henry's infatuation with Anne started around Christmas 1524–25. At first things did not go smoothly. In May 1527 Henry and Anne appeared in public together for the first time at the reception given at Greenwich for the French ambassadors. Cavendish noted her rise and remarked that she was 'very haughty and stout [self-confident] having all manner of jewels or rich apparel that might be gotten with money'.[34] Even so, the first extant reference to the king providing her with expensive gifts of clothes and jewellery dates from three years later. On 21 May 1530 Henry paid £59 18*s* to his tailor and skinner for items for Anne.[35] Six days later a warrant was issued to Sir Andrew Windsor for a number of saddles and other items to be provided for Anne, including three black and gold saddles and other harness, in addition to harness for the mules carrying her litter.[36] One of the saddles was of the French fashion, so reflecting Anne's Francophilia, with a pillow of down covered with black velvet, the head of copper and gilt. On 29 May Henry presented her with archery equipment including bows, arrows, a shooting glove and a bracer costing £1 3*s* 4*d*.[37] In the following month additional bows were supplied at a price of 13*s* 4*d*.[38] Later, in November, Henry spent £16 on 19¾ yards (18 m) of crimson satin for Anne at 16*s* the yard and a dozen budge skins.[39] This would have been enough cloth to provide her with a new gown.

Henry's gift to Anne at the New Year 1531 was a set of cloth of silver, cloth of gold and embroidered crimson satin hangings for her bed and bed chamber.[40] The gifts continued throughout 1531 and the work was undertaken by craftsmen either in the employment of the king or Catherine of Aragon. In April 1531 William Ibgrave was paid £18 14*s* 9*d* in April 1531 for stuff for Anne.[41] In December Thomas Addington received £80 8*s* 8*d* towards furs and furring Anne's gowns and undertook further work 1531 for £40 15*s* 8*d*.[42] In the same month John Scut was paid £28 6*s* 4*d* for making apparel for her.[43] He received a further payment of £7 11*s* 4*d* dated 26 May 1532. 1531 was a turning point in Anne's ousting of Catherine. From then onwards items were ordered for her on the king's own warrants. Items ordered on the king's warrant dated 16 June 1531 included a nightgown of black lukes velvet embroidered with gold thread, lined with black taffeta and the sleeves lined with buckram, 16 pairs of velvet shoes and two pairs of night slippers.[44]

There are two portrait types of Anne Boleyn, both of which survive only in various versions from after her death. In the first, Anne wears the French hood, with the velvet hanging down her back and it is decorated with upper and nether biliments of pearls. This use of pearls is echoed in her two necklaces of pearls, with a B with three pendant pearls hanging from the short necklace and a square of pears decorating the neckline of her gown (Pl. Vc).[45] She was dressed in a black gown with a low square neckline which is not infilled with a partlet. The width of the neck pushes the sleeve heads

of her very tight-fitting sleeves slightly off her shoulders. Her oversleeves of a dark brown fur, possibly of sable, are just visible. In the second portrait type, Anne wears a gable headdress and a carcenet of rubies and pearls with the AB monogram pinned to the square neckline of her bodice.[46] Both portraits indicate that she used her jewellery to promote her own status and that of her family.

A list of jewels delivered to the king by Cornelius Hayes since 1 August of an unspecified year included a list of pieces made for 'Mistress Anne' has traditionally been dated to May 1531.[47] However, this document has been tentatively dated to 1527 because the list included a ring set with emeralds given to Anne by Henry at Beaulieu and the king did not return there after 1527.[48] Other items included two borders of gold set with ten diamonds and eight pearls for her sleeves, a girdle of crown gold, two diamonds set upon hats and 19 diamonds set in trueloves of crown gold.

In June 1532 Henry bought clothes for Anne out of his privy purse. The list included an open-sleeved cloak of black satin, lined with the same and trimmed at the hem and the collar with black velvet, made by John Malt for 5*s*.[49] In addition there was a nightgown of black satin lined with black taffeta and edged with velvet, also made by Malt.[50] A second nightgown was made for her from 16 yards (14.6 m) of green damask costing £6 12*s* and made up by John Scut.[51]

On 1 September 1532 Anne was ennobled as marchioness of Pembroke and a month later George Tailor was paid £56 for 'certeyne silkes by him provided for Apparell'.[52] In December John Parker of the robes received £16 16*s* 'for suche stuf as he dud bye of locke and of barker for my lady marques'.[53] During the autumn Anne had accompanied Henry for his meeting with Francis I at Calais and he had a lot of jewellery reset for her prior to the visit.[54] On 27 October Anne led the ladies who danced before the two kings: 'After supper came in the Marchiones of Penbroke, with vii ladies in Maskyng apparel of straunge fashion, made of clothe of gold, compassed with Crimosyn Tinsell Satin, owned with Clothe of Siluer, linyng lose and knit with laces of Gold.'[55]

Anne married Henry in January 1533 but another four months elapsed before her coronation. An antagonistic view of her coronation stated that 'the crown became her very ill, and a wart disfigured her very much. She wore a violet velvet mantle, with a high ruff of gold thread and pearls, which concealed a swelling she has, resembling goitre'.[56] In this view, her clothes were used to conceal her physical deformity. There is one warrant that has been listed in *Letters and Papers* with the coronation documents, but the editors acknowledged that it may not be linked with this event. The document includes payments for 3 yards (2.7 m) of crimson taffeta to line Anne's velvet gown, 5 yards (4.5 m) of white satin for a kirtle and 2½ yards (2.2 m) of red cloth to line the kirtle.[57]

According to the Jesuit Nicolas Sander, writing a long time afterwards, Anne was very interested in her appearance and consequently 'every day she made some change in the fashion of her garments'.[58] Unfortunately, there are very few references to clothes being ordered by Henry for Anne after their marriage. A rare example is a gift ordered for 'our derest wyffe' in June 1535 on his own warrant consisting of 20⅞ yards (19 m) of green satin and 13⅝ yards (12.4 m) of checked green cloth of gold which was supplied by the great wardrobe.[59]

George Tailor, receiver-general to Anne Boleyn, prepared his accounts on 29 September for the year ending Michaelmas 1535. The account summaries recorded that £68 17*s* 6*d* had been spent on the wardrobe of the robes and £44 7*s* 8*d* on the wardrobe of the beds.[60] These figures added together were a sixth of what Anne's horses had cost. The modesty of the totals is striking and suggests that many items ordered during the 12 months involved were either still unpaid for or were paid for from a different source. The list of her debts at her death provides further details about her expenditure on textiles and dress. Amongst the unsettled bills, three are of particular interest. On 19 and 20 February 1536 Henry Cryche, the clerk of her wardrobe, received four tassels of fine Florence gold costing 4*s* 6*d* each and he paid 3*s* for laying in new satin into an old bonnet. In March eight of her frontlets had been repaired at a cost of 12*d* each.[61] A bill from William Lock, mercer, for the last four months of her life shows her spending about £40 a month with Lock on cloth plus a further £68 4*s* 1½*d* on trimmings.[62] On 17 May 1536 Anne's marriage was annulled and two days later she was beheaded. Elegant to the last, Anne wore for her execution a mantle of ermine over a loose gown of dark grey damask trimmed with fur and a crimson petticoat. Under her headdress she had a white linen coif covering her hair which she revealed on removing her headdress just before being beheaded.[63]

Jane Seymour

Jane Seymour came from a Wiltshire gentle family. She caught Henry's eye while serving Anne Boleyn as one of her ladies. On 1 April 1536 Eustace Chapuys referred to Jane as 'the lady whom he [i.e. Henry] serves'.[64] He described her as being 'Of middle stature and no great beauty; so fair that one would call her rather pale than otherwise. She is over 25 . . . The said Seymour is not a woman of great wit, but she may have good understanding. It is said that she inclines to be proud and haughty'.[65] She married the king on 30 May 1536, 11 days after the execution of Anne Boleyn, and she died on 24 October 1537 shortly after giving birth to Prince Edward. Her motto was 'Bound to obey and serve'.

The evidence of her wardrobe indicates that she used it to define her role as queen. On 23 December 1536 'Yesterday the king and Queen, with all the dukes and lordes and the Emperor's ambassador, rode through London and were honourably received. Such a sight has not been seen since the emperor was here'.[66] A selection of Jane's clothes is recorded in the 1542 inventory of Whitehall. It represents a significant percentage of the clothes that were made for her during the 17 months of her marriage to the king. Her wardrobe included a wider range of garments to those found in Catherine of Aragon's wardrobe. Jane's clothes were also made from a larger range of colours but a similar range of fabrics. A fragmentary set of accounts for her clothing possibly includes

Table 10.4: *Analysis of Jane Seymour's clothes by textile type*

	Gowns	Outside of a gown	Kirtles	Foreparts	Cloaks	Sleeves	Stomachers	Frontlets
Capha	1	~	~	~	~	~	~	~
Cloth of gold	~	1	3	~	~	16	3	~
Cloth of silver	~	~	1	~	~	10	3	~
Composite	~	~	~	~	~	1	~	~
Damask	6	~	2	~	~	~	~	~
Linen	~	~	~	~	~	2	~	~
Satin	4	2	1	1	1	12	3	15
Taffeta	3	~	1	~	~	1	~	~
Tissue	~	~	~	~	~	8	3	~
Velvet	9	~	6	~	~	14	~	~
	24	3	**14**	1	1	**64**	12	15

Table 10.5: *Analysis of Jane Seymour's clothes by colour*

	Gowns	Outside of a gown	Kirtles	Foreparts	Cloaks	Sleeves	Stomachers	Frontlets
Black	5	1	1	~	~	8	~	~
Carnation	1	~	1	~	~	2	~	~
Cloth of silver	~	~	1	~	~	3	1	~
Cloth of gold	~	~	~	~	~	3	~	~
Crimson	3	~	4	1	~	10	1	10
Gold/silver	~	~	~	~	~	1	~	~
Green	2	~	2	~	~	4	~	~
Orange	~	~	~	~	~	1	~	~
Orange/tawny	~	~	1	~	~	~	~	~
Purple	4	~	3	~	~	13	7	2
Russet	1	~	~	~	~	~	~	~
Tawny	~	1	~	~	1	2	~	~
White	3	~	1	~	~	16	3	3
Yellow	3	~	~	~	~	1	~	~
	24	2	**14**	1	1	**64**	12	15

payments for some of the items listed in the 1542 inventory: ¾ of a yard (0.68 m) of white velvet for a pair of sleeves for a kirtle of white velvet for 10*s* and 1 ¾ yards (1.6 m) of white satin for the upper parts of a kirtle of embroidered white velvet costing 11*s* 8*d*.[67]

Nineteen of Jane's 23 recorded gowns were described as being 'turned up' meaning bordered, with just two gowns described as being without borders. Of these all but four were turned up with fabric of the same colour, while three had a different colour. In eight cases they had used the same fabric and in ten they had not. Only one gown was turned up with fur. Her accounts include payments for two kirtles, neither of which figure in the 1542 list:

1 ½ yard of crimson satin for the upperbodies of a kirtle of carnation coloured velvet embroidered 18*s*
1 ½ yard of purple satin for the upperbodies of a kirtle of purple velvet embroidered 18*s*

In addition to having kirtles with bodies, she also had 'one base of a kirtle' (11272) and a forepart (11275).

Sleeves provided an excellent means of display. Jane had sleeves adorned with gold aglets or rather pairs of gold aglets. Forty-nine pairs of sleeves were decorated in this way and the descriptions indicate that the aglets had a function: 'oone peir of Slevis of white cloth of golde reyzid with golde and Silver tissue / tyed with viij peir of Aglettes of golde' [2144]. After aglets, embroidery was the next most favoured form of adornment, being employed on 16 pairs. It appears to have chiefly been carried out in metal thread or black silk, and a few naturalistic designs are recorded: acorns [2180], honeysuckle [2178] and 'a barnacle and traile' [2175]. There are also four instances of decorative quilting, and in each case the work was executed in black silk in floral designs of the type recorded in portraits including 'oone peir of Slevis paned overth~~warte~~ <arme> with golde and Silver quiltid with blac Silke ruffed at thande with strawberye Leavis and flowers of golde and blac Silke' [2181].[68]

Just one pair of sleeves was decorated with the king's initial made in gold: 'oone peir of Slevis of crymsen Satten thowtesides of either of them sett with iiij .H. of golde And in every H. ix peerles' [2174]. It is possible that Jane wore these sleeves when Henry wore the doublet, the foresleeves and placard of which, had been decorated with 18 emeralds and 29 letter of I, each containing nine pearls, all set in gold.[69] The stones and letters were delivered by Sir Anthony Denny on 14 June 1536 to William Ibgrave, embroiderer to the king. Jane also owned two pairs of linen sleeves of the type seen in the portrait from the Mauritshuis (Pl. VIA), one pair being more luxurious than the other:

oone peir of Lynen slevis paned with golde over tharme quiltid with blac ilke and flowers betwixe the panes and at the hande. [2182]
oone peir of Lynen Slevis enbraudred alover with blac silke and venice golde tuffed owte with Lynen cloth. [2183]

Holbein painted Jane once, and he and his studio produced several versions of her portrait (Pl. VIb). Her crimson velvet gown has a tight-fitting bodice with a waistline slightly below normal with a square neckline and tight-fitting sleeves worn in conjunction with large oversleeves. The embroidered or couched grid pattern of gilt metal thread on the cuffs or oversleeves that matches the narrow embroidered border around the neckline of her gown and the triangular front opening of her skirt. The square of clusters of four pearls alternating with rubies echoes the composition of her two necklaces. In addition, Jane wore a large ruby pendant and a jewelled IHS monogram pinned to her bodice.[70] Her girdle, also of rubies and pearls, follows her natural waistline.

Anne of Cleves

On 18 March 1539 Cromwell informed the king how Christopher Mount 'presses the matter every day, and that meanwhile the picture may be sent. The Duke promised to send it, but said that his painter Lucas [Cranach] was sick at home. Everyone praises the lady's beauty, both of face and body. One said that she excelled the Duchess [of Milan] as the golden sun did the silver moon'.[71] Nicholas Wotton focused more on her accomplishments, noting that 'She occupieth her time much with the needle. She can read and write her own [language] but French and Latin, or any other language she knoweth not; nor yet can sing or play on any instrument, for they take it here in Germany for a rebuke and an occasion of lightness, that great ladies should be learned or have any knowledge of music'.[72] At the time she was not the only candidate. Henry also considered Mary of Guise very seriously. Gaspard de Coligny, sieur de Castillion, reported that 'the king of England would have given half his kingdom for her'. Henry felt she would be appropriate because he needed a big wife as he himself was large.[73]

Henry VIII and his advisors considered another candidate, Christina of Denmark, the recently widowed duchess of Milan (Fig. 9.1).[74] Holbein's full-length portrait of the duchess depicts her dressed in a black, fur-lined loose gown with a stand collar, worn over a black kirtle, drawn in with a silk girdle tied at the waist. Her white linen chemise is decorated with a small frill which showed at the neck of her kirtle, edged with black silk. In addition, she wears a tight-fitting black silk bonnet and she holds a pair of leather gloves. The portrait is of particular interest as the king kept it, being listed in both the 1542 and 1547 inventories of his possessions. Once it became apparent that Henry's fourth marriage would not last, gossip linked his name with that of the duchess again. On 13 July 1540 Richard Pate mentioned to the duke of Norfolk the current rumours that 'the Queen [Anne of Cleves] will be secluded in an abbey, and the King marry either the duchess of Milan or an English duke's daughter'.[75]

The marriage treaty signed on 6 October 1539 by several privy councillors allowed the following: point 2 'that the duke of Juliers shall within two months, if he can obtain safe conduct, convey, at his own expense, the lady Anne his sister honourably to Calais'; point 3 that the king is to meet her and 'marry her publicly'; point 4 that she is to receive a dowry of 100,000 florins of gold; and point 5 that Henry is to give her dower lands worth yearly 20,000 golden florins of the Rhine, the equivalent to 5,000 marks and after the king's death, if she has no children she was to receive a pension of 15,000 florins to be paid half-yearly, as well as her dresses and jewels.[76]

10.3 *Anne of Cleves, attributed to Barthel Bruyn the Elder. The President and Fellows of St John's College, Oxford*

The English were not enamoured of the high-necked Netherlandish fashions for women favoured in Cleves, such as those she wore and in which she appears in her portrait attributed to Barthel Bruyn the elder (Fig. 10.3). In Holbein's portrait of her (Fig. 10.4) she wears the fashionable dress and jewellery of the Netherlands: a jewelled coif, a jewelled pendant, a short necklace worn about the throat made up of enamelled floral links, her square made of similar floral links.[77] Anne and her sister Amelia were presented to the English ambassadors in 'monstrous habit and apparel'. In defence as much as anger, the chancellor of Cleves asked, 'Why, would you see them naked?'.[78]

Lady Lisle heard how, for her meeting with the king at Blackheath, Anne was 'shifted ... wondrous gorgeously in cloth of tissue, and a rich attire upon her head of her own country fashion'.[79] The French ambassador observed that 'she was clothed in the fashion of the country from which she came' (Fig. 10.4) and went on to add that 'she looks about

10.4 *Miniature of Anne of Cleves by Hans Holbein the Younger. P.153–1910. © V&A Images, Victoria and Albert Museum London*

30 years of age, tall and thin, of medium beauty, and of very assured and resolute countenance. She brought 12 or 15 ladies of honour clothed like herself — a thing which looks strange to many'.[80] He found Anne's women 'inferior in beauty even to their mistress and dressed so heavily and unbecomingly that they would almost be thought ugly even if they were beautiful'.[81]

The divorce settlement agreed on 21 July 1540 allowed Anne an income, clothes, jewels and pearls and a sufficient household to her status.[82] Three days later the king told his envoys abroad that Anne had 'confessed the integrity of her body and refusing mother and brother and all who would move her to the contrary, committed herself wholly to the King to remain as his servant and subject'.[83] The separation did not make Anne downcast. The French ambassador observed that she was 'as joyous as ever, and wears new dresses every day'.[84]

Following the arrest of Catherine Howard, Anne of Cleves speculated as to whether Henry would accept her again as his wife. But on 29 January 1542 Chapuys informed Charles V that 'There seems less hope than ever of his taking back the lady of Cleves, though on New Year's day she presented him with some pieces of crimoisy cloth, and he gave her some glass pots and flagons'.[85] Even so, rumours persisted. Four years later, Stephen Vaughan in the Netherlands was questioned 'Whether the King had taken again the Lady Anne of Cleves and she was brought abed with two children and why she was put away at first. Somewhat abashed I answered that I had heard this of the Emperor's subjects, but knew only that she goes and comes to the Court at her pleasure and has an honest dowry to live upon'.[86]

Catherine Howard

Catherine was the second cousin of Anne Boleyn. She began her career at court as a maid of honour to Anne of Cleves. On 28 July 1540 she married Henry VIII. On 8 August she was presented at court as queen and a week later the public prayed for her as their queen. Following the revelations about her sexual misconduct before and after marriage, she was beheaded 13 February 1542.

Even before his divorce from Anne of Cleves, Henry showed Catherine favour. The first was on 24 April 1540 when he gave Mistress Howard land and several weeks later he presented her with 23 lengths of quilted sarsenet.[87] On 6 July the French ambaasador reported that there was 'some diminution of love [for Anne of Cleves] and new affection to another lady, this queen has been sent to Richmond. The King, who promised to follow her in two days, has not done so, and his going thither is not spoken of, for the route he has proscribed for his progress does not lie in that direction'.[88] About the same time the 'courtiers first observed that he was much taken with another young lady, very small of stature . . . whom he was seen crossing the Thames to visit, often in the day time and sometimes at night'.[89] Archbishop Cranmer's secretary observed that 'The King's affection was so marvellously set upon the gentlewoman, as it was never known that he had the like to any other woman'.[90] Ever a source of gossip, the French ambassador described Catherine on 3 September 1540 as being 'a young lady of moderate beauty but superlative grace. In stature she is small and slender . . . She is dressed after the French fashion like all the other ladies of this court and bears her device round her arm, "Non aultre volonté que le sienne" "No other will than his"'.[91]

Catherine, like her cousin, favoured French fashions and as such this would denote a change in style that would have distinguished her both from Jane and Anne of Cleves. Until recently, it was held that there are no known authentic portraits of Catherine Howard. The half-length portrait that is often identified as being of her is probably a member of the Cromwell family.[92] A miniature of an unknown lady by Holbein has been identified as Catherine Howard by her jewellery (Fig. 10.5). She wears a pendant ruby jewel similar to that in the portrait of Jane Seymour in the Kunsthistorisches Museum, Vienna.[93] In addition, the king's gifts to her at the New Year in 1541 included 'an upper habiliment containing eight diamonds and seven rubies' very similar to those depicted in the miniature.[94]

Little has come to light about Catherine's wardrobe. Francis Dereham gave her small gifts and she reciprocated. He gave her a silk flower of a type known as a 'French fennel' which he bought from 'a little woman in London . . . skilled in making all sorts of silk flowers'.[95] In 1547 there was 'a braunche of flowers wrought vppon wyer' (9548) in the closet over the waterstair at Greenwich which may have been one of these sprays of flowers. In 1541 Catherine exchanged New Year's gifts with Dereham. She gave him a band and sleeves for a shirt that were decorated with embroidery. He gave her a silk heart's ease and sarsenet for a quilted cap which was

10.5 *Portrait of a lady, possibly Catherine Howard, by Hans Holbein the Younger. RCIN 422293 GR 6 Cust19101/13. The Royal Collection © 2004, Her Majesty the Queen Elizabeth II*

delivered 'to a little fellow in my lady's house to embroider, as I remember, his name was Rose, an embroiderer, to make it what patterns he thought best, and not appointing him to make it with friar's knots, so he can testify if he be a true man'.[96]

In October 1541 Catherine was arrested and she lost her clothes, her jewels and her royal status. Henry VIII ordered that:

> Mr Seymour shall remain there [Hampton Court], with all the jewels and other things of the queen's, till she be gone and then to bring them hither. As to the queen's grace you must appoint six French hoods, with the appertenances, with edges of goldsmiths' work, so there be no stone or pearl in the same; likewise, as many pair of sleeves, six gowns, and six kirtles of satin, damasks and velvets, with such things as belong to the same, except always stone and pearl.[97]

Late in January 1542 Chapuys mentioned to the emperor that 'She is still at Syon, making good cheer, fatter and more beautiful than ever, taking great care to be well apparelled and more imperious and troublesome to serve than ever she was with the King'.[98] Two weeks later, on 10 February, Catherine was taken to the Tower and 'on their arrival at the Tower, the lords landed first; then the Queen, in black velvet, and they paid her as much honour as when she was reigning'.[99] She was executed on the 13th.

Catherine Parr

Holbein incorporated Catherine Parr's maiden head badge into a design for a brooch which consisted of the maiden (wearing a French hood and a gown with a square neckline and large hanging oversleeves) holding a scroll with the queen's motto 'Well Lovydi well' and three pendant pearls.[100] This illustrates Catherine's careful development of her royal image, making full use of contemporary designers. Catherine came from a Westmorland gentle family with midlands links and a traditional service at court. Her godmother was almost certainly Catherine of Aragon. On 12 July 1543 she took Henry VIII as her third husband. She was described as being 'of small stature' and as being 'graceful and of cheerful countenance; and is praised for her virtue'.[101]

A number of portraits of Catherine Parr are known, of which the most striking is a full-length portrait *c.* 1545 attributed to Master John.[102] Catherine is dressed in a gown of cloth of silver tissue woven with a very large repeat pomegranate design. The tight-fitting bodice has a square neckline and a low pointed waistline, while the conical shape of the skirt is created by her farthingale (Fig. 9.3). In the portrait attributed to William Scrots, *c.* 1545, Catherine wears a bonnet or cap which is very masculine in style (Fig. 10.6). The bodice of her gown or kirtle is made of crimson satin with a Medici-style collar and V-neck with bands of couched metal thread embroidery worked in geometric designs in double bands down the sleeves, at the shoulders and cuffs and a quadruple band up the front of the bodice. The bodice is less tight-fitting with the fabric formed in loose pleats, while the one-piece sleeves are full at the sleeve heads running down to tight cuffs.

10.6 *Catherine Parr, attributed to William Scrots, 1545. National Portrait Gallery, London (NPG 4618)*

Catherine's interest in clothes in the latest styles is indicated by her engagement of John Scut, who had been tailor to all of Henry's previous queens, prior to her becoming queen. A bill with a marginal note dated 16 February 1543 included gowns in the French, Dutch, Italian and Venetian styles along with hoods to a total value of £8 *9s 5d* made by Scut for her stepdaughter Margaret Neville.[103] After her marriage, Scut worked for her directly.[104]

For her first year as queen, Catherine chose to dress in crimson and cloth of gold. On 18 February 1544 for the reception of the duke of Najera she wore 'an open robe of cloth of gold, the sleeves lined with crimson satin, and trimmed with three piled crimson velvet, the train more than two yards long. Suspended from the neck were two crosses, and a jewel of very rich diamonds, and in her headdress were many rich and beautiful ones. Her girdle was of gold, with very large pendants'.[105] Catherine was attended by Princess Mary, Lady Margaret Douglas and 'other ladies [who] were dressed in different silks with splendid headdresses'. Later, she wore purple for all important occasions.[106] A bill dated 29 November 1544 submitted by Symond Loo, a mercer, for stuff delivered to the queen confirms this. In the previous nine months Arthur Belfield had delivered 8½ yards (7.7 m) of purple velvet for a kirtle at 25*s* the yard and 2 yards (1.8 m) of purple satin for the bodies at 12*s* the yard, and to Ralph Worsley, 10 yards (9.1 m) of purple satin for a kirtle with French sleeves and Venetian stocks at 15*s* the yard; 1¾ yards (1.6 m) purple satin for a forepart of a kirtle of purple satin 'pownste'; 2½ yards (2.2 m) of black velvet for turning up of a gown of camlet for Mrs Dorothy Fountain at 13*s* 4*d* the yard and 10 yards (9.1 m) of yellow satin for a kirtle at 8*s* 6*d* the yard (0.91 m).[107]

Catherine shared her husband's fondness for shoes, ordering pairs in a range of colours including black, crimson, white and blue, all trimmed with gold at 14*s* a pair, quarter shoes at 5*s* a pair and corked shoes lined with red at 5*s* a pair.[108] Two of her cordwainer's bills (Table 10.6) give a good indication of the quantity and variety of shoes that she was wearing.

A short account for Catherine's wardrobe of the robes dating from 1544–45 includes a range of entries that were not dated individually, but a number relate to livery given by the queen at the New Year and to gifts of clothing given to Edward. It is possible that Catherine sought to celebrate the New Year in style. This seems to be the most likely occasion that she would have ordered matching clothes for herself, Princess Mary, Princess Elizabeth, Prince Edward and Anne of Cleves at a cost of £65 16s. Dominico Erizo provided 16 yards (14.6 m) of plain cloth of silver for 'a frenche gowne for the Quenes grace' costing £22 8*s*, and 8 yards (7.3 m) of the same for a kirtle with French sleeves and Venetian stocks for £11 4*s*.[109] In addition, there were kirtles of the same cloth for Mary, Elizabeth and Anne, while Edward was given a doublet and a pair of highly fashionable slops. It is possible that Catherine had a particular liking for cloth of silver for the New Year as there exists a second order for a kirtle with Venetian sleeves made from 8 yards (7.3 m) 'of fine clothe silver braunched' at 40*s* the yard, along with her second order for black satin livery given as New Year's gifts.

Mark Milliner made regular deliveries to the queen's wardrobe, as shown by two accounts running from 13 July 1543 to 22 January 1546 and 17 July 1543 to 4 January 1546 with a total value of £26 3*s* 4*d*.[110] Items were supplied in small, but regular, deliveries with some several times a month. The queen bought large quantities of silk ribbon for aglets, short lengths of black velvet and black sarsenet, gloves, both Spanish and English and hats. The latter included 'a felthe for a woman covered with satin with laces of gold delivered to Mr Forten at Deptford' for 4*s*, 1½ yards (1.3 m) of gold lace and a tassel of silk and gold for a hat and 'a cap of red and yellow velvet with four feathers and four tassels of gold and silk' costing 6*s* 8*d*.

Like the king and his children, Catherine received large deliveries of cloth from the silk house at Whitehall from the time of her marriage until the king's death (Table 10.7). Crimson and purple certainly feature prominently amongst the lengths, supplemented with a range of other colours.

In the spring of 1547, following Henry VIII's death, Catherine married Lord Seymour of Sudeley.[111] Following her death in September 1548 and Seymour's execution in February 1549, clothes which may have been hers or Henry's were returned from Sudeley to Whitehall. These clothes included a gown, a coat, a cassock and two coats which were described as 'but a Cassocke' (17645–49) that could have been Henry's or Seymour's. There were no gowns or kirtles amongst the clothes sent from Sudeley, possibly because these were given away to Catherine's ladies-in-waiting at her death. However, what remained was of very high quality and gives an indication of her taste and of what was fashionable. Of the 14 partlets (17653–66), 33 placards (17667–97) and 55 pairs of sleeves (17698–751), velvet, cloth of silver and satin were the most frequently used fabrics, while purple, crimson and black were the most common colours. Most of these garments were heavily decorated with metal thread embroidery or applied cutwork. The sleeves were similarly decorated, often edged with a contrasting fabric or with fur. Distinct types were identified including 37 pairs of French sleeves, 11 pairs of trunk sleeves, two pairs of Turkey sleeves and five pairs of an unspecified type, including 'another paier of frenche Sleaves of greane velvet richelie embraudred withe flowres of

Table 10.6: *Shoes delivered to Catherine Parr*

Type of shoes	July 1543–August 1544	August 1544–March 1545
Buskins	1 pair	~
Shoes	56 pairs	4 pairs
Shoes, for the Maundy	32 pairs	~
Shoes, for walking	2 pairs	~
Shoes, lined	4 pairs	~
Shoes, lined and corked	4 pairs	6 pairs
Shoes, low voided	2 pairs	~
Shoes, quartered	10 pairs	28 pairs
Shoes, trimmed with gold	~	9 pairs
Slippers	2 pairs	~
Slippers, lined	4 pairs	~
	117 pairs	**47 pairs**

Table 10.7: *Cloth delivered to Catherine Parr from the Whitehall silk house*

Type of cloth	Quantity	Type of cloth	Quantity
Tissue	26¼ yards (24 m)	*Damask*	
Cloth of gold		– Black	1½ yards (1.4 m)
– Crimson	23¾ yards (21.7 m)	– Orange	34⅞ yards (31.9 m)
– Yellow	21 yards (19.2 m)	*Taffeta*	
Cloth of silver	9 yards (8.2 m)	– Black	10 yards (9.1 m)
Velvet		– Incarnate	11 yards (10.1 m)
– Black	315⅝ yards (288.6 m)	– Purple	10 yards (9.1 m)
– Crimson	64¾ yards (56.5 m)	*Sarsenet*	
– Green	23¼ yards (21.3 m)	– Black	78½ yards (71.2 m)
– Murrey	12 yards (10.9 m)	– Crimson and red	48 yards (41.9 m)
– Purple	28⅝ yards (26.2 m)	– Green	5 yards (4.6 m)
– Russet	29 yards (26.5 m)	– Murrey	12 yards (10.9 m)
– Tawny	29 yards (26.5 m)	– Purple, blue and violet	18 yards (16.5 m)
Satin		– Russet	12 yards (10.9 m)
– Black	95¼ yards (87.1 m)	– Tawny	18 yards (16.5 m)
– Blue	1 yard (0.9 m)	– White	12 yards (10.9 m)
– Changeable	17¾ yards (16.2 m)	– Yellow	12½ yards (11.4 m)
– Crimson	6½ yards (5.9 m)	*Baudekin*	104½ yards (95.5 m)
– Incarnate	2 yards (1.8 m)	*Normandy cloth*	12 ells (8.3 m)
– Murrey	1 yard (0.9 m)	*Passementerie*	5 lb 7 oz (2.5 kg)
– Purple	4½ yards (4.1 m)	**Totals: 1,102⅜ yards (1,003.3 m); 12 ells (8.3m); 5 lb 7 oz (2.5 kg)**	
– White	4¼ yards (3.9 m)		

damaske golde pirle of morisco worke withe knoppes of veanice golde cordiaunte raised euery sleave hauing vj small Buttons of golde and in every Button a peerle and the Traines of the flowres set withe peerle' (17706).

Catherine seems to have liked aglets which appeared on 22 pairs of sleeves, but not quite to the same extent as on Jane Seymour's sleeves. However, a new feature was the use of enamelled aglets on 14 pairs. Embroidery was also important, appearing on 11 pairs: six were worked with floral designs but there were also designs incorporating large numbers of seed pearls, cutwork, antiques and 'moresco work'. Nineteen pairs of sleeves were edged with fabric, often velvet. One reason why the use of embroidery may have been restricted somewhat was the increased use of patterned fabrics: 22 pairs made from floral fabrics, five with 'works' and two with roundels.

Catherine's accounts reveal how her clothes were stored in the queen's wardrobe which continued to be housed at Baynard's castle. In October 1544 Mr Frytton was paid 4*s* 6*d* for riding from Woking to London 'for certeyn the Queen's Graces ffurde gownes from Baynardes' and from Eltham to London for pins, starch and other necessaries. In the following month John Morley, sumpterman, received 2*s* 8*d* 'for his ch[arges going] with the sumpter horse from Ok[ing for certain] gowns for the Queen's [grace from Ba]ynardes Castell'.[112]

Catherine's coffer brought from Sudeley on 16 November 1549 contained a white ostrich feather (3537) and five caps made from black velvet (3592–96), 'a Cappe of black vellat garneshed with xxij paire of Aglattes of gold and xj Buttons of gold enameled black' (3594). The caps may have belonged to either the king or Seymour, but equally Catherine may have been their owner. Her jewel coffer contained four biliments of gold that she would have worn with French hoods (3531–34).

Table 10.8: *Analysis of Catherine Parr's clothes by textile type*

Textile	Partlets	Placards	Sleeves
Baudekin	~	1	~
Camlet, gold	~	~	1
Cloth of gold	1	4	6
Cloth of silver	3	3	12
Damask	~	1	~
Satin	1	9	11
Taffeta	~	1	~
Tinsel	~	~	4
Tissue	~	6	6
Velvet	9	8	15
	14	33	55

Table 10.9: *Analysis of Catherine Parr's clothes by colour*

Colour	Partlets	Placards	Sleeves
Black	~	9	7
Blue	~	2	2
Carnation	~	~	1
Cloth of gold	~	3	1
Cloth of silver	3	3	8
Crimson	4	4	11
Green	~	2	5
Murrey	2	2	1
Purple	4	2	13
Red	1	2	3
Tawny	~	3	~
Unspecified	~	1	1
White	~	~	2
	14	33	55

Catherine also owned 'a Fanne or a Skryne for to holde in thande of black Oistriche feathers sett in golde garneshed with vj counterfett stones and some peerles' (3591). The introduction of the ostrich feather fan to northern Europe has been cost of bringing his sister from Berwick to London, at a price of £130 3*s*. This included £7 for sending a tailor and skinner to Berwick 'to make the apparrelle of the seid quene and her husbond' and 19*s* 4*d* 'to dyverse shepsters for makyng of iij smockes for the seid quene and twoo shirtes for her husbond'.[142] She also asked her tailor in Edinburgh to make more and in the meantime was 'going to have in all haste' a gown of purple velvet lined with cloth of gold, a gown of crimson velvet furred with ermine, three other gowns and three satin kirtles.[143] A portrait of Margaret 'Painted ... in a Black habbitt with yallow sleeves with a litle Monkey houlding uppon her hands' belonged to Charles I.[144] The portrait was painted in 1515–17 during her stay in England.[145] It is now lost and is known from the copy by Mytens (Fig. 10.7).

An inventory compiled in September 1516 listed the jewels in a coffer at the castle of Templetone that were delivered to Margaret's commissioners when she was in England.[146] Margaret's treasures included rosaries, habiliments, chains and unset jewels such as:

A cheffroun with a chenze of 57 links; another with points of gold, with 61 pearls in crammesy velvet; one set with 21 rubies and 33 pearls in gold and 'ane burde of gold and twa smallbeltis with hedes and pendatit of gold'
A collar of gold enamelled with white and red roses, two other collars of gold;
A pair of sleeves of cloth of gold lined with crammesy satin, another pair of sleeves
'the King of France's great diamond set in a red hat' that was valued at 8,000 crowns
a ruby balatt on a black hat with three pearls
a partlet of gold fret set upon crammesy satin with 12 diamonds, 14 rubies, 25 pearls
a partlet of cloth of gold
a partlet of white taffeta goldsmith work
a pair of sleeves of black velvet; one bust with damask gold with ten prinnys of gold wire
a pair of coral beads with six pearls
a pair of beads of jasper with four gaudies.[147]

However, her furs could not be obtained from Stirling until after the bishop of Galloway returned from the north.

On 17 April 1517 the young James V granted his mother permission to return Scotland with a suitable suite and to receive all the profits from her dowry, her jewellery and her property.[148] On her return in May 1517, Edward Hall noted she was 'richely appointed of all things mete to her estate both of Jewells, plate, tapissry, Arras, coyne, Horsses, and all other thinges of the kynges gift and liberalitie'.[149] Unfortunately, the improvement in Margaret's situation was only temporary. Three years later she confessed that she was 'in a sore case'. She had had to pawn the jewels given by her brother on her departure from England and she had turned away her servants apart from her comptroller Robin Barton who had laid out £500 of his own to support her. Otherwise she would 'have been compelled to live like a poor gentlewoman'.[150] In 1523 she looked to her brother for assistance. She asked the earl of Surrey 'how soon the King wishes her to come, where [she was] to be met and by whom', adding that she 'will send her gowns and cobord before her and bring her jewels with her'.[151]

In 1526 Margaret married Lord Methven. Henry continued periodically to send gifts to his sister but these became increasingly sporadic. In August 1535 Cromwell noted that he was to receive cloth of gold and cloth of silver, crimson and purple satin and black velvet from Anthony Denny to be forwarded to Margaret in Scotland.[152] A month later Cromwell had not received these, and he asked, 'What silk and money the King will send to the Scotch Queen'.[153] Margaret became increasingly isolated. On 14 October 1537 she told Cromwell that 'I am now forty nine years old ... I shall never have another husband ... The King my son is more unkind to me daily, and I had liever be dead than treated as I am'.[154] She survived another two years, dying on 19 October 1539.

10.7 *Margaret Tudor, by Daniel Mytens. RCIN 401181, OM 115. The Royal Collection © 2004, Her Majesty the Queen Elizabeth II*

MARY, QUEEN OF FRANCE

Mary was acknowledged as a beauty. Erasmus observed that 'nature never formed anything more beautiful as she exceeds no less in goodness or wisdom'.[155] The Venetian ambassador admitted that she was 'very beautiful and has not her match in England; she is tall fair, of a light complexion with a colour, and most affable and graceful'.[156] Henry clothed Mary from his accession in 1509 until her marriage to Louis XII in 1514.[157] Seven warrants survive, three of which can be matched with the accounts.[158] There is also one entry in the accounts for which the warrant does not survive. Of the four entries in the accounts, the three for clothing cost £297 5*s* 1½*d*.

Many of the new gowns made for Mary had wide sleeves, such as a gown of cloth of gold lined with sarsenet, while the sleeves were lined with velvet and edged with the same. These gowns required 16 yards (14.6 m) of fabric as in the case of a gown made of russet satin costing £7 4*s*, with 5¾ yards (5.2 m) of cloth of gold to line the sleeves costing £17 5*s*. She also received two gowns with narrow sleeves. Each was made from 11 yards (10 m) of cloth. Her gown of black velvet was bordered with 1½ yards (1.3 m) of crimson satin and lined with 5 yards (4.5 m) of black sarsenet. Each warrant included two or three kirtles that were predominantly made from 7 yards (6.4 m) of satin, with just two being made from tilsent or tilsent satin. The kirtles were often bordered or hemmed with velvet and they could be worn with matching sleeves.

Most warrants ordered gowns and kirtles, but the warrant of 7 December 1511 also included a nightgown of black velvet furred with coney.[159] The warrants regularly listed 12 pairs of knit hose, as well as shoes, slippers and a pair of furred night buskins, as well as pinsons on one occasion. Mary also received linen for underclothes in the form of 30 ells (20.6 m) holland for smocks, rails, kerchers and biggins, sipers for head and neck, ribbon and lacing ribbon, 10,000 pins, 12 dozen gloves, one bonnet ermine and sarsenet for tippets for her head and neck.[160]

While Henry provided his sister with new garments, many of which were sumptuous, he also paid to have a number of her clothes remade or repaired. In May 1510 he gave instructions for 'new bodying and sleeving' six of her gowns: one each of black velvet, tawny cloth of gold upon satin, black satin and velvet upon velvet pirled and two of crimson velvet, 7 yards (6.4 m) of green velvet were provided to make a purfil for the tawny cloth of gold gown and 4½ yards (4.1 m) of black sarsenet for lining, while 1½ yards (1.3 m) of tawny satin was needed for the vents, collar and cuffs of the black velvet gown and a roll of buckram to reline it.[161] In December 1511 gowns of crimson and black velvet were translated, new-bodied and new-sleeved.[162] Henry also made payments for making up a gown and kirtle from cloth 'from her own store' and for furring gowns with furs already in her possession.[163] He also gave her items for her wardrobe of the beds. On 3 July 1511 the king signed a warrant granting his sister bed sheets, a traverse of crimson sarsenet and a fold bed with four vanes and a celure, tester, valance and counterpoint of blue and crimson velvet paned costing in all £68 14*s* 5*d*.[164]

One of the last warrants prior to those preparing her wedding clothes dates from 3 December 1513. This included a gown of cloth of gold of tissue with wide sleeves lined and edged with crimson satin and the body of the gown lined with black sarsenet, a gown of crimson satin with wide sleeves lined and edged with cloth of gold tissue four kirtles of crimson satin, white satin, black damask and velvet, four pairs of sleeves of white cloth of silver, tinsel, crimson satin and white satin.[165]

On 12 February 1515, Mary married the duke of Suffolk secretly, without consulting either Henry VIII or Francis I (as she ought to have). Suffolk informed the king, 'Sir, I never saw woman so weep'.[166] He urged Wolsey to help them, adding that 'I fyer me layes that sche be with chyld'.[167] On 16 April 1515 Mary acknowledged receipt of a number of the jewels that she had received as queen of France, including the 'Mirror of Naples', a large diamond, with a pearl and 20 diamonds, eight large pearls as buttons for sleeves and eight pearls for a carcanet.[168]

On their return to England, and this time with the approval of the king, they married publicly at Greenwich on 13 May 1515. At the tournaments to celebrate the marriage, Suffolk carried a banner with the motto:

> Cloth of gold, do not despise,
> Though thou hast wedded cloth of frieze;
> Cloth of frieze, be not too bold,
> Though thou hast wedded cloth of gold.

On 11 March 1516 Mary gave birth to a son who was named Henry after her brother. Two days later the child was christened with the king and Wolsey standing as the boy's godfathers, and his great-aunt, Lady Catherine, as godmother. Henry's role was central: 'The King gave the name Henry . . . The King then served water . . . the King's gift borne next before the child.'[169] The young Henry died in 1527 but was survived by his sisters, Frances and Eleanor.

Mary figured prominently at court. On 3 May 1515 she attended the arrival of her sister in London from Scotland. On 15 November that year she sat at the top table with Henry and Catherine of Aragon at the banquet held to celebrate Wolsey receiving his cardinal's hat. In the same month the king named a new ship after her and held a special dinner on board with Mary, Suffolk and Catherine. In 1520 Mary was present at the reception of Charles V and when she attended mass on Whit Sunday she was 'dressed in silver lama, in pleats, joined throughout with gold cords at the extremities of which were fine pearls instead of tags'.[170] She also attended the Field of Cloth of Gold where her apartments made much of her former status as queen of France:

> The first hall was hung with very exquisite tapestry of gold and silk as above; the other with crimson velvet and gold tissue, the velvet being embroidered with the letters ML within a gold knot; and in certain other places were embroidered sundry porcupines, the hangings having been made when she was the wife of king Lewis . . .[171]

Three years later she witnessed the reception of Charles V's sister, the queen of Denmark. In 1525 she attended the ennoblement of her illegitimate nephew as duke of Richmond. Her last major appearance at court was for the signing of the treaty of Greenwich in 1527. There are reasons to believe that she did not care for Anne Boleyn. She refused to attend the meeting at Calais when neither the queen of France nor the queen of England was present, but Anne Boleyn was. Sickness prevented her from attending Anne's coronation, and several weeks later, on 25 June 1533, she died, being buried at Bury St Edmunds.

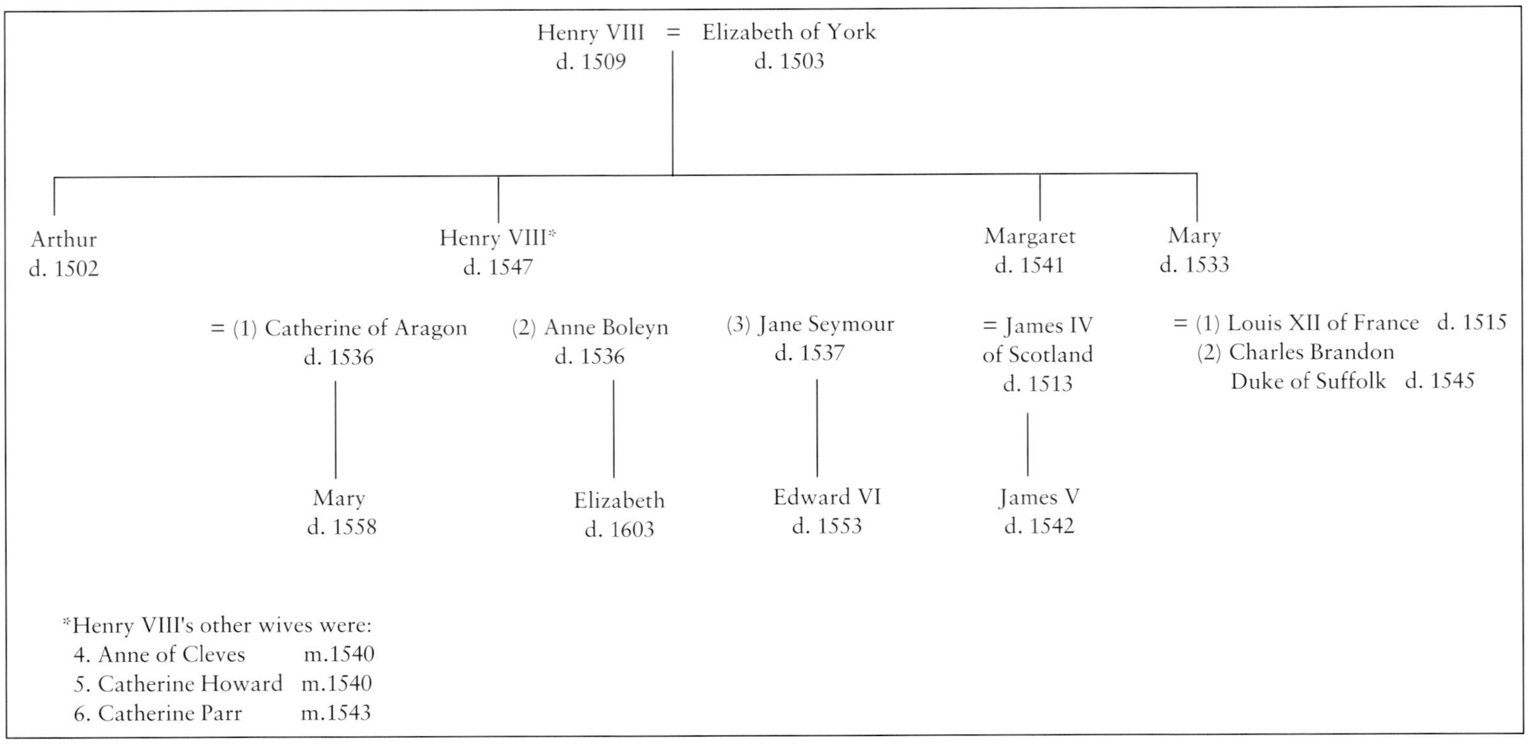

Family tree 3 Henry VIII's wives and children

The question of whether a marriage had been consummated could be answered by the individuals concerned, although, as the conflicting answers recorded above indicate, they might have reason to lie. The question could also be addressed by members of their households. Charles V sought evidence to support Catherine of Aragon's case of non-consummation, including the testimony of the wife of Juan de Cuero, a former lady of the bedchamber to Catherine who lived in Madrid, Donna Maria de Rojas 'who slept in the Queen's bed after the death of Prince Arthur', and Catalina, 'the Queen's slave and bed maker'.[9] When the ladies of Anne of Cleve's household asked her to describe her married life with Henry, she told them, 'When he comes to bed . . . he kisses me and taketh me by the hand, and biddeth me "good night sweet heart" and in the morning, kisses me and biddeth me "Farewell, darling". Is this not enough?'. To which the countess of Rutland replied, 'Madam, there must be more, or it will be long ere we have a Duke of York which all this realm most desireth'.[10] Anne never pretended that her marriage had been consummated, and during its annulment she admitted to Henry that she was still a virgin, with 'my body preserved in the integrity which I brought into this Realm'.[11]

Husbands, and potential husbands, were sometimes concerned that their spouses, real or yet to be realised, might seriously damage their ability to conceive and carry a child to term through fasting and religious observance. On 20 October 1505 Julius II outlined to Henry, then prince of Wales, his marital rights with regards to Catherine of Aragon:

> it is sufficiently clear that, according to divine and human laws, that a wife does not have complete authority over her own body apart from her husband, and that her vows and fasts, so long as they are considered to interfere with her bodily health, the procreation of children, and the customary usages of her life, can be revoked and undone by her husband.[12]

It is possible that Catherine of Aragon's inability to carry most of her pregnancies to term may have resulted from her severe fasting. As a less extreme mark of devotion, prior to the Reformation, wealthy women often undertook a pilgrimage if they wished to have a child or to pray for the safety of their children. Elizabeth of York visited the shrine at Walsingham in 1495 and this may have been linked to the death of her daughter Elizabeth, aged four, and the premature birth of a son.[13] Henry's sister Margaret went on a number of pilgrimages in the hope of conceiving a child, and her husband James IV who was deeply religious accompanied her.[14] Catherine of Aragon went on pilgrimage on a number of occasions, including February 1521, 'to fulfil a vow' possibly in the hope of conceiving a male child.[15]

A royal or noble pregnancy was a very significant event and often warranted a visit from foreign ambassadors or emissaries. However, such a visit could also be used as a cover for other political considerations as indicated in a letter sent by Charles V to his son Philip on 2 August 1545. Charles stated that he had 'despatched Dandolo, ostensibly to visit the Duchess of Camarino, who is pregnant, but really to learn the exact amount of assistance to be expected from His Holiness'.[16] Such visits were also intended to assess the validity of the news and sort fact from fiction. Rumours that Catherine Howard was pregnant, or 'already enceinte', were circulating in July 1540.[17] Further rumours abounded in the following year on 10 April 1541: the French ambassador reported 'this Queen is thought to be with child, which would be a very great joy to this King'.[18]

Once a pregnancy was confirmed, the news spread quickly. On 30 April 1537 John Husee told Lady Lisle that 'it is said that the Queen is with child'.[19] On 27 May 1537 which was Trinity Sunday, Jane Seymour's pregnancy was proclaimed by a *Te Deum* sung at St Paul's.[20] The news was worthy of celebration, 'And also the same night various great fires were made in London, with a hogshead of wine at every fire for the poor people to drink as long as it lasted'.[21] Henry cancelled his progress to the north, because Jane might be concerned by 'some sudden and displeasant rumours and bruit that might by foolish or light persons be blown abroad in our absence'.[22] Her pregnancy may explain why her coronation was postponed, although Anne Boleyn was known to be six months pregnant at her coronation in 1533. On 1 September 1537 Husee told Lady Lisle that Jane would take her chamber in 20 days.[23]

Concern was often voiced at the queen travelling during pregnancy. On 1 July 1518 Henry wrote to Wolsey that he hoped Catherine was with child. He continued that this was why he was reluctant to remove, 'because about this time is partly of her dangerous times and because of that I would remove her as little as I may now'.[24] Four days later Richard Pace informed Wolsey that 'The King arrived this night; the Queen is with him with a big belly. *Te Deum laudamus* is to be sung at St Paul's'.[25] By the following October the Venetian ambassador noted that 'The Queen is near her delivery which is anxiously looked for'.[26] On 10 November, 'This night the Queen was delivered of a daughter ... the entire nation looked for a prince. Had this event taken place before the conclusion of the betrothal that event might not have come to pass; the sole fear of this kingdom being that it may pass into the power of the French through this marriage'.[27] Henry was not the only anxious father to take care of his pregnant wife. Isobel of Portugal conceived within a few months of her marriage to Charles V in 1526. Travelling to Valladolid she was carried by 24 men in a litter, and an observer noted it was 'just as they usually carry a corpse to the burial place. I have never seen anything like it'.[28]

Both Jane Seymour and Catherine Parr recorded their thoughts on being pregnant.[29] On 12 October 1537 Jane Seymour prayed:

> And for as much as by the inestimable goodness and grace of Almighty God, we be delivered and brought in childbed of a prince ... we have thought good to certify you of the same. To the intent you might not only render unto God condign thanks and prayers for so great a benefit, but also continually pray for the long continuance and preservation of the same here in this life.[30]

In 1548 Princess Mary wrote to Catherine Parr on hearing of her pregnancy to say that she would be back from Norfolk by Michaelmas, 'at which time, or shortly after, I trust to hear good success of your Grace's great belly, and in the meantime shall desire much to hear of your health'.[31] Catherine described her pregnancy to Lord Seymour: 'I gave your little knave your blessing, who like an honest man stirred apace after and before. For Mary Odell being abed with me had laid her hand upon my belly to feel it stir. It hath stirred these three days every morning and evening so that I trust when ye come it will make you some pastime.'[32]

News concerning the health of a queen during pregnancy was highly prized. On 26 November 1515 Sir Robert Wingfield wrote to Henry, stating that he 'understood that the King was in good health and the Queen great with child'.[33] On 24 June 1535 Sir William Kingston told Lord Lisle that 'The King and Queen are well and the Queen has a fair belly as I have seen'.[34] Concern for queens in the later stages of pregnancy was common. For example, on 13 July 1515 Lord Dacre informed the council that Henry's sister Margaret was 'great with child' and of his anxiety about her health.[35]

The entire kingdom had an interest in the queen giving birth to a healthy child. For the royal household the significance of the queen's pregnancy was more acute. On 6 January 1511 a payment of £6 *13s 4d* was made to the gentlemen of the chapel for praying 'for the quenes grace for hir goode delyuveraunce'.[36] On 5 March 1516, Lord Mountjoy wrote to Wolsey from Tournai, noting that he had given thanks for Catherine's safe delivery with a procession and bonfires.[37] When Jane Seymour's labour lasted several days, a procession was held in London 'to pray for the Queen that was then in labour of child'.[38] On 12 October Prince Edward's birth was celebrated with another *Te Deum* sung in all London churches and a procession to St Paul's.[39] Antonio de Guaras recorded that Henry cried when he first held his son.[40]

The use of relics to reduce the pains of labour and to protect the mother and child was quite common in pre-Reformation England. During the last months of Elizabeth of York's final pregnancy, a monk was given *6s 8d* for bringing 'our Lady gyrdelle to the Quene' on 13 December 1502.[41] The practice was common throughout Europe, as indicated by a series of letters sent by Sir Thomas Boleyn to Wolsey from the French court. Early in March 1519 Boleyn reported that he had been taken to see the queen who was dressed 'in a nightgown, and noting [upon her] head, but only a kerchief, looking always for her ho[ur when she shall] be brought in bed'.[42] On 16 April he noted that 'yesterday was a solemn procession in the court, attended by the King and his mother, in honour of the holy cord with which our Lord was bound to the pillar, with other relics sent to the Queen on her delivery'.[43] Following the birth of the baby, Boleyn informed Wolsey that he had distributed £100 between the nurse, the four rockers, the gentlewomen of the queen's chamber and made an offering at the christening.[44]

Death following childbirth was the fate of many. One of the most famous fatalities was Elizabeth of York in 1503. On the night of Candlemas, 'the Quene that nyght was delyuered of a doughter ... and vpon the Saterday folowyng was the said doughter Cristened within the parisshe chirche of the Towre and named Kateryn'.[45] Elizabeth died nine days later. Jane Seymour died after giving birth to Prince Edward.[46] The dynastic implications of such events ensured the rapid transmission of news. Edward Carne wrote to Henry from Brussels on 3 August 1545, informing him that 'The Princess of Spain died in child-birth of the young prince lately born'.[47] The news of the birth of a son spread quickly — in March 1541 Henry gave a gold chain worth £65 *2s 6d* to the gentleman that brought him tidings of the birth of 'a prince of Scotland'.[48]

Establishing the queen's chamber and the royal nursery

A key moment in a royal pregnancy was the withdrawal by the queen from court life to prepare for the birth of her child.

The *Ryalle Book* includes detailed instructions on how the queen's chambers were to be prepared for when she 'took her chamber'. This marked the point when a queen relied predominantly, but not exclusively, upon the female members of her family and her household. Lady Margaret Beaufort took a leading role when Elizabeth of York withdrew from court.[49] The *Ryalle Book* describes the queen's bed, the pallet bed used for childbirth, the associated bedding and the canopy placed over the pallet bed. In 1486 the canopy ordered for Elizabeth of York was made from cloth of gold and velvet, furred with ermine and embroidered with Tudor roses.[50] Elizabeth's confinement was described: 'And so she departed to her inner Chambre, which was hanged and seyled with riche Clothe of blew arras, with Flourdelissis of Golde, without any ouder Clothe of Arras of Ymageryе, which is not convenient aboute Wymen in suche Cas.'[51] It has been suggested that the ordinances concerning the preparations for royal births were drawn up by Lady Margaret Beaufort, but there is no evidence of this.[52]

The birth chamber was almost invariably a female preserve. There were occasional intrusions. Four ambassadors from France were admitted to see Elizabeth of York 'in her awne Chambre' shortly before the birth of Arthur, 'but ther entred no mor then ben affore rehersed, saving my Lord the Quenes Chamberlain, and Garter Principal of Armes'.[53]

The necessary furnishings for the royal nursery were provided by the great wardrobe at the king's expense. These were not old stock in store, but new items freshly made. The king also paid for the building work necessary to prepare the queen's apartments prior to the birth of her child and provided the livery for the women employed within the nursery.

As part of the preparations for the expected birth of a prince, two warrants were issued to the great wardrobe on 12 March 1510. The first warrant concerned the christening.[54] The second warrant requested Sir Andrew Windsor to deliver to Oliver Holland, yeoman usher with our 'most dearest wife the Queen', a 'silour and testour with dobull valaunces with three curteynes large and long of blewe and dobull sarcenet accordingly to hang over the cradell of estate within our noucery' which was to be lined with buckram.[55] On 27 May 1510 Catherine wrote to her father to tell him that she had been 'delivered of a daughter, still-born, an event which in England is considered unlucky, and therefore she has not written sooner'. She went on to describe that while in labour she had 'vowed a rich head-dress to St Peter the Martyr, of the Franciscan Order; and sent it to the niece of the Treasurer Morales who wishes to become a nun of that Order. The girl's father has detained both Catherine's letter and the headdress, as his daughter's property'.[56]

A document relating to the great wardrobe accounts for the year 1509–10 contained a reference to some additional items bought for the nursery.[57] These included 8 yards (7.3 m) of purple velvet costing £6 for a 'berying payne' with a long train, and two pieces of green say of the smallest size for hanging the chamber of the lady mistress of the nursery at a price of 26*s* 8*d*. Another order for the royal nursery dated 16 December 1510 consisted of 30 ells (20.6 m) of linen for two pairs of sheets costing 30*s* and a piece of green saye of the middle sort costing 25*s*.[58] A further two orders were dated 23 December 1510. The first warrant was for blue say, hooks and curtain rings.[59] The second listed ten pieces of blue Normandy say, hooks, crochets, rings and trashes, lior and nails, blue sarsenet for a traverse that was hung from 160 latten rings, blue sarsenet for three large curtains trimmed with blue silk ribbon and lined with blue lockeram. Reeds for drawing the curtains cost £40 5*s* 2*d*.[60]

New preparations were made for a laying in chamber when on 4 October 1514 a warrant was issued to Henry Roper, yeoman of the beds with the queen, for blue say to cover the walls, a traverse and a large curtain of blue sarsenet and a traverse of purple sarsenet. He was expected to provide the queen's bed with two Brussels ticks of the largest size and to repair the ermine trimmed counterpane with new fur 'where it shall be requisite'.[61] At the same time other items including a cradle covered with scarlet without a frame, a couch of wool and several sets of linen sheets 'for the use of our nursery, God willing' were delivered to William Lambert.[62] For the baby there were four cradle bands 'of very fine wollen wrought in the frame', each of them 4 yards (3.6 m) long and ⅜ of a yard (0.33 m) wide and six swaddling bands 3 yards (2.7 m) long and ⅜ of a yard (0.33 m) wide. Once again the preparations were in vain. In December 1514 Andrea Badoer informed the Venetian republic that 'the Queen was delivered of a stillborn child of eight months — a great grief to all the Court'.[63] It was premature, the birth of the child having been brought on by Catherine's unhappiness at the breach between her husband and her father.[64]

Following Henry's marriage to Anne Boleyn, hope for a male heir revived. On 24 July 1533 Lord Mountjoy wrote to Cromwell: 'I send you certain remembrances of things to be provided against the Queen's taking her chamber, of which I had experience of when I occupied the room. Please send it to her chamberlain.'[65] On 6 August 1533 Sir John Russell told Lord Lisle that 'soon after the Queen removes thence to Greenwich to take her chamber'.[66] On 3 September Chapuys informed Charles V that 'The King has taken from his treasures one of the richest and most triumphant beds which was given for the ransom of a duke of Alencon'.[67] The implication was that the bed was given to Anne because the king was confident that she would have a son. In view of Anne's pro-French stance, the choice of the Alencon bed was most significant (9035). In 1534 the preparations made during Anne's pregnancy included commissioning a silver cradle from Cornelius Hayes, embroidered bedding and cloth of gold baby clothes.[68] Other preparations undertaken at Eltham 'against the coming of the prince' included putting up an iron canopy over the cradle, the repainting of the rooms with yellow ochre and work to keep the draughts out.[69]

While most of the building works focused on the temporary provision of a suitable suite of rooms for the queen to give birth in, further work was necessary once a child had been born. The building accounts for Greenwich from 31 August to 28 September 1533 included payments to carpenters for making tables, trestles and forms for the nursery and, more specifically, a joined table 'for the norysshe to Roale

the princes clothes upon'.[70] Three years later the accounts included 'the new makyng of a Jonede bede for my lady prynces made after the fawcion of a cradell'. A London mercer provided 3 ¼ yards (2.9 m) of crimson satin for the embroiderers for 48*s* 9*d* and other materials used to make the bed including an ell (0.68 m) of tuke (15*d*), 1 ½ oz (42.5 g) of sewing silk (18*d*) and 1 ½ oz (42.5 g) of crimson silk fringe (21*d*). In addition, two travelling cases covered with calf skin and lined with yellow cotton were provided for the bed.[71]

The provision of blue hangings was a common feature of the furnishings provided for English queens as they awaited the birth of their children. The choice of colour is an interesting one, as in other situations blue was associated with royal mourning. The implication is that the choice was deliberate. Another feature of the furnishings was the emphasis on quality. This can also be seen from the preparations made by Lady Lisle, she borrowed textiles from the wardrobe of the beds in 1536–37. All of these carefully managed preparations ensured the creation of a temporary gendered space where female interests and concerns were dominant.

The staff of the nursery

The household ordinances of 1493 stated that a lady mistress, a nurse and four rockers were sufficient to staff a royal nursery for a newborn child.[72] Both Henry VII and Henry VIII rigorously observed the regulations. However, one other individual, not mentioned in the ordinances, played an important part: the midwife. The midwife was a vital, if short-term appointment and was invariably included in the group of staff rewarded after the birth of a child. Alice Massy was midwife to Elizabeth of York. She was retained between 1486 and 1503 on a salary of £10 per year.[73] In 1537 Princess Mary gave a gift of £30 to 'the myddewife and Nurce and Rockers at the Cristening of the Prince'.[74] Three years later, in January 1540, she gave 7 yards (6.4 m) of yellow damask costing 52*s* 6*d* to Edward's nurse and a gilt spoon to each of his rockers at a price of 11*s* each.[75]

The lady mistress oversaw the running of the royal nursery. On 19 November 1517 Elizabeth Denton, lady mistress to Mary, received an annuity of 40 marks, for her service to the princess, but on her death the post was to revert to Margaret Bryan.[76] Margaret was the widow of the recently deceased Sir Thomas Bryan of Ashridge. Her removal seems to have been contemplated by Cardinal Wolsey who wrote to the king on 25 July 1521 about whom would make a good lady governess for the princess. He had:

> written to my lady of Oxford and those about her, to induce her to undertake the governance of the Princess. Expects she will refuse on account of her ill health; if so [he] will write to Sir Philip Calthorp and his wife. Will speak to my lord of Oxford's mother, if your grace pleases. She is right discreet, and of a good age, and is near at hand. She can, at any rate, be tried for a season.[77]

Nothing came of this. Lady Bryan was to care for all of Henry's children. In 1536 she recalled: 'When my Lady Mary was born it pleased the king's grace [to make] me Lady Mistress, and make me a baroness, and so I have been a mother to the children his grace had since.'[78] In January 1538 Mary gave her a New Year's gift of 'a Bonet and a frountlet' which cost 28*s*.[79]

The employment of wet nurses and dry nurses was standard practice. Catherine of Aragon broke with tradition when she insisted upon attending on the Princess Mary personally: 'There is no need of any other person but myself to nurse her . . . I will put her in my own bed when I sleep, and will watch her when is needful.'[80] The royal children became attached to their nurses. In July 1509 Henry granted to Anne Luke, his old nurse, and her husband Walter, an annuity of £20 for life out of the revenues from Cambridgeshire and Huntingdonshire.[81] This grant was renewed in July 1515 when it was augmented by a further £20 from the treasury.[82] The nurses were also rewarded by the grateful parents. In September 1511 Henry VIII gave £20 for life to Elizabeth Poyntz, 'late nurse unto our dearest son the Prince'.[83] Six years later, he awarded two annuities of £10 to Catherine Pole, nurse to the Princess Mary on 2 July 1517.[84]

Care was exercised in the selection of the women who acted as wet and dry nurses. In October 1538 Sybil Penne was appointed as Prince Edward's dry nurse. She was the sister-in-law of Sir William Sidney who was chamberlain of the prince's household. Sidney was asked by Cromwell to 'signify to you the ability of my wife's sister for the room of the Prince's dry nurse'. He replied, 'I doubt not but that she is every way an apt woman for the same'.[85] A pearl necklace exists that family tradition says was given by the king to Sybil for her service to Edward.[86]

Henry VIII appointed four rockers for Princess Mary. They received livery. On 5 November 1516, four unnamed women were given gowns of broadcloth furred with poots at a cost of £16 17*s* 4*d*.[87] A year later they received four gowns of russet broadcloth furred with black budge costing £18 5*s* 4*d*.[88]

Children's dress

The preparations for a baby included making clothes and nappies for the infant. These preparations were mentioned by Sir Brian Tuke in a letter of 16 June 1539 to Lady Lisle: 'My poor daughters being all in Essex, [are] preparing clouts for my daughter Audelai's very great belly.'[89] Infancy, spanning from birth to the age of three, was divided into two main phases: the first as a swaddled babe in arms, lasting for the first three to six months of life and the second, the change to short coating (i.e. clothing that reaches the ankles), from six months to three years.[90] Swaddling could leave the arms free or bind the arms to the body.

The double portrait of the *Cholmondeley Sisters*, *c*. 1600–1610, depicts the twins sitting in bed holding their swaddled infants.[91] Their babies were dressed in a shirt, a clout or nappy, a bed (a cloth wrapped round the body, covering from the chest to below the feet), swaddling bands and a bib (a piece of cloth worn below the chin to keep other clothing clean).[92]

This ensemble was intended to provide warmth and to keep the limbs straight. Amongst Henry VIII's possessions at his death there were 'A litle boxe of crymson Satten embrodred contayninge shertes and other thinges for yonge children' (11073) and 'a boxe of glasse of dyuers colowes conteyninge a Swathinge bande of brode white Taphita fringed with golde' (11092) in the study next to the king's old bedchamber at Whitehall. It is very likely that these had belonged to one of the king's children.

This style of dressing infants acted as a means of displaying clean, fine quality white linen, over which would be placed a bearing cloth, which combined warmth with grandeur. It also required the services of a laundress and access to a plentiful supply of linen. Swaddling was also highly distinctive of the early months of life — the only parallel being the binding of the wrists and ankles of the dead — and it was not gender specific. Clothing of this type was provided for Henry, while a baby, his siblings and his children and with almost no differentiation between the sexes.

On a baby's starting to crawl and learning to walk it was provided with short coats. The exact timing depended upon the individual child, but it usually took place between six to nine months of age. Children, irrespective of gender, were placed into a coat with ankle-length skirts as a practical response to their need for freedom of movement. This style of dress can be seen in the double portrait of Lady Catherine Grey (1540–67), daughter of Henry VIII's younger sister Mary, and her son, Lord Beauchamp, who was born in September 1561. He was dressed in a back fastening sleeveless coat with hanging sleeves which could act as leading strings. He also wore a close-fitting cap and a bonnet with a feather, along with a linen bib and handkerchief.[93] Elements of these clothes derived from adult dress, but other features such as the back fastening, the use of the hanging sleeves as leading strings and the bib and handkerchief were all concessions to childhood, which were easy to launder and kept the other clothing clean. Boys and girls wore a close-fitting cap, often in conjunction with a bonnet, as it was felt to be important to keep their heads warm.

Neither the great wardrobe accounts nor the privy purse refer to knitted baby clothes, although archaeological finds prove that they were produced: for example, a knitted wool vest with short sleeves, a square neckline and slit opening at the centre back (Fig. 11.1).[94] A baby's mitten with a decorative band around the cuff worked in three rows of black two-ply wool has also been found (Fig. 11.2).[95] In the autumn of 1548 Bess of Hardwick bought clothes for her five-month-old daughter, Frances, including 'a knete waste cote' costing 3*s* 4*d* and two 'knete capys' costing 6*d* each. In the following year, Bess also bought 'ij yerdes of holande to make her begenes hedclothes and partletes', 'fusten to make har ij gones vij yerdes' and 'ij yerdes of carsey to make har ij petycotes'.[96]

Once an infant started to walk it was considered a child.[97] In September 1538 Lord Audley visited Prince Edward and noted that 'he shotyth owt in length, and wexith ferme and stiff, and can stedfastly stond, and wold avaunce hym self to move and go, if they would suffir hym'.[98] Six months later Lady Bryan told Cromwell that 'My lord Prince is in good health and merry. Would to God the King and your Lordship had seen him last night. The minstrels played, and his Grace danced and played so wantonly that he could not stand still'.[99]

Increasing mobility did not result in specific changes in clothing. But, as children got older, their clothing was gradually influenced more by adult styles. Boys continued to wear long skirts until the end of childhood, when they were then breeched.[100] On a purely practical level, a skirt was far easier to manage than hose pointed to a doublet, for dressing

11.1 *Child's knitted wool vest or waistcoat. Finsbury, 39.108/1, Museum of London*

11.2 *Infant's knitted wool mitten. A1989, Museum of London*

and undressing. There is a very rare survival of a boy's short coat dating from 1660 and a picture of the future Charles IX wearing it in the Swedish royal collection.[101] While wearing the skirted coat, boys superficially appeared closer in style to their mother, sisters or the women who staffed the nursery. However, they were clearly differentiated from girls and older and younger male siblings by subtle details and the accessories they carried, as indicated by Holbein's drawing of a woman with four children (Fig. 11.3).[102]

Portraits of children generally included indications of their youth such as a piece of coral or a rattle, pet animals or birds, toys and an apron or a muck minder, while a sense of scale was provided by depicting them with adults, older siblings or furniture. Boys were particularly highlighted by their carrying a sword, dagger or bow, by having their heads uncovered (to make them more hardy), by the length and style of their hair, by their skirts not being supported with underpinnings as those of their sisters were, by their doublets fastening at the front rather than at the back and by wearing a sash diagonally across the chest.[103] When in 1567 Lord Cobham was painted with his wife, his three daughters and three sons, the eldest son dressed in black was clearly differentiated from his younger brothers dressed in white satin.[104]

Archaeological evidence has yielded a number of children's leather shoes from the Tudor period. Most had square toes, following the style favoured for adult shoes. The uppers were often decorated with vertical or horizontal slashes and had a low-cut vamp and versions with and without a strap to keep them on.[105] Other finds, including a girl's bonnet, 8½ inches (0.22 m) in diameter and made of a lightweight, plain weave silk, with a wired front and gathered into pleats at the back, have been recovered.[106]

While long skirts appear feminine to modern eyes, small details distinguished these garments from female attire. Even while boys remained in the care of their mothers and female servants, they started to learn skills taught to them by men for later life. These included riding and archery, as well as rudimentary education, which in Prince Edward's case began shortly after his fourth birthday with the appointment of Richard Cox as tutor. Boys aged between five and seven made the transition from being cared for predominantly by women to spending their time in the company of men. This transition was marked by two events, which often took place at the same time but did not have to coincide. First, a boy gave up his skirted coat and put on a doublet and hose by a process known as breeching. This was a highly visual sign of a boy's transition. Second, he came under the authority of his male tutors and it signified that he was ready for education.

There is some debate as to whether any concessions to youth were made in terms of the colour, cut or type of cloth of the clothes of royal children. Suzanne de Bourbon was the granddaughter of King Louis XI of France. When *c.* 1493 she was painted aged two by the Master of Moulins, she was dressed all in white, as indeed was her cousin, the dauphin.[107]

11.3 *Drawing of a woman and four children, by Hans Holbein the Younger. 1852-5-19-1, reproduced by courtesy of the Trustees of the British Museum*

Suzanne was dressed in a gown with long sleeves with turned-back fur-edged cuffs with a square-necked bib. Her gown was made from silk or linen damask with a large pomegranate design and she wore a bonnet over a coif which fastened under her chin. Seemingly simple, with no surface decoration, these white clothes would have needed very regular laundering to keep them presentable.

Clothing the king's children

Henry ordered clothes for Mary, Elizabeth and Edward from the great wardrobe fitfully, with the scale and the regularity of the orders reflecting their current standing with him. Their mothers and stepmothers also provided them with clothing. As they got older, they ordered their own clothing with purchases of clothes, jewellery and accessories being recorded in their own accounts. The surviving privy purse accounts of Mary and Edward both provide insights into their personal tastes in clothes. Like their father, they also received deliveries of silk and linen from the silk house at Whitehall, as did Lady Margaret Douglas, the king's niece and her husband, Lord Lennox (Table 11.1). Their clothing was intended to reflect their status, as the king's children, as his representatives and as the head of their own households. Over the last five-year period of Henry's reign, Mary, Elizabeth and Margaret received comparable quantities of cloth which is surprising in view of their relative ages and status. In contrast, Edward received surprisingly little cloth, but this may reflect that, though young, he was receiving large orders from the great wardrobe.

LADY MARGARET DOUGLAS

Lady Margaret Douglas (1515–78) was the daughter of Margaret Tudor, queen of Scots, by her second husband, Lord Archibald Douglas. She was Henry VIII's niece. In 1521 she accompanied her father into exile in France for several years. She arrived in England in 1528 and two years later she joined Catherine of Aragon's household. During 1530 Lady Margaret received two grants of clothing, which were fairly similar in their composition. On 6 April 1530 she was given a gown of tawny velvet lined with the same velvet, a gown of black damask lined with black velvet and a gown of black satin lined with tawny velvet, two kirtles with sleeves, one of black velvet and the other black satin and two partlets, one of crimson satin and one of white satin which cost £64 4*s* 8*d*.[108] On 14 December 1530 Lady Margaret received a gown of crimson velvet lined with cloth of gold, a gown of black velvet lined with black velvet and a nightgown of Turkey satin furred with black coney, a kirtle of crimson velvet and a kirtle with sleeves of black velvet, a cloak of black cloth, the vents of black satin, a partlet of crimson satin, habiliments of black velvet and crimson velvet, rails, kerchers and smocks and two French hoods of black velvet costing £96 17*s* ¼*d*. In both instances, provision was made for her two ladies-in-waiting: gowns of tawny camlet, lined with tawny velvet, kirtles of worsted and sleeves of worsted and of tawny velvet; gowns of black cloths, the sleeves lined with tawny velvet, kirtles of worsted, velvet sleeves and velvet partlets lined with sarsenet.

During 1531 Lady Margaret transferred from the household of Catherine of Aragon to that of Princess Mary. Later she became a lady-in-waiting to Anne Boleyn. A warrant dated 26 October 1531 ordering clothing for Margaret from the great wardrobe included gowns of 'tynsyn', black velvet furred with powdered ermine and black damask lined with the same; sleeves and kirtles of crimson satin, black velvet and black satin, partlets of crimson and white satin, habiliments of black velvet and crimson satin, two black velvet French hoods, 12 pairs of gloves, black velvet and leather shoes. She also received livery for her two gentlewomen of black cloth gowns lined with tawny velvet, worsted kirtles, black velvet sleeves and a partlet, a gown of black velvet with a crimson frontlet, six pairs of hose, eight pairs of shoes, linen for smocks and two pounds of pins and for her manservant, a cloth coat, a doublet of black satin, three shirts, three pairs of hose, eight pairs of shoes and a bonnet.[109] The clothes ordered by the warrant cost £190 18*s* 9*d*.[110]

In 1534 Lady Margaret was described by the French ambassador as being 'beautiful and highly esteemed here'.[111] The symbolic value of cramp rings was indicated when the king discovered the clandestine marriage of Margaret Douglas and Thomas Howard. As a consequence, they were imprisoned in the Tower on 8 June 1536. Under examination Howard declared that the only token he had given to Margaret was a cramp ring. In return she had presented him with a diamond and her portrait.[112] Even so, on 31 December 1536 William Green received for her use silver fringe at 5*s* an ounce and crimson silk fringe at 14*d* the ounce to a total cost of £12 7*s* 7*d*. At the same time he submitted a bill for making for her a chair covered with crimson velvet.[113] In 1537 Lady Margaret assured Thomas Cromwell that her romance with Lord Howard had come to an end:

> And my Lord, where it is your pleasure that I shall keep but a few here with me, I trust ye will think that I can have no fewer than I have: for I have but a gentleman and a groom that keeps my apparel, and another keeps my chamber, and a chaplain that was with me always in the Court . . . I beseech you to be so good as to get my poor servants their wages.[114]

A list of people dependent on the king's generosity in 1537 included £40 a year for Lady Margaret towards her attendants and dress.[115] Further payments were made in March and at midsummer 1538 to Lady Margaret for the wages of her servants and gentlewomen, coming to £24 7*s* 10¼*d*.[116]

Following Anne of Cleves's marriage she was appointed as a lady-in-waiting to the new queen. But her liaison with Charles Howard led to her banishment from court. In 1542, a list of tasks drawn up by John Gates included knowing the king's answer for 'My Lady Margaret's apparel'.[117] Between 1542 and 1547, Lady Margaret received a substantial quantity of cloth from her uncle's silk store at Whitehall: 1,040¼ yards (951 m) of silk and 247¾ ells (169.9 m) of linen. This quantity of fabric was on a par with the amounts given to the king's daughters and highlights the political and personal value

Table 11.1: *Cloth issued from the Whitehall silk store to Lady Margaret, her husband Lord Lennox, Princess Mary, Princess Elizabeth and Prince Edward between 1542–47*

Type of cloth	Lady Margaret	Lord Lennox	Mary	Elizabeth	Edward
Tissue	½ yard (0.4 m)	~	2 yards (1.8 m)	11 yards (10.1 m)	~
Cloth of gold					
– crimson	19⅜ yards (17.7 m)	12 yards (10.9 m)	24¼ yards (22.2 m)	35¾ yards (32.7 m)	~
– incarnate	7½ yards (6.8 m)	~	15½ yards (14.2 m)	8 yards (7.3 m)	~
– purple and blue	3 yards (2.7 m)	~	6½ yards (5.9 m)	~	~
– yellow	~	~	9 yards (8.2 m)	~	~
Cloth of silver	59½ yards (54.4 m)	25 yards (22.8 m)	16¼ yards (14.8 m)	9½ yards (8.7 m)	20½ yards (18.7 m)
Tinsel	~	~	~	~	7 yards (6.4 m)
Velvet					
– black	154½ yards (141.3 m)	~	351⅛ yards (321.1 m)	242⅝ yards (221.8 m)	6 yards (5.5 m)
– crimson	27⅜ yards (25.0 m)	~	71⅛ yards (65.1 m)	52¼ yards (47.8 m)	~
– incarnate	⅜ yard (0.3 m)	~	~	~	~
– murrey	~	~	4⅞ yards (4.5 m)	~	~
– purple	10½ yards (9.6 m)	~	24¾ yards (22.6 m)	5⅝ yards (5.1 m)	~
– russet	18 yards (16.5 m)	~	~	~	~
– tawny	34¾ yards (31.8 m)	~	38½ yards (35.2 m)	37⅝ yards (34.4 m)	~
– white	~	~	~	2½ yards (2.3 m)	~
– yellow	15 yards (13.7 m)	~	9 yards (8.2 m)	5 yards (4.6 m)	~
Satin					
– black	129½ yards (118.4 m)	~	207¾ yards (189.9 m)	136 yards (124.4 m)	~
– crimson	46 yards (42.1 m)	13 yards (11.9 m)	65⅝ yards (60.1 m)	57¼ yards (52.3 m)	~
– incarnate	26 yards (23.7 m)	~	~	4 yards (3.7 m)	~
– purple	18⅜ yards (16.8 m)	~	~	21¼ yards (19.4 m)	~
– tawny	39 yards (35.6 m)	~	16 yards (14.6 m)	~	~
– white	40 yards (36.6 m)	~	42⅜ yards (38.7 m)	14½ yards (13.3 m)	~
Damask					
– black	75½ yards (69.0 m)	~	183¼ yards (167.6 m)	50 yards (45.7 m)	~
– blue	15 yards (13.7 m)	~	~	~	~
– crimson	29½ yards (26.9 m)	9 yards (8.2 m)	16 yards (14.6 m)	23⅛ yards (21.2 m)	~
– murrey	18 yards (16.4 m)	~	16 yards (14.6 m)	1½ yards (1.3 m)	~
– purple	~	~	16 yards (14.6 m)	16¼ yards (14.8 m)	~
– tawny	22½ yards (20.6 m)	~	84 yards (76.8 m)	84 yards (76.8 m)	22½ yards (20.6 m)
– white	9½ yards (8.9 m)	~	13½ yards (12.4 m)	27¾ yards (25.37 m)	~
– yellow	11 yards (10.1 m)	~	16¾ yards (15.3 m)	11½ yards (10.5 m)	~
Taffeta					
– black	35 yards (32 m)	~	40 yards (36.6 m)	11⅜ yards (10.4)	~
– crimson	~	~	~	3⅜ yards (3.1 m)	~
– incarnate	10½ yards (9.6 m)	~	6 yards (5.5 m)	3⅜ yards (3.1 m)	~
– purple	~	~	18½ yards (16.9 m)	19½ yards (17.8 m)	~
Sarsenet					
– black	70 yards (64.0 m)	~	85½ yards (78.2 m)	63⅜ yards (57.9 m)	~
– crimson and red	53 yards (48.5 m)	~	64½ yards (58.9 m)	59⅝ yards (54.5 m)	~
– murrey	6 yards (5.5 m)	~	~	~	~
– purple, blue and violet	12 yards (10.9 m)	~	15 yards (13.7 m)	19½ yards (17.8 m)	~
– russet	6 yards (5.5 m)	~	~	~	~
– tawny	5½ yards (5.1 m)	~	6 yards (5.5 m)	4½ yards (4.1 m)	~
– white	12 yards (11 m)	9 yards (8.2 m)	6 yards (5.5 m)	4⅜ yards (4.0 m)	~
– yellow	~	~	3 yards (2.7 m)	~	~
Bridges satin	~	~	3 yards (2.7 m)	6 yards (5.5 m)	~
Holland	76 ells (52.4 m)	~	243⅜ ells (168.9 m)	255⅝ ells (176.4 m)	408 ells (281.5 m)
Normandy cloth	146¾ ells (101.3 m)	~	72 ells (49.7 m)	270 ells (186.3 m)	~
Cambric	25 ells (17.3 m)	~	42⅜ ells (29.3 m)	13 ells (8.9 m)	~
Passementerie	~	~	3 lb ½ oz (5.2 kg)	8 lb 5⅝ oz (1.4 kg)	~
Totals	**1,040¼ yards (951.2 m) 247¾ ells (170.5 m)**	**68 yards (62.2 m)**	**1,498⅝ yards (1,370.3 m) 357¾ ells (246.8 m) 3 lb ½ oz(5.2 kg)**	**1,307 yards (1,195.1m) 538⅝ ells (371.65 m) 8 lb 5⅝ oz(1.4 kg)**	**464 yards (424.3 m) 408 ells (281.5 m)**

Henry placed on his niece. On 29 June 1544 'this morning at Mass, the King and Queen attending' she married the 'lusty, beardless' earl of Lennox.[118] Sir Ralph Sadler described Lennox as 'being hitherto noted a good Frenchman, is now become a good Englishman and will bear his heart and his service to Your Majesty'.[119] As indicated in Table 11.1, Henry gave some silk to Lennox. With the exception of the white sarsenet, that was possibly used as for lining, the fabric was crimson in colour and it may have been given to him at the time of his marriage.

PRINCESS MARY

On 18 February 1516 Catherine of Aragon wrote to the provost of Tournai to inform him of the birth of Princess Mary.[120] The Venetian ambassador noted how the news of the death of her father had been kept from Catherine because she 'was on the eve of her delivery'.[121] After the christening, when he was rash enough to observe that 'the Signory would have been more satisfied if it had been a boy', Henry VIII replied, 'The queen and I are both young and if it is a girl this time, by God's grace the boys will follow'.[122]

On reaching the age of 11, Mary was 'so thin, spare and small as to render it impossible for her to be married for the next three years'.[123] Four years later in 1527 she was described as 'not very tall, has a pretty face, and is well proportioned, with a very beautiful complexion'.[124] The French ambassador summed her up as 'of middle stature and is in face like her father, especially about the mouth, but has a voice more man-like for a woman than he has for a man . . . with a fresh complexion, she looks not past 18 or 20, although she is 24. Her beauty is mediocre . . . Have tried to get a portrait of her, but no painter dare attempt it without the King's command'.[125]

As Henry's only surviving child and heir by Catherine of Aragon, she was dressed appropriately. On 14 December 1516 she was given 10 yards (9.1 m) of white gold tinsel, 10 yards (9.1 m) of white silver tinsel, 12 yards (10.9 m) of white satin and 11 yards (10 m) of white damask for four gowns. Three of the gowns were furred with two timbers and ten skins of ermines, 40 timbers of miniver and 2,900 powderings. They were lined with white fustian and flannel. In addition to single and double sipers, she also received six pairs of hose, six pairs of sleeves, six pairs of shoes covered with crimson, tawny and black velvet, two bonnets of ermine, 3,000 pins. The cost of the items ordered came to £106 2*s* 4*d*.[126] A year later she received a comparable order on a warrant dated 4 December 1517. She was given crimson tinsel for a gown furred with ermine, crimson satin for a gown lined with cloth of gold tissue, a russet velvet gown furred with ermine, violet tinselled satin for a gown, crimson velvet for a gown lined with cloth of silver, black velvet for a gown furred with pampilion and green satin for the sleeves of a kirtle. Smaller items included two bonnets of ermine, linen for smocks, rails, night-kerchers and red, yellow, green, black satin for kirtles. These totalled £115 3*s* 4*d*.[127]

Catherine of Aragon's wardrobe account includes a list of garments made for the four-year-old girl in March 1520 (Fig. 11.4). The entries only give the costs for making, but they describe the pieces and so give a good indication of what Catherine was ordering: a gown of crimson velvet lined with crimson satin, a gown of black velvet lined with satin, a gown of purple velvet embroidered with damask gold of French fashion, a kirtle of purple velvet embroidered with damask gold, a French hood of black velvet, two frontlets of black velvet, a gown of black sarsenet French fashion, a pair of sleeves of white silver paned and a kirtle of black tissue with yellow satin for the bodies. This list is followed by a selection

11.4 *Miniature of Princess Mary, by Lucas Horenbout,* c. *1521. National Portrait Gallery, London (NPG 6453)*

of garments that were described as being 'of the king's gift': a gown of crimson velvet furred, a kirtle of white satin, a gown of purple velvet, a kirtle of crimson satin, a pair of sleeves of crimson satin pleated, a gown of blue damask gold, a pair of sleeves of white satin, a gown of black velvet furred with black budge, a kirtle of black satin and a pair of sleeves of black satin.[128] There is a single glimpse of her wardrobe in the following two years, when the king ordered 4 yards (3.6 m) of crimson satin for a kirtle, 9 yards (8.2 m) of black sarsenet for lining various gowns and a yard (0.91 m) of crimson satin for a pair of sleeves, costing £6 9*s*.[129]

On being made princess of Wales and her departure for the Welsh marches, her governess, the countess of Salisbury, was given detailed instructions concerning 'the cleanliness and well wearing of her apparel, both of her chamber and her person, so that everything about her be pure, sweet, clean and wholesome'.[130] Nothing comes to light about her clothing in the late 1520s. Our knowledge improves in 1530. On 10 April 1530 a range of clothes were ordered for the *domina principissa* at a cost of £392 14*s* ½*d*.[131] The warrant allowed for eight gowns, one of purple velvet furred with powdered ermine, another of crimson velvet furred with black budge in the sleeves and purfil and the body, three of cloth of gold, one each of purple tinsel, cloth of silver and tawny cloth of gold; five kirtles with sleeves of cloth of gold tissue, cloth of silver, crimson satin, crimson velvet and of black velvet and upperbodies and oversleeves of black satin for the kirtles and a cloak of broad cloth, the hood and vents lined with black satin. She also received a range of accessories including 12 lawn partlets, two French hoods of black velvet lined with satin, one partlet of black velvet lined with sarsenet, tippets of sarsenet and a selection of shoes and girdles. A month later she received a second warrant which ordered a range of linen items including sheets, pillowberes and smocks.[132] Lord Andrew Windsor was the recipient of a warrant dated 27 September 1531 listing clothes to be supplied for Mary, starting with a gown of silver tissue lined with plain cloth of silver. She received five gowns of cloth of silver tissue, purple velvet, black tinsel, crimson satin and black velvet, a nightgown of black velvet, kirtles with sleeves of cloth of gold, crimson velvet, black tinsel and two of cloth of silver, a cloak of fine black cloth, two partlets and linen for smocks and rails.[133]

Two items were ordered for Mary on her father's warrant of 9 January 1532: a gown of black satin with two welts of black velvet furred with black coney, and a cloak of black cloth with two welts of black velvet, the sleeves lined with buckram.[134] She received a more sumptuous order of clothes later in the year. A warrant dated 27 September instructed John Scut to make garments and Thomas Addington to fur them, costing £457 17*s* 8*d*.[135] The clothes were gorgeous and fully emphasised her rank. The key items comprised the following garments: 11½ yards (10.5 m) of cloth of silver tissue for a gown costing £86 5*s*, lined with 3 yards (2.7 m) of plain cloth of silver costing £10, 14½ yards (13.2 m) of purple velvet for a gown lined with the same costing £21 15*s*, 14½ yards (13.2 m) of black tinsel for a gown lined with the same costing £48 6*s* 8*d*, 11½ yards (10.5 m) of right crimson satin for a gown costing £10 7*s* lined with 3 yards (2.7 m) of cloth of gold costing £20 and 11½ yards (10.5 m) of black lukes velvet for a gown furred with ermine costing £10 7*s*. She was given five kirtles, all made with sleeves: of cloth of gold with works (£25), of cloth of silver tissue (£56 5*s*), of cloth of silver with works (£20), of crimson velvet (£11 5*s*) and of black tinsel (£20). The upperbodies, upperstocks and sleeves of the kirtles were all made from tawny satin. A black velvet nightgown furred with black coney and a black cloth for a cloak, the sleeves lined with tawny satin.[136]

On her death in 1536 Catherine of Aragon left Mary two specific items in her will: a gold collar with a cross that she had brought from Spain and the furs from her gowns.[137] The imperial ambassador informed Charles V that the collar was withheld from her, adding that 'I think there are not 10 crowns worth of gold in the said cross nor any jewellery but within is a portion of the true cross, towards which the Princess felt great devotion'.[138] He described Mary being in mourning for her mother, noting 'the heavynes of her apparel'. Who paid for this mourning is not recorded, but further items costing £172 10*s* 6*d* were paid for by Henry VIII.[139] The opening entry was for two gowns made from 32 yards (29.2 m) of black lukes velvet costing £30 8*s* for which Scut charged 42*s* 8*d* for making and lining. She had another two gowns made from 26 yards (23.7 m) of black damask which were lined and edged with black velvet. The gowns could be worn with three partlets of velvet and another three of satin. Mary also received two kirtles with sleeves of 14 yards (12.8 m) of the same black velvet for velvet costing £13 6*s* and another two made from 14 yards (12.8 m) of black satin costing £6 6*s*, all of which were upperbodied with black satin. For informal wear Mary was allowed two nightgowns, one made from 13 yards (11.8 m) of black velvet, lined with taffeta and the other made from 13 yards (11.8 m) of black satin furred with 90 black squirrel skins.[140] In June 1536 Mary was visited by Viscount Beauchamp, Jane Seymour's older brother, as a mark of her intention to treat Mary well. Mary assured Thomas Cromwell on 1 July, 'Sir, as touching mine apparel, I have made no bill, for the king's highness's favour is so good clothing unto me, that I can desire no more; and so I have written to his grace, resting wholly in him, and willing to wear whatsoever his grace shall appoint me'.[141] In December 1536 Henry VIII gave Mary a border of goldsmith's work for a gown. She later paid a goldsmith £4 3*s* 4*d* to lengthen it.[142]

In April 1537 Henry wrote to Richard Pate with regards to the conduct of Mary, observing that 'we shall not only know our daughter, but use her besides in all things as to the degree of the daughter of so great a Prince'.[143] Later that autumn and winter, Mary played a key role in court ceremonial. For the christening of her young brother, Edward, her privy purse included a payment of £10 'to peycocke for a kyrtle of Clothe of Siluer agaynst the Cristening of the prince'.[144] She was the chief mourner at Jane Seymour's funeral. Thomas Palmer, groom of the robes, spent two weeks going to Hampton Court to view her apparel and to London to provide mourning at a rate of 8*d* a day and 16*d* paid for boat hire, coming to 10*s*.[145] Further items for mourning were obtained in December: black velvet for a nightgown, a bonnet of powdered ermines, cambric for kerchers, rails and holland for smocks, black silk ribbon for belts, shoes, pins, needles, thread and holland for sheets costing £55 2*s* 8*d*. Following the end of mourning at court, Mary secured a warrant allowing her, amongst other things, six bonnets of velvet, six frontlets with cauls of gold, black velvet for a French partlet and two partlets, a cloak, 20 pairs of kersey hose, two dozen lawn partlets, two dozen lames for partlets, six pieces of ribbon for belts and 10,000 pins, along with gowns for the women of her household costing £106 5*s* 8*d*.[146]

The lavish provision for Mary continued throughout 1539. Under the king's own warrant dated 6 January 1539 she was allowed the furring of a gown of black satin with 144 furs of black squirrel, another of black velvet with 166 black budge skins, a gown of tawny cloth of gold with sables and a gown of tawny velvet with 25 timbers and seven ermine skins powdered with 18,000 pinks and powderings.[147] Two months later, she was provided with six velvet bonnets, six frontlets with cauls of gold, black cloth for a cloak, 20 pairs of hose, two bonnets of powdered ermines, right crimson velvet for a gown turned up with the same, black velvet for a gown turned up with the same, black satin for a gown turned up with black velvet, crimson damask for a gown turned up with the same damask, black damask for a gown turned up with the same damask, black taffeta for a gown turned up with the same taffeta, black 'lukes' velvet for a nightgown, lined with black satin and black damask for a nightgown furred with 136 black coney skins. Her kirtles were made from cloth of silver, crimson velvet, yellow satin, white satin, black satin and black velvet coming in all to £275 2*s* 7*d*.[148]

Not withstanding the 20-year gap in age between Mary and her two siblings, and her demotion following the birth of Princess Elizabeth, there is evidence that she held the pair in some affection, tempered by political prudence. She exchanged gifts with Princess Elizabeth and Prince Edward and also with Lady Margaret Douglas. In December 1537 she paid 65*s* for 'a Cappe for a New yeres gyfte to the Prince grace' and in April 1540 she gave 53*s* 4*d* 'to the kinges Braudrer for Enbraudring a Cote for the Prince grace'.[149] Princess Elizabeth lacked Mary's financial resources, and as a child she often made her presents for her family. In 1540 she gave Edward a cambric shirt as a New Year's gift 'of her owne woorkynge'.[150]

Mary's privy purse accounts record the New Year's gifts received by her. The list of gifts for 1543 indicates the extent of the recognition at court of her fondness for clothes:

Lady Margaret — a gown of carnation satin 'of the vencie fascion'
Lady Frances Dorset — a wrought smock and half a dozen handkerchiefs
Lady Suffolk — a pair of wrought sleeves and 'pullers out for an Italian gown wrought'
Lady Calthrop — two pairs of sleeves, one of gold with passamayne lace and the other off silver, wrought
Earl of Hertford — a ring with a diamond
Lady Russell of Worcestershire — half a dozen handkerchiefs
The Young Lady Norfolk — two pairs of sleeves, half a dozen handkerchiefs.[151]

This list presents a very similar pattern of gifts to those given to her sister Elizabeth when she was queen.

For the reception of the duke of Najera in 1543 she wore a kirtle of cloth of gold and an open robe of violet velvet with three heights of pile. In 1544 Donna Maria of Aragon, having heard she was very fond of Spanish gloves as befitted her Spanish heritage sent Mary some 'which she hopes will suit her highness'.[152] In November 1545 Henry sent a warrant to the great wardrobe authorising the keeper 'to deliver stuff and apparel for My Lady Mary' (Pl. VIIA).[153] This was followed by a warrant for clothes and saddles for Mary in May 1546.[154] Six months later in November 1546, a warrant for Mary's clothing for Christmas was signed by the stamp.[155] A bill for clothing which was supplied on 7 December 1546 costing £26 19*s* may relate to this warrant.[156] In keeping with the winter season, Mary received four furred gowns: a gown of black velvet guarded with three timbers of ermines and decorated with six bundles of powderings, a gown of black satin guarded with black velvet furred with 132 black coney skins, a gown of black satin with breadths of gold with three lusern skins and 40 white lamb for the body and sleeves and a gown of black velvet furred with twelve pampilion skins.

An account for Mary's wardrobe of the robes from 1545–46 recorded a number of garments being altered, embroidery and tailoring costing £79 5*s*. The garments were very luxurious but some of the items were being translated either in terms of being enlarged or refashioned. The refashioning often included extensive embroidery worked with metal thread, so combining a labour intensive technique with expensive materials.[157] The reworking or translating of a gown of black velvet involved the gown being decorated with 16 oz (453 g) of damask gold pirls or pipes at 6*s* the oz. Three new gowns were also embroidered: a gown of black velvet of 'pastment' gold with braid of fine Venice gold; a gown of purple satin wrought with 'pastment' of gold and silver with a braid of gold and silver and a gown of black satin embroidered with 'pastment' of gold and silver and with a braid of 'pastment' of gold and silver. This account provides evidence of the speed with which fashions changed and the keenness with which she followed these. She had three pairs of sleeves altered to make them into French sleeves: one pair of black tilsent, one pair of purple satin and one pair of crimson satin, fringed with Venice gold and wrought with Venice gold and pirls of damask gold. The workmanship cost 20*s* a pair. In much the same way, a pair of French sleeves was translated to turn them into Venice sleeves of black velvet guarded with passementerie of gold and great wreaths of Venice gold costing 10*s*.

Mary shared her father's passion for jewellery. This is demonstrated by the extant inventory listing her jewels.[158] The document recorded jewels in the care of Mary Finch which had been 'Receyved of my lady Maryes grace into my Custodie' in December 1542 and it was updated on 1 January 1543 and 20 July 1546. It was reviewed on 25 January 1547, three days before her father's death.[159]

THE DUKE OF RICHMOND

Henry Fitzroy, born in 1519, was the only illegitimate son that Henry VIII acknowledged. His mother was Elizabeth Blount, who after his birth married Sir Gilbert Tailboys and later Lord Clinton.[160] Little is known about his childhood until his creation as duke of Richmond in 1525 when he was made president of the council in the north. At the same time he was provided with his own household. The records from this include the charges of his wardrobe of the robes and beds and the stable from 12 June 1525 to 31 March 1526, with £88 1*s* 2*d* spent on his apparel and £8 5s 10½*d* on washing his napery.[161] His own accounts included a payment for 'the duke's robes of estate, of crimson velvet, and blue velvet lined with sarsenet, with other appertenances belonging to the garter'.[162] Henry VIII placed an order for green and purple sarsenet for the wardrobe of the beds of the duke costing £14 2*s* 4½*d* from the great wardrobe in the accounting year 1525–26.[163] For the creation of his son as duke of Richmond in 1525, the king distributed largesse of £5, and for his installation as a knight of the Garter, he paid £10 for setting up his banner, helm and crest.[164]

On 14 January 1527 Richmond thanked his father for a New Year's gift of plate.[165] A year later he asked for a suit of armour 'for his exercise in arms, according to his learning in Julius Caesar' and begged Cardinal Wolsey to support this request.[166] Whether he was successful is unknown, but on 20 July 1528 the duke acknowledged 'your letters and the goodly apparel you sent me by Master Magnus'.[167] In autumn 1528, then aged nine, he stayed at the home of the earl of Northumberland at Topcliffe where he 'did not use himself, like a child of his tender age, but more like a man in all his behaviours'.[168] For two years he lived at Windsor in the company of the earl of Surrey with whom from October 1532 to September 1533 he visited the French court.

'The view of the said wardrobe taken by John Uvedale, secretary to the duke [taken] on 23 June in the xxiijth yere (1531) by the commandment of Sir William Parre Chamberlain to the said Duke' begins with his 'Robes of Estate made at my Lordis Creacion'.[169] The fact that they take pride of place in the inventory, and no other robes of estate are listed, suggests that these robes had been made with plenty of room for growth. As in his father's inventories, his Garter robes 'with a great cross of saint George embroidered with the garter about it' came next. Of the pieces in the main part of the inventory, many such as a 'doublet of cloth of gold of tissue, sore worn, colour yellow' were described as heavily worn. The decorative details are the most interesting feature of the duke's clothes, in particular the buttons, which were numerous and were often decorated with roses, either plain or enamelled. Embroidery, guards and fur linings all feature heavily. The number of hats and bonnets owned by the duke is significant but no shoes, boots or buskins were listed in this inventory. References are lacking to his jewels, which may suggest that they were recorded separately. However, he now had 'one goodly dagger the hafte, cross and pomell and sheath all silver and gilt with a knife and a bodkin' and 'a little woodknife hafted with ivory the sheath black velvet the chape gilt on iron with two knives and one hammer'.

Like his father, his clothes were made from a range of colours (Table 11.2). The reference to some items being in the 'new colour' is suggestive of the new colour of the king's livery.[170] His hose were predominantly in black or white, with two in a neutral ash colour.

The number of items made from cloth woven with metal thread is conspicuously small with only two gowns of tinsel, one doublet of cloth of gold tissue and one of cloth of silver (Table 11.3). Equally, there are no matching sets of doublets and hose. As the textile used for the hose is not described, it can be inferred that it was wool, although in most cases the hose do have silk linings that are either self-coloured or in a contrasting colour. Where the hose are in a contrasting colour, this suggests that the lining was visible through slashing. There are also no sets of matching doublet, hose and gown which is different to the king's wardrobe. The most frequently used fabric is velvet, with satin a close second.

On 26 November 1533 Richmond married Mary, daughter of the duke of Norfolk and the sister of his companion the earl of Surrey. Holbein drew Mary. In the portrait she wears a male-style bonnet with a feather and sketched an alternative design for her hat, showing it decorated with an *R* for Richmond.[171] Whether the duke was depicted by Holbein is not known. His miniature was painted by Lucas Horenbout: the duke appears informally dressed in his shirt, with its high collar left undone, and a close-fitting black work cap (Fig. 11.5). Richmond went into a decline in the summer

Table 11.2: *Analysis of Richmond's clothes in 1531 by colour*

Colour	Gowns/nightgowns	Riding cloaks	Spanish cloaks	Riding coats	Jerkins	Doublets	Hose
Ash colour	~	~	~	~	~	~	2
Black	5	~	1	3	2	5	15
Blue	1	~	~	~	~	~	~
Crimson	1	~	~	1	~	2	~
Green	~	~	~	3	~	~	~
New colour	~	~	~	1	~	~	~
Purple	2	~	~	1	~	5	~
Russet	1	~	~	~	~	~	~
Scarlet	~	1	~	~	~	~	~
Tawny	2	~	~	~	~	1	~
Unspecified	~	~	~	~	~	2	2
White	~	~	~	~	~	1	13
	12	1	1	9	2	16	32

Table 11.3: *Analysis of Richmond's clothes in 1531 by textile*

Textile	Gowns/nightgowns	Riding cloaks	Spanish cloaks	Riding coats	Jerkins	Doublets	Hose
Cloth	~	~	~	1	~	~	31
Cloth of gold tissue	~	~	~	~	~	1	~
Cloth of silver	~	~	~	~	~	1	~
Cotton	~	~	~	1	~	~	~
Damask	1	~	~	~	~	~	~
Frisado	~	~	~	1	~	~	~
Sarsenet	~	~	~	~	~	6	~
Satin	2	~	~	~	1	6	~
Scarlet	~	1	~	~	~	~	1
Taffeta	2	~	~	2	~	1	~
Tinsel	2	~	~	~	~	~	~
Velvet	5	~	1	4	1	1	~
	12	1	1	9	2	16	32

Shortly after Henry VIII's death in 1547, Elizabeth was described by her tutor Roger Ascham in a letter to John Sturm. He noted that 'She has just passed her sixteenth birthday and shows such dignity and gentleness as are wonderful at her age and in her rank . . . In adornment she is elegant rather than showy, and by her contempt of gold and head-dresses, she reminds one of Hippolyte rather than Phaedra'.[193]

11.7 *Edward VI as a child, by Hans Holbein the Younger,* c. *1539. Image © Board of Trustees, National Gallery of Art, Washington (1937.1.64)*

PRINCE EDWARD

Two months before his birth, Francis I heard that Henry VIII meant to name the baby, if a boy, either Edward or Henry.[194] Edward was born at Hampton Court on 12 October 1537, the vigil of St Edward's day, and was named in honour of Edward the Confessor, the English royal saint. He was the long-awaited son and he was described as 'our moost noble and moost precyous joyelle'.

When in September 1538 the king's council declared its intention to visit the prince, Lady Bryan felt that she lacked suitable clothes for him to wear then. She would 'acompleche et to the best of my power with syche thynges as her es to do et with al, wyche es but very bare for syche a time. The best cot my Lord Princses grace hath es tensel, and that he shal have on at that teym; he hath never a good jewel to set on his cape howbet I shal order al things for my lordes honer the best I can'.[195]

In the following months Holbein undertook a preparatory sketch for a painting of the young prince, possibly given to Henry as a New Year's gift on 1 January 1539 (Fig. 11.7).[196] If this is the case, then Edward was aged about 14 months, when he would have been short-coated.[197] He wears a coat of scarlet wool cut trimmed with black cloth of gold. The coat, which fastened at the back, had a square neck and hanging sleeves, which could act as leading strings if he was unsteady on his feet, with separate sleeves of cloth of gold.[198]

Perhaps not surprisingly, Henry VIII ordered clothes for his son on his own warrants. The first such order was made on 6 January 1539, when the boy was 15 months old. It consisted of a coat of crimson velvet with three welts of cloth of gold, a coat of tawny velvet with two welts of cloth of gold, a coat of black velvet with a single welt of cloth of gold, all lined with scarlet and the sleeves lined with sarsenet, two coats of scarlet, two bonnets of white satin and two nightgowns of black velvet lined with buckram.[199] There are also three larger warrants for Edward dated 21 July 1539, 27 March 1544 and 26 February 1545 when he was 21 months, six and a half and almost seven and a half.[200] The last warrant was issued on the same day as a warrant for the king which also included a small amount of work for the prince. Catherine Addington provided a selection of furs for Edward including 30 sable skins, 16 luzards and four panes and four vents of libards.[201]

Table 11.6 indicates that there was a marked increased in the number of different types of garments ordered for Edward over the course of these three warrants, reflecting his increasing age and maturity. The variety of items echoes the contents of his father's wardrobe and parallels the development previously of Richmond's wardrobe. The second and third warrants both date after the time of his breeching and adoption of clothing worn by adults. In 1547 Edward recalled his transition from the nursery at the age of six in his journal, noting that he was brought up by women until he was six. He continued, 'At the sixth year of his age he was brought up in learning by Dr Cox . . . and John Clerke . . . Master of Arts'.[202]

The warrant from March 1544 provided the prince with some very fancy items, with rich surface decoration often making use of contrasting colours and a variety of techniques (Fig. 11.8). The order included two doublets with matching slops, of crimson velvet and black satin, slashed, one full of wreaths of crimson satin, the other with black velvet, with buttons and loops of Venice gold, the vents and collar of velvet and a coat without sleeves for archery of plain gold tissue with welts of lukes velvet laid on with silk and gold cord, lined with sarsenet and fastening with 'claspes and Eis' of silver.[203] The emphasis on highly decorated clothes continued in the warrant from February 1545: a frock of black tinsel with one wide and two narrow guards of crimson velvet put on with gold and silk cord and lined with crimson sarsenet and a coat of purple cloth of gold with five guards of purple velvet, also put on with gold and silk cord.[204]

of gold braid and the button loops were made from 'braided golde lace'.

Richard Cecil, yeoman of the king's robes, subscribed a warrant dated January 1546 'for certain stuff and workmanship delivered for the prince's grace's apparel'.[209] Edward's wardrobe contained clothes for everyday wear as well as court and state occasions. On 8 May 1546 he told his older sister how he 'puts on his best clothes very seldom and yet he loves them more than the others; even so he rarely writes to her but loves her most'.[210] A letter addressed to his father on 4 August 1546, in which his tutor's hand may be detected, Edward thanked him 'for his kindness and for the great and precious gifts, as chains, rings with balls, jewels, collars and brooches, necklaces and dresses, which show his fatherly affection and are given not to make his son proud but urge him on in virtue and piety'.[211] At the reception of the French admiral five weeks later, Edward rode out to meet him at Hampton Court with a retinue dressed 'in velvett cots on horsebacke'.[212] The imperial ambassador noted that the horsemen accompanying him were 'mostly in cloth of gold'.[213]

A list of weapons and accessories delivered for the prince included three sword girdles of white, tawny and purple velvet, one girdle for a wood knife of black velvet, 'a new rapier for my lord prince with four scabbards to the same' costing 20*s*, along with a hammer for 16*d* and a pair of compasses costing 20*d*.[214] These items were necessary for the prince's education and part of his dress.

William Thomas, while in exile, described Edward in his book entitled *Perygrine*, noting that 'he hath suche a grace of porte and gesture in gravitye when he commeth to any presence, that it shold seme he were all redy a father, and yett he passeth not the age of x yeres'.[215] At the time, Thomas could not have seen the prince for two years. That he was not exaggerating is clear in a three-quarter-length portrait of Edward, in which he wears a jewel surmounted with the prince of Wales feathers, painted in *c.* 1546. The artist was a member of the Flemish School, possibly William Scrots (Fig. 11.9), and thought to have been painted at Hunsdon.[216] A second, slightly later, version of the painting at Petworth, this time full-length, presented Edward as king.[217] Edward had adopted the stance favoured by his father and wore fashionable male dress: a white satin doublet and tight-fitting hose, embroidered with gold thread and guarded down the front and round the skirts with gold passamayne lace, with a lynx lined russet velvet gown guarded with a double embroidered guard of the same. Once king, he ordered armour, as a further means of emulating his father (Fig. 11.10).

11.9 *Edward VI, unknown artist. RCIN 404441 OM 44 WC 69. The Royal Collection © 2004, Her Majesty the Queen Elizabeth II*

11.10 *Three-quarter armour for a boy of about 12 years old, possibly Edward VI, front view, Greenwich, c. 1550. The Royal Armouries, Leeds. © The Board of Trustees of the Armouries*

Table 11.6: *Overview of the type and number of clothes ordered for Prince Edward*

Garments	21 July 1539	27 March 1544	26 February 1545
Outer garments			
Cloaks	~	1	1
Coats	4	11	6
Coats for archery	~	5	~
Coats, short	2	10	2
Frocks	~	~	2
Jerkins	~	1	2
Gowns	~	~	2
Nightgowns	~	1	~
Spanish gowns	~	~	1
– Doublets			
Doublets	~	28	5
Doublets with bases	~	~	11
– Hose and slops			
Hose	4	72	4
Slops	~	28	8
– Headwear			
Bonnets*	43	19	8
Night bonnets	6	12	9
Hats	1	~	2
– Footwear			
Velvet covered shoes	4	Numbers not given	~
– Accessories			
Ruffs and bands	6 sets	24	~
– Cases			
Cases for bonnets	1	~	~
Cases for cloaks	~	~	1
Cases for doublets, gowns, hose and slops	~	51	8
– Translating garments			
Translating cloaks	~	~	1
Translating coats	~	~	1
Translating doublets	~	1	~
Translating frocks	~	~	1
Translating slops	~	~	6
Items for Thomas Brown			
Coats	~	1	1
Riding coats	~	~	1
Doublets	~	~	2
Slops	~	~	2
Translating/enlarging coats	~	1	1
Cost	**£91 10s 8*d***	**£325 7*s* 1*d***	**£181 9*s* 10*d***

* Included bonnets, superior bonnets and sub bonnets

11.8 *Edward continued to favour the use of rich surface decoration in contrasting colours after he became king, as indicated by this portrait of Edward VI, attributed to Guillim Stretes. RCIN 405751 OM 49 HC 1246. The Royal Collection © 2004, Her Majesty the Queen Elizabeth II*

Edward received clothes as gifts from other members of his family. Mary's present to him for New Year 1539 was 'a cote of crymosen satten enbrowdered with gold with paunses of pyrles and sleves of tynsell and iiij aglettes of gold'.[205] His gift roll for January 1540 recorded from his father a pair of flagons, 178 oz (5,046 g), a pair of salts with covers, 38¾ oz (1,098 g); from Mary a gold brooch with the image of St John the Baptist set with a ruby and from Elizabeth a bracer of needlework of her own making.[206] Anne of Cleves' accounts of 1540 include a payment of £4 16*s* 4*d* for a crimson velvet bonnet set with bullion of gold and fringed with gold bought from William Tailor, haberdasher, and given to the prince.[207] His stepmother Catherine Parr bought him clothes for his New Year's gift in 1545 which cost £18 21*d*.[208] Her gift consisted of a gown of crimson satin in grain, richly embroidered and lined with crimson satin in the body, vents, cape and taffeta to line the rest; white satin for a coat, doublet and a pair of slops, the coat was embroidered and the coat, doublet and hose were edged with white velvet, the coat lined with white striped satin, while the doublet and slops were lined with fine holland. The coat and doublet both had eight gold buttons with stalks

Just as a few of Prince Arthur's clothes survived in Henry VIII's possession some of Edward's clothes remained in his sister Elizabeth's wardrobe of the robes in 1600. These included his parliament robes, as well as the robes for the orders of the Garter and St Michael, three gowns, three frocks, two coats, two riding coats, one jerkin and three sets of matching doublets and hose, as well as a small selection of jewels and weapons.[218] While the sample is small, cloth of gold, cloth of silver, velvet and satin predominate and crimson and purple were most common.

Lady Jane Grey

Lady Jane Grey was born in October 1537, about the same time as Edward VI. She was the daughter of Henry's niece, Frances Brandon and Henry Grey, later duke of Suffolk. Her tutor, John Aylmer, who later became bishop of London, described Jane in his book *A Harbour for Faithful Subjects*. Aylmer made a connection between her nobility and the simplicity of her clothing:

> The king left her rich clothes and jewels; and I know it to be true, that in seven years after her father's death, she never in all that time looked upon that rich attire and precious jewels but once, and that against her will. And that there never came gold or stone upon her head, till her sister forced her to lay off her former soberness, and bear her company in her glittering gayness. And then she so wore it, as every man might see that her body carried that which her heart misliked. I am sure that her maidenly apparel which she used in King Edward's time, made the noblemen's daughters and wives to be ashamed to be dressed and painted like peacocks; being more moved with her most virtuous example than with all that ever Paul or Peter wrote touching that matter.[219]

However, Edward VI rejected her as a potential bride, stating that he favoured 'a foreign princess, well stuffed [with an impressive wardrobe] and well jewelled'.[220]

When on 6 July 1553 Edward VI died, Jane was at her parent's home in Chelsea. Two days later she travelled down the Thames to the Tower after being proclaimed queen. A Genoese merchant witnessed her arrival. His description records that she had dressed befitting her new dignity. In his opinion, Jane was:

> very short and thin but prettily shaped and graceful. She has small features and a well-made nose, the mouth flexible and the lips red. The eyebrows are arched and darker than the hair, which is nearly red . . . She wore a dress of green velvet stamped with gold, with large sleeves. Her headdress was a white coif with many jewels. She walked under a canopy, her mother carrying her long train, and her husband, Guildford, walking by her, dressed all in white and gold, a very tall, strong boy with light hair, who paid her much attention. The new Queen was mounted on very high chopines to make her look much taller, which were concealed by her robes, as she is very small and short.[221]

Jane and her husband were dressed in the Tudor colours of green and white, so stressing her legitimate right to the throne. In order to make her stand out from the crowd, Jane wore the highly fashionable Italian high-heeled shoes or chopines.[222]

Notes

1 *CSP Venetian, 1509–19*, p. 561.
2 F. Fernández-Armesto, *Ferdinand and Isabella* (1975) p. 118; Fraser, *Six Wives*, p. 11.
3 *LP* IV.iii, 5774.
4 *LP* II.i, 80.
5 According to Campeggio, Catherine assured him that 'from the embraces of her first husband she entered this marriage as a virgin and an immaculate woman'; *LP* IV.iii, 5681.
6 R. Holinshed, *Chronicles of England, Scotland and Ireland*, III (1807), p. 527.
7 Fraser, *Six Wives*, p. 29.
8 Knecht, *Rise and Fall*, p. 80.
9 *LP* V, 362.
10 Strype, *Memorials*, VI, pp. 221–22.
11 *LP* XV, 898.
12 Bruce, *Making Henry*, p. 167.
13 Harvey, *Elizabeth of York*, pp. 169–70; Laynesmith, *Last Medieval Queens*, p. 111.
14 For example, Strickland, *Queens of Scotland*, I, pp. 63–68.
15 *CSP Venetian, 1520–26*, p. 104.
16 *LP* XX.ii, 19.
17 *LP* XV, 901.
18 *LP* XVI, 712.
19 *LP* XII.i, 1069.
20 Wriothesley, *Chronicle*, I, p. 64.
21 Loades, *Chronicles*, p. 188.
22 *SP* I.ii, p. 551; *LP* XII.ii, 77.
23 *LP* XII.ii, 626.
24 *LP* II.ii, 4279.
25 *LP* II.ii, 4288.
26 *LP* II.ii, 4529.
27 *LP* II.ii, 4568.
28 H. Soly, ed., *Charles V and His Time, 1500–1558* (Antwerp, 1999), p. 67.
29 Catherine Parr's pregnancy occurred during her fourth marriage.
30 Crawford, *Letters*, p. 199 (*LP* XII.ii, 889).
31 Weir, *Six Wives*, p. 558.
32 Fraser, *Six Wives*, p. 405.
33 *LP* II.i, 1198.
34 *LP* VIII, 919.
35 *LP* II.i, 705.
36 TNA E36/215, p. 100.
37 *LP* II.i, 1622.
38 Wriothesley, *Chronicle*, I, p. 65.
39 Ibid., I, pp. 66–67.
40 M. Hume, *Chronicle of King Henry VIII of England* (1889), p. 73.
41 *PPE Elizabeth*, p. 78.
42 *LP* III.i, 145.
43 *LP* III.i, 189.
44 *LP* III.i, 289.
45 Pollard, *Henry VII*, I, p. 231.
46 See above, pp. 94–95.
47 *LP* XX.ii, 31.
48 TNA E315/249, f. 52v.
49 Leland, *Collectanea*, IV, p. 249.
50 Ibid., p. 179; TNA E101/410/12.
51 Leland, *Collectanea*, IV, p. 249.
52 Staniland, 'Royal entry', p. 299.
53 Leland, *Collectanea*, IV, p. 249.
54 See above, p. 58.
55 TNA E101/417/3, no 84 (*LP* I.i, 394.2).
56 *LP* I.i, 473.
57 *LP* I.i, 578.
58 TNA E101/417/4, unfoliated.
59 BL Additional MS 18,826, f. 12 (*LP* I.i, 647).

60 TNA E101/417/4, unfoliated.
61 TNA E101/418/5, no. 43 (*LP* I.ii, 3332). Two counterpoints of estate 'of powderde armyns' which are very similar to those made for Catherine of Aragon were listed with the goods of Catherine Parr (17641–42).
62 TNA E101/418/5, no. 44 (*LP* I.ii, 3333).
63 *LP* I.ii, 3500.
64 *LP* I.ii, 3581.
65 *LP* VI, 890.
66 *LP* VI, 948.
67 *LP* VI, 1069.
68 TNA SP1/88, f. 116 (*LP* VII, 1668).
69 Colvin, *HKW*, IV, p. 82.
70 Bod Lib Rawlinson MS D.775, ff. 95r, 96r.
71 NUL MS Ne01, unfoliated.
72 *HO*, p. 127; Murphy, *Bastard Prince*, p. 34.
73 TNA E404/79, 168; *PPE Elizabeth*, p. 102.
74 *PPE Princess Mary*, p. 42.
75 Ibid., p. 85
76 *LP* II.ii, 3802.
77 *LP* III.ii, 1439.
78 BL MS Cotton, Otho, CX, f. 234.
79 *PPE Princess Mary*, p. 53.
80 *CSP Spanish*, V.i (1534–35), p. 134.
81 *LP* I.i, 132.39.
82 *LP* II.i, 658–59.
83 *LP* I.i, 885.8.
84 *LP* II.ii, 3429.
85 *LP* XIII.ii, 524; in July 1539 she was granted, along with her husband David, an annuity of £40 a year; *LP* XIV.i, 1354.54.
86 Private collection; illustrated in Scarisbrick, *Tudor*, p. 76.
87 TNA LC9/51, f. 9r.
88 Ibid., f. 62v.
89 *LP* XIV.i, 1121.
90 J. Wilson, 'The noble imp: the upper-class child in English Renaissance art and literature', *The Antiquaries Journal*, 70 (1990), pp. 360–78.
91 Tate Britain, London.
92 Buck, *Clothes*, pp. 21–26.
93 Ibid., p. 58; Doran, *Elizabeth*, pp. 64–66.
94 MoL 39.108.1.
95 MoL A1989. Found in Hill Street, Finsbury. Worked at 8½ stitches and 13½ rows per inch.
96 S. M. Levey, 'References to dress in the earliest account book of Bess of Hardwick', *Costume*, 34 (2000), p. 16.
97 For an example of a chair modified to help a young child stand, see The Daughters of Philip II, *c.* 1571, by Alonso Sànchez Coello in the Monasterio de las Descalzes Reales, Madrid. Illustrated in Ortiz, *Resplendence*, p. 16.
98 *LP* XIII.ii, 306.
99 *LP* XIV.ii, 9.
100 For an example of adult hose, see the yellow silk knitted hose with cod piece made for elector Augustus of Saxony, illustrated in Rangström, *Lions*, pp. 34–35.
101 Ibid., pp. 200–01.
102 Rowlands, *Age of Dürer*, pp. 230–31.
103 See, for example, the portrait of Marcus Gheeraerts of Anne, Lady Pope, with her children; private collection.
104 British School; in the collection of the Marquess of Bath, Longleat House, Warminster, Wiltshire.
105 Examples can be seen in the collection of the Museum of London, e.g. (MoL 4703). M. de Neergaard, 'Children's shoes in the thirteenth to the sixteenth centuries', *Costume*, 19 (1985), pp. 14–21.
105 MoL A26591.
107 Musée du Louvre, Paris; Scott, *Visual History*, p. 129.
108 TNA E101/420/14, unfoliated.
109 TNA E101/420/1, no. 37 (*LP* V, 498).
110 TNA E101/421/3, unfoliated.
111 *LP* VII, app. 13, see *DNB*, 16, pp. 697–701.
112 *LP* XI, 48.
113 *LP* XI, 1396.
114 M. A. E. Green, ed., *Letters of Royal and Illustrious Ladies*, II (1846), pp. 292–93.
115 *LP* App. I.i, 1284.
116 *LP* XIII.2, 1280.
117 *LP* Additional I.ii, 1573.
118 *LP* XIX.i, 799.
119 A. Clifford, ed., *The State Papers and Letters of Sir Ralph Sadler*, I (1809), p. 183.
120 *LP* II.i, 1556.
121 *LP* II.i, 1563.
122 *LP* II.i, 1585.
123 *CSP Venetian*, 1527–33, p. 58.
124 Ibid., p. 288.
125 *LP* XVI, 1253.
126 TNA LC9/51, ff. 9v–10r.
127 Ibid., ff. 59r–v.
128 The making costs were as follows: 5*s* for a gown, regardless of style, 3*s* 4*d* for a kirtle, 20*d* for a French hood, 12*d* for a partlet and 12*d* for a pair of sleeves; JRL Latin MS 239, f. 17v.
129 TNA E101/418/4, f. 3v.
130 Strickland, *Queens of England*, II, p. 371.
131 TNA E101/420/14, unfoliated. Later in the same year, on 20 December, Mary received an order of bedding consisting of 32 pairs of linen sheets, four bolsters and four ticks costing £27 13*s* 8*d*; E101/420/14, unfoliated.
132 TNA E101/418/1, no. 1.
133 The warrant also included ribbon for points, garters and girdles, velvet shoes, hose, gloves, French hoods and a night bonnet of ermine; TNA E101/418/1, no. 6 (*LP* V, 439).
134 TNA E101/421/3, unfoliated.
135 Ibid., unfoliated.
136 The warrant also included a clock case of bridges satin, a black velvet partlet, a black satin partlet, both lined with sarsenet, holland for smocks and cambric for rails. She received a similar warrant dated 25 March 1534; TNA E101/417/3, no. 48.
137 *LP* X, 40, 141; also *PPE Princess Mary*, p. lxvi; I am grateful to Alison Carter for this reference.
138 *LP* X, 351.
139 TNA E36/455, ff. 31r–v.
140 The order also included three bonnets of black velvet, three frontlets for the same bonnets, two dozen lawn partlets, two dozen partlet pastes, twelve pairs of hose, twelve pairs of velvet shoes, 30 ells holland (20.6 m) for smocks and rails.
141 *LP* XI, 6.
142 *PPE Princess Mary*, p. 4.
143 *SP* VII, p. 685.
144 *PPE Princess Mary*, p. 43.
145 TNA SP1/126, f. 208r (*LP* XII.ii, 1147).
146 TNA LC9/51, f. 265v.
147 TNA E36/456, f. 17v.
148 TNA E36/456, ff. 31v–32r.
149 *PPE Princess Mary*, pp. 49, 89.
150 BL Cotton MS App. 89, f. 41r.
151 *PPE Princess Mary*, pp. 96–99.
152 *LP* XIX.i, 422.
153 *LP* XX.ii, 909.16.
154 *LP* XXI.i, 963.149 and 150.
155 *LP* XXI.ii, 475.115.
156 TNA E101/424/7, f. 3r.
157 TNA E101/424/7.
158 BL MS Royal 17B.XXVIII, ff. 136r–49v (*PPE Princess Mary*, pp. 175–201).
159 *LP* XXI.i, 1333.
160 RL 12198, Parker 42; Holbein sketched in his clothes in some detail, annotating his drawing.
161 *LP* IV.i, 2063.2.
162 *LP* IV.i, 1530.
163 TNA E101/418/4, f. 9v.
164 *LP* IV.i, 1431.
165 *LP* IV.ii, 2502.
166 *LP* IV.ii, 3860–61.
167 *LP* IV.ii, 4534.
168 Murphy, *Bastard Prince*, p. 97.
169 Longleat Miscellaneous MS 17, unfoliated. I am most grateful to Chris Woolgar for bringing this document to my attention.
170 See below, pp. 248–49.
171 RL 12212, Parker 16; see Millar, *Holbein*, p. 70. Holbein's notes refer to her wearing *samet rot* and *schwarz felbet* (red and black velvet).
172 BL Royal MS 7F, XVI, f. 83 (*LP* XI, 163), *LP* XI, 174.
173 Nichols, 'Inventories', p. 5.
174 Ibid., pp. 5–6.
175 Murphy, *Bastard Prince*, pp. 191–93.
176 Nichols, 'Inventories', p. 2.
177 For a full discussion of Elizabeth's appearance and life beyond 1547, see Arnold, *Queen Elizabeth*; for her early life, pp. 3–4.
178 *LP* VII, 469.
179 TNA SP1/103, ff. 322r–327v (LP X, 913); W. Loke, Account of materials furnished for the use of Anne Boleyn and Princess Elizabeth, 1535–6', *Miscellanea of the Philobilion Society*, 7 (1862), cited in Ives, *Anne Boleyn*, p. 269.
180 *LP* XI, 860.
181 TNA SP1/103, f. 323v (*LP* X, 913).
182 Ibid., ff. 324v, 327r.

183 H. Ellis, *Original Letters, Illustrative of English History*, Second Series, II (1827), pp. 78–83 (*LP* XI, 203).
184 TNA LC 5/31, p. 8.
185 TNA E36/456, f. 18r.
186 BL Stowe MS 559, f. 58. Catherine also gave her some beads 'of golde that is to say x Longe stones enamuled with white and garneshed with peerle & redstones every of them havyng peerlles and x other stones ennamuled with blewe like cuppes havyng also a pillar garnesshed with peerll and redstones and a buttone of golde with divers small cheynes of golde with black knoppes'.
187 *PPE Princess Mary*, pp. 194, 197.
188 TNA E101/423/12, unfoliated.
189 *LP* XX.ii, 909.18.
190 *LP* XXI.i, 963.37 and *LP* XXI.i, 963.86.
191 *LP* XXI.ii, 475.117.
192 RC; J. Arnold, 'The "Pictur" of Elizabeth I when princess', *The Burlington Magazine*, 123 (1981), pp. 303–04.
193 J. A. Giles, *The Whole Works of Ascham*, I (1864), p. lxiii.
194 *LP* VI, 1070.
195 Nichols, *Literary Remains*, p. xxxvij.
196 RL 12200, Parker 46.
197 For a drawing by Holbein showing Edward's skirts (and shoes) see Foister, *Holbein*, p. 196.
198 Monnas, *Merchants*, ch. 8 (forthcoming). The portrait was inscribed with verses in Latin, which translate as 'Little boy, take after your father and also inherit his virtues. The world in its immensity contains nothing greater. You are to surpass the deeds of such a father!'. National Gallery of Art, Washington D C, 64; Rowlands, *Holbein*, pp. 146–47. Rowlands questions the date and suggests that the painting was given on 1 January 1540.
199 TNA E26/456, f. 15r.
200 TNA E36/456, ff. 30r–31v and E101/423/10, ff. 26v–34v and ff. 55v–62v. An analysis of the clothes made for Edward in the first of these has been undertaken, comparing these with what he had worn for his picture several weeks before; J. L. Nevinson, 'Prince Edward's clothes', *Costume*, 2 (1968), pp. 3–8; includes a transcript of the entry in TNA E36/456.
201 TNA E101/423/10, f. 37r.
202 W. K. Jordan, ed., *Chronicle and Political Papers of Edward VI* (1966), p. 3.
203 TNA E101/423/10, ff. 30v and 31v.
204 Ibid., ff. 56r and 55v.
205 BL Cotton MS App. 89, f. 41r. Edward was fond of Mary and on 11 January 1546 he reminded her that his 'affection for her and his mother [would] ever hold the chief place in his heart'; *LP* XXI.i, 50.
206 *LP* XV, 1.
207 TNA E101/422/15, unfoliated.
208 TNA E101/423/12, unfoliated.
209 *LP* XXI.148.71.
210 *LP* XXI.i, 770.
211 *LP* XXI.i, 1416.
212 *LP* XXI.i, 1384; Wriothesley, *Chronicle*, I, p. 173.
213 *LP* XXI.ii, 14; *CSP Spanish*, VIII, 316.
214 TNA E101/424/16, f. 1v.
215 Nichols, *Literary Remains*, I, p. lxxxi. Girolamo Cardano, the Milanese philosopher, described him in 1553 the following terms, 'His stature was below the medium ... his general appearance dignified and formal'.
216 H. Colvin, 'Edward VI and Hundson House', *Burlington Magazine*, 113 (1971), p. 210.
217 Hearn, *Dynasties*, p. 50.
218 BL Stowe MS 557, ff. 5r–7v; Arnold, *Queen Elizabeth*, pp. 252–53.
219 C. Falkus, ed., *The Private Lives of the Tudor Monarchs* (1974), p. 76.
220 Strickland, *Queens of England*, II, p. 339.
221 D. M. Ashdown, *Tudor Cousins: Rivals for the Throne* (Thrupp, 2000), p. 90.
222 For examples of chopines or calcagnetti, see D. D. Poli, *The Arts and Crafts of Fashion in Venice, from the 13th to the 18th Century* (1997), p. 86.

At the time of his death, Wolsey was still a wealthy man, as indicated by the valuation of his goods: in ready money £3,000, in plate £1,753 3*s* 7½*d*, the contents of the wardrobe £800, 80 horses and geldings with their harness £150, four mules for the saddle with their harness £60 and six mules for carriage with their harness £40, with a total value of £6,374 3*s* 7½*d*.[45] The inventory of his goods included cloth of silver and green satin 'sometime the lining of two gowns' which may have been remnants of his wardrobe when cardinal.[46] A list of effects included 'silks and cloths of gold that my lord his Grace hath of Richard Gresham' and other fabric from John Gresham, but it is uncertain whether this was all bought for making vestments or whether some was for Wolsey's personal wardrobe.[47] While his funeral was less magnificent than it would have been, Wolsey was still accorded the honour of having a canopy carried over his coffin as it was borne to the chapel of Our Lady at Leicester abbey.[48]

THOMAS CROMWELL

Holbein's portrait of Cromwell was painted some time after his appointment as master of the king's jewels on 12 April 1532. The letter in the foreground is addressed to him as 'our trusty and right well biloved Counsaillor Thomas Cromwell Maister of our Jewell House' (Fig. 12.6).[49] In contrast to the duke of Norfolk (an aristocrat) and Sir Henry Guildford (a gentleman), Cromwell was well aware of his humble background and he had himself presented in the understated dress of a lawyer.[50] On 21 November 1535 Eustace Chapuys outlined to Charles V his origins and rise to power, commenting that he 'speaks well in his own language, and tolerably in Latin, French and Italian; [he] is hospitable, liberal both with his property and with gracious words, magnificent in his household and in building'.[51]

12.6 *Sir Thomas Cromwell, by Hans Holbein the Younger. © The Frick Collection, New York*

Cromwell employed the king's livery and his own household with its livery to assert his position. On 20 March 1539 Andrew Baynton excused himself, stating 'I beg you will take no displeasure for my long absence not for my departing; for when your Lordship rode from St James's to the Court, my fellows told me that I was not appointed to ride with you, not having your livery'.[52] In the following month, Nicholas Thorne reported to Cromwell on ships being made ready for the king's service in Bristol. He noted that 'Among which is the *Saviour*, wherein I have appointed 60 mariners besides officers, with the flags and streamers of your Lordship's colours and arms'.[53] Cromwell's accounts included an entry for his 'robbys of the Exchequyre for the xxvij and xxviij yere of king Henry the viijth', which had cost £25 13*s* 8*d*.[54]

Cromwell's position at court was reflected in the number of gifts that he received to secure his favour and patronage. The network of individuals who exchanged gifts with Cromwell at the New Year or who sent him gifts that could be construed as bribes highlight his perceived role as a conduit for access to and patronage from the king. On 3 October 1536 the earl of Northumberland thanked him 'especially for getting the king to give the writer certain gorgeous and sumptuous apparel of his own wearing'.[55] Three years later, Sir William Penzon sent 'a diamond set in a slender gold ring, meet to be set in the breast of a George, which though, not the best, he desires Cromwell to accept'.[56] So it is not surprising that Cromwell dramatised his arrest by symbolically removing his head gear. The French ambassador reported that, on being arrested on 10 June 1540, 'Cromwell, roused to fury, took his bonnet and having ripped it from his head, threw it in rage to the ground'.[57]

Symbols of status: the significance of noble robes

Noble robes were overt symbols of noble status. They were presented at the peer's creation and they were worn at coronations and during parliament (Pl. VA). They were very traditional in their materials and construction, and the fur used to trim them codified the rank of the wearer. The finer details were recorded in the 'Memorandum that all manner of Estates shall ware there Apparell Powdred As ys Abouesaide'.[58] This memorandum included two pages of diagrams recording the placement of the ermine tails:

The queenes Bonnette ¼ inch, the queenes sleves Inch ½, the gounes of the quene Inch ½, the Princes Bonnett Inch, the Princes gowne ij Inch, the Princes sleves Inche ½, the duchis bonnette Inche 4 by Suffrounce, a duches sleves ij Inch ¼, the duches goune 3 inch full, the Marques sleues 2 Inch, for a Marques goune 3 Inch ½, a Countesse Sleues 3 Inches Full, a Vice Contes sleves 4 Inch Full, a Vice Contes goune 5 Full And the laste that alter, a Baronnes by Suffraunce alter in her sleves where as by olde custum she shulde haue but iij Rowes and alter 4 Inch ¾, where as a Baronnes by Sufferaunce dothe alter in the sleues a question to be knowen she shall were in her goune vij full. Memo A Baunerette wyfe shall were ij Rowis in hir sleve inch thinch And A knighte wyfe shall were But j rowe in lykewyse, a Baunerettes wyfes bonnet 3 full, a knightes wyfe in her bonnette 3 & ¼.

These rules were followed closely to express the subtleties of rank. On 21 August 1532 the duke of Norfolk wrote to Cromwell and referred to an earlier letter in which he had asked him to provide crimson velvet for three countesses. The king had changed his mind and his 'pleasure now is that no robes of estate shall be now made but only for my wife. I send you the pattern'.[59] Consequently, peers' robes could be recycled and reused, as happened on 10 August 1540 when 'a robe with the kertell and whod of astate for the creation of an earl of right crimson velvet furred with miniver which was the late earl of Essex' was delivered to the earl of Sussex and the lord chamberlain.[60]

The significance attached to the symbolism of these robes can be seen in the following example which shows how every detail was recorded in contemporary accounts. On 12 March 1542 Sir John Dudley was created Viscount Lisle at Whitehall:

After the sacring of the King's mass, he went to the Page's Chamber nigh to the King's Great Chamber and did on his surcote and hoode and was led between the earl of Hertford, in habit of estate, and the lord admiral In his parliament robe and his habit called the mantle having ij barres and a halfe of lectues was borne by lord Delaware'

and then processed to the king's privy chamber.[61]

The ennoblement of peers

These ceremonies were designed to celebrate a peer's changed status, while emphasising that their position was conferred by the monarch, who would always be their superior. Consequently, the ceremonies of ennoblement almost invariably took place in a royal house or parliament. An exception occurred on 2 February 1514 when they were held at Lambeth, the residence of the archbishop of Canterbury, as the palace of Westminster had not been rebuilt following a fire there two years before. Observers noted that:

First, after the King and Queen had offered and other lords and ladies as accustomed, the said Lords went into two chambers that was prepared for them: that is to say, one chamber for the dukes , another chamber for the earls; which were in a gallery at the great chamber end, where they did on their robes of estate. And when the high mass was done, the King came to the said great chamber and there stood under his cloth of estate, not being crowned, accompanied by the great part of the nobles of the realm, and also the Duke of Longueville of France which was prisoner. The Queen and the ladies stood there as they might see all the order of their creations.[62]

Henry favoured group creations, which made the occasions more spectacular, while also reinforcing the idea that the new peers were members of a group. The process of creating a new peer was designed to involve the existing peers so creating a group identity. This was particularly evident in 1525 when the records of the heralds recorded the elevation of the following individuals:

the marquess of Exeter: to convey him to the king, the duke of Suffolk and the earl of Northumberland, to beare his Swerde, Therle of Oxforde [and] to beare his Circulet, Therle of Westmoreland
the earl of Lincoln: to beare hym, Sir Philip Vere, to lede hym, the earl of Arundel and the earl of Oxford [and] to beare his sword, the earl of Northumberland
the earl of Rutland: to lede hym, the earl of Arundell, the earl of Oxford [and] to bear his sword, the earl of Westmoreland
the earl of Cumberland: to lede him, the earl of Oxford and the earl of Northumberland [and] to bear his sword, the earl of Shrwsbury
the viscount Fitzwalter: to lede him, the earl of Shrewsbury and the lord of Burgeveny [and] to beare his mantel, the lorde dacre
the viscount Rocheford: to lede hym, therle of Westmorelande, The Lord Ferrers [and] to beare his mantell The Lorde Hastinges
As these patentz presented to the kynges persone by Sir Thomas Wriothesley gartier principall kyng at Armes.[63]

Most ennoblements were rewards for services done and for services to be done. There were notable exceptions, including the ennoblement of Henry Fitzroy in 1525 and Anne Boleyn in 1532. On 18 June 1525 the king's son, Henry Fitzroy, aged six, was made duke of Richmond at the Bridewell in London. He was the male heir apparent, albeit illegitimate. No concessions were made to his youth:

and when it came to the words 'Gladdii Cuituram' then the young Lord kneeled down and the king's grace put the girdle about the neck of the young Lord the sword hanging bendwise over the breast of him when the patent was read the king took it to the said Earl and this Earl of Nottingham accompanied as before entered the said Gallery.[64]

Henry's elevation of Anne Boleyn on 1 September 1532 was intended to remove the stigma of her being the king's mistress in advance of her introduction several weeks later to Francis I. She was created the lady marquess of Pembroke at Windsor castle.[65] The ceremony followed the same format as that for the creation of male peers, indicating that she held the title in her own right and not through marriage. Anne was accompanied by the dukes of Norfolk and Suffolk and the French ambassador. Garter herald carried her patent of creation, while Mary, the daughter of the duke of Norfolk, carried her mantle of crimson velvet furred with ermine and her coronet. Anne was described as being 'in her hair' (she wore her hair loose) and she was dressed in a surcote of crimson velvet with straight sleeves that was furred with ermine. She gave Garter herald £8 for her apparel and £11 13*s* 4*d* for the office of arms. An indication of the cost of her robes can be gauged from Cromwell's 'bills and obligations' which included a warrant from the king dated 16 September for £82 9*s* 8*d* for silks and other materials provided for the creation of the lady marquess.[66]

The 1540s saw Henry making strategic use of these ceremonies in an attempt to build support amongst the Irish peers. On 24 September 1542, Henry raised Con Bacagh O'Neill to the earldom of Tyrone. Robes of estate were to be made at the king's charge for the creation. A gold chain worth £100 was also to be prepared for O'Neill, along with other apparel as the king thought appropriate.[67] In 1543, John Malt, the king's tailor, made robes for the creation of Murrough O'Brien, as earl of Thomond, Ulrick Burgh, as earl of Clanricarde and Donghe O'Brien, baron of Ibrakan, at the command of the duke of Norfolk.[68] Malt's bill dated 28 June 1543 costing in total £59 3*s* 10*d* included 3 yards (2.7 m) of crimson velvet delivered to a cutler to make girdles and scabbards for the two and precious stones; and also the precious Relique of oon of the leggs of Saint George set in silver gilte' to the altar next to his tomb at Westminster abbey.[110] Earlier in 1416 the Emperor Sigismund had presented Henry V with the heart of St George. It was kept in a monstrance 'of golde closyd in byrall' which was carried in procession by the Garter knights until the Reformation.

Court politics and foreign policy

The interaction between England, France and Spain lay at the centre of European politics. The question was whether England could hope to be an equal player or whether she could seek to tip the balance of power between France and Spain. The factions at court all sought to influence English foreign policy. However, it was the occasions when Henry VIII met Charles V or Francis I that provided the greatest opportunity for emphasising his magnificence through his dress and the furnishings at his court.

MEETINGS WITH THE EMPEROR, 1520 AND 1522

Henry VIII met with Charles V twice in 1520, once on English soil just on the eve of the Field of Cloth of Gold, and again at Gravelins after his encounter with Francis I.[111] Charles arrived at Dover on 26 May 1520 and landed under a 'cloth of his estate of the blacke Egle all splaied on riche clothe of golde'.[112] He met Henry VIII in Dover castle and they travelled to Canterbury. Henry was dressed in 'cloth of silver with a raised pile, and wrought throughout with emblematic letters', a 'stiff brocade in the Hungarian fashion'. Later he 'was dressed in white damask in the Turkish fashion, the above-mentioned robe all embroidered with roses, made of rubies and diamonds' and 'wore royal robes down to the ground, of gold brocade lined with ermine'. The Venetian ambassador noted that 'all the rest of the court glittered with jewels and gold and silver, the pomp being unprecedented'.[113] During the festivities Catherine of Aragon wore a 'petticoat of silver lama, the gown of cloth of gold lined with violet velvet with raised pile, on which the roses of England were wrought in gold'.[114] Charles sailed home shortly after from Sandwich, not Dover, because Dover was where Henry was embarking for his trip to Calais and then on to meet Francis I near Guisnes.

Charles V returned to England again two years later. He landed at Dover on 28 May 1522. On 6 June 1522 Henry and Charles made their joint entry into London dressed in identical outfits of cloth of gold embroidered with silver.[115] They were entertained by a series of pageants in the city.[116] Charles and his retinue stayed in Bridewell palace and the Anglo-Imperial alliance was marked by his betrothal to the Princess Mary. Jousts were prepared by Richard Gibson and the prince of Orange, the count of Vascourt, Monsieur Whavery and Monsieur Egmond were given their costumes which consisted of long gowns of tinsel satin, with double sleeves, with hoods of the same, velvet buskins and satin bonnets.[117] Charles travelled with the king to Hampshire and on 6 July he returned home.

THE FIELD OF CLOTH OF GOLD, 1520

A meeting between Henry and Francis was contemplated as early as 1515. The Venetian ambassador reported a meeting at Calais was being planned and that 'his majesty of England has despatched a messenger post haste to Florence for a great quantity of cloths of gold and silk' so as to meet this most Christian King with honour'.[118] Five years later a meeting came to realisation. On 12 March 1520 Wolsey issued a proclamation outlining the agreed etiquette for the meeting between the two kings at the Field of Cloth of Gold (Fig. 12.7).[119]

The size and composition of the English retinue is recorded in a list drawn up on 26 March.[120] A memorandum drawn up at the same time considered, amongst other things, what was to be worn and by whom: the king's clothes were to be 'ordered according to his own pleasure and desire', the leading officers of the household were to attend 'in their best manner, apparelled according to their status and degree', 200 of the guard were to attend with doublets, hose, caps and two coats, one of goldsmith's work with the king's badges and one of red 'as the riding coats now be', 50 noblemen and women would participate in the masque and 'their apparel is referred to the king's pleasure'.[121] Warrants that were to be completed with the name of the individual and the number of their attendants were drawn up commanding them to attend upon the king. They were to be 'conveniently apparelled and horsed'.[122] A French ordinance concerning dress produced at the same time noted that the 'dames and damoyselles shall be dressed as they please . . . [and the] gentlemen [in] cloth of gold and silver, . . . satin, damask, brocade and velvet'.[123] The French colours were of 'white underneath black and tawny wreathed'.[124] In spite of these attempts at regulation, Hall observed that 'he were miche wise that could haue tolde or shewed of the riches of apparel that was amongst the Lordes and Gentlemenne of Englande Clothe of Golde, Cloth of Siluer, Veluettes, Tinsins, Sattins embroidered and Crymosyn Sattens'.[125]

As part of the preparations for the Field of Cloth of Gold, Henry wrote to Sir Adrian Fortescue asking him to attend upon Catherine of Aragon. Henry stated that he was:

> willing therfor and desiring you, not oonly to put your self in arredinesse with the nombre of ten tall personnages well and conveniently apparailled for this pourpose, to passe with you over the see, but also insuch wise to appointe your self in apparaill as to your degree, the honour of us, and this our reame it apperteigneth.[126]

The king provided livery for some members of the household, including items amounting to £8 13*s* 4*d* for Thomas Carvanell and three others, items costing £9 15*s* for George Pole and five others, items costing £39 18*s* 4*d* for John a Wyncle and four

12.7 *The Field of Cloth of Gold, unknown artist, c. 1545. RCIN 405794 OM 25. The Royal Collection © 2004, Her Majesty the Queen Elizabeth II*

others, 16 yards (14.6 m) of black sarsenet to line two gowns costing 69*s* 4*d* for James and William Knyvet, 48 yards (43.8 m) of black damask for four gowns costing £16 16*s* for Nicholas Dabovall and three others, 13 yards (11.8 m) of crimson satin for a gown £11 12*d* for Elizabeth Brown and 30 yards (27.4 m) of green damask to make half of six coats for 'vj Stilpipers'.[127]

Not surprisingly, Catherine of Aragon was opposed to this meeting with the French and voiced her disapproval. Consequently, the king's councillor's informed him that the queen had 'made such representations, and shown such reasons against the voyage [to France], as one would not have supposed she would have dared to do'. However, the French ambassador noted that 'on this account she is held in greater esteem by the King and his council than ever she was'.[128] She emphasised her stance by wearing Spanish dress. On 12 June 1520 'the headdress of the English Queen was in the Spanish fashion, with a tress of hair over her shoulders and gown, which last was all of cloth of gold; and round her neck were most beautiful jewels and pearls'.[129] On another occasion she wore 'round her neck were five large strings of pearls, with a pendant St George on horseback slaying the dragon, all in diamonds'.[130] Henry did not create any female ladies of the Garter in the way that English kings from Richard II to Henry VII had, so Catherine wearing the Lesser George was very significant. It also allowed her to make an overtly English statement.

The two kings used their dress as a form of competitive magnificence (Pl. VIIb). When the two kings first met in the valley of Ardes, Francis I wore 'a chemew of clothe of siluer culpond with clothe of gold, of damaske cantell wise, and garded on the bordours with Burgon bendes . . . [and] a cloak of broched satten, with gold of purple coloure, wrapped aboute his body trauerse; beded from the shulder to the waste, fastened in the lope of the first fold'.[131] Francis and his supporters for the joust on 20 June were 'apparelled their bard couerd with purple sattin broched with gold and purple velvet, ouer all brodered couerd with galondes of friers' knottes of white satten and in every garland liiij paunse flowers, whiche signified 'thinke on Fraunces''.[132] Henry also employed symbolism to good effect at their meeting. He rode a bay horse in a new style of harness 'of fyne Golde in Bullion, curiously wroughte, pounced and sette with anticke woorke of Romayne Figures'.[133] Similar ideas prevailed at the jousts where the Tree of Chivalry was made from hawthorn and raspberry, symbolising the union of England and France.[134]

Wolsey played his part, dressed 'in a robe of velvet upon crimson velvet figured, the rochet of fine linen all over, and a red hat upon his head, with large hanging tassels; mounted on a barded mule with a headstall, studs, buckles and stirrups of fine gold, and the trappings of crimson velvet'.[135] In March 1521 Wolsey informed Sir William Fitzwilliam that he should tell Francis I that Henry 'not only loves him above all other princes, most esteeming his amity and constant dealing but also cannot be quiet and contented in his mind till he shall eftsoons attain the sight of his person by a new, secret, loving and familiar interview'.[136]

THE MEETING AT CALAIS IN 1532

Henry's second meeting with Francis was timed between sessions of the 1529 parliament because 'he is obliged to return

12.8 *Jean de Dinteville and George de Selve (*The Ambassadors*) by Hans Holbein the Younger, 1533.* © *National Gallery, London (NG 1314)*

Ambassadors (Fig. 12.8).[177] Jean de Dinteville, the French ambassador, was a member of the French royal household and he served as the French ambassador in England repeatedly in the 1530s.[178] He was painted wearing a pink satin doublet, a black velvet jerkin with long skirts, a black satin gown guarded with black velvet and lined with lynx. George de Selve was bishop of Lavaur, and was dressed in a long gown of dark brown damask with a very large pattern repeat. While de Selve had been appointed as bishop of Lavaur in 1526, he was not consecrated until 1534, the year after this picture was painted, and so this was why he was not painted dressed as a bishop.[179]

A year after painting *The Ambassadors*, Holbein painted Charles de Solier, Sire de Morette, who was ambassador from 3 April until 26 July 1534.[180] His cap badge depicts St John the Baptist and is inscribed *Doce me facere volunt atem*. He was dressed all in black — a black gown with elbow-length sleeves, lined and faced with dark brown fur, probably sable and decorated with gold aglets. Under the gown he wore a black jerkin with patterned gold buttons over a black doublet, the sleeves of the doublet visible from wrist to elbow and slashed to reveal white cloth, either of the shirt or puffs of white cloth stitched behind the slits.

Godparenting

Children were often named after Henry VIII, as in the case of the firstborn son of the duke and duchess of Suffolk, his brother-in-law and sister, as a sign of loyalty and deference. The king was sought frequently as a godfather. When Henry Brandon was born on 11 March 1516, he and Cardinal Wolsey stood as his godfathers. On 17 July 1517 Thomas Alen reported the birth of a daughter to the duchess of Suffolk, and noting that 'the Queen and my lady princess will be godmothers, and the Abbot of St Albans, godfather'. In reality, two of the duchess's ladies stood proxy for Catherine of Aragon and Mary. In contrast, in February 1537 Jane Seymour acted as godmother along with the Princess Mary and Thomas Cromwell to her nephew, son of her brother Viscount Beauchamp by his second wife, Anne Stanhope.

The king was reluctant to be godfather to all of his courtiers' children, but he could show favour at the birth of a child in other ways. On 4 February 1530 he gave the nurse and midwife to the countess of Worcester £4 and on 6 March 1532 he sent £3 *6s 8d* to the nurse and midwife of Sir Nicholas Harvey's child.[181] In August 1535 the king rewarded the midwife and nurse with £4 at the christening of his to namesake recently born to the duke of Suffolk and his fourth wife.[182]

Henry became godfather to the second son of Francis I, who was also named Henry. On 19 March 1519 Sir Thomas Boleyn informed Henry that 'if the Queen be delivered of a son, Francis hopes the King will stand godfather; if of a daughter, the Queen to be godmother'.[183] On 20 April 1520 Sir Robert Wingfield reported how 'I saw him out of all his clouts. I assure your highness it is as fair a babe as can be, and as large for his age'.[184] On 1 May 1526, while the boy was being held hostage in Spain, Cheyney and Tayler informed Wolsey that Orleans 'much resembleth his Highness'.[185]

The king continued to stand godfather to members of the French royal family. On 1 May 1546 a correspondent told Prince Philip of Spain that 'the infant daughter of the Dauphiness is not yet christened. If peace is made with England the king of England will be godfather. The Queen [of France] will be one of the godmothers'.[186] A month and a half later, a patent was issued to Sir Thomas Cheyney, treasurer of the household, to act as his proxy at the baptism of Elizabeth, the dauphin's daughter.[187] The privy council approved gifts at the following rates: for the lady mistress £66 13*s* 4*d*, the midwife £40, the nurse £40, and the rockers 120 angel.[188] Another list provides additional detail, noting that he gave 'to Madame de la March, gouvernaunte, a chain and girdle, 233 cr. at 5*s* 6*d* £64 4*s* 4*d* [to] Madame de Penon, gouvernaunte, a like chain and girdle . . . [to] Trois femmes de chambre qui borsent Madame, £30'.[189] On 3 July Cheyne described how the dauphin (Prince Henry) was 'daily apparelled in white and green' in honour of his godfather and, on meeting the king, Francis made him 'keep his cap on'.[190]

Gifts of clothing

Clothing was given as gifts by the king on a number of occasions. While plate was the most common gift given by the monarch at the New Year, clothing or cloth could also be given. A warrant dated 4 January 1499 recorded the following New Year's gifts given by Henry VII: 6 yards (5.4 m) of black satin for a kirtle to Dame Catherine Grey, 3 yards (2.7 m) of tawny damask for a doublet to both John Vendy and John Grace, 3 yards (2.7 m) of black velvet to Piers Barber and 2 yards (1.8 m) to James Braybrooke.[191]

More usual were gifts of clothing given against a marriage. On 26 December 1510 John Hette, yeoman almoner of the chamber, was given broad cloth for a gown 'to be taken of our gift and reward to the marriage of our said servant'.[192] Other examples include a gown of violet cloth containing 4 broad yards (3.6 m), furred with black Irish lamb and tawny camlet for a jacket for Richard Mayre, one of the yeomen of the Ewery, on 12 January 1512. His bride was also given 3 broad yards (2.7 m) of violet cloth for her gown.[193] Two days later John Black, a trumpeter, was given a gown of violet cloth, a bonnet and a hat.[194] William Toke, page of the laundry, also received a gown, jacket, doublet and a bonnet at the time of his marriage.[195]

The king often made an offering at the marriages of members of the nobility. On 2 December 1509 Henry made an offering of 6*s* 8*d* 'at my lord Hasting's marriage'.[196] On 16 February 1511 the king's offering at Lady Anne Percy's marriage was 6*s* 8*d*.[197] In some instances he made more generous provision, in terms of providing entertainment. On 20 October 1519 Henry provided jousts at Greenwich to celebrate the marriage of the earl of Devon which cost £200 4*s* 9*d*.[198] However, these entertainments did not always go as planned. When Lord William Howard married Mrs Gamage in the chapel at Whitehall on 29 June 1533, the king mounted a small battle on the river Thames, where one man drowned and two others broke a leg jousting.[199]

Gifts of dress were also distributed as part of royal charitable provision because clothing the naked was one of the Seven Acts of Mercy. For example, the allowances made by Henry for Ralph Lyons 'that was gevyn owr Latte souerayne Lorde Kynge' and who was 'put to teache to Robartte Phyllyppes of the king's chapel.[200] The provision for Lyons lasted from Christmas 1545 until Lady day 1547. In that time he received three sets of clothing, each consisting of a lined coat, two shirts, two pairs of hose, three pairs of shoes, one doublet, two dozen points, a girdle, a cap and a purse. He got board wages. Gifts of dress could also be given as a reward for service. On 1 October 1514 Sir Walter Devereux received £25 for a 'gown of tynsel for Mistress Anne Devereux, sent over with the French Queen'.[201]

Dress as an expression of treason

On 10 May 1540 the earl of Essex presented the case for the attainder of the countess of Salisbury and the marchioness of Exeter, in the house of lords. The evidence against the countess of Salisbury included her possession of an item of clothing that was embroidered with imagery deemed to be treasonable. The details were specified in the letter John Worth sent to Lord Lisle:

> there was a cote armor fownde yn the duchys of Salysbyrrys coffer, and by the on syde off the cote there was the Kynges Grace ys armes of Ynglonde, that ys the lyons withowt the flowar delysses, and abowte the holl armys was made paneys for Powll [Cardinal Pole], and marygoldes for my lady Mary. Thys was abowte the cote armer. And betwyxt the marygolde and the pancye was made a tree to rys yn the myddes, and on the tree a cote off purpell hangyng on a bowgh, yn tokynyng off the cote of Cryste, and on the other syde of the cote all the Passchyon of Cryste. Powll yntendyd to havee marryd my lady Mary and betwyxt them boythe shuld agen rys the olde Doctryne off Cryste.[202]

While there were many underlying factors behind the conviction of these women, this piece of coat armour was deemed to imply aspirations to the throne.

For others, such as the duke of Buckingham, it was his use of expensive clothes as a means of drawing support away from the king that was emphasised when he was tried for treason in May 1521. One of the accusations brought against him was that on 20 October 1515 he had sent his chancellor from Thornbury to London and on a number of other occasions to buy cloth of gold, silver and silk to the value of 300 marks.

The lengths of cloth were bought with the intention of giving 'them to the knights and gentlemen of the King's guard to procure adherents'.[203] More specifically he was charged with having given a doublet of cloth of silver to Sir Edward Neville, and boasting that he had his support to Lord Bergavenny.

Buckingham was also guilty of dressing in a style that outshone the monarch. When Henry met Maximilian in 1513, the duke attracted comment when he wore 'purple Satten, his apparel . . . full of Antelops and Swannes of fine gold Bullion and full of Spangles, and little Belles of golde, marueylous costly and pleasant to behold'.[204] The rest of the nobility were described as a group: 'the noble men of the kynges campe were gorgeously apparelled, ther coursers barded of cloth of gold, of damask & broderie, there apparel all tissue clothe of gold and syluer and golde smithes worke, great cheynes of balderickes of gold and belles of bullion.'[205] As long as the duke only rivalled the king on such occasions, the risk was acceptable.

Henry Howard, earl of Surrey, however, sought to use his wardrobe in the 1540s to rival that of the king on a daily basis. During his trial, Alice Flaner recalled an episode in March 1543 when 'my lord of Surrey was deceived in buying cloth, her mistress expressed marvel "that they will deceive a prince"'.[206] His sumptuous clothes and interest in continental fashions were charges brought against him. However, in addition to assuming the king's style of dress, he was also foolish enough to aspire to the king's style of address. This was reflected in his full-length portrait (Pl. VIIIA).

Noble prisoners and executions

Throughout his reign, Henry maintained a number of prisoners in the Tower of London. While some were only held captive there for a matter of days, others were detained for years. Amongst the prisoners in June 1537 were Lady Anne Hungerford held for ten months at 10*s* a month and her sister for the same at 5*s* the month, and George Hayes, a Scot, secretary to the duke of Albany, two years at 6*s* 8*d* the month.[207] The total came to £757 10*s*. A further list was drawn up on 31 March 1538.[208] In addition, ongoing payments were made, as in the case of £25 5*s* 4*d* supplied in July 1539 for the diets of the marchioness of Exeter and her women and 'for her apparel, fuel and other necessaries'.[209] Other supplies delivered to the Tower of London included 150 'elming boards that made bedsteads for iij gentlemen that were prisoners' costing 3*s* 6*d* and three pieces of timber that made a frame in the gentlemen's chamber to hang arras upon costing 21*d*.[210]

Henry also maintained a number of influential prisoners of war, most notably the duke of Longueville and the seigneur de Bayard, who were captured at the battle of the Spurs. The duke was sent to England to lodge in Catherine of Aragon's household, but as she was fighting in the north he was placed in the Tower with six others at a cost of £13 6*s* 8*d*. While hostage, he played a key role at the proxy marriage of Princess Mary to Louis XII in 1513 and Henry provided him with a gown of cloth of gold.[211] In a similar way, at Christmas 1542 Scottish prisoners released from prison were 'called to Court at Christmas and had great cheer, being permitted to carry swords and daggers and do as they liked'.[212] Not all military prisoners were in the king's hands. On 20 August 1544 the archbishop of York wrote to Shrewsbury Herald concerning three Scottish prisoners, all relatives of the earl of Cassilis, whom he had held for a year and a half without receiving any money. He had been 'constrained to give then both robes and gowns and other things'. While he was happy to keep them and their horses, he expected the earl to 'provide them with apparel, or else, with winter coming on, they will lack many things'.[213]

Both Henry VII and Henry VIII kept several members of the de la Pole family in the Tower. These were relatives whose descent from Edward III was superior to the Tudors. Clothing was delivered to Sir Richard Cholmeley, lieutenant of the Tower, for Edmund de la Pole (executed in 1513) and his brother William on a warrant dated 23 July 1509.[214] An earlier warrant for Edmund dates from 28 May 1506.[215] He was provided with a gown of tawny cloth furred with black budge, a gown of russet cloth, two black satin doublets, hose, shirts, a bonnet, a hat, slippers, points and sheets. Another order for him made on 28 October 1510 was for two gowns of russet furred with six fox furs, two gowns of tawny medley furred with black budge, two doublets of black satin and another two of black velvet, six pairs of hose, six shirts, two black bonnets costing £35 10*s* 7*d*.[216] Eleven warrants are extant for William dating between November 1516 and October 1538 which are similar to those for Edmund, except half the amount of each garment type ordered until 1527 when he received two extra doublets, after that point just one extra doublet of black damask.[217] Another brother, Richard, lived in exile in France where, to the Tudor's chagrin, Louis XII recognised him as the king of England and Francis I considered placing him at the head of an army to invade England.

While the countess of Salisbury was a prisoner in the Tower in 1540, the privy council asked John Scut, the queen's tailor, to make clothes for her: a nightgown furred with a kirtle of worsted and a furred petticoat, another gown in the fashion of a nightgown of say lined and faced with satin, a bonnet, a frontlet, four pairs of hose, four pairs of shoes and a pair of slippers.[218] These items were paid for out of the king's book of payments and they cost £11 16*s* 4*d*.[219] Sir Edmund Walsingham, lieutenant of the Tower, also paid £6 4*s* 6*d* for the board wages of a woman to attend her for 83 weeks at 18*d* the week and 60*s* for her charges for half a year.[220] When on 28 May 1541 she was executed, the imperial ambassador noted 'as the ordinary executioner of justice was absent, doing his work in the north, a wretched and blundering youth was chosen, who literally hacked her head and shoulders to pieces in the most pitiful manner'.[221]

On 19 May 1540 Arthur Plantagenet, Lord Lisle, was arrested for treason. The French ambassador told Francis I that 'Lord Lisle is in a very narrow place, from which no one escapes unless by miracle'.[222] On 1 March 1541 the privy council instructed John Malt, the king's tailor, to provide Lisle with a large gown of damask furred with black coney, a

12.10 *Henry Brandon, second ~~earl of Surrey,~~ duke of Suffolk by Hans Holbein the Younger. RL 422294 GR7. The Royal Collection © 2004, Her Majesty the Queen Elizabeth II*

12.11 *Charles Brandon, third duke of Suffolk, by Hans Holbein the Younger. RCIN 422295 GR8. The Royal Collection © 2004, Her Majesty the Queen Elizabeth II*

were aged five and four respectively. Neither had been breeched, so Henry wears a black, short-sleeved short coat, over a doublet of shot green silk, while Charles has a grey gown with applied red guards over a black doublet.[239] They were the sons of the duke of Suffolk (d. 1545). The two were made knights of the Bath at Edward's coronation, and Henry, the next duke, carried the orb during the service. However, they died within half an hour of each other in 1551 of the sweating sickness.

Revels, disguisings, mummeries and jousts

Revels, like disguisings and mummeries, combined a sumptuous visual display with a variety of entertainments including a banquet.[240] More specifically, disguisings often involved music, ornate costumes, a narrator to explain the events and dancing by the ladies and gentlemen of the court. In the early sixteenth century this was a hybrid type of entertainment that would develop in England into the court masque.[241] Indeed, by the middle of the century, the terms mummery and disguising were replaced by masque in the accounts.[242] While revels were often held indoors and in the evening, jousts and tournaments were outdoor occasions. The types of combat could vary, but generally included pairs of knights armed with lances riding towards each other separated by a barrier.[243]

The organisation and design of revels and jousts could provide the opportunity for individuals at court to develop and plan the proceedings, as indicated by the preamble to Richard Gibson's account for the jousts held on 29 December 1524. Gibson recorded that 'Our soverayn lord kyng . . . grauntyd hys gracyus favor to the nobyll lord Leonard Gray . . . that the sam lord Lenard and hys bend scholld edyfy a kastell In the lysts or tyllt yerd at Greenwyche In the Kynges ground at the Kyngs charge'.[244] An invitation to participate in the jousts and revels held at court was a sign of royal favour.

Henry regularly furnished new costumes for the revels and jousts held at court. The wearers often received part or all of their costumes in reward. On 5 June 1522, Richard Gibson's revels accounts record that Mrs Danet, Mrs Darrell and Mrs Carew, who danced with the duchess of Suffolk, all retained their bonnets of black velvet, gold coifs of tristram knots and their 'syers'.[245] However, this was not always the case. On 6 May 1534 John Husee wrote to Viscount Lisle, who had received armour from the king, noting that 'Loffkyne says you are his debtor for a doublet of satin, or 20s in money'.[246]

The costumes were made by skilled tailors, so while their design might have been a little frivolous, the basis construction methods were sound. These costumes had to function as proper clothes, as the wearers had to move unencumbered and to dance and joust. They had to look striking when viewed from a distance. The clothes for jousts were worn outdoors in daylight, while the revels costumes were largely worn indoors and were seen by candlelight.

Henry was not alone in entertaining splendidly. In 1518 Cardinal Wolsey organised the:

> most sumptuous supper the like of which, I fancy, was never given by Cleopatra or Caligula . . . After supper . . . twelve male and twelve female dancers made their appearance in the richest and most sumptuous array possible, being all dressed alike . . . They were disguised in one

long nightgown of cloth at 10*s* the yard furred with black lamb and faced with budge, two jackets, one of satin and one of damask, two doublets of satin, four pairs of hose, six pairs of shoes, one pair of slippers, four shirts, two nightcaps of velvet and satin, two upper caps of cloth and two nightkerchiefs, with the bill to be paid by the council.[223] On 1 March 1542 the miraculous happened and Lisle learnt that he was to be freed but he died two days later, probably of a heart attack, without gaining his liberty. Six days later the privy council sent a letter to the deputy and council of Calais to free Lady Lisle and her daughters, and to see to 'the restoring to the same off theyre apparail and jewels'.[224]

On 14 December 1546 Chapuys's successor as imperial ambassador wrote to Mary of Hungary about the arrest of the duke of Norfolk and his son the earl of Surrey. He noted that they had both been taken to the Tower on 12 December, even though the earl had previously been under arrest at the house of Chancellor Wriothesley. He believed that 'their chance of liberation is small, as the Garter and staff were taken from the father, and the son was led publicly through the streets'.[225] An account of the costs of the earl of Surrey being in the Tower from 8 December to 19 January made by Sir William Stonore included £24 for the earl's attendants, coal and the delivery of a 'right sattyn' coat for him to attend his arraignment in.[226]

Nevertheless, the king did not clothe all of his prisoners. Among the less fortunate was Silken Thomas, who had led a failed rebellion in Ireland and whose followers wore a silk ribbon. In 1536 he described his conditions in a letter to a servant:

> Since I came into prison . . . I have had neither hose, doublet nor shoes nor shirt . . . nor any other garment but a single frieze gown instead of velvet furred with bowge . . . This I write to you . . . that you should be the more diligent in going unto O'Brien and in bringing me the before said £20, whereby I might the sooner have here money to buy me clothes, and also for to amend my slender commons and fare, and for other necessaries.[227]

Male youth culture at court

Still 17 at his accession in 1509, Henry VIII betrayed a marked preference at court at the start of his reign for people of his own age. In October 1510 he held a banquet for 24 young men who, for an entertainment, fought before him with axes. He provided 200 marks for the feast held at the Fishmongers' hall and the young men were all dressed in the Almain fashion: 'their vitter garmentes all of yealow Satyne, yealow hosen, yealow shoes, gyrdels, scaberdes and bonettes with yealow fethers, their garmentes and hosen all cutte and lyned with whyte Satyn.'[228]

As the king grew older he grew bored with his initial companions, and by 1515 he was turning to a younger group nicknamed the minions. Edward Hall recorded how Henry took pleasure 'to set forth young gentlemen'.[229] But not everyone shared his enthusiasm. It was noted that 'certain young men in his private chamber not regarding his estate or degree, were so familiar and homely with hym, and plaied suche light touches with hym that they forgat themselves'.[230] The king showered clothes on these young men.[231] Francis Weston was still a recipient of these favours when in July 1532 the king's warrant included a coat for him of black damask bordered with black velvet and furred with 120 black budge skins and a doublet of black velvet lined with fustian and canvas.[232]

Sir Nicholas Carew was the principal beneficiary from among the minions. He was described as 'well mannered and having the French tongue' and being of the king's 'own upbringing'.[233] Carew figured prominently in the royal jousts (Fig. 12.9). His portrait of around 1528, based on a drawing by Holbein, depicted him in armour.[234] On 19 May 1511 and 19 March 1512 he received his livery as a groom of the privy chamber, along with William Gower, Christopher Rochester and John Dingley.[235] Carew also received a regular annual warrant for clothing for himself personally, which was set up as a warrant dormant from the outset. The earliest extant warrant of this type dates from 9 December 1516. He received the fabric but not the making-up costs for a black velvet gown lined with black sarsenet, a black velvet coat, a russet velvet gown furred with budge and a russet velvet riding coat which cost £44 3*s* 8*d*.[236] The last surviving warrant dates from December 1538 but that was delivered at Michaelmas and it is unusual in that Carew only received 15 yards (13.7 m) of russet velvet for a gown, 120 black budge skins and 12 yards (10.9 m) of russet velvet for a coat costing £26 5*s*.[237] In spite of his close friendship with the king, he was indicted for treason as a member of the Exeter conspiracy and executed early in 1540.

A number of boys, usually from a noble background, were attached to the household of Prince Edward as he grew up. These included the prince's kinsmen, Henry and Charles Brandon (Figs 12.10 and 12.11).[238] Their portraits were painted by Holbein, probably on 10 March 1541, when they

12.9 *Sir Nicholas Carew, by Hans Holbein*, c. *1528. SNPG O NO 18. By kind permission of the duke of Buccleuch & Queensbury, KT*

suit of fine green satin, all over covered with cloth of gold, undertied together with laces of gold, and had masking hoods on their heads; the ladies had tires made of braids of damask gold with long hairs of white gold. All these maskers danced at one time, and after they had danced they put off their visors, and they were all known ... The two leaders were the King and the Queen Dowager of France, and all the others were lords and ladies.[247]

On 24 April 1540 the French ambassador told Francis I that 'the lords and gentlemen of this Court who are not summoned to Parliament are preparing for the jousts and tourneys to be held all next month'.[248] These began on 1 May.[249] Not everyone relished the prospects of participating. On 5 March 1517 the duke of Buckingham explained to Wolsey that he had been invited to a tournament on May day but he was unhappy about jousting. He begged Wolsey to put him on the king's team, 'but if that cannot be, that he may be excused from running against the king's person. He would rather go to Rome than do so'.[250]

At a banquet held at Greenwich on 7 July 1517 to mark the signing of the League of Cambrai, Henry VIII sat on the top table with Cardinal Wolsey, Catherine of Aragon, the duchess of Suffolk and the imperial ambassador.[251] The diners were seated with men and women alternating. The Venetian ambassador also noted that the jousts held that day had 'new and costly decorations'. The King jousted with Suffolk 'like Hector and Achilles'.[252] Nicholas Sagudino described in greater detail the clothes worn at the jousts. The marshal had a surcote of cloth of gold, 30 footmen were dressed in blue and yellow livery, the drummers and trumpeters wore white damask, while 40 knights were in cloth of gold, the king was 'in silver bawdkin' and 30 gentlemen in velvet and white satin.[253] On 7 March 1519 the king held a revel which the revel's account called a masque 'after the manner of Italy'. The revel was followed by a joust and the king provided clothing for 46 individuals costing £60 7*s* 3*d*.[254]

Jousts were held by the king to celebrate the marriage of the earl of Devon which took place on 20 October 1519. Richard Gibson prepared two bases and trappers of russet velvet and cloth of silver engrailed, lozenged and cross-lozenged with cloth of gold, every lozenge embroidered with trueloves of cloth of gold with saddle covers and harness of the same and of a harness, trapper and base of russet velvet and cloth of silver on one side and purple velvet on the other which were worn by the king, Sir William Kingston and William Carey.[255]

Giving the costumes away as gifts was a frequent sequel to court occasions. After the revel on 23 August 1519 Gibson noted that 'all the apparel was given to the wearers. Nothing remaining'.[256] However, a full set of new costumes was not made for every revel, as in the case of when on 5 January 1520 Henry decided to visit Wolsey with 19 gentlemen dressed in masquing apparel 'from the King's store', along with a small group of new items.[257] The accounts for the revels held on 14 January 1526 recorded the provision of black velvet gowns for eight ladies and eight bonnets of purple velvet, as well as gowns for the men. A number of the items came from the king's store.[258] Costumes could be recycled and remade, as was the case for a revel held on 3 January 1521 at York Place by Wolsey. Eight garments of cloth of gold and crimson velvet were made from seven cloaks and eight doublets that had been made for a masque as part of the Field of Cloth of Gold in 1520, and from seven half coats from the masque performed at the subsequent meeting with the emperor.[259] The costumes and accessories could be damaged, as in the case of the jousts held in June 1520 at Guisnes when eight bards and bases were 'sore worn in the hurtling of horses'.[260]

The entertainments at court sometimes bore a political message. At a triumph held on the Thames in front of Whitehall on 17 June 1539, 'two barges were prepared with ordnance of war . . . one for the bishop of Rome and his cardinals, and the other for the king's grace . . . at last the pope and his cardinals were overcome, and all his men cast overboard into the Thames'.[261] This sort of event was not restricted to England. On 26 January 1540 Sir William Eure described to Cromwell an interlude performed before the king and queen of Scots on Epiphany, 'all turning upon the naughtiness in religion, the presumption of bishops, the collusion of spiritual courts called in Scotland the consistory courts and misusing of priests'.[262]

Celebrating Advent and Christmas

Advent marked a period of fasting before the feasting and celebrations associated with the Nativity.[263] During the season of Advent the king was free to dress as he pleased. However, Advent did include the celebrations associated with the election of the boy bishop on 6 December, St Nicholas's day. The chosen boy played the role of the boy bishop from 6 December until Holy Innocents (28 December).[264] In December 1500 William Newark, master of the children of the chapel, was paid 53*s* 4*d* 'for Saint Nicholas'.[265] On 3 December 1502 Elizabeth of York presented 40*s* 'to the Bisshop of the Kinges Chappelle on Saint Nicholas even at Westminster'.[266] On 6 December 1511 a reward of £6 13*s* 4*d* was given to St Nicholas's bishop.[267] As late as 1540 the children of the chapel received £6 13*s* 4*d* 'on St Nicholas Day as hath been heretofore accustomed'.[268] This inversion of the usual adult child order echoed the role taken by the lord of misrule at the Tudor court where a junior member of the court entertained their superiors.

The 12 days of Christmas ran from Christmas eve to Twelfth day or Epiphany, including the feasts of St Stephen (26 December), St John the Evangelist (27 December), Holy Innocents or Childermass (28 December) and St Thomas of Canterbury (29 December). At court, the lord of misrule, or 'master of merry disports', oversaw the Christmas entertainment. His official duties ran throughout the 12 days of Christmas, although elsewhere, in some noble households, his duties might cover a much longer period from All Hallows (1 November) to the day after Candlemas (3 February).[269] His duties were to organise 'fine and subtle disguisings, masks and mummeries'.[270] The best description of the range of events organised at this time of year appears in the letter of George Ferrers to Thomas Cawarden for the Christmas period 1553.[271] Ferrers ended his letter by focusing upon his own

13.1 *Henry VIII dining, surrounded by courtiers and members of his household. Unknown artist, late sixteenth century. 1854-6-28-74. Reproduced by courtesy of the Trustees of the British Museum*

13.2 *The king, surrounded by his footmen and pages, as he processes before Catherine of Aragon. Le heulme du Roy/Le Roy desarmey. The Westminster Tournament Roll, College of Arms*

The financial benefits of royal service included the receipt of wages or fees (not infrequently in arrears), livery, bouche of court and potential access to perquisites and legacies. A list of expenses for the royal household for the year ending in April 1527 included liveries for the guard and household servants costing £321 3s.[9] Thomas Cromwell's remembrances for March 1540 had an entry for 'Appointment to be made for £6,000 for the Household, and money for weekly, monthly and quarterly wages, for which I have taken appointment with Mr Tuke'.[10]

Whether as a royal or noble institution, the household was essentially male in composition, and mainly single men at that

13.3 *Miniature of Francis I with his three sons and members of his household including Cardinal Duprat on the king's left, by an unknown artist. Museum of the Condé region, Chantilly, France*

(Fig. 13.3). Those who were married left their wives at home. A sizeable household provided opportunities for several members of the same family to work together, but this feature was not as evident in the Tudor royal household as it had been under the late Plantagenets.[11] The household also had a charitable role, expressed by the provision of support for elderly members once they were no longer able to work. On 11 February 1542 William Webster, 'pencioner of the stable', received £3 for three-quarters of his annuity.[12]

The roles for women were limited to the ladies attendant on the mistress of the household, women working in the nursery or laundresses. Indeed, the royal laundresses were the only permanent female members of the king's household. At Henry VIII's funeral they received black livery. Queen consorts had their own households and they were expected to maintain these from their own funds. The opportunities for women were equally limited. The households of queens regnant, such as that of Elizabeth I, were different in this respect, causing an interruption in the normal patterns of patronage.[13]

Royal and noble households were large, making them expensive to maintain and consequently a highly visible expression of conspicuous consumption. As such, the household was a very good way of displaying wealth, both real and assumed. Sir William Fitzwilliam wrote to Wolsey on 31 July 1527:

> The King is keeping a very great and expensive house, for there are lodged here the duke of Norfolk and his wife, the duke of Suffolk, the marquis of Exeter, the earls of Oxford, Essex and Rutland, viscounts Fitzwalter and Rocheford, both the ladies of Oxford and others. He and the other officers intended to have reduced the expenses this summer, but he does not see how it can be done.[14]

Henry's household consisted of approximately 1,500 individuals and it had two forms: the full household which was present with the king from autumn to spring, and the smaller or riding household which travelled with the king when he went on progress or 'the geists'.[15] During this period the household was reduced by about half. Equally, the size and presence of the chapel royal was a very good indicator of whether the household was in its full or reduced form.[16] Another factor that could influence the size of the household was an outbreak of disease. In November 1517 the Venetian ambassador noted that 'The King is abroad and moves from place to place on account of the plague, which makes great ravages in the royal Household. None remain with him except three favourite gentlemen and Memo'.[17]

Many individuals held more than one office within the household, together with one or more posts in the government or the administration of royal lands. In August 1517, a good example of this involved Sir Nicholas Vaux. Cardinal Wolsey, on hearing a report of Vaux's sickness, raised with the king the possibility of Sir Henry Guildford asking for Vaux's captaincy at Guisnes and their response to Guildford's suit. Wolsey reminded Henry that the captaincy was incompatible with several of Guildford's current posts, which could be given to others. He proposed the following redistribution: 'the Mastership of the Horse to Sir William Sandys or Sir Maures Barkley, the Mastership of the Henchmen to one well mannered and having the French tongue, as Mr Carew, of your own bringing up, the Standard Bearer to some goodly tall personage as Sir William Kingston.'[18]

Like all the king's ministers, Wolsey used his position to exercise patronage on behalf of his master. On 4 August 1526 he informed the king that the new earl of Oxford was 'humble, constant and faithful and [he] will furnish that room as well as any of his predecessors have done'.[19] Indeed, many individuals sought to gain offices for themselves or others. On 18 July 1527 the duke of Norfolk wrote to Wolsey after the death of George Lawson who had 'many offices and fees of the king's gift'. The duke asked him to remember Richard Cavendish who was in the ducal service 'but has neither office nor fee'.[20]

The provision of clothing to members of the household formed an important part of the remuneration of many appointees. This clothing ensured that the members of the household had a specific appearance which could be either uniform or with a range of variants to highlight the household's hierarchy. The livery also acted as an expression of the wealth of the head of the household in terms of the colours and types of fabrics worn by their retainers. Livery added to the royal household's conspicuous consumption and it was especially evident when the king was travelling, entering London or processing to parliament.

13.5 *Detail of an embroidered Tudor rose from Henry VII's hearse cloth,* c. *1504–05. Fitzwilliam Museum, Cambridge, © The Textile Conservation Centre, University of Southampton*

13.6 *Sir Thomas More, by Hans Holbein the Younger. © The Frick Collection, New York*

13.7 *Sir Henry Guildford, by Hans Holbein the Younger, 1527. RL 12266 P10. The Royal Collection © 2004, Her Majesty the Queen Elizabeth II*

LIVERY COLLARS AND OTHER SYMBOLS OF OFFICE

Some members of the household were issued with livery collars as a symbol of their office.[73] Edward IV and Richard III had developed the SS livery collar. Examples of these can be seen in the Donne triptych of *c.* 1477 by Hans Memlinc.[74] Sir John Donne and his wife wear gold collars of alternating links of suns and roses with a pendant white enamelled lion, the badge of Edward IV.[75] The Tudors substituted Tudor roses and portcullises for the Yorkist badges. In March 1541 Morgan Wolf was paid £73 17*s* 8½*d* for 'a collar of gold with esses'.[76] A collar of this type can be seen in Holbein's portrait of Sir Thomas More (Fig. 13.6). A few surviving examples of these collars are known. A silver collar of SS was found on the Thames foreshore with a trefoil loop with a pendant ring as the central link.[77] A collar made up of 28 gold SS's alternating with Tudor roses and friar's knots with a central link of a portcullis belonged to Sir John Alen, one of the king's councillors in the 1530s.[78] Sometimes livery collars were given as gifts to foreign visitors to the court. On 2 June 1510 13*s* 4*d* was given in compensation to Vincent Marshall of the king's hall for his livery collar which was 'given to Lusborne that came from Flanders'.[79]

Leading officials in the household had staffs as the symbols of their positions: the chamberlains, the comptroller, the great master and the treasurer. Sir Henry Guildford holds his white staff as comptroller in his portrait of 1528 by Holbein (Fig. 13.7), while Lord St John holds his as great master in the allegory *Edward VI and the Pope* (Fig. 7.2).[80] The staff held by the duke of Norfolk in his portrait by Holbein relates to his tenure of the office of lord treasurer of England (Fig. 16.8). The admiral had a whistle, not a staff. When the earl of Southampton, great admiral of England, went to meet Anne of Cleves, he was dressed 'in a coate of purple veluet cut on cloth of golde & tyed with great aglettes and treilfoiles of golde, to the number of iiijC & baudrickwise he ware a chayne, at the whyche did hang a whistle of gold set with ryche stones of great value'.[81]

Notes

1 Myers, *Black Book*, p. 89.
2 Mertes, *English Noble Household*, p. 5.
3 J. Huizinga, *The Waning of the Middle Ages* (Harmondsworth, 1979), p. 39.
4 Loades, *Tudor Court*, p. 1.
5 See below, pp. 301–16.
6 Woolgar, *Great Household*, ch. 2.
7 Mertes, *Noble Household*, pp. 26–31.
8 *LP* x, 908.
9 *LP* iv.ii, 3084.
10 *LP* xv, 322.
11 For examples within noble households, see Woolgar, *Great Household*, p. 36.
12 TNA E315/251, f. 68r.
13 See P. Wright, 'A change in direction: the ramifications of a female household, 1558–1603', in D. R. Starkey, ed., *The English Court from the Wars of the Roses to the Civil War* (London and New York, 1987), pp. 147–72; also see C. Howey, 'Busy Bodies: the Role of Women at the Court of Elizabeth I, 1558–1603' (unpublished PhD thesis Rutgers, State University of New Jersey, 2007).
14 *LP* iv.ii, 3318.
15 Thurley, *Royal Palaces*, p. 70.
16 F. Kisby, 'Kingship and the royal itinerary: a study of the peripatetic household of the early Tudor kings 1485–1547', *The Court Historian*, 4.1 (1999), pp. 32–33.
17 *LP* ii.ii, 3788.
18 TNA SP1/232, f. 43 (*LP* Additional i, 196).
19 *LP* iv.ii, 2372,
20 *LP* iv.ii, 3276.
21 *LP* iii.i, 491.
22 *LP* iv.ii, 3084.
23 *LP* xvi, 394.
24 *LP* ii.ii, 3100.
25 *HO*, pp. 150–51 and 148.
26 *HO*, p. 150.
27 *LP* xvi, 61.
28 Hall, *Chronicle*, p. 673.
29 D. R. Starkey, 'Intimacy and innovation: the rise of the privy chamber', in Starkey, *European Court*, pp. 75–76.
30 R. L. Storey, *The Reign of Henry VII* (1968), p. 153.
31 D. Luckett, 'Crown office and licensed retinues in the reign of Henry VII', in R. E. Archer and S. Walker, eds, *Rulers and Ruled in Late Medieval England* (1995), pp. 230–31.
32 BL Harley MS 442, f. 29 (*LP* i, 5493).
33 C. Rawcliffe, *The Staffords, Earls and Dukes of Buckingham 1394–1521* (Cambridge, 1978), p. 99; Harris, *Stafford*, p. 167; Hall, *Chronicle*, pp. 599–600.
34 *LP* xvii, 714.21.
35 Myers, *Black Book*, pp. 127–28.
36 *LP* vii, 256.
37 *LP* ix, 1135.
38 R. Horrox and P. W. Hammond, eds, *British Library Harleian Manuscript 433*, 1 (1979), p. 236.
39 *LP* xx.ii, 706.
40 A. Dyce, ed., *The Poetical Works of John Skelton*, 1 (1843), p. 13.
41 Kipling, *Receyt*, p. 10.
42 TNA E36/1, f. 27v (*LP* i.i, 3608). Similar provision was made by Robert Brigandine for the *Peter Pomegranate* which was moved at the same time. However, the coats cost 6*s* 8*d*; ibid., f. 28r.
43 TNA E101/417/6, f. 29 (*LP* i.i, 1184).
44 Ibid., f. 20 (*LP* i.i, 1195).
45 *LP* iii.l, 870, p. 309.
46 The other designs are for black, decorated with gold and crimson, embellished with gold, BL MS Cotton Augustus III, 11, 18 and 19; illustrated in Starkey, *European Court*, p. 53.
47 *LP* i.i, 728.
48 CoA MS M16bis, f. 15v.
49 See below, pp. 295–96.
50 Sutton and Hammond, *Coronation*, p. 53.
51 Ibid., p. 57.
52 TNA LC 9/50, f. 140r.
53 Ibid., f. 219v.
54 Ibid., f. 12v; Sutton and Hammond, *Coronation*, p. 92.
55 TNA LC 9/50, f. 219v.
56 Ibid., f. 219v.
57 TNA LC2/3.i, ff. 73–129. I am most grateful to Lisa Monnas for providing me with her summary of this data.
58 TNA LC2/3.i, f. 130.
59 BL MS Harley 69, f. 57v; Nichols, *Chronicle of Calais*, p. 116 (*LP* v, 1232).
60 *LP* v, 1323. On the reverse were the names of those to receive livery at a cost of 15*s*: yeomen — Giles Churchill, Edward Floyd, Robert Little, John Pate, Roland Rigley, William Rigley; grooms — John Anthill, Walter Badham, John Crunde, John Curson, Richard Daye, John Geslyn, John Parker, John Throgmorton; pages — William Oxonbridge, William Reskimmer, John Rigley, Jerome West.
61 Hall, *Chronicle*, p. 793.
62 *PPE*, p. 120.
63 Ibid., p. 125.
64 TNA LC 2/3.i, p. 66.
65 The second portrait of an unidentified man is in the collection of the Kunsthistorisches Museum, Vienna, along with a companion portrait of an unidentified woman; see Foister, *Holbein*, p. 16; and Rowlands, *Holbein*, p. 141.
66 *LP* ix, 413.
67 In France, the royal salamander device of Francis I was carved onto the fireplaces at the château of Blois and represented the monarch even when the king was not present.
68 Musée des Beaux-Arts, Troyes and the BM, London.
69 BM; J. Cherry, 'The Dunstable swan', *The Journal of the British Archaeological Association*, 32 (1969), pp. 38–53.
70 *PPE*, p. 16.
71 Ibid., p. 187.
72 D. Gaimster and J. A. Goodall, 'A Tudor parcel-gilt livery badge from Chelsham, Surrey', *Antiquaries Journal*, 79 (1999), pp. 392–99.
73 J. G. Nichols, 'On collars of the royal livery', *The Gentleman's Magazine*, 17 (1842), pp. 157–61, 250–58, 378–79; Scarisbrick, *Jewellery*, pp. 21–27.
74 Hinton, *Gold and Gilt*, p. 247.
75 NPG; Scott, *Visual History*, pl. 115.
76 TNA E315/249, f. 52v.
77 B. Spencer, 'Fifteenth century collar of SS and hoard of false dice with their container, from the Museum of London', *Antiquaries Journal*, 65 (1985), pp. 449–51.
78 In the collection of the Lord Mayor and Corporation of London; illustrated in Somers-Cocks, *Princely Magnificence*, p. 52; Scarisbrick, *Tudor*, pp. 36–37.
79 TNA E36/215, p. 62.
80 M. Aston, *The King's Bedpost: Reformation and Iconography in a Tudor Group Portrait* (Cambridge, 1993), p. 18.
81 Hall, *Chronicle*, p. 832.

Table 14.1: *Number of grants of livery for individuals, groups, departments and events*

Recipients	1 warrant	2 warrants	3 warrants	4 warrants	5 warrants	More than 5
Warrants						
Individuals	53	8	5	~	~	1: 10 warrants 1: 47 warrants
Groups/ events/departments	21	4	2	~	2	1: 6 warrants 4: 7 warrants 1: 9 warrants 1: 12 warrants
Accounts						
Individuals	61	11	4	1	1	1: 11 warrants 1: 13 warrants 1: 51 warrants
Groups/ events/departments	15	7	~	3	2	1: 8 warrants 1: 11 warrants 1: 20 warrants

This level of provision was not cheap but, according to Pedro de Ayala, Henry VII was a wealthy man. This was partly because 'If gold coin once enters his strong boxes, it never comes out again'. De Ayala elaborated on this, saying that, 'His ordinary expenses for his house, table, kitchen, pension, council, chapel, servants, liveries, hunting etc., for his own person, the Queen, the Prince of Wales, and all his children together, is about one hundred thousand scudos a year'.[7]

The livery issued by Henry VII to his household falls into two distinct types. First, there was his dynastic livery of green and white. This colour combination was largely limited to jackets and coats and given to a range of individuals, including George Grey, a spear of Calais, receiving 12 yards (10.9 m) of green damask and 12 yards (10.9 m) of white damask on 13 June 1503, Worley Herman, master gunner at Calais, was given 2½ yards (2.2 m) of green and white cloth for a livery coat, 24 members of the yeomen of the guard received jackets with bases of green and white and four French minstrels received coats of white and green camlet with sleeves.[8] Its use extended to the staff of the royal stable, the men rowing the royal barge and the crew of the king's balinger. Henry VII's use of it also incorporated the two footmen accompanying Margaret north for her marriage to James IV.[9] Her footmen and littermen also received a black velvet livery with crowned portcullises. This was possibly a variant of the type of livery worn by the king's almsmen in the illustration in the indenture for founding the king's chantry chapel in Westminster abbey in 1504. Behind Abbot Islip kneel monks of the abbey and the king's almsmen, who had long hair, no tonsure and were dressed in black with the crowned Tudor rose on their left shoulder (Fig. 14.1). Henry VII was the first English king to use the closed imperial crown on his coins. The illustration indicates that it was also displayed on the king's livery. This practice is further confirmed by the presence of the closed imperial crown on the hearse cloths commissioned during 1504–05 by the king and now preserved in the Fitzwilliam and Ashmolean museums (Fig. 14.2). On 4 May 1490 John Fligh paid William Moreton and John Smith for embroidering 21 jackets and for goldsmith's work, and William More for work on 20 jackets, along with 60 jackets costing 18*s*, giving a total of £115 6*s*.[10]

14.1 *Illuminated initial of the founding indenture of Henry VII's chantry chapel, Westminster abbey, 1504, showing Henry VII and Abbot Islip and the almsmen who wear the crowned rose badge on their left shoulder. The National Archive, E33/1*

The second type of livery was much less defined in terms of colour or cloth, and was given to members of the king's household, the quantity and quality of the clothing usually dependent on their social standing and position within the household. Much of the clothing was black or tawny, but not all. For example, Ralph Pudsey received a tawny cloth gown furred with white lamb in January 1503, and the same furred with black lamb in January and November 1505.[11] In contrast, on 4 March 1499 Guiliam Maynard was given a gown of violet wool dyed in grain and furred with white lamb and a black satin doublet.[12] As with the king and his immediate family, a limited range of fabrics and colours were used. Woollen fabrics were used quite consistently and included russet and motley for watching livery, broad cloth and kersey. The provision of fur was limited both in the varieties used and the

14.2 *Detail of the royal arms supported by a dragon and a hound from Henry VII's hearse cloth, c. 1504–05. Fitzwilliam Museum, Cambridge, © The Textile Conservation Centre, University of Southampton*

number of recipients. The watching livery issued in six years between 1486–87 and 1502–03 was russet, but in 1504–05 and 1505–06 it was tawny.[13]

The livery provided for Henry VII's footmen and the henchmen is subtly different from that provided for most other groups both in terms of the quantity and quality (Table 14.2). For example, in December 1487 the four footmen were given a gown of crimson in grain furred with black shanks, a doublet of black velvet, a jacket of crimson velvet, a red bonnet and a crimson hat while in March 1488 the seven henchmen received riding gowns of crimson velvet and cloth of gold, two black satin doublets, a demi-gown of murrey in grain and fine tawny, two pairs of hose of unspecified colour and a cloak of scarlet.[14] While there are parallels in the livery given to the footmen and henchmen, the latter always received more, of greater variety and more up to date in fashion including the demi-gown and cloak. They also received riding jackets, boots and spurs, in keeping with their role as a highly visible part of the royal entourage when the king appeared in public. The henchmen were also provided with bedding.[15] The footmen received a less generous provision and their role walking with the king's retinue was emphasised by their receipt of double-soled shoes rather than boots and no spurs. Henry VIII continued his father's provisioning, but as elsewhere he was compelled to expand upon it. Henry VIII usually had nine henchmen and six to eight footmen and lavished more clothes upon them.

The chief sections of the household to receive livery and textiles from the great wardrobe included musicians, trumpeters, officers of the chamber or *domus magnificencie* and the offices of the stable and the chapel. Much of this continued unchanged under Henry VIII, although there were some subtle differences. The privy chamber and its associated staff emerged during Henry VII's reign, but it did not develop fully until after 1509. Just one warrant surviving in the extant accounts provided livery for a group of officers from the privy chamber: dated 15 January 1504 it awarded black damask gowns and doublets of black damask and black satin to Richard Clement, John Green, Peter Narbonne and Robert Wingfield, grooms of the privy chamber.[16] This black livery continued in use throughout Henry VIII's reign. The musicians in Henry VII's service formed a smaller group with more traditional instruments than the individuals retained by Henry VIII. The livery provided for them was also conservative in its form. A warrant dated 17 June 1504 allowed red cloth gowns for five trumpeters, 'viij stille mynstralles & v lowed mynstralls' and jackets of green and white damask for six minstrels.[17]

Equally, the various facets of the royal chapel were well provided for both in terms of livery and textiles, as indicated from the expenses of William Tebbe, the sergeant of the vestry, from 30 September 1490 to 1 October 1491 (Table 14.3). A vestment maker at Windsor was paid 68*s* 3*d* for working on items for the chapel: for 38 days labour at 4*d* the day, 12*s* 8*d*; for 1 lb (0.4 kg) of fine thread of various colours, 2*s* 3*d*; 18 oz (0.5 kg) of ribbon, 18*s*; for making six vestments, 14*s*.[18] A warrant for the king's chapel dated 4 January 1499 commissioned William More and John Martin, embroiderers, to provide three copes of green velvet, each with 16 portcullises,

Table 14.2: *Expenditure on livery issued to the footmen, the henchmen, the guard and on watching and Tower livery*

Year	Footmen	Henchmen*	Watching livery	Tower livery	The Guard
1498–99	4: £32 5*s* 2*d*	3–4: £148 5*s* 5¼*d*	?: £94 17*s* 11*d*	12: £12	20: £24 9*s* 0
1502–03	4: £33 11*s* 0*d*	5–6: £84 3*s* 7*d*	?: £81	No entry	No entry
1504–05	4: £20 18*s* 6*d*	3: £54 9*s* ob	63: £73 8*s* 8*d*	No entry	No entry
1505–06	3–4: £55 2*s* 6½*d*	5: £159 7*s* ½*d*	74: £75 12*s*	12: £12	No entry

* The figure given is for the number of henchmen. It does not include the master or their page, one or both of whom sometimes appear on the warrants.

Table 14.3: *Expenditure on livery issued to the chapel, the closet, the vestry, the barge and the stable*

Year/account	The Chapel	The Closet	The Vestry	The Barge	The Stable
1498–99	£25 7*s* 5½*d*	~	£1	£21 0*s* 4*d*	£102 16*s* 10½*d*
1502–03	~	~	~	£3 15*s* 3*d*	£12 4*s* 11¼*d*
1504–05	~	£4 7*s* 5*d*	~	~	£20 4*s* 2*d*
1505–06	~	~	~	~	£78 10*s* 6*d*

XV

Henry VIII's Household: The Domus Magnificencie *and the* Domus Providencie

THE ROYAL HOUSEHOLD in the late Middle Ages consisted of three sections: the household above stairs under the lord chamberlain, the household below stairs under the lord steward, and the stable, under the governance of the master of the horse, who had primacy when the monarch was outside the household. The reign of Henry VII witnessed the rise of the privy chamber, initially as a subsection of the chamber and then as a separate household department. Each section of the household had its own staff, its own set of responsibilities and distinct areas within the physical structure of the king's houses and palaces where they were expected to provide service. The household above stairs or the *domus magnificencie*, as its name suggests, was intended to reflect the king's own magnificence and to impress all that saw it. This was indicated by the quantity and quality of the livery provided for the offices of this department and the furnishings deployed there. The same applied to the stable with its staff and horses, being highly visible when the king travelled. In contrast, the household below stairs, or *domus providencie*, was expected to manage its resources carefully and care for the king's needs, while very little provision was made for livery because the staff were rarely seen outside the areas where they worked.

On 1 August 1524 the commissioners appointed to collect the subsidy noted those members of the royal household authorised to act as their deputies. The list highlights the key offices within the household and gives a sense of their hierarchy: the steward of the king's household, the chamberlain, the chamberlain of the queen's household, the king's treasurer, comptroller and chamberlain, the captain of the king's guard, the cofferer and the two clerks of the greencloth. Similar notes were drawn up in relation to the households of the Princess Mary, the duchess of Suffolk and Cardinal Wolsey.[1]

The Act of Precedence of 1539 modified and clarified the hierarchy:

> In all parliaments as in the Star Chamber, and in all other assemblies and conferences of Council, the lord chancellor, the lord treasurer, the lord president, the lord privy seal, the great chamberlain, the constable, the marshal, the lord admiral, the grand master or lord steward, the king's chamberlain, shall sit and be placed in such order and fashion as is above rehearsed, and not in any other place.[2]

The act, which dealt specifically with where office holders sat in the house of lords, did not mention the master of the horse because he customarily sat in the house of commons. His place in the order of things was recognised in a warrant authorising the appointment of a second secretary to the privy council in 1540:

> His Majesty ordaineth that in all Councils, as well in his Majesty's household as in the Star Chamber and elsewhere, all lords, both of the temporality and clergy, shall sit above them [the secretaries]; and likewise the treasurer, comptroller, master of the horse, and vice-chamberlain of His Highness's Household; then after that to be placed the said principal secretaries.[3]

The household above stairs

The provision of body service increased in status during the fifteenth century. Consequently the standing of those providing such service also increased. The physical space occupied by the *domus magnificencie* consisted of the chamber which incorporated a number of rooms: the guard chamber, the presence chamber and the privy chamber. The household above stairs came under the control of the lord chamberlain. The Black Book of Edward IV noted that the chamberlain received winter and summer robes, delivered at Christmas and Whitsun. These robes were to be paid for out of the counting house at a cost of 8 marks each.[4] This post was often held by a close friend of the king: Richard III's chamberlain was Lord

Lovell. Under Henry VII the post was enjoyed by Sir William Stanley (1485–95) and Giles, Lord Daubeney (1495–1508) and under Henry VIII by the earl of Worcester (1509–26), Lord Sandys (1526–40), Lord St John (1543) and the twelfth earl of Arundel (1543–47).[5]

The great wardrobe accounts include a number of entries for long velvet gowns, decorated with a double border or guard for the lord chamberlain. On 17 February 1527 he was given a gown of black velvet with two borders of the same velvet, a coat of russet cloth guarded with two broad borders of russet velvet and a hat lined with sarsenet.[6] On 31 December 1527 he was supplied with a similar gown of black velvet with two double borders of the same velvet furred with black budge, the upper sleeves lined with buckram.[7] The colour, if not the form, of the gown sometimes varied. Thus by the warrant dated 1 January 1529 he got a gown of russet velvet with two borders of the same velvet and on 26 February 1545 a long gown of tawny velvet guarded with two burgion guards of the same, furred in the body.[8]

Sir Henry Wyatt (d. 1537), was treasurer of the chamber from 1524–28 (Fig. 15.1). In his portrait, the original of which by Holbein is lost, he wears a black velvet gown furred with sable, a gold chain on his shoulders of round links with a pendant cross.[9] The sleeves of his doublet of black damask or satin are fur-lined at the cuffs, while his close-fitting black cap comes down over his ears.

THE CHAMBER

A number of different groups of royal servants, including the king's footmen, the henchmen and the yeomen of the guard, belonged to the chamber (Fig. 15.2). Consequently, expenditure on livery for this group of household staff was high (Table 15.1). The issue of Tower livery (livery to be worn at the Tower of London) was very consistent.[10] There were 15 recipients in every year listed with the exception of 1510–11. The numbers in receipt of watching livery fluctuated, with 84 recipients in 1527–28 and 153 in 1543–45. The name of the livery is suggested by the tasks undertaken by the yeomen of the chamber which included 'to make beddes, to bere or hold torches . . . to apparayle all chamres . . . to wache the king by course'.[11] While watching livery was usually issued as a block grant, on occasion individuals were omitted or admitted to the office after the grant was made, and so were issued with a separate warrant. The same method was followed for the guard with the variant that the guard did not receive new livery every year. As the livery received by the guard was issued in a range of grades, so the total cost does not always directly correlate with the number of recipients. The numbers

15.1 *Sir Henry Wyatt, after Hans Holbein the Younger, sixteenth century. Photograph courtesy of the National Gallery of Ireland*

15.2 *Drawing of an unknown young man by Hans Holbein the Younger, 1532–40. The style and quality of the clothes would have been comparable with the livery issued to the king's yeomen. Reproduced by courtesy of the Trustees of the British Museum*

Table 15.1: *Livery supplied to the footmen, henchmen, as watching and Tower livery and to the guard*

Where applicable/known, the number of recipients is given and then the cost of the livery.

Year	Footmen	Henchmen*	Watching livery	Tower livery	Guard
1510–11	£97 14*s* 5*d*	£154 11*s* 8*d*	£6	£13	£8 15*s* 8*d*
1516–17	£247 11*s* 8*d*	£919 3*s* 10*d*	£133 8*s*	£15	£192 6*s* 5*d*
1517–18	£228 8*s* 11*d*	£660 19*s* 5*d*	£131 8*s*	£18 15*s*	£147 8*s*
1521–22	£232 7*s* 1½*d*	£722 15*s* 11*d*	~	£15	£151 11*s* 2*d*
1523–25	£243 6*s* 2½*d*	£216 19*s* 6*d*	£121 8*s*	£15	£12 19*s* 6*d*
1526–27	£99 16*s* 2*d*	£150 0*s* 7*d*	~	£15	~
1527–28	£173 1*s* 11*d*	£255 13*s* 10*d*	£98	£15	~
1530–31	£222 5*s*	£447 10*s* 5*d*	~	£15	£86 8*s*
1531–32	£222 7*s* 8*d*	£696 0*s* 8*d*	£98 8*s*	£15	£178 10*s*
1533–34	£220 13*s*	£508 7*s* 1*d*	£98	£15	~
1535–36	£213 18*s*	£457 14*s* 1*d*	£100 8*s*	£15	£70 7*s*
1537–38	£170 18*s*	£200 17*s*	£116 8*s*	£15 6*s* 3*d*	~
1538–39	£317 12*s* 9*d*	~	£125 14*s* 3*d*	£15 6*s* 3*d*	£109 14*s* 7*d*
1543–45	~	£65 2*s* 8*d*	£163	£15	~

* The figure given is for the number of henchmen. It does not include the master or their page, one or both of whom sometimes appear on the warrants.

in receipt of livery range between 40 in 1531–32 and 200 in 1521–22. The number of henchmen fluctuates quite widely between 13 or 14 during 1516–18 and four during 1531–32, and the costs are always high. The number of footmen tended to be stable at six but occasionally it rose to seven or eight. The number rose to ten during 1538–39 when Thomas Cromwell was undertaking his review of the royal household.

Under the Black Book of Edward IV, the 40 squires of the household were entitled to clothing in winter and summer, or 40*s* and 'Hit hath euer byn in speciall charge to squiers in this court to were the kinges lyuery custumably, for the more glory and in worshipp this honorable houshold'.[12] Large-scale deliveries of livery were made on an annual basis to the officers of the chamber in the form of watching livery. Under Edward IV, there were four yeomen of the crown, one being the yeoman of the robes and another being the yeoman of the beds, who received changes of clothing half-yearly or 16*s*. In addition they received watching clothing, and in accordance with the statutes dating from the reign of Edward III they were allowed 10*s* for a gown and 4*s* 8*d* for hose and shoes.[13] Other groups of officers in the chamber also received watching livery.

On 13 December 1510 livery was ordered for 12 yeomen ushers, 73 yeomen, 15 grooms, seven pages.[14] On 30 January 1514 12 daily waiters received 5 yards (4.5 m) of broad cloth of tawny medley for watching livery.[15] In December 1514 192 yeomen ushers, yeomen, grooms and pages of the chamber were given watching livery of London russet.[16] In 1545 two orders were placed for watching livery. In October a warrant signed by the comptroller of the household was issued to the great wardrobe for 'watch lyveries to the yeoman waighters' in the Tower and another, signed by the vice-chamberlain, in December benefited the yeomen, grooms and pages of the chamber.[17] The last issue of watching livery for the yeomen, grooms and pages of Henry's household was ordered on a warrant shortly before the king died in January 1547.[18] Some informal provision of clothing was made to the staff of the chamber from the king's privy purse. On 14 January 1531 the wife of William Armourer was paid £5 11*s* 4*d* 'for ij dousin of handekerchers and Shertes for them of the Chambre being at the kines finding'.[19] Six months later six pairs of hose were bought for the king's children of the chamber costing 30*s*.[20]

There are occasional references to livery being provided for gentleman ushers. On 5 November 1513 a gown of black camlet was ordered for William Cotton.[21] Seventeen years later Christopher Rochester, gentleman usher, under a warrant dated 8 April 1531, received fabric for a gown of black damask, a jacket of tawny satin and a yellow velvet doublet costing £11 10*s*.[22]

The grooms of the chamber mostly received gowns or coats. On 21 June 1510, motley for coats and black velvet for doublets were delivered to Christopher Rochester and William Gower.[23] On 28 January 1511 a gown of tawny camlet was given to William Wise.[24] On 8 December 1513 Christopher Rochester and John Dingley, 'grooms of our chamber', received 14 yards (12.8 m) of russet damask for a gown furred with black budge and guarded with crimson velvet, black velvet jackets, crimson velvet doublets.[25] In 1514 a gown of camlet was supplied to Peter Malvesey.[26] In April of that year, William Gower was given 15 yards (13.7 m) of russet damask for a gown furred with black budge and 7 yards (6.4 m) of black velvet for a jacket.[27]

The lack of evidence relating to the sewers of the chamber is perhaps indicative of their declining role in the household. On 31 July 1510 Nicholas Lode was provided with a coat.[28] Four years later William Wise was given a black damask gown.[29] The second warrant also provides evidence of Wise's advancement, as he had risen from being a groom to a sewer of the chamber.

In the fifteenth century the royal footmen had risen in importance and they continued to be important in the Tudor period. Curiously, their tasks are not described in the Black Book, but their primary role was to attend upon the head of the household while riding and at events outdoors, such as jousts. The footmen also accompanied the king when hunting. In 1525 a footman saved the king's life when he fell into a ditch while hunting. The man jumped into the water and 'lift up his head, whiche was fast in the clay'.[30]

Over the space of a year in 1510–11 (November, May and October), the king's six footmen received gowns of tawny medley.[31] The timing suggests that this was their regular livery. However, for special occasions they received more sumptuous attire. On 11 October 1513, the Milanese ambassador wrote to the duke of Milan about the jousts in which Henry VIII and Lord Lisle had taken part: 'The king's footmen wore doublets of gold and black velvet, his favourite's had white.'[32] In December 1513, William Gore, footman, was given livery consisting of a gown of tawny medley furred with black Irish lamb, one black and one tawny doublet, a jacket of crimson velvet, six pairs of hose and six shirts with drawn work.[33] This increased grant of livery was echoed in the following year by the grant of livery on 19 April 1514 to Andrew de Fosse, William Gower, David Philips, Stephen Toote, Thomas Trestram and John Williams: gowns of tawny camlet lined with camlet, green and black velvet doublets, a jacket of crimson velvet, two velvet caps, a coat of green velvet, a cloak of scarlet, eight pairs of shoes and six shirts.[34]

While the colours and fabrics changed slightly from year to year, the basic order remained the same. From April 1522 the footmen also received short coats of crimson velvet decorated with roses of crimson and white satin and silver and gilt spangles.[35] Similar provision continued to be made after that date, although in some years they received an embroidered crimson jerkin rather than a coat.[36] However, in October 1545 Edward Same was appointed to be one of the ten ordinary footmen and he was given an allowance of £40 a year instead of the accustomed apparel from the great wardrobe, subscribed by the master of the horse.[37] The same was granted to Thomas Edmund.[38]

The Black Book provided a detailed description of the role of the henchmen or the pages of honour who rode or walked next to the king in processions and on progress. Edward IV and Richard III usually had seven henchmen, while Henry VIII had between four and nine.[39] The henchmen were allowed bedding, a servant each to keep their harness and their chamber, 'And all other finding for theyre bodyes they take of the kinges warderober, by sewte of the master of henxmen made to the kinges chambrelayn for warrauntez'.[40] The role of the master of the henchmen was:

to show the scoolez of vrbanitie and nourture of Inglond, to lern them to ride clenly and surely, to drawe them also to justes, to lern them were theyre harneys; to haue all curtesy in wordez, dedes and degrees, dilygently to kepe them in rules of goynges and sittinges, after they be of honour. Moreouer, to teche them sondry languages and other lernynges vertuous, to herping, to pype, sing, daunce, and with other honest and temperate behauing and pacience; and to kepe dayly and wykely with thees children dew conuenitz, with correcions in thyere chambres according to suche gentylmen; and eche of them to be vsed to that thinges of vertue that he shalbe most apt to lerne, with remebraunce dayly of Goddes seruyce accustomed.

Like the squires of the household, the master received clothing, harness and livery for his horse.[41]

As the henchmen played an important ceremonial role the king did not stint on their livery. They were prominent in processions, notably at royal coronations and funerals. At Henry VII's funeral, there were nine henchmen riding:

on coursers trapped with black velvet the three foremost bearing caps of maintenance which three Popes had sent the King, the next three bearing rich swords point downwards, the seventh bearing target of the arms of England otherwise called a shield crowned, the eighth a helmet with a lion of gold on it, the ninth a spear covered with black velvet.[42]

The identical number of henchmen attended Henry VIII's funeral.[43] They also took part in the king's revels and jousts. The 1547 revels list includes 'ij olde cotes for henchemen of Tilsent and Crymsen satten in panes with twoo Cappes of Tilsent' (8640).

The henchmen received two substantial warrants a year. The winter warrant dating from November 1510 consisted of gowns of tawny medley furred with fox poots and of tawny damask furred with black budge, doublets of black velvet and tawny satin, linen shirts decorated with drawn thread work, hose of scarlet and tawny, double-soled shoes and pinsons, caps, hats with sarsenet hatbands, silk girdles, silk and leather points.[44] For Henry's meeting with Francis in 1532, they had coats made from purple, black and white velvet, and hose made from black, white and purple cloth.[45] They also received some highly fashionable items such as short cloaks, jackets with bases and riding coats, made from their very best quality materials. In April 1517 their jackets with bases for riding were made from crimson velvet and bordered and guarded with cloth of gold.[46] In May 1525 the crimson velvet jackets with bases were trimmed with green cloth of gold. In July 1534 the henchmen received crimson velvet coats, clocked and guarded with white tilsent.[47] As a group, they were the most expensively and well-dressed of the king's household that were paid for out of the king's purse.

THE PRIVY CHAMBER

The privy chamber originated under Henry VII. Its staff initially came under the control of the groom of the stool, but its structure evolved under Henry VIII. The staff included the king's barber and the officers of the wardrobe of the robes and they were often provided with livery on the king's own warrants. The king spent time in his privy chamber with his friends and advisors. As discussed above, the officers of the privy chamber received two types of livery from 1527, one of which changed colour every year.[48] The evidence here relates to the other set of livery these officers received.

The Eltham Ordinances of 1526 stated that:

The gentlemen of the privy chamber [were] to be ready by 7 o'clock ... to help to dress him, putting on his garments in reverent, discrete and sober manner. None of the grooms or ushers to touch his person without special command or meddle with the dressing, except it be to warm clothes and carry them to the gentlemen; the garments to be brought to the privy chamber door by the yeoman of the robes and received by one of the grooms, who shall deliver it to one of the six gentlemen to put upon the King's person.[49]

The gentlemen helped the king to dress, working with the officers of the robes. No references to the provision of livery for the gentlemen have been discovered earlier than 1527.

The grooms of the privy chamber seem to have been more fortunate. Two warrants for the grooms survive from the start of the reign. On a warrant dated 19 May 1511 Nicholas Carew, John Dingley, William Gower and Christopher

Rochester received gowns of tawny cloth and gowns of tawny camlet on another warrant dated 19 March 1512.[50] By the time of the next batch of warrants, the order was larger. There are three warrants dated 22 November 1529, 22 November 1530 and 20 November 1531 for four grooms (Urian Brereton, William Brereton, John Carey and Walter Walsh) and John Penne, the barber.[51] There is also a warrant dated 14 December 1533 for Urian Brereton, William Brereton, John Carey, Anthony Denny, Nicholas Simpson, and John Penne.[52] All four warrants ordered damask gowns furred with budge, velvet jackets and doublets. The warrant dated 9 May 1538 was slightly different and not repeated. It consisted of broadcloth gowns guarded with black velvet and furred with black budge, jackets of damask, doublets of satin and fustian, white kersey hose, shirts and bonnets.[53]

The warrant issued on 28 November 1539 made provision for six grooms, but otherwise it reverted to the standard form.[54] A warrant issued at Hampton Court on 28 November 1542 for livery to be issued at Christmas for the grooms of the privy chamber gave details of the quantity and the price of the damask for a gown and velvet for a coat and doublet, with black budge and other materials for trimming and lining costing in total £27 15*s*.[55] A similar order was placed in November 1543.[56] A warrant signed with the stamp in November 1545 authorised the great wardrobe to provide apparel to every groom of the privy chamber and the barber for the coming year.[57]

The officers of the wardrobe of the robes, originally under the control of the chamberlain, had transferred to the jurisdiction of the chief gentleman of the privy chamber. However, the basic structure and rationale remained the same as it had been when it was described in the Black Book of Edward IV. The staff of the wardrobe of the robes consisted of a yeoman, who was to be dressed like a yeoman of the crown, a groom who was given clothing within the household yearly, or 6*s* 8*d* along with watching clothing from the wardrobe, and a page who was also allowed clothing.

A few warrants for staff from the wardrobe of the robes survive from early in Henry VIII's reign. For example, on 20 November 1514, John Copinger, page of the robes, was provided with black damask for a gown.[58] A few weeks later Richard Smith, yeoman of the robes, was given tawny camlet for a gown.[59] After the mid 1520s, the officers of the robes came to be thought of as part of the privy chamber staff, and accordingly they were included in the block warrants for this section of the household.

The king's barber was also a member of the privy chamber. His role was described in the Black Book:

> the King's barber shall be dayly by the King's uprising ready and attendant in the privy chamber; there having in readinesse, his water, cloths, knives, combes, sissors, and such other stuffe as to his roome doth appertayne, for trimming and dressing the King's head and beard. And that the said barbor taken especiall regard to the pure and cleane keeping of his own person and apparell.[60]

His livery was included on the warrants for the grooms of the privy chamber.[61]

Provision was made for the barber's livery and the 1547 inventory included references to a silver basin for shaving in the Tower (1457) and another received from Hampton Court (1534). Shaving cloths were kept in removing coffer M (2584), while shaving cloths 'trymmed with golde' (11588) and 'trymmed with blacke silke' (11593) were at Whitehall and Hampton Court respectively. The king also had a selection of combs, including 'a Combe of golde garnysshed with course stones and perle lacking some stones' (2922), 'a horse tayle to make cleane Combes' (11208) and hair brushes (9471, 9582). Other tools for the king's personal hygiene included 'a shorte case of gold enameled full of to the pikes' (2318) and 'an Eare picke of Siluer' (2618).

THE FOOL

There were two types of fool to provide amusement at court: the clever fools and the innocents who needed care.[62] Fools could use their own dress to make a satirical point, as in the episode involving a jester at Edward IV's court described in the *Great Chronicle*. The jester appeared before the king carrying a pike. He was dressed in a short coat cut in points along the hem and a long pair of boots that were tied to the points. When asked to explain his appearance, he replied: 'I have passed thorwth many Cuntrees of your Realm, and in placys that I have passid Ryvers been soo hieh that I coude hardly scape throw theym, But as I was fayn to serch the depth wyth this long staff.'[63] This comment was a veiled attack on the all pervasive influence of Earl Rivers, the king's father-in-law.

The accounts from Henry VIII's reign suggest that the king's fool was provided with clothing rather than having to supply his own. The clothes were often brightly coloured. The king also provided his fools with a horse and horse harness. On 12 December 1509 William Worth, keeper of the fool, received a gown of tawny medley furred with lamb and a doublet of fustian for Thomas Cliff.[64] Two years later, another warrant ordered the delivery of a fustian coat to Thomas Cliff and a gown of broad cloth to Thomas Tailor, who had replace Worth as Cliff's keeper.[65]

Philip Sexton, familiarly known as Patch, started his career in Wolsey's household. According to George Cavendish, Wolsey made a gift of his fool to Henry at the time of his fall from grace. The cardinal asked Henry Norris to 'present the kyng with this poore foole . . . suerly for a noble mans pleasure he is worth a M[l] li'.[66] A selection of clothing was bought for him from the king's privy purse, including a coat of kendal and a doublet of fustian made by Cotton in June 1530 costing 15*s* 4*d*.[67] He also received fabric for garments costing £3 11*d*, a doublet and hose of worsted and sarsenet with the making (33*s* 10*d*), 'a perwyke' (20*s*), washing his shirts (9*s* 8*d*), a Milan bonnet and a night cap (8*s*), cloth and making of a coat (21*s* 8*d*), a night cap, washing his shirts, shoes (6*s* 8*d*) and two pairs of hose, a doublet and a pety coat.[68] Sexton had a servant called Skinner who received wages of 15*s* 2*d* a quarter and who was given 22*s* 6*d* for his own livery.[69] The servant was provided with a livery coat costing 23*s* 4*d*.[70]

In July 1535 the imperial ambassador reported that the king had 'nearly murdered his own fool, a simple and innocent man, because he happened to speak well in his presence of the Queen and Princess and called the concubine "ribaude" and her daughter "bastard". He has now been banished from Court, and has gone to the Grand Esquire who has sheltered and hidden him'.[71] Seven months later, one Thomas Bedyll wrote to Cromwell about Sexton's worsening increpitude and suggested a replacement. He knew of a suitable young candidate at Croyland who was 'very fit for the Court, and will afford the king much pastime which he shall make both with gentlemen and gentlewomen'.[72] Nothing came of the proposal.

Will Somer, an innocent, was the king's last appointee as fool. The first entry for clothes for him dates from 28 June 1535. He was given two doublets of worsted lined with canvas and cotton, a coat and cap of green cloth fringed with red crewel and lined with frieze, a coat of green cloth with a hood fringed with white crewel and a demi-coat with a hood of green cloth fringed with white and red crewel. He also received two pairs of hose of blue cloth, guarded with red and black cloth.[73] A set of three undated bills provided him with a range of small items and also paid for his laundry: one bill for 12*s* including washing (11*s*), a pair of boot hose (8*d*) and shaving (4*d*); one bill paid for 40*s* for a number of pairs of black hose and stocks; and a third bill for 14*s* 2*d* provided three pairs of lined shoes (10*d* each), seven pairs of unlined shoes (8*d* each), two pairs of summer buskins (2*s* a pair) and a pair of winter boots (3*s*).[74]

There are two portraits of Will Somer. The group portrait of *The Family of Henry VIII* by an unknown artist *c.* 1545 includes a portrait of Will Somer on the far right, with a monkey on his shoulder (Fig. 16.1). Somer also appeared in the miniature illustrating psalm 52 in Henry's psalter by David Mallard c. 1540 (Fig.15.3). The king was represented in the role of the Old Testament king David, playing the harp, with Somers dressed in a short green coat and hood in attendance. Henry's own collection of paintings included

15.3 *Henry VIII and his jester Will Somer, 1537–38, in Henry VIII's Psalter. By permission of the British Library, Royal MS 2A XVI, f. 63v*

'oone table with the Pictures of the Frenche king the Quene his wiff and the foole standing behing hym' [734].[75]

Fools were not always men. There were some female fools, usually attached to female households, such as those of Jane Seymour, Catherine Parr and Princess Mary.[76] There are several references in Henry VII's accounts from 1502 to 'the great woman of Flanders' and a satin gown was provided for 'the grete Flemyng called Anne' which suggests that he retained a female giant in his service.[77]

THE MUSICIANS

Music formed an important part of court life: as part of court ceremony, for religious services, for private pleasure and for court entertainments.[78] Musicians could also teach the royal children how to play instruments such as the lute or virginals. On 4 July 1546 Prince Edward thanked his father for sending Philip van der Wilder, noting that he 'is both a musician and a gentleman, for his improvement in playing the lute'.[79] There were several distinct groups of musicians who were provided for differently in terms of livery. This is highlighted in the Black Book of Edward IV which describes the provision made to musicians: four minstrels, 'some use trumpets, shawms and small pipes' were given clothing with the household, in winter and summer, or 20s and a wait was given clothing with the household.[80]

Most of the musicians were employed in groups, playing instruments such as the trumpet, sackbut or viol. There were a number of soloists including 'blynde Dikke, our harper' who, on 6 December 1511, was granted a tawny gown furred with black Irish lamb and a black satin doublet.[81] Henry also employed an organist — the best known being the Venetian Dionisius Memo who was in England from 1516–17. Most of the royal chapels possessed organs. At St James's there was 'a payer of Organes standing in the chapple' (15325) and at Beaulieu there was 'a paier of faier greate Organes in the Chappell with A curten afore them of lynnen cloth stayned Redd and blewe paned' (13686).[82] Periodically, Henry retained an organ maker. On 16 January 1530 John de John, 'our organ maker' was given 4 yards (3.6 m) of puke-coloured broad cloth for a gown and black budge to fur it, a black damask jacket lined with black cotton and a doublet of black velvet lined with white cotton.[83] On 23 December 1535, John Jones, described as the king's organ mender, was given a black puke gown lined with say and a damask jacket lined with cotton, costing £5 13*s* 10*d*.[84]

The number of trumpeters under the direction of the sergeant or marshal ranged between 14 and 16. The trumpeters were sometimes given clothing in preparation for specific events. On 25 April 1512 green and white camlet for coats was delivered to Francis Knyf for the trumpeters.[85] Two years later the trumpeters of the king and the earl of Surrey were given coats of green and white camlet and banner cloths with the king's arms.[86] Similar provision was made towards the end of the reign. On 21 September 1545 the king issued a warrant to the great wardrobe for a livery coat and banner to each of

15.4 *Les Trompettes/The trumpeters, wearing short coats and with trumpet banners with the king's arms. The Westminster Tournament Roll, The College of Arms*

the trumpeters.[87] In the following November a warrant for the trumpeters' liveries was preferred by Sir Ralph Sadler, probably in connection with the visit of the French Admiral.[88]

On 12 February 1511 the great wardrobe supplied 15 painted trumpet banners with fringe and tassels costing £42 19*s* 1*d* (Fig. 15.4).[89] These banners could be paid for via the chamber, as in the case of Pieter de Casa Nova, marshal of the king's trumpeters, upon a warrant for 12 banners for trumpets against Christmas 1512 costing £12.[90] On 25 April 1512 four trumpet banners were delivered to Francis Knyf, 'one of our trumpets, painted in oil on sarsenet with fine gold'.[91] Shortly after, banners were delivered to Thomas Gardiner, Francis Knyf, Christopher Papa and John Sturt, 'our trumpets of war'.[92] The orders for the trumpeters got larger as the reign progressed, partly because they often received two warrants a year from 1531–32.

The king's trumpeters provided fanfares and ceremonial music. They participated at events held in the outer rooms of the king's palaces and in public occasions outside the royal houses. In 1521, when Henry received the title of Defender of the Faith (*defensor fidei*), Hall described how 'the Bull eftsonnes declared ... trumpettes blew, the shalmes and saggebuttes plaied in honour of the kynges newe style'.[93]

While the accuracy of Holbein's drawing of a group of musicians, *Musicians on a balcony* (Fig. 15.5), has been doubted because the straight trumpet was not played in polyphonic groups, it still indicates how other musicians playing sackbuts and shawms might have performed at court events.[94]

Throughout his reign Henry VIII provided livery for a group of minstrels playing for his entertainment. Until the late 1520s, these men received livery individually, as happened in January 1511 with William Borow, on 6 May 1512 with Pety John Cokeron and Richard Denis and on 14 November 1514 with Blind Dick, Thomas Evans and William Kechyn.[95] From 1529 group warrants were issued to the musicians. On 1 December 1529 Petre de la Planshe, Nowell de la Sale, John de

15.5 *Musicians on a balcony, attributed to Hans Holbein the Younger. 1852-5-19-2. Reproduced by courtesy of the Trustees of the British Museum*

Shevernak and Gregory Vasher were issued with livery, while two weeks later a similar warrant was given to Mark Anthony, John de Anthony, Jasper de Barnard, Petre Mary, Ipolito de Salvator and Pilgrim de Symon.[96] During the period covered by the privy purse accounts, a number of payments were made for the minstrels, including new livery coats on 21 July 1531 for Pety John and his fellows, costing £6 15*s*.[97] On 24 October 1531, £13 6*s* 8*d* was given to four of the king's 'new mynstrelles for ther costes going to Southampton to fetch ther stuf'.[98] In April 1540 the king made a grant to his minstrels, the musicians of the privy chamber, the sackbuts and the viols: Alinxus, John, Anthony, Jasper and Baptista de Basam, 'brothers in the science or art of music' were given stipends: to Alinxus £50 a year, to John 2*s* 4*d* a day and to

167 Ibid., p. 43.
168 Kipling, *Receypt*, p. 73.
169 TNA E101/418/4, f. 1r.
170 This cost £6 10*s* 4*d*; TNA E101/421/3, unfoliated.
171 This cost £5 14*s* 4*d*; TNA E101/421/16, unfoliated.
172 D. Loades, *Power in Tudor England* (Basingstoke, 1997), p. 107.
173 NUL MS Ne01, unfoliated.
174 *HO*, p. 148.
175 TNA E101/417/4, unfoliated.
176 BL Additional MS 18,826, f. 46r.
177 TNA LC 9/51, f. 10r.
178 Ibid., f. 59v, and E36/224, p. 55.
179 *LP* VI, 694.
180 *LP* XIV.ii, 781.
181 R. Lockyer, ed., *Thomas Wolsey Late Cardinal his Life and Death*, The Folio Society (1962), p. 46.
182 *LP* XIV.ii, 781.
183 BL Arundel MS 97, f. 185r (*LP* XVI, 1489).

XVI

Outside the Household: The Stable, the Hunts and Beyond

HENRY VIII provided livery for the men involved in the stable and the king's hunts. They formed a highly visible group, and accordingly great attention was bestowed upon their clothing. This clothing and the equipment they were provided with was expensive, and represented a significant percentage of the great wardrobe's expenditure (Table 16.1).

The stable and the master of the horse

Under the direction of the master of the horse, the royal stables provided the horses needed during the military campaigns and social unrest. They more routinely provided the horses needed to transport the king and court from one destination to another, for his riding out and hunting. The royal stable was funded out of the exchequer. According to the Eltham Ordinances of 1526, its staff numbered 104 individuals. These comprised the master of the horse with a fee of £66 13*s* 4*d* a year, the avenor with £40, five squires with £40 or £20, and 97 others. The core staff consisted of the avenor, three squires, the clerk of the avenery, a surveyor, a purveyor, a yeoman garnitor, a yeoman of the stirrup, a yeoman farrier, a yeoman saddler and ten footmen.[1]

The officers of the stable performed four primary duties. First, they fed and cared for the horses, which included grooming before and after they were ridden or worked, and for this they were provided with comb, brushes and cloths. Sixteenth-century manuscript illustrations show grooms currying horses with curry combs with angular blades and semi-cylindrical blades of the sort found during archaeological excavations in London.[2] Second, the blacksmith kept the horses shod. The late medieval style of horseshoe had an angular inner profile and square nail holes that tapered inwards from the profile of the shoe. They usually had three or four holes on each side, with the maker's stamp on the tapering heals.[3] Third, medical care was administered whenever necessary. The stable had an allowance of £10 a year for 'Medusons and drinks' for horses which was supplemented as necessary.[4] On 22 March 1531 £8 18*s* was paid to Hannibal Zinzano for 'drynkes and other medicynes for the kinges horses', and in 1532 one Burdet received £3 6*s* 8*d* for putting the king's horses out to grass and for medicine.[5] Fourth, the officers of the stable were expected to provide the king with horses. This could be by purchase, as illustrated by those acquired in 1546–47 by Gilbert Compert and Richard Gibson: £5 for a black grey gelding bought at Uxbridge Fair to serve as a bottle horse, £5 for a white grey gelding for Princess Mary, delivered to Mr Hungate, £5 for a white ambling gelding for the king's saddle and 10*s* for Gibson's expenses.[6] Henry also bred horses. In 1547, the inventory of the late king's goods listed the horses at four royal studs: two in England at Warwick and Malmesbury, two in Wales, at 'Eskermayne' and an unspecified location.[7]

According to the Eltham Ordinances, some of the stable staff received money to cover the costs of their livery coats. This explains why livery coats for them do not feature in the great wardrobe accounts.[8] Three different types of coat were allowed and these were valued at 17*s* 4*d*, 15*s* and 10*s*. They were allocated as follows: coats of 17*s* 4*d* to the yeoman of the stirrup, three surveyors of the stable, one yeoman purveyor, the yeoman of the mules, the yeoman bit maker, one yeoman, the yeoman of the close car of the robes and a packman; coats of 15*s* to five grooms of the stirrup, one courser man, the groom of the close car of the robes and the page of the close carriage; and coats of 10*s* to a groom ferriour. The following did not receive livery: three surveyors of the stable, three yeomen garnitors, two yeomen ferrors, 28 courser men, keepers of the barbery horses, stallions, mules, hobbies and geldings, six sumpter men, one bessage man, two groom ferrors, 13 keepers of the carriage mules and ten footmen. Henry VIII made charitable provision for elderly members of the stable's staff. On 1 April 1515 he gave 100*s* to William

Table 16.1: *Expenditure on the stable and the royal hunts*

Year	The stable	The buckhounds	The leash	The toils
1510–11	£465 2s 6d	£15 16s 7d	£30 16s 8d	~
1516–17	£336 2s 10½d	£47 12s 4d	£51 6s 2d	£18
1517–18	£504 13s 7d	£42 13s 9d	£40 2s 5d	~
1521–22	£305 9s 10d	£40 19s 6½d	£42 9s 8d	~
1523–25	£134 15s 5½d	£40 11s 0d	£42 1s 8d	~
1526–27	~	£19 4s 11d	£31 15s 0d	~
1527–28	£593 7s 3d	£30 15s 7d	£42 11s 4d	~
1530–31	~	£116 8s 6d	£18 14s 8d	£2 8s
1531–32	£942 18s 7d	£115 18s 7d	£66 9s 4d	£2 10s 8d
1533–34	£651 17s 2d	£75 19s 3d	£57 7s 4d	£26 3s 3d
1535–36	£769 8s 8½d	£92 17s 4d	£42 13s 4d	£70 16s 11½d
1537–38	£931 2s 4d	£76 15s 0d	£42 13s 4d	£2 3s 4d
1538–39	£850 7s 3½d	£76 15s	£42 13s 4d	£2 3s 4d
1543–45	~	£65 2¼d	£51 19s 4d	~

Kebet, late sumpterman, 'fallen into poverty and decay', and a year later a further £4.[9]

Some provision was also made for the stable staff via the privy purse. A number of the payments relate to clothing for the boys of the stable who seem to have a range of clothes on a sporadic basis. On 29 December 1529 £3 10s 11*d* was 'paied to Ogull for shertes Cappes, hosen pointes and shoes for the boyes of the stable'.[10] Other payments included 'a paire of quarterd hosen for the boye of the stabull' costing 9*s*, three nightcaps for the boys, and shoes and boots and coats for the riding boys of the stable, provided by John Scot costing £3 5*s* and delivered to the master of the horse.[11] In October 1532 eight pairs of hose were provided for three running boys with the king's geldings at 3*s* 4*d* a pair and shoes costing 14*s*.[12] In the following month, Lancelot and Leonard, two of the riding boys, received coats and doublets costing £3 19*s* 4*d*.[13] Some of the clothing provided for the officers of the stable was delivered to the master of the horse. On 23 December 1530 he received £3 14*s* 'for Cotes doubelettes for the Ryding boyes and for making and lynyng of the same'.[14] On 31 December 1546 Sir Anthony Browne signed a bill submitted by Alexander asking allowance for £6 9*s* for clothes, shoes for Robert Gounbe of the stable and for board wages for 35 weeks at 2*s* 4*d* a week.[15] The list of clothes consisted of 15*s* for a coat, cloth, lining, making and embroidery, 8*s* for two doublets of fustian including lining and making, 8*s* for two pairs of hose, 4*s* for two caps, 4*s* 8*d* for two shirts, 2*s* 4*d* for a pair of boots and 5*s* 4*d* for eight pairs of shoes. For three months from 1 July 1546 Anthony Vannabrowke, one of the king's boys with the stable, was allowed 43*s* 2*d* for 13 weeks' board, four pairs of shoes, repairs to his shoes and washing his clothes.[16] For the next three months, the bill for him rose to £2 17*s* 6*d*, the increase largely explicable on account of items bought against winter: a cap, a frieze coat and a pair of winter boots.[17]

A small amount of provision was made for the officers via the great wardrobe. Three such warrants are known. John de Naples, keeper of 'our little jennet', received a gown of violet furred with black lamb, a doublet of bridges satin, a coat of tawny medley lined with yellow cotton, two shirts, two pairs of tawny hose, a hat and cap.[18] The other two provided the more standard issue of a gown, jacket and doublet, on a par with what was issued to the officers of the privy chamber. On 31 December 1527 Hannibal, the king's blacksmith, and five others (who might have been from the stable), were given gowns of black cloth guarded with black velvet, jackets of black camlet, doublets of black velvet.[19] Nearly five years later, on 15 September 1532, the king issued a warrant to Robert Acton, saddler, Alexander Rider and John Owensted, surveyor of the stable, the first two of whom received 10 yards (9.1 m) of damask for a gown guarded with 3 yards (2.7 m) of velvet), while the third got 14 yards (12.8 m) of damask for a gown, guarded with velvet, and furred with black budge, 10 yards (9.1 m) of velvet for a jacket and 3 yards (2.7 m) for a doublet.[20] The main provision for the stable from the great wardrobe was in the form of saddles, harness, horse blankets and other items for the care of the horses.

The master of the horse was one of the three leading offices within the household, and the most important when the king was out of doors.[21] It was also a ceremonial role. Sir Thomas Brandon, as master of the horse to Henry VII, officiated at his funeral in 1509: 'Then followed Sir Thomas Brandon, Master of the Horse, leading a courser trapped with black velvet embroidered with the arms of England.'[22] Sir Anthony Browne, appointed in 1538, was to have stuff from Henry VIII's stable and the harness used at the king's funeral (Fig. 16.1).[23] Sir Francis Knollys, who had been master of the horse to Prince Edward, but did not continue to serve the new king in this role, received 'all the furniture of the stable apperteigning to his charge at that tyme within charge of thequirye'.[24]

In general, the warrants granted to the master of the horse were to provide saddles and harness for the horses rather than livery for himself.[25] On 23 February 1510 Thomas Knyvet received 20 horse houses of green and white cloth lined with canvas, linen for bags and dusting cloths for the king's horses, as well as for his own four horses.[26] On 29 June 1532 the master of the horse received money in full payment of a bill of £26 11*s* for horses and saddles.[27] On 8 July 1533, a mail saddle and harness covered with blue velvet, three saddles covered white velvet, six pad saddles covered with Spanish leather and four saddles covered with black velvet were delivered to Nicholas Carew or George Lovekyn.[28] Under a warrant dated 11 March 1539, Robert Acton received stuff provided at the instigation of Carew, costing £89 9*s* 9*d*. On 21 September 1545 Sir Anthony Browne signed a warrant for saddles and necessaries for the stable, and another for saddles and other stuff 'for your geldings and the prince's geldings'.[29] Early in 1546 he signed a saddler's bill headed 'Mr Gates' bill' for the previous 26 April to 3 November 1545, totalling £6 12*s* 7*d*.[30]

The king's ape

In the closing years of his reign Henry VIII had a pet ape. This is perhaps the animal depicted on the shoulder of Will Somer in the Tudor family portrait of Henry VIII with his children and the dead Jane Seymour (Fig. 16.2). In this the ape wears a

16.1 *Sir Anthony Browne, unknown artist,* c. *1550. National Portrait Gallery, London (NPG 5186)*

red hooded gown. The king's own warrant dated 27 March 1544 records the manufacture of four gowns for the ape of red and green striped satin, lined with buckram costing 4*s*.[31] In the following a year another four coats were made for him from Spanish leather, three red and one blue, welted with passamayne lace.[32]

The king's hunts

Henry was a very enthusiastic huntsman. In 1520 Richard Pace described how the king rose 'daily, except on holy days, at 4 or 5 o'clock, and hunts till 9 or 10 at night. He spares no pains to convert the sport of hunting into a martyrdom'.[33] It was an enthusiasm that he shared with much of the European élite. In March 1523 Sir Thomas Boleyn and Richard Sampson reported from Valladolid that Charles V was 'very assiduous in deliberating with his council, except one day in each week, when he hawks or hunts'.[34] It was also a subject that had been written about by other enthusiasts. Gaston III, count of Foix, known as Gaston Phoebus, wrote his *Livre de Chasse* between 1387–89. In the period 1406–13, Edward, duke of York, translated and extended Phoebus's work as *The Master of the Game*. So it is not surprising that the Eltham Ordinances that 'whensoever the King's grace hath gone further in walking, hunting, hawking, or other disportes, the most parte of the noblemen and gentlemen of the court have used to passe with his grace, by reason whereof, not onely the court hath been left disgarnished, but also the King's said disports lett, hindered and impeached'.[35]

Henry VIII's interest in the sport is indicated by the sheer quantity of hunting paraphernalia he owned. In 1521 the wardrobe of the robes included two of his hunting trophies: 'a great tuske of a bore in a case of crimosyn veluete' [B387] and 'a Roobuckes hed in a case of crimosyn veluete' [B388].[36] While some of the items were stored in boxes, others were on open display, such as the 'Cx hawkes hoodes embrawdered hanging vppon the wall' of the closet next to the privy chamber at Greenwich (9494).[37] He had a bed specially made, which was described in the warrant ordering it dated 6 July 1526, as 'a bed for hunting for the use of the king'. The great wardrobe provided 25 yards (22.8 m) of crimson gold baudekin damask for the testor, celure and counterpoint costing £57 10*s*, and

16.2 *Detail of a male servant with a monkey on his shoulder, from* The Family of Henry VIII, *unknown artist, c. 1545. The monkey is dressed in a coat and cap, of the type listed in the great wardrobe accounts. RCIN 405796 OM 43. The Royal Collection © 2004, Her Majesty the Queen Elizabeth II*

8½ yards (7.7 m) of green baudekin with flowers for the same valued at £14 3*s* 4*d*.[38] It had matching curtains made from 10 yards (9.1 m) of red and 12¾ yards (11.6 m) of green sarsenet. The king's goldsmith, Cornelius Hayes, made and gilded four pommels decorated with the arms of England, roses and cyphers for £16 4*s* 9*d*. The bed could be dismantled, and to transport its components one cloth-sack and two coffers were provided. The total cost for this bed came to £133 18*s* 9½*d*.

The royal hunting parks were kept stocked with deer. The long-established royal parks at Clarendon, Windsor and Woodstock were supplemented by the creation of new parks at Westminster in 1536 and Hampton Court in 1539.[39] A number of the lesser royal houses built by the king were intended primarily as bases for hunting with hounds, often described at the time as hunts and with falcons. The three main types of sight hound used at this period were the greyhound, the alaunt and the mastiff, while the scent hound was referred to as the running hound, rache or *chien courant*. Three main groups of hounds were maintained by the king: hart hounds, otter hounds and buck hounds. Of the men who cared for these dogs, only the officers of the buck hounds received regular issues of livery from the great wardrobe. Like the stable, the hunts were funded through the exchequer. In addition to the hounds and their carers, the exchequer also footed the bill for the falcons with the falconers, bowmen expert with longbows and crossbows, and the men of 'the toils', that is specialists in creating traps or driving animals into the path of the king, to be slaughtered by him and his companions.

Many of the illustrations in Gaston Phebus's *Livre de Chasse* show the huntsmen dressed in green, grey or a combination of the two, indicating that these colours were considered suitable for hunting livery.[40] However, John I of Portugal believed that the cut and type of clothing were more important than the colour. The gown or coat should not come to below the knee and the sleeves should be fitted, either from the elbow to wrist or for the whole length, 'provided this does not conflict too grossly with fashion'.[41] He also considered boots to be obligatory for hunt staff.

THE BUCKHOUNDS

The general staffing of the hunt can be gauged from the quantities of livery issued. A change in the hunting staff took place in about 1536. Before that date there were two yeomen of the buckhounds, assisted by four or five grooms. On 23 November 1513, Edward Lyne and Thomas Borne were given tawny broad cloth for a gown furred with black lamb, camlet for a doublet, three pairs of hose, Holland for three shirts, bonnets, hats and shoes.[42] The grooms also received livery twice a year. The basic order consisted of a gown, doublet, hose, shirts, shoes and bonnets (Figs 16.3 and 16.4). In the winter warrant, the gown (either of motley or broad cloth) was quite often furred with lamb, while the summer gown was not.

The changes put in place late in 1535 or 1536 resulted in a staff of two sergeants, two yeomen prickers and five grooms. The changes were completed by the issue of a warrant dormant dated 23 May 1536 for livery to be delivered at Christmas and at Pentecost. In the final year of the reign, livery was also provided for two pages. For their winter wardrobe, the sergeants received camlet coats lined with cotton, two doublets, one of tawny satin and the other of fustian, linen shirts and bonnets. In the summer the order remained the same, except for their coats being made from green broad cloth. The yeomen received a similar allocation, except their winter coats were made from russet cloth, while those for summer were cut from kendal. The grooms received the same as the yeomen, but their coats contained 5 (4.5 m) rather than 6 yards (5.4 m) of cloth, and they also were provided with three pairs of hose and five pairs of double-soled shoes each (Fig. 16.5).[43] The office also had two pages, for whom the earliest extant pair of warrants date from 3 September 1535 and 20 January 1536. Ralph Mountjoy and Owen Doddesworth received a similar livery to the yeomen

16.3 *Knitted, felted and fulled cap for a child or young man worked in stocking stitch using 2-ply yarn. Worship Street, London, 5008. Museum of London*

16.4 *Man's knitted cap with a brim and a silk ribbon chin strap. Worship Street, London, A26566. Museum of London*

16.5 *Two adult leather square-toed Tudor shoes with slashed decoration,* c. *1550. The officers of the hunts may have worn shoes of this type, and more hardwearing, double-soled versions. RS222. Museum of London*

and grooms, but with no hose, two bonnets and seven pairs of double-soled shoes.[44]

Some additional costs for the buckhounds were covered by the king's privy purse. In June 1530 Ralph Mundy received two pairs of hose, a leather jerkin and a doublet of white fustian costing 14*s*.[45] In the following June the king paid for a pair of hose for Ralph costing 3*s* 5*d*.[46] Livery coats costing £3 7*s* 6*d* were provided for Walter Doddesworth, Ralph Mundy and Humphrey Raynesford in December 1531.[47] A month earlier, Mundy had received 15*s* for 'bringing of whelpes to the kinges grace'.[48] The king showed his closeness to his huntsmen when in June 1531 he paid 16*s* for the burial of William Doddesworth.[49]

The master of the buckhounds directed the staff of the office. In 1516, when the office of master was not liveried, the appointment was enjoyed by Sir Edward Neville and he received a payment of £30 on 21 September.[50] In 1528, George Boleyn was appointed as master with a salary of £33 6*s* 8*d*, with the onus of the work undertaken by the sergeants who received 9*s* a month. In June 1529 Boleyn, received 60*s* 'for finding the hounds meat'.[51] In January 1519, Thomas Borne, yeoman of the buckhounds, was paid at a rate of £2 13*s* 4*d* (4 marks) a year.[52]

The hounds were provided with collars, leashes or liams, and possibly coats, certainly for those hounds given as gifts. On 5 November 1545 Bishop Gardiner announced his intention to Paget to give the regent of the Netherlands Henry's gift of hounds and greyhounds, 'which will be a gorgeous matter when their colours be on, which be very gay'.[53] In addition to the regular issues of liams, leashes and collars made to the officers of the hunts with their grants of livery, further purchases were made during the king's progress. These were listed in the accounts according to the purchaser, location and date. Between 17 June and 30 September 1546 Wheeler made seven purchases of collars, liams and couples costing 39*s* 10*d*.[54]

The hounds were transported by cart from one hunting place to another. On 22 September 1510 a cart for the hounds was bought from Thomas Pole of Stratford at Bow for 61*s*.[55] Sometimes the cart was hired, as the accounts of the privy purse reveal. In September 1531 a cart was hired for 2*s* 6*d* to carry the hounds 15 miles from Grafton to Ampthill; in October another cart took the hounds from Ampthill to Waltham at a cost of 5*s* and also from Ampthill to Knebsworth (5*s*).[56] In addition to the carts, linen canvas covers were provided in order to keep the hounds protected from the elements during the journey. The hounds also had collars and other equipment wherever they went. On 26 June 1510 a cart cover and other stuff was delivered to Thomas Carnyval and William Royte.[57]

THE LEASH

The leash was the second of the king's hunts and unlike the buckhounds its staffing was consistent throughout the reign. Few specific details are recorded about their duties. However, there are no payments for transporting their greyhounds, indicating that the leash did not follow the king on his progresses in the way that the buckhounds did. On 21 July 1510, John Colinson, groom of the leash, received 40s for kennels, leashes, chains and collars for greyhounds.[58] The office was staffed by a yeoman, groom and four pages, or children of the leash, all of whom received livery. Each of these received their livery on separate warrants, with the yeoman and groom included on a warrant with the yeoman and groom of the bows. On 28 June 1514 William Harwood, yeoman, and John Colinson, groom, received a coat of motley made from 8 yards (7.3 m) of cloth and a number of collars and leashes.[59] On 23 April 1513, Richard Dunmont, Richard Simpson, John Singleton and John Williams, the children of the leash, received a coat of motley, a camlet doublet, three shirts, three pairs of hose, along with double-soled shoes, bonnets, collars and leashes.[60]

Generally the staff received their livery twice a year, once between October to November and then again between April and May. They received a full set of clothing, including shirts, hats, bonnets, shoes, as well as outer garments, also collars and leashes and two doublets, usually one of camlet and one of fustian. In November 1510 the colour was given as tawny, and in November 1517, black; in March 1517 and May 1528 they received three pairs of hose of green kersey. They were given two gowns, often of motley or broad cloth and generally furred with black Irish lamb, or a gown and a coat, with the latter made from motley and once of red broad cloth embroidered with the king's initials. They also received three shirts decorated with openwork on the collar, and double-soled shoes. In May 1538 the pages were John Barwick, Richard Bolton, William Hammond and Hugo Lee. In January 1546 a warrant dormant was issued to Thomas Moyle, yeoman of the leash, for yearly apparel as previously enjoyed by John Willesdon.[61]

THE TOILS

The office of the toils maintained and deployed the pieces of canvas and nets that were positioned to direct the game being hunted. The office came under a master whose staff included keepers and setters. In March 1519 Francis Bryan, master, received half-year wages of £33 6*s* 8*d*.[62] Two months later he got £20 for repairing the toils.[63] In 1514 Thomas Morris and Nicholas Harris, the toil keepers, were recipients of 16*s* a month.[64] In December 1520 the toil setters, Charles Waleston and William Nicholson, had wages of 32*s*.[65] There are only a handful of references to livery being issued to the officers of the toils. In the 1530s Hector Pirton and William Turner, grooms of the toils, were given red livery coats of broad cloth, lined with cotton or frieze and embroidered with the king's initials.[66]

The toils were a drain on time and money. On 4 April 1512 Simon Balake was given £16 4*s* 6*d* to pay the wages of the persons who had been employed to mend the toils.[67] On 9 July 1515 Wistan Brown was appointed as the keeper of the 'great carol' for the king's hunting called the toils or the 'pale of canvas' which was to be repaired at the king's cost.[68] Repairs to the toils were also undertaken within the great wardrobe. On 27 February 1517 Richard Cokkes supplied canvas costing £18.[69] In 1519 large-scale repairs were made to the toils. The numerous tailors and 17 cordwainers used 1,531 fathoms of net at 4*d* the fathom. Payments totalling £158 10*s* 4*d* were made to John Butler, Richard Gibson and William Guisnam.[70]

The entry on 4 August 1536 for repairs totalling £66 4*s* 11½*d* provides a good insight into the range of people and materials required: wages of tailors at 6*d* a day coming to £11 14*s* 3d, 726 ells (497.8 m) of canvas bought from William Lock for £18 3*s*, with a further 61½ ells (42.1 m) canvas from the great wardrobe stores, thread at 104*s* 2½*d*, black wax 7*s* 4*d*, wages of the net makers 46*s*, while William Shrief, net maker, and supplier of cord, head line and other materials, received £20 9*s* 8*d*, the wages of William Green, coffer maker, 31*s*, and leather wombs, thread, wax and nails £6 9*s* 6*d*.[71]

The toils were important throughout Henry's reign. But when the king stopped riding out after hounds after 1536, the toils took on a slightly different role. Once the king started to shoot deer from a standing, that is, a raised, platform, the careful placement of the nets and canvas to direct the deer towards where the king stood became more significant.[72] Catherine Parr rewarded William Alyn, groom of the stable, with 2*s* for riding to Langley and Old Windsor for the keeper of the toils, and then on to Guildford for a buck and a doe for the queen.[73] The toils continued to be used by Edward VI and Mary I, but evidently less was spent in maintaining them. On 6 June 1552 a warrant signed by Sir John Gates and five others noted that 'we be enformed that the kinges maiesties toiles be out of reperacion and therefore meate to be sent vnto and remied the rather for that his highness progresse is at hand wher the same toiles ar to be emploied'.[74] In June 1556 the privy council told Sir Thomas Cawarden that the toils were unfit for the use of Philip of Spain and instructed him to 'overlooke it and therevpon to make report vnto what provision may be made for the repairing of it that is may be dispatched accordingly'.[75]

THE BOWS AND THE LONGBOWS

Not withstanding the increasing use of handguns, bows, longbows and crossbows remained popular for hunting. The officers of the bows continued to be important throughout Henry VIII's reign. According to *The Master of the Game*, the early morning preparations for hunting included 'the maister forstere or parker oweth to shewe hym the kyngges stond, and if the kyng wold stonde with his bowe and where al the remenaunt of the bowes shuld stond and the yemen for the kynges bowe owen to be ther to kepe and make the kynges stondyng and abide ther without noyse to the kyng come'.[76]

Livery was provided for a group of six hunt servants on the same annual warrant: the groom and page of the long bows, the cross bows and the leash.[77] Each of them received a coat made from 8 yards (7.3 m) of motley lined with cotton, a pair of kersey hose and a bonnet. From 6 May 1536 this order was established as a warrant dormant, and at this point the colour of the hose was specified as being green.[78] In 1546 John Abre and Giles Churchill received from William Green a standard for 'the keeping and carrying safe of the king's crossbows benders and for all quivers arrows bolts and a till within the said standard for thread cord wire and all manner of tools to the said office belonging and for the said standard three locks and four keys', along with two great quivers of leather and four leather cases costing £4 10s.[79]

16.6 *Robert Chesman, by Hans Holbein the Younger. It is uncertain whether Robert Chesman was royal falconer, but this portrait indicates how popular falconry was in Tudor England amongst the élite. The Hague, inv. no. 276. Royal Picture Library, Mauritshuis, The Hague*

THE FALCONERS

Henry VIII was an avid falconer. In September 1533 Sir William Kingston remarked that he 'hawks every day with goshawks and other hawks ... lanners, sparhawks and merlins, both afore noon and after'.[80] A number of these birds came from Europe. On 11 June 1526 Christopher de Schidlowijecz, chancellor of Poland, wrote to Henry explaining how he had met the duke of Norfolk's falconer, who was travelling on the Continent to buy hawks. He had previously sent birds to Maximilian, the king of Hungary and the emperor, and now he wished to give the king a great saker with an injured claw 'which does not fly from the fist, but on high and kills not only wild ducks but cranes and other large birds' and four young falcons 'from an approved nest'.[81] The king's personal choice of falcons is indicated by the payments made in his privy purse. On 8 December 1529 Walsh bought a goshawk and two falcons for £3 and seven days later five falcons and a tarsel for £8.[82]

Curiously, no formal provision was made for the king's falconers by the great wardrobe (Fig. 16.6). Their livery was provided by other means. On 26 March 1529 the king paid for coats for ten falconers, nine at a price of 22*s* 6*d* and one for Old Hugh costing 25*s*.[83] In December 1529 the king's privy purse allowed 20*s* to provide livery of an unspecified type to 'Elys, the falconer'.[84] In April 1530 another payment of 20*s* was made for clothing young Ellis 'ayenst Easter', and Ellis the elder received a livery coat.[85] In the previous month, Richard Brandon, falconer, took receipt of a livery coat costing 22*s* 6*d*, and Christopher, falconer, and Haukyn also got livery coats.[86] Later in the year, John Scot was paid 20*s* 4*d* for 'ij Cotes of freze And for ij doubelettes of fustyan And for making and lynyng of the same for henry Elys the fawcon'.[87] Some of the king's falconers specialised in the care of specific types of bird. In 1529 Nicholas Clamp, falconer, was paid for keeping a lanner falcon called Cutte for a year at 1*d* a day.[88] In April 1531 he was sent overseas by the king and he received £10 for his costs, and at the same time he received a new livery coat.[89]

In the summer of 1546 John Harris made a number of purchases on behalf of the king. On 26 August when he was hawking at Hampton Court, Harris paid 2*s* 8*d* for a pair of lines of red silk and gold for the king's hawk, 2*s* 6*d* for a hawking glove and 4*d* for a hawk hood. Later, when Henry was hawking at Windsor, Harris bought a hawking bag (16*d*), a hawking glove embroidered with silk (2*s* 6*d*), a pair of fine lines for the king's hawk (2*s*), a hawk hood (Fig. 16.7) and two pairs of fine bells for the king's hawk (18*d*).[90] The prices indicate that these were functional gloves bought to meet a specific need. A bill from Mark Milliner included a more luxurious hawk glove trimmed with crimson velvet and embroidered with gold and silver, and another trimmed with white velvet, also embroidered with gold and silver, both costing 15*s*. Hawking bags were made to have internal divisions, as in the case of a bag lined with white velvet with three purses set in and the whole trimmed with gold lace.[91] More magnificent items were delivered by Mark Milliner in 1546–47: three saddles 'gilt and engraved' £10 each; a pair of stirrups to match (£3), 11 dozen hawk hoods at 8*d*, 24 dozen hawk bells at 6*d*, 18 hawking bags of silk with gilt rings at 15*s*, one dozen large hawk hoods (7*s* 6*d*) and 28 pairs of hawk bells (28*s*).[92]

The 1547 revels list includes a set of hawking stuff, a group of 'viij shorte garments or cassocks for fawkeners', supplied with hats of red gold sarcenet trimmed with white ribbon and feathers, double-ringed hawking bags and lures (8628). These garments had wide sleeves lined with green satin and ending in cuffs of white and green checked velvet. They were conspicuously elaborate. Even so, the double-ringed bags and lures suggest that these had been functioning hawking outfits, intended for use on a state occasion such as the meeting with Francis I in 1532 or during the reception of the French admiral in 1546.

16.7 *Henry VIII's hawk hood covered in cloth of tissue. Ashmolean Museum, Oxford*

HUNT OFFICERS NOT PROVIDED FOR BY THE GREAT WARDROBE

Not everyone retained by the king for the hunt benefited from issues of clothing from the great wardrobe. The dog keepers, with the exception of the officers of the leash, the spaniel keepers and the keepers of the buckhounds were among the non-beneficiaries.[93] Henry II had enjoyed otter hunting and his Tudor namesakes also kept a pack of otter hounds.[94] In January 1519 Christopher Rochester, page of the chamber, was appointed as the king's otter hunter with 3*d* a day, 4½*d* a day for the king's six dogs, 1½*d* a day for a boy and 9*d* for 12 dogs, as held previously by Sir Edward Bensted.[95] In September 1533 Sir Nicholas Carew was granted the reversion of the office, then held by Rochester, with 3½*d* a day for himself, 4½*d* for keeping six otter hounds, 1½*d* for wages for a page and 9*d* for keeping 12 hounds. These expenses were to be paid by the collectors of the customs of the port of Southampton.[96]

The king's harriers were used to flush the young and small deer, including the fallow deer, out of the way of the hunt, but they could also be used to course hares.[97] The organisation of the office and the number and type of hounds employed are clearly indicated by the grant in April 1543 appointing Sir Anthony Browne as master of the king's harriers. Like his uncle, the earl of Southampton, he held the office with 12*d* a day, and wages for a yeoman barners of 4*d* a day, 3½*d* a day for the keep of a horse, two yeomen barners and two yeomen veautiers at 2*d* a day each, two lads at 1¼*d* a day each, food costing ½*d* a day for 36 running dogs and nine greyhounds.[98] Other offices in the king's harriers were occasionally mentioned. In November 1520 Richard Bigge, the riding yeoman of the king's harriers, received an annuity of £3 10*d*.[99]

Henry also kept some other dogs for hunting: namely mastiffs, beagles, greyhounds and spaniels. Prized for their strength and ferocity, if not for their appearance, mastiffs took their place in the hunts. In January 1532 William Ford was paid £10 17*s* 10*d* for collars and muzzles for the king's mastiffs.[100] Beagles and greyhounds were used for hare coursing, depending on whether the rest of the field followed on foot or not.[101] On 12 April 1531 Robert Shere, keeper of the privy beagles, was given a livery coat.[102] On 25 November 1509 livery was ordered for Richard Dunnoll, Richard Simpson, John Singleton and John Williams, the four keepers of the greyhounds.[103] The livery consisted of a gown of tawny furred with black lamb, a camlet doublet, two pairs of hose, two shirts, two pairs of double-soled shoes, a hat and a French bonnet.

Spaniels were used largely for retrieving the prey caught by hawks, but Henry had at least one for a pet. In 1528 Thomas Comper, keeper of the king's goshawks and three pairs of spaniels, received £5 10*s* 4*d*.[104] In November 1529 a servant of the earl of Westmorland delivered a gift of a spaniel to the king.[105] His spaniel was lost at least twice in May 1530 and February 1531.[106] In August 1546 John Gates received a liam and collar for Greke, the king's spaniel. In the same year Robin, the king's spaniel keeper, received a range of clothes including a canvas doublet (2*s* 8*d*), a doublet and pair of upper stocks made from three doe skins (8*s* 7*d*), a coat of grey frieze (2*s* 8*d*), a pair of satin hose with nether stocks (5*s*) and a doublet and hose made of fustian (8*s*). He also bought hair cloth to rub the spaniels with and several pairs of couples, as well money for transporting the spaniels, such as 8*d* for 'coming with the spaniels from Sion to Guildford and home again'.[107]

As well as keeping parks stocked with deer, Henry also reared pheasants for his hawks to catch and for him to shoot. On 22 December 1532, he paid 40*s* paid to a French priest known as 'the fesaunt breder' for a gown and other items.[108] Ten years later John Fries, taker of pheasants and partridges, was supplied with a livery coat for one year due at Michaelmas last past.[109] Some keepers specialised in the care of hen pheasants, as in the case of 'the hen taker' who on 28 April 1530 was given a livery coat costing 20*s*.[110]

The barge

The royal barge played an important part in the king's travel arrangements while he was in London or visiting his houses along the Thames.[111] It could also be made available for visiting dignitaries, as in the case of Lorenzo Pasquaglio, a Venetian diplomat in England in 1515, who described how he went down to the Thames 'where a large barge had been prepared, precisely like a bucintor covered with the royal colours in cloth, the cabin being hung in arras'.[112] Access to and control over the queen's barge played a significant part in the struggle between Catherine of Aragon and Anne Boleyn.

In September 1529 Thomas Spert was paid £28 for making the king a new barge, and in the following month John Johnson, master of the king's barge, received 40*s* for 24 new oars.[113] An illustrated copy of George Cavendish's *Life of Cardinal Wolsey* included a sketch of 'My lorde goes by water to grenewiche'. The image depicted the cardinal being transported down the Thames in his barge with a textile awning.[114] On 5 November 1514 two tilts, one for the barge and one for the boat, were delivered to John Thurston, master of the barge.[115] New green and white cloth covers were ordered for the king's two barges on 13 April 1522.[116] Not all of the covers were made from just textile. In March 1518 a new cover was made for the king's boat from 38 skins of 'portingal' leather and two pieces of tick (one green and one white) by his saddler, Nicholas Mayor.[117] In December 1531 Carter, the king's boatman, was paid 20*s* for dressing the king's barge, and 20*s* for cotton for lining the king's boat. William Green delivered a barehide to cover the king's barge, costing £8.[118]

The other textiles associated with the barge were the clothes worn by the watermen. On 22 December 1529 livery for six new watermen was bought at a price of £6.[119] Two years later on 10 December 1531 the king 'paied to xvj of the kinges watermen for ther lyverays to every of them xxij*s* vj*d*', costing £18.[120] The number of men needed to row the barge depended on who was travelling and whether the barge was going with or against the tide. John Johnson, master of the king's barge, received 17*s* 4*d* for conducting the king to and from parliament with 24 men on 31 March 1531.[121]

Livery issued 'out of court'

A number of individuals who were considered to be 'out of court' were provided with livery at the king's expense. These included the chancery, the exchequer, the law courts, the great wardrobe and the privy wardrobe and the king's works.

THE GREAT WARDROBE

The great wardrobe was a satellite of the royal household, independent of it but subsidiary to it.[122] It provided employment for a range of individuals including the keeper, auditors, clerk, yeoman tailors, two other clerks, the porter and the rent gatherer. The provision of livery remained almost unchanged throughout our period. In 1480 the livery issued was as follows: 10 yards (9.1 m) of violet in grain and a piece of tartaryn, to Piers Courteys, keeper, 4 yards (3.6 m) of musterdeviliers to William Misterton, clerk, two yeomen tailors, Thomas Stanes, porter, the two clerks and the rent gatherer, and 3 yards (2.7 m) of the same to the two auditors.[123] In 1499 Robert Lytton, keeper of the great wardrobe, received winter livery of 10 yards (9.1 m) of cloth in grain, a hood of 32 wombs of miniver gross, two furs of byse and a fur of made of 120 furs of miniver gross and a further 10 yards (9.1 m) of cloth in grain for his summer livery at a cost of £15. In contrast, Laurence Gower, clerk of the wardrobe, received 5 yards (4.5 m) of dyed cloth in the winter and the summer costing 50*s*.[124] Similar provision was made in Henry VIII's great wardrobe accounts.

THE KING'S WORKS

The office of the king's works was responsible for building new properties for the king, or the structural maintenance and extension of old ones.[125] Its staff also oversaw a regular programme of repairs, most of which were undertaken just prior to his arrival. A small number of specialist craftsmen were employed by the king's works, while larger numbers of craftsmen were employed on a daily or weekly basis to complete the tasks in hand. In September 1519 William Vertue and Henry Redman, masons, were appointed as master masons of the king's works in the Tower and elsewhere, with 12*d* a day and a robe like those issued to the esquires of the household.[126]

The prestige enjoyed by works' officers can be seen by the establishment of a warrant dormant on 16 March 1533 for a red livery coat embroidered with the king's initials delivered at Michaelmas to a group of leading craftsmen: Thomas Cune, sergeant plumber, John Molton, the king's master mason, Christopher Diconson, master mason of the king's works at Windsor castle, John Ripley, the king's master joiner, John Russell, master carpenter, and Henry Kumming, the king's builder.[127]

A number of the craftsmen employed by the king also worked for others. James Nedehan began his career as the king's carpenter and in 1532 he was promoted to the clerk and overseer of the king's works at the Tower. In 1532 he worked on Thomas Cromwell's new house at Austin Friars, London.[128] On 17 October 1532 John Williamson wrote to Cromwell to inform him that, 'Your works go well forward. Mr Alwerd, Mr Heretage, Mr Russel, Nedam, Armstrong, Whalley and divers other carpenters and Bricklayers bestow great diligence upon them'.[129] Thomas Alvard was paymaster of the works at Whitehall, Thomas Heritage surveyor of the works there, and James Nedeham surveyor general of the king's works.

The building accounts for the work at Tournai compiled by Arthur Lovekyn, clerk to William Pawne, master of the king's works, ran from 29 March 1517 to 28 March 1518. His accounts included payments for a kendal coat costing 20*s* 'for my master', 20*s* to Nicholas van Haye, mercer of Tournai, for 2 yards (1.8 m) of black velvet to guard a gown of tawny velvet, 20*s* to John Fenn towards the outside of his 'plak' gown, 4*s* 4*d* to John Cawswell, hosier of Tournai, for hose and 2*s* to John Fenn for a cape 'for my master'.[130]

OTHER GOVERNMENT OFFICIALS

The Black Book of Edward IV made provision for the following officers: the lord chancellor of England, none delivered; the great chamberlain, his winter and summer robes, at Christmas and Whitsun, payable out of the counting house at a rate of £10 13*s* 4*d* for both; the chief judge of common pleas received none, but the barons were allowed that 'Though the king geue clothing embrawdid, yet these lordez nor knytes haue none but a speciall sute or warraunt vnder priuy seale directed to the kinges warderober of chaumber'.[131]

At the end of the yearly great wardrobe account there is a block of provision to a leading group of officials, including the treasurer of England (Fig. 16.8), the under-treasurer, the chamberlain of the receipt, the four barons of the chancellery, the clerks of the receipt, the teller of the receipt and the auditors of the exchequer. Amongst the others were the officers of the great wardrobe who received livery at Christmas and Whitsun in reward for clothing the king and his household.[132] The orders were standardised and symbolic of their offices. The great wardrobe account for 1543–44 included the following provision:

16.8 *Thomas Howard, third duke of Norfolk, by Hans Holbein the Younger. RCIN 404439 OM 30 WC 59. The Royal Collection © 2004, Her Majesty the Queen Elizabeth II*

> To the duke of Norfolk, treasurer of England, 10 yards (9.1 m) of crimson cloth in grain furred with 300 wombs miniver pure for his winter clothing and 10 yards (9.1 m) of cloth in grain for his summer clothing (£15 7*s* 8*d*).
> To the four barons of the chancellery, Richard Lister, John Smith, Thomas Welsh and Nicholas Luke, 10 yards (9.1 m) of cloth in grain, one hood of 32 wombs miniver pure and a fur of 120 wombs miniver pure each for their winter clothing. and 10 yards (9.1 m)of cloth in grain each for their summer clothing (£74 6*s*)
> To the count of Salop and [blank], two chamberlains of the king's receipt, 10 yards (9.1 m) of cloth in grain, a hood of 32 wombs miniver pure and a fur of 120 wombs miniver pure each for their winter clothing. and 10 yards (9.1 m) of cloth in grain each for their summer clothing (£26 13*s*).
> To Richard Weston, the undertreasurer of England, 6 yards (5.4 m) of cloth of colour and a fur of buse for winter, and 6 yards (5.4 m) of cloth of colour for summer (£4 6*s* 8*d*).
> To Thomas Danyell and John Wodall, clerks of the receipt, 6 yards (5.4 m) of cloth of colour each for winter, and the same for summer (£5 8*s*).
> To Thomas Tamworth and the sub clerk, auditors of the exchequer, winter clothing only of 6 yards (5.4 m) of cloth each and two counting cloths (£6 2*s*).[133]

On 21 April 1517 the treasurer and barons of the exchequer and the surveyors of crown lands received an order. They were required to allow £61 20*d* to John Heron, clerk of the hanaper, for the master of the rolls and 11 other chancery officials for robes for the year starting Michaelmas 1515. In view of the very high cost of woollen cloth, and because they had received no further payment from the king apart from their robes, Heron was to pay whatever additional costs they had incurred as long as this did not exceed £43 a year.[134] In April 1533 Thomas Cromwell was appointed as chancellor of the exchequer 'with the fees, robes and vesture' belonging to the office from the death of the previous office holder, Lord Berners.[135]

In March 1540 Thomas Wriothesley and Sir Ralph Sadler were appointed as the king's principal secretaries. The warrant outlined their privileges which included that 'the principal secretary shall sit in the Upper House of Parliament on one of the Woolsacks, as Wriothesley and Sadler may do the King's service in the Nether House where they now have places'.[136]

Other officials also enjoyed the occasional provision of livery (Fig. 16.9). On 12 July 1509, the accounts of George Kirkham, the keeper or clerk of the hanaper in chancery, included a receipt of 32*s* 8*d* for a single special livery.[137] In 1531 the expenses of chancery included 46*s* 8*d* for summer and winter gowns of the keeper, a winter gown for 13*s* 4*d* for John Judde, underkeeper of the hanaper, the gowns for Thomas Alberd, Spigernel, William Skyte and one Portjoy for 40*s*, a winter robe for John Hill 10*s* and for his shoes 4*s*. Additional costs included six bags for writs, patents and charters costing 3*s*, velvet for a bag for the great seal embroidered with the king's arms, £5 5*s* 8*d* and £4 10*s* 10*d* for green say, cushions and other items stolen from the house of John Hill.[138] Cromwell's accounts on 29 September 1534 included a payment of £42 15*s* for winter and summer robes for the

16.9 *Sir John Godsalve, by Hans Holbein the Younger. Sir John's fur-lined gown and turned-back cap are typical of the style of dress favoured by government officials. RL 12265B P22. The Royal Collection © 2004, Her Majesty the Queen Elizabeth II*

master of the rolls and 11 masters in chancery. He made special allowance for the high cost of the cloth used for the summer and winter robes received by the clerk of the hanaper. Other payments included 12*s* for skins of vellum for the jointure of Anne Boleyn and garnishing, 6*s* for silk and gold to the same, along with two cushions with the king's arms and the garter, 12 yards (10.9 m) of green say to hang behind the lord chancellor's back in chancery and a green cloth to keep the wax warm.[139]

On 12 July 1536 the account of Henry Polsted, receiver of Thomas Cromwell, included money for summer and winter robes and a payment for 12 yards (10.9 m) of broad cloth given yearly by the comptroller of the household.[140] The fees associated with some royal offices were intended to cover the costs of paying junior staff and providing them with clothing. However, these payments were not always sufficient, as indicated by a grant made in August 1536 to John Gostwick, treasurer and general receiver of the court of first fruits and tenths. Gostwick was given an annuity of £200, over his yearly fee of £100, to cover the cost of the diets of himself, his clerks and servants and for robes.[141] In May 1541 Thomas Massey was appointed as the usher of the court of first fruits and tenths during good conduct with fees of 40*s* 7½*d* a year and 10*s* for his livery.[142]

LINKS WITH CITIES: CAPS OF MAINTENANCE

The grant of a cap of maintenance by the English monarch was seen as a symbol of loyal service to him. The cap, often in conjunction with a sword, was granted by the king to the municipal authorities of his cities and towns; in 1388, for example, Richard II granted a cap of maintenance to York.[143] From the closing years of Edward III's reign and 1497, 17 English and Irish cities (including London, Calais, Dublin and Drogheda) were granted this honour, and one feature that linked them all was their mercantile and strategic importance.[144] The sword and cap of maintenance were given to the mayor and corporation of Exeter by Henry VII in 1497 after the unsuccessful siege of the city by Perkin Warbeck (Fig. 16.10) 'to encourage the mayor and citisens to be

16.10 *The Exeter cap of maintenance, 1497. Royal Albert Memorial Museum and Art Gallery. Reproduced by kind permission of Exeter City Council*

16.11 The *Waterford Cap of Maintenance, 1536. By kind permission of Waterford Museum of Treasures*

embroiderer, was paid for embroidering 123 coats of green cloth at 6*s* 8*d* each.[13] Embroidery figured prominently on the guard's livery. In December 1528, the treasurer of the chamber paid £18 4*s* to Mortimer, for embroidering 62 coats of red cloth for the guard with roses and the crown imperial at 5*s* each, and for 5 yards (4.5 m) of crimson satin for the roses at 8*s* the yard and 2 yards (1.8 m) of white bridges satin at 4*s* the yard and 24 ells (16.5 m) of canvas at 5*d* the ell.[14] Early in 1547, William Ibgrave received £57 7*s* 4*d* for embroidering the coats of the guard, the footmen and the messengers.[15] This level of expenditure on embroidery ensured that their attire was splendid, rich and costly. In 1522 Sir Andrew Windsor was paid £300 for 124 coats for the guard.[16] The danger of possible shabbiness was avoided by a regular programme of cleaning and airing. In February 1538 a payment, authorised by the vice-chamberlain, of 6*s* was made to John Piers and John Belson, yeomen of the guard, for themselves and four women 'to brush and a yere for the rich cotes of the Garde'.[17]

The yeomen of the guard accompanied Henry VIII wherever he went. As a result, information about the removal and storage of their clothes features frequently in the accounts of the royal household. In the early years of his reign, the jackets were transported in two standards by cart at a rate of 2*d* per mile. During the spring and early summer of 1510 most of the journeys saw the movement of the jackets between Greenwich, Richmond, Westminster, Windsor and the Tower.[18] Then, between July and October the guard and their jackets went with the king on his summer progress over 262 miles at a cost of £2 6*s* 2*d*.[19] In other years the accounts record less detail, giving just a blanket payment to cover the travel costs, as in the case of a payment of 29*s* 2*d* from October 1514 to October 1515.[20] However, it is clear from this total that the jackets were moved far less in this year than they had been in 1510.

Provision was made for the guard's clothes and weapons. On 13 July 1516 John Champnes of Greenwich received 5*s* 4*d* for the hire of a room for 17 weeks at 4*d* the week and then 8*d* for moving them into his own home.[21] In 1517 and 1518 the guard hired a house in Greenwich from John Amadas at the same rate.[22] A year later the bailiff of Greenwich was paid for houseroom, and John Digby let a room in Windsor for four weeks.[23] When the king went to the Field of Cloth of Gold, Laurence Eglesfeld spent £6 2*s* in taking the jackets from London to Calais and Guisnes and back, and for 12 weeks of house hire in Calais for the jackets, standards, halberds, arrows and bows.[24]

For ceremonial occasions, the guard was armed. In July 1538, 77 sheaves of arrows and bows and three javelins were issued from the Tower 'for the yeomen of the Guard to ride with the King in his progress and for the carriage of it thence to the White Friars in Fleet Street for the King's use by the space of iij days'.[25] In December 1545 arrows, bows, javelins as well as new coats were ordered for the guard.[26] In January 1547, as the king lay dying, the master of the ordinance supplied 130 livery bows, and William Temple, fletcher, was paid £34 3*s* 4*d* for 130 sheaves of arrows.[27]

The band of spears or pensioners

The band of spears was established by Henry VIII at his accession in 1509. He

> ordeined fiftie Gentlemen to be Speres, euery of theim to have an Archer, a Demilaunce, and a Custrell, and whiche bende the Erle of Essex was Lieuetenaunt and sir Jhon Pechie Capitain, who endured but for a while, the apparell and charges so greate, for there were none of theim but they and their Horses were appareled and trapped in Cloth of Golde, Siluer, and Golde Smithes worke and their seruauntes richely appareled also.[28]

Members had to provide their own arms, 'have three greate Horses' and to equip their own attendants. In addition, the band provided a source of participants at court jousts. References of members of the spears receiving clothing are rare. On 30 June 1510, Gyot was given a gown of black velvet and a gown of black satin, both lined with black sarsenet, a doublet of crimson satin guarded with cloth of gold and a doublet of tawny satin guarded with purple tilsent.[29] In the following November, Edward Neville, described as 'one of our speyers', got 18 yards (16.4 m) of black velvet by a warrant.[30] Following the king's return from the Tournai campaign in 1513, the spears were disbanded.

The gentleman pensioners

The establishment of a new royal guard was first mooted in 1537, but it was not instituted for another two years.[31] On 20 December 1538 it was noted that the royal guard were expected 'in their livery coats to wait upon his Grace in his chamber to the great setting forth and honour of his house'. The yeomen of the guard were not always present and to meet new ideas of magnificence a new guard was required 'with one captain, and ... they should wait in his chamber, and where the yeomen bear bills or halberds the gentlemen might bear poleaxes, and go before the King when he goes to mass or evensong'. They were to receive livery gowns of silk twice a year and the average cost per gentleman would be £50 a year.[32] Where they obtained their clothes has not been established, beyond the fact that the great wardrobe was not the source. It is conceivable that they provided their own clothes.

The membership was initially restricted to 50.[33] Sir Anthony Browne, who was also master of the horse, was appointed as their first captain. Their first public appearance was on 3 January 1540 when they attended the reception of Anne of Cleves at Blackheath. They were dressed in a black velvet coat and doublet and Milan bonnet, and wore a gold chain with the badge of the pensioners on it. It has been suggested that the clothing, medallion and hat badge depicted in the drawing by Holbein of William Parr, marquess of Northampton, are those of the gentlemen pensioners (Fig. 17.1).[34] Northampton joined Browne in the captaincy late in 1541 or early in 1542. While the medallion and hat badge fit with this suggestion, the colours of his garments, that Holbein identifies as *wis felbet* (white velvet), *burpor felbet* (purple velvet) and *wis satin* (white satin), do not.[35]

17.1 *William Parr, first marquess of Northampton, by Hans Holbein the Younger. RCIN 12231P57. The Royal Collection © 2004, Her Majesty the Queen Elizabeth II*

The portrait of one of the gentlemen pensioners, Sir William Palmer, by Gerlack Flicke dating to 1546, does accord with what is otherwise known. Palmer wears a high-necked, black doublet, a black gown trimmed with dark fur and a black bonnet. In his right hand he clasps a poleaxe, while his left rests on his sword hilt.[36]

Royal messengers

The royal messengers delivered the king's personal letters as well as more routine government letters to their recipients.[37] The Black Book of Edward IV recorded that four royal messengers received winter and summer clothing worth 13*s* 4*d* (1 mark) and each man received 'for his chaunces 4*s* 8*d*'.[38] In May 1519 John Hune was appointed one of the four messengers in the exchequer at the rate of 4½*d* a day and a grant of livery as worn by the yeomen of the chamber, and on surrender of his patent in January 1532 Robert King, a king's messenger of the chamber, succeeded him.[39] On a warrant dated 2 June 1539, Robert Smith, messenger, received an embroidered red livery coat made from 3 yards (2.7 m) of wool and 6 yards (5.4 m) of frieze costing 22*s*.[40] Two years later, John Ward and Jasper Punt, messengers, received £3 towards the cost of their liveries. This was a fair sum, covering the cost of the materials and making it up.[41]

The kings of arms, heralds and pursuivants

The Black Book noted that the kings of arms, heralds and pursuivants were to take largess from the jewel house, but were not to receive any wages, fees or clothing, while the four sergeants of arms were given clothing paid for from the profits of diverse counties of England.[42] By 1509 these arrangements had changed. By the accession of Henry VIII there were three kings of arms (Garter, Clarencieux and Norrey), six heralds (Somerset, York, Richmond, Chester, Lancaster and Windsor) and four pursuivants (Rouge Cross, Bluemantle, Rouge Dragon and Portcullis).[43] The offices were hierarchical and there was a clear sense of progression from pursuivant to king of arms. On 17 May 1522 John Joiner, alias Richmond, was appointed as Norrey, king of arms and principal herald of the north, with £20 a year and a livery from the great wardrobe as worn by kings of arms in the time of Edward III.[44] On 5 November 1522 Thomas Byseley, alias Rouge Dragon, was made Bluemantle pursuivant at arms with £10 a year.[45]

One of the traditional functions of the heralds was the declaration of war. In February 1528 Clarencieux herald informed Cardinal Wolsey that he had 'made declaration of war against the Emperor . . . sitting in a great hall in the siege royal, accompanied with all the nobles and gentlemen of his court'. He had returned with the emperor's reply, 'which I have carried in clews of silk wherfore they be evil to read'.[46] The coats that the heralds wore were seen as symbolic of their office and as such gave them a degree of protection, but their distinctive livery could also endanger them. On 19 August 1544 Secretary Paget informed Lord St John how the French had 'shot a piece of ordnance at one of our heralds sent to them in his coat armour, and slew his horse under him'.[47]

Heralds did not invariably wear their coats of arms. On 1 September 1524 Tomasso Hannibal, the papal ambassador, who was the bearer of a gold rose from the pope to the king, landed at Dover. On his journey to London he was met by many dignitaries, including Sir Andrew Windsor, Lord Fitzwater, Lord Roos and 'others of the King's servants, and certain officers of arms without their coats of arms, for it is not usual for them to be worn when the King is not present at such ceremonies'.[48] This could prove dangerous. In January 1543 Somerset Herald was murdered on his return from Scotland. According to his killers, he was 'withowt coitt armore, bagges on his brest or saffe cundithe contrary to ye lawe of armis'.[49]

The heralds orchestrated ceremonial at court. Tournaments were their preserve: they made the announcements, proclaimed the challenges, introduced the combatants and kept score. They also maintained the partition books. For example, on 5 January 1511 the heralds issued articles of the challenge on behalf of the four knights of the queen for tilts to be held at Richmond to celebrate the birth of Prince Henry.[50] In 1520 English heralds proclaimed the jousts to be held at the Field of Cloth of Gold at the courts of Zeeland, Holland and France, while the French heralds performed the same task in Artois and Flanders, as well as Greenwich.[51] Heralds managed revels in much the same way.

The heralds ensured that etiquette was maintained. They were fastidious about coats of arms being displayed at any time. They oversaw coronations, weddings and funerals. At the burial of Prince Arthur, his own pursuivant 'sore weeping' threw his tabard into the prince's grave, symbolic of his own grief as well as his loss of office.[52] In contrast, at Henry VII's funeral, the heralds all threw down their tabards with the king's arms and then put on coats with his son's arms and proclaimed Henry VIII. On 2 March 1511 the heralds presented 'A bill of peticion to ye Kinge touching the rights, annuities and largesses appertaineing of auntient custome to the Officers of Armes after the usage of England' including their rights at a tourney, preparation for the creation of a prince, the creation of estates for the degree of an earl and upwards.[53] The same day John Heron, treasurer of the chamber, received a warrant to pay Garter, king of arms and the others £40 for their rights and duties at the tournament.[54] On 29 September 1514 Sir John Dauntsey gave £8 to Garter king of arms, for his expenses at 8*s* a day for 20 days when attending the marriage of Princess Mary to Louis XII of France.[55] In 1534 the executors of Thomas Benout, Clarencieux king of arms, petitioned Thomas Cromwell for satisfaction of fees amounting to £14 6*s* 8*d* from the burial of Sir Robert Johns, promised by Sir John Alen and Sir John Mylborne but still unsettled: for Clarencieux's mourning livery, 5 yards (4.5 m) of black cloth or 33*s* 4*d* and 40*s* for his pains; for the herald at arms 5 yards (4.5 m) of black cloth or 33*s* 4*d* and 20*s* for his pains; for black cloth to set round the hearse 40*s*; for the hatchments to be set on John's tomb 40*s*, for amending and reforming John's arms and crest £4.[56]

According to Jean Coutois, Sicily herald in the 1430s, the heralds' tabards were long in the body and short in the sleeves, while those of the pursuivants, the junior heralds, were the reverse, with long sleeves and short in the body. The tabards were the same but worn in a different orientation and, when pursuivants were promoted to heralds, they rotated their tabards through 90 degrees to achieve short sleeves and a longer section at the front and back.[57] By the mid fifteenth century the herald's tabard had developed into the form that can be seen in the Westminster tournament roll of 1511: a loose tabard usually split at the sides with open sleeves. The front, back and sleeves of the tabard would be decorated with coats of arms.

New livery was ordered for the heralds from the great wardrobe when they were sent on diplomatic missions or when attending events such as coronations and royal funerals. All the kings of arms at Anne Boleyn's coronation received embroidered coats.[58] A dearth of diplomatic tasks and certain court rituals sometimes resulted in garments having to last for far longer than perhaps envisaged. In May 1532 Garter herald asked for a coat of arms 'considering that these 17 years passed the said garter hath had no new coat of our said arms'.[59] They also received perquisites. In 1520 Henry gave 'to Clarenceaux a Cote of purpull veluete opon veluete pirled frenged with Ermyns' [A244]. In June 1541 Henry Ree, pursuivant, wrote to the king from Scotland where he had taken secret letters to Margaret. She 'sent secret word that she durst not speak with him and he sent her the letters by her servant; and received letters from her again and a black velvet doublet as reward'.[60]

The coats of arms could be produced by painting and stamping the royal arms and badges onto the cloth. For Henry VII's coronation, the king's painter decorated 'xij cotes of armes for herauldes, beten and wrought in oyle colers with fyne gold' at a cost of 30*s* each.[61] In May 1541 a payment of £39 6*s* 8*d* made to Andrew Wright, the king's sergeant painter, for 'painting of certain coats of arms for the heralds at arms'.[62] On occasion they were embroidered, as indicated by Garter receiving a tabard with embroidered arms for Henry VII's funeral and the delivery made in August 1518 'to mortemer the brawderer ij yerdes of tawny cloth of gold opon saten for thenbraudryng of a Cote armor for one of tharoldes at armes' [A397].[63] The distinctions of rank were made by the choice of fabric used: the tabards of the kings of arms were made from velvet, those for the heralds were made from damask and those for the pursuivants were made from sarsenet.[64] The coats were often decorated with fringe, as indicated by the warrants dated 8 May 1512 which ordered a coat with the king's arms of damask beaten with fine gold and 'enoyled', fringed with red and blue silk for Somerset Herald.[65]

Military roles for Henry VIII's nobility

The nobility was expected to lead the king's forces on land and sea in times of war and social unrest. At such time noblemen represented the king and they were equipped accordingly. In March 1511 Lord Darcy was provided with two horse cloths, one of green velvet and white cotton with green silk tassels and the other of red and yellow, costing 43*s* 7*d*.[66] It seems very likely that these horse cloths were provided for Darcy's expedition to aid Ferdinand of Aragon against the French. On 12 April 1514 William Bull, Thomas Cappe, Thomas Kirtewon, Thomas Last and William Newman, trumpeters with 'our cousin the earl of Surrey, admiral', were given a coat of white and green camlet containing 4½ yards (4.1 m) of each colour of fabric and lined with yellow cotton and a banner cloth with the king's arms 'beaten with gold and in oil'.[67]

Not all royal armies were sent abroad. On 15 October 1536, at the time of the Northern rebellion, the earl of Surrey informed his father, the duke of Norfolk, that 'The gentlemen have doubled and trebled the numbers limited to them by the king's letters, so that the livery you provided was too little by 1,500 coats for which I have sent unto Suffolk'.[68] Norfolk passed this information on to Henry VIII: 'those who have brought men ask for money for coats; it is said that 8*d* a day is not enough for a man and horse now that horses are on hard feed.'[69] About the same time, the earl of Shrewsbury raised men to help restore order in Lincolnshire and Yorkshire. Payments made by his paymaster Anthony Neville included 3,917 coats at 2*s* 6*d* each, with a total cost of £498 7*s* 6*d*.[70]

Between 1540 and 1545, Suffolk acted as the king's lieutenant. He had wide-ranging military responsibility including oversight of the northern border, the defence of southern England and the expedition to Boulogne (Fig. 17.2). He also took a leading role on the king's council, advising on military issues.[71] The king summed up Suffolk's standing when he described him as 'o[ur] chief minister in the wynnyng of Bulleyn', which had increased the 'sp[ec]iall love, confidence and good affection w[hich] we beare to you before others'.[72]

Acting as a royal commander could prove fatal. In April 1513 Sir Edward Howard engaged the captain of the French galleys, Prégent de Bidoux. When Howard realised that the fight could only end in disaster, he threw the gold whistle which was the symbol of his office overboard. He was killed and his body stripped. His clothes were sent to Claude, the French king's daughter, while his gold chain was given to her mother.[73] Prégent de Bidoux noted in his letter dated 28 April that 'As the Queen gave him a whistle he sends her the Admiral's'.

The rank and file of the king's military forces

In the absence of a standing army, the royal household continued to provide the backbone for armed forces whenever needed, even though by the end of Henry VIII's reign this function had been overstretched and was breaking down, with the result that alternative means were being investigated. In times of need, groups of soldiers were mustered to fight for the king, either abroad or at home (Fig. 17.3). Some of the forces assembled were sizeable. In August 1523 the list of diets and wages of the army beyond the sea under the duke of Suffolk included 100*s* a day for the duke, 12*d* a day for his standard bearer, 4*s* for a herald, 2*s* each for two pursuivants and 16*d* a

17.2 Charles Brandon, first duke of ~~Surrey~~ Suffolk, *unknown artist,* c. 1545. *National Portrait Gallery, London (NPG 516)*

17.3 *Detail showing the soldiers in the fort and mariners on board ship in Dover Harbour from* The Embarkation of Henry VIII at Dover, *unknown artist. RCIN 405793, OM 24. The Royal Collection © 2004, Her Majesty the Queen Elizabeth II*

day each for eight trumpeters. The total size of the army amounted to 10,688 men.[74] John Brown, the king's painter, made Suffolk a standard on double sarsenet costing £3, two banners of the king's arms costing £5 6*s* 8*d*, ten gittons at 13*s* 4*d* each, 50 escutchions on paper and two dozen on buckram, 40 flags and pencils for the duke's baggage and a coat of arms for his herald, costing in all £24.[75] The account of Suffolk's campaign in France included a reference to how 'Monsieur Lyne won Bowgard by a train, and put out the French in their doublets and hose'.[76]

Brigandines were also provided for some of the troops. In January 1547 there were 19 pairs of brigandines (5062) in the armoury at Calais and 24 'Mayhurtes for brigandynes', which may have been shoulder pads (5069). The items in the armoury at Westminster were described more fully: 210 'Briggendines couered with blacke fustian and white lynnen Clothe called Millen Cootes' (8198). There were another 50 jacks at Dover (4154), four in the wardrobe at St John's Clerkenwell (13862) and 'one Northerne Jacke couered with lynnen' at Westminster (8200).

FLAGS AND BANNERS

During the hostilities the great wardrobe provided flags and banners for the king's armies and his ships. The warrants supplied to the great wardrobe indicate that new banners were made for each major campaign or engagement, although these could be supplemented with existing banners. On 2 August 1514 the earl of Surrey was supplied with one new standard and two flags of crimson and white sarsenet with the cross of St George and two flags on double sarsenet painted in oil and gold.[77]

Henry VIII's wars with France and Scotland early in his reign provide copious evidence relating to the provision of banners. A series of eight payments totalling £290 was made to Dominick Cyny for flags and streamers for the king's ships.[78] On 25 and 26 April 1512, 200 'pencelles wrought upon buckram, white and green, and upon every of them a red rose with a crown imperial yellow colour inoyled' that were to be set upon the carriage of 'our treasure of war' were delivered to Sir Henry Willoughby.[79] In the following July, flags were delivered to the marquess of Dorset, lieutenant general of the army in Guyenne.[80] A month later, banners and standards were delivered to the earl of Surrey, 'lieutenant of our army now to be sent Northwards'.[81] In the following year, further large-scale provision of banners was made. On 7 August 1513 John Dauntsey acknowledged a payment of 7*s* 2*d* made to James Glydo, servant of Sir Andrew Windsor, for carrying a hamper with the king's standards, banners and streamers from London to Canterbury.[82] A month later, two standards of the lion crowned imperial according to 'my lord's standard and pattern', two banners of the arms of England, two with those of England and Spain were delivered to Richard Justice, groom of the robes.[83]

In 1544 a set of banners and standards were ordered for the Boulogne campaign which was 'delivered into the hands of the king's majesty'. The religious iconography of some of the banners reflected Henry's religious conservatism in combination with his promotion of St George as the national saint of England and patron of the order of the Garter:

One great banner of crimson and blue satin with the king's arms embroidered richly with cutwork of cloth of gold
Six banners of blue and crimson damask with the king's arms painted in gold and oil
Four banners of the king's arms painted upon double sarsenet in oil and gold
Four banners of the cross of St George of white and crimson sarsenet
One standard of the lion of England with crown imperial upon the king's arms painted upon double sarsenet in oil and gold
Three banners of the Holy Trinity of crimson and blue damask likewise painted
Three banners of the Holy Mary the Virgin of crimson and blue damask likewise painted
One banner of St George of crimson and blue sarsenet likewise painted.[84]

Banners could be pieced to make the design, as in the case of a banner with a cross of St George made from white and crimson sarsenet and then fringed with crimson and white silk fringe.[85] However, the designs were often painted by one of the king's painters working in oil on a silk or linen canvas ground.[86] The range of materials in use can be seen from a payment made on 2 June 1514 for streamers and banners painted by Vincent Volpe for the king's newly built ship the *Henry Grace a Dieu*, costing £112 19*s* 8*d*.[87] William Botry provided cloth for making the streamers and pennants: 11 pieces of red buckram, seven pieces of 'bressell', five pieces of blue buckram, 12 pieces of green buckram and five pieces of black buckram costing in all £20 5*s* 4*d*.[88] Flags and streamers were often trimmed with fringe, as in the case of a streamer supplied for the *Henry Grace a Dieu* that was 51 yards (46.6 m) long and edged with cadow fringe.[89]

While banners were a potent symbol for identifying the king's forces, they were not always provided as promptly as the commanders wished. On 27 March 1546 the earl of Hertford, who was in Calais, desired 'a banner of the King's arms and another of St George, to be had from Mr Sadleyr out of the Great Wardrobe, which the heralds have forgotten to bring'.[90] A month later he had to repeat his request.[91]

CONDUCT COATS

Some of the levies, that is the troops raised, were issued with a conduct coat or jacket to identify their being in the king's service. The coats were usually green and white but the colour was not always specified. Coats were also provided occasionally for men serving in the garrisons at Calais and Berwick and for mariners taken into the king's service.

Occasionally the king provided armour for the troops. On 20 May 1513 Robert Bolt, a London grocer, received £1,040 for 1,300 sets of armour already delivered by him to John Blewberry in the king's armoury.[92] Four days later, Giovanni Cavalcanti, acting on Bolt's behalf, contracted with Edward Guildford, the master of the armoury, to supply 1,700 complete sets of harness for foot soldiers. In the following month, William Jekell, one of the king's commissioners, provided cart horses for the army and 145 jackets for carters costing £43 10*s*.[93]

Henry VIII also employed mercenary companies and the leading mercenaries were given livery to indicate that the whole company was in his service. On 3 July 1513, Thomas Trye and Richard Cotton were issued with a receipt for necessaries bought 'for the retinue of the Almayns', including green and white sarsenet to make a standard.[94] On 19 July further provision was made for this group of soldiers: 13*s* 4*d* each for the 23 drumslades and fifes as a reward, and jackets of green and white damask for the three standard bearers at a cost of 7*s* 6*d* a yard, and taking 12 yards (10.9 m) in all.[95]

France

Livery costs were supplied in large numbers for the king's troops fighting in France. For example, in August 1522, 6,928 coats at 3*s* 4*d* each were supplied for an expedition under the command of the earl of Surrey at a cost of £1,154 13*s* 4*d*. In the following August 1,700 coats costing £840 were provided for the army under the leadership of the duke of Suffolk. A further 6,608 coats were supplied at 3*s* 4*d* and 1,331 coats at 2*s* 4*d*, costing £1,256 12*s* 4*d*. Money was also given to Lord Mountjoy for 214 coats, to Sir Edward Croft for 102 coats, to Sir George Throckmorton for 102 coats, to Sir Thomas Tyrrel for 50 coats, to Sir Thomas Tey for 50 coats, to William Fermor for 20 coats and to John Pye of Oxford for 20 coats all at 3*s* 4*d*; and 'For so many men which were appoynted to have gone over the see for the reenforcing of the seid army and afterward retorned home from diverse places as the were commyng up from London. Wherfor the seid cotes been to be restored to the kynges use iiijxx xiij li' — £1,349 12*s* 4*d*.

The invasion of France in 1544 was planned meticulously.[96] The livery worn by the soldiers gives a clear indication of the composition of the core of the king's army for this campaign and so it is worth citing it in some detail. The men who came directly under the king's control were given a special issue of red and yellow livery. A warrant signed by the stamp authorised Sir Ralph Sadler to provide 'certain coats and stuff for captains, horsemen and footmen' to be supplied by the great wardrobe against the king going to Boulogne.[97] This red and yellow livery gave emphasis to the men of the household as the core of the royal army; it also stressed the importance of the heralds and musicians amongst the king troops. Interestingly, the livery was uniform in that it was cut from standard patterns. The campaign accounts included a large delivery of kerseys to Sir Thomas Cawarden to make these patterns: 15 pieces of red kersey 'for to cut out part of the patrons for the fashion of all the forenamed coats for the foot guard, stand guard, demi lances, javelins and divers others' costing £20 5*s*; 11 yards (10 m) of yellow kersey for the same cause, £14 17*s* and two pieces of blue kersey for the same cause, 54*s*, with a total cost of £37 16*s*.[98]

The king also paid for some items on his own warrant: cassocks for 11 gentlemen of the privy chamber, one part of crimson velvet new making and the other cloth of gold welted with cloth of gold and velvet, lined with sarsenet, cassocks for 'singing pages' in the privy chamber of red cloth guarded with yellow velvet, lined with buckram and cotton and 20 doublets for the same, ten of red damask and ten of yellow satin, the satin doublets slashed and lined with red sarsenet and all lined with fustian and canvas. Will Somer, the king's foot, also received a cassock of red cloth guarded with yellow velvet, pulled out with sarsenet and lined with buckram, six hoods of yellow buckram and two cassocks, part of red cloth and part of yellow bridges satin paned and lined with buckram.[99]

Cloth was used to indicate rank. Decorative techniques such as welting and slashing were also employed. For example, in 1544 the king ordered two cassocks of crimson velvet welted with cloth of gold and lined with buckram on his own warrant for Mr Throckmorton, captain of 100 cavalry and Mr Wentworth, captain of 100 foot.[100] Under this pair, there were 18 petty captains who each received a coat of crimson and yellow velvet guarded with like colour velvet. These coats were slashed and the cuts were welted with taffeta and lined with crimson and yellow sarsenet. They were lined with black buckram. Beneath them, the king allowed for:

18 standard bearers each having a coat of the same type made from yellow velvet and crimson damask;

140 men at arms each having a coat of crimson and yellow damask guarded with a cut guard of crimson and yellow velvet;

110 demi lances, gentlemen each receiving a coat of yellow damask and red kersey full of cuts;

334 demy lances each having a coat of red kersey full of cuts welted with yellow satin and tuffed out with yellow sarsenet;

487 of the stand guard and the foot guard each receiving a coat of red kersey full of cuts welted with yellow satin and tufted out with yellow sarsenet;

403 javelins each having a cassock of red kersey guarded with a cut guard and welted all of satin bridges; to every cassock four yards kersey and 1½ yards satin bridges for the guard and welts;

374 Northern men and demi-hakes each having a cassock of red kersey guarded with a cut guard of yellow satin bridges to every cassock three yards kersey and ⅜ yard satin bridges for the guard;

four grooms of the king's majesty's privy chamber each having a coat of crimson and yellow velvet guarded with crimson and yellow velvet and lined with buckram;

25 officers each receiving a coat of crimson damask guarded with yellow velvet and lined with black buckram;[101]

48 officers each having a coat of red kersey all guarded with yellow satin or yellow kersey from four yards of red kersey for each coat;[102]

11 trumpeters, with the sergeant of the trumpets received a coat made of scarlet and red damask, guarded with yellow velvet, while the ten trumpeters received coats of red broad cloth guarded with yellow velvet;

ten singing children having scarlet kersey for hose;

six drum players [of] crimson and yellow satin for doublets and hose;

two officers of the stable and four mule men — incarnate damask for the coats for the officers of the stable guarded with yellow velvet; incarnate damask for jerkins for mule men, guarded with yellow damask and lined with buckram; crimson velvet for guarding the jerkins and hose;

692 pairs of crosses of crimson velvet and roses of crimson satin cloth of silver and cloth of gold for captains, petty captains, men at arms, standard bearers, demi lances with others;

473 pairs of crosses of crimson velvet and roses of crimson satin and white satin embroidered with spangles of silver and gilt embossed with eight holes to every coat for the king's stand guard and foot guard;

881 pairs of crosses of crimson satin and roses of crimson and white satin and cloth of gold for javelins and northern men, demi hakes and others;

king's at arms, heralds and pursuivants at arms — coats of incarnate double jean velvet guarded with yellow velvet for coats for Garter and Clarenceux kings at arms;

coats of incarnate damask guarded with yellow damask for Windsor and Somerset heralds; a coat of blue damask guarded with incarnate damask for a coat for Richmond herald; a coat of blue damask guarded with yellow damask for a coat for York herald;[103]

coats of red camlet guarded with yellow camlet for Portcullis, Blue Mantle, Risbank, Hammes and Guynes pursuivants at arms; a coat of blue camlet guarded with red camlet for a coat for Rouge Dragon pursuivant; a coat of blue camlet guarded with yellow camlet for a coat for Rouge Cross pursuivant.

A letter sent from the privy council to Thomas Chamberlain on 1 May 1544 about the livery to be worn in the ward that Monsieur Buren would fight in reveals that different sections of the army wore different colours. The colours for Buren's section were red and blue with 'the body of the garment blue and a broad guard of iij fingers' broad red, and one of the sleeves: every man maketh his own colours'.[104] The troops under the command of the duke of Norfolk in the vanguard of the army were equipped as follows:

Furste euery man Sowdyer [is] to haue a Cote of blew clothe After suche fasshyon as all footemens cotes be made here at London / to serve his maiestie in this Jorney / And the same to be guarded with redde clothe / after suche sorte as others be made here And the beste serve to be trymmed after suche sortes as shall please the Cappetaine to deuyse.

Provyded allwaies that no gentelman nor other wore any manner of sylke vpon the garde of his cote / Save oonely vpon his lefte sleves / And that no yomen were any manner of sylke vpon his said cote nor no gentelman nor yoman to were any manner of badge.

Item euery man to provyde A payre of hose for euery of his men the Right hose to be all redde and the lefte to be blew / with oone strype of iij fingers brode of redde vpon the owtesyde of his left legge from the stockes dounewarde.

Item that euery man have an arminge Dowblette of fustyan or canvas.

Item every man to haue a cappe to be made to putte his Sculle or Sallette in after suche fasshyon as I haue deuysed with Sir William Tayllor Capper within Ludgate doth make for me / where you may have as many of them as ye lyste for — viijd the pece.

The king also specified which banners were to be made. In addition, some of the heralds and pursuivants received the traditional coats of arms while others received two coloured liveries on three warrants dated 2 to 9 June 1544:

for Richmond Herald (Gilbert Dethink) 'viij yardes of blew And ij yardes of redde damaske / And to Roug Dragon (Martin Marroffe) purcevant viij yardes of blew / And ij yardes of redde chalett for their lyverys' in the vanguard under the duke of Norfolk

for York Herald (Bartholomew Butler) 'viij yardes of blew And ij yardes of yelowe damaske / And to Rougecrosse (William Flower) purcevant viij yardes of blew / And ij yardes of yelowe chalett for their lyverys' in the vanguard under the duke of Norfolk

to Garter and Clarenceaux kings of arms 8 yards of red and 2 of yellow velvet, to Windsor and Somerset heralds, 8 yards of red and 2 of yellow damask and to Portcullis, Bluemantle, Risebank, Hampnes and Guisnes, 8 yards red and 2 yellow of sarsenet.[105]

Finally, on 24 June 1544 two auditors compiled an account for Sir Francis Lovell for money he had received from Sir Richard Rich, treasurer of the king's wars against France, for horses to draw the king's carts. The account included payments for 399 horses costing £498 13*s* 4*d*, for red and yellow cloth to make 114 coats for the carters at 4*s* each and conduct money for 114 carters at ½*d* a mile from Norwich to Dover (140 miles). Horse meat was provided for seven days at 8*d* the day a horse. With various other expenses included, the total account came to £656 6*s*.[106]

Two examples of textiles survive from the Boulogne campaign and provide further evidence of how pervasive the red and yellow livery was. The suit of armour made for the king's use as commander, known as the Wilton armour, has red and yellow piccadills or textile borders.[107] At the other end of the spectrum, a gun-shield *c.* 1540, from the royal arsenal, has a yellow upholstered pad on the reverse and fragments of red 2/2 twill woollen textile on the proper right of the gun mount over a plain weave hemp textile stuck to the wood under the red top fabric.[108]

Scotland

Relations with Scotland, the kingdom's northern neighbour, were rarely harmonious. Warfare was periodic and a few examples will serve to show the range of provision made for the king's troops. The accounts of Edward Bensted, late treasurer of the king's war northward, record the money spent by the earl of Surrey as commander, for 84 days up to 27 October 1522. The accounts include payments to the earl for 500 green and white coats at 4*s* each, coming to £100.[109] Green and white coats were also provided for Edward Bensted, in his official capacity as treasurer, and Thomas Wharton, as clerk of the wars.[110] Other recipients included William Butler, sergeant of arms, and two soldiers, John Millett, comptroller of the war, and his six soldiers, all at the same price of 4*s*. Sir William Sands' expenses included a payment to 'Guyot Heull for retaining 400 Almayns for six weeks, wages, cloth for coats and houses (hose)'.[111] On 31 May 1524 Lord Dacre acknowledged receipt of some money but he went on to say that he needed a further £3,000 to cover the wages for the garrisons and the jackets to be given them at the command of the king and Wolsey.[112] The accounts for the northern borders declared on the death of the abbot of St Mary's York, covering the ten years up to 31 May 1526, include payment for 1,000 jackets costing 3*s* 4*d* each on 5 September 1522 to the earl of Shrewsbury, as lieutenant in the north.[113]

On 1 May 1541 Henry VIII sent troops north dressed in 'the old fashion with jacks or coats of mail'.[114] Makers of jacks were welcome in England, as indicated by letters of denization given in June 1544 to John and Patrick Howye of Bamborough, jack makers. The letters described them as Scots by birth who had lived in England for 14 years.[115] Conduct coats were simpler to make than jacks but they still took time to prepare. On 30 September 1543 Henry informed the duke of Suffolk that, although he had been told that the making of conduct coats and delivering them to the borders would take 15 days, he thought 12 to 14 was more likely. He added that 'to save expense, they may wear only red crosses, to which they will be easily persuaded if Borderers are told that nothing else is meant but a raid into Scotland, and inland men that they are levied for the defense of the Borders, which the Scots are ready to enter and burn'.[116] The king was not always so stingy. On 13 November 1543 he agreed to Viscount Lisle, warden of the marches against Scotland, being awarded £407 16*s* 8*d* for his own diets, coats and conduct money for himself, five captains, five petty captains and 500 men.[117]

When in March 1544 the earl of Hertford entered Newcastle upon Tyne in procession, he took the opportunity to display his authority and the magnificence of the royal army:

first rode 3,000 Northern horsemen in jacks with spears, then 8 score nobles and gentlemen in coats of black velvet and chains of gold, 3 trumpets and 3 clarions, 3 officers of arms in their coats of arms, a gentleman bearing a naked sword, then the Earl himself in very rich apparel, 3 pages of honour richly clothed, 8 score of his servants in his livery, and last, 5,000 men on foot.[118]

In the following month a series of warrants were issued by the earl of Hertford to pay Sir George Conyers, Lancelot Neville, George Stafford and John Winter for wages and conduct coats for the expedition against Scotland.[119]

Ireland

Disorder, civil unrest and open rebellion in Ireland recurred throughout Henry VIII's reign. In 1520 Sir William Bulmer received £213 6*s* 8*d* for wages, conduct money and coats for 100 light horse sent there from Calais.[120] By 24 September 1520 Kite, archbishop of Armagh, reported to Cardinal Wolsey that peace had been restored. He continued that 18 of the 220 men accompanying the lord lieutenant were dead and 117 had been given licence to return home and only 95 remained. Although he noted that all of the Irish captains were at peace, he warned that 'of a surety, and it pleaseth your grace, the people of this land be variable, subtle and crafty, naturally; in whom is little confidence or trust to be taken, otherwise than for their proper advantages; and be people of fair promises and words and marvellous vainglorious and covetous'.[121]

Further troops were sent in 1563 as the accounts of William Brabason, treasurer of the army in Ireland, record. Payments were made to Edward Aglionby, Thomas Dacre, Laurence Hamerton and Leonard Musgrave for 300 coats at 3*s* 4*d* each.[122] About the same time, the earl of Derby wrote to Thomas Cromwell, 'In times past ever man has had an allowance of 4s for a jacket in time of war and this time they have paid for them at their own costs'.[123] Derby's remarks seem to have been noticed. On 9 July 1540 John Gostwick informed the king that he had given £200 to William White for coats, wages and conduct money for 100 horsemen sent to Ireland.[124]

Naval expeditions

At the king's accession the ships owned by the crown were in the charge of the keeper or the clerk of the king's ships, assisted by the clerk controller and the clerk of the storehouses.[125] However, by Henry's death a group of seven officers known as 'the admiralty' or 'the council for marine causes' had been established.[126] A memorandum, probably dating from February or March 1545, outlined the membership of the council. The three existing clerks were supplemented with the lieutenant or vice-admiral, the treasurer, the surveyor and rigger and the master of the naval ordinance.[127] A list of the king' ships taken at the end of the king's reign recorded that Henry had 53 'sheppes, barkes, Galles, pynnassis' with 11,065 tonnes and capable of carrying 7,995 men. Each ship was listed in turn giving details of the crew: For example, *The Jesus* had 158 mariners, 24 gunners and 118 soldiers, while *The Brigandine* had 40 mariners and 4 gunners.[128]

The sailors and soldiers on the king's ships were provided with livery. For example, in November 1511 William Hilton, tailor, received £42 12*s* 11*d* for 100 white and green cloth jackets for the mariners of *The Peter Pomegranate* against her voyage into Zeeland.[129] On 8 April 1512 Sir Edward Howard, admiral, undertook to command the fleet with 3,000 men in addition to the 700 soldiers, mariners and gunners in *The Regent*. The coats for each captain and soldier cost 4*s*, while those for mariners and gunners cost 20*d*.[130] Several months later, William Mortimer and Thomas Foster, embroiderers of London, were paid £6 6*s* 4*d* upon a bill signed by Howard, for badges with roses and crosses that they made for the masters and mariners of the king's ships, the *Mary John* and the *Anne of London*.[131] On this occasion, no reference was made to the colour of the fabric of the coats, but they appear to have been of two different qualities as there were two prices: 3*s* 4*d* and 2*s* 4*d*. They were issued in large numbers. By the autumn Howard was still receiving coats for his troops. On 28 October 1512 he was allowed coats for the soldiers at 4*s* each and to the mariners at 20*d* each.[132]

Coats were also supplied to those involved in building the king's ships. The shipwrights working on Henry VIII's new ships between 1509 and 1512 were paid from 2*d* to 6*d* a day, as well as being provided with an allowance of 2½*d* a day for food and a livery coat.[133] In all, 141 coats were supplied at a cost of £24 11s.[134] Provision was also made for their bedding, including 60 mattresses, bolsters, coverlets, pairs of sheets and blankets, and 60 feather beds were hired at Woolwich and Erith for £68 11*s* 2½*d*.[135]

Garrisons

The king maintained garrisons at several outposts of the kingdom: Boulogne, Berwick, Calais and Tournai. The evidence is spasmodic but it suggests that he provided some livery under some duress when the soldiers were disaffected. At other times, the costs appear to have been defrayed by the commander of the garrison or by the civic or municipal authorities.

On 14 September 1509 a warrant issued to Fox, bishop of Winchester, authorised him to pay wages for 100 men sent to reinforce the Calais garrison under Sir John Peche. The men were issued with jackets costing 2*s*, with Peche's jacket priced at 6*s* 8*d* and those for his petty captains at 3*s* 4*d*.[136] In 1516 the accounts of the treasurer of the Calais garrison included several payments relating to livery: to Sir Richard Jerningham for red cloth for bends for the guard, £2 4*d*, and to Simkin de Rode, draper, for red cloth for bends for the soldiers, 'the same day that the great rebellion was like to be', £6 10*s*.[137] In May 1522 the soldiers received 1,523 coats at 3*s* 4*d* each, totalling £253 16*s* 8*d*. Two months later, the king's own warrant dated 22 July included making the body of 22 coats of red cloth for soldiers embroidered with gold and goldsmiths' work and a red and white rose.[138] The pale of Calais included the fort at Guisnes. In July 1524 the garrison there numbering 232 got coats costing £38 13*s* 4*d*. Eighteen years later, Peter Swift was given £63 16*d* for coats and conduct money of a captain, petty captain and 100 soldiers to serve there under Lord Sandys.[139]

The items allowed to garrisons went beyond conduct coats. For example, in October 1545, £135 8*s* ½*d* was spent on 'frysses and mattresses' for the men at Boulogne.[140] There was often a delay between an outlay being incurred and reimbursement. In May 1546 Sir Ralph Sadler received a warrant 'for certain coats and stuff for captains, petty captains, horsemen and footmen, delivered out of the Great Wardrobe against your majesty going to Boloigne' two years earlier.[141]

As part of the scheme to protect the marches from Scottish incursions in 1542, the castle at Alnwick, then in the crown's possession, was manned. Coats were supplied for 12 men costing £2, while Thomas Browne, Edmund Friar, Arthur Scarlet and John Toke received 6 yards (5.4 m) of white camlet for their coats.[142] The management of the larger garrison at Berwick was laid down in a set of statutes drawn up in May 1542. Two of the points related directly to the livery worn by the troops: point 26 noted that every soldier admitted to wages was to wear a jacket of the king's colours, viz. white and green, whenever summoned by the captain; point 35 required soldiers wearing any other livery that was not the king's or his captain's to forfeit it and lose their room. In addition, point 23 linked the ownership of armour to social standing. Any soldiers of the garrison 'taking an enemy which is a gentleman of coat armour' and not presenting him first to the captain was to be fined.[143]

Royal entries as part of military campaigns

Royal entries under the Tudors derived from Roman triumphs in classical antiquity and took their inspiration from Petrarch's *Trionfi*. The theatrical pageants and triumphal arches combined to celebrate royal magnificence and military power.[144] Tudor entries consisted of a formal procession. Such entries were into London as the capital of England. Henry VIII also made entries elsewhere in the kingdom and abroad in 1513 and 1544.

His entry into Therouanne on 24 August 1513 was recorded by a number of observers. Laurent de Gorrevod wrote to Margaret of Savoy, noting that, 'the King and the Emperor entered Terouenne at vespers. The Lords with them were all in cloth of gold and accoutred as if for a triumph'.[145] The entry was described by Hall:

> the kyng ... entered into the cytye ... his persone was apparelled in armure gilt and grauen, his garment and barde purple veluet full of borders and in all places trauersed with branches in ronnyng worke of fyne golde, the branches of hauthorne wrought by goldsmythes crafte wounde with a braunche of Roses, and euery flower, lefe and bury were embossed.[146]

On 12 September Henry made his entry into Lille:

> which the King entered with as much pomp as ever he did at Westminster with his crown on, to visit Lady Margaret of Savoy . . . Between the gate of the town and the palace the way was lined with burning torches, although it was bright day . . . Tapestries were hung from the houses, a tent erected at frequent intervals, where histories of the Old and New Testament and of the poets were acted.[147]

When on Sunday 25 September he made his entry into Tournai, he entered the city through the main gate and passed along the main street, into the street of Our Lady before reaching the main church and his lodgings. On his return 'through the same streets (which were hung with tapestry), all the bells were rung and the officers of the said town, holding flambaux in their hands conducted him ... to his lodgings'.[148] Three decades later, following a tried and tested model, the king entered Boulogne in 1544:

> the kinges highnes, hauyng the sworde borne naked sword before him by the Lorde Marques of Dorset, like a noble and valyaunt conqueror rode into Bulleyn, and the Trompetters standyng on the walles of the toune sounded their Trompettes, at the same time of his entring, to the great comfort of al the kynges true subiectes, the same beholdyng.[149]

Notes

1 Hall, *Chronicle*, p. 539.
2 *LP* I.i, 2157.
3 Hall, *Chronicle*, p. 544.
4 *LP* I.ii, 2391.
5 *CSP Venetian, 1509–19*, 662.
6 Norris, *Costume*, p. 51; for a detailed analysis of the yeomen of the guard, see A. R. Hewerdine, 'The Yeomen of the King's Guard 1485–1547' (unpublished PhD thesis, University of London, 1998).
7 *PPE*, p. 269.
8 Hall, *Chronicle*, p. 774.
9 TNA E101/417/6, 22 (*LP* I.i, 1033).
10 Hall, *Chronicle*, p. 539.
11 TNA SP1/230, ff. 289–90 (*LP* I.ii, 3373).
12 Brown, *Four Years*, I, p. 90.
13 TNA SP1/232, f. 79 (*LP* Additional I.i, 214).
14 *LP* V, p. 306.
15 *LP* XXI.ii, 770.33.
16 *LP* III.ii, 2750.
17 *LP* XIII.2, 1280.
18 TNA E36/215, pp. 43, 44, 47, 68.
19 Ibid., pp. 70, 72, 73, 77, 78, 84, 85.
20 Ibid., p. 406.
21 Ibid., p. 460.
22 Ibid., pp. 493, 543, 562.
23 Ibid., pp. 80, 104.
24 TNA E36/216, pp. 197, 241.
25 *LP* XIII.2, 1280.
26 *LP* XX.ii, 1067.4, 6 and 7.
27 *LP* XXI.ii, 770.31 and 32
28 Hall, *Chronicle*, p. 512.
29 TNA E101/417/3, no. 76.
30 BL Additional MS 18,826, f. 3.
31 Starkey, *European Court*, pp. 136–37.
32 *LP* XIII.ii, 1111.
33 *LP* XIV.ii, 783.
34 RL 12231, Parker 57.

35 Millar, *Holbein*, pp. 90–91; Roberts, *Holbein*, pp. 72–73.
36 Nevinson, 'Portraits', p. 6; private collection, illustrated in Starkey, *European Court*, p. 137.
37 For an insight into their working lives, see the accounts of William Brereton, Edward Leighton and Thomas Wriothesley while working as royal messengers; *LP* IV.iii, 6489.
38 Myers, *Black Book*, p. 133.
39 *LP* V, 766.11.
40 TNA E36/456, f. 32v.
41 *LP* XVI, 745.
42 Myers, *Black Book*, pp. 130–31.
43 For more information, see A. Wagner, *Heralds and Heraldry in the Middle Ages. An Inquiry into the Growth of the Armorial Function of Heralds* (1939), and A. Wagner, *Heralds of England: A History of the Office and the College of Arms* (1967).
44 *LP* III.ii, 2261.
45 *LP* III.ii, 2654.
46 *LP* IV.ii, 3940.
47 *LP* XIX.ii, 112.
48 *LP* IV.i, 614.
49 *LP* XVIII.i, 26.5.
50 *LP* I.i, 671.
51 Young, *Tournaments*, p. 44.
52 A. Ailes, '"You know me by my Habit": Heralds' tabards in the fourteenth and fifieenth centuries', *The Ricardian*, 13.1 (2003), pp. 7–81.
53 Ashmol MS 857, ff. 504–10 (*LP* I.i, 711).
54 BL Additional MS 6,113, f. 208v (*LP* I.i, 710).
55 TNA SP1/230, f. 256 (*LP* I.ii, 3309).
56 TNA SP1/239, f. 89 (*LP* Add. I.i, 956).
57 Ailes, 'Heralds' tabards', p. 4.
58 TNA E36/113, f. 35r; LC2/1, ff. 102v, 98v.
59 TNA E101/420/1, no. 38.
60 *LP* XVI, 946.
61 Campbell, *Materials*, 2, p. 14.
62 BL Arundel MS 97, f. 188r (*LP* XVI 1489).
63 TNA SP1/229, f. 4v (*LP* I.i, 20.2).
64 TNA LC 2/1, f. 98v; E36/113, f. 34.
65 TNA E101/417/6, f. 30 (*LP* I.i, 1185).
66 TNA SP1/229, f. 25 (*LP* I.i, 728.ii). The bill was annotated to record that Francis Howlson had received 28*s* in part payment.
67 BL Additional MS 18,826, f. 50r.
68 *LP* XI, 727.
69 *LP* XI, 754.
70 *LP* XI, 930.
71 Gunn, *Charles Brandon*, pp. 183–98.
72 *LP* XIX.ii, 483.
73 *LP* I.ii, 1825; A. Spont, ed., *Letters and Papers Relating to the War with France in 1512–13*, Navy Records Society, 10 (1897), pp. 132–39.
74 *LP* III.ii, 3288.
75 *LP* III.ii, 3517.
76 *LP* III.ii, 3516.
77 TNA LC 9/51, f. 120v.
78 TNA E36/1, ff. 43v–44r.
79 TNA E101/417/6, f. 36 (*LP* I.i, 1159.3).
80 Ibid., f. 2 (*LP* I.i, 1283).
81 Ibid., f. 7 (*LP* I.i, 1313).
82 TNA SP1/230, f. 22r (*LP* I.ii, 2148).
83 TNA E101/417/3, no. 9 (*LP* I.ii, 2243). The warrant was signed by the queen and countersigned by Canterbury, Rochester, Englefield and Southwell.
84 TNA E101/423/10, f. 92r.
85 TNA LC 9/51, f. 120v.
86 M. A. Hayward, 'The flags: Fabric', in C. S. Knighton and D. M. Loades, eds, *The Anthony Roll of Henry VIII's Navy*, NRS (Aldershot, 2000), pp. 31–33.
87 BL Stowe MS 146, f. 124 (*LP* I.ii, 2967).
88 TNA E101/56/10/6, no. 56.
89 BL Stowe MS 146, f. 111 (*LP* I.ii, 2799).
90 *LP* XXI.i, 471.
91 *LP* XXI.i, 637.
92 *LP* I.ii, 1920. Also see *LP* I.ii, 1935, for a similar order placed with Guido Portenary.
93 *LP* I.ii, 2054.
94 TNA SP1/230, f. 13r (*LP* I.ii, 2062).
95 TNA E101/56/10/6, no. 226.
96 *LP* XIX.i, 272–73.
97 *LP* XXI.i, 963.123.
98 TNA E101/423/10, f. 91v.
99 Ibid., f. 48v.
100 Ibid., f. 37r.
101 Three for the officers of the wardrobe of the robes, one for the king's clerk, three for the barbers, three for the surgeons, one for the apothecary, one for the armourer, eight for the officers of the wardrobe of the beds, three for the officers of the jewel house, one for the groom porter, one for the sergeant painter.
102 For the yeoman armourer, the morris pike maker, their coats guarded with yellow satin, 16 armourers, seven grooms of the chamber, four messengers, 12 officers of the stable, four horse keepers, two grooms of the stirrup, the fool keeper, their coats guarded with yellow kersey.
103 A warrant dated 9 June 1544 required Ralph Sadler to deliver the following: to Garter and Clarenceux kings of arms, 8 yards (7.3 m) of red and 2 yards (1.8 m) of yellow velvet each, to Windsor and Somerset heralds, 8 yards (7.3 m) of red and 2 yards (1.8 m) of yellow damask each, to Portcullis, Blue Mantle, Risbank, Hammes and Guisnes pursuivants, 8 yards (7.3 m) of red and 2 yards (1.8 m) of yellow camlet each; *LP* XIX.i, 651.
104 *LP* XIX.i, 448.
105 CoA MS M16bis, ff. 97v–101r.
106 *LP* XX.i, 134.
107 Blair and Pyhrr, 'The Wilton "Montmorency" armour', pp. 96–97.
108 V&M M 507–1927; S. Metcalf, A. R. E. North and D. Balfour, 'A gun-shield from the armoury of Henry VIII: decorative oddity or important discovery?', *V&A Conservation Journal* (Autumn 2001), pp. 14–16; and S. Metcalf, A. R. E. North and D. Balfour, 'The conservation of a gun-shield from the arsenal of Henry VIII. Textiles meet arms and armour: the benefits of a multi-disciplinary approach', in R. D. Smith, ed., *Make All Sure: The Conservation and Restoration of Arms and Armour* (Leeds, 2005), pp. 76–90.
109 TNA E36/1, f. 52v.
110 Ibid., f. 53r.
111 *LP* I.i, 1463.
112 *LP* IV.i, 383.
113 *LP* IV.i, 2216.
114 *LP* XVI, 785.
115 *LP* XIX.i, 812.23.
116 *LP* XVIII.ii, 234.
117 *LP* XVIII.i, 436.
118 *LP* XIX.i, 534.
119 *LP* XIX.i, 408.
120 *LP* IV.i, 2216.
121 *LP* III.ii, App. 15.
122 *LP* XI, 934.
123 *LP* XI, 1066.
124 *LP* XV, 862.
125 M. Oppenheim, *A History of the Administration of the Royal Navy, 1509–1660*, 1 (1896), p. 3; D. Loades, *The Tudor Navy* (Aldershot, 1992), pp. 15–16.
126 C. S. L. Davies, 'The administration of the Royal Navy under Henry VIII', *EHR*, 78 (1963), p. 170.
127 Loades, *Tudor Navy*, p. 81.
128 Bod Lib Rawlinson MS C. 846, pp. 85–92; also see Knighton and Loades, *Anthony Roll*.
129 TNA E36/1, f. 33r.
130 *LP* I.i, 1132.
131 TNA E36/1, f. 41v (*LP* I.i, 1463).
132 *LP* I.i, 1453.
133 TNA E36/5, ff. 20v–25v.
134 Ibid., f. 177v; ten coats at 5*s*, 38 coats at 4*s*, 48 coats at 3*s* 4*d*, 39 coats at 3*s* and six coats at 2*s*.
135 Ibid., ff. 69r–80v.
136 *LP* I.i, 168.
137 *LP* II.i, 1514.
138 TNA LC 9/51, f. 123r.
139 BL Arundel MS 97, f. 133v (*LP* XVI, 380).
140 *LP* XX.ii, 558.
141 *LP* XXI.i, 963.123.
142 *LP* XVII, 726.
143 *LP* XVII, 343.
144 Strong, *Splendour at Court*, pp. 23–37.
145 *LP* I.ii, 2201.
146 Hall, *Chronicle*, p. 552.
147 *LP* I.ii, 2391.
148 *LP* I.ii, 2302.
149 Hall, *Chronicle*, p. 862.

Catherine's household accounts for 1543–44 record her distribution of livery at the New Year: 45 yards (41.1 m) of black satin for 15 doublets at a cost of £16 10*s*; 60 yards (54.8 m) for 20 doublets for £22 10*s*; 48 yards (43.8 m) of 'fyne bolloyn satten blacke' for 16 doublets costing £18. William Lock provided a further 57 yards (52.1 m) for 20 doublets costing £21 7*s* 6*d*.[110] The earl of Essex received a gown of black satin guarded with black velvet. She also distributed red cloth for her livery: 128 yards (117 m) of red cloth for £38 8*s* and 10⅝ yards (9.7 m), costing 63*s* 9*d*.[111]

Anne Herbert (her sister), Maud Lane and Elizabeth Tyrwhitt (her cousins) were Catherine's ladies of the chamber. They were described by John Foxe as being 'great with [the queen] and of her blood; [and] the chiefest whereof, as most of estimation and privy to all her doings, were these'.[112] They were issued with gowns of black double jean velvet: Lady Herbert and Lady Tyrwhitt received 28 yards (25.6 m) of black double jean velvet for £21 for a gown each and 7½ ells (5.1 m) of black sarsenet for lining costing 35*s*. A similar gown was given to Lady Lane 'of the Quenes graces gifte'. These women wore 'the queen's badge on their caps displaying the head of St Katherine adapted from the woodblock print in the old Horae ad Usum Sarum'.[113] Lady Herbert was given 3½ ells (2.4 m) of blue sarsenet for lining a gown of blue velvet. In addition, Mistress Kendal received 13½ yards (12.3 m) of black damask for a gown costing £4 14*s* 6*d* and 2½ yards (2.2 m) of black velvet to trim the gown at 33*s* 4*d*. She was also given 7½ yards (6.8 m) of russell worsted for a gown and ¾ yard (0.7 m) of black bridges satin priced at 12*s* 11*d* in all, and 2½ yards (2.2 m) of russet lukes velvet. By the 1540s the regular provision of black livery to the women of the queen's chamber echoes the livery issued by the king to the offcers of his privy chamber.

Two of Catherine's ladies in waiting, Anne Basset, the stepdaughter of Viscount Lisle executed for treason in 1540, and Dorothy Bray, the daughter of a minor nobleman (whose name had briefly been linked in the early 1540s with Catherine's brother), seem to have received greater provision for their clothing than the others.[114] They were in receipt of a number of lengths of silk from the silk house at Whitehall (Table 18.1). The lengths they received were clearly specified as for their use. Catherine's accounts for 1543–44 also include payments for the carriage of Anne's stuff from Guildford to Sutton, 6*d*, from Sutton to Reading, 3*s* 8*d*, from Reading to Dorchester, 3*s* 9*d*, and from Dorchester to Woodstock, 2*s* 6*d*.[115] In January 1546 two warrants were signed by the stamp for apparel delivered to her last Whitsun and for apparel at Christmas.[116] She received two more, similar warrants in her favour, in June 1546 against Whitsun and in the following November for clothing against Christmas.[117]

On 8 December 1543 Catherine bought livery for John Symonds and John Coke, her two littermen, at a cost of £20 7*s* 2*d*. Their livery consisted of a long frock of camlet lined with black cotton, a jerkin of crimson velvet, a doublet made half from yellow velvet and half from crimson velvet, four pairs of black kersey hose, four holland shirts, one bonnet and six pairs of shoes.[118] On 10 June 1544 Peter Richardson received £20 from Wymond Carew in part payment for a delivery of spangles for the coats of the queen's footmen.[119] Catherine's account for 1543–44 records that Hugh Apparry, groom of the queen's stable, rode to London with the footmen's coats for four days at 12*d* the day, boat hire from Lambeth to Baynard's Castle and back again cost 4*d*, fetching the coats again cost 6*d*, while fire to air and lavender to scant the coats cost 4*d*.[120] On 1 December 1545 livery was issued to Laurence Leigh, Giles Bateson, Robert Tyrthrey and [...], footmen, consisting of

Table 18.1: *Cloth distributed to Anne Basset and Dorothy Bray from the silk store at Whitehall, 1542–7*

Type of cloth	Anne Basset	Dorothy Bray	Type of cloth	Anne Basset	Dorothy Bray
Cloth of silver	5 yards (4.6 m)	7½ yards (6.86 m)	*Damask*		
Tinsel	~	6 yards (5.5 m)	– black	42½ yards (38.8 m)	29½ yards (26.9 m)
Velvet			– blue	~	15 yards (13.7 m)
– black	94½ yards (86.4 m)	144 yards (131.7 m)	– crimson	16¼ yards (14.8 m)	43½ yards (39.8 m)
– blue	⅜ yard (0.3 m)	3¾ yards (3.4 m)	– murrey	15 yards (13.7 m)	~
– crimson	10½ yards (9.6 m)	43¼ yards (39.5 m)	– orange	9 yards (8.8 m)	~
– green	~	18¼ yards (16.7 m)	– tawny	12½ yards (11.4 m)	~
– orange	⅜ yard (0.3 m)	~	– white	18 yards (16.5 m)	36¼ yards (33.1 m)
– purple	~	18 yards (16.5 m)	– yellow	10½ yards (9.6 m)	10½ yards (9.6)
– tawny	48½ yards (44.4 m)	18 yards (16.5 m)	*Sarsenet*		
– white	⅜ yard (0.3 m)	1 yard (0.9 m)	– black	49½ yards (45.3 m)	41½ yards (37.9 m)
– yellow	7½ yards (6.8 m)	7⅞ yards (7.2 m)	– crimson and red	6 yards (5.5 m)	21¼ yards (19.4 m)
Satin			– green	~	6 yards (5.5 m)
– black	42 yards (38.4 m)	67 yards (61.2 m)	– murrey	6 yards (5.5 m)	~
– blue	9 yards (8.2 m)	10½ yards (9.6 m)	– purple, blue and violet	~	12¼ yards (11.2 m)
– crimson	10 yards (9.1 m)	25 yards (22.9 m)	– tawny	6 yards (5.5 m)	14 yards (12.8 m)
– incarnate	1 yard (0.9 m)	2¾ yards (2.5 m)	– white	6 yards (5.5 m)	6 yards (5.5 m)
– tawny	30 yards (27.4 m)	10½ yards (9.6 m)	*Bridges satin*	~	7¾ yards (7.1 m)
– white	20 yards (18.3 m)	29½ yards (26.9 m)	*Holland*	72 ells (49.7 m)	90½ ells (62.5 m)
Taffeta			*Normandy cloth*	61 ells (42.1 m)	~
– black	14 yards (12.8 m)	16⅜ yards (14.9 m)	*Cambric*	26 ells (17.9 m)	44⅜ ells (30.8 m)
– tawny	1¼ yards (1.1 m)	9 yards (8.2 m)	**Totals**	**491⅝ yards (449.5 m) 159 ells (109.7 m)**	**681¾ yards (623.4 m) 135⅛ ells (93.2)**

a scarlet cloak guarded with crimson velvet and a crimson velvet running coat and hose, the latter being lined with kersey and sarsenet. They also received doublets, shirts, hats, Milan and French bonnets, ribbon points and shoes, costing £56 10*d*.[121]

Catherine retained the service of a fool called Jane who had previously been attached to the Princess Mary. In 1543–44 she bought her a red petticoat.[122] In June 1546, Jane was described as 'the Queen's fool' and she was provided with 'two gowns and two kirtles' by the great wardrobe.[123] Jane could be the figure in the background of the group portrait of Henry and his family (Fig. 18.2). She is dressed in a tight-fitting cap in white and red, a red patterned gown and an unusual pleated kirtle.

The expensive materials used to make the clothes worn at court inevitably proved too much of a temptation for some. A letter from the queen's council to the king's council written on 28 September 1544 concerned a boy waiting upon one of the queen's maids who had 'picked certain pieces of goldsmith's work from his mistress'. The queen's councillors asked the king's pardon for the boy on the grounds of his youth, his penitence and 'the fact is but hardly construed felony'.[124]

18.2 *Detail of a female servant, possibly Jane the fool, from* The Family of Henry VIII, *unknown artist*, c. *1545. RCIN 405796 OM 43. The Royal Collection © 2004, Her Majesty the Queen Elizabeth II*

Short-term provision for the king's sisters

Princess Mary's household had been augmented in 1508 by Henry VII. On her engagement to the prince of Castile, the king consented to the appointment of 'certayn . . . ladies' to Mary's household, 'the which with thear attendaunce gevyng uppon the said ladie maistres, and by her advise have the charge to devise for thapparelle of her person'.[125] He also allowed her 'iij or iiij fotemen with riche cotes of goldsmyth worke to goo aboute her litter, or about her palfray'.[126] On his accession, Henry VIII assumed responsibility for his younger sister and her household. He provided some livery via the great wardrobe, in addition to grants of land and offices. For example, in September 1509 Henry Calise, her yeoman of the robes, was appointed during pleasure, as keeper of Okehampton park, in Devon, a post which had reverted to the crown on the death of the earl of Devon.[127]

Henry VIII maintained Mary's household until her marriage in 1514. There are a few fleeting references to individuals who were in her service: on 14 November 1509, William Studdon and Thomas Hill, yeomen of the chamber, were appointed to wait on her.[128] Two warrants dated 5 November 1509 and 12 December 1510 refer to Thomas Parker, 'footman with our sister'.[129] In the first of these he was granted a gown of tawny cloth. Equally, there was a passing reference to Arnold Chollerton, Mary's servant, in a warrant dated 3 July 1511, ordering sheets and other bed linen for her.[130] In March 1512, Alexander Duwes and John Tremayle were named as grooms of her chamber.[131] The same year saw Anne Jerningham in Mary's service as a gentlewoman attendant on her.[132] In April John Wellys, yeoman of the king's chamber, was appointed to give attendance on her and he was granted watching livery of London russet.[133] Rewards issued in 1514 indicate that a number of the women in her service had also served her mother, suggesting, that on the death of Elizabeth of York in 1503, certain women transferred to her household: in September 1514 Elizabeth Saxby, widow, received an annuity of £20 for her services to the king's father and mother and his sister, Mary, while Elizabeth Catesby, the king's kinswoman, was given an annuity of 40 marks for services to both mother and daughter.[134] On 2 March 1515, Jane Barners, chamberer, received 12 yards (10.9 m) of damask at 8*s* the yard (0.91 m) for a gown, and as much calabre as was required to fur the gown and mink to edge the collar and cuffs.[135]

One of Mary's maids of honour was Jane Popincourt. She was a Frenchwoman who had entered the service of Henry VII to look after his daughters as a companion. By 1502 she was a maid of honour to Mary and she received two grants of livery in this capacity from Henry VII. On 20 December 1504 the warrant was quite small and cost 57*s* 10*d*. She received a frontlet of tawny velvet, linen for kerchers, smocks and rails, sipres, silk for girdles, 1,000 pins, a selection of French and English ribbons and 1¼ yards (1.1 m) of kersey for hose.[136] A year later her provision was more generous: a gown of tawny cloth lined with buckram, black cotton and linen and with black velvet for the collar, cuffs and purfil, a kirtle of black worsted lined with black cloth and linen, three pairs of hose and three pairs of shoes which cost 64*s* 4*d*.[137] Following his they undertook large volumes of work for the king, and it was impossible for one person to complete it all.

Under Henry VIII, the royal armourers were only allowed to work for external clients if the king had consented to this with a warrant from him authorising it. Sir Robert Southwell, who died on 30 March 1514, was such a client, and his final set of household accounts included a payment of *26s 8d* to 'The King's armourer for a pair of leg harness and a pair of aubarcs'.[7] Other royal artificers do not appear to have been constrained in the same way as the armourers were. There is evidence that many of them undertook commissions from members of the court, the royal household and wealthy Londoners. For some, these commissions may have been a route to royal service. In 1526 the duke of Suffolk had work done by the painters John Browne and Clement Urmeston, and the embroiderer, William Ibgrave. Ibgrave, who was already working for the revels, would become the king's embroiderer in two years' time.[8] When Syrres Gwynello, a former French servant of the duke's, died in 1534, the witnesses of his will included Ibgrave.[9] For others, such as John Scut, the queen's tailor, there is evidence of him working for a range of external clients. The best documented of these was Lady Lisle. On 21 August 1538 John Husee informed her that he had delivered to Scut 'for the upper bodies and plackards j yard iij quarters of Lucca velvet and for the lining of the sleeves ij yards di of the best black satin I could get . . . I have further delivered him xv yards of Lucca velvet and a roll of buckram for your gown and vj yards of Lucca velvet for your kirtle and sleeves'.[10] In September he told her that Warley had 'the books and bills of reckonings of Skut' as well as 'the piece of cloth of gold Skutt sent'.[11] In the following April 1539 he assured her that 'as touching your ladyship's taffeta gown, Mr Skut hath promised to make it according to your ladyship's desire. It is not much worse for the wetting'.[12]

The crafts people working for the king were predominantly male, but with a few notable exceptions: his silk women and one female skinner. Most of their skills were labour intensive, repetitive and learned by watching and working with others through a formal training. While paid at a much higher rate than unskilled workers, the value of their labour was invariably exceeded markedly by the cost of their materials. Equally, some offices were kept within family groups such as the king's cordwainer and silk woman, while in others such as the king's tailor there was no continuity. Many of these individuals spent a long period in the king's service, often dying in office. This suggests that such posts were seen as the pinnacle of a craftsman's career. These offices certainly brought advantages including wealth, access to royal patronage and patronage from the wider court circle. The queen's tailor was often in demand and the clothes that came out of his workshop provided a very direct means of disseminating court fashion.

The role of European, as opposed to English, craftsmen at Henry VIII's court was small but highly significant. The transmission of skills and ideas on fashion and fashionable design was linked to the migration of craftsmen. When in 1503 Henry's sister Margaret went to Scotland to marry James IV, she took a London skinner with her and he was referred to in Scottish records as 'the Inglis Furrour'.[13] On 3 December 1528 a certificate was issued to the commissioners appointed to enquire within the city of London and within a two-mile radius into the number of alien artificers and the number of their stranger servants, especially focusing on cordwainers.[14]

The records providing information about Henry VIII's artificers are more detailed and more numerous than those for his queens. This is partly because the queen's household was not continuous, although what evidence there is suggests that there was a surprising degree of continuity of service between all six wives.[15] In many of the accounts the names of the officers were either familiar to the clerk so they did not need naming, or such details were felt to be redundant and payments were often recorded against an office rather than a named individual. The accounts of Lady Margaret Beaufort include the names of a number of individuals who made her clothes and shoes: for example, in 1498 her cordwainer was named as Rowland, who received *21d* for shoes and slippers.[16] However, an entry in Catherine Parr's accounts from June 1544 recorded that Thomas Berk received *7s 6d* in part payment for 12 yards (10.9 m) of yellow cotton, this was for trussing jewels going to 'her grace's goldsmith and her silkwoman at sondry times'.[17]

The principal artificers

THE KING'S TAILOR

The *scissori regis* or king's tailor would have been a familiar figure to Henry VIII. Not only did he know the king's dimensions, he knew his taste in clothes. He was well placed to be an arbiter of fashion, by promoting new ideas while dissuading the king from breaking with long favoured styles. The royal tailor made the king's clothes to measure as opposed to ready-to-wear items. A number of clothes, especially hose, hats and shoes, could be bought off the peg for some members of the household, but not for the king. The king's tailor generally appears to have undertaken the work on a garment from start to finish. However, sometimes he would complete a job started by another, as in the case of William Hilton, inserting linings into riding coats of kendal and cottoned cloth [A1582, 1587]. Royal tailors also undertook some of the decorative work that embellished the king's clothes, using a variety of techniques listed in the accounts and wardrobe books, including bordering, edging, guarding, hemming and welting. Fur linings were taken out [A111, B26, 34] and put back in [B96] on a regular basis.

Most of the royal tailors had strong links to the company of Merchant Taylors which had been established under Henry VII. It had received a charter in 1503 that recognised the links between the tailors and linen armourers. On 6 January 1503, Richard Smith, yeoman of the robes with the queen and master of the company, and four men, who were the wardens of the guild of tailors and linen armourers, were granted the right to be called the guild of Merchant Taylors after payment of £10 in hanaper.[18] The cost of the tailor's labour was small in comparison to the value of the materials he worked with.

Indeed, most tailors kept a modest stock of materials, as the customer generally provided the cloth. However, in the case of the king's tailor, the cloth came either from the great wardrobe, the wardrobe of the robes or the silk store at Whitehall, or it was supplied by the tailor himself. In this respect the role of the king's tailor underwent a change during Henry VIII's reign and it is linked to the new concept of the merchant taylor. In this context, the distinction between a 'household tailor', or one who worked for a specific patron and lived in their home, and the 'salesman tailor' who produced off-the-peg garments is an interesting one. While tailors were not officially distinguished in this way in contemporary records until the mid Elizabethan period, the Henrician great wardrobe accounts make it clear that the different types had existed earlier than this. By the Elizabethan period the salesman tailor was often associated with producing cheap, sub-standard clothing.[19] This association does not appear to have been made overtly during the mid Tudor period, but the king's tailor was essentially a 'household tailor', while 'salesman tailors' only provided goods to the lower ranks of the household.

The range of garments a tailor made defined the extent of his craft. During the fifteenth century and the early decades of the sixteenth, the tailor's repertoire included gowns, doublets, jackets and mantles (Fig. 19.1). Both William Hilton and John de Paris also made hose for the king but only in limited quantities: on 31 December 1516 John de Paris was provided with 4 yards (3.6 m) of black tilsent [A723], and 7½ yards (6.8 m) of blue velvet on 12 February 1517 towards making up two sets of matching doublet and hose [A909], while on 1 June 1518 Hilton received 1¼ yards (1.1 m) of cloth of damask to make stocks for a pair of hose [A388]. However, from 1504 William Croughton, the king's specialist hosier, had been making hose for Henry VII, and he and his son held the post of king's hosier throughout Henry VIII's reign. A similar trend in the specialisation of the tailor's skills resulting in a new sub-group of artisans can be seen during Elizabeth I's reign. Towards the end of Henry's reign, tailors started making farthingales for women. However, in 1567 there was the first reference in the great wardrobe accounts to 'John Bate verthingale maker' who was paid for making a farthingale of crimson satin edged with crimson velvet for the queen.[20]

19.1 *John More, by Hans Holbein the Younger. John More's doublet and highly decorative gown are good examples of the Tudor tailor's craft. RL 12226 P6. The Royal Collection © 2004, Her Majesty the Queen Elizabeth II*

The warrants for Henry VII and his son reveal that the king's tailor made a growing number of garments for the king, while also making some pieces for members of the household. There were set prices for different types of garments, and standard amounts of fabric were distributed to make them. Most of the garments were outer garments for the upper body, but the king's tailor also made some headwear, including bonnets and hats, as well as occasionally overlapping with the work of the king's hosier and the king's skinner, particularly in the area of inserting or removing fur linings. By the 1530s, the king's tailor also often provided a substantial amount of the fabric used for making the orders of clothes supplied for the king. It is not possible to tell from the accounts whether the king's tailor claimed any of the trimmings as a perquisite, which later came to be known as cabbage.[21]

In fifteenth century London the main distinction was between tailors who made new clothes and had 'the experience or Cunnying to Cutt or shape Garmentes of the newe & diverse fashions', and botchers who modified and repaired existing clothing or second-hand clothing.[22] However, by the early sixteenth century this distinction had effectively ceased to exist. In 1518 the Merchant Taylors' company petitioned the mayor of London about elderly tailors with poor eyesight who 'are fain to fall to the said feat of botching'.[23] Recycling and refurbishing or, to use contemporary terms, 'new making' and 'performing' Henry's clothing became an increasingly significant part of the royal tailors' work as the king became older and bigger. While this work might be technically regarded as coming close to the tasks undertaken by the botcher, these alterations needed to be undertaken with a very high level of skill and attention to detail in order to ensure that these modifications were discreet.

While the great wardrobe accounts leave little doubt as to Henry VIII's passion for new clothes, he also had garments repaired and altered, albeit on a much lesser scale. Linings were replaced chiefly as a means of keeping clothing fresh smelling, but it could also have been in response to a lining becoming worn through use. Like was not always replaced with like, as in the case of 'a Jaquet of blacke tylsent lined with blacke saten' against which there was a marginal note recording that 'the saten woren & new with sarcenet' [B179]. Some pieces were refurbished, including 'a Jaquet of siluer tissewe newe clocked ay guysnes with crimosyn cloth of gold tissewe lined with blacke saten' [B177]. Garments could also be unpicked and made up as something else, as in the case of 'a Gowne of Russet veluete single' delyuerd to Richard Gibson in 1519–20 to make 'half a trapper & half a horsharnes panes with venis siluer' [A153] and 'a mantel of white tylsent single to make iij doblettes & iij payr of hose for the king' [A143].

Many people kept their clothes long after they were past their best, partly because of their retained value and possibly for sentimental reasons. At her death in 1509 Lady Margaret Beaufort had 'an olde Broken gown of white damaske in ix peces' in her 'bede chambre' and one of her coffers contained 'a litill olde broken gown of tynselde satin' and 'an olde purphill of velwet', valued at 20*s*, 6*s* 8*d* and 14*s* respectively.[24] In contrast, Henry VIII gave away a lot of his clothes, but he did keep a few items, including 'a very olde shorte gowne of blacke Damaske embroidered with golde and iiij Cordauntes black silk & gold furred with Budge' (14218).[25]

The revels accounts often record the translation of garments and other textiles. The men working on the jousts held on 29 December 1524 were paid at the rate of 8*d* and 6*d* the day for the 'translacyun of garments', while the sleeves of six rich garments were enriched with 'cut work of the broken cloth of gold in the king's store'.[26] In May 1519, George Lovekyn, clerk of the stable, stored embroidered bards decorated with the arms of England and France within the armoury at Greenwich.[27] Ten of these pieces were selected to be reworked by Richard Gibson and Thomas Forster who were to 'Ryppe' off the embroidery and to remount it 'vppon Russet and white'. In other instances, the valuable materials were removed. A trapper 'enbrawdered with dragons and powdered with dragons winges of goldsmythes worke' was dismantled and the dragons' wings were delivered to George Senesco and John Burton, gold wire drawers.[28]

As Henry VII had spent 14 years in exile before his accession in 1485, he had no familiarity with London craftsmen on coming to the throne. During his 12 years in Brittany and two in France, he knew Breton ducal court dress and the styles favoured at the French royal court. This may have influenced his choice of George Lovekyn as his tailor. Lovekyn originated from Paris but he had worked for both Edward IV and Richard III and knew how an English king was expected to dress. Henry VII retained only two royal tailors, and after Lovekyn's death in 1504 he chose Lovekyn's apprentice, Stephen Jasper. Jasper also made the clothes of Henry, prince of Wales, and on his accession in 1509 Henry VIII made Jasper his tailor.

The value of having a foreign tailor was obvious. They had first-hand experience of and familiarity with the cut and construction of fashionable styles and garment shapes from other areas of Europe. Gustavus Vasa's tailor, George Ballinger, was German, which was highly appropriate as Vasa favoured clothes cut in the German style: long, paned hose with lots of slashing and worn with a codpiece, a doublet, also decorated with slashing and a short gown. In the 1540s a new item appeared in Vasa's wardrobe, the French coat or *mantlar*, which may have been as a result of Gustavus sending an embassy to Francis I in 1542.[29]

When in 1567 Elizabeth I was looking for a new tailor, Sir William Cecil wrote to Sir Henry Norris in Paris, saying, 'The Queen's Majesty would fain have a tailor that had skill to make her apparel both after the Italian and the French manner, and she thinketh that you might use some means to obtain some one that serveth the French Queen, without mentioning any manner of request in our queen's majesty's name'.[30] Elizabeth was unsuccessful. While queen, she engaged only two tailors, both of whom were English: Walter Fyshe (1558–82) and William Jones (1582–1603).[31]

George Lovekyn had been king's tailor under Edward IV and Richard III, but in 1483 he had been temporarily displaced by Henry Davy. He went on to make clothes for Henry VII and his eldest son, Arthur.[32] His reappointment by Henry VII thus accorded with the king's general policy of benevolence towards Yorkist appointees, while being cool to Ricardian nominees. Born in Paris, by 1470 he was working for Edward IV in London and in 1475 he was designated as the king's sergeant tailor.[33] In the following year, he received letters of denization. Following his reappointment in 1485, he made Henry VII's coronation clothes at a price of £15 4*s* 4*d*.[34] On 7 November 1485 Lovekyn was appointed for life as the sergeant tailor of the great wardrobe with 12*d* a day, and given 100*s* for the rent of a house in the city of London.[35] The following November when the grant was repeated, it noted that he had held the office since the previous October and that he was entitled to summer and winter livery.[36] In October 1489 Lovekyn, along with two others, received the grant of two messuages in the parish of St Martin le Grand during the minority of the earl of Northumberland.[37] Two years later he was paid £175 11*s* 8*d* 'for apparel for our person and our son, our cousin, the earl of Northumberland, henchmen, footmen and other persons, from the beginning of the reign'.[38] On 19 October 1493 he received a smaller payment of £83 16*s* 4*d*.[39] When Lovekyn married for a second time in 1497, Henry VII gave him 5 yards (4.5 m) of 'good scarlet to be taken of our gieft towardes his wedding clothing'.[40] His apprentices included Stephen Jasper, who he remembered in his will of 1504, and who succeeded him as the king's tailor. During 1486–87 he was the warden of the Merchant Taylors' company.[41] His eldest son and namesake also entered royal service: by 1503 he was a clerk in the king's stable.[42]

Stephen Jasper succeeded Lovekyn as king's tailor and the great wardrobe accounts from 1504–05 and 1505–06 provide a good insight into his role. His work fell into four main categories: furring garments and laying in furs; laying in linings; making new garments including doublets, glaudekins, gowns, jackets, jerkins, maundy gowns, palls, partlets, riding gowns and tippets; and mending and translating gowns and glaudekins. On 21 May 1509 Henry VIII appointed him, during pleasure, to be the king's tailor in the place of one George [Lovekyn].[43] On 11 October 1509 Jasper, a native of Hainault, was granted English denization. In the margin was a note that he had sworn that his goods did not exceed £20 in value.[44] The first warrant for his work as king's tailor dates from 6 May 1510. His work features in the wardrobe account covering 1510–11, where it is evident that he alone made new garments for the king, including arming doublets, bases, cloaks, coats for harness, doublets, gabardines, glaudekins, gowns, hunting coats, jackets, nightgowns, partlets with sleeves and riding coats, as well as supplying a very small amount of cloth including violet in grain. He also received livery. On 28 June 1511 he was granted 4½ yards (4.1 m) of violet in grain for a gown furred with 132 black lamb skins, 3 yards (2.7 m) of black velvet for a doublet lined with canvas and fustian and 7 yards (6.4 m) of black damask for a jacket costing £10 18½*d*.[45] He died the same year.

William Hilton started his work as king's tailor on 29 September 1511, but it was not until 23 November of that year that he was officially appointed as the king's tailor, with 12*d* a day.[46] A list of fees and annuities paid by the king in 1516 listed William Hilton as the king's tailor, receiving a salary of £18 5*s*.[47] The range of his work can be seen from two warrants from 1513 and 1514. On 12 December 1513 a warrant was issued to pay Hilton, 'our tailor', for making a bard of purple velvet and other items for Lord Lisle.[48] On 1 January 1514, Hilton was paid £40 12*s* 11*d* for 100 white and green cloth jackets for the mariners of the *Peter Pomegranate* against her voyage into Zeeland.[49]

Hilton is listed as the king's tailor in two extant accounts: 1516–17 and 1517–18. He supplied a fairly modest range of materials: budge, buff leather, canvas, coney, damask, frieze, fustian, satin and velvet. However, the vast majority of Hilton's work consisted of making new garments for the king: arming doublets, bonnets, cloaks, coats, doublets, doublets with bases, gabardines, gowns, jackets, jackets with bases, mantles, maundy gowns, night bonnets, night caps, partlets, riding coats, riding coats and caps, short coats, stalking coats, stomachers and tennis coats. In addition, he put in a small number of linings and undertook the translation of several gowns. Hilton also appears as the king's tailor in Worsley's wardrobe book and between 24 December 1516 and 10 September 1519 he received cloth on numerous occasions.[50] In 1519 he was listed as the king's tailor, but against his name was a marginal note 'mortuus est'.[51]

Not long after his receipt of the last documented quantity of cloth, Hilton died. On 20 October 1519 John de Paris was appointed the king's tailor with 12*d* a day.[52] However, he had then been in the king's service at least three years. He appears in December 1516 in James Worsley's wardrobe book as making two sets of doublets and hose of black tilsent and blue velvet. The start of his tenure and the range of work undertaken by him for the king can be charted in detail within BL Harley MS 2284. Cloth was delivered to him to be made up into clothing for the king on the following dates in Worsley's book: 13 October, 5, 6, 13 and 30 November 1519 and 26 March, 19 April, 4 May, 2, 14 and 27 June, 6 August, 7 October and 17 December 1520. John, as his name suggests, was of French origin, and in January 1521 he was granted denization.[53] De Paris was named in only one extant great wardrobe account, that for 1521–22, in which he provided broad cloth, buckram, cloth, leather belts, velvet and made bonnets, cases, chammers, cloaks, coats, doublets, frocks, gowns, jackets, night bonnets, riding coats, sleeves and stalking coats. In addition to making up complete garments he also applied borders, put in linings, new made, performed and welted items. The date of Paris's death has not been established. He died some time between 1528 and January 1532, when John Malt was named as his successor.

On 21 February 1528 John Malt, described as 'our tailor', received along with Henry Johnson, 'our shoemaker', a 40 mark fine levied on Felix Macerosa, clerk of chancery.[54] In January 1532 he was formally granted the office of the king's tailor with fees of 12*d* a day.[55] By 1533 he kept a large enough establishment to require a foreman called William Holt who brought evidence against Andrew Hewet, an apprentice tailor accused of heresy.[56] In November 1534, Malt succeeded the recently deceased Richard Gibson as yeoman tailor in the great wardrobe with 6*d* a day and livery.[57] Along with John Scut and Thomas Addington, he was assessed on goods worth £1,000 in the subsidy of 1535.[58] In 1536 he was listed as one of those owed money by Anne Boleyn.[59] In 1539–40 or 1540–41 he was master of the Merchant Taylors' company.[60] In 1540 he was appointed to a commission of five aldermen and five commoners who were ordered to appear before the commissioners for the first payment of the subsidy.[61]

Unlike his predecessors, the scale of his business with the great wardrobe was substantial. On 27 April 1541 the court of augmentations settled a bill of £1,778 3*s* 5*d* owing to John Malt for silk and other stuff delivered by him to the great wardrobe between Michaelmas 1539 and Michaelmas 1540.[62] He converted his profits into properly, for example, in May 1541 he acquired the reversion and rent of the rectory of Uffington, Berkshire, and a selection of other property in the area.[63] Three years later he bought the manor of Andresey (otherwise Nyland), Somerset, for £1,824 16*s* 8*d*.[64] In 1546 he purchased further property in Somerset for £1,311 2*d*.[65] Several of his purchases were made in conjunction with his illegitimate daughter Audrey and they provide a clear indication of his prosperity.

He continued to have very strong links with the great wardrobe, right to the end of his life. There is a warrant signed by the stamp dated 21 September 1545 and presented at the suit of Richard Cecil, yeoman of the robes, granting a joint patent to Richard Egliston and John Malt, for the office of cutter and botcher in the great wardrobe with 6*d* a day.[66] A warrant dated 1546 and signed by Sir Ralph Sadler authorised Sir John Williams to pay Malt £1,162 1*s* 8¾*d* for stuff and workmanship delivered into the great wardrobe in the previous two years ending in Michaelmas.[67]

Malt was Henry VIII's longest serving royal tailor. He appears in ten of the extant great wardrobe accounts: those for 1521–22, 1523–25, 1526–27, 1527–28, 1530–31, 1531–32, 1533–34, 1537–38, 1538–39 and 1543–44. Over the years he supplied increasingly greater amounts of the fabric used to make the king's clothes, culminating in 1543–44 when he supplied the following: bridges satin, broad cloth, brushes, buckram, budge, cambric, camlet, canvas, cloth, cloth of silver, cord, cotton, crest cloth, damask, frieze, fringe, fustian, linen, passamayne, ribbon, rubbers, sackcloth, sarsenet, satin, taffeta, velvet, silk buttons, Venice gold and silver buttons (Figs 19.2 and 19.3). The range of clothes he made was similar to those produced by Hilton and Paris, but there were a few additional items, including shirts and livery coats embroidered with HR and the royal arms. From the account in 1521–22, he undertook a small amount of translation work, but this increased markedly in volume as the reign progressed.

THE KING'S HOSIER

In the first half of the sixteenth century hose became increasingly complex garments. As a consequence, specialist hosiers developed alongside tailors, some of whom still continued to make hose. Hosiers made a variety of types of hose, including 'almain' hose. The hosier liaised closely with the king's tailor as doublets and hose were often made as matching pairs. Hose were also made to match jerkins. The standard fabric allowance made to the king's hosier for a pair of upper stocks was 1¼ yards (1.1 m), as in the case of 'a yerde quarter of cloth of gold after baudkyn for the stocking of a payr of hose for the kinges grace' [A387] in April 1518.

From 1498–99 until 1505–06 Thomas Mount provided hose, including ready-made hose for Henry VII's household. However, a man called William Croughton or William hosier appears in the great wardrobe accounts for 1504–05 and 1505–06 making hose for the king. Croughton also features in all of Henry VIII's accounts, starting with the account from 1510–11. A payment of £4 made to Davy Francis, the king's hosier, on Whit Sunday 1514 for his whole year's wages, 'as received by the late William Croughton', suggests that there were two William Croughtons, probably father and son, who held the office.[104] In March 1521 Croughton's wages, which had been paid daily at a rate of 2*d*, were then paid quarterly (15*s* 2*d*).[105] However, as the reign advanced his wages increased. Croughton received quarter wages of 35*s* at Lady Day 1539.[106] On 9 October 1539, Croughton's house in St Giles in the Fields burnt down and he lost goods to the value of £200. To assist him, Henry VIII licensed him to collect alms through England and Wales.[107]

Occasionally other hosiers are mentioned in the royal accounts. In 1530 John Pyne, hosier, made three pairs of hose for Weston, three pairs for Mark, six pairs for the two Williams, three pairs for Philip's boy, two pairs for Henry Ellis and three pairs for Patch, at 5*s* per pair, with a total cost of £5.[108] The revels account for 23 August 1519 included a payment of 8*s* to Gabriel the French hosier for making four pairs of hose for Frenchmen.[109]

THE QUEEN'S HOSIER

The hose made for women differed from those supplied for men. In essence, the hose for women were like stockings or long socks, and they could be made either from woollen cloth or by knitting.[110] It is possible to trace the names of some of the queen's hosiers, but little is known of their careers. While he is never named as her hosier, in November 1502 Thomas Humberston, hosier, supplied the cloth and made up seven pairs of socks for Elizabeth of York at a price of 6*d* a pair.[111] In 1536 Thomas Hardy was named as Anne Boleyn's hosier in the list of debts of her wardrobe of the robes. He was owed 22*s*.[112] Robert Hardy was described as hosier to Anne of Cleves when he received wages of £4 18*s* on 11 May 1540.[113] He was also hosier to Catherine Parr.[114]

THE KING'S SKINNER

The first king's skinner was appointed in 1405 and his name was Henry Barton. His role was to supply or purvey the furs required by the king and his household and to oversee the work being undertaken by skinners employed within the great wardrobe. He received a fee of 12*d* a day and livery.[115] Like the royal tailors, the skinners could be required to work through the night to get clothes ready in time. John Ryng was given 8*s* 4*d* for fuel for the cutters, skinners and other workers working in the winter time in the great wardrobe.[116]

In some instances, the skinner evidently undertook the preparation of the skins, as the accounts include payments for tawing. For example, a bill for work carried out by Nicholas Barley for Henry VII in the first year of his reign includes payments of 100*s* for making a lining of ermine for a purple velvet gown, £22 10*s* for 22½ timbers of ermine and 22*s* 6*d* for tawing the skins.[117] However, there were also specialists such as John Massey, the tawyer, who was paid 40*s* for tawing seven timbers of whole sables at 5*s* the timber.[118] The skinners also periodically provided damask powder used to scent the furs and keep them clean. As indicated above, some work with furs could be undertaken by tailors, such as the insertion of linings or the addition of fur borders. Consequently, disputes could arise between tailors and skinners over who had the right to fur garments. In 1555 the lord deputy in Ireland had to intervene in such a dispute, ruling that it was illegal for a tailor to undertake such work.[119]

Sixteenth-century skinners worked with quite a small range of furs. These included budge, sable, coney and lynx. Some of the skins were small — the usable section of a sable skin measures 12 × 3½ in. (0.30 × 0.09 m) — meaning that large numbers were required to fur a full garment, so making full fur linings were very labour intensive to make. On 26 December 1517 Thomas Jenyn received 80 budge skins that were 'delyuerd by the kinges commandement . . . for a mantell of purpull tylsent for the king' [A354]. A black satin gown that was furred with sable for the king had 110 skins for the front, 130 for the back, 64 for the upperstocks and breeches, 32 for the fore-sleeves and 14 for the cape and collar.[120] The skins were usually stitched together using silk thread, and they were sometimes stitched onto canvas to give them extra strength. The edges of large sections of fur could be bound with strips of fine leather.

On 10 November and 4 December 1485 Nicholas Barley, skinner of London, received grants of the sergeant skinnership with wages from Michaelmas of that year.[121] He was succeeded by Thomas Jenyn, also a London skinner, who was appointed as the king's skinner with 12*d* a day, on the death of Barley, from 6 November 1511.[122] On 9 April 1514 Sir John Dauntsey paid Jenyn £54 8*s* for furs bought for the king in Calais.[123] While there, he furred three gowns: a gown of russet velvet with black ermine at £5 6*s* 8*d* for the fur, a gown of yellow velvet with libard wombs at £17 13*s* 4*d* for the fur, and a gown of white velvet with powdered ermine costing £31 8*s* for the fur. On his death in August 1518 his widow wound up his affairs. James Worsley's inventory included an entry for 'Item xiij fyne bugie skynnes. Mistress Jenyns must answer for theim' [B327]. Jenyn worked in close association with John Ring who worked in the great wardrobe from 1483, selling furs to the crown. Ryng played a very important role in preparing the furs for Henry VIII's coronation. In 1514 Ring undertook all of the work on Mary Tudor's trousseau, and he died in 1516.[124]

In 1516 Nicholas Jenyn, leather dresser of London, was described in a list of fees and annuities as the king's leather dresser and as being in receipt of £18 5*s* a year for life.[125] In the same year, Jenyn was listed on a bill of receipt by Dauntsey as paying £6 for a year's rent of the king's armoury in Tower Street, presumably, as his place of business.[126] On 22 September 1518 he received a grant of the office of the king's leather dresser or sergeant furrier, after the death of Thomas Jenyn, with 12*d* a day.[127] In 1523 he was elected as an alderman of the Skinners' company, but he was exempted from office as he was not worth £1,000. However, by the time of his death in 1533 he owned property in at least nine London parishes, and throughout the home counties and a manor in Surrey.[128]

On 23 April 1533 Jenyn was succeeded by Thomas Addington as 'the king's leather dresser, alias sergeant of the *pelletria*'.[129] However, as with his predecessors, he had been undertaking work for the king prior to his appointment as king's skinner. On 30 December 1530 he had been paid £80 8*s* 8*d* 'for furres & furring of my lady Annes gownes'.[130] In the following year he was paid £40 15*s* 8*d* for work undertaken for Anne.[131] His wife, Catherine, also undertook work for the great wardrobe, and on Addington's death in December 1543 she succeeded him as king's skinner.[132]

In April 1544 Catherine and Thomas Addington (posthumously) bought the lordship of the manor of Harlow in Essex, along with the rectory there and other property for £1,549 14*s* 10*d*.[133] In February 1546 Catherine Addington and Richard Brykett, skinner of London, were granted the office of the king's skinner in survivorship. Catherine was granted the fee of 12*d* a day.[134] The scale of her business with the king is further indicated by a document signed by the stamp in August 1546 which authorised the treasurer of the tenths to pay her £781 14*s* 2*d* 'for stuff and workmanship delivered to your Majesty's use before Michaelmas last'.[135]

THE QUEEN'S SKINNER

The nature of the female wardrobe meant that the queen's skinner had a much more limited range of garments to work with than the king's skinner. The work consisted chiefly of furring gowns, sleeves and buskins, taking out and putting in fur linings, making fur bonnets and trimming garments with fur (Fig. 19.4). In 1485 Richard Storey was listed as skinner to Elizabeth of York, but the patchy nature of the accounts reveals little about the work he undertook.[136] The same is true of Richard Hanchet who in 1520 was listed as skinner to Catherine of Aragon when he received livery of 4½ yards (4.1 m) of tawny broad cloth for a gown.[137] It is very likely that Thomas Addington was Anne Boleyn's skinner, because he was listed as being owed money (£29 19*s* 2*d*) in her wardrobe of the robes at the time of her execution.[138] Addington was also skinner to Catherine Parr, as is shown by a payment for his work made to his widow.[139]

19.4 *Lady Butts wears a fur-trimmed loose gown over her kirtle. Lady Butts, by Hans Holbein the Younger. Isabella Stewart Gardner Museum, Boston*

THE KING'S EMBROIDERER

The embroiderers in the king's service undertook a range of different embroidery techniques and produced a variety of items, including embroidered motifs, often with heraldic overtones, such as roses, garters and initials. These motifs could be made up in advance of when they were needed. Earlier extant examples of motifs of this sort include a badge of the order of the Dragon worked in couched gold or gilt metal thread and in the context of a whole garment, on the 'Eagle Dalmatic' which forms part of the regalia made in *c.* 1320.[140] Comparable pieces appeared in the wardrobe of the robes in 1547, including 'twoo crownes embrawderid vppon crimesen vellut' (14548), a fleur-de-lis worked in the same way (14549) and 'iij skutchions embrodrid with tharmes of Inglonde & Castell' (14550). Appliqué and couched thread work were also used to decorate the king's own clothes, revels costumes and furnishings. In addition, royal embroiderers undertook repairs, as in the case of ⅜ yard (0.33 m) of plain cloth of gold being delivered to William Mortimer 'for mending of the bordors of enbraudry of iij doblettes & iij Jaquettes for ye king' [A501].

The embroiderers' working methods are hinted at in the payments made for Henry VII's coronation. Cristian Peynter received 20*s* 'for devising of xij trappours of the kinges armes, portred on papir with diuers colours for the brauderers and the hexmenes jaketts'.[141] Further details are provided in letters sent to Lady Lisle. On 19 June 1539 John Husee told her about her sleeves:

> wherin with the broiderer's advice I shall do my best. Yet the pattern your Ladyship shall understand, will serve no purpose, as far as I can see, for it is too little for the whole sleeve and too large for the half sleeve. I will not be too busy in cutting of it till I see the broiderer's ways; of which, if it frame not to my purpose, shall not be cut till I know further of your Ladyship's pleasure.[142]

The embroiderer engaged by Lady Lisle was William Ibgrave, the king's embroiderer who travelled to Calais, and 'he will signify your ladyship, I doubt not, at his coming to Calais'. Ibgrave did not undersell himself: 'the broiderer will have no less for his labour than xx*s* . . . he hath promised to do it as well as any man can do it'.[143]

While the king had one royal tailor, he regularly appointed a pair of craftmen to the office of the king's embroiderer. In December 1485 William Moreton, citizen and mercer, vestment maker and embroiderer, and William More were granted the office of the king's embroiderer in survivorship.[144] Following Morton's death, More enjoyed the office solo until on 3 October 1518 he surrendered his patent of 6 December 1509 in favour of a new one, naming him in survivorship with William Mortimer.[145] A year later, on 2 October 1519, More gave up his interest. In March 1528 Mortimer was joined by William Ibgrave.[146] Mortimer died in the next 15 months and Ibgrave remained in office until the king's death in January 1547. The embroiderer was paid at a rate of 1*s* a day.

Other individuals also feature in the accounts. For example, on 7 September 1516, Thomas Forster was paid £84 13*s* for embroidering certain pieces of horse harness which were sent to the emperor.[147] Foster was listed as an embroiderer in Worsley's wardrobe book where he undertook a small amount of work between May and December 1520. His commissions included bases and trappers for three men at arms decorated with 25 yards (22.8 m) of cloth of silver, and a gift of collars and muzzles for mastiffs made from 1¼ yards (1.1 m) of crimson velvet sent to Francis I.

William Mortimer appears in Worsley's wardrobe book as receiving 4 yards (3.6 m) of tawny cloth of gold on satin damask for embroidery on a mantle on 24 December 1516 [A371]. The last amount of embroidery recorded by him in the book was in May 1520 when he received ½ yard (0.45 m) of purple velvet for an embroidered border on a cloth of estate [A1170]. In all of the entries listed in Worsley's wardrobe book, Mortimer was undertaking an appliqué technique because he was supplied with cloth in all cases. He was given cloth of gold and velvet for embellishing the king's clothes and satin for making embroidered roses and crowns to decorate coats for the yeomen of the guard. On 31 December 1516 he received 6¼ yards (5.7 m) of crimson satin for roses and crowns to put on 120 coats for the guard [A1190].

On 8 July 1518 Mortimer received payment for embroidering three red satin coats at 5*s* each and the breast of a doublet of crimson satin 'with pearls of damask, gold and silver' for the king's own wear, costing 26*s* 8*d*. He also worked on a pair of hose to the same doublet, costing 26*s* 8*d*, and quilted a night cap of black satin for the king, 2*s*.[148] In 1520 he made a mule harness in anticipation of Charles V's visit to Calais.[149] Eight years later, he is mentioned in the accounts of the treasurer of the chamber for embroidering 62 coats of red cloth for the guard with roses and the crown imperial at 5*s* each, and for 5 yards (4.5 m) of crimson satin for the roses at 8*s* the yard and 2 yards (1.8 m) of white bridges satin at 4*s* the yard and 24 ells (16.5 m) of canvas at 5*d* the ell, costing £18 4*s*.[150] In 1529 his executors, William Botry, Richard Gresham, John Malt and Ralph Worsley, received £491 2*s* 1*d* owed by the king for velvets, silks and embroidery.[151]

By July 1529 William Ibgrave was listed as the king's embroiderer in the treasurer of the chamber's accounts for embroidering coats of red cloth.[152] In January 1530 he received £21 3*s* 4*d* for embroidery for the king and nearly three years later he was paid £257 5*s* 4*d* for embroidery.[153] For special commissions Ibgrave incorporated jewels and pearls into his designs for the king. A list of items delivered to Thomas Alvard on 16 November 1534 included 'a doublet of crimson velvet Inbroyderyd with cordons of gold the forslevys and placard garnysshed with eighteen gret Emerodys set in gold and twenty and nyne letters of gold and in euery of them nyne perlys'.[154] On 10 May 1536 he signed a receipt for 516 pearls from the king, to be bestowed upon his doublet and the queen's sleeves, and the rest to be returned to the king.[155] A little over a month later, Ibgrave received 1,562 pearls to decorate 'the hinder part' of the queen's kirtle.[156] He also signed a receipt for 18 emeralds and 29 letters of I [that is for Jane], each containing nine pearls, all set in gold to be put upon the foresleeves and placard of a doublet delivered by Anthony Denny.[157] He could also undertake work for the king's children. In April 1540 Princess Mary 'payed to the kinges Braudrer for Enbraudring a Cote for the Prince grace 54*s* 4*d*'.[158] On 6 May 1540 he was paid £391 9*s* 4*d* upon a warrant by John Gostwick for work in preparation for the arrival of Anne of Cleves.[159] Five years later he got £71 for embroidering coats for the yeomen of the guard, footmen, four ordinary messengers and others.[160] A month later in January 1546, he was paid the extraordinarily high figure of £698 3*s* 2*d* 'for stuff and workmanship employed upon your Majesty's apparel'.[161]

Like John Malt, William Ibgrave prospered sufficiently to become a country gentleman with a domicile at Abbots Langley in Hertfordshire.[162] In May 1540 he received a grant of the rectory and church there for £460 10*s* 10*d*.[163] Three years later in July 1543 he received a grant in fee for £87 2*s* 3*d* of lands elsewhere in the country.[164]

A number of other embroiderers were working in London, many of whom were not English. In May 1524 Guillaume Breyllant of London, an embroiderer and a native of Normandy, was granted denization, while in June Martin Graunde, embroiderer, native of Tournai, received denization.[165] However, there was work for English-born embroiderers too. In March 1530 the treasurer of the chamber's accounts record a payment of £126 9*d* to Stephen Humble, embroiderer, 'for embroiderings' made for the king.[166] In the following year Stephen, described simply as the king's embroiderer, received £100 from the privy purse on his bill which was paid on 9 April 1531.[167] While some tasks were small, as in the case of a payment on 12 January 1531 of 40*s* made to 'one peter Chadwyke, the kinges enbrawderer', others could provide longer-term employment.[168] On June 1538 Edmund Hodgeson, embroiderer, was paid on a warrant of 18 April 1538 for 6*d* a day for a quarter from 2 April to 30 June, 45*s*.[169]

THE QUEEN'S EMBROIDERER

The evidence is uneven, but what there is suggests that Henry's queens often had several embroiderers in their service at any one time. The bulk of their work would have been to decorate clothes made for the queen or to make badges to place on her household's livery. Like the king's embroiderer, the queen's embroiderer could work for others. On 22 November 1533 Leonard Smith wrote to Lady Lisle to tell her that 'I have also this day ... delivered your frontlet to the Queen's broiderer, who saith you shall have one of other fashion shortly after Christmas, to be at your pleasure and commandment'.[170] Three weeks later he assured Lady Lisle that the frontlet would reach her, and in the meantime he enclosed the bond from the queen's embroiderer.[171]

Robinet was embroiderer to Elizabeth of York. In November and December 1502 he received payments of £6 18*s* 11*d* and 113*s* 1*d* to reimburse him for money spent on wages for embroiderers and others working on the 'Queen's rich bed', and on 2 January 1503 he claimed 30*s* for his house rent for three-quarters of a year, for a period ending in Christmas 1502.[172] Shortly after Henry VIII's accession he entered the service of Catherine of Aragon . He was paid for making fleur-de-lis, great and small, wreathes, clouds, roses and rose buds of gold for nine jackets for the henchmen, which were ordered on 15 November 1509.[173] No further references to the queen's embroiderer have been discovered until 1520 when Arnold Lock was described as holding the post.[174] A payment of 22*s* 6*d* was made to him for 4½ yards (4.1 m) of tawny broad cloth for a gown.

In parallel with his work for the king, William Ibgrave also worked for Anne Boleyn long before she became queen: on 16 April 1531 the king settled on her behalf a bill from Ibgrave for £18 14*s* 9*d*.[175] Ibgrave was one of the three embroiderers, along with Guillaume Brellant and Stephen Humble, to whom she owed money to at the time of her execution. She owed Ibrgave, Brellant and Humble £31 2*s* 6*d*, £10 4*s* 8*d* and £13 13*s* 4*d* respectively.[176] Ibgrave and Brellant are both mentioned as embroiderers in Anne of Cleve's accounts.[177] Brellant then went on to embroider for Catherine Parr.[178] While he is never named as Catherine Parr's embroiderer, two quite substantial payments were made to him in her bills recorded in the 1547 inventory: 'an acquitaunce of Cxx[li] paid to Guillam the Embroderer' (17752) and 'an Acquitaunce of William Smithe broderer for C[li] receaued of Sir Anthonie Coope knight to the behalfe of Gillam Braibot the Emborderer' (17760). He continued to be engaged by the royal family. In 1559, he was listed as working for Elizabeth I's coronation, along with William Middleton and David Smith.[179]

THE KING'S SILK WOMAN

Notwithstanding the assertion that royal silk women did not exist until the reign of Mary I, such women can be traced back to the reign of Richard III.[180] Of these, Alice Claver supplied 6 oz (170 g) of red ribbon for the coronation of Henry VII.[181] Even so, very little is known about how the silk women were organised for business purposes. However, it has been demonstrated that they did work together in order to protect their business interests. In particular, the silk women sought to prevent the import of twined silk and ready-made silk goods such as laces and ribbons.[182] The silk women mainly bought the raw silk from the mercers which they then made into a range of small, fancy goods including buttons, laces, ribbons, fringe and tassels. However, other activities that silk women were associated with were highlighted in the 1547 inventory: 'a litle purse of lether with iiij Registre pynnes whereof twoo Silke womens worke' (2587) and 'one Coiffe Venice golde Sylkewomans worke' (8730).

Elizabeth Langton was listed as the king's silk woman in Henry VII's accounts for 1502–03, 1504–05 and 1505–06. She was perhaps the widow of Thomas Langton who had supplied the king with silk in 1498–99. Thomas and Elizabeth provided a range of goods including bonnets, buttons, frontlets, girdles, lacing ribbon, round silk ribbon, silk laces, silk points, sipers and tassels (Fig. 19.5). The name Elizabeth Langton does not recur after 1506, but the appearance early in Henry VIII's reign of Elizabeth Worship, the king's silk woman in 1510–11, suggests that in the interval she may have married, or more likely, remarried. Elizabeth Worship appears as the king's silk woman in the accounts for 1510–11, 1516–17, 1517–18, 1520–21 and 1523–25. Her career overlapped with that of Catherine Worship who figures in the accounts for 1523–25 and 1526–27, on the latter occasion with John Worship. From 1527–39 Lettice Worship features and in 1540 she received £177 10*s* from John Gostwick in connection with Anne of Cleves.[183] From the rehearsal of the facts it is tempting to see Catherine, John and Lettice of the children of Elizabeth Worship, née Langton.

Catherine Addington, wife of Thomas Addington of London, and widow of Thomas Jenyn, was granted the room of silk woman to the king on 25 May 1524.[184] However, she was not listed in her own right in the great wardrobe accounts as the king's skinner, until after the death of her second husband in 1543–44. Anne and Agnes Grey are also listed in the account for 1543–44. They supplied a very similar range of goods including arming points, buttons, cord, Guernsey hose, hose, needles, passamayne, English ribbon, ribbon for stocks, shirts for day and night and silk thread. They may make been related but it is also possible that Agnes was an alias used by Anne. A warrant dated September 1545 allowed William and Anne Grey £1,158 13*s* for stuff delivered to the great wardrobe in the year ending Michaelmas 1544 which was paid to Sir John Williams for land they had bought.[185]

Coffers could be made to house particular items, as in the case of 'one coffer . . . to put in hur graces plakards', 'on Juell coffer with xx drawing tylles and partycyons', 'a coffer with xij drawing tylles & a Rome a bowe to put yn yowr graces sleves' and 'on coffer for hur graces lyneng'.[241] An extant example of a coffer of this type is provided by Lady Margaret Beaufort's coffer at Westminster abbey (Fig. 8.2 and 8.3). The coffer is subdivided with 18 wooden partitions covered with blue, plain weave linen, while the inside of the coffer is lined with red linen. The coffer makers also undertook a range of related activities, such as covering and upholstering chairs.

The names of two of Henry VIII's coffer makers are known: Philip Evaker or Sewaker and William Green. In 1520 Philip Evaker made three short standard chests costing £9 and one long one costing £6 for the revels.[242] He was described as 'our coffer maker' in a warrant dated 16 February 1522 when he supplied two standards, a coffer, a cloth sack and two 'mayles'.[243] By 8 February 1526 William Green was described as 'a coffer maker' and he was granted 'a red coat of our livery'.[244] A warrant dormant dated 8 February 1536 ordered a red livery coat for Green to be delivered annually at Michaelmas at a cost of 29*s* 6*d*.[245] In 1539 Green gave the king 'a small coffer couered with blakk veluet with H and R and Rooses and floure deluces' as a New Year's gift. In return he received a gilt cruse weighing 12⅜ oz (0.35 kg).[246] The great wardrobe accounts record regular deliveries made by Green of coffers, chests and barehides to the offices of the wardrobe of the robes. Two of his accounts survive from 1545–46.[247] He also supplied the king with close stools, as indicated by his bill from December 1546 for a close stool delivered to Sir Anthony Denny, including black velvet to cover it, 3 lb (1.36 kg) of down for padding the seat, elbows and side pieces, 2,000 gilt nails and 26 'bolyeon' nails at 6*d* each, in total £4 10*s* 6*d*.[248] There is also a bill from Elizabeth Slanning for silk fringe and ribbon delivered by her to Green for a close stool costing 27*s* 7½*d*.[249] Other bespoke items included a standard for the king for keeping and carrying his crossbows costing £4 10*s*.[250] The Green family continued to work in royal service under the later Tudors and transported into the service of James I in 1603.[251]

THE QUEEN'S COFFER MAKER

The queen's coffer maker preformed much the same work for the queen as the king's coffer maker did for the king. Indeed the two posts seem to have been performed by the same man. William Green was also coffer maker to Anne of Cleves.[252] Later he served Catherine Parr in the same capacity.[253]

THE KING'S CORDWAINER

Cordwainers worked with cordwain, which was a type of leather that had originated in Cordoba. Originally, in the eighth century, it had been made from mouflon, a native Spanish sheep breed, but by the sixteenth century it was more commonly goat skin. There were several types including those tanned with sumac or alum and dyed, most particularly to produce scarlet leather by dying alum tawed skins with kermes. Cordwainers derived their name from the leather that they worked, and at one time they had produced a broad range of goods, but by the Tudor period they had specialised as shoe makers. The king's cordwainer made shoes, boots and slippers, chiefly for the king, but he also provided footwear for certain groups within the royal household, such as the footmen, the henchmen and the officers of the royal hunts. The latter generally received double-soled shoes as these were more hardwearing.[254]

Sixteenth-century shoes had a fairly simple construction and were not durable. Fashionable shoes of the sort worn at Henry's court would have been made from dyed goatskin or with textile uppers. The shoes of this period had a welted construction. The toes were round or more usually square and this feature became very exaggerated by the middle of Henry VIII's reign, with shoes being over 6½ in. (0.17 m) wide. This style of shoe was known as a high shoe and they could fasten at the front with a buckle, toggle or lace. Lower cut shoes were also available with an ankle strap as a means of attaching them and a square or horned toe. By the 1550s the pointed toe started to become fashionable again. Leather shoes were often decorated either with slashing that usually ran parallel to the end of the toes, stamping, piercing or incising.[255] Fur linings could be supplied for boots and buskins, but these were usually made and inserted by a skinner.

The position of king's cordwainer during Henry VIII's reign was monopolised by Cornelius and Henry Johnson, who were probably father and son. Both men worked with the high quality Spanish leather and the less esteemed English leather, for shoes, buskins and boots, and they also made shoes and slippers with textile uppers, chiefly silk velvet. Their descendants remained in royal service until the early seventeenth century: Garrett Johnson was Elizabeth's cordwainer from 1552 until 1590, while his son Peter worked for Elizabeth and later made shoes for James I and Anne of Denmark.[256]

Cornelius Johnson is mentioned within the great wardrobe accounts for 1510–11, 1516–17, 1517–18, 1521–22 and 1523–25. On 16 June 1510 he submitted a bill for five pairs of winter boots, nine pairs of riding buskins of Spanish leather, four pairs of hunting shoes, two pairs of arming shoes and five pairs of tawny velvet shoes.[257] He regularly supplied shoes, boots and buskins with the variety of footwear increasing from boots, double-soled shoes, pinsons, shoes and slippers in 1510–11, to arming shoes of red Spanish leather, boots, boots of English leather, boots of Spanish leather, buskins of Spanish leather, buskins of velvet, double-soled shoes, night slippers, pinsons, shoes made from English leather, shoes for football, shoes made from Spanish leather and velvet-covered shoes. In addition, in 1523–25 he also supplied skins of Spanish leather for making a coat for the king and he undertook the sewing. Henry Johnson was listed in the royal accounts for nine years between 1523–23 to 1543–45. As well as making a wide variety of shoes, slippers, pinsons and boots, he also made leather-covered cases and supplied leather on occasion. In addition, in December 1531 he was sent on a journey with Anthony Anthony by the king and he was paid £6 6*s* 4*d* for his costs.[258]

Others occasionally made shoes for or sold shoes to the great wardrobe. These were mostly sales in a single year and involved double-soled shoes for the officers of the hunt or the king's footmen: Roger Allen, haberdasher, provided double-soled shoes in 1523–25; Andrew Carre, double-soled shoes in 1537–38; William Hewetson, double-soled shoes in 1543–45; Ralph Warren, shoes, double-soled shoes and velvet shoes in 1533–34, and John Witpain, double-soled shoes in 1543–45. Sometimes the shoes purchased were of velvet: Thomas Mount sold velvet shoes to the great wardrobe in 1533–34, shoes of an unspecified type in 1538–39 and double-soled shoes in 1543–45, and Henry Mints made velvet shoes in 1538–39. Shoes were also bought for the king's revels, as in the case of the revels held on 23 August 1519 when 12 pairs of shoes 'overhylled with satin' were bought from 'divers persons at Southwark, St Martin's, Temple Bar and Bak Chapyllton' for 16*s*.[259]

THE QUEEN'S CORDWAINER

The wardrobe accounts indicate that the queen's cordwainer offered a more limited range of footwear than that provided to the king. Most of the references are to shoes, slippers and fur-lined buskins for sleeping. A pair of accounts for shoes made for Catherine Parr, Mistress Neville (her stepdaughter) and Jane, her fool, from 1544–45 lack the name or signature of the cordwainer, but they are signed off by Sir Thomas Arundel and Sir Robert Tyrwytt, and they come to £25 12*d* and £17 19*d*.[260]

Rutte was described as Elizabeth of York's cordwainer when on 2 January 1503 he supplied a large order of shoes and buskins for the queen, in addition to shoes given to poor women on Maundy Thursday, a pair of buskins for the countess of Suffolk and shoes for the queen's footmen.[261] By 1520 Lybart Vaughan had become cordwainer to Catherine of Aragon, and in this capacity he received 4 yards (3.6 m) of tawny broad cloth costing 20*s* for a gown.[262] At the time of her execution in 1536, Anne Boleyn owed her cordwainer Anilee 42*s* 6*d* for shoes.[263] Other references indicate that in 1531–32 John Scut provided shoes for Anne Boleyn.[264] Anne of Cleve's cordwainer is mentioned but not named in her household accounts. Amongst others, Philip Ryves and Francis Woodville, supplied shoes for Anne.[265] Godfrey Lowley was shoe maker to Catherine Parr.[266]

THE KING'S CUTLER

Swords and daggers, although still a necessity for self-protection, had also become fashion accessories. The authorities, including Henry VIII, were concerned about their use in brawls and duelling. On 18 October 1524 it was stated that 'no manner of person, of whatsoever estate, degree or condition he be, except the sheriff of Middlesex, the warden of the Fleet and his officers, bear or wear any manner of weapon, that is to say bills, swords, bucklers, wood knives, daggers or other weapons, within his palace or hall of Westminster or the precincts of the same, upon pain of forfeiture of the same weapon'.[267] Hunting knives also had a practical use, especially as Henry's court, where hunting was such a popular pastime. Finally, swords could have a processional role, when they would be carried before the monarch as he processed. All such items that were in regular use by the king were kept within the wardrobe of the robes or in the keeping of the king's cutler.

The role of the king's cutler included making scabbards, sheaths and girdles, undertaking repairs or refurbishing items when they became worn or dirty, in addition to maintaining the weapons and their sharpness. Even so, he did not have a monopoly on these tasks. In 1489 John Smith, armourer, received 6*s* 8*d* for covering two swords and a scabbard with cloth of gold.[268] Alternatively, they could work with materials provided by other craftsmen: in 1486 Nicholas Warley, a London goldsmith, was paid £6 for 'the gyrdille harneys of the kynges swerd, weieth iij oz', and 6*s* 8*d* 'for a cors for the same swerd'.[269]

An undated bill from the closing years of Henry VIII's reign for 'armourer's work' signed by Richard Cecil, Thomas Sternold and John Rowland recorded payment for a range of work. This included making girdles and scabbards, cleaning weapons and 'for gilding a dagger with a crystal haft and a knife gilt to the same dagger'.[270] The bill also itemised payments of 12*d* for travel for 'my costs and charges for my horses and myself to Hampton Court one day', as well as to Oatlands and Guildford.

In May 1513 Marinus Garet was described as the king's cutler. He was a native of Normandy but resident in London, and he was granted a licence to employ English or foreign apprentices.[271] He may well have been the Marion listed in James Worsley's wardrobe book as having received velvet to make girdles, sheaths and scabbards for wood knives and swords. These deliveries of cloth, usually of 1 or 1¼ yards (0.91 m or 1.1 m), were made between 4 June 1517 and 2 June 1520.[272] He was also described as 'the blade Smythe' when on 3 February 1531 he was paid £6 16*d* on his bill.[273] On 11 November 1532, 31*s* 1*d* was 'paied to the Cutler for dressing of the kinges swerdes at Calays'.[274] On 10 October 1537 John Gates, page of the robes, listed the 'daggers and swords remaynyng with Maryon'.[275] This included a large number of items, similar in range to the group of weapons held by the wardrobe of the robes in 1547. Entries include 'a dagger with an ivory haft plain the sheth all siluer with ij men wrestlyng the one breaking the back of the other', and 'a sword the hilt flat the pommel and hilt gilt the hilt and haft covered with velvet and robed with silk'. In March 1542 John Videe was appointed as the king's cutler and worker in iron, with fees of 4*d* a day.[276] Little else is known about him. Philip Lenthall, cutler, was granted by the king a red gown guard with black velvet, lined in the bases with frieze and in the vents and collar with satin, with one pocket. The gown was ordered for Lenthall on the king's own warrant dated 27 March 1544 at a cost of 3*s* 4*d* to make.[277]

The king's most famous cutler was the Spanish damascener and swordsmith Diego da Çaias (Fig. 19.8). By March 1543 he metals, as in the case of those supplied in June 1502 for disguising jackets for Elizabeth of York by William Antyne, coppersmith, for 56*s* 8*d*.[312]

Fernando Gawo appears as Catherine of Aragon's goldsmith in her wardrobe book of 1520. He was given 4 yards (3.6 m) of tawny broad cloth for a gown costing 20*s*, which was furred with black budge worth 46*s* 8*d*. He also received 3 yards (2.7 m) of black velvet for a doublet priced at 30*s*. His wife was also issued with livery consisting of 14 yards (12.8 m) of tawny camlet for a gown costing 37*s* 4*d*, 2 yards (1.8 m) of black velvet to line the sleeves and purfil for 20*s* and a roll buckram worth 3*s*. In all, the warrant came to £7 17*s*.[313] This indicates that it was an important enough post to warrant the provision of livery, and his name indicates that Catherine favoured a Spanish goldsmith who would create traditional Spanish designs. In 1536 Richard Silcock is listed as Anne Boleyn's gold wiredrawer in the list of debts owing to her wardrobe of the robes and she owed him £38.[314]

In September 1536 Henry granted Peter Richardson, an alien goldsmith, 'a native of Holland in the Emperor's dominions', a licence to have six servants or journeymen, natives or foreigners, for the making of 'juells, works an dyvyses' for Queen Jane.[315] Richardson transferred to Anne of Cleves's service and as her goldsmith on 27 May 1540 he received £46 18*s* for jewels. However, Cornelius Hayes also undertook work for her, providing spangles for coats for her guard at a cost of £20. Her accounts also refer to John Hawes, the queen's gold cutter, and Robert Copper, goldsmith, who provided items for her saddles.[316] Richardson entered into partnership with the goldsmith Hans of Antwerp and after Catherine Parr's marriage to Henry VIII he became her goldsmith.[317]

THE KING'S JEWELLER

A jeweller can be both a maker of jewellery and a vendor of it and jewelled fastenings. The word was often used interchangeably with goldsmith. Hans of Antwerp is often described as a goldsmith, but his skills included cutting hardstones. Hans arrived in England in 1513. In 1537 he was admitted to the Goldsmiths' company. As a friend and colleague of Hans Holbein the younger, he was soon drawn into the king's service and he married an English woman. A girdle prayer book depicting the worship of the brazen serpent and the judgement of Solomon has been attributed to Hans' workshop.[318]

The monetary value of jewels is made clear in a letter of Charles V dated 2 August 1545: 'The emeralds and precious stones from Cartagena, and the pearls, came just in time to provide payment for Prince Doria and other matters.'[319] Consequently, jewellery was highly prized by most European monarchs and, as with other desirable commodities, Henry often granted licences to foreign merchants to encourage them to bring their wares to England. In April 1524, Nicoluccio Ninaicciesi, merchant of Florence, was granted a licence to import jewels, which were to be shown to the king first, and to export those unsold without paying customs and then to proceed into foreign parts with one servant and two ambling or trotting horses.[320]

Henry's accounts emphasise the significance of Parisian goldsmiths and jewellers as producers and sellers of high quality items. Paris was the largest European court city throughout the sixteenth century. The range of goods is evident from the licence issued to Jean Langue, jeweller of Paris and Gilles, his son, in July 1546. Father and son were authorised by Henry VIII to bring in to England all manner of 'juelles, perlles, precious stones, as well set in gold and embrawdred in garments as unsett, almoner goldsmythes worke of golde and sylver, almanner sortes of skynnes and furres of sables and lusardes, clothes, newe gentlelesses of what facion or value the same be, wrought and set or unwrought and not set, in gold or otherwise'.[321] In the following month Jean Langue received a discharge for the custom duties on the jewels that the king had bought from him 'in recompense whereof he did give your Highness a ring with a fair sapphire'.[322]

The sources of jewellery designs, many deriving from Islamic ornament, included published engravings by Virgil Solis (1514–62) and Hans Brosamer (1506–52) and books such as Thomas Geminus's *Moryse and Damashin renewed and encreased very profitably for Goldsmythes and Embroderers* published in 1548. The jewellers working for Henry often worked from specially commissioned designs produced by artists of Holbein's calibre (Fig. 19.9). Holbein also designed a brooch for Catherine Parr incorporating her personal badge.[323] How items were commissioned is the subject of a letter dated 24 October 1535 from Richard Blount to Lady Lisle. He described his discussions with a jeweller in Bruges who would be making a jewel for her: 'He demands three weeks to make it, and 4 angels 12 styvers for the work . . . I enclose a pattern of the goldsmith's doing and the xx with spottes be the plassys wer the dyamondes shullde stoned.'[324] Another Lisle letter which survives only in a damaged condition discusses a variety of jewellery, particularly a flower like a gillyflower 'which it is desired shall be made of more substance, for it breaketh oft times because the branches be slender . . . [it is to] be rich and goodly, and of the best and newest fashion that you can devise, though it were for some person being under a cloth of estate'.[325]

Antwerp was the north European centre for the sale and purchase of gemstones. In 1551 Edward VI bought 'a fayer flower of golde having sett in the same three ballace a perle sett withowte foyle and betwene euerey ballace a perle and in the myddes betwene the three ballaces a large pointed Diamounte and a perle pendaunt at one of the ballaces' (3686) from Anthony Fulker in Antwerp. Erasmus Skeetz, merchant of Antwerp, sold jewellery to Edward VI using Thomas Gresham as an intermediary. On 10 March 1552 he delivered 'a fayer greate table Dyamounte ring sett in fayer worke enameled blacke redd white and blewe And in a case of Leather gilte and veluet within' (3687).

As with other specialist skills, jewellery making and stone cutting were areas where Henry was dependent upon foreign craftsmen. This was highlighted by a petition made to the king's council in 1524 by Hubert Busman, factor of Leonard Hyrsfogel and his fellow merchants who were transporting

19.9 *Design for a cipher combining the letters HI, almost certainly for Henry and Jane Seymour for a pendant, by Hans Holbein the Younger. 5308.116, reproduced by courtesy of the Trustees of the British Museum*

unpolished diamonds on a ship, the *Martyn*. When the ship sank near to Chichester, the passengers lodged with Arnold Stoltz, beer brewer of Portsmouth. The master of the ship died in Stoltz's house and, when the diamonds were asked for, Stoltz denied any knowledge of them, but his wife allegedly offered them for sale in London, 'but as no man here could polish and dress them, none would buy'. Stoltz, assisted by Mr Skeffington, the master of the king's ordinance, then took the diamonds to Flanders, but returned hastily when he feared he might be discovered. Undeterred, his wife took some of the diamonds to Cornelius Hayes, whereupon the Stoltzes were arrested.[326]

The ambiguous use of the term jeweller makes it hard to plot the careers of the men who became the king's jewellers, a process that is not facilitated by the post apparently being an Henrician development in the reign and it sometimes being left vacant. John Lengram was a merchant of 'Valenayne beyond the sea', and he was described as the king's jeweller in a licence issued in April 1524 allowing him to come to England for six years and to import jewels of which the king was to have first choice.[327] In September 1536, £180 was paid to Henry Salvage, merchant of Genoa, for three emeralds bought by the king, while 'Jenyns Longraunt' received £1,000 for jewels.[328] In July 1538 a passport was issued to Peter van der Waal, of Antwerp, which described him as the king's jeweller.[329] He was allowed to leave the country with six horses, baggage and servants.[330] However, he was described as a goldsmith in the 1547 inventory and examples of his work were recorded (281, 948–49, 1039) along with the other luxury goods he dealt in. (12157–58).

Alvard Plumber received a grant in March 1542 to import 400 tons of Toulouse woad and Gascon wine.[331] In November 1546 he was described as a merchant and jeweller of Paris, and he was trading in partnership with his son-in-law, Thomas Sible, and they received a licence to import jewellery and stones into England, for the pleasure 'of us, of our dearest wief the Queen, our nobles, gentlemen and other'.[332]

There were several other highly specialised offices that were closely related to the post of the royal jeweller. In June 1541 Peter Francis Benall, engraver of precious stones, was given a salary of £10 a year plus 22*s* 6*d* for a livery coat, and in May 1546 Thomas Geminus, engraver, received a salary of £10 a year.[333] Very shortly after in September 1546 Everard Everdes received a safe conduct for his wife, children, household stuff and necessaries.[334] He was listed as a goldsmith and the king's lapidary in the 1547 inventory. In July 1547, at the commandment of the Lord Protector, Everdes was sent a large sapphire 'to cutt' which he supplied for Edward VI's use 'cutt in squares' (2849). These men would have probably been producing similar work to that undertaken by Richard Astyll, who was employed by the king to produce portrait cameos.[335]

THE KING'S MILLINER

The king's milliner made bonnets, caps and hats for the king. In addition, milliners also sold fancy goods and consequently they came into competition with haberdashers. According to Sir Thomas Smith in his *Discourse of the Commonweal of this Realm of England*, written in 1549, haberdashers sold 'white paper, looking glasses, pins, pouches, hats, caps, brooches, silk and silver buttons, laces and perfumed gloves', noting that 'the list descends from luxuries to frivolities'.[336] However, milliners did not have a monopoly on élite hat making in the first half of the sixteenth century. Some headwear was made for both the king and other members of the household, including the henchmen and footmen, by the king's tailor. Worsley's wardrobe book records that William Hilton made a range of hats for Henry VIII: bonnets made from 1¼ yards (1.1 m) of velvet [e.g. A921], night bonnets made from ⅜ of a yard (0.33 m) of velvet or satin and hoods made en suit with riding coats and demi-coats [A937]. On 28 June 1535 John Malt, the king's tailor, was required to make one green velvet hat, three velvet caps of yellow, orange and green and a cap for Henry VIII, along with a hood for William Somer, the king's fool.[32] However, some hats for members of the household were bought in ready made and consequently were cheaper than the bespoke items.

Christopher Milliner was probably the Christopher Carcano listed in the accounts relating to expenditure within the king's privy purse.[337] On 21 July 1539 he provided hats, feathers and aglets for Prince Edward costing £18 14*s* 11*d*.[338] Carcano was not the only milliner serving the king. Two bills submitted by Mark Milliner indicate a similar pattern of goods and expertise. The bills itemised a number of caps and night caps, amongst a profusion of gloves, buttons, aglets and hunting equipment.[41] The range of goods that Carcano dealt with can be assessed from a list of jewellery imported by him under licence via the port of London on 4 February 1544. The list includes 'one martron skynne with the head and claws of gold, the head garnished with iij emeralds, ij diamonds and iij rubies. A carcan of gold garnished with iiij great table diamonds, iiij great rocke rubies, viij great pearls and a pearl pendant, a chain, a girdle, two crosses and two rings'.[339] He is also mentioned in the 1547 inventory supplying knitted doublets and hose to the king.[340]

Francis Albert, milliner, the king's servant, was granted a licence to bring a range of luxury goods into the realm for sale, including:

> all manner of jewels, pearls, precious stones as well set in gold and embroidered in garments as unset, all manner of goldsmiths' work of gold and silver, all manner of cloth of gold, tinsel, tissue, velvets, damask and such other like silks, mixed with gold or silver or with silk or otherwise, all manner of garments as hose, doublets or other garments or things embroidered with gold and silver or silk, of what making or new fashion so ever they be and all manner sorts and making of fringes and passamayne wrought with gold and silver or otherwise all manner of sorts and ribbons . . . [and] all manner of caps of whatsoever foreign country making they be of.[341]

There was also the related office of the king's capper. The king's capper does not often appear to have made caps for the king, but for members of his household. Cappers worked with non-woven materials such as felt and felted knitting, as well as woven textiles.[342] In May 1514, according to the king's book of payments, money was paid to Bartholomew Whale of London, the king's capper, for bonnets and to other unspecified individuals for kersey and other cloth for the king's cordwainer. It is not clear from this reference what materials Whale was working with, but there is a suggestion that he was working with wool. He also provided 18 hats for the members of the yeomen of the guard who accompanied the duke of Suffolk to France for Princess Mary's marriage to Louis XII. The hats cost 2*s* 4*d* each, coming to a total of 42*s*.[343] About the same time Whale supplied 18 hats for the yeomen of the guard which were delivered to Laurence Eglesfeld, clerk of the check with the guard.[344] However, the king's capper had competition. For example, in December 1514 John Hendry of London, 'attending upon our court with haberdash wares', was granted a licence for to import 500 dozen caps and 100 dozen hats.[345]

THE KING'S SADDLER

On 28 October 1495 Henry VII granted a charter to the Saddlers' company confirming an earlier one and in 1540 Henry VIII reconfirmed it. In 1537 the Saddlers' company was 26th in the list of London companies, with a membership of 60.[346] The king's saddler made saddles, covered saddles and harness in velvet and undertook repairs. The styles of saddle and horse harness were influenced by fashion and national taste (Fig. 19.10). For example, on 9 April 1519 Alfonso d'Este wrote to Henry VIII about horses, and added that he had sent him '200 patterns of bridles'.[347]

The great wardrobe accounts demonstrate that the king's saddler also provided buckles, hooks, pendants (quatrefoil, octofoil, lozenge, cruciform, circular and rectangular that could be gilded, enamelled, engraved or have punched decoration) and suspension mounts. These fittings were recorded in inventory entries as in the case of 'A bridell of Cloth of tissue and Ruset vellet and two collers of belles siluer and guilte conteyninge xvj great belles' (8393). These could be their own work or they could be selling on the work of lorimers. Lorimers made the metal elements of horse harness and so they worked in close conjunction with the saddler who incorporated the metal elements into the finished harness. In 1377 the lorimers were listed amongst the group of crafts sending representatives to the common council, and in 1504 they contributed to the guildhall kitchens, although they were not

19.10 *An example of the style of saddle and harness fashionable in the early sixteenth century.* La selle d'honneur/Le grant Escuyer/Le maistre des pages *(The saddle of honour/the master of the horse/the master of the pages). The Westminster Tournament Roll, The College of Arms*

appointed to keep the watch in 1518.[348] A list of payments for horses bought for the king's armouries in 1520 included a payment for 22 laten buckles and 22 pendants costing *11s 6d*, cleaning off the sprue *11d* and gilding *36s 9d*.[349]

The 1547 inventory includes a reference to 'one stele Sadle of redd Lether with A Seat of Crimsen Vellet embrodered with grene Silke' (8385).[350] This compares well with a very good example of a complete Italian saddle from slightly later — *c.* 1570–80 — with a wooden saddle tree, gilded saddle steels and a padded saddle cover of red silk velvet which is decorated with cord and braid and embroidered with a small foliate motif in metal thread.[351] This saddle is very similar in construction (with the pommel and cantle joined by two semicircular arches which are connected by two metal sidebars) to the saddle made for the 'Genouilhac' armour which was possibly made for Henry in 1527.[352]

English kings often kept a mule for riding, as well as horses. Consequently, presents of mules and mule harness were most welcome. On 22 May 1526 Cardinal Wolsey reported that the king had received two mules sent to him by the Regent of France that were 'fair, goodly and well trained beasts as hath been seen and their garnishing was rich and of the best fashion'. He added that he had received two similar mules that 'might have been a right honourable present to have been sent unto the Pope's holiness'.[354] Henry periodically employed a specialist saddler to make mule harness. For example, in September 1533 Michael Borsert, the maker of saddles for the king's mules, was granted a passport because the king planned to send him abroad on business.[353] By 1547 the king's possessions included 'a footeclothe for a Moile of purple vellat allouer embraudered with veanice and damaske golde perle and blewe stones with a Border likewise embruadered with perle and garnettes fringed with a narrowe frindge of veanice golde with heddestall patrell Rsyne and hinder parte . . . with Bockells and penauntes of siluer and gilte' (9924).

The king's saddler is rarely mentioned in Henry VII's great wardrobe accounts. In the account for 1498–99 there are references to John Lere, saddler, supplying items including bridles, buckles, harness, saddles and stirrups (Fig. 19.11). A payment

19.11 *Two stirrups thought to have been made for Henry VIII. 1685-B449-50, Ashmolean Museum, Oxford*

of £4 *16s 8d* was made to him for covering a saddle with crimson velvet and decorating it with gold and silk fringe, for 16 yards (14.6 m) of crimson velvet and labour for covering four other saddles in July and November 1498.[355] William Stile seems to have succeeded Lere as saddler, as he appears in the accounts of 1502–03, 1504–05 and 1505–06, making similar provision.

Stile's period in office overlapped with that of Nicholas Mayor, a saddler of Southwark, who served as both the king and queen's saddler. Mayor's work features in the great wardrobe accounts from 1502–03, 1504–05, 1505–06, 1510–11, 1516–17, 1517–18, 1521–22, 1523–25 and 1527–28. Between 9 May 1516 and 2 June 1520, he received cloth of gold, tilsent and velvet from James Worsley to cover harness for the king's horses. He undertook a range of tasks including covering horse harness with 1½ yards (1.3 m) of purple tilsent [A782], making a trapper from 12 yards (10.9 m) of russet cloth of gold [A439] and performing a saddle house for the king's mule with ½ yard (0.45 m) of russet velvet [A1173]. Examples of his accounts survive, countersigned by George Lovekyn and entitled, 'The Reperacyon of the grete warrant done by me Nycholas Maior that wasse gyuyn at Stony Stratford the x day of September anno xvij° Regis H VIII^mo^' and 'The Reperacyons of the kynges horses in Gloseter and in abyngton and in oxefforde', which come to £3 *3s 11d*.[356]

Robert Acton was born into a family of Worcestershire gentry. How he gained his first post at the Tudor court is unknown. However, by 22 October 1518 he was a groom of the chamber and by 1528 he was a gentleman usher. By May 1528 he was married to Margery Mayor, daughter of Nicholas Mayor of Southwark, and in September of that year Acton was appointed as the king's saddler with *12d* a day on the death of his father-in-law.[357] He sat as MP for Southwark in three parliaments. He was listed as the king's saddler in the extant great wardrobe accounts for 1531–32, 1533–34 and 1535–39. He made and covered saddles and horse harness as well as supplying buckles and pendants, usually the preserve of the lorimer, and brushes and combs. He also undertook repairs and the restuffing of saddles. In August 1540 he obtained a grant of the abbot of Hailes's lodging at Coscombe, Gloucestershire.[358] On 15 March 1542 he received £661 *14s 8d* for saddles and other stuff delivered to the great wardrobe.[359] By September 1543 he had been knighted.

John Gitto or Gytto, the king's saddler, appears in the accounts for 1527–28, 1531–32, 1533–34, 1537–38 and 1538–39. He seems to have been subsidiary to Acton, with his primary role being to undertake repairs and to re-stuff saddles. However, in 1538–39 he also covered saddles with leather as well as supplying buckram, harness, reins, slop houses, stirrup leathers and velvet. A set of his accounts survives for a year from Michaelmas 1525 which has been dated in another hand to the year from Michaelmas 1527.[360] The accounts record a steady pattern of repairs and sales of buckles, buttons and small pieces of tack at a range of locations as the king removed from one property to the next, including Windsor, Eltham, Greenwich, Richmond, Waltham, Guildford and the More. The total came to £11 *6s 7d*.

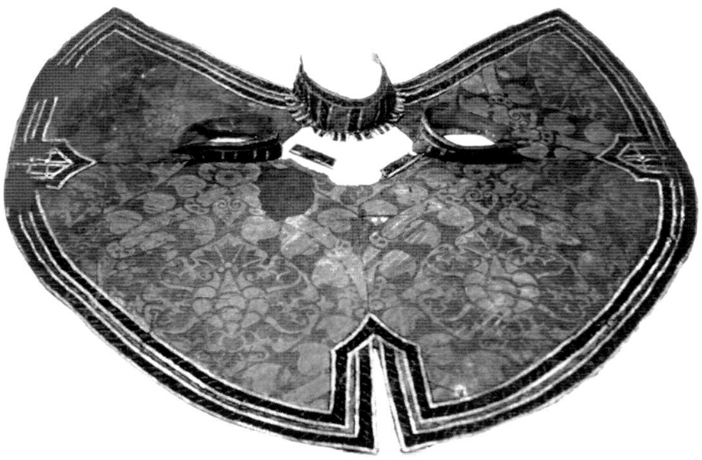

20.1 *Don Garzia de'Medici's cloak, after conservation, giving a very clear indication of the cut and piecing of the fabric and placement of the guards. Reproduced with the permission of Mary Westerman for the Janet Arnold slide archive, Galleria del Costume, Palazzo Pitti*

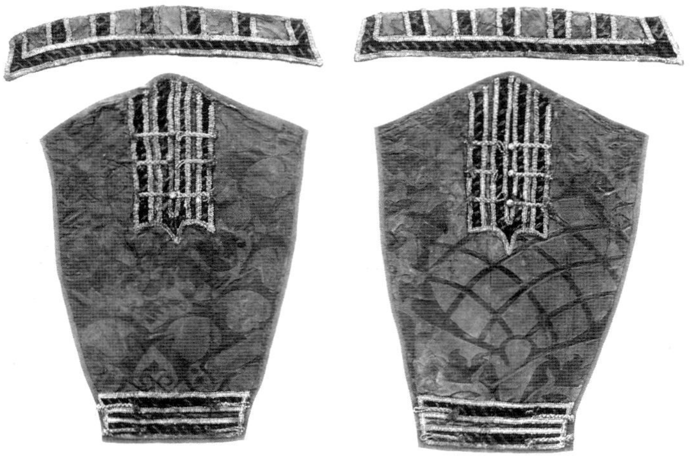

20.2 *Detail of the sleeves of Don Garzia de'Medici's cloak, after conservation. Reproduced with the permission of Mary Westerman for the Janet Arnold slide archive, Galleria del Costume, Palazzo Pitti*

contained 'a blake kyrtill clothe redy shaped price vjs'.[9] While these examples indicate that patterns were in use in a noble household, there were very few references to patterns or toiles being made within the great wardrobe in the early and mid Tudor period. This suggests that there were either existing patterns that were used and modified, or that the tailors cut the pieces by eye, aided by experience.[10] However, there were a few exceptions, such as the patterns used for making the king's coronation robes. This may reflect that coronation robes were not made very frequently. Henry VII's coronation accounts included a payment to Thomas Windwood, mercer of London, for 4 yards (3.6 m) of crimson cloth 'for a patron for the kinges gowne' costing 13*s* 4*d*.[11] Twenty-three years later, on 1 June 1509 Elizabeth Swayne supplied 118½ ells (81.3 m) of canvas for 'patterns for robes of coronation, long gowns, glawdekins, riding coats and jackets', costing 41*s* 11½*d*.[12]

After Henry VIII's accession, the evidence suggests the sporadic use of patterns both for revels costumes and items for the king's personal wardrobe. The account for a revel held on 23 August 1519 included a payment of 3*s* 2½*d* for 7 ells (4.8 m) of canvas 'for a pattern for a garment of the King's device, and kept by him'.[13] Some years later, on 26 February 1545 John Malt received 20*d* for making a pattern of canvas for a coat of mail or *tunica de maile*.[14] Royal patterns could be disseminated in various forms and stored in unlikely places. On the fourth shelf of the little study next to the king's old bed chamber at Whitehall were 'diuerse plattes and paternes of gownes' (11142) and 'A booke of parchement conteyninge dyuerse paternes' (11164).[15] This may indicate that Henry VIII consulted the pattern books and had his fittings in his bedchamber. This would certainly fit with the development of special dressing rooms for the king at Whitehall in the 1540s.[16]

Exchanging patterns was one way of spreading ideas about what was fashionable, especially for women's dress, from one country to another. On 13 April 1513 Princess Mary wrote to Margaret of Savoy, thanking her for 'some patterns of costume of the ladies of her court', adding that she hoped 'to introduce the same fashion for herself'.[17] An account for Catherine of Aragon from March 1520 included a number of gowns made in the 'Milan' fashion, including a gown of black velvet lined with quilted black satin. It also contained an entry for 2 yards (1.8 m) of canvas that was used for 'patrons of myllon facion', costing 6*d*.[18] The suggestion is that these gowns were for inclusion in her wardrobe at the Field of Cloth of Gold.

An account for Princess Mary in 1546 included 3*s* 4*d* 'for drawing of the lining of a partlet upon cambric'.[19] Patterns were not exclusive to women in royal circles, although they could sometimes prove to be elusive. On 9 November 1539 John Husee wrote to Lord Lisle to inform him that he could 'get no new pattern for my lady's frontlet'.[20] By Elizabeth I's reign, the frequency with which patterns were made, or at least recorded and charged for, had changed and a number of references to the taking and making of patterns and toiles appear in the great wardrobe accounts.[21]

Equipment

Tailoring did not require the use or acquisition of expensive or extensive equipment.[22] Scissors were the most important tool and they feature both in written and visual sources. A manuscript illumination of *c.* 1320–30 depicts a tailor using a pair of shears to cut out a garment, possibly a coat.[23] The same activity was captured in Giovanni Moroni's portrait of *The Tailor*, *c.* 1570–79, which presented the tailor, fashionably dressed in a doublet, holding a pair of scissors and in the process of cutting out a garment.[24] Shears could be bought for a specific project, as in the case of the preparations for the revels held on 12 and 13 February 1511 when Richard Gibson bought 'of fyen sesors of breges kolen makyng xxiiij payer . . .

ix payer of kolen scheres . . . iiij fyen tolovs scheres'. These scissors were given heavy use, as Gibson's comments recorded that they were all 'spent and vtterly worn to nothing . . . and svm borkyn yn the revets and svm in the bowes'.[25] Purchases of shears feature in other revels accounts, such as Gibson's account dating from 25 April 1527. William Botry, mercer, supplied two pairs of tailor's shears costing 3*s* 4*d*.[26] The king also had scissors in his possession: there were 'a small paier of sheres and a paier of Sisars' (2363) in removing coffer E. These may have been for the officers of the robes to undertake emergency repairs or alterations while the king was on progress.

Needles were essential. The revels account for February 1511 listed 'sowyng nedylls and pap [pack] nedylls as mene as kost iij[d]', while the 1547 inventory contained a range of needles including 'vij papers of Nedelles of dyuers sortes' (2561).[27] At the opposite end of the scale there were much coarser needles, such as 'a Bodkynne' (3480) and the 150 sail needles listed in the account of Walter Crane for 'repairing, riggyng and emperolyng' *The Great Nicholas* moored in the Thames at Woolwich from 17 January to 9 March 1513.[28] Good quality needles were imported. On 26 February 1546 Stephen Vaughan wrote to Lord Cobham from Antwerp and he enclosed 'a little clout with needles for Cobham's daughter, whom he heard wish she might somewhere find some good needles'.[29] Pins were used to temporarily join pieces of fabric while they were being stitched together. The *History of Jack of Newbury* produced during Henry VIII's reign records how clothiers and tailors stored their pins: 'He had on a plain russet coat, a pair of kersey breeches, without welt or guard, and stockings of the same piece sewed to his slops which had a great codpiece on which he stuck his pins.'[30] Whether professional tailors used a thimble may well have been a matter of personal preference. However, noble women evidently did use them, because a number of examples were listed in the 1547 inventory, including 'a Thimble Siluer gilte' (2411) and a 'thimble of gold garnished with small stones as Rubies Emerades Dyamountes' (2612).

George Lovekyn left some of the tools of his trade to his apprentices in his will dated 1504: 'unto Stephyn Jasper, late my servaunt . . . my great cofer which standith in my shaping hous and also one of my shaping bordes . . . to Stevyn Lumbard, late my serevaunt, a nother shaping borde.'[31] However, there were no references to chalk for marking the cloth, or measures for taking a client's measurements.

Tailors and other royal craftsmen were periodically supplied with candles to allow them to work during the evenings, so extending the working day. Tailors did not require purpose-built premises, although access to the optimal amount of natural daylight would have been advantageous. This allowed tailors to make use of a wide variety of work spaces.

Selection and orientation of the top fabric

It seems most likely that the king's tailor was personally involved in the selection of the fabrics used to make the king's clothes, and in many instances he also supplied them. Alternative supplies of fabric came from the great wardrobe, the silk house at Whitehall and the store of cloth kept within the wardrobe of the robes (see Tables 6.5, 10.7 and 11.1). The type of fabric selected could be influenced by a range of factors such as: the intended use of the garment, and if it was required for a specific occasion that required a certain colour or type of cloth to be used; availability; cost and the type and style of the garment requiring cloth with a specific drape or handle. Many of the warrants issued to the great wardrobe only provided the top fabric, meaning that the recipient would have had to pay for the linings, fastenings, decoration and making up themselves.

The amounts of cloth allocated for specific types of garment reveal that the tailors of the great wardrobe had standard lengths of material to work with: for example 3 yards (2.7 m) for a doublet, 4 to 5 yards (3.6 m–4.5 m) of woollen cloth and 8 to 11 yards (7.3 m–10 m) of silk for a man's gown and 7 yards (6.4 m) for a kirtle. Similar ideas can be found in other sources. References to 'gown cloths' appear in Stephen Vaughan's letter to Sir William Paget dated 13 September 1545, suggesting that there were approximate yardages of cloth felt to be necessary to make up particular garments. However, as Vaughan observed, an individual's dimensions could have a bearing on this: 'I send you 12 ells of the best gros greyn to make you a night gown. The tailors tell me that 10 ells of that breadth is too much; and Mr Chamberleyn made one with 9 ells, not fully of your length but he made it to the half leg with less that ix ells.'[32]

Extant garments indicate that, while the individual pieces were generally cut on the straight grain, the fabric could also be used cut on the bias. Hose provide one example where bias-cut cloth could enhance the fit, although cloth cut on the straight grain was also used. The strips used for making guards were often cut on the bias, as in the case of the decorative bands applied to the yellow damask gown of Maurice of Saxony or the black damask cloak with sleeves owned by Don Garzia. The cuffs of Mary of Hungary's wedding dress were cut on the bias, so enhancing the way the fabric fell over her hands.[33] Equally, extant clothing and textiles from this period often reveal a very economical use of fabric which took little regard of the orientation of the warp and weft or matching the pattern. Certainly fabric from several different sources could be used to make one garment. Three different satin damasks, with three slightly different loom widths, were used to make a sixteenth century doublet.[34] Even lengths of fabric could be pieced, such as a piece of white baudekyn with flowers of gold 'sowen togeders cont xviij yerdes at xxxiijs iiijd — xxx li' [B410]. However, some objects, such as the yellow damask gown of Maurice of Saxony, which was made from a yellow silk damask with a very large pattern repeat, reveals very careful piecing of the fabric which balanced and matched the design.

The idea of conspicuous waste or the use of excessive fabric in garments, either through pleating or lengthy trains, has been considered by a number of authors. Anne Hollander has linked the excessive use of fabric in the Renaissance period clothing to the fact that cloth was 'the primary worldly good'. Consequently, cloth, as the most important contemporary manufactured product, was used to emphasise social standing and moral worth, and this was why angels and saints were often painted dressed in the styles favoured by the élite.[35] Taking the idea one step further, the use of slashing, cutting and pinking as a means of embellishing very expensive woven textiles that were often highly patterned in their own right, both enhanced the decorative impact while potentially undermining the structural integrity of the weave.

Linings

A range of different materials were used as linings and the final choice of fabric could be dependent upon a number of factors. Lightweight fabrics such as sarsenet could be used to give additional body and so assist with the drape of the top fabrics. A bard made for the king embroidered with eglantines, a hand, trueloves and H and K was lined with 18 yards (16.4 m) of white sarsenet.[36] Smooth fabrics of this type would slide over any other garments worn as under layers. Linings of this type could be easily and quite cheaply replaced in order to keep the garment fragrant. Linings could be the same colour as the outer fabric, but more frequently they were a contrasting colour. The type of lining could be changed to reflect seasonal requirements. Items worn in the summer, which were sometimes unlined, were often described in inventories as 'single', while fur linings were used to provide warmth so fur linings were put in for the autumn and winter and taken out in the summer. On 14 September 1539 Lord Lisle wrote to his wife, asking her to 'Send me the furs of my tawny velvet gown and the sables; for from what I have heard they may be needed'.[37]

Heavier weight, cellulosic fabrics could be used as linings to give added bulk and definition to a garment. The revels account of Richard Gibson from 12–13 February 1511 included 'koton cloothe xxiij yerdes de . . . spent and in ployd for lynyng of iij kyrtylles of rvsset damaske . . . for lynyng of iij gownes . . . for lynyng and stvffynge of the plyght of the iij gowns' and 'ij ells iij qvarters of lynnyn clothe . . . for lynyng of the vj garments for the iij maydyns'.[38] The lining fabrics used for a doublet made from red gold brocade in lampas for Gustavus Adolphus (1594–1632) were a red silk taffeta in a tabby weave and a yellow-grey tabby weave linen.[39] More specifically, the Hever doublet was lined with plain weave linen with a thread count of 18 warps and wefts per 10 mm.[40]

Twenty-five different types of fabric were identified as being used as lining fabrics in Worsley's wardrobe book, ranging from canvas [A84], buckram [A269] and felt [B111] to cloth of gold [A133], cloth of silver [B41] and tissue [A27].[41] Satin and sarsenet were the most commonly used materials, with sarsenet recorded on 91 occasions and satin placed in 120 garments. These linings were recorded in 27 different types of garment and sets of garments, indicating that linings were an integral part of the construction of the king's clothes. Most information was provided about the linings used in doublets, gowns and jackets which is not surprising as these was the most commonly made items recorded in Worsley's book. A key point raised by this list is the use of rich, heavyweight fabrics as linings, which suggests that the lining was going to be seen.

The evidence recorded in the 1547 inventory indicates that two decades later a much smaller range of materials was being used as linings. Just six types of lining were identified: capha damask, damask, sarsenet, satin, taffeta and velvet. Linings are recorded in 13 types of garment.[42] Frocks could be lined throughout with a single fabric, but they were often lined with velvet in the body and satin for the bases. There were 13 Spanish capes, all of which were lined, most with velvet. Only 17 of the 39 gowns were described as being lined. However, some of the gowns had had the linings removed, leaving only 'thowtside of a gowne with a square cape of Russett Satten' (14221). Even so, some were probably never lined, indicating that they were made for summer use.

In addition to providing warmth, fur linings were also worn as an expression of wealth and status. During Henry VIII's reign fur was usually applied, either as a decorative edging or border or a full lining, to a range of outer garments, although not all outer garments were furred; for example, none of the king's cassocks in 1547 were either faced or lined with fur. Equally, fur was not usually found on doublets, jerkins or hose. Fur linings could be inserted into boots, buskins and slippers for warmth. In contrast, women's sleeves provided a very good vehicle for the display of fur, especially the large hanging-over sleeves of the 1540s that could be lined with fur, as in the full-length portrait of Catherine Parr (Fig. 9.3). In most cases, inventories, warrants and bills make a distinction between the furs used for 'furring' and 'facing' because different colours, types and qualities of fur were normally used for the two functions.

Henry VII and Henry VIII both spent heavily on fur, especially sable. During 1543–44 Henry VIII spent £166 on 80 sables for a gown of damask with guards of velvet embroidered with gold thread.[43] A gender bias in the type of furs purchased can also be observed. Royal men favoured sable, while the women tended to wear pale furs such as ermine, lettice and miniver.[44]

Worsley's wardrobe books record the use of 13 types of fur used on 134 garments (Table 20.1): 35 occurrences for budge, 27 for sable, 19 for coney including black and of unspecified colour, 17 of ermine, nine each for luzards and miniver, eight of jennets including black and grey, two each for mink, pure, shanks and wolf skin and one each for ostrich skin and pampilion. It is not surprising that sable features so prominently, but the prevalence of the cheaper furs such as budge and coney presents a very different use of fur to that seen in the fourteenth century.

Ten types of fur, some of which are different to those used in Worsley's book, were recorded in 1547: budge, calabre, coney, ermine, lamb, libard wombs, luzards, pampilion, sable and squirrel. The fur was used to line and trim just three types of garments: 11 out of 20 coats, three out of 17 frocks and 15 out of 39 gowns. The clerks provide details about the type and placement of fur linings, as in the case of a short gown 'furred with lowe Boudge' (14205), a gown of 'fresed veluett with a square cape' 'saving the cape whiche hath noo furr in it' (14185) and a gown which may have been lined and faced with fur but was described as 'lacking the facing therof' (14217).

Table 20.1: *Fur-trimmed and -lined garments in Worsley's wardrobe books*

Garment	Number furred and the types of fur
Bases	(1) Coney B309
Caps of maintenance	(1) Ermine B325
Chammers	(14) Budge B134; luzards B24, 95, 131; sable A20, 22, 139, B23, 25, 31, 34, 94, 119, 121,
Cloaks	(2) Sable B96; wolf skin B137
Coats	(11) Budge A175, 240, 251; coney A155–6, 164–5, 205 B140; ermine A244, B334
Coronation robes	(1 set) Ermine B1–2, 4; miniver B3
Demi-coats	(1) Fox B143
Four-quartered jackets	(3) Budge A122, 246, 248
Frocks	(6) Budge A114, B99, 124; coney B126–7; sable B83
Gowns	(52) Budge A3–4, 9, 12, 14, 23, 34, 103, 138, 144, B38–9, 86, 92, 113–4, 116–7, 122; coney A101, B33; ermines A11, 18, 121, 328, 330, 332, B19; jennets A10, 145, B20–1, 29, 120; luzards B27, 36, 85, 93, 118, 123; mink A124; pampilion A 31; sables A15, 21, 127, B22, 26, 28, 30, 32, 37, 84, 115, 132; shanks A123
Gowns for women	(3) Ermine A119; mink A78; shanks A118
Jackets	(7) Budge A238, B142; coney A171, 199, B141, 144, 333
Mantles	(3) Budge A1–2; ermine B331
Nightgowns	(4) Coney, B110; sable B35, 100, 133
Parliament robes	(1 set) Ermine B5–6; miniver B7–8
Robes with a train for a child	(1) Pure B323
Short four-quartered jackets	(2) Budge A69, 71
Short gowns	(2) Budge A64, 66
Tabards	(2) Miniver A67; pure B324
Trappers	(1) Ermine A269

Interlinings and facings

Interlinings were extra layers of a heavyweight fabric, such as buckram or canvas, that were added to provide additional weight to part or all of a garment or to ensure that a garment hung correctly. The interlining in the red doublet of Gustavus Adolphus is of a grey-black plain weave or tabby linen which has been coated with an unidentified stiffening substance.[45] These fabrics were usually stitched to the top fabric, in order to ensure that the interlining moved with the top fabric. Interlinings were not necessarily used for a whole garment. Rather they tended to be used for specific elements that needed extra stiffness such as collars, cuffs and the skirts of doublets and coats. A collar, possibly from a coat, made from silk velvet and edged with a silk braid, with a jute interlining and a wool lining, was found on the *Trinidad Valencera* which sank on its return to Spain in 1588.[46] The front and back of the Hever doublet had a coarse plain weave linen interlining with a thread count of 15 warps and wefts per 10 mm, while the sleeves did not.[47]

References to the fabrics used as interlinings are rare in inventories, chiefly because the interlinings are not visible on the finished garment and so not accessible for the clerk to record. However, the particular accounts of the great wardrobe and the wardrobe warrants do include references to the range of fabrics that were used as interlinings in garments such as doublets, frocks and coats. There are rarely any specific references made to the use or placement of interlinings or facings in the accounts. However, extant garments and archaeological finds indicate that facings were used to reinforce edges, especially those that had large numbers of buttons, buttonholes or lace holes.[48]

Heavy canvas was used to line bodices of women's gowns to create a very smooth surface. There were no darts either in the side seams or underarm area in these bodices in order to accommodate the bust.[49] The pleats at the back waistband of the skirt of a woman's gown were supported by the use of additional sections of fabric.[50] Generally one layer of fabric was used, but multiple layers could be used for collars or sleeve heads. Small sections of linen acting as an interlining were used to support puffs of fabric inserted into slashes on doublets and hose.

Padding and stiffening

There are very few references in the great wardrobe accounts to materials being used to pad garments to create a specific shape or for warmth. However, there are a few payments for down and wool used as padding materials for saddles and close stools, as well as more unusual items such as '8 felltes ostrege woll' at 12*d* each.[51] This creates the presumption that the bulky male images of the first half of the sixteenth century were created by wearing a number of layers rather than by wearing padded clothes. There are also passing references to padding being used to provide protection. Wool padding could be incorporated into garments and armour, as indicated by payments made for the jousts held on 20 October 1519 to celebrate the marriage of the earl of Devon: 2½ lb (1.1 kg) of carded wool at 4*d* the pound, for the headpieces, gauntlets, maundvers, borlets, and 9 yards (8.2 m) of Cheshire cotton at 7*d* the yard for lining the king's pasguard, great guard and 'great mayn de fer', all of which were then lined with 3½ yards (3.2 m) of crimson satin bought from William Botry at 9*s* the yard.[52]

A revels account from March 1519 included 'ladies petticoats of Spanish work' made with four dozen pasteboards to make hoops for the petticoats and to stiffen bonnets costing

16*d*, and 6 lb (2.7 kg) of wire 'for wiring the hoops' costing 2*s* 6*d*.[53] A revels account for August 1519 included the purchase of 16 pasteboards for bonnets at 3*d* each.[54] The accounts for a mummery held at Greenwich on 31 December 1519 included 12 Paris pasteboards for the 'turffys' of the lords' bonnets for 4*s*.[55]

Sewing thread

Sewing thread does not feature on the general warrants issued to the great wardrobe. However, references to silk and linen thread do occasionally appear on the warrants for the wardrobe of the beds, on some of the king's own warrants from the later part of the reign, and the exchequer accounts for 1518–19 included payments for small needles and white thread costing 1*d* and 2*d* respectively.[56] Some of the dyed threads were not colourfast, as indicated by the letter that John Husee sent to Lady Lisle on 23 April 1539. On one of the voyages from Calais to London, some of Lady Lisle's goods including an embroidered stool were damaged and Husee had to report that 'The colours are faded. It is of crewel'.[57]

Large quantities of thread were bought for the livery made for 1544 campaign: Thomas White supplied 83 bolts of black thread for sewing the coats, £10 7*s* 6*d*; 126 lb (57.15 kg) of red thread, £16 16*s*; 99 lb (44.9 kg) of yellow thread, £9 18*s*; 22 lb (9.9 kg) of grey thread, 18*s* 4*d*; 26 lb (11.8 kg) of grey thread, 26*s*, and 37 oz (1.04 kg) of yellow silk, 37*s*, costing in total £41 2*s* 10*d*. Such large scale purchases were unusual and most orders were for small bundles or skeins of thread, as indicated by the following entries from the 1547 inventory: 'thre bundelles of silke of blacke and grene' (11165), 'v bunches of white thred' (2556) and 'four bobynnes siluer gilt' (2902).

There is no direct evidence that the royal tailors waxed their sewing thread. However, it is possible that they did, providing their own wax, thus explaining why it did not feature in the accounts. The technique was certainly in use, as indicated by a fifteenth century manuscript which illustrates how a knight was armed. The author described how arming points were made, noting that the best material was 'fine twine such as men make stryngis for crossbowes' which were then waxed in order to make them pass through the lacing holes more easily.[58]

Seams and hems

Hand-sewn seams are usually formed with one or two lines of stitching.[59] The need for the stitching to withstand wear and cleaning, including the laundry process for linen items such as shirts and shifts, meant that small, closely placed stitches were the ideal. Extant garments provide examples of simple seams worked in running and back stitch, the latter generally making a stronger seam. The back seam of a pair of sixteenth century hose, made from a worsted 2.2 twill, was stitched with running or back stitch and the seam allowance was stitched flat, also with running stitch.[60] The seam allowance could be stitched down with lines of a fine running stitch worked a few millimetres away from the seam, on more prestigious garments such as on the yellow damask gown of Maurice of Saxony. Equally, the cut edges of seams could be rubbed with wax to reduce the likelihood of fraying. While there are no references to the purchase or provision of wax for such purposes in the great wardrobe accounts, the practice clearly was undertaken. Residual traces of wax can be seen on the turnings of the velvet panes of Nils Sture's *pluderhose*.[61] The quality of finish on the seam turning becomes much less important if a garment is fully lined, as most of the king's clothes were. Where possible, and especially on shirts, and shifts, selvedges appear to have been utilised to avoid fraying and to provide additional strength. Finally, some seams were left open intentionally, either for a short section or along the whole length, as a feature of the design.

Decorative finishes to seams were not uncommon, especially on collars or bands and cuffs on shirts. An interesting and highly decorative technique was used on some of the main seams on the boy's shirt in the Victoria and Albert Museum. A similar technique can be seen on the shoulder seams of the king's shirt in Holbein's portrait (Pl. IC). Richard Gibson's record of a masque held on 23 August 1519 included a reference to 12 pairs of 'wide shirt sleeves with reban semys of fine cloth'.[62] Additional decorative finishes included frilled edges that could be created either by gathering or pleating a strip of cloth, or the cloth could be shaped using techniques such as starch and crimping.[63]

Most hems were finished very simply with the fabric turned up once or twice. However, a range of more decorative finishes was also used. In the early Tudor period, decorative bands of contrasting fabric were often placed round the hems of gowns and kirtles. Such bands would have the added benefit of strengthening the edge. Even so, there are no references in the great wardrobe to the practice of padding hems with felt, an example of which can be seen on the crimson gown *c.* 1560 in the Museo di Palazzo Reale, Pisa, which is thought to have possibly belonged to either Eleanor of Toledo or one of her ladies in waiting.[64] Fancy edgings such as jagging were rare in Henry VIII's wardrobe, but the use of contrasting edging to embellish a range of garments including gowns, doublets and hose was used throughout Henry's reign.[65]

Fit and shaping

Cut is the initial factor in achieving a good fit. By the sixteenth century tailoring skills were highly developed in London.[66] Many important developments were perfected in the fourteenth century, as indicated by the *pourpoint* of Charles of Blois, *c.* 1364. The depth of the armhole can be varied to give greater ease of movement with tight-fitting sleeves, and the solution with the *pourpoint* was to cut the armholes very deep at the front and back.[67] In addition, gussets were inserted at the top of the sleeve to create further ease.[68] However, when looking at the ways a garment is made, it is also important to distinguish between pattern pieces being cut to create a specific shape as opposed to just making efficient use of expensive fabric.

In addition, to adjusting the cut of the armhole, the formation of sleeves became increasingly sophisticated. Shaped sleeves could be cut in two pieces, so giving a closer fit than a one-piece sleeve. With the Hever doublet, the inside seam was left open at the cuff end to provide a little ease.[69] The large, puffed sleeves, which often formed the top section of a long sleeve could have stay tapes stitched inside the puffed section to create the volume.

Many clothes in the early sixteenth century were sophisticated in cut and construction. They depended on a good fit to shape and define the wearer's body which was achieved by piecing fabric. This is especially evident in the construction of the doublet and hose. Consideration of the hose from the three members of the Sture family in Uppsala cathedral or the Medici burial clothes emphasises the importance of the seams at the centre-front, centre-back, the shaping of the back, the positioning of the shoulder seams and the padded cod-piece. The first half of the sixteenth century saw the development of certain features such as the transition from the one-piece sleeve with the sole seam on the underside of the arm to the two-piece sleeve, and creation of the collar, with the back section of the stand collar being cut in one with the garment back while the front sections of the collar were separate from the main body of the doublet. The positioning of the waistline moved from taking the natural level to below the natural waistline and from being cut in the round or in a downwards point. Indeed, the development of a seam at the waist provided further options for shaping garments and choices in the height (above, at or below the natural waistline) and shape of the waistline (round or pointed).[70] The skirts of the doublet or the jerkin got shorter.

In general, gussets were not used to shape garments. However, there are a few examples of their use, including a pair of hose cut from woollen cloth excavated in Finsbury. These hose were essentially cut in one piece for the foot and leg, with a separate sole and two small triangular inserts or gussets to create ease around the ankle.[71]

One of the interesting features of the great wardrobe accounts from the closing years of Henry VIII's reign is the appearance of references to pockets being made from bridges satin in a range of the monarch's clothes including coats, frocks and gowns. The garments provided for Prince Edward also had pockets.[72] Other references to pockets can be found elsewhere. The examinations taken in January 1541 of Richard Pate's servants after his flight include the comment of William Langland, page, that he had been asked to bring the keys to Pate's privy coffer out of the 'powake of Richard Attowan's coat to get a letter out of the coffer'.[73] Equally, there is a pocket slit in the crimson satin lining of the hose of Don Garzia de'Medici which would have provided access to the pocket between two of the velvet panes. Although traces of linen were found in the turnings of the slit during conservation, no remnants of the pocket bag were discovered.[74]

Initially pockets appear to have been restricted to men's clothing. By Mary I's reign the situation had changed. The queen's wardrobe accounts show that pockets were put into some of her gowns.[75] The clothes preserved in Eleanor of Toledo's grave of 1562 include two pieces of yellow taffeta that Janet Arnold believed to be the remains of a pocket, attached to the front waistband of her gown.[76] This construction is supported by evidence recorded in the portrait of Anna Eleonora Sanvitali, 1562, by Girolamo Mazzola Bedoli.[77] The slit opening of the pocket was depicted as being placed just below the slightly downward pointing waistline on the left front of her skirt.

Not all garments from this period, such as the gown and the shirt, were fitted. Rather they needed only to fit in specific places such as around the neck and across the shoulders. Less shaped garments could make very effective use of the full loom width of the fabric that they were made from. However, in such instances, a degree of gathering or pleating could be employed to accommodate the excess fabric and create some shaping. Pleats could also be used to improve the fit, as in the back of a riding gown of black velvet made for the king and given away on 26 December 1519 to the clerk of the kitchen [A74] or at the back of the skirts of women's gowns and kirtles. This is especially evident in the accounts of Elizabeth of York, where extra fabric was supplied to support the pleats. Pleats could also be used to provide decorative interest, as in the case of 'a lytell short gowne of purpull veluete . . . drawen with playtes' [A60].

Fastenings: buttons, clasps, hooks, latchets and pins, dress hooks, lacing, points and girdles

A range of different fastening was used on the clothes of this period, including laces, aglets or points, buttons, dress hooks, pins and girdles (Table 20.2). These fastenings can be divided

Table 20.2: *Fastenings on Henry's clothes in 1547*

Garment	Details
Cloaks	**Buttons**: 10 round buttons, set with specks of counterfeit ruby and sapphire; 10 buttons of gold
Coats	**Aglets**: 12 pairs of gold on the sleeves
Frocks	**Aglets**: 37 pairs of gold on the bases and sleeves, 40 pairs of gold on the bases and sleeves; **Buttons**: 32 round, of gold; 36 round, of gold; 40 of gold like roses
Gowns	**Aglets**: 28 pairs, of gold; 32 pairs; 42 pairs, of gold; **Aglets and buttons**: 21 aglets and 21 buttons of gold; 26 pairs of aglets and 4 buttons of gold; 34 round aglets of 2 sorts and 10 round buttons of gold; 36 pairs of aglets and 4 buttons of gold; **Buttons**: 28 of gold, on sleeves; 32 of gold; 77 of gold, round, black enameled
Spanish capes	**Troches**: 8 troches of pearls, each with 5 pearls

into two groups: edge-to-edge fastenings and overlapping fastenings. With overlapping fastenings, the clothes tended to fasten left over right, but two extant doublets from the sixteenth century fasten right over left, as can also be seen in some portraits.[78] While a selection of fastenings was listed in Worsley's wardrobe book and inventory and the great wardrobe accounts, the number of references is not large. The greatest detail can be gleaned from the 1547 inventory.

Table 20.2 highlights that references to fastenings were generally restricted to outer, male garments for the upper body and that they frequently combined functional and decorative roles. Although buttons were known in prehistoric times, they then went out of use. It has been argued that buttons were reintroduced in the British Isles in the 1330s, but it has been shown conclusively that the date was much earlier.[79] Archaeological evidence suggests that they were reintroduced from the East.[80] Buttons were both functional and decorative. Their different usage can be seen in the *pourpoint* of Charles of Blois, *c.* 1364, which has 31 fabric-covered buttons down the centre-front. The buttons are flat at the neck and from the waist down, with more spherical buttons on the chest.[81] Gold and silk buttons are occasionally mentioned in Edward IV's great wardrobe accounts, including 'a mantel lace of blue silk with botons of the same' costing 17*s*, and 'xvj botons of blue silk and gold', price 4*s*.[82] In 1509 Lady Margaret Beaufort's collection of jewellery included 'iij buttons of golde'.[83] Many of the buttons used on the king's own clothes were made from gold and were produced in sets, such as 'x buttons of golde carcan fasshion having vppon euerie button a small table dyamounte' (2100). These may well have been similar to the four gold buttons found on the wreck of the *Girona*, which range in diameter from 11 mm to 14 mm, and were decorated with different styles of stamped, geometric designs.[84] Examples of lengths of gold metal thread braid worked into four button loops dating from the 1580s have been recovered from the wreck of the *Trinidad Valencia*, another ship in the Armada fleet which sank in 1588.[85] A rather fine set of 12 spherical gold buttons decorated with stamping, engraving and white, red, black and blue enamel was found in the tomb of Count Palatine Friedrich (1557–97).[86]

Buttons can be seen in a number of portraits from the first from the later 1520s half of the sixteenth century. There are relatively few references to buttons in Worsley's wardrobe book. The examples were gold or enamelled and found on three chambers (with one having small gold buttons [B134]), three doublets, a doublet and hose and six gowns. References to them also appear in the great wardrobe accounts from the late 1520s. In the account dated 14 July 1527 John Worship supplied just ten buttons of Venice gold for 5*s*.[87] In the late 1530s, decorative buttons were placed on the shoulders of the king's doublets. By the 1540s, the number of buttons placed on specific garments suggests that they were placed down the centre-front and at the cuffs of sleeves.

By then the number of buttons being bought had risen substantially. Anne Grey supplied 285 dozen buttons of gold silver and coloured silk costing £106 14*s* on a warrant dated 27 March 1544, and 342 dozen buttons of gold, silk and silver (56 dozen at 16*s* per dozen, 54 dozen at 12*s* per dozen, 120 dozen at 6*s* the dozen, and 112 dozen at 2*s* the dozen), coming to £124 8*s* on the subsequent warrant dated 26 February 1545.[88] In addition, she supplied 36 buttons of blue silk at a price of 12*s* for the night gown of purple velvet made for Edward while he was in mourning for his father. In order to create the means of fastening, Anne also provided 18 yards (16.4 m) of passamayne lace in blue silk to make applied loops for the buttons at a cost of 36*s*.[89] The 1547 inventory reveals a variety of types of button including carcan fashion (2098), enamelled (3657), with inscriptions (e.g. *Amor vincit omnia* (3658)), shaped 'like katherin wheles' (3516), triangular (3656), Stafford knots (2884), with faces (5) and gem set, with pearls for example (2173).

By the 1530s buttons were more commonplace on doublets, coats and jackets. When, following Henry VIII's marriage to Anne Boleyn, Pope Clement VII threatened the king with excommunication, the duke of Norfolk told him 'to not care a button'.[90] Many of the buttons put on the king's clothes consisted of silk thread wrapped round a wooden or a fabric core. There is a single row of silk buttons on the Hever doublet. Each button has a long shank ending with a fabric-covered disc decorated with three circles of embroidery with a bullion in the centre. Buttons of this type can be seen in Holbein's portrait of Sir Richard Southwell painted in 1537.[91] There are 11 silk-wrapped buttons on the body of Don Garzia's doublet and two on the collar, and 14 buttons on Cosimo I's doublet, with none on the collar. In contrast, the outer doublet of Count Friedrich von Stubenberg had 16 buttons stitched down the front edge. These were just for decoration and all but three remain. The buttons were made from wool cloth covered with wool thread, and then decorated with radiating threads and buttonhole stitch. There are no buttonholes and the doublet actually fastened with hooks and eyes.[92]

A range of precious and non-precious metal dress hooks have been recorded and they may well have been used in both decorative and functional roles (Fig. 20.3).[93] Pairs of metal hooks appear to have been used to hook up women's skirts, while larger number of hooks may have been used with a more decorative function. In 1506 a pair of hooks was made for Lady Margaret Beaufort weighing half an ounce which cost 18*s* for the metal and 18*d* for the fashioning and gilding.[94] At the time of her death, a number of Lady Margaret's jewels were in the keeping of Mistress Fowler. These included 'ij hokys siluer vpon a rybande for the Tuckyng of a gown'.[95] This echoes the use Holbein recorded in his sketch of a woman walking (Fig. 18.1). Dress hooks may also have been used for securing the laces and tassels worn with formal robes.[96]

Jean Fouquet's portrait of Gonella, the jester at the Ferraran court, *c.* 1445, provides one of the earliest representations of hooks and eyes. The metal hooks and eyes are stitched to the inside front edge of the collar of Gonella's doublet.[97] There are a few references to hooks in Henry VIII's inventories, such as hooks of gold (14543) and silver gilt hooks (2317), but as they are loose and not attached to garments it is hard to get a sense of scale or their specific function. Hooks of this type are similar to latchets which were made of metal, in pairs, with one half having a hook and the other having an

20.3 *Three sixteenth-century silver-gilt dress hooks, private collection. Photo: Mike Halliwell*

eye. However, while the term latchet does not feature in the king's accounts, clasps do. James Worsley's wardrobe book included a doublet and hose [A202] and a pair of hose with clasps [A194]. Clasps of this kind could be highly ornamental, as in the case of 'v Claspes gold having vppon euerie claspe A roose of Diamountes and twoo Rubies' (2096), and made in larger groups such as 'tenne claspes of golde enameled euerie of theym sett with three dyamountes and vj rubies having written vppon euery of theym Dieu et mon Droit' (2119). The queen's jewels contained seven gold clasps, all decorated with gemstones, including 'one Claspe with a fair Ballais' (2665) and 'one Claspe with an Emerode' (2666). Clasps periodically required repair. A letter sent early in February 1538 by John Husee to Lady Lisle refers to repairs he had undertaken on her behalf: 'I do further send ij pair of clasps, whereof I have caused iij to be new made, and the other new annealed.'[98]

Large orders of pins were often included in the warrants for the king's wives and daughters because they were essential for constructing the complex outfits and head-dresses women wore. They could be made from precious metals, as in the case of 'a pynne of silver' (3313) and 'two pynnes of siluer guilte' (3455), and decorative items such as these could be kept in 'a Pynnecase of golde with ij tassels fullie garnysshed with redde stones' (2791). However, pins were made more usually from brass and iron for all ranks of society. The quantities that were bought indicate that large numbers were lost or bent, making them unusable. A pinner delivered the following order for Jane Seymour's use: 10,000 pins for 16*s* 8*d*, 8,000 pins for 15*s* 8*d*, 1,000 pins for 15*d*, 1,000 for 12*d*, 5,000 for 4*s* 2*d* and 6,000 small pins costing 4*s*, coming to 37*s* 9*d* in total.[99] This list also indicates that a variety of sizes and qualities were available. On occasion specific types of pins were listed in the accounts: for a revel in March 1522 1,000 velvet pins were bought for 10*d*.[100] Pins could have solid heads or wire heads that could be spherical or flat in shape.[101]

Laces consisted of a length of silk ribbon, cord or possibly a thin leather thong that would be threaded through a series of eyelet holes. The ends of the lace were finished with chapes or tags, so making the ends easier to insert into the eyelet holes that they were threaded through. Most of the chapes or tags for the king and his immediate family were made from precious metal, while those ordered for other members of the royal household might well have been made from a cheaper metal. All of the examples found in archaeological contexts in London are of copper alloy sheeting formed into a tapering tube with a straight overlapping seam.[102] The contents of five excavated chapes have been analysed with two certain examples of leather and three possible examples of textile laces.

Lacing allows quite simply shaped clothes to be closely fitted to the body of the wearer. The eyelet holes on the garment were worked using buttonhole stitch or reinforced with a mail, a metal eyelet for passing a lace through. Richard Gibson recorded the following purchase in the accounts of a revel held in February 1511: 'bowght by me . . . CCC laten maylls, the C jd spend vn iij kyrtylles for the iij maydyns.'[103] The result of lacing a garment closed was similar to stitching the wearer into it. Lacing was particularly important for female dress, partly because of the added curves of the female body, partly because of the need to make clothing adaptable to changes in body shape, especially as a consequence of pregnancy, and it is most commonly seen in portraits running down one side of the bodice. This can also be seen on the bodice of the grave clothes of Eleanor of Toledo. The bodice laces down both of the curved back seams (Fig. 20.4).

Descriptions of people dressing and undressing are infrequent. When they do occur, they shed light on how clothes fitted together. At the execution of Sir Thomas Wyatt, 'he put off his gown, untrussed his points, and plucked off his doublet and waistcoat'.[104] Points were used to attach sleeves to bodices, jerkins or doublets and they were used to join doublet and hose. The points were threaded through worked eyelet holes, which were often positioned in pairs, on a supplementary strip at the waistband of a doublet and the waistband of the hose. The eyelet holes were often placed very close together. There were nine pairs of eyelet holes on each front of Cosimo de'Medici's doublet and four pairs on either side of the back, making 26 pairs in all.

Aglets were recorded on a range of garments in Worsley's wardrobe books: chammers [A102], cloaks [B138], doublets [A11], frocks [B67], gowns [B32], hose [A11], jackets [A11], mantles [B125], placards and foresleeves [A256], on capes [B125], on sleeves [B131] and with a specific function such as tying a collar [B225]. The aglets were predominantly made from gold [A11], with a few examples decorated with enamel [B322] and several made from silver [B225–26]. A few clues were given with regards to their shape, including flat [B138], long [B322], small [A259] and 'wrethen' [B134]. Worsley also made occasional references to arming points of silk and gold [A268] with aglets [B322] and placed on doublets [B322].

20.4 *Lacing was used to close the side opening of Eleanor of Toledo's bodice, 1562. Reproduced from the Janet Arnold Collection by courtesy of her executors*

Also referred to as aglets and tags, points were used in a similar way to laces, but generally they were shorter in length and they were often bought in sets. Points consisted of a length of silk ribbon, cord or tape, a silk and metal thread combination or a leather thong; a similar effect and function to lacing. Examples of a round silk cord made from S-plied silk threads with copper alloy tags on each end were excavated at Fast castle in Scotland. The free ends of the cord extended beyond the tags to form a fringed end. In this example, the round cord was not constructed from the usual eight-strand plait. The length of cord used to make points can indicate use — short cords were used to tie sleeves, while longer cords were used for lacing up the sides of garments, or joining doublets and hose. For the latter, the cords could be tied in decorative loops, so requiring the longer length of cord.[105]

Arming points were a specialised form and they were periodically listed in the wardrobe of the robes. In 1547 six sets of points were described as arming points, including 'xij arminge points of purple silke and silver having Aglettes of golde enameled purple and white' (14574) and 'twelve pointes of black silke and golde thaglattes of Silver gilte' (3423). All types of points were frequently purchased in bulk: Lettice Worship supplied three gross of ribbon points of divers colours costing 42*s* and a piece of ribbon for pointing for Cornelius Hayes costing 4*s* on a warrant dated 22 January 1534, and six gross and a half-dozen of ribbon points costing £4 4*s* on the next warrant for the king dated 24 June 1534.[106] Henry's warrants often allowed for hundreds of points, while Catherine Parr received very large numbers of points from Mark Milliner between 1543 and 1546.[107]

The regulations of the girdlers' guild indicate that there were four or five standard widths of girdle with no leather below the quality of ox leather used to make them. Leather girdles were mostly worn with the grain side out. The buckles and strap ends were decorated using a range of techniques including stamping, incising, engraving, punched openwork and the use of inlaid pins.[108] At the luxury end of the market, gold enamelled buckles were popular.[109] Girdles were often made by using techniques such as tablet weaving. However, the number of textile girdles preserved in London is very small: eight of silk, one of worsted and one of silk and worsted. The guild's charter of 1321 banned the use of inferior metals by girdlers and promoted latten, copper, iron and steel. The use of more precious metals was restricted to the Goldsmiths' company and strictly limited by the sumptuary law of 1363.[110]

Girdles could be very simple in their construction, and they were worn around the waist or hips. They were often made of a length of a lightweight silk such as sarsenet. Girdles of this type were worn by the king, as can be seen in his portraits (Pl. IIA). Lengths of sarsenet were supplied for this purpose and just tied round the waist of the wearer and knotted at the front. On 2 May 1502 Elizabeth of York purchased 12 yards (10.9 m) of sarsenet in eight colours for girdles, costing 48s.[111] Lengths of wide silk ribbon or cord could also be used in the same way to make simple but effective girdles. Girdles that were intended to hang swords or daggers from were often made from leather, covered with a textile and then decorated with metal elements. Girdles of this type were largely functional, in that they drew the clothes in at the waist or could be used to suspend items around the wearer's waist. The most spectacular London find of this type is a nearly complete waist belt of leather with most of its 154 copper alloy mounts in place.[112] The belt was possibly a sword belt, and there are traces of textile on the front and back of the leather.

When in 1544 Master John painted Princess Mary, she wore at her waist a pearl and gem set girdle (Pl. VIIA). Many of the girdles worn by the female élite were fine examples of the goldsmith's craft, such as 'a girdell conteyning xxxij Dyamountes and lxiiij perles set by cowples' (2716) and 'a Girdell conteyning xxj Rubies and Clx perles set by eightes' (2721). The girdle was a decorative item, but it could also be functional, and a range of items could be hung from it including small girdle books and pomanders. In April 1543 Princess Mary paid a goldsmith £3 9*s* for 'lengthtyning of a girdle of goldesmyth worke a pomandr'.[113]

A range of decorative and functional items were hung from a woman's girdle including pomanders, girdle books, rosaries and 'twoo womens purses one of crymsen satten thither white lether with buttons and tasselles of golde' (9654). The quality of such items can be gauged from a late fifteenth century pierced gilded silver round pomander made up of four segments which open to reveal a figure of the Virgin Mary.[114] In 1547 the queen's jewel coffer included 'a Tablet of golde being a Clock fashioned like an Hartee garnysshed with iij Rubies and one fair dyamounde lozenged' (2653) that might have hung from a girdle.

Decorative techniques: paning, slashing, cutwork, pinking and clocking

A range of decorative effects were used by the king's tailors to embellish his clothes. Some of these techniques were quite short-lived, and only featured in Henry VIII's wardrobe for up to a decade, while others were used throughout his reign. Paning was a term that could be used to describe two different types of construction: alternating solid panels of cloth of contrasting colour or weave (used to make a range of garments for the king, for example, a 'Cote panyd with cloth of golde of baudkyn & crimosyn saten lyned with sarcenet' [B253]); or thin strips of fabric (this effect could be created in two ways, either by joining separate strips of cloth at the top and bottom only or by slashing a single piece of fabric to create the same effect). A second fabric, usually of contrasting colour and weight, was stitched behind the paned strips and pulled out in puffs. When the colours used contrasted, the effect created could be striking.

Worsley's wardrobe book indicates that between 1516 and 1521 paning was used to decorate a range of garments. In a number of cases only one or two examples of a specific type of garment is recorded: chammers [B119], frocks [B71], gowns [B79] and riding coats [B255]. However, other garments, especially doublets either made singly [A162] or with matching hose [A182] and jackets [A180] were clearly favoured for this style of decoration. For an especially striking effect, the king ordered a matching set of doublet, hose and frock [A208]. By 1547 paning had ceased to be an important decorative technique in the king's wardrobe.

Slashing was the term used for making longer cuts in the fabric, while short cuts and small holes were referred to as pinking and decorative cut edges were often called cutwork or jagging.[115] Towards the end of the fifteenth century, slashing was predominantly placed on sleeves. It was applied to the doublet and then the hose. As a technique, slashing was at its height in England between 1520 and 1535.[116] The positioning of the cuts required careful planning, as in the case of a jerkin worn by Charles V in 1517 which was made from cloth of gold and cloth of silver, both of which were slashed to reveal the crimson satin lining underneath: 'there must have been a hundred slashes and more in the jerkin, all so well set out that one could not have arranged them better.'[117]

Slashing could be in the form of long or small cuts all over the surface of the cloth. The cuts were worked in lines or geometric patterns and the fabrics chosen were usually plain silks such as satin or velvet rather than patterned cloths. Small diagonal cuts were also used to decorate the edges of cuffs and collars, as on the collar and cuffs of Jean de Dinteville's doublet in Holbein's *Ambassadors*. This technique was used on the cuffs of Don Garzia's doublet and was created by stitching in place a doubled-over length of bias-cut satin that was cut.

Slashing could be combined with a range of other fancy cutwork techniques and the effect (as with paning) was enhanced by placing linings of contrasting colours under the cuts. In 1541 the king's wardrobe included 'a cote with slevys of Russet vellet embrouderyd and frogged with venyce gold cut and pulled owt with crymsen taphata lined with black satten'.[118] The linings could have an interlining to ensure that the puffs of fabric stood out. This technique was not confined to the king's wardrobe, and it was used extensively on the livery provided for the 1544 campaign. For example, each of the 110 demi-lances received:

> 1 coat of yellow damask and red kersey full of cuts; 2¾ yards yellow damask and ¼ yard for guarding, 2½ yards red kersey and ⅛ yard for guarding, welted with ¼ yard yellow taffeta for one half and ¼ yard red damask for the other half, the cuts lined with 1 yard of sarsenet of like colour to the cuts and 3½ yards of black buckram to line.[119]

The term cutwork was used to describe a range of decorative techniques that involved cutting the fabric into decorative shapes (also see appliqué).[120] It often required the garment to be made from several layers of fabric, so allowing the lower layer or the lining to show through. Cutwork was a very common technique in the 1510s and early 1520s, and as such it features strongly in Worsley's wardrobe book (Table 20.3). It was used to embellish a wide variety of garments and worked on a range of different textiles, many of which were very expensive.

Related to the technique of slashing was pinking (Table 20.4).[121] This consisted of making a series of small cuts worked over the surface of the cloth, and became fashionable in the 1540s (Figs 20.5 and 20.6). It is found on a range of items in Henry VIII's wardrobe at his death in 1547, including Spanish capes (14305) and coats (14289). In Princess Mary's accounts for 1546 there was an entry 'for pinking of 2 yards of velvet', indicating that the fabric was pinked before being made up into a garment.[122]

Clocking is a decorative technique associated in the second half of the sixteenth century with wedge-shaped embroidery worked on hose. The terms appear occasionally in the records of the king's wardrobe from the early part of his reign and, when it does appear, the context suggests a slightly different approach: 'a Jaquet of crimosyn tissewe clocked with siluer tilsent with dropes lined with blacke saten' [B172]. However, the warrant dated 27 March 1543 includes a number of new items decorated with this technique, including a frock of black damask 'cut with clocks and with welts for the clocks of velvet and guarded with three guards' and lined with sarsenet, and a doublet of crimson satin with 'clocks in the sleeve, the clocks lined with sarsenet'. Older garments were translated and enlarged and made more fashionable by clocking: two doublets of satin lined with velvet, one of crimson and the other of white, 'made with clocks in the sleeves and the clocks lined with crimson and white velvet' and slashed.[123]

Table 20.3: *Positioning of cutwork on clothes listed in Worsley's wardrobe book and inventory*

Garment type and number of examples	Details
Outer garments	
Bases	Cut with letters B150
Bases and short coats	Cut upon velvet A268
Bases and trappers	Cut work of blue velvet A271
Chammers	Cut upon cloth of silver A20; cut upon cloth of gold A102; cut upon cloth of gold lozengewise B81–2
Coats	Cut upon velvet and cloth of gold A183, 189
Frocks	Covered with satin cut A113
Gowns	Cut upon cloth of gold A19; cut and set with points B21
Mantles	Cut in a rich border A107; cut upon cloth of gold A371
Riding coats	Cut upon cloth of gold B168
Doublets, jackets and hose	
'Almain' doublets and hose	Cut and paned A182
Doublets	Cut upon cloth of silver A11, 53; cut and tied A259; cut upon cloth of gold B193; cut upon velvet B194; cut and edged B195; cut in panes B201
Doublets and hose	Cut upon tilsent A193; cut after the 'Almain' fashion A196; cut upon cloth of gold A202; cut upon damask silver A201; covered with cut satin A234, 237; cut all over A253; cut and tied A260
Doublets, hose and jackets	Cut over upon cloth of gold A169, 198; cut upon cloth of gold and embroidered A184, 217; cut over satin A188, 190, 207; a cut of velvet A219; cut upon cloth of silver A11, 220; cut all over on satin A229
Doublets and jackets	Cut all over A224
Jackets	Cut upon cloth of silver A48, B163; cut upon cloth of gold B151; cut upon velvet B160

Guards, borders, crests and edges

Decorative borders or guards were a very popular form of ornamentation throughout Henry VIII's reign. They were applied to a number of different types of garments (Table 20.5). The quantities of fabric given to the tailors to perform particular decorative techniques indicate the scale of the various forms of embellishment. Edging took the least fabric with 1¼ yards (1.1 m) of cloth of gold damask to edge a cloak [A440] and 1¼ yards (1.1 m) of green velvet to edge a coat and demi-coat [A964]. Welting also required fairly modest amounts of cloth: 2 yards (1.8 m) of black silver tissue to welt a coat [A622] and 2 yards (1.8 m) of black velvet to welt a gown [A1156]. In contrast, decorative borders were on a grander scale: 4 yards (3.6 m) of crimson velvet to border a cloak [A1169], 6 yards (5.4 m) of plain cloth of silver damask to be drawn through the border of a coat, and 5 (4.6 m) [A499] or 5¼ yards (4.8 m) of damask silver for the border on a frock [A486]. Decorative borders that were made for specific types of garment were often detachable and could be moved from one item to another, or were left detached in the wardrobe:

> a bordor of stole werke yt was opon a Riding gowne of russet veluete [B350].
> a bordor of stole werke of a womans gowne of crimosyn saten [B351].
> a bordor & cuffes of stole werke of a womans gowne of tawny veluete [B352].

Guards were decorative borders applied to the front edges, cuffs and hems of garments, usually gowns, coats and cloaks. They were also used to cover and embellish seams. Guards were found on a range of garments in Worsley's wardrobe book, including bases [A200], cloaks [B138], coats [A161], doublets [B208] frocks [A29], half-coats [A200] and mantles [B125]. They were usually made from expensive fabrics such as cloth of gold after baudekin [B223], satin [A164] and velvet [A29] and they could be decorated with scrollwork [B208]. There were also references to the less commonly used burgeon guards, which were recorded on cloaks [B111] and gowns [B101], made of velvet [B108]. Guards continued to feature on the king's clothes, as indicated by 'a gowne with a square cape of purple satten embroidered with gold upon a brode garde of purple vellut and lined with purple vellut' from 1541.[124]

Garments could have single or multiple guards of the same or varying width. The guards could be made from contrasting material or the same and were often embellished with embroidery, metal braid or slashing: 'a brode garde and twoo narrowe gardes of blacke vellut embrawderid with blacke Silke and golde' (14295), 'twoo burgonion gardes of the same [blacke vellut] welted with weltes of blacke satten cut' (14299) and 'twoo burgonion garde of blacke vellut cut with diuerse cuttes' (14300). An example of a single guard, with diagonal slashing and noted as being of 'sam' (satin), that were applied to the front and on the sleeves of a gown, can be seen in Holbein's portrait drawings of the earl of Wiltshire and Ormond and Lord Vaux (Figs 20.7 and 20.8).

The use of applied borders was a very common decorative technique for the male wardrobe, and a number of instances were recorded in Worsley's book. Not surprisingly, borders were used on outer garments including chammers, cloaks, coats, gowns, riding coats and short coats. Velvet was the most popular material for these borders [B86], followed by satin [A107] and stoolwork [B350], but some were made from cloth of gold [B156] and cloth of silver [A97]. Several distinctive types were recorded. The first type used cutwork [B273], while the second used multiple borders to create effect. Double [B109], triple [B118], quadruple [B275] and sextuple versions [B291] are listed.

There is a rare example of an extant border or guard in the collection at Hardwick Hall that could have been used on clothing or furnishing textiles. This guard consists of a strip of crimson silk velvet 0.06 m wide, and originally over 7 m long,

20.5 *A fragment of a sixteenth-century silk satin with slashing, 1869. Photo: Abegg-Stiftung, CH-3132 Riggisberg, (Christoph von Viràg)*

20.6 *A fragment of stamped and slashed sixteenth-century silk satin, 1864. Photo: Abegg-Stiftung, CH-3132 Riggisberg, (Christoph von Viràg)*

Table 20.4: *Instances of pinking and cutting in 1547*

Item of dress	Details
Outer garment	
Cloaks	cut (2)
Coats	cut and tufted with sarsenet (3); pinked (1)
Gowns	cut (1)
Spanish capes	cut (1); pinked (1)
Doublets and hose	
Doublets	cut and raised with threads of Venice gold (1); cut and tufted with sarsenet (2); tufted with sarsenet (1)
Hose	cut (2); cut and tufted with sarsenet (2); cut with divers cuts (1); tufted with sarsenet (1)

worked with metal wrapped thread and spangles in a scrolling S-shaped design ornamented with stylised leaves and flowers.[125] Borders of this type can be seen on the gown that Eleanor of Toledo was buried in. They were used to decorate the bodice, centre front and hem of her skirt. The borders were made by couching metal-wrapped threads and silk cord onto the ground fabric (Fig. 20.9). Simpler examples have been found in London made from strips of cut wool cloth (Figs 20.10 and 20.11). These decorative techniques were felt to be both frivolous and costly. In 1537 Charles V passed an edict to control the number and width of decorative borders: he lay down one border was to be of no more than four fingers wide or two to four narrower strips of the same overall width.[126]

Another type of applied decorative band was the crest. It was used on a similar range of outer garments to those decorated with borders, including cloaks [B102], coats [B254], gowns [B104] and Spanish capes [B107]. Crests were also put on doublets [B264] and jackets [B283]. They were made from a similar range of materials as borders, with velvet being the most popular material and no stoolwork examples. As with borders, they were also used in groups, usually either double [B267] or triple [B276].

20.7 *James Butler, ninth earl of Wiltshire and Ormond, 1530–35, by Hans Holbein the Younger. RL 12263 P23. The Royal Collection © 2004, Her Majesty the Queen Elizabeth II*

Edging is sometimes referred to as hemming. By the time that James Worsley compiled his inventory, edging had passed its sartorial heyday. Only five examples occur in Worsley's wardrobe book, and these indicate that it was used

Table 20.5: *Decorative borders, edges and guards on Henry VIII's clothes in 1547*

Garment	Type of decoration and materials
Outer garments	
Cassocks	**edged** (3): velvet; **welts** (1): velvet
Cloaks	**burgeon guards** (3): velvet; **guards broad and narrow** (2): velvet
Coats	**borders** (8): cord, velvet formed down with cord and embroidered, Venice gold, Venice gold striped with cord, Venice gold and silk striped with cord; **edged** (1): knots, velvet; **guards** (3): passamayne, velvet embroidered with Venice gold
Frocks	**borders** (1): Venice gold; **guards** (6): passamayne, velvet; **welts** (1): passamayne
Gowns	**borders** (10): damask and Venice gold, embroidered, passamayne and cord, silver, velvet formed down with a double knot of Venice silver, Venice gold, Venice gold like goldsmiths work, Venice gold like passamayne with knots; **burgeon guards** (1): Venice gold and silk; **edged** (1): velvet; **guards** (16): passamayne of silk and gold, velvet embroidered with silk, velvet, velvet embroidered with Venice gold, velvet formed down with cord, Venice gold, Venice gold and silk; **passamayne** (1): Venice gold and silver; **welts** (7): passamayne of silk and gold, velvet; **wreaths** (1): damask and Venice gold
Spanish capes	**borders** (4): passamayne, velvet; **burgeon guards** (1): velvet; **guards** (2): velvet; **passamaynes** (3): flat Venice gold, Venice gold and silver
Doublets and hose	
Doublets	**borders** (3): damask gold, Venice gold; **edged** (2): passamayne; **guards** (1): passamayne
Hose	**borders** (3): damask gold, Venice gold; **edged** (2): passamayne

20.8 *Thomas, Lord Vaux, by Hans Holbein the Younger, 1532–35. RL 12245 P 24. The Royal Collection © 2004, Her Majesty the Queen Elizabeth II*

on outer garments: cloaks [B51, 112], doublets [B195], gowns [B115] and jackets [B312]. As with other techniques of this type, expensive fabrics were favoured: cloth of gold [B51], tissue [B195] and velvet [B112, 115, 312]. Jagging is a technique related to edging. It involved cutting the hem or edge of a garment into points. There are only a handful of references to jagging. When it is mentioned, it occurs on the clothes of members of the royal household, rather than the king, which suggests that these garments of lesser officials harked back to older decorative techniques no longer fashionable with the élite.

Applied trimmings or passementerie

In addition to embroidery, the Tudor tailor had access to a range of fancy goods supplied by the silk women that he could use to further embellish garments. These silk and metal thread trimmings could take a range of forms and they were often listed using rather vague terms such as 'Sundry Remnauntes of deape silke fringe of sundrye Cullour weying in all ij poundes' (15135).

Ribbon was produced in an extensive range of types, widths and colours, and sometimes it incorporated metal thread. It was intended for a range of specific uses, some of which were functional as well as decorative: cap ribbon, garter ribbon, ribbon for belts and girdles and ribbon for hanging keys on. Ribbon was also used for making aglets.

In the first half of the sixteenth century the terms 'lace' and 'passamayne' were not generally used to denote the type of open lace that was made with bobbins from the late sixteenth century.[127] Rather, these terms generally denoted a braid lace, as in the case of 'viij peces yelowe lace for the Kings Grace' bought in 1530.[128] Many of the descriptions are quite vague, making it difficult to distinguish the specific technique used, but the entries suggest that there was variety. The 1547 inventory listed several different types of passamenterie, including 'passamayne of golde and siluer', 'golde and Silke' and 'of blacke silke. . .raised like newe making veluett in bredthe di quarter of a yarde and in lengthe xij yards di' (15132–34). Braids of this type were used to embellish guards and borders or were used alone to cover seams.

However, there is some evidence of bobbin lace being made in England by the mid sixteenth century. The earliest known reference so far discovered for bobbin lace appears in the 1547 inventory where a small purse is decorated 'with bone worke lace gold' (2504). References to bobbin lace also appear in the account books of Bess of Hardwick, who in the winter of 1548 bought 'Wyte bowene worke for coufes for my smokes' and 'bone lace and pynke lace for the shyrtes'.[129]

Silk and metal thread fringes became increasingly popular as decoration for clothing as the sixteenth century progressed. They were used both in a matching or a contrasting colour to the main garment. From the outset, there are sporadic references to fringe: on 15 July 1510 a riding hood of black sarsenet fringed with silk and gold was ordered for the king.[130] There are fairly limited references to the use of fringe to decorate clothing in Worsley's wardrobe books, with examples being located on bases and placards [A264–65], coats [A244] and trappers [A266]. There were also a small number of instances when fringe was applied to furnishings: altar cloths [A325] and curtains [A326–27]. Fringe was also used to special effect on revels costumes, as in the case of 'twelve Almain coats with Italian sleeves, [six] of yellow satin, and six of green satin, the latter . . . and set with scales like scales of a dragon or a sturgeon, each scale of flat god damask fringe fretted; the yellow coats, the same in silver', supplied by Richard Gibson in 1519.[131] By the 1540s the use of fringe had increased, often in conjunction with embroidery or other passementerie.

Tassels were often used to decorate furnishing textiles, including cushions, but they were also found in certain contexts within the king's wardrobe of the robes (Fig. 7.3). Large tassels decorated the ends of the cords used to fasten the ceremonial robes worn for the Garter and parliament. Tassels, often very complex in their design, were also worn hanging from the hilts of daggers, as in the case of the blue and gold tassel on Jean de Dinteville's dagger in Holbein's *The Ambassadors*. Henry owned several examples at his death in 1547, including 'oon Tassell for a dagger of blacke silke and veanice golde garneshed with peerle' (9966). Sometimes the tassels were stored separately or became detached, as in the case of 'an olde tassel of crymsen Silke' (9476). A fragmentary golden-yellow silk tassel that may have been worn in a similar way was recovered from the wreck of the *Trinidad Valencera*.[132]

Passementerie was predominantly made of silk, but sometimes cheaper and more hardwearing wool and linen products were used. These alternatives included caddis, a wool tape made from the 'cadace' or flocks of wool that was used for

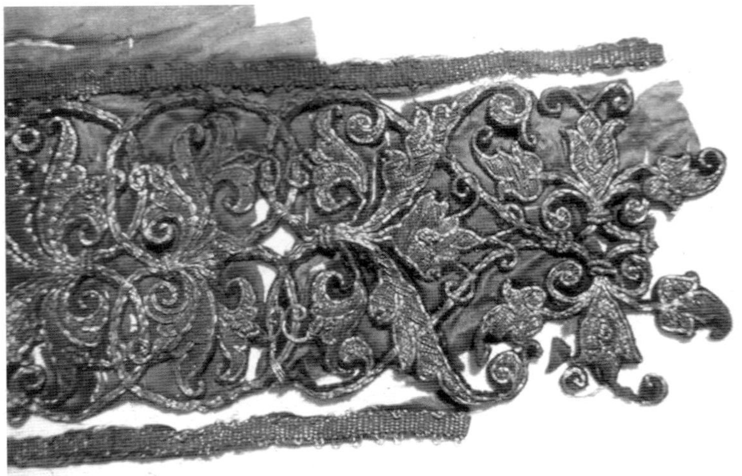

20.9 *An embroidered guard from Eleanor of Toledo's gown, part of the Medici burial clothes, 1562. Reproduced from the Janet Arnold Collection by courtesy of her executors*

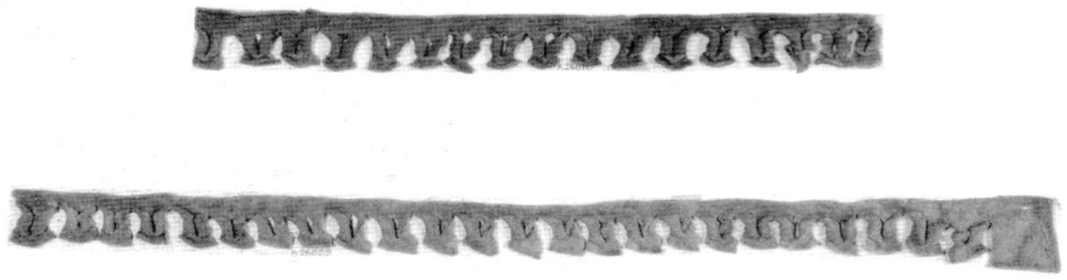

20.11 *Decorative edgings on a fulled, wool fabric, found at Worship Street, London. A26809-10, Museum of London*

making garters and for trimming furnishings.[133] Crewel yarns were used to make fringe or woven into tapes and braids. Inkle was a tape made from linen thread and produced in a range of widths and weights. Most of the narrow-wares supplied to the great wardrobe were made by silk women, but some came from other sources. On 21 December 1515, Anthonio Vivaldi, merchant of Genoa, was granted a licence to export cords, girdles, ribbons and laces made in England, notwithstanding the Act of 1509.[134]

Surface decoration: embroidery, quilting, stoolwork and goldsmith's work

The king's clothes were often highly ornate. A variety of decorative techniques were used, of which embroidery played a central role. Embroidery was used to embellish many of the king's clothes.[135] In particular it was used to provide bands of ornament around the hem or on guards or for overall decoration. Embroidery, as opposed to needlework, used expensive materials for both the ground and the stitched decoration, and a range of words were employed to describe this form of decoration in the accounts, including 'wrought'. Embroidery was a slow, skilled technique, and many of the professional embroiderers were highly skilled. Both men and women earned their living by producing embroidery, the men generally earning more than the women. The king's

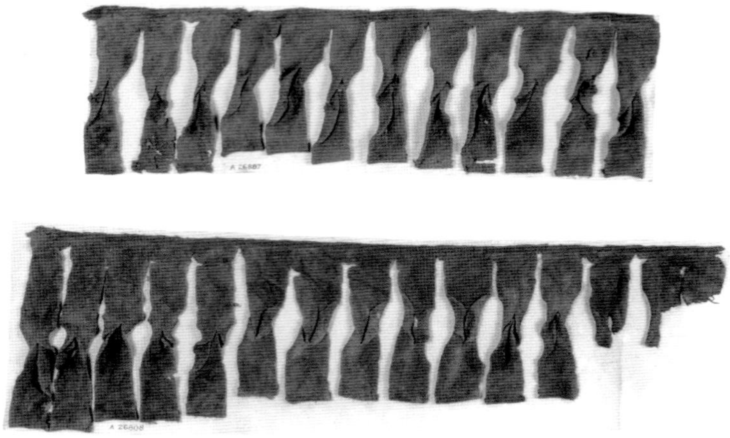

20.10 *Decorative edgings on a fulled, wool fabric, found at Worship Street, London. A26807-8, Museum of London*

embroiderer worked on and completed objects that had been started by other craftsmen in the king's employment. Embroidery was also undertaken by women from the middle and higher ranks of society as it was considered to be a suitable pastime that was both modest and useful.

Even though Worsley's wardrobe book indicates the range of uses to which embroidery was put, it played a limited role in embellishing the king's clothes. William Mortimer, the king's embroiderer, undertook embroidery on a fairly small range of garments: chammers [A478], coats [A384], doublets and jackets [A409, 474], doublets, jackets and hose [A431, 433], gowns, doublets and jackets [A398] and mantles [A371]. He also embroidered coats for the king's guard [A1569] and mended damaged work including a set of embroidered borders [A501]. By 1547, just over half the 224 garments listed in the wardrobe of the robes (Table 20.6) were embroidered (51.7%). This reveals a significant evolution in the importance of this technique for embellishing and enhancing the king's clothes during his reign. Embroidery was applied to all the major groups of clothes within the king's possession and could be used to create suits of garments that were linked by colour, fabric type and surface decoration.

Working in conjunction with artists such as Holbein, the king's embroiderers drew upon the new corpus of Renaissance motifs to create distinctive patterns to enrich the surface of Henry VIII's clothes. 'Moresques', Islamic interlace designs and grotesques all became highly popular in applied decoration on dress and accessories in the first half of the sixteenth century. In Holbein's portrait of Henry VIII, *c.* 1536, (Pl. Ic) there are four bands of embroidered decoration worked in laid thread couching on the body of his doublet and also on the sleeves. A simpler band of embroidery was worked in a classical scroll pattern, outlining the very low neckline of his jerkin.[136] Holbein also depicted a deep band of embroidered scroll work around the hem of the skirts of Henry VIII's doublet in the Barber Surgeons' portrait (Fig. 20.12).

Designs circulated in Europe through the medium of books such as Antonio Tagliente's *Opera Nuova ... intitolata esempio di raccammi* of 1527. This embroidery pattern book presented a series of Moresque designs in a black and white scheme, including borders and strips of ornaments. The influence of Renaissance ornament on embroidery designs and styles was also influenced by Alessandro Paganino's *Libro primo … de rechami*, published in the same year, which provided instruction on the techniques, mainly cutwork, and included designs. Three years later Francesco Pellegrino published *La Fleur de la science de pourtraicture* as a textbook for embroiderers who were looking for 'Patrons de Broderie'. Pellegrino's exotic designs included interlaced bandwork, often angular in style, and delicate, foliate stems. Embroidered bands of interlaced designs became fashionable in Italy, France and England. About 1540, a Frenchman, Thomas Geminus, came to England and he was instrumental in the dissemination of Moresque design. In 1548 Geminus produced the first book of designs, aimed at embroiderers and goldsmiths, to be published in England. The book, titled *Morysse and Damashin renewed and encreased Very profitable for Goldsmythes and Embroderars*, was to be very influential.[137]

Strapwork was an innovation at Francis I's chateau of Fontainebleau where borders of interlaced designs made from strips of leather were used to create decorative schemes. Similar interlaced designs were adapted for use in embroidery and were used to create decorative borders or guards on clothing. Elements of the design could be raised by the use of padding.[138] Embroidery at the Henrician court also included a range of naturalistic and heraldic motifs that in origin predate the Renaissance. A range of decorative motifs are recorded in Worsley's inventory. These include heraldic images such as arms of England [B391], religious motifs such as the Holy Ghost [B336] and designs based on nature such as roses [A267, 302, 312; B362, 394] and oak leaves [B260, 308].

Henry VIII was often consulted about the choice of design. For example, in October 1533 Thomas Cromwell wrote an *aide-mémoir* to himself 'To show the King the patterns for the embroidery for the Queen'.[139] Once a choice had been made, patterns were made for the craftsmen to follow. In 1519–20 Catherine of Aragon's tailor provided 2 ells (1.4 m) of canvas to make patterns for stoolwork at a price of 8*d*. Further down in the same account was an entry for the making of a gown of purple velvet lined with stoolwork.[140]

A range of embroidered techniques was in use to embellish clothing. Appliqué was a relatively quick technique that could make very effective use of strong contrasts in colour between

Table 20.6: *Analysis of the use of embroidery in the king's wardrobe, 1547*

Item of dress	Number and percentage embroidered	Item of dress	Number and percentage embroidered
Outer garments		7 jerkins	7 (100%)
13 capes, Spanish	8 (61.5%)	1 pair of slops	1 (100%)
10 cassocks	1 (10%)	*Associated items*	
8 cloaks	2 (25%)	4 partlets	4 (100%)
20 coats	12 (60%)	*Headwear*	
17 frocks	3 (17.6%)	3 hoods	1 (33%)
41 gowns	22 (53.6%)	*Accessories*	
Doublets, jerkins and hose		24 girdles	10 (41.6%)
25 doublets	18 (72%)	21 lyams and collars	9 (42.8%)
25 pairs of hose	18 (72%)		

20.12 *Infrared detail from* Henry VIII and the Barber Surgeons *by Hans Holbein the Younger, c. 1540, showing scrollwork embroidery on the skirts of the king's doublet. Reproduced with permission of the Department of Conservation and Technology, Courtauld Institute of Art*

the applied layer and the ground fabric. The cut pieces were often edged with metal thread, self-coloured silk thread or thread of contrasting colours to conceal the raw edge and reduce the problem of fraying. It was used to produce bold designs based on fashionable Renaissance ornament and so the technique was especially suited to pieces for use at royal jousts and for furnishings. For the jousts held in March 1522, 3½ yards (3.2 m) of blue satin at 8*s* the yard (0.91 m) were supplied for embroidering fetters or shackles on the costume of Sir Nicholas Carew, along with ½ yard (0.45 m) of black velvet costing 6*s* for letters on the bards and bases.[141] Appliqué was used on a finer scale to embellish the king's own clothes. Worsley's wardrobe book recorded a delivery to William Mortimer of 'iiij yerdes of tawnye cloth of gold opon satten damaske gold for thembrauderyng of a mantell of white satten cutte opon cloth of gold for the kinges grace' [A371].

Of the monochrome embroidery techniques prevalent from the fifteenth to the seventeenth centuries, blackwork is the best known. It is strongly associated with English sixteenth-century dress. The blackwork designs favoured in the mid Tudor period were typified by interlacing, small geometric shapes and meander scrollwork, with the scrolling terminating with floral and fruit forms.[142] By the 1540s naturalistic motifs, including trailing plants, animals, birds, flowers and fruits were frequently combined with the more traditional geometric forms.[143] The same years also saw the introduction of 'speckling', little stitches to infill the naturalistic motifs, replacing the more formal diaper fillings. Blackwork could be embellished with gold thread for heightened affect. The introduction of the technique to England is associated with Catherine of Aragon and her household, and her liking for it resulted in it being called Spanish work.[144] Examples of it can be seen in her portraits on her cuffs. Blackwork can be carried out using a variety of stitches including back, chain and buttonhole stitch. A fine example worked in blue silk can be seen on the cuffs of a boy's shirt *c.* 1550 (Fig. 20.13).

Strapwork was also influential for embroidered designs executed on fine linen which was decorated with a range of designs including narrow borders of simple geometric designs and more complex naturalistic motifs. Patterns that were predominantly linear in their form, such as those used on guards or cuffs, could be executed in a range of stitches including cross stitch, back stitch and stem stitch, along with double running or Holbein stitch.[145] Double running was used to create the double-sided designs that worked to such good effect on collars and cuffs. Holbein's portraits and preparatory drawings provide a very good overview of the range of blackwork designs favoured by the élite. The portrait of Simon George, *c.* 1535, shows a double-sided blackwork design on the collar and cuffs of his shirt (Fig. 1.9). The shirt worn by the earl of Surrey *c.* 1542 has a delicate floral design on the collar and cuffs.[146]

Couching, or laid thread work, consists of a silk cord or metal wrapped thread laid down on the surface of the textile and secured using stitches worked using another thread. This thread could be either the same or a contrasting colour. It was worked in the form of decorative bands or as all over decoration. This style of decoration is shown in contemporary portraits. Moretto's *Portrait of a Young Man*, *c.* 1542, shows the sitter wearing a black satin doublet with couched embroidery, and the *Portrait of a Boy*, *c.* 1545, by an unknown Italian artist depicts him with a short, crimson satin gown with bands of couched gilt metal thread embroidery.[147]

20.13 *Detail from Fig. 6.13 of the shirt's embroidered cuff, showing the double-sided floral design. T.112-1972 © V&A Images, Victoria and Albert Museum London*

An entry in the great wardrobe account for 1545 records payments for 'vj virg de laques hispani nigri pro edginge j smocke'. This black Spanish cord was probably for couching into a geometric design to produce an effect similar to blackwork.[148] The quantity of cord required for decorative work of this type was substantial. In the 1543–45 account, Anne Grey made two deliveries. On the first occasion she supplied 402 oz (11.4 kg) of cord, passamayne and ribbon (£100 10*s*), 9 lb 14 oz (4.47 kg) of silk (£13 3*s* 4*d*) and 17 oz (0.48 kg) of hollow and round cord of black Spanish silk and other colours (34*s*). The second order was on a similar scale: 352 yards (321.8 m) of passamayn and ribbon, 11 lb (4.9 kg) of silk, 22 pieces of round, hollow cord, 10½ oz (0.29 kg) of round cord, twisted, of Spanish silk and 47 pieces of silk of 'Rakemayne'.[149]

Samples of couched embroidered decoration can be seen in two of Holbein's portraits, on the doublet of Count Morette and on the sleeves of Simon George's doublet (Fig 1.9). Similar guards to those on George's doublet appeared on the king's gowns including 'A gowne of fresed black veluett withe a brode garde of blacke veluett embraudered with venice golde and Silke' (14118) and another with embroidery 'like vnto Clowdes' (14194). While the 1547 inventory entries provide very few details concerning the designs and materials, there are some clues including a doublet 'enbrodered with golde and iiij Cordauntes blacke silke & gold' (14218), another 'all over embrawderid with pirles of damaske golde and Silver' (14227) and an arming doublet 'all over embrawderid with a busie woorke' (14233). Couched cord was also used to create a striped effect as in the case of the metal wrapped cord stitched to the pink satin doublet worn by Prince Carlos when he was painted by Sanchez Coello *c.* 1556. The same effect can be seen on the crimson satin doublet of Don Garzia and the velvet panes of his hose. The technique was used to embellish items for Henry VIII, including 'a jaquet of carnacion vellut embroderyd with damaske golde pyrled lydd with black satten'.[150]

Goldwork developed out of the blackwork tradition. It was more expensive, on account of the higher value of the materials used. The metal threads were also often used in combination with polychrome silk threads. A deep band of embroidery of this type worked in an interlaced design can be seen on the collar of Henry's shirt in Holbein's portrait (Pl. Ic) and on the neckline of Prince Edward's shirt (Fig. 11.7). Whitework was a solid embroidery technique worked in a white thread on a white open ground. It was much less common than blackwork at this period, but examples can be seen on the turned-back collar of Catherine Parr's shift (Fig. 10.6). There is whitework embroidery, worked in a small, floral design, on the small stand collar of Jean de Dinteville's collar, one of Holbein's *Ambassadors*.

Drawn thread work was usually worked on tabby or plain weave linen because of the distinct weave that makes it easier to remove the necessary threads. The technique was often used to decorate shirt collars for the henchmen and the officers of the hunts. Related to this are the thread-counting techniques that are worked by counting the warps and wefts of a cloth, usually linen, with a pronounced weave. The technique can be quickly mastered, producing geometric designs of the type, often found on edges of chemises and shirt collars. Examples of the latter have been found at the Alpirsbach monastery.[151]

Additional surface decoration could be applied, in the form of pearls, small gemstones, beads, spangles (sequins), oes (small metal rings) which could be stitched on singly, seeded over the ground fabric or in patterns and doublets, small pieces of glass backed with a coloured metal foil. Catherine Parr's wardrobe of the robe's account for 1544–45 includes an entry for 9⅜ oz (0.27 kg) of small pearls bought from Laurence Warren for £18 15*s* and delivered to 'Guillam brauderer for a border of a Gowne of Crimsin veluett for the queens grace'.[152] In the royal wardrobe the effect was often enhanced by the use of numerous jewels, as in the case of a 'a doblet of blacke veluete enbrauderd lyned with blacke saten and tufte with lynen cloth cut in panes tyed togeders with CC perles set in gold' [B201]. The effect was highly valued and items featuring it in the 1547 inventory included 'one paier of Sleaves of white vellat all over embraudered with damaske golde and garneshed with peerle and set with diuerse stones in Collettes silver gilte' (9946) (Fig. 20.14).

A variety of decorative techniques could be deployed on a single garment. In 1547 'a Litell Coofer' held 'xlj Buttons of golde vij small Rubies sett in Collettes of golde tenne paire and one Aglatt of gold cetayne small garneshing peerle in a paper and ceten small garneshing Beades of golde in a paper' (3410). This last moment reserve selection is strikingly like the range of decoration found on doublets and pairs of sleeves during the 1530s and 1540s that could be added at random, even while the king was dressing. In 1547 the king's coffers also included 'vj Roopes of small beedes to garnish between perles' (2230), 'a Beede of silver' (3480), but it is not clear whether these were small beads used to ornament clothes or beads used to make rosaries.

Quilting is a stitched technique for joining two, three or more layers of cloth that was both functional and decorative. Layers of padding or wadding could be placed between the outer layers of fabric for added warmth or to provide a degree of protection, as in the case of the 8 ells (5.4 m) of holland that were provided 'for quilting to match under the yellow satin that lined the King's pieces of harness'.[153] Alternatively, the padding is replaced by cord, which is stitched between two layers of fabric, to create a design in relief. In addition to securing the layers, the stitching is also decorative, often worked in repeating, geometric patterns. The stitching can be worked in thread the same colour as the ground fabric or in a contrasting colour.

How quilting was used decoratively, while giving body to a garment (or an element of a garment) can be seen in Titian's portrait of *A man with a quilted sleeve*, *c.* 1510.[154] The profile of the sitter's richly quilted right sleeve is presented to the viewer. Quilting was worked to good effect on the sleeves of the red satin Hever doublet. The quilting was padded with wool, while the stitching was worked in back stitch using red

20.14 *Infrared detail from* Henry VIII and the Barber Surgeons *by Hans Holbein the Younger, c. 1540, showing the king's sleeve embellished with slashing, embroidery and jewels. Reproduced with permission of the Department of Conservation and Technology, Courtauld Institute of Art*

silk thread in double rows that were placed 6 cm apart.[155] Quilting was used on a small range of garments made for the king including bonnets, gowns and waistcoats. A list of the king's clothes dated 1541 included 'a gowne of quilted sarsenet black with a brode garde of black new making of vellut' while in 1547 he had 'a long gowne of blacke Taphata quilted' (14187).[156] The accounts of Mark Milliner reveal that on 23 September 1546 he delivered 'a lynynge of crymysyn satten lined with redd sarcenet and quilted wythe cotton' costing 4*s* to Mr Alsop at Windsor.[157] Quilting was also used on female clothing, such as a kirtle belonging to Jane Seymour 'of clothe of Siluer quilted with blacke silke' (11262).

Stoolwork was applied, often in the form of borders or cuffs, on both male and female clothing. It was put on gowns [B352], placards [B281], four-quartered jackets [A72], foresleeves [B281], doublets and hose [A255]. When pieces of clothing were worn out or given away, the stoolwork borders were retained [A77] and stored for reuse. This is what happened with 'a bordor of stole werke yt was opon a Riding gowne of russet veluete' [B350] and 'a bordor of stole werke of a womans gowne of crimosyn saten' [B351]. It was also used to decorate hunting accessories including dog collars [B391–92], greyhound collars [A313] and hawk hoods [B389].

137 VAM 19009; a page from the book is illustrated in Snodin and Styles, *Design*, p. 46.
138 S. Levey, 'Embroidery', in J. Harris, ed., *5000 Years of Textiles* (1993), p. 205. Designs based on this theme were produced for Henry VIII, possibly for use at Whitehall, as indicated by a preparatory design in the Musée du Louvre, Paris.
139 *LP* VI, 1382.
140 JRL Latin MS 239, f. 15v.
141 *LP* III.ii, p. 1558.
142 A slightly later woman's bodice embroidered with blackwork designs belongs to the Victoria and Albert Museum. The design is worked in running stitch with a design of scrolls infilled with birds, animals and insects. It is illustrated in Symonds and Preece, *Needlework*, pl. XLI.1.
143 G. Speirs and S. Quemby, *A Treasury of Embroidery Designs: Charts and Patterns from the Great Collections* (1985), pp. 50–54.
144 Symonds and Preece, *Needlework*, p. 240.
145 Levey, 'Embroidery', p. 205.
146 In the Museo de Arte, São Paolo, Brazil; Reynolds, *Holbein*, no. 76, pp. 147–48.
147 NG299 and 694.
148 TNA E351/3025.
149 TNA E101/423/10, ff. 25r, 54v.
150 TNA SP1/168, f. 199r.
151 Stangl and Lang, *Mönche und Scholaren*, p. 49.
152 TNA E101/423/12, unfoliated.
153 *LP* III.ii, p. 1555.
154 NG 1944.
155 Nevinson, 'Sixteenth century doublet', p. 371.
156 TNA SP1/168, f. 201v.
157 TNA E101/424/4, f. 3r.
158 Hall, *Chronicle*, p. 514; Anglo, *Great Tournament Roll*, p. 50.
159 Egan and Pritchard, *Dress Accessories*, p. 336.
160 Ibid., pp. 235–37.
161 *LP* I.ii, 2562.

XXI

Transcription Notes

The transcripts of BL Harley MS 2284 and BL Harley MS 4217 follow the approach and conventions used in *Queen Elizabeth's Wardrobe Unlock'd*, *The 1542 Inventory of Whitehall: the Palace and its Keeper* and *The 1547 Inventory of King Henry VIII*. Each entry has been numbered for ease of reference, with BL Harley MS 2284 numbering 1–1648 and the entries in BL Harley MS 4217 numbering 1–741. In order to distinguish between the two manuscripts, an A has been inserted before the entries in BL Harley MS 2284 and a B before the entries in BL Harley MS 4217.

The text of both manuscripts is written in a single column down the middle of each folio and the block of text is delineated by two black lines. Each group of objects listed in the main section of both documents is introduced by a heading. The headings are centred above the main column of text and written in an engrossing hand. The heading is repeated on each subsequent folio, sometimes in an abbreviated form, until a new group of items starts. These headings are printed in bold and in larger font than the main text of the transcript to denote the use of an engrossing hand.

Extensive marginal comments appear on both manuscripts, detailing the dispersal of the objects. They have been transcribed in full. Marginalia is shown in a smaller font than the main text and its original location on the document is denoted by LM for left margin and RM for right margin. A number of the marginal notes relate to groups of entries, and the clerk used brackets to denote this on the manuscript. In the transcript this is expressed by placing the note immediately after the first entry of the group with the range of entry numbers encompassed by the brackets: for example:

[A369] R — Item delyuerd by the kinges commaundement to John Scut the quenes taillor iiij yerdes of white cloth of golde of tissewe for a gowne for my lady princess.

[A369-72] LM: anno viij° xxiiij° die decembris.

All of the main text and part of the marginal notation is in English, but a small amount of the additional notation (mainly dates and notes relating to the formal accounting process) is in Latin. The original spelling has been followed and words that are particularly unusual have been clarified with a note. The major difference between sixteenth-century and modern spelling is in the use of *i*/*j* and *u*/*v*, which now have distinct roles but then were interchangeable. While the modern usage of *i*/*j* has been followed for the English text, the *i* has been retained, just in the short form, for the Latin text, with one exception: in the transcription of Januarii, Junii and Julii. The ampersand (&) for *and* appears frequently and it has been retained.

The original punctuation has also been retained but the placement of full-stops has been standardised to follow current usage. Where expansion marks had been used to denote a contraction, the word has been expanded and given in full, when the sense and spelling is known. Where either is in doubt, the word has been left in its contracted form, as in the case of *Ex* (for *Ex'r* or *Ex'ur*). Possible expansions and translations include *examinetur* (examined) or *excipietur* (checked), *extrahitur* or *extrahuntur* (removed), or *exitus* or *exitum* (issued).[1] While the exact translation proves illusive, the general meaning is clear: the object in question had been given away.

In a few places, the clerk made errors in the text of the manuscript during production, and these have been replicated in the transcript. Inserted words have been placed within angled brackets <>, while words or phrases that were crossed out are shown struck through with a line, ~~word~~. When a word was omitted, and the sense is clear, it has been inserted within square brackets, for example [and]. [. . .] denotes omissions where the word cannot be supplied from the context of the sentence. A small number of mistakes were not corrected by the clerk. Where a word or phase was duplicated and not amended, this has been highlighted using a note.

The king and the commissioners signed the manuscript and their signatures have been marked in the transcript. The dates in the main text and the marginal notes are in given regnal years. A list of the relevant regnal years has been given below and the dates have been converted into calendar years in the notes: 8 Henry VIII: 22 April 1516–21 April 1517; 9 Henry

VIII: 22 April 1517–21 April 1518; 10 Henry VIII: 22 April 1518–21 April 1519; 11 Henry VIII: 22 April 1519–21 April 1520; 12 Henry VIII: 22 April 1520–21 April 1521.

Roman numerals were used to denote lengths, money and weights, and these have retained. This includes the *i-longa*, or *j*, for one and for the last component of a number, when it is an *i*: e.g. *iij* rather than *iii*. By the sixteenth century certain numbers no longer followed the classical Latin form — four was usually written *iiij* rather than *iv*, and *xiiij* was used for *xiv*. Many of the lengths of cloth include fractional measurements. The words *qrt* and *iij qrt* have been expanded as *quarter* and *iij quarters*, while *di* (*dimidium*), meaning half, and *cl* (*clavus*), for a nail, have been left. The divisions of a yard are as follows: di quarter = ⅛; quarter = ¼; quarter di = ⅜; di = ½; di di quarter = ⅝; iij quarters = ¾; iij quarters di = ⅞. Other key units of measure for cloth are: the Flemish ell (27 in. [0.69 m]), the English ell (45 in. [1.14 m]), the nail (*clavus*) (2¼ in. [0.06 m]).

Notes

1 For a discussion of this point, see Hayward, *1542 Inventory*, II, p. 9, n. 8.

The Wardrobe Book of the Wardrobe of the Robes prepared by James Worsley in December 1516, edited from British Library MS Harley 2284

THE BOKE of delyueraunce and dis charge of the kinges standyng warderobe of his Robes withyn the towre of london newe made anno Regni Regis Henrici Octaui viij^ui^

f. 1r[1]

Memorandum that herafter in this present boke ensueth alle suche parcelles of the kinges Riche Robes with gownes glawdekyns Jaquettes & doblettes / as also Cloth of gold baudkyns tilsenttes velwetes dammaskes satens sarcenettes and other stuff that hath bene delyuerd oute of the kinges standing warderobe of his Robes within the towre of london by the commaundement of his grace at diuerse tymes by thandes of James Worsley yoman of our said souueraigne lordes Robes & kepre of his said warderobe sithen the xx^th^ day of december the viij^th^ yere of our said souuerane lordes moost noble Reigne.[2]

[A1] Furst delyuerd by the kinges commaundement to Nicolas Carewe a mantelle of purpull tilsent furred with blacke bugie.

[A1] LM: x^mo^ die augusti anno x^mo^.[3]

[A2] Item delyuerd by the kinges commaundement to a frenche man a mantelle of blake veluete furred with blake bugie.

[A2] LM: anno x^mo^ xxiiij^o^ die Octobris.[4]

Henry R

f. 1v[5] [blank]

f. 2r[6]

Gownes of cloth of gold & of velwete delyuerd by the kinges commaundement at diuerse tymes

[A3] Item delyuerd to the kinges grace at the grome porters a Gowne of crimosyn velwete with a high coller furred with bugie to my lorde Ferrers at Casnell marte.

[A3–7] LM: anno ix^o^ x^o^ die Julii.[7]

[A4] Item delyuerd to Mr Tyler by the kinges commaundement a Gowne of blacke velwete furred with bugie.

[A5] Item delyuerd by the kinges commaundement to my lorde of Suffolk a Gowne of white chamlet damaske siluer lyned with white velwete.

[A6] Item delyuerd by the kinges commaundement a Gowne of grene tylsent lyned with grene velwete to Mr Carewe.

[A7] Item delyuerd to the kinges grace at the grome porters a Mantelle of yelowe velwete lyned with yelowe satten to Mr Coffyn at casnall marte.

Henry R

[A8] Item delyuerd by the kinges commaundement to Sir William Sandes knight a Gowne of grene velwete lyned with grene satten with xvj buttons of gold with a Jaquet of grene tylsent & doblet & hose to the same.

[A8–9] LM: anno ix^mo^ xx^mo^ die Octobris.[8]

[A9] Item delyuerd by the kinges commaundement to Mr Carewe a Gowne of blacke velwete with a high coller furred with bugie.

[A10] Item delyuerd by the kinges commaundement to my lorde barnes a Gowne of Russet tylsent furred with grey Jenettes.

[A10] LM: anno ix^mo^ xx^mo^ die Februarii.[9]

Henry R

[A11] Item delyuerd by the kinges commaundement to the ducke[10] of Bukingham a Gowne of purpull tylsent furred with Ermyns a Jaquet a doblet & a payre of hose of purpull velwete enbrawderd & cutte withpon white cloth of siluer with aglettes of golde.

[A11–14] LM: anno ix^mo^ xxiij^to^ die marcii.[11]

[A12] Item delyuerd by the kinges commaundement to Mr Norres a Gowne of blake velwete furred with blacke conye with a high coller & strayte slyves with a doblet of crimosyn satten lyned with scarlet.

[A13] Item delyuerd by the kinges commaundement to my lorde Chamberlayn a Gowne of blake satten lyned with crimosyn clothe of gold of damaske.

[A14] Item delyuerd by the kinges commaundement to Mr More a Gowne of blacke velwete furred with blacke bugie with a high coller.

Henry R

[A15] Item delyuerd by the kinges commaundement to Mr Shatyllyon a Gowne of purpull tilsent furred with sabulles / the sabulles Remaignyng.

[A15] LM: anno x^mo^ x^mo^ die augusti.[12]

Henry R

f. 2v

Gownes of Diuerse makinges

[A16] Item delyuerd by the kinges commaundement to Mr Norres and Paynes a Gowne of purpull velwete lyned with crimosyn cloth of gold of dammaske.

[A16–17] LM: x^mo^ die augusti anno x^mo^.[13]

[A17] Item delyuerd by the kinges commaundement to Mr Wentworth & Carre a Gowne of purpull cloth of gold after baudkyn lyned with purpull saten.

Henry R

[A18] Item delyuerd to my lorde admyral a Gowne of crimosyn saten and cloth of gold partie and embrauderd furred with Ermyns.

[A18–20] LM: xxvj^o^ die Septembris anno x^mo^.[14]

[A19] Item delyuerd to the lorde admyral of fraunce a Riche Gowne of white syluer cut opon cloth of gold opon saten damaske gold with a Riche border embrauderd lyned with crimosyn saten.

[A20] Item delyuerd by the kinges commaundement to one of thembassadors of Fraunce a chammer of yelowe tilsent cut opon white siluer furred with sables.

Henry R

[A21] Item delyuerd by the kinges commaundement to Mr Carewe a gowne of crimosyn veluete with a high coller and furred with sabullus.

[A21–23] LM: anno x^{mo} xxiiij^{o} die Octobris.[15]

[A22] Item delyuerd to Mr Bryan by the kinges commaundement a chammer of blacke saten with iij borders of blake veluete furred with sabullus.

[A23] Item delyuerd to Sir Edward Nevelle by the kinges commaundement a Gowne of blake veluete with a Rounde Cape furred with blake bugie.

[A24] Item delyuerd by the kinges commaundement to my lorde Chamberlayn a Gowne of Russet veluete opon veluete <pirled> lyned with Russet tylsent.

[A24–25] LM: anno x^{mo} xx^{mo} die aprilis.[16]

[A25] Item delyuerd by the kinges commaundement to Syr Thomas bollayn a Gowne of purpull baudkyn damaske gold lyned with purpull veluete.

Henry R

[A26] Item delyuerd by the kinges commaundement to Sir William Fitzwilliam a Gowne of Russet veluete lyned with russet saten with a high coller.

[A26–30] LM: anno xj^{mo} primo die decembris.[17]

[A27] Item delyuerd by the kinges commaundement to the ducke of buckingham a Chamber of crimosyn veluete opon veluete pirled enbrauderd with freres knottes & lyned with Russet cloth of tissewe & crimosyn saten.

[A28] Item delyuerd to sir William Sandes a Gowne of grene veluete opon veluet pyrled with syluer lyned with cloth of gold diaper werke & damaske werke gold.

[A29] Item delyuerd to sir William S John[18] Copynger a Frocke of blacke veluete with ij gardes of the same and lyned with blacke sarcenet.

[A30] Item delyuerd to my lorde of devonshire a mantell of purpull tylent lyned with purpull saten.[19]

[A30] LM: Ex hic.

Henry R

f. 3r

Gownes of diuerse makinges

[A31] Item delyuerd to Nicolas Carewe by the kinges commaundement a Gowne of blacke [. . . .] with a high Coller furred with Pampyons.

[A31–34] LM: anno xj^{mo} iiij^{to} die decembris.[20]

[A32] Item delyuerd to mastres Cole by the kinges commaundement ij peces of ij fore quarters veluete brede & one of the slyves of crimosyn veluete opon veluete of a gowne.

[A33] Item delyuerd by the kinges commaundement to James Worsley a Gowne of Russet veluete syngle withoute furre.

[A34] Item delyuerd by the kinges commaundement a Gowne of blacke veluete furred with blacke bugie to master Carewe.

Memorandum yeuen by the kinges owne handes at the warderobe of his Robes within the tower of london all thies parcelles ensuyng to thies personnes folowyng xxj^{o} die decembris anno xj^{o} Regni Regis henrici viijui[21]

[A35] Furst to the ducke of Suffolk a Gowne of russet cloth of golde tissew lyned with Russet saten of D. S.

[A35–51] LM: anno xj^{mo} xxj^{mo} die decembris.[22]

[A35–45] LM: Gownes

[A36] Item to Sir Nicolas Waux knight a Gowne of crimosyn bawdkyn lyned with crimosyn saten of D. S.

[A37] Item to Sir Robert Wyngfeld a Gowne of crimosyn saten syngle.

[A38] Item to Sir William Compton a Gowne of crimosyn veluete lyned with cloth of gold tissewe.

[A39] Item to Mr Wyngfeld and Mr Weston a longe gowne of crimosyn cloth of gold tissewe syngle.

[A40] Item to Sir Richard Gernyngham and Sir William Kingston a Gowne of purpull cloth of gold tissewe syngle.

[A41] Item to Nicolas Carewe a Gowne of white tylsent syngle.

[A42] Item to ~~Nicolas~~ <Henry> Norres a Gowne of crimosyn tylsent syngle.

[A43] Item to Mr Carewe a Gowne of crimosyn baudkyn syngle.

[A44] Item to James Worsley a Gowne of russet veluete syngle.

[A45] Item to John Porth an olde Gowne of blacke saten single.

[A46] Item to Henry Page a iiij quarterd <Jaquet> of crimosyn veluete lyned with blac saten.

[A46–51] LM: Jaquettes

[A47] Item to ye same Henry a Jaquet of blac saten lyned with scarlet.

[A48] Item to Master Care a Jaquet of white veluete cut opon cloth of siluer enbrauderd <of D. S.>

[A49] Item to Mr Worsley a Jaquet of white cloth of siluer baudkyn lyned with blacke sarcenet of D. S.

[A50] Item to Sir William Tyler a Jaquet of purpull tylsent syngle.

[A51] Item to Mr bryan a Jaquet of tawny cloth of gold of damaske lyned with blacke saten.

Henry R

f. 3v

yet yeuen by the kinges owne handes at the tower of london within the warderobe of Robes there all thies parcelles ensuyng to thies personnes folowyng xxj^{mo} die decembris xj^{mo} Regni Regis Henrici viij^{mo}[23]

[A52] Item to Henry Norres a doblet of crimosyn tylsent lyned with blacke sarcenet of D. <S.>.

[A52–59] LM: anno xj^{o} xxj^{o} die decembris.[24]

[A52–54] LM: Doblettes

[A53] Item to Mr Care a doblet of white veluete cut opon cloth of siluer enbrauderd.

[A54] Item to Mr Worsley a doblet of grene tylsent dammaske siluer of D. S.

[A55] Item to Mr Compton a Remnaunte of blacke veluete opon veluete of xvij yerdes.

[A55–59] LM: Veluetes

[A56] Item to Mr Gernyngham & Mr kyngston a Remnaunte of russet veluete pyrled conteignyng xxiiij yerdes iij quarters for either of theim a gowne.

[A57] Item to Mr Wyngfeld & Mr Weston a Remnaunte of tawny veluete <pyrled> conteignyng xxv yerdes for either of theim a gowne.

[A58] Item to Mr Carewe & Mr bryan a Remnaunte of russet veluete opon veluete pyrled conteignyng xxvj yerdes di for either of theim a gowne.

[A59] Item to Mr Norres & Mr Care a Remnaunte of tawny veluete conteingyng xxviij yerdes di for either of theim a gowne.

[A55–59] Summa totalis — Cxxj yerdes iij quarters

[A60] Item a lytell short gowne <or Cote> of purpull veluete lyned with blac saten drawen with playtes.

[A60–78] LM: anno xj^{o} xxvj^{o} die decembris.[25]

[A60–72] LM: delyuerd to John Copynger and to William Whyse of ye kinges Robes.

[A61] Item a longe gowne of purpull veluete syngle.

[A62] Item a short gowne of purpull veluete syngle.

[A63] Item a womans gowne of purpull veluete syngle.

[A64] Item a shorte gowne of purpull veluete syngle furred with bugie.

[A65] Item a short gowne of crimosyn veluete lyned with blacke saten.

[A66] Item a short gowne of crimosyn veluete furred with bugie.

[A67] Item a lytell taberd & a kyrtell of crimosyn veluete with a hoode furred with menever for a Childe.

[A68] Item a short iiij quarterd Jaquet of crimosyn cloth of gold lyned with blac saten.

[A69] Item a short iiij quarterd Jaquet of yelowe cloth of gold opon saten furred with bugie.

~~[A70] Item a short iiij quarterd Jaquet of crimosyn cloth of gold lyned with blac saten~~.

[A70–71] LM: Thies ij percelles to be voyde here for they be enterd next afor.

~~[A71] Item a short iiij quarterd Jaquet of yelowe cloth of gold opon saten furred with bugie~~.

[A72] Item a short iiij quarterd Jaquet of crimosyn veluete with slyves lyned with blac saten borderd with stole werke / the border Remaynyng.

[A73] Item to Jamys Worsley ij lytell short Jaquettes of stole werke syngle.

[A74] Item to Mr Clerk of [the] kechyn a Riding gowne of blake veluete with playtes on the backe lyned with backe[26] saten.

[A75] Item to Mr Meryman a short gowne of blake veluete lyned with blac sarcenet.

[A76] Item to Mistress Norres a kyrtell of crimosyn saten.

[A77] Item to Mistress Worsley a gowne of tawny veluete with a bordor of stole werke Remaynyng.

[A78] Item to Mistress Coke a furre of mynkes for a womans gowne.[27]

Henry R

f. 4r

yet youen by the kinges owne handes thies parcelles ensuing to thies personnes folowyng xxvj^{to} die decembris anno xj^{o} Henrici viij^{ui}[28]

[A79] Item a Ryding Gowne of blac veluete borderd with stole werke lyned with blacke saten. The border of stole werke Remagnyng.

[A79–82] LM: anno xj^{mo} xxvj^{o} die decembris.[29]

[A79–82] LM: youen by the kinges grace to Rauf Worsley.

[A80] Item a short Gowne of blacke veluete lyned with blake sarcenet.

[A81] Item a iiij quarterd Jaquet of blake saten with slyves lyned with blac sarcenet.

[A82] Item a short iiij quarters Jaquet of blake saten lyned with sarcenet without slyves.

[A83] Item to Copynger & Wyse a Riding Gowne of blac veluete lyned with blac saten.

[A83–84] LM: anno xj^{o} xiiij^{o} die decembris.[30]

[A84] Item a doblet of purpull veluete rychely set <with> stones lyned with cloth of gold with wyde slyves lyned with canvas and purpull sarcenet delyuerd to the kinges owne handes at Richemounte by Jamys Worsley with a bill of the nomber of ye stones.

[A85] Item delyuerd at the kinges commaundement to the sergeaunt of the vestry a Cope of crimosyn veluete enbrauderd with nedyll werke with an orfevas of nedyll werke.

[A85–88] LM: anno xj^{mo} primo die Januarii.[31]

[A85–88] LM: Chapelle stuf delyuerd to the sergeaunt of the vestry by the kinges commaundement anno xj^{mo}.

[A86] Item delyuerd by the kinges commaundement to the said sergeaunt a Riche Cope of crimosyn cloth of gold tissewe with a vestamente & ij Tunicles and ij albes to the same.

[A87] Item delyuerd by the kinges commaundement to the said sergeaunte a fayre aulter cloth of crimosyn veluete enbrauderd with a fayre Crucifix Mary & John.

[A88] Item delyuerd by the kinges commaundement to the said sergeaunte a Frounte for an aulter of crimosyn veluete opon veluete enbrauderd with the salutacion of our ladye.

[A89] Item delyuerd by the kinges commaundement to my lorde Chamberlayn a Glaudkyn of Russet tylsent lyned with Russet veluete.

[A89] LM: anno xj^{mo} xviij^{o} die Januarii.[32]

Henry R

[A90] Item a Riche Gowne of crimosyn cloth of gold tissewe syngle.

[A90–98] LM: delyuerd to Sir Andrew Wyndesore knight for the kinges vse by my lorde Cardynalles commaundement anno xj^{mo}.

[A91] Item a nother Gowne of crimosyn cloth of gold tissewe lyned & welted with cloth of siluer.

[A92] Item a Gowne of purpull cloth of gold of baudkyn syngle.

[A93] Item a Gowne of crimosyn cloth of gold of damaske syngle.

[A94] Item a Gowne of purpull cloth of gold opon saten syngle.

[A95] Item a Gowne of crimosyn cloth of gold after baudkyn syngle.

[A96] Item a Gowne of grene tylsent lyned with grene saten.

[A97] Item a Gowne of riche crimosyn cloth of gold tissewe damaske gold with a border of white siluer lyned with crimosyn veluete.

[A98] Item a Gowne of purpull cloth of gold tissewe venis gold syngle.

Henry R

f. 4v

Gownes delyuerd by the kinges commaundemnt ut patet

[A99] Item delyuerd by my lorde Cardynalles commaundement to my lorde Armagh for the kinges vse a Riche Gowne of stole werke syngle.

[A99–104] LM: anno xj^{mo} mensis marcii.[33]

[A100] Item delyuerd by the kinges commaundement to Sir Richard Wyngfeld a gown of blacke tylsent lyned with blacke saten.

[A101] Item delyuerd by the kinges commaundement to master Norres a gowne of Russet dammaske furred with conye.

[A102] Item delyuerd to the kinges owne handes vj buttons of gold & iij aglettes of gold that were opon a Chammer of crimosyn saten cut opon cloth of gold.

[A103] Item delyuerd to Moye a frencheman a gowne of blacke veluete with a square <cape> furred with blacke bugie with xvj buttons of gold blewe enameld.

[A104] Item delyuerd to Sir William Tyler a gowne of blacke veluete with a high collor lyned with blacke saten.

Memorandum yeuen by the kinges graces owne handes thies parcelles folowyng to thies personnes ensuyng anno xij^{mo}

[A105] Item to sir William Kingston knight a Glaudkyn of cloth of gold baudkyn lyned with crimosyn saten.

[A105–13] LM: anno xij^{mo} vltimo die Aprilis.[34]

[A106] Item to Nicolas Carewe a Gowne of crimosyn tilsent with byrdes Ies.

[A107] Item to Sir William Compton knight a mantelle of cloth of gold of damaske couerd with white saten cutt with a ryche border enbrouderd and lyned with white tylsent.

[A108] Item to sir Richard Weston knight a mantelle of purpull tilsent syngell.

[A109] Item to Jamys Worsley a Frocke of crimosyn veluete enbrauderd with sylke.

[A110] Item to Antony knyvet a Gowne of purpull veluete the slyves with Rolles syngle.

[A111] Item to Sir Edmond Walsyngham a Frocke of grene saten garded with grene velut <ye furre Removed>.

[A112] Item to Sir William Tyler a Frocke of Russet veluete enbrauderd with silke.

[A113] Item to John Copynger a Frocke of grene tylsent couerd with grene saten cutt.

Henry R

[A114] Item delyuerd by the kinges commaundement vnto Wyse page of ye Robes a Frocke of Russet veluete pyrled furred with bugie.

[A114–19] LM: anno xij^{mo} iiij^{to} die Maii.[35]

[A114–19] LM: delyuerd by the kinges commaundement at grenewyche anno xij^{o}.

[A115] Item to James Worsley & John Parker a Gowne of crimosyn saten syngle.

[A116] Item to Rauf Worsley a Gowne of purpull veluete syngle.

[A117] Item to James Worsely a lytelle di gowne of crimosyn veluete opon veluete <single>.

[A118] Item to Mistress Fynche a gowne of crimosyn veluete furred with shankes.

[A119] Item to Mistress Norres a gowne of crimosyn veluete furred with Ermyns.

[A118–19] RM: of q. e.

Henry R

f. 5r

Gownes delyuerd by the kinges commaundement ut patet

[A120] Item to Copynger and Wyses seruauntes a Gowne of white veluete syngle.

[A120–26] LM: anno xij^{mo} xiij^{mo} die Maii.[36]

[A120–25] LM: delyuerd by the kinges commaundement at grenewyche anno xij^{mo}.[37]

[A121] Item to Gaddes Hill churche a Gowne of blewe veluete furred with Ermyns the Furre of Ermyns Remaignyng.

[A122] Item to Jenyns of the pastry John Verdon & George Lovekyn a iiij quarters Jaquet of crimosyn cloth of gold with slyves furred with bugie.

[A123] Item to William Hogson Henry Ages Thomas Parker & John Dale a Gowne of crimosyn saten with ij clockes of cloth of gold furred with shankes of Q. E.

[A124] Item to William Thyn & Thomas Atclyf a Gowne of crimosyn saten with a bordor of stolewerke egged with mynkes the stolewerke Remaignyng.

[A125] Item to Davy Fraunces & Cutberd blackden a gowne of blac veluete single.

[A126] Item to Sir Richard Cornwall a Frocke of crimosyn saten lyned with sarcenet.

Henry R

[A127] Item to monsir Lestue[38] a frencheman a Gowne of siluer tissewe furred with sabullus youen to hym by the kinges grace.

[A127–34] LM: anno xij^{mo} xxiij^{o} die Junii.[39]

[A128] Item delyuerd to Sir Richard Cornwall a Frocke of crimosyn saten with weltes of the same lyned with sarcenet.

[A129] Item delyuerd by the kinges commaundement to Mr Carewe a Frocke of blacke veluete welted with the same lyned with sarcenet.

[A130] Item delyuerd to Jamys Worsley a Frocke a F[40] of blacke veluete enbrauderd with sylke lyned with blacke sarcenet.

[A131] Item delyuerd to monsir labattie a frenchemen at guysnes a gowne of crimosyn veluete opon veluete pirled lyned with crimosyn tylsent.

[A132] Item delyuerd to monsir bryanne a frenchman at Guysnes a Gowne of Russet tylsent lyned with cloth of siluer.

[A133] Item delyuerd to monsir de la Roche Pot a gowne of cloth of siluer ~~gold~~ lyned with cloth of gold of carnacion collor.

[A134] Item delyuerd to monsir de la Palays a gowne of yelowe tissew lyned with crimosyn ~~veluete~~ <saten>.

Henry R

[A135] Item delyuerd by the kinges commaundement vnto Mr Carewe a shammer of tawny tilsent with a high collor welted with siluer tissew lyned with purpull saten.

[A135–38] LM: anno xij^{mo} xxvj^{o} die Julii.[41]

[A136] Item delyuerd to Hanyball de carr with themperor a shammer of blacke tylsent with a high collor welted with cloth of siluer lyned with purpull saten.

[A137] Item delyuerd to Rochepot a gowne of blacke tylsent lyned with cloth of siluer of damaske.

[A138] Item delyuerd to Mr Wysse by the kinges commaundement a gowne of blacke veluete with a high collor furred with blacke bugie.

Henry R

f. 5v

[A139] Item delyuerd by the kinges commaundement to Mr Carewe a shammer of blacke veluete furred with sabullus.

[A139–45] LM: Anno xij^{mo} vj^{o} die Octobris.[42]

[A140] Item delyuerd to Mr Wyse by the kinges commaundement a Frocke of blac saten lyned with sarcenet with iij weltes of the same.

[A141] Item delyuerd to Mr Wyse the same tyme a nother Frocke of blacke damaske lyned with sarcenet.

[A142] Item delyuerd to Sir William Fitzwilliam a gowne of purpull cloth of gold of baudkyn lyned with purpull saten.

[A143] Item delyuerd to John deparres a mantelle of whyte tylsent syngle to make iij doblettes & iij payres of hose for the king.

[A144] Item delyuerd by the kinges commaundement to John Hopton a gowne of blac veluete with a high collor furred with blacke bugie.

[A145] Item delyuerd to Sir Richard Gernyngham knight a gowne of white siluer tyssewe furred with blacke Jenettes y^{t} ye king had of Mr Norres and not in the Infra.

[A146] Item delyuerd by the kinges commaundement to Mr Carewe a Gowne of cloth of siluer playne syngle youen in anno x^{mo}.

[A146–53] LM: anno xij^{mo}.[43]

[A147] Item a Gowne of blacke saten syngle delyuerd by the kinges commaundement vnto Jamys Worsley in anno x^{mo}.

[A148] Item a Gowne of blacke saten syngle delyuerd by the kinges commaundement to Sir John Sherpe knight in anno viij^{mo}.

[A149] Item a Gowne of Russet veluete syngle delyuerd by the kinges commaundement to Mr Compton in anno x^{mo}.

[A150] Item a Gowne of crimsyn veluete syngle delyuerd by the kinges commaundement to Sir Henry Guyldforde knight in anno x^{mo}.

[A151] Item a Gowne of blake veluete syngle delyuerd by the kinges commaundement to Mr Worsely in anno x^{mo}.

[A152] Item a Shammer of blacke saten syngle borderd with vj borders of blake veluete ~~sy~~ delyuerd by the kinges commaundement to Jamys Worsley anno x^{o}.

[A153] Item a Gowne of Russet veluete syngle delyuerd to Richard Gibson to make half a trapper & half a horsharnes paned with venis siluer anno xj^{o}.[44]

Henry R

f. 6r[45]

Cotes and Jaquettes and doblettes delyuerd by the kinges commaundement at diuerse tymes

[A154] Item delyuerd by the kinges commaundement to Sir Edwarde Guylford a Riding Cote of crimosyn cloth of golde of tissewe lyned with ~~hit~~ white cloth of siluer damaske siluer and welted with the same.

[A154–59] LM: anno ix^{o} xij^{mo} die Julii.[46]

[A155] Item delyuerd to the kinges grace at grome porters a Coote of blake velwete furred with blake cony to my lorde Ferres at Casuel marte.

[A156] Item delyuerd by the kinges commaundement to Sir Edwarde Gilford a Coote of Russet velwete furred with cony garded with Russet satten.

[A157] Item delyuerd by the kinges commaundement to my lorde of Suffolk a doblet of white tissewe couerd with white satten.

[A158] Item delyuerd by the kinges commaundement to Mr Carewe a doblet of yelowe baudkyn couerd with yelowe satten with hose & Jaquet to the same.

[A159] Item delyuerd by the kinges commaundement to Sir John Peche knight a doblet of cloth of tissewe couerd with crimosyn satten.

Henry R

[A160] Item delyuerd by the kinges commaundement to my lorde of Suffolk a Riding Cote of grene velwete lyned with grene sarcenet with a di Cote to the same.

[A160–65] LM: anno ix^{no} xx^{mo} die Octobris.[47]

[A161] Item delyuerd by the kinges commaundement to Mr Carewe a Cote of grene velwete garded with grene satten at Holy Rode day.

[A162] Item delyuerd by the kinges commaundement to Mr Compton a doblet of crimosyn tilsent & crimosyn velwete paned with a payre of scarlet hose to ye same.

[A163] Item delyuerd by the kinges commaundement to lytell Carewe a doblet and a Jaquet of of blake tylsent & blewe velwete paned.

[A164] Item delyuerd by the kinges commaundement to Mr Arthor Poulle a Cote of Russet velwete with ij gardes of russet satten furred with blacke Conye.

[A165] Item delyuerd by the kinges commaundement to Sir Arthor Plante[agenet a][48] Cote of blake velwete furred with blacke Cony.

[A166] Item delyuerd by the kinges commaundement to Mr Wyse a Jaquet of crimosyn satten lyned with redde sarcenet.

[A166] LM: anno ix^{no} xx^{mo} die Februarii.[49]

[A167] Item delyuerd by the kinges commaundement to Mr Carewe a Jaquet of crimosyn tylsent lyned with crimosyn satten with a doblet [&] hose of crimosyn tylsent richely enbrauderd with gold of damaske for the same.

[A168] Item delyuerd by the kinges commaundement vnto Arthor Pole a doblet & a payr of hose of crimosyn tylsent enbrauderd.

Henry R

Cotes & Jaquettes

f. 6v[50]

[A169] Item delyuerd by the kinges commaundement to Mr Arthor Pole a Jaquet a doblet & a payr of hose of Russet velwete cutt ouer opon cloth of gold.

[A169–70] LM: anno ix^{mo} xx^{mo} die Marcii.[51]

[A170] Item delyuerd by the kinges commaundement the same tyme at Riche mount to Mr Bryan a doblet & hose of blacke tilsent of byrdes Eys.

Henry R

[A171] Item delyuerd by the kinges commaundement to Mr Wyse a Jaquet of Crimosyn satten furred with blacke conye.

[A171–73] LM: anno ix^{mo} xxix^{mo} die maii.[52]

[A172] Item delyuerd to Mr Carewe by the kinges commaundement a doblet and hose of white cloth of siluer couerd with crimosyn satten.

[A173] Item delyuerd by the kinges commaundement to the ducke of Suffolk a Jaquet a doblet & hose of blake tilsent damaske gold.

Henry R

[A174] Item delyuerd by the kinges commaundement to Sir Edwarde Nevelle knight a Cote with a di Cote of grene velwete garded with grene saten.

[A174–82] LM: anno x^{mo} x^{mo} die augustii.[53]

[A175] Item delyuerd by the kinges commaundement to Mr Carewe a Cote of blacke velwete & blewe tilsent paned furred with blacke bugie.

[A176] Item delyuerd by the kinges commaundement to Sir Henry Guylford knight a doblet hose and Jaquet of crimosyn cloth of gold playne lyned with crimosyn saten.

[A177] Item delyuerd by the kinges commaundement to Mr Norres a doblet & hose of purpull cloth of gold tissewe couerd with purpull saten.

[A178] Item delyuerd by the kinges commaundement to Mr Poynes a doblet and hoses of cloth of gold couerd with grene veluete.

[A179] Item delyuerd by the kinges commaundement to Mr Carre a Cote of grene tylsent Raysed with gold by Mr Wentworth.

[A180] Item delyuerd by the kinges commaundement to James Worsley yoman of the Robes a doblet hose and Jaquet of blacke tilsent & blewe velwete paned.

[A181] Item delyuerd to John Copynger grome of the Robes a doblet and a Jaquet of grene tilsent and grene velwete by the kinges commaundement.

[A182] Item delyuerd by the kinges commaundement to William Wyse an almayn doblet and hose of blacke tylsent & purpull velwete paned & cutte.

Henry R

[A183] Item delyuerd by the kinges commaundement to the ducke of Suffolk a Cote of crimosyn velwete cutte opon grene cloth of gold & velwete.

[A183–84] LM: xxvj^{o} die Septembris anno x^{mo}.[54]

[A184] Item delyuerd to my lorde of devonshire a doblet a Jaquet and hose of blacke velwete cutte opon cloth of golde and enbrauderde.

Henry R

f. 7r

Cotes Jaquettes doblettes & hose

[A185] Item delyuerd by the kinges commaundement to Mr Carewe a doblet & hosez of crimosyn cloth of gold the ground of damaske golde.

[A185–97] LM: anno x^{mo} xxiiij^{o} Octobris.[55]

[A186] Item delyuerd by the kinges commaundement to Mr Weston a Jaquet of crimosyn cloth of gold tissewe lyned with crimosyn saten.

[A187] Item delyuerd by the kinges commaundement to Mr Carewe a Jaquet of blake tylsent lyned with blake saten.

[A188] Item delyuerd to Mr Bryan a Jaquet doblette & hosez of ~~yelowe~~ <crimosyn> cloth of gold after baudkyn with cutts ouer all of crimosyn saten & lyned with crimosyn saten.

[~~A189~~] ~~Item delyuerd to my lorde of Suffolk by the kinges commaundement a Cote a Cote of crimosyn velwete cutt opon cloth of gold & welted~~.

[A189] LM: vac hic qz entrat antea in altra parte.

[A190] Item delyuerd to Sir Thomas Boleyn by the kinges commaundement a Jaquet doblet & hosez of cloth of gold with a cutte ouer all of russet saten.

[A191] Item delyuerd to Mr Compton by the kinges commaundement a doblet of blake tilsent square lyned with scarlet.

[A192] Item delyuerd to Arthor Pole a doblet of blake tylsent lyned with scarlet by the kinges commaundement.

[A193] Item delyuerd to Mr Norres a doblet of crimosyn saten cutt opon crimosyn tylsent with hosez to the same.

[A194] Item delyuerd to Mr Carewe a doblet hosez & Jaquet of blewe tilsent dammaske gold with claspes & aglettes of gold at the hosez.

[A195] Item delyuerd to the same Mr Carewe by the kinges commaundement a Jaquet of Russet tissewe chekerd with dammaske gold lyned with russet saten.

[A196] Item delyuerd by the kinges commaundement to a frencheman a doblet & hosez of purpull veluete & blake tilsent paned & cutt after thalmayn facion.

[A197] Item delyuerd by the kinges commaundement to Mr Bryan a doblet of russet cloth of gold of tissewe chekerd with hosez to the same.

[A198] Item delyuerd to William Woodhowse spere of Calais a doblet hose & Jaquet of purpull velwete enbrauderd & cutt opon cloth of gold lyned with blac saten.

[A198–99] LM: anno xj^{mo} xviij^{o} die maii.[56]

[A199] Item delyuerd to Morres of the Celler a Jaquet of Russet satten furred with blacke Conye.

Henry R

[A200] Item delyuerd by the kinges commaundement to Sir Henry Guylford a Coote of grene veluete with the base & di Coote to ye same garded with grene saten.

[A200–03] LM: anno xj^{mo} primo die decembris.[57]

[A201] Item delyuerd to Sir William Fitzwilliam a doblet & hose of crimosyn saten cutt opon damaske siluer with a playne Jaquet of crimosyn saten.

[A202] Item a doblet of cloth of siluer cut opon cloth of gold enbrauderd with hoses to the same & claspes & auglettes of gold delyuerd to the ducke of buckyngham.

[A203] Item delyuerd by the kinges commaundement to William Wyse a Coote of grene veluete with ij gardes of the same with the di coote.

Henry R

f. 7v

[A204] Item delyuerd by the kinges commaundement to Mr Carre a doblet hoses & a Jaquet of cloth of gold of damaske gold with a cutt ouer all of purpull veluete.

[A204–05] LM: anno xj^{mo} xxx^{mo} die Septembris.[58]

[A205] Item delyuerd by the kinges commaundement to Mr Carewe a Coote of crimosyn veluete furred with blake conye.

[A206] Item delyuerd to my lord of devenshire by the kinges commaundement a Jaquet a doblet & hose of purpull veluete enbrauderd & lyned with purpull saten.

[A206] LM: anno xj^{mo} primo die aprilis.[59]

[A207] Item delyuerd by the kinges commaundement to bewveys a Frencheman a doblet a Jaquet & a payre of hose of purpull tylsent with a cut ouer all of purpull saten.

[A207–08] LM: anno xj^{mo} xviij^{mo} die Novembris.[60]

[A208] Item delyuerd by the kinges commaundement to Henry Norres a doblet hose and Frocke of blacke tylsent & blewe veluete paned.

Henry R

Memorandum delyuerd by the kinges commaundement sithen the viewe taken vltime die Nouembris xj^{mo} by the ducke of Suffolk and other the kinges commissioners thies parcelles ensuyng parcel of the clerc Remaigne of the said viewe.[61]

[A209] Furst delyuerd by the kinges commaundement and my lorde Cardynalles to Robert Amadas goldsmythe for the kinges vse CCCCxlviij oz iij quarters of fyne gold and DCCClj perles of a sorte that was takyn of from the kinges cote thone syde of purpull veluete pyrled and thoder syde of white cloth of siluer tyssewe.

[A209–16] LM: anno xj^{mo} xxvij^{o} die maii.[62]

[A209] LM: delyuerd to Robert Amadas of london goldsmyth anno xj^{mo}.

[A210] Item v short cotes of blewe veluete with goldsmythes werke for thenchemen.

[A210–11] LM: delyuerd by my lorde Cardynalles commaundement to my lorde arma chauer for ye kinges vse anno xj^{mo}.

[A211] Item xxv placardes of white cloth with x[...] crosses set with goldsmythes werke.

[A212] Item delyuerd by the kinges commaundement to Sir Richard Wyngefeld a doblet of purpull tissewe lyned with blake sarsenet.

[A213] Item delyuerd to the same Sir Richard Wyngefeld a Jaquet of purpull tilsent lyned with purpull saten.

[A214] Item delyuerd to the sergent porter a doblet of crimosyn cloth of gold of baudkyn damaske gold lyned with crimosyn sarsenet of d. s.

[A215] Item delyuerd to the kinges owne handes v payres of aglettes & vj bottons of gold that were set opon the same doblet.

[A216] Item delyuerd to John deparres a riche Jaquet & a doblet of purpull veluete garnisshed alouer with spangelles of fyne gold to be paned with riche white tissewe the border of the same Jaquet and the foreslyves of the doblet was not spent butt delyuerd to the kinges grace.

Henry R

f. 8r

Memorandum youen by the kinges owne handes at Grenewiche thies parcelles folowynge to thies persons ensying mensis aprilis anno xij^{mo}

[A217] Item to Sir William Kingston a doblet hose and Jaquet of blacke veluete cut & enbrauderd opon with cloth of gold of damaske.

[A217–36] LM: anno xij^{mo} vltimo die aprilis.[63]

[A217–36] LM: delyuerd by the kinge commaundement in mensis aprilis & maii anno xij^{mo}.

[A218] Item to Nicolas Carewe a doblet hose & Jaquet of purpull tissewe enbrauderd with white siluer hose & Jaquet.

[A219] Item to Cary a Jaquet doblet & hose of crimosyn tylsent with a cutt of Crimosyn veluete.

[A220] Item to Cary a Jaquet doblet & hose of cloth of gold of damaske cutt opon white siluer.

[A221] Item to Sir Richard Gernyngham knight a doblet hose & Jaquet Cote with di slyves of Russet cloth of gold drawn with lynen cloth.

[A222] Item to the same Sir Richard a doblet hose and Jaquet of white siluer tissewe Reysed.

[A223] Item to Henry Norres & Care a doblet & hose of cloth of golde of banden with [a] Jaquet of the same lyned with crimosyn saten.

[A224] Item to the said Harey & Cary a doblet and a Jaquet of cloth of gold of damaske with a cutt ouer all of purpull veluete.

[A225] Item to Sir William Compton knight a doblet hose & Jaquet of purpull saten enbrauderd.

[A226] Item to Sir William Tyler a doblet <hose> and a Jaquet of purpull tyssewe.

[A227] Item to the same William a doblet and hose of Russet veluete enbrauderd.

[A228] Item to Sir Richard Weston a doblet hose & Jaquet of crimosyn saten enbrauderd.

[A229] Item to Mr Bryan a doblet hose and Jaquet of crimosyn tylsent with cutts all ouer of crimosyn saten.

[A230] Item to Sir Gyles Capell a doblet hose & Jaquet of grene saten enbrauderd.

[A231] Item to Mr Knolles a doblet hose & Jaquet of cloth of gold baudkyn.

[A232] Item to James Worsley a doblet & hose of crimosyn veluete enbrauderd with sylke.

[A233] Item to Antony Knyvet a doblet & hose of purpull tylsent tissewe with Rolles couerd with purpull saten.

[A234] Item to John Copynger a doblet & hose of grene tylsent couerd with grene saten cutte.

[A235] Item to monsir barges an Almayn Cote of purpull veluete & blacke tylsent Richely enbrauderd lyned with blacke saten.

[A236] Item to Mr Bryan a doblet and hose of blewe veluete & blacke tilsent Richely enbrauderd.

Henry R

f. 8v

[A237] Item to Sir Edmonde Walsyngham a doblet and hose of grene tylsent couerd with grene saten cutt.

[A237–39] LM: anno xij^{mo} vltimo aprilis.[64]

[A238] Item to Richard Gibson a Riche Jaquet of stole worke scaled furred with blacke bugie for parte of a trapper & a base for the king the furre Remaignyng.

[A239] Item to Richard Gibson thone half of a cote of Riche siluer tissewe that was parte with purpull veluete pirled for the performyng of a base & a trapper for the king.

Henry R

[A240] Item to Mr Beryman a Cote of purpull chamlet gold furred with blake bugie.

[A240–49] LM: anno xij^{mo} iiij^{to} die maii.[65]

[A241] Item to Mynors sergeant of ye cellor a Jaquet of crimosyn veluete opon veluete pirled syngle.

[A242] Item to Morres of the cellor a Jaquet crimosyn cloth of gold after chamlet makyng synkell.[66]

[A243] Item to Henry Page a Jaquet of Russet tylsent syngle.

[A244] Item to Clarenceaux a Cote of purpull veluete opon veluete pirled frenged with Ermyns.

[A245] Item delyuerd to the kinges owne handes a small border of wrethes of goldsmythes werke y^{t} was set opon a doblet & a payr of hose of grene saten.

[A246] Item to Jamys Worsley for a iiij quarter Jaquet of purpull cloth of gold of Chamlet with slyves furred with white bugie.

[A246–49] LM: delyuerd by the kinges commaundement at grenewiche anno xij^{mo}.

[A247] Item to John Porth a iiij quarterd Jaquet of crimosyn veluete with slyves the border enbrauderd with nedyll werke the border Remaingnyng.

[A248] Item to John Copynger a iiij quarterd Jaquet of crimosyn cloth of gold of damaske with slyves furred with bugie.

[A249] Item to John Porth a iiij quarterd Jaquet of crimosyn veluete with slyves borderd with stole werke the bordors remaignyng.

Henry R

[A250] Item delyuerd to Mr Carewe a doblet of blacke veluete enbrauderd that Anthonye Browne gave the kinge.

[A250–52] LM: anno xij^{mo} xxiij^{o} die Junii.[67]

[A251] Item delyuerd to Mr Bullayn a Cote of crimosyn veluete furred with blacke conye.

[A252] Item delyuerd to Cornysshe of the kinges Chapelle a Coote of blacke veluete lyned with sarsenet.[68]

Henry R

f. 9r

[A253] Item delyuerd by the kinges commaundement to Mr Wyse a doblet of crimosyn tylsent with a cut ouer all of crimosyn veluete with hose to the same.

[A253–57] LM: anno xij^{mo} vj^{o} die Octobris.[69]

[A254] Item delyuerd by the kinges commaundement to Mr Carewe a Jaquet doblet & hose of purpull cloth of gold tissewe playn.

[A255] Item delyuerd to Mr Wyse by the kinges commaundement a doblet and hose of blacke veluete with siluer stole werke.

[A256] x — Item sent to the Frenche king a doblet of cloth of gold of baudkyn the placard & foreslyves wrought with flate gold with viij payre of aglettes.

[A257] Item delyuerd by the kinges commaundement to Mr Wyse a doblet of blacke dammaske lyned with sarsenet.

[A258] Item delyuerd to Mr Merymann by the kinges commaundement a Jaquet of Russet saten Furred with blacke bugie.

[A258–60] LM: anno xij^{mo} xij^{mo} die Januarii.[70]

[A259] Item to Mr Wyse a doblet of blake saten cut & tyed with small buttons & aglettes of gold with hose to ye same the buttons & aglettes of gold delyuerd to the king by thandes of the said Mr Wyse.

[A260] Item to the same Mr Wyse a doblet of crimosyn saten cut & tyed with small buttons and aglettes of gold with hose to the same the buttons & aglettes of gold was delyuerd to the king [by] the hands of the said Mr Wyse.

[A261] Item a doblet of Russet cloth of gold.

[A261–63] LM: Sent vnto ye French king in Januarii anno xij^{o}.[71]

[A261–63] RM: The placardes & foreslyves of euery of theim Richely enbrauderd with dammaske gold.

[A262] Item a doblet of Crimosyn satten.

[A263] Item a doblet of dammaske syluer.[72]

Henry R

f. 9v [blank][73]

f. 10r[74]

Placardes bases trappers & bardes delyuerd by the kinges commaundement at dyuerse tymes

[A264] Item delyuerd by the kinges commaundement to Sir Henry Guylford knight to be kept for the kinges vse a Base with a placard of white cloth of gold of tissewe to were opon harnes with a riche trapper of the same lyned with grene saten frenged with white silke & gold & laces of silke & gold.

[A264–67] LM: anno x^{mo} xxviij^{o} die augusti.[75]

dammaske for stocking of a payre of hose couerd with crimosyn velwete cut opon [. . . .].

[A415] g — Item delyuerd to William Hilton xj yerdes di of cloth of gold of dammaske dammakse gold to be vnder the said velwete cutt opon for a doblet and a Jaquet for the kinges grace.

[A416] g — Item delyuerd to William Hosyer a yerde quarter of cloth of gold of dammaske playn for the stocking of a payre of hose couerd with blacke velwete cutt & enbrauderd opon for the king.

[A417] g — Item delyuerd by the kinges commaundement to my lorde John grey & my lord Leonard his brother xij yerdes of blewe cloth of gold towardes a trapper and a base for either of theim to prepare themself for the kinges Justes ayenst the commyng of thembassadors of Fraunce.

[A417] LM: primo die Spetembris anno x^{mo}.[124]

[A418] s — Item delyuerd by the kinges commaundement to William Hilton xj yerdes di of cloth of siluer dammaske siluer for a Jaquet & a doblet for the king.

[A418–24] LM: vij^{mo} die Septembris anno x^{mo}.[125]

[A419] g — Item delyured by the kinges commaundement to the said Hilton xj yerdes di of yelowe cloth of gold dammaske gold to couer the same Jaquet & doblet.

[A420] s — Item delyuerd to William Hosier by the kinges commaundement a yerde quarter of cloth of siluer for the stockes of a pair of hose for the king.

[A421] g — Item delyuerd to William Hosyer a yerde quarter of cloth of gold dammaske golde to couer the said stockes of the same payr of hose for the king.

[A422] g — Item delyuerd to William Hosyer by the kinges commaundement to William a yerde quarter of cloth of gold for stockes of a pere of hose for ye king.

[A423] g — Item delyuerd to Hilton a yerde iij quarters di of cloth of gold dammaske gold to welte a coote of crimosyn velwete cut opon cloth of gold for ye king.

[A424] g — Item delyuerd to Hilton by the kinges commaundement xvj yerdes di of purpull baudkyn dammaske gold for a gowne for for the kinges grace.

Henry R

g — iij^{C} xlv yerdes quarter di

f. 17r

Cloth of gold of diuerse collors

[A425] g — Item delyuerd by the kinges commaundement to the ducke of Suffolk my lorde admyrall Syr Henry Gilford and Mr Carewe in white cloth of gold of ~~gold of~~ dammaske towardes a base and a trapper for eueryche of theim the somme of xl yerdes.

[A425–29] LM: vltimo die Septembris anno x^{mo}.[126]

[A426] g — Item delyuerd by the kinges commaudement to Richard Gibson a yerde quarter di quarter of clothe of gold opon saten to performe the kinges disguysing aforesaid — a yerde quarter di quarter.

[A427] g — Item delyuerd by the kinges commaundement to Robert Gernyngham. Mr Hanserd Mr Henry Mr Parker and to Mr [. . . . .] vj yerdes of blewe cloth of gold for a base and a trapper for euyerche of theim in all xxx^{ti} yerdes.

[A428] g — Item delyuerd by the kinges commaundement to Richard Gibson for the kinges riche mumrye in grene cloth of gold at ij tymes the somme of xxviij yerdes di & iij nayles.

[A429] s — Item delyuerd to Richard Gibson by the kinges commaundement in cloth of siluer for the kinges riche mumry at ij diuerse tymes the somme of Cxxvj yerdes di di quarter.

[A430] t — Item delyuerd by the kinges commaundement di yerde of white cloth of siluer of tissewe for a stomager for the quenes grace.

[A430–40] LM: primo die Octobris anno x^{mo}.[127]

[A431] s — Item delyuerd by the kinges commaundement to Mortemer iiij yerdes of white cloth of siluer for thenbraudring of a doblet a Jaquet & hose for the king.

[A432] g — Item delyuerd to Hilton a yerde of yelowe bawdkyn to performe a Cape of a gowne of crimosyn saten cut & latessed opon cloth of gold after baudkyn for ye king.

[A433] g — Item delyuerd to Mortemer a yerde di of tawny cloth of gold dammaske gold to performe thenbraudring of a doblet a Jaquet & hose of blake velwete for ye king cut.

[A434] t — b — Item delyuerd by the kinges commaundement to Hilton di yerde of crimosyn cloth of tissewe to performe a Cape a cape[128] of a gowne of crimosyn tissew for ye king.

[A435] g — Item delyverd to Hilton di yerde of purpull cloth of gold after bawdkyn to performe a Cape for a gowne of purpull bawdkyn for the king.

[A436] g — Item delyverd to Hilton xij yerdes of cloth of gold opon saten dammaske gold for a doblet & a Jaquet for the kinges grace.

[A437] g — Item delyuerd to John Wheler by the kinges commaundement v yerdes of crimosyn cloth of gold of bawdkyn for a gowne for my lady Princes.

[A438] t — Item delyuerd to the said John a yerde di of white cloth of tissewe for to lyne the same gowne of bawdkyn for my lady Princes.

[A439] t — Item delyuerd by the kinges commaundement to Nicolas maior xij yerdes of russet cloth of gold tissewe for a trapper for the kinges grace.

[A440] g — Item delyuerd to Hilton a yerde quarter of cloth of golde dammaske gold to egge[129] a cloke of crimosyn velwete opon velwete for the kinges grace.

Henry R

f. 17v

Cloth of gold of diuerse collors

[A441] g — Item delyuerd by the kinges commaundement to William Hosyer a yerde quarter of purpull ~~v~~ cloth of gold opon saten for stocking of a payre of hose for ye king.

[A441–44] LM: x^{mo} die Octobris anno x^{mo}.[130]

[A442] t — Item delyuerd by the kinges commaundement to Hilton xij yerdes of Russet cloth of gold tissewe for a Chammber for the kinges grace.

[A443] s — Item delyuerd to Hilton by the kinges commaundement xiiij yerdes of dammaske siluer for a Chammer for the king after baudkyn making.

[A444] Item delyuerd by the kings commaundement to Richard Gibson lviij yerdes quarter & the nayle of grene cloth of gold for the kinges ryche mumrye.

Henry R

[A445] t — Item delyuerd by the kinges commaundment to mr Carewe a Remnaunt of grene cloth of gold tissewe conteignyng a yerde quarter long.

[A445–60] LM: anno x^{mo} xxij^{do} die Octobris.[131]

[A445–60] LM: xvj lytell Remnauntes of cloth of gold.

[A446] t — b — Item delyuerd by the kinges commaundement to Syr Edwarde Nevelle knight a Remnaunte of crimosyn cloth of gold tissewe conteignyng di yerde di quarter.

[A447] t — b — Item delyuerd by the kinges commaundement to Syr Edwarde Nevelle aforsaid a Remnaunte a Re[132] of crimosyn cloth of gold tissewe conteignyng iij quarters & di nayle.

[A448] g — Item delyuerd to Fraunces poynes by the kinges commaundement a Remnaunte of yelowe baudekyn conteignyng a yerde quarter.

[A449] g — Item delyuerd by the kinges commaundement to Mr Norres a Remnaunte of yelowe baudkyn conteignyng di yerde di quarter.

[A450] g — Item delyuerd by the kinges commaundement to Syr Edwarde Nevelle knight a Remnaunte of purpull cloth of gold after chamlet conteignyng iij yerdes caz di nayle.

[A451] g — Item delyuerd by the kinges commaundement to Syr Edwarde Nevelle a Remnaunte of damaske siluer conteignyng a yerde iij quarters.

[A452] s — g — Item delyuerd by the kinges commaundement to Fraunces Poynes a Remnaunte of venys siluer conteignyng a yerde di & nayle.

[A453] t — a — Item delyuerd by the kinges commaundement to Mr Carewe a Remnaunte of purpull cloth of gold of tissewe conteignyng di yerd di nayle.

[A454] g — Item a yerde di caz ye nayle of purpull cloth of gold.

[A455] g — Item a yerde quarter di quarter of crimosyn cloth of gold.

[A456] g — Item a yerde of crimosyn cloth of golde.

[A454–56] RM: delyuerd to the kinges owne handes for ye said persons.

[A457] g — Item delyuerd by the kinges commaundement to Mr Carewe a Remnaunte of purpull baudkyn dammaske gold conteignyng a yerde di di quarter.

[A458] g — Item delyuerd by the kinges commaundement to Syr John Walloppe knight a Remnaunte of crimosyn cloth of gold opon saten conteignyng iiij yerdes iij quarters of venis gold.

[A459] s — Item delyuerd by the kinges commaundement to mistress Carewe a Remnaunte of white cloth of siluer chekerd dammaske siluer conteignyng iij yerdes iij quarters di.

[A460] g — Item delyuerd by the kinges commaundement to Antony browne a Remnaunte of tawny cloth of gold opon saten conteignyng iij yerdes di.

Henry R

f. 18r

Cloth of gold of diuerse collors

[A461] g — Item delyuerd by the kinges commaundement to Hilton a yerde of damaske gold to edge a Chammer of crimosyn saten latise & cut opon cloth of gold.

[A461–66] LM: anno x^{no} primo die Nouembris.[133]

[A462] t — b — Item delyuerd to Mr Carewe by the kinges commaundement ij yerdes of cloth of golde of tissewe.

[A463] s — Item delyuerd to Henry Norres by the kinges commaundement xiiij yerdes of white cloth of siluer venys siluer to lyne a gowne for him.

[A464] g — Item delyuerd to Mortemer a yerde di of tawny cloth of gold opon saten venis gold to performe a Coote of armes for Norrey the harrold.

[A465] s — Item delyuerd to Mortemer by the kinges commaundement iij yerdes of cloth of siluer for thenbraudring of Carres cote.

[A466] s — Item delyuerd by the kinges commaundement two yerdes di of white cloth of venis siluer for to lyne a gowne for Mistress Mary Fynes.

[A467] g — Item delyuerd by the kinges commaundement to Hilton iiij yerdes of tawny cloth of gold of damaske damaske gold for a doblet for the king.

[A467–73] LM: anno x^{mo} iiij^{to} die Februarii.[134]

[A468] g — Item delyuerd to William Hosier a yerde quarter of cloth of gold of damaske damaske gold for the stocking of a payre of hose for the king.

[A469] t — Item delyuerd by the kinges commaundement xj yerdes of blacke cloth of tissewe for a gowne for the quenes grace.

[A470] g — Item delyuerd to Hilton by the kinges commaundement xij yerdes of cloth of gold of dammaske reysed for a Chamber for the king.

[A471] t — Item delyuerd to Hilton by the kinges commaundement x yerdes of blacke tissewe for a Chammer for the kinges grace.

[A472] g — Item delyuerd to Hilton by the kinges commaundement ix yerdes of Russet cloth of gold for a Jaquet for the king.

[A473] s — Item delyuerd to John Schut x yerdes of dammaske siluer for lynyng of a Gowne for the Quenes grace.

Henry R

[A474] g — Item delyuerd to Mortemer vj yerdes di of dammaske gold for thenbraudryng of a Jaquet & doblet of blake veluete for the king.

[A474–77] LM: anno x^{mo} viij^{mo} die marcii.[135]

[A475] g — Item delyuerd to Richard Gibson lij yerdes of cloth of gold aswell for the Justyng as also for the Revelles of maskelyn after the manner of Italye kepte at the kinges manor of grenewyche.

[A476] s — Item delyuerd to Hilton a yerde di of cloth of siluer towardes a doblet for Carre for thone half therof.

[A477] g — Item delyuerd to Hilton xv yerdes di of yelowe cloth of gold after bawdkyn for lynyng of a gowne of crimosyn saten for the king.

Henry R

f. 18v

Cloth of gold of diuerse collors

[A478] t — Item delyuerd by the kinges commaundement to Hilton & to Mortemer vj yerdes of Russet cloth of gold of tissewe for lynyng & enbraudryng of a Chammer of crimosyn veluete pirled for the king.

[A478–79] LM: anno x^{mo} xvj^{o} die maii.[136]

[A479] g — Item delyuerd to Hilton iij yerdes of cloth of gold for a doblet for the king couerd with white tylsent cutt opon the same cloth of gold.

Henry R

[A480] s — Item delyuerd to Hilton by the kinges commaundement xv yerdes di of damaske siluer for lynyng of a gowne of damaske siluer for the king.

[A480–83] LM: anno xj^{mo} xxvj^{o} die maii.[137]

[A481] g — Item delyuerd to Hilton by the kinges commaundement xj yerdes di of cloth of gold of dammaske dammaske gold for a Riding Cote for ye king.

[A482] g — Item delyuerd to Hilton iij yerdes of cloth of gold for weltyng of a Coote of crimosyn saten cutte opon cloth of gold for the king.

[A483] g — Item delyuerd by the kinges commaundement to William hosyer a yerde quarter of cloth of gold for stocking of a payre of hose for ye king.

[A484] g — Item delyuerd to Hilton xj yerdes of tawny cloth of gold after baudkyn for a Jaquet & a doblet for the kinges grace.

[A484–88] LM: anno xj^{mo} xvj^{mo} die Julii.[138]

[A485] g — Item delyuerd to William Hosyer a yerde quarter of tawny cloth of golde for stocking of a payre of hose for the kinges grace.

[A486] s — Item delyuerd to Hilton v yerdes quarter of dammaske siluer to lyne the border of a Frocke of purpull veluete enbrauderd with venys gold the cloth of siluer drawn through the border losynge wyse.

[A487] t — Item delyuerd to John Scutte the quenes taillor iiij yerdes di & nayle of Riche white siluer tissewe for a gowne for my lady Princes.

[A488] s — Item delyuerd to Hilton x yerdes of cloth of siluer dammaske syluer for to lyne the bordors of ij Frockes thone of blake veluete & thoder of blake saten both enbrouderd with venys gold the cloth of siluer drawen through the border losynge wyse for the kinges grace.

[A489] s — Item delyuerd to John de paris x yerdes of white cloth of siluer reysed after tissewe for a Jaquet & doblet for the kinges grace.

[A489–90] LM: anno xj^{mo} xiij^{mo} die Octobris.[139]

[A490] t — Item delyuerd to John de parres xiiij yerdes di of riche purpull cloth of gold of tissewe with perles of damaske gold & ye grounde dammaske gold for a gowne for the kinges grace.

[A491] s — Item delyuerd to Richard Gibson by the kinges commaundement ~~to R~~ xxxij yerdes of cloth of siluer for ye performyng of ij bases & ij trappers for ye king.

[A491–93] LM: anno xj^{mo} xxiiij^{o} die Octobris.[140]

[A492] g — Item delyuerd to the same Richard iiij yerdes of cloth of gold of venis gold towardes the performyng of a base and a trapper for the king.

[A493] g — Item delyuerd to Richard Gibson iij yerdes of cloth of gold opon saten dammaske gold towardes the performyng of a base & a trapper for ye king.

Henry R

f. 19r

[A494] g — Item delyuerd by the kinges commaundement to Richard Gibson ij yerdes di of cloth of gold of dammaske gold to performe a base & a trapper for the kinges grace.

[A494–96] LM: anno xj^{mo} xxiij^{o} die Octobris.[141]

[A495] g — Item delyured by the kinges commaundement to the same Richard a yerde of cloth of gold of venis to performe a base & a trapper for the king.

[A496] g — Item delyuerd by the kinges commaundement to the same Gibson a yerde di of cloth of gold of dammaske dammaske golde towardes the performyng of a bace[142] & a trapper for the kinges grace.

g — iij^{C} xlv yerdes quarter
t — Cxliij yerdes di quarter
g — Summa totalis — vj^{C} iiij^{xx} x yerdes di quarter
s — Summa totalis — iiij^{C} lviij yerdes iij quarter & naile

Henry R

[A497] t — Item delyuerd by the kinges commaundement to the quenes grace iij yerdes of riche cloth of gold tissewe dammaske gold reised with pyrles damaske siluer for to lyne a gowne for the quenes grace.

[A497–98] LM: anno xj^{mo} vij^{mo} die Nouembris.[143]

[A498] t — Item delyuerd by the kinges commaundement xiij yerdes of cloth of siluer tissewe reysed with damaske gold for a gowne for ye quene.

t — totalis — Clix yerdes di quarter

Henry R

Memorandum delyuerd by the kinges commaundement sithen the viewe taken vltimo die Nouembris anno xj^{mo} by the ducke of Suffolk & other the kinges commissioners / thies parcelles ensuyng parcell of the clere Remaigne of the said viewe[144]

[A499] s — Furst delyuerd by the kinges commaundement to John de pares vj yerdes of playne cloth of siluer dammaske siluer to be drawen through a bordor of a Cote of russet veluete enbrauderd for the king.

[A499–502] LM: anno xj^{mo}.

[A500] g — Item delyuerd to the said John xiiij yerdes di of white cloth of gold of dammaske & dammaske gold for a gowne for the king.

[A501] g — Item delyuerd to Mortemer a quarter di of playne cloth of gold for mending of the bordors of enbraudry of iij doblettes & iij Jaquettes for ye king.

[A502] t — Item delyuerd to John de Parrys xj yerdes quarter di of riche cloth of gold tissewe with pyrles of damaske siluer for a Jaquet with di slyves and a doblet for the kinges grace.

Henry R

t — xj yerdes quarter di
g — xiiij yerdes iij quarters di
s — vj yerdes

f. 19v

[A503] t — Item delyuerd to William Hosier by the kinge commaundement to William Hosyer[145] a yerde di quarter of riche cloth of gold tissewe with pyrles of damaske siluer for stocking of a payr of hose for the king.

[A503–07] LM: anno xj^{mo} viij^{o} die decembris.[146]

[A504] t — Item delyuerd by the kinges commaundement to my lorde Cardynalle a Remnaunte of russet cloth of gold of tissewe conteignyng viij yerdes di quarter.

[A505] s — Item delyuerd by the kinges commaundement to Richard Gibson xiij yerdes of playne damaske siluer for a base a trapper a horsharnes & a sadell.

[A506] g — Item delyuerd to Richard Gibson xij yerdes quarter of playn cloth of gold of damaske gold for to enbrauder opon the said base trapper horse harnes & sadell for the king.

[A507] Item delyuerd to the kinges grace xix yerdes quarter of white cloth of siluer damaske siluer for Mistress Carewe.

Certan peces & Remnauntes of Clothes of gold of diuerse collors and makynges delyuerd by the kinges commaundement by Jamys Worsley yomen of his Robes to Syr Andrewe Wyndesore knight master of the kinges warderobe for the kinges vse anno xj^{o} Crimosyn cloth of gold tissewe for the Chapelle

[A508] C — a pece conteignyng xx yerdes di.

[A508–21] LM: delyuerd to Syr Andrewe Wyndesore knight for the kinges vse xxvj^{to} die marcii anno xj^{mo}.[147]

[A509] C — a pece conteignyng xxxj yerdes iij quarters.

[A510] C — a pece conteignyng xxj yerdes iij quarters.

[A511] C — a pece conteignyng xx yerdes iij quarters.

[A512] C — a pece conteignyng xxxj yerdes.

[A513] C — a pece conteignyng xx yerdes iij quarters.

Blewe cloth of gold tissewe for the Chapelle

[A514] C — a pece conteignyng xxj yerdes.

[A515] C — a pece conteignyng xxxij yerdes quarter.

[A516] C — a pece conteignyng xxxj yerdes di.

Tawny veluete pyrled paled with cloth of gold

[A517] v — a pece conteignyng xv yerdes.

[A518] v — a pece conteignyng xxxj yerdes.

Blacke veluete pyrled paled with cloth of gold

[A519] v — a pece conteignyng xxix yerdes di di quarter.

Crimosyn veluete pyrled paled with cloth of gold

[A520] v — a pece conteignyng vj yerdes quarter.

[A521] v — a pece conteignyng iij quarters.

Henry R

t — ix yerdes quarter at iiij^{li} ye yerde — xxxvij^{li}
g — xij yerdes quarter at xl^{s} ye yerdes — xxiiij^{li} x^{s}
v — iiij^{xx}ij yerdes di di quarter at xlviij^{s} ye yerde — CCxix^{li} iiij^{d}
s — xxxij yerdes quarter xlvj^{s} viij^{d} ye yerdes — lxxiij^{li} v^{s}
C — CCxxxj yerdes quarter at xl^{s} ye yerde — iiij^{C} lxij^{li} x^{s}

f. 20r

Purpull veluete pyrled paled with cloth of gold

[A522] v — a pece conteignyng ix yerdes.

[A522–44] LM: delyuerd to Syr Andrew Wyndesore knight for the kinges vse xxvj^{o} die marcii anno xj^{mo}.[148]

Blewe cloth of gold cheveralle

[A523] g — a pece conteignyng xix yerdes quarter.

Blacke cloth of gold cheveralle

[A524] g — a pece conteignyng xix yerdes quarter.

[A525] g — a pece conteignyng x yerdes iij quarters di.

Grene cloth of siluer cheveralle

[A526] s — a pece conteignyng vj yerdes quarter.

Grene cloth of tissewe with velwete

[A527] v — a pece conteignyng xxv yerdes.

Blew cloth of gold cheveralle

[A528] g — a pece conteignyng xix yerdes di.

Crimosyn cloth of gold of damaske enbosed

[A529] g — a pece conteignyng xxij yerdes.

Crimosyn cloth of gold quylted

[A530] g — a pece conteignyng ix yerdes.

Grene cloth of gold quylted

[A531] g — a pece conteignyng ij yerdes.

Grene cloth of gold of damaske damaske making

[A532] g — a pece conteignyng xxj yerdes quarter.

Grene cloth of gold of damaske

[A533] g — a pece conteignyng xvij yerdes.

[A534] g — a pece conteignyng vj yerdes di di quarter.

[A535] g — a pece conteignyng xiij yerdes.

[A536] g — a pece conteignyng xxvj yerdes.

[A537] g — a Remnaunte conteignyng v yerdes di.

[A538] g — a Remnaunte conteignyng vj yerdes di.

[A539] g — a Remnaunte conteignyng ij yerdes di quarter.

[A540] g — a Remnaunte conteignyng ij yerdes di.

Blacke cloth of gold of damaske

[A541] g — a Remnaunte conteignyng j yerdes iij quarters di.

White cloth of gold of dammaske making

[A542] g — a pece conteignyng xix yerdes di.

[A543] g — a pece conteignyng xx yerdes quarter.

Crimosyn cloth of gold tissewe

[A544] t — a Remnaunte conteignyng iij quarters di.

Henry R

t — iij quarters di at iiij^{li} ye yerde — iiij^{li} x^{s}
g — CCxliiij yerdes at xl^{s} ye yerde — iiij^{C} iiij^{xx} viij ^{li}
v — xxxiiij yerdes at xlviij^{s} ye yerde — iiij^{xx} j^{li} xij^{s}
s — vj yerdes quarter at xl^{s} ye yerde — xij^{li} x^{s}

f. 20v

Blacke cloth of gold tisewe with veluete

[A545] v — a Remnaunte conteignyng j yerde di.

[A545–65] LM: delyuerd to Syr Andrewe Wyndesore knight for the kinges vse xxvj^{o} die marcii anno xj^{mo}.[149]

Grene cloth of gold tissewe with veluete

[A546] v — a Remnaunte conteignyng ij yerdes.

[A547] v — a Remnaunte conteignyng ij yerdes.

[A548] v — a Remnaunte conteignyng ij yerdes.

White cloth of gold quylted

[A549] g — a Remnaunte conteignyng iij yerdes.

White cloth of siluer damaske siluer

[A550] s — a Remnaunte conteignyng iiij yerdes.

Purpull cloth of gold of venis

[A551] g — a pece conteignyng xvj yerdes quarter.

Blewe bawkyn with flouers of gold

[A552] b — a pece conteignyng xxxv yerdes di.

[A553] b — a pece conteignyng v yerdes.

White baudkyn with flouers of gold

[A554] b — a Remnaunte conteignyng vj yerdes iij quarters di.

Grene baudkyn with flouers of gold

[A555] b — a pece conteignyng xxxiij yerdes di.

Crimosyn baudkyn with flowers of gold

[A556] b — a Remnaunte conteignyng ij yerdes.

Grene baudkyn with sterres of gold

[A557] b — a pece conteignyng xix yerdes quarter.

Crimosyn baudkyn with flouers of gold

[A558] b — a pece conteignyng xxiiij yerdes iij quarters.

Grene bawkyn with portcules

[A559] b — a pece conteignyng xx yerdes.

White baudkyn with portcules

[A560] b — a pece conteignyng xx yerdes.

Satens Rawed with gold of diuerse collors

[A561] g — a pece of crimosyn — xvj yerdes di quarter.

[A562] g — a pece of blacke — xxiij yerdes di.

[A563] g — a pece of Russet — xxij yerdes quarter.

Grene cloth of gold of damaske chekerd

[A564] g — a pece conteignyng xiij yerdes di di quarter.

Blewe cloth of gold of damaske makyng

[A565] g — a pece conteignyng vj yerdes di.

Henry R

g — Cj yerdes quarter at xl^s the yerde — CCij^li x^s
s — iiij yerdes at xl^s the yerde — viij^li
b — Clxvj yerdes iij quarters di at xxxiij^s iiij^d — CClxvj^li xvij^s vj^d
v — vij yerdes di at xlviij^s ye yerde — xviij^li

f. 21r

yelowe cloth of gold opon saten venys gold playn

[A566] g — a pece conteignyng xix yerdes di di quarter.

[A566–88] LM: delyuerd to Syr Andrew Wyndesore knight for the kinges vse xxvj^o die marcii anno xj^mo.[150]

Grene cloth of siluer damaske siluer

[A567] s — a pece conteignyng xiiij yerdes iij quarters.

[A568] s — a pece conteignyng xix yerdes quarter di.

[A569] s — a Remnaunte conteignyng iij yerdes.

[A570] s — a pece conteignyng xvij yerdes iij quarters di.

Tawny cloth of siluer dammaske siluer

[A571] s — a pece conteignyng xix yerdes.

Crimosyn baudkyn damaske gold

[A572] g — a pece conteignyng x yerdes iij quarters di.

[A573] g — a pece conteignyng xv yerdes quarter di.

[A574] g — a pece conteignyng xiij yerdes iij quarters.

[A575] g — a pece conteignyng iij yerdes quarter di.

Crimosyn cloth of gold baudkyn venys gold

[A576] g — a pece conteignyng xix yerdes quarter di.

Purpull cloth of gold baudkyn damaske gold

[A577] g — a Remnaunte conteignyng iij yerdes quarter.

Grene cloth of gold of dammaske damaske makyng

[A578] g — a pece conteignyng xvij yerdes iij quarters di.

Grene baudkyn venis gold

[A579] g — a pece conteignyng xiij yerdes iij quarters di.

Crimosyn cloth of gold opon saten venis gold

[A580] g — a pece conteignyng xvij yerdes quarter di.

Crimosyn cloth of gold of venis damaske making

[A581] g — a pece conteignyng ix yerdes di.

yelowe cloth of gold of venis damaske making

[A582] g — a pece conteignyng ix yerdes iij quarters.

yelowe cloth of gold of damake damaske making

[A583] g — a pece of conteignyng xij yerdes di di quarter.

Crimosyn cloth of gold of dornix

[A584] g — a pece conteignyng xxiiij yerdes quarter.

Blacke cloth of gold of dornix

[A585] g — a pece conteignyng xvij yerdes.

Crimosyn cloth of gold playn

[A586] g — a pece conteignyng xxxj yerdes di.

[A587] g — a pece conteignyng x yerdes iij quarters di.

Crimosyn cloth of gold playn

[A588] g — a pece conteignyng xiij yerdes.

Henry R

g — CClxiiij yerdes quarter at xl^s per yerde — Cxxviij^li x^s
s — lxxiiij[151] yerdes ~~iij quarters~~ at xl^s — Cxlviij^li

f. 21v

Blew cloth of gold playn

[A589] g — a pece conteignyng xxvij yerdes iij quarters.

[A589–97] LM: delyuerd to Syr Andrew Wyndesore knight for the kinges vse xxvj^o die marcii anno xj^o Henrici viij^ui.[152]

[A590] g — a pece conteignyng xvij yerdes iij quarters.

Blew cloth of gold of venis

[A591] g — a pece conteignyng x yerdes di.

yelow cloth of gold of venis playn

[A592] g — a pece conteignyng v yerdes iij quarters.

[A589–92] at xl^s — Cxxij^li x^s

White cloth of siluer venis siluer

[A593] s — a pece conteignyng xj yerdes at xl^s — xxj^li.

Cloth of gold braunched with crimosyn veluete opon veluet pirled

[A594] v — a pece conteignyng xx yerdes quarter di.

[A595] v — a pece conteignyng xx yerdes quarter di.

Cloth of gold braunched with blew veluete opon veluete pirled

[A596] v — a pece conteignyng xix yerdes iij quarters.

[A597] v — a pece conteignyng xx yerdes quarter.

[A594–97] at xlviij^s — Ciiij^xx xiij^li xvj^s

[A598] t — Item vij yerdes of Riche cloth of gold tissewe with fleur de luces and one quarter di quarter & nayle of the same cloth of gold for iiij quisshons.

[A598–602] LM: delyuerd by my lorde Cardynalles commaundement for to make vij quisshons for ye king anno xj^o.

[A599] g — Item ij yerdes and the nayle of grene cloth of gold venis gold for the backe syde of ij of the said quisshons.

[A600] t — Item ij yerdes di di quarter of tawny cloth of gold tissewe for a quisshon.

[A601] t — Item ij yerdes of grene cloth of gold tissewe for thone syde of ij quisshons.

[A602] g — Item ij yerdes of grene cloth of gold for thoder syde of the said ij quisshons.

[A603] t — Item vj yerdes di di quarter of blacke cloth of tissewe for a kyrtelle for ye quene.

[A603–08] LM: delyuerd to John Wheler for the quenes grace xxvij^{o} die aprilis anno xj^{o}.[153]

[A604] t — Item ij yerdes & nayle of purpull cloth of tissewe for <lyning of> gownes for the quene.

[A605] t — Item ij yerdes di of chekerd tissewe for lynyng of a gowne for the quene.

[A606] g — Item vij yerdes of purpull cloth of gold dammaske gold for a kyrtelle.

[A607] g — Item vij yerdes of blake baudkyn damaske gold for a nother kyrtelle.

[A608] g — Item vij yerdes of white cloth of gold damaske for a nother kyrtelle.

[A609] t — Item xviij yerdes of cloth of siluer tissewe.

[A609–12] LM: To George Lovekyn by the kinges commaundement mensis aprilis anno xj^{mo}.[154]

[A610] s — Item xij yerdes of cloth of siluer of damaske.

[A611] g — Item xv yerdes of cloth of gold of damaske.

[A612] g — Item ij yerdes di of cloth of gold of damaske.

[A609–612] For horsharnes and fotemens doblettes.

[A613] g — Item xiij yerdes quarter di of cloth of gold after baudkyn damaske gold.

[A613–14] LM: To John Powney yoman of thenchemen anno xj^{mo}.

[A614] g — Item xx yerdes di of cloth of gold after baudkyn damaske gold.

[A613–14] for thenche men.

[A615] s — Item delyuerd to the kinges grace xij yerdes iij quarters di of white cloth of siluer damaske siluer.

[A615] LM: mensis Februarii anno xj^{mo}.[155]

Henry R

t — xl yerdes iij quarters & naile
g — Cxxxvij yerdes iij quarters & nayle
s — xxxv yerdes iiij quartrs di
v — iiij^{xx} yerdes iij quarters

f. 22r

[A616] s — Item xj yerdes di of white siluer tissewe to couer a Jaquet & a doblet of purpull tissew.

[A616–34] LM: delyuerd to John de pares for the kinges vse xix^{mo} die aprilis anno xj^{mo} Regni Regis Henrici viij^{ui}.[156]

[A617] t — Item iiij yerdes di of riche white tissewe pyrled with damaske gold for half a Jaquet and a doblet paned with purpull veluete set with spangelles of gold.

[A618] s — Item xiiij yerdes of white cloth of siluer damaske siluer for a gowne.

[A619] g — Item xiiij yerdes of cloth of gold carnacion collor damaske gold to lyne a gown of cloth of siluer for the king.

[A620] t — Item xiiij yerdes quarter of yelowe cloth of tissewe for a gowne.

[A621] t — Item viij yerdes di of blacke tisssewe damaske gold for a Riding Cote.

[A622] t — Item ij yerdes of blacke siluer tissewe to welte a cote of blacke tissewe.

[A623] g — Item ij yerdes of cloth of gold of damaske gold to welt a Jaquet and a doblet of siluer tylsent for the king.

[A624] t — Item x yerdes di of tawny cloth of gold tissewe for a Jaquet & a doblet.

[A625] s — Item v yerdes iij quarters of blake cloth of damaske siluer for a Jaquet & a doblet.

[A626] s — Item ij yerdes of blacke cloth of siluer damaske siluer for weltyng of a Jaquet and a doblet of blacke cloth of siluer & blacke tylsent paned.

[A627] t — Item x yerdes di of white siluer tissewe for a Jaquet & a doblet.

[A628] s — Item ij yerdes di of blacke cloth of siluer damaske siluer for weltyng of a Jaquet and a doblet of tawny cloth of gold tissewe.

[A629] g — Item ij yerdes of cloth of cloth[157] of gold playn for weltyng of a Jaquet and a doblet of cloth of siluer tissewe.

[A630] t — Item xij yerdes of riche crimosyn tissewe for a gowne.

[A631] g — Item xiiij yerdes of white cloth of gold damaske gold for a gowne.

[A632] t — Item ix yerdes quarter of white siluer tissewe for a Jaquet & a doblet.

[A633] t — Item xvj yerdes quarter of siluer tissewe for a Riding Cote a Jaquet & a doblet.

[A634] g — Item vj yerdes of yelowe cloth of gold damaske gold to welt a Ridyng Cote ij Jaquttes and ij doblettes of siluer tissewe.

[A635] t — Item a yerde quarter of purpull tissewe to stocke a payre of hoses.

[A635–42] LM: delyuerd to William hosyer for ye kinges vse xix^{mo} die aprilis anno xj^{mo} Regni Regis Henrici viij^{ui}.[158]

[A636] t — Item a yerde di quarter of siluer tissewe to stocke a payre of hoses.

[A637] t — Item a yerde quarter of siluer tissewe to stocke a payre of hoses.

[A638] s — Item a yerde quarter of blake cloth of siluer damaske to stocke a payre of hoses.

[A639] s — Item iij yerdes quarter di of cloth of siluer tissewe for stocking of iij payres of hoses.

[A640] g — Item a yerde of yelowe cloth of gold of damaske gold to welt iij payres of hoses of siluer tissewe.

[A641] s — Item iij quarters of cloth of siluer damaske siluer to be panyd with blacke tilsent for stocking of a payre of hoses.

[A642] t — Item for a yerde quarter of tawny cloth of gold of tissew for stockyng of a payre of hoses for the king.

Henry R

t — Cvij yerdes di
g — xxxix yerdes
s — xxvj yerdes quarter

f. 22v

[A643] t — Item delyuerd to John depares by the kinges commaundement ix yerdes quarter of purpull cloth of tissewe for a Jaquet & a doblet for the king.

[A643] LM: anno xj^{mo} xix^{mo} die aprilis.[159]

Memorandum delyuerd by the kinges commaundement to Richard Gibson at diuerse tymes a xix^{mo} die marcii anno xj^{mo} vsque iij^{o} diem maii anno xij^{mo} for the kinges Justes prepared ayenst the metyng of the frenche king at Calais thies parcelles ensuyng that is to saye[160]

[A644] t — Furst delyuerd xiiij yerdes of white tissewe damaske gold.

[A644–51] LM: To Richard Gibson for the kinges Justes at Calais.

[A645] t — Item delyuerd xiiij yerdes of blacke tissewe damaske gold.

[A646] t — Item delyuerd lxviij yerdes j quarter & naile of white tissew venis gold.

[A647] t — Item in white tissewe damaske siluer — xvij yerdes.

[A648] g — Item in yelowe cloth of gold damaske gold — Dxix yerdes di.

[A649] g — Item in cloth of gold of venis playn — Clxij yerdes quarter & nail.

[A650] s — Item in cloth of siluer damaske siluer playne — CCCxlix yerdes di.

[A651] s — Item in cloth of siluer of venis playne — CCClv yerdes j quarter.

Delyuerd for thenparelyng of certan gentilmen & other attending opon the king at his forsaid Justes

[A652] g — Item in damaske gold playn — xviij yerdes.

Blacke tylsent damaske gold

[A822] a pece conteignyng vij yerdes quarter.

Blacke tylsent venis gold

[A823] a pece conteignyng xxvj yerdes iij quarters di.

[A824] a pece conteignyng xxiij yerdes iij quarters di.

[A825] a pece conteignyng viij yerdes di quarter.

[A826] a pece conteignyng xix yerdes di.

[A827] a pece conteignyng vj yerdes quarter di.

[A828] a pece conteignyng ij yerdes iij quarters di.

Tawny tylsent venis gold

[A829] a pece conteignyng ix yerdes quarter di.

[A830] a pece conteignyng xxij yerdes.

[A831] a pece conteignyng xvij yerdes iij quarters di.

[A832] a pece conteignyng xxiij yerdes quarter di.

[A833] a pece conteignyng iij yerdes di di quarter.

[A834] a pece conteignyng j yerde iij quarters.

[A835] a pece conteignyng j yerde di di quarter.

yelowe tylsent venis gold

[A836] a pece conteignyng xxiij yerdes di quarter.

[A837] a pece conteignyng x yerdes iij quarters.

White tylsent venis gold

[A838] a pece conteignyng xxj yerdes.

[A839] a pece conteignyng xv yerdes quarter.

White tylsent damaske siluer

[A840] a pece conteignyng v yerdes.

Henry R

Summa pagine — CCCxlvj yerdes iij quarters di

f. 28r

White tylent venis siluer

[A841] a pece conteignyng v yerdes iij quarters.

[A841–55] LM: delyured to Syr Andrew Wyndesore knight for the kinges vse xxvj° die marcii anno xj^mo^ Henrici viij^ui^.[201]

[A842] a pece conteignyng vij yerdes di.

[A843] a pece conteignyng iiij yerdes di di quarter.

[A844] a pece conteignyng iij yerdes quarter.

[A845] a pece conteignyng iiij yerdes iij quarters.

Crimosyn tylsent venis gold

[A846] a pece conteignyng iij yerdes iij quarters di.

[A847] a pece conteignyng iiij yerdes iij quarters di.

[A848] a pece conteignyng ij yerdes quarter.

Russet tylsent venis gold

[A849] a Remnaunte of iij yerdes di di quarter.

yelowe tylsent venis gold

[A850] a pece conteignyng viij yerdes quarter.

[A851] a pece conteignyng vj yerdes di quarter.

White tylsent

[A852] a pece conteignyng ij yerdes di quarter.

[A853] a pece conteignyng iij yerdes iij quarters.

Crimosyn tylsent venis gold

[A854] a pece conteignyng j yerde di quarter.

Purpull tylsent

[A855] a pece conteignyng v yerdes iij quarters.

[A856] Item vij yerdes of blacke tylsent damaske gold for a kyrtelle.

[A856–58] LM: delyuerd to John Wheler for ye quenes grace xxvij^mo^ die aprilis anno xj^mo^.[202]

[A857] Item vij yerdes of russet tylsent for a kyrtell for the quene.

[A858] Item vij yerdes of tawny tylsent for a kirtell for the quene.

[A859] Item delyuerd to John Powney by the kinges commaundement vj yerdes of yelow tylsent for the kinges henchemen.

[A860] Item xv yerdes quarter of white tilsent dammaske siluer to lyne a gowne of white tissewe for the king.

[A860–66] LM: delyuerd to John de paris for the kinges vse mensis aprilis anno xj° Regni Regis Henrici viij^ui^.[203]

[A861] Item xj yerdes quarter of blacke tylsent for a Jaquet & a doblet for ye king.

[A862] Item xiiij yerdes quarter of blacke tylsent for a gowne for the king.

[A863] Item xiiij yerdes di of white tilsent to lyne a gowne of blacke tylsent.

[A864] Item xj yerdes of blacke siluer tylsent for a Jaquet & a doblet.

[A865] Item v yerdes iij quarters of blacke tylsent for a Jaquet and a doblet to be paned with blacke cloth of siluer.

[A866] Item ij yerdes of blacke tylsent for weltyng of a Jaquet & a doblet of blacke cloth of siluer & blake tylsent paned.

Henry R

Summa Pagine — Clxxij yerdes

f. 28v

[A867] Item delyuerd by the kinges commaundement to John de pares xv yerdes iij quarters of siluer tylsent with dropes to lyne a gowne of crimosyn cloth of gold tissewe for the king.

[A867–69] LM: anno xj^mo^ xix^no^ die aprilis.[204]

[A868] Item delyuerd to William Hosyer iij quarters of blacke tylent to be panyd with blacke cloth of siluer for stockyng of a payr of hoses for the king.

[A869] Item delyuerd to William Hosyer a yerde quarter of blake tylsent to stocke a payre of hoses for the kinges grace.

Delyuerd to Richard Gibson by the kinges commaundement for themparelle of the kinges maskers at diuerse tymes sithen the xix^th^ day of marche anno xj^mo^ vnto the iij^de^ day of maye anno xij^mo^ thies parcelles of tylsenttes ensuyng[205]

[A870] Furst in yelowe tylsent — xxxix yerdes.

[A870–72] LM: To Richard Gibson for the kinges maskes.

[A871] Item in blake tylsent riche — xxj yerdes di di quarter.

[A872] Item in Russet tylsent riche — xxviij yerdes quarter di.

[A873] Item di yerde of blacke tylsent to performe the weltyng of a doblet and a Jaquet of blacke tylsent & blacke cloth of siluer paned for ye king.

[A873–74] LM: To John de Parres for the kinges vse anno xij°.

[A874] Item xj yerdes of crimosyn tylsent for a Jaquet & a doblet ~~of~~ couerd with crimosyn saten for the king.

[A875] Item to William hosyer a yerde quarter of crimosyn tylsent for stocking of a payr of hose for the kinges grace.

Henry R

[A876] Item delyuerd by the kinges commaundement to my lorde of devon iij yerdes quarter di of white tylsent dammaske siluer.

[A876–80] LM: anno xijmo iiijto die maii.[206]

[A877] Item delyuerd by the kinges commaundement to mr Carewe a Remnaunte of Russet tylsent conteignyng v yerdes di quarter.

[A878] Item delyuerd to mastres Norres by the kinges commaundement of white tylsent damaske siluer conteignyng iiij yerdes di quarter.

[A879] Item delyuerd by the kinges commaundement to John de Paris vj yerdes di of blacke tylsent for a Riding Cote paned with crimosyn tissewe.

[A880] Item delyuerd to the kinges grace by thandes of Carre v yerdes quarter di of tawny tylsent.[207]

Henry R

[A881] Item to mastres Fynes vj yerdes of tawny tylsent for a kyrtell.

[A881–83] LM: anno xijmo xiiijmo die maii.[208]

[A882] Item to ye Lady Elizabeth grey vij yerdes of blacke tylsent for a kyrtell.

[A883] Item to ye Lady Oxforde <x>iij yerdes of blacke tylsent for a gowne.

Henry R

Summa pagine — CCxx yerdes

f. 29r

[A884] Item delyuerd by the kinges commaundement to the quenes grace a pece of blacke tylsent with kateryn whelys xvj yerdes di di quarter.

[A884–85] LM: anno xijmo xixno die maii.[209]

[A885] Item delyuerd by the kinges commaundement to the quenes grace a pece of blacke tylsent damaske gold conteignyng xj yerdes.

Henry R

[A886] Item xiiij yerdes of blacke tylsent damaske gold for a doble Clocke for the kinges grace.

[A886–93] LM: anno xijmo ijdo die Junii.[210]

[A886–93] LM: To John de Paris.

[A887] Item xix yerdes of blacke tylsent for a double Cloke for the kinges grace garded with the same.

[A888] Item vij yerdes of russet tylsent to be cutt & paned with crimosyn baudkyn for a Cote for the king.

[A889] Item xv yerdes of Russet tylsent to lyne a doubille mantelle with slyves of blacke cloth of gold after baudkyn for the king.

[A890] Item iiij yerdes of blacke tylsent damaske gold for a doublet garded with the same for the kinges grace.

[A891] Item xv yerdes iij quarters of tawny tylsent for a frocke for the king.

[A892] Item xvj yerdes of blacke tilsent for a frocke for the king.

[A893] Item ij yerdes quarter of russet tylsent for a doblet for the king paned with cloth of siluer paned.

[A894] Item ij yerdes iij quarters of blake tylsent damaske gold for the vpper partes of a payre of hose to the knee all of tylsent garded with the same.

[A894–95] LM: To William Hosyer.

[A895] Item ij yerdes di of siluer tylsent with dropes for stockyng of a payr of hose for the kinges grace.

[A896] Item delyuerd by the kinges commaundement to mosyr Morret a Frenche man xvj yerdes of Russet tylsent for a gowne.

[A897] Item delyuerd to Pulleyn a frencheman iiij yerdes quarter of Russet tylsent and ij yerdes iij quarters of tawny tylsent for his owne vse.

[A898] Item delyuerd to William Hosyer a yerde iij quarters of russet tylsent for stocking of a payre of hose for the king.

Henry R

Summa partes — C~~xlv~~j yerdes di di quarter

Summa totalis of Tilsentes delyuerd a viijmo die decembris anno xjmo Regni Regis Henrici viijui vsque xxvui diem Julii anno xijmo euisdem Regis[211]

— Ml CCxxiiij yerdes quarter di

[A899] Item delyuerd to John de Paris xj yerdes iij quarters of crimosyn tylsent dammask gold for panyng of a Frocke & a doblet of crimosyn saten for the king.

[A899–900] LM: anno xijmo iiijto die septembris.[212]

[A900] Item delyuerd to William Hosyer a quarter of crimosyn tylsent damaske gold for stockyng & weltyng of a payre of hose for the king.[213]

Henry R

Summa — xij yerdes

f. 29v [blank]

f. 30r[214]

Baudekyns of dyuerse collors delyuerd by the kinges commaundement at diuerse tymes

[A901] Item[215]

[A901] LM: anno.[216]

Baudkyn

f. 30v [blank][217]

f. 31r[218]

Veluettes of diuerse collors delyuerd by the kinges commaundement at diuerse tymes

[A902] Item delyuerd to Hilton vij yerdes of blake velwete for a Cote paned with purpull tylsent for the kings grace.

[A902–07] anno viijo ijdo die Januarii.[219]

[A903] Item delyuerd by the kinges commaundement to Hilton iij yerdes of blewe velwete for a doblet for the kinges grace.

[A904] Item delyuerd by the kinges commaundement to Hilton xv yerdes of crimosyn velwete for a gowne for the kinges grace.

[A905] Item delyuerd by the kinges commaundement to Hilton iij yerdes quarter of blacke velwete for a Tenes Cote for the kinges grace.

[A906] Item delyuerd to Hilton iij yerdes quarter of blew velwete delyuerd by the kinges commaundement for a Tenes Cote for the king.

[A907] Item delyuerd by the kinges commaundement to one Russell Capten of Torney a pece of Russet velwete conteignyng xxij yerdes di.

[A908] Item delyuerd by the kinges commaundement to Hilton xj yerdes of riche Crimosyn velwete for a Riding Cote for the kinges grace.

[A908–15] anno viijo xijmo die Februarii.[220]

[A909] Item delyuerd to John de Pares vij yerdes di of blewe velwete for a doblet & a payre of hose partie with blake tilsent for the kinges grace.

[A910] Item delyuerd by the kinges commaundement to John Scut iiij yerdes of crimosyn velwete for a gowne for my lady Prynces.

[A911] Item delyuerd by the kinges commaundement to John Scut iiij yerdes of blake velwete for a gowne for my lady Princes.

[A912] Item delyuerd by the kinges commaundement to Hilton xiij yerdes of blake velwete for a gowne for the kinges grace.

[A913] Item delyuerd by the kinges commaundement to Syr Richard Tempes xv yerdes of blake velwete for a gowne.

[A914] Item delyuerd by the kinges commaundement [to Hilton] xiij yerdes of blake velwete for a gown for the kinges grace.

[A915] Item delyuerd to Hilton xj yerdes of blake velwete for a Ridyng Cote for the kinges grace.

velwete pirled for a glaudkyn for the kinges grace.

[A992] Item delyuerd to William Hilton xxvij yerdes of purpull velwete pirled for a longe gowne with greate wyde slyves for the king.

[A993] Item delyuerd to Hilton xij yerdes iij quarters of crimosyn velwete cut opon cloth of gold of dammaske enbrauderd with goldsmyth [werke] for a doblet & a Jaquet.

[A994] Item delyuerd to William Hosyer a yerde quarter of crimosyn velwete cut opon cloth of gold of dammaske for stocking of a payre of hoses for the king.

[A995] Item delyuerd to William Hilton xj yerdes di of blacke velwete cut opon cloth of damaske enbrauderd for a doblet & a Jaquet for the king.

[A996] Item delyuerd to William Hosyer a yerde quarter of blacke velwete for to couer the stockes of cloth of gold of damaske playn cutt opon of a paire of hose.

[A997] Item delyuerd to Richard Justes iij quarters of a yerde of crimosyn velwete for the fentes bordor & Cuffes for a gowne for my lady princes.

[A998] Item delyuerd by the kinges commaundement to my lorde John Grey and to my lorde Leonardes brother xvj yerdes of yelowe velwete towardes a base and a trapper for either of theim for to prepare themse2lf for the kinges Justes ayenst the commyng of the forsaid embassadors of Fraunce.

[A998] LM: primo die Septembris anno x^{mo}.[244]

[A999] Item delyuerd by the kinges commaundement to Hilton xj yerdes of crimosyn velwete for to couer a Cote of cloth of gold cutt & welted for the king.

[A999–1000] LM: vij^{mo} die Septembris anno x^{mo}.[245]

[A1000] Item delyuerd to William Hosyer a yerde quarter of purpull velwete to couer the stockes of cloth of gold of a payr of hose for the kinges grace.

Henry R

Ciiij^{xx} yerdes iij quarters

f. 34r

Velwetes of diuers collors

[A1001] Item delyuerd by the kinges commaundement to Robert Gernyngham mr Hansard mr Hervy mr Parker mr [. . .] viij yerdes of blewe velwete towardes a base and a trapper for eueryeche of theim in all xxxx yerdes.

[A1001–17] LM: xviij^{o} die Septembris anno x^{mo}.[246]

[A1002] Item delyuerd by the kinges commaundement to Syr Edward Gilford xv yerdes of blacke velwete towardes a base & a trapper — xv yerdes.

[A1003] Item delyuerd by the kinges commaundement xiij yerdes di of tawny velwete opon velwete for a gowne for the quene.

[A1004] Item delyuerd by the kinges commaundement to Care xiij yerdes <di> of blac velwete.

[A1005] Item delyuerd by the kinges commaundement for the childryn that waytes on the king vj yerdes of yelowe velwete & vj yerdes of blacke velwete.

[A1006] Item delyuerd to Hilton iiij yerdes quarter of purpull velwete pirled for slyves and to performe a Cape of a gowne of purpull velwete pirled for the king.

[A1007] Item delyuerd to Hilton iiij yerdes quarter di of crimosyn velwete for slyves to performe a Cape for a gowne of crimosyn velwete for the king.

[A1008] Item delyuerd to mastres Mary Fynes ij yerdes di of crimosyn velwete to lyne a gowne of crimosyn tylsent.

[A1009] Item delyuerd by the kinges commaundement to John Scutt xj yerdes of tawny velwete for a gowne for mastres Carewe.

[A1010] Item delyuerd to Hilton xiiij yerdes of crimosyn velwete opon velwete pirled for a chammer for the king.

[A1011] Item delyuerd by the kinges commaundement to mastres Carewe iij yerdes of crimosyn velwete to lyne the same gowne.

[A1012] Item delyuerd to Hilton xiiij yerdes of purpull velwete for a doblet and a Jaquet cut opon cloth of gold for the kinges grace.

[A1013] Item delyuerd by the kinges commaundement xiiij yerdes of crimosyn velwete opon velwete for a Cloke for the kinges grace.

[A1014] Item delyuerd by the kinges commaundement to William Hosyer a yerde <quarter> of purpull velwete for stockes for the kinges grace.

[A1015] Item delyuerd by the kinges commaundement to Hilton a yerde di of crimosyn velwete for a bonet for the kinges grace.

[A1016] Item delyuerd by the kinges commaundement to Hilton a yerde di of blake velwete for a bonet for the kinges grace.

[A1017] Item delyuerd by the kinges commaundement to Hilton vij yerdes quarter of blacke velwete for a Jaquet for the kinges grace.

Henry R

[A1018] Item delyuerd by the kinges commaundement to the quenes grace a Remnaunte of purpull veluete opon velwete pirled conteignyng iij quarters & [a] nayle.

[A1018–19] LM: anno x^{mo} xxij^{do} die Octobris.[247]

[A1019] Item delyuerd by the kinges commaundement to my lady Guylford a Remnaunte of tawny veluete pirled conteignyng xij yerdes for a gowne.

Henry R

Ciiij^{xx} v yerdes quarter di

f. 34v

Veluetes of diuerse collors

[A1020] Item delyuerd by the kinges commaundement to Hilton xij yerdes of Russet veluete for a Jaquet & a di Coote for the king.

[A1020–25] LM: primo die Nouembris anno x^{o}.[248]

[A1021] Item delyuerd by the kinges commaundement to Syr Thomas Chenye knight xiiij yerdes of russet veluete pirled for a gowne.

[A1022] Item delyuerd by the kinges commaundement to Mr Harry Norres xiiij yerdes of russet veluete for a gowne.

[A1023] Item delyuerd to mastres Mare Fynes by the kinges commaundement xj yerdes of russet veluete for a gowne.

[A1024] Item delyuerd by the kinges commaundement to Hilton vj yerdes of russet veluete for ij doblettes for the kinges grace.

[A1025] Item delyuerd by the kinges commaundement to mastres Carew x yerdes of tawny veluete for a gowne for hir.

Henry R

[A1026] Item delyuerd by the kinges commaundement to Hilton xvj yerdes quarter of blake veluete for a Jaquet & a doblet for the kinges grace.

[A1026–35] LM: anno x^{mo} iij^{o} die Februarii.[249]

[A1027] Item delyuerd to William Hosyer a yerde quarter di quarter of blacke veluete for the stocking of a payre of hose for the kinges grace.

[A1028] Item delyuerd by the kinges commaundement to the duck of Suffolk two yerdes of blake veluete for a payr of buskyns.

[A1029] Item delyuerd to mr Carewe by the kinges commaundement ij yerdes of blake veluete for a payr of buskyns.

[A1030] Item delyuerd to mr Bryan by the kinges commaundement ij yerdes of blake veluete for a payr of buskyns.

[A1031] Item delyuerd to Syr Henry Guylford knight by the kinges commaundement ij yerdes of blake veluete for a payr of buskyns.

[A1032] Item delyuerd to mr Norres by the kinges commaundement ij yerdes of blake veluete for a payr of buskyns.

[A1033] Item delyuerd to Syr Edwarde Nevelle knight by the kinges commaundement ij yerdes of blac veluete for a payr of ~~hos~~ buskyns.

[A1034] Item delyuerd to Syr Gyles Capell ij yerdes of blake veluete for a payr of buskyns by the kinges commaundement.

[A1035] Item delyuerd to Hilton a quarter of blake veluete for to ege the slyves of gowne of blake saten for the king.

[A1036] Item delyuerd to Hilton by the kinges commaundement iiij yerdes of blac veluete for a doblet for the kinges grace.

[A1036–38] LM: anno x^{mo} vj^{o} die marcii.[250]

[A1037] Item delyuerd to Hilton by the kinges commaundement iiij yerdes of Russet veluete for a doblet for the kinges grace.

[A1038] Item delyuerd to William Hosyer a yerde <quarter> of russet veluete for stocking of a payre of hose for the king.

Henry R

Cliij yerdes di quarter

f. 35r

Veluettes of diuerse collors

[A1039] Item delyuerd by the kinges commaundement to William Hosyer a yerde quarter of Russet veluete for stocking of a payre of hose for the king.

[A1039–40] LM: anno x^{o} viij^{o} die marcii.[251]

[A1040] Item delyuerd by the kinges commaundement to Richard Gibson CCxiij yerdes of blake veluete aswell for the Justynges as also for the Revelles of maskelyn after the manner of Italy at grenewyche.

[A1041] Item delyuerd to Hilton xij yerdes di of blake veluete for a frocke for the king with ij narowe gardes of the same veluete.

[A1041–47] LM: anno x^{mo} xvij^{mo} die marcii.[252]

[A1042] Item delyuerd to Hilton xij yerdes of Russet veluete for a frocke with a border enbrauderd with russet silke.

[A1043] Item delyuerd to Hilton xij yerdes of blake veluete for a Frocke of lyke werke for the kinges grace.

[A1044] Item delyuerd to mastres Carewe by the kinges commaundement vij yerdes of blewe veluete.

[A1045] Item delyuerd to Hilton xij yerdes of crimosyn veluete for a frocke for ye king.

[A1046] Item delyuerd to Hilton by the kinges commaundement iiij yerdes of crimosyn veluete for a doblet for the kinge with ruff slyves.

[A1047] Item delyuerd to William Hosyer a yerde quarter of crimosyn veluete for stockes for a payre of hose for the king.

[A1048] Item delyuerd to Hilton xviij yerdes of blake veluete for a shammer and a Cote for Carre.

[A1048–52] LM: anno x^{o} iij^{o} die aprilis.[253]

[A1049] Item delyuerd by the kinges commaundement to Syr Edward Guylford xiiij yerdes of blake veluete for a gowne.

[A1050] Item delyuerd by the kinges commaundement to mr Henry Norres xj yerdes of blake veluete for a Frocke.

[A1051] Item delyuerd by the kinges commaundement to Babam sergeaunt of the confecionary nichill hic quz entrat in alio loco.

[A1052] Item delyuerd by the kinges commaundement to Fraunces Poynes xiiij yerdes of blake veluete for a gowne.

[A1053] Item delyuerd by the kinges commaundement to William Hilton xv yerdes di of crimosyn veluete for the kinges grace for a gowne.

[A1053–57] LM: anno x^{mo} xviij^{o} die maii.[254]

[A1054] Item delyuerd to William Hilton a yerde of crimosyn veluete to couer and to cutt opon a doblet of crimosyn tylsent for the king.

[A1055] Item delyuerd to William Hilton viij yerdes of blewe veluete for a Frock partye with blacke tylsent for the kinges grace.

[A1056] Item delyuerd to William Hilton ij yerdes of blewe veluete for a doblet paned with blake tylsent for the kinges grace.

[A1057] Item delyuerd to William Hosyer iij quarters of blewe veluete for stockyng of a payre of hose paned with blacke tylsent for the king.

Henry R

iiij^{C} xxj yerdes quarter

f. 35v

Veluetes of diuerse collors

[A1058] Item delyuerd by the kinges commaundement to Hilton xv yerdes di of blake veluete for a gowne for the kings grace.

[A1058–60] LM: anno xj^{mo} xxvj^{o} die maii.[255]

[A1059] Item delyuerd by the kinges commaundement to Hilton xv yerdes di of blake veluete for a mantelle for the king.

[A1060] Item delyuerd to William Hosyer a yerde quarter of crimosyn veluete to be sett opon a payre of stockes of crimosyn tylsent for the king.

[A1061] Item delyuerd to Hilton by the kinges commaundement iij yerdes of crimosyn veluete for a longe partelet for the king.

[A1061–67] LM: anno xj^{o} xxiij^{o} die Juni.[256]

[A1062] Item delyuerd to Hilton by the kinges commaundement iij yerdes of grene veluete for a longe partelet for the king.

[A1063] Item delyuerd to Hilton by the kinges commaundement iij yerdes of blac veluete for a longe partelet for the king.

[A1064] Item delyuerd by the kinges commaundement to Syr Edwarde Cobham by the kinges commaundement[257] xiiij yerdes of blake veluete for a gowne.

[A1065] Item delyuerd to William Hosyer a yerde quarter of grene veluete for stocking of a payre of hose for the king.

[A1066] Item delyuerd to William Hosyer a yerde quarter of crimosyn veluete for stocking a payre of hose for the king.

[A1067] Item delyuerd to Hilton by the kinges commaundement xxv yerdes of blake veluete for a frocke & a mantelle for the king.

[A1068] Item delyuerd to Hilton by the kinges commaundement iiij yerdes quarter of russet veluete for a di Cote for the kinge.

[A1068–72] LM: anno xj^{mo} x^{mo} die Septembris.[258]

[A1069] Item delyuerd to Hilton by the kinges commaundement xv yerdes of blake veluete for a frock and a doblet for the king.

[A1070] Item delyuerd to William Hosyer by the kinges commaundement a yerde quarter of blake veluete for stockyng a payre of hose for the king.

[A1071] Item delyuerd to Hilton by the kinges commaundement xvj yerdes of blake veluete for a gowne for the king.

[A1072] Item delyuerd to John Scutte ye quenes taillor v yerdes of Russet veluete

lukes for a nyght gowne for the king[259] my lady princes.

[A1073] Item delyuerd by the kinges commaundement to John de parris tailor xiiij yerdes di of russet veluete for a gowne for the kinges grace.

[A1073] LM: anno xj^mo xiij^mo die Octobris.[260]

[A1074] Item delyuerd by the kinges commaundement to Richard Gibson vij yerdes quarter of Russet veluete to the performyng of a bace & a trapper for ye king.

[A1074–76] LM: anno xj^to xxiiij^to die Octobris.[261]

[A1075] Item delyuerd by the kinges commaundement to Richard Gibson x yerdes iij quarters of Russet veluete to the performyng of a bace & a trapper for the king.

[A1076] Item delyuerd by the kinges commaundement to Richard Gibson iiij yerdes of Russet veluete towardes ye performyng of a bace & a trapper for the king.

Henry R

Clx yerdes iij quarters

f. 36r

[A1077] Item delyuerd to Hilton by the kinges commaundement Cl yerdes of blacke veluete for garding of Cxx Cootes of ye ij^de sorte of redde cloth for ye garde.

[A1077] LM: anno viij^o xxvj^o die aprilis.[262]

[A1078] Item delyuerd by the kinges commaundement lxiij yerdes of blake veluete for to make fyve gownes for fyve gentylmen of the quene of scottes.

[A1078–79] LM: anno viij^o ix^o die maii.[263]

[A1079] Item delyuerd by the kinges commaundement to iij gentylmen of the quene of scottes chamber xlij yerdes of blacke veluete for euery of y^em a gowne.

[A1080] Item delyuerd by the kinges commaundement to Richard Gibson CCxiij yerdes iij quarters of white veluete spent for the kinges Justes.

[A1080] LM: anno ix^mo vij^mo die Julii.[264]

[A1081] Item delyuerd by the kinges commaundement xiiij yerdes of blacke veluete for a gowne for the sergeaunte porter.

[A1081–82] LM: anno x^mo viij^o die Junii.[265]

[A1082] Item delyuerd by the kinges commaundement to mr Coffyn xiiij yerdes of blake veluete for a gowne.

Henry R

[A1083] Item delyuerd by the kinges commaundement to John deparys ij yerdes of russet veluete for a doblet & weltyng of a gowne of russet dammaske.

[A1083–88] LM: anno xj^mo v^to die Nouembris.[266]

[A1084] Item delyuerd to the same John xiij yerdes of russet veluete for a Cote with di slyves and a doblet for the king.

[A1085] Item delyuerd to William hosyer by the kinges commaundement a yerde quarter of russet veluete for stocking of a payre of hose for the king.

[A1086] Item delyuerd to mastres Worshop by the kinges commaundement iij quarters of russet veluete for ij pursses for the kinges grace.

[A1087] Item delyuerd by the kinges commaundement to John de pares a yerd di quarter of crimosyn veluete for the newe making of the half quarters & ouer bodyes of a Jaquet & a doblet of crimosyn veluete opon veluete.

[A1088] Item delyuerd to John de paris a yerde di quarter of crimosyn veluete for ye newe making of half quarters & ouer bodyes of a Jaquet & a doblet of crimosyn veluete for the kinges grace.

Henry R

Summa totalis — M^l M^l iiij^C xiij yerdes quarter di quarter

Dxiij yerdes iij qurater

f. 36v

Memorandum delyuerd by the kinges commaundement sithen the view taken vltimo die Nouembris anno xj^mo[267] by the duck of Suffolk and other the kinges commissioners thies parcelles ensuing parcelles of the clere Remayne of the said viewe

[A1089] Furst delyuerd by the kinges commaundement to mastres Coke xij yerdes of blacke veluete tawny veluete for a gowne.

[A1090] Item delyuerd by the kinges commaundement to John de parrys xiij yerdes of blacke veluete for a Cote for the kinge.

[A1091] Item delyuerd by the kinges commaundement to Syr Rauf Ellerear xiiij yerdes of blacke veluete for a gowne.

[A1092] Item delyuerd by the kinges commaundement to maryan a yerde ~~a yerde~~ of blacke veluete for coueryng of iij scaberdes for the king.

[A1093] Item delyuerd to John de pares ij yerdes of russet veluete for doble weltyng of a gowne of russet dammaske for the king.

[A1094] Item delyuerd to Maryon by the kinges commaundement a yerde quarter of blacke veluete for coueryng of scaberdes of the kinges swerdes.

[A1095] Item delyuerd by the kinges commaundement to the quenes grace xiij yerdes of crimosyn veluete opon veluete for a gowne.

[A1096] Item delyuerd by the kinges commaundement to John de parrys xv yerdes di of purpull veluete for a Frocke & a doblet for the king.

[A1097] Item delyuerd by the kinges commaundement to lytell Carre a pece of Russet veluete conteignyng xxv yerdes.

[A1098] Item delyuerd by the kinges commaundement to mr shatyllion xiij yerdes di of blacke veluete for a gowne.

[A1099] Item delyuerd to John de parres xv yerdes of Russet veluete for a shammer doubill welted with iij weltes of the same for the king.

[A1100] Item delyuerd to the said John xv yerdes of blacke veluete for a shammer doubill welted with iij weltes of the same for the king.

[A1101] Item delyuerd to Richard Gibson xiij yerdes of russet veluete for to mache cutwerke & engreyle with cloth of siluer for a base a trapper a horsse harnes and a sadelle for the king.

[A1101–02] LM: anno xj^mo xxvj^o die Januarii.[268]

[A1102] Item delyuerd to the lady Guylfordes seruaunt by mr Compton [on] his bill xij yerdes of blac veluete to be had to Calais for the kinges vse.[269]

Henry R

Summa pagine — Clxv yerdes quarter veluete enterd amonges gownes — Cxxj yerdes iij quarters

f. 37r

Certan peces & Remnauntes of veluetes of diuerse collors & makinges delyuerd by the kinges commaundement by Jamys worsley yomen of his Robes to Syr Andrewe Wyndesore knight master of the kinges greate warderobe for the kinges vse anno xj^mo

Blew & grene mottely veluete pyrled

[A1103] a pece conteignyng xij yerdes iij quarters.

[A1103–28] LM: delyuerd to Syr Andrewe Wyndesore knight for the kinges vse xxvj^o die marcii anno xj^o.[270]

Russet veluete opon veluete pyrled

[A1104] a pece conteignyng xiiij yerdes.

[A1105] a pece conteignyng viij yerdes di quarter.

Tawny veluete opon veluete pyrled

[A1106] a pece conteignyng vij yerdes di quarter.

Tawny veluete opon veluete

[A1107] a pece conteignyng vj yerdes di.

Grene veluete opon veluete pyrled

[A1108] a Remnaunte conteignyng ij yerdes di.

Purpull veluete

[A1109] a pece conteignyng iiij yerdes iij quarters di.

[A1110] a pece conteignyng vj yerdes.

[A1111] a Remnaunte conteignyng j yerde di quarter.

[A1112] a Remnaunte conteignyng iij quarters di.

[A1113] a Remnunte conteignyng iij quarters.

[A1114] a Remnaunte conteignyng iiij yerdes di di quarter.

[A1115] a Remnaunte conteignyng v yerdes di.

[A1116] a Remnaunte conteignyng iiij yerdes quarter.

[A1117] a Remnaunte conteignyng j yerdes quarter di.

[A1118] a Remnaunte conteignyng iiij yerdes quarter di.

[A1119] a Remnaunte conteignyng v yerdes di.

[A1120] a pece conteignyng xxiij yerdes iij quarters.

[A1121] a pece conteignyng xv yerdes di.

[A1122] a pece conteignyng xij yerdes quarter.

Grene veluete

[A1123] a pece conteignyng xvj yerdes quarter.

[A1124] a pece conteignyng ix yerdes.

[A1125] a pece conteignyng ix yerdes quarter.

[A1126] a pece conteignyng vj yerdes.

[A1127] a Remnaunte conteignyng j yerde di.

[A1128] a Remnaunte conteignyng ij yerdes quarter.

Henry R

Summa pagine — Ciiij^xx vj yerdes

f. 37v

Grene veluete

[A1129] a Remnaunte conteignyng iij yerdes di di quarter.

[A1129–41] LM: delyuerd to Syr Andrewe Wyndesore knight for the kinges vse xxvj^o die marcii anno xj^o.[271]

[A1130] a Remnaunte conteignyng j yerde di di quarter.

[A1131] a Remnaunte conteignyng j yerde di.

[A1132] a Remnaunte conteignyng iiij yerdes di di quarter.

Veluete white & grene chekerd

[A1133] a pece conteignyng xvj yerdes di di quarter.

[A1134] a pece conteignyng v yerdes iij quarters di.

[A1135] a pece conteignyng xv yerdes di di quarter.

Veluete orynge collor

[A1136] a pece conteignyng xij yerdes di quarter.

[A1137] a pece conteignyng xxiij yerdes.

[A1138] a pece conteignyng xvij yerdes.

Yelowe veluete

[A1139] a pece conteignyng xiij yerdes iij quarter.

[A1140] a Remnaunte conteignyng vij yerdes.

[A1141] a Remnaunte conteignyng ij yerdes quarter.

[A1142] Item delyuerd Cl yerdes of crimosyn veluete.

[A1142–48] LM: To George Lovekyn by the kinges commaundement mensis aprilis anno xj^mo.

[A1143] Item delyuerd xlij yerdes di of right crimosyn veluete.

[A1144] Item delyuerd l yerdes of blake veluete.

[A1145] Item delyuerd xix yerdes di of russet veluete.

[A1146] Item delyuerd xij yerdes of purpull veluete.

[A1142–46] RM: For horsharnes with all thinges necessarie to ye same and fotemens doblettes.

[A1147] Item delyuerd xij yerdes of right crimosyn veluete.

[A1148] Item delyuerd iiij yerdes of right crimosyn veluete.

[A1147–48] For fotemens doblettes and hoses

[A1149] Item delyuerd xvj yerdes iij quarters of crimosyn veluete pirled.

[A1149–50] To John Powney yeman of thenchemen anno xj^mo.

[A1150] Item delyuerd xx yerdes di quarter of crimosyn veluete pirled.

[A1150–51] For the henchemen

[A1151] Item delyuerd by the kinges commaundement to Henry Norres xiij yerdes of blacke veluete for a gowne.

[A1152] Item delyuerd by the kinges commaundement to John de paris xiiij yerdes quarter of crimosyn veluete to lyne a gowne of yelowe tissew for ye king.

[A1153] Item delyuerd to Wiliam mortemer iiij yerdes of purpull veluete to enbrawder the border of the Riche cloth of estate of crimosyn tissewe.

[A1154] Item delyuerd to John de paris xiiij yerdes quarter of purpull veluete to to[272] lyne a gowne of white cloth of gold of damaske for the king.

[A1155] Item delyuerd to John de paris by the kinges commaundement ij yerdes of blacke veluete to welt a gowne of blacke tylsent for the king.

Henry R

Summa pagine — CCCCiiij^xx xix yerdes di

f. 38r

Memorandum delyuerd at diuerse tymes to Richard Gibson by the kinges commaundement from the xix^th day of marche anno xj^mo vnto the iij^de may anno xij^mo thies parcelles of velvetes ensuyng spent towardes the preparyng of the kinges Justes ayenstes the metyng of the french king at Calais[273]

[A1156] Furst in Russet veluete pyrled — xxiiij yerdes.

[A1156–58] LM: To Richard Gibson For Justes at Calais.

[A1157] Item in Russet veluete — DCClxv yerdes quarter.

[A1158] Item in white veluete — Cviij yerdes.

Delyuerd For gentelmen wayters & other attenders opon the kinges on horsbacke & on fote thies parcelles

[A1159] Item in Russet veluete — lxviij yerdes di quarter.

[A1159–60] To Richard Gibson for the kinges waiters.

[A1160] Item in yelowe veluete — xlv yerdes.

Delyuerd for themparell of the kinges maskers thies parcelles of veluete ensuyng / that is to say

[A1161] Furst in right crimosyn veluete — iiij^xx yerdes.

[A1161–63] LM: To Richard Gibson for the kinges maskers.

[A1162] Item in yelowe veluete — xv yerdes.

[A1163] Item in blacke veluete — iiij yerdes.

Henry R

Delyuerd by the kinges commaundement to Doctor Rawson clerke of the kinges Closet for vestmentes & frontes for aulters anno xij^mo

[A1164] Furst lv yerdes of crimosyn veluete opon veluete.

[A1164–65] LM: anno xij^mo viij^mo die maii.[274]

[A1165] Item xix yerdes quarter di of crimosyn veluete opon veluete pirled.

[A1166] Item xij yerdes of blacke veluete delyuerd to the kinges grace by thandes of Care.

Henry R

[A1167] Item to John de paris xij yerdes quarter of russet veluete for a nyght gowne.

[A1167–69] LM: anno xij^mo xiiij^mo die maii.[275]

[A1168] Item delyuerd to the said John de paris iiij yerdes of crimosyn veluet to border a Cloke of scarlet for the kinges grace.

[A1169] Item delyuerd to Mortemer di yerde of purpull veluete to performe the border of the ryche cloth of estate of crimosyn tissewe.

Henry R

Summa pagine — M^l CCxj yerdes di

f. 38v

Delyuerd by the kinges commaundement at diuerse tymes thies parcelles of veluetes ensuyng of diuerse collors

[A1170] Item xxvij yerdes of blewe veluete delyuerd to Forster for ye kinges vse.

[A1170–74] LM: anno xij^mo ij^do die Junii.[276]

[A1171] Item delyuerd to George Lovekyn xij yerdes di of blacke veluete for a fote mantelle & a sadelle house for the king.

[A1172] Item delyuerd to Nicolas majer a di yerde of russet veluete to perform the coueryng of a sadelle howse for the kinges mule.

[A1173] Item delyuerd to George Lovekyn xvij yerdes of Russet veluete for fote clothes & harnes for the kinges mewlys.

[A1174] Item delyuerd to the king xix yerdes quarter di of blacke veluete.

[A1175] Item delyuerd to John de pares xiij yerdes of blacke veluete for a Frocke for the kinges grace.

[A1175] LM: anno xij^mo xxvij^to die Junii.[277]

Henry R

Summa partes — iiij^xx ix yerdes quarter di

Summa totalis of veluetes of diuerse collors a vij^mo die decembris anno xj^mo RR Henrici viij^ui vsque xxv^mo die Julii anno xij^mo RR euisdem domini Regis[278]

M^l M^l CClxxiij yerdes quarter di

[A1176] Item delyuerd by the kinges commaundement to John de paris xvj yerdes of blacke veluete for a Frocke for the king.

[A1176–81] LM: anno xij^mo vj^o die augusti.[279]

[A1177] Item delyuerd to the said John de paris ij yerdes of Russet veluet for dobill weltyng of a Cote of Russet cloth for the king.

[A1178] Item delyuerd to John de paris ij yerdes iij quarters of blac veluete for a longe partelet & for weltyng of a doblet of blac saten for ye king.

[A1179] Item delyuerd to Maryan a yerde quarter of blacke veluete for coueryng the skabardes and gyrdelles of certan woodeknyves & swerdes for ye king.

[A1180] Item delyuerd to John de paris xiij yerdes of blacke veluete for a gowne for the king with a high coller.

[A1181] Item delyuerd to John de parris xvj yerdes of Russet veluete for a gowne for the king.

[A1182] Item delyuerd to John de paris xxxij yerdes of blac veluete for a gowne and a shammer for the king.

[A1182–84] LM: anno xij^mo vij^mo die Octobris.[280]

[A1183] Item delyuerd to the said John ij yerdes of blacke veluete for weltyng of iij doblettes of white tylsent & a gowne of blacke saten for ye king.

[A1184] Item delyuerd to William Hosyer di yerde & di quarter of blacke veluete to welte the stockes of a payre of hose for the king.[281]

Henry R

f. 39r

[A1185] Item delyuerd by the kinges commaundement to Forster a yerde quarter di of crimosyn veluete for collers & moselles for mastyes sent to the frenche king.

[A1185–87] LM: anno xij^mo xvij^mo die decembris.[282]

[A1186] Item delyuerd to William Hosyer di yerde di quarter of blac veluete for weltyng of iij payre of hoses of white tylsent for the king.

[A1187] Item delyuerd to John de paris xiij yerdes of blac veluete for a gowne with a high collor for the kinges grace.

Henry R

Summa — C yerdes di di quarter[283]

f. 39v [blank][284]

f. 40r[285]

Sattens of dyuerse collors delyuerd by the kinges commaundement at dyuerse tymes

[A1188] Item delyuerd by the kinges commaundement to Hilton xvj yerdes iij quarters of white satten for a mantelle for the kinges grace.

[A1188–99] LM: anno viij^o xxxj^o die decembris.[286]

[A1189] Item delyuerd by the kinges commaundement to Mortemer iiij yerdes of crimosyn satten for thenbrauderyng of Roses & crownes for six score Riche Cootes of Redde cloth for the garde.

[A1190] Item delyuerd by the kinges commaundement to Hilton iij yerdes of Crimosyn satten for a doblet for the kinges grace.

[A1191] Item delyuerd to mortemer ij yerdes quarter of Crimosyn saten for the performyng of Roses for vj Riche Cotes of red cloth for the garde.

[A1192] Item delyuerd to John Scutt a yerde of blacke satten for Coller Cuffes and Fentes to a gowne of blake veluete for my lady Prynces.

[A1193] Item delyuerd by the kinges commaundement to Syr Thomas bollayn iij yerdes of crimosyn satten for a doblet.

[A1194] Item delyuerd by the kinges commaundement to the Quenes grace ij yerdes of crimosyn satten.

[A1195] Item delyuerd to Hilton by the kinges commaundement iij yerdes quarter of crimosyn satten for a doblet for the kinges grace.

[A1196] Item delyuerd to Hilton by the kinges commaundement iij yerdes of grene satten for a doblet for the kinges grace.

[A1197] Item delyuerd [to] Hilton iij yerdes quarter of Crimosyn satten for a doblet for the kinges grace.

[A1198] Item delyuerd to Hilton by the kinges commaundement iij yerdes quarter of blake satten for a doblet for the kinges goode grace.

[A1199] Item delyuerd to Richard Gibson by the kinges commaundement ix yerdes of white satten to be put in to a base & a trapper partie with cloth of red and blewe tylsent for the kinges grace.

[A1200] Item delyuerd to Richard Gibson ix yerdes of blake satten for half a base & half a trapper for the kinges grace.

[A1200–03] LM: anno ix° xxiiij° die Junii.[287]

[A1201] Item delyuerd to Richard Gibson xlv yerdes di of Russet satten for iiij half bases iiij half trappers for iiij men of armes on the kinges side at Justes.

[A1202] Item delyuerd to Richard Gibson ix yerdes of blacke saten for half a base and half a trapper for Syr Jeffrey Gates.

[A1203] Item delyuerd to Richard Gibson lxiiij yerdes quarter of blewe satten for vj half bases & vj half trappers for vj men of armes on the kinges syde at Justes.

Henry R

Ciiijxx j yerdes di *Saten*

f. 40v

Sattens of dyuerse collors

[A1204] Item delyuerd to Richard Gibson xj yerdes di of grene satten for half a base and half a trapper for Sir William knighton.

[A1204–08] LM: anno ix^{mo} xxviiij^{mo} die Junii.[288]

[A1205] Item delyuerd to Richard Gibson xx yerdes di of tawny saten for ij half bases & ij half trappers for ij men of armes on ye kinges syde at Justes.

[A1206] Item delyuerd to Richard Gibson CCCxxv yerdes of white satten for bases and trappers for xiiij knightes and gentilmen for their half Cotes & for x hole Cootes for x officers spent at Justes.

[A1207] Item delyuerd to Richard Gibson xlj yerdes di of crimosyn satten for iiij half bases & iiij half trappers for iiij men of armes on the kinges syde at the same Justes.

[A1208] Item delyuerd to Richard Gibson liij yerdes of yelowe satten for vij half bases and trappers for vij men of armes on ye kinges syde at [the] Justes.

[A1209] Item delyuerd to William Hosier ij yerdes di of grene saten for ye stockes of ij payre of lether hose for the kinges Grace.

[A1210–21] LM: anno ix^{no} primo die Julii.[289]

[A1210] Item delyuerd to Hilton iiij yerdes iij quarters of grene satten for the garding of a Riding Cote and a stalking Cote of grene veluete.

[A1211] Item delyuerd to William Hosier one yerde quarter of crimosyn satten for ye stockes of a payre of hose for the king.

[A1212] Item delyuerd by the kinges commaundement to Hilton v yerdes quarter of crimosyn satten for a doblet Ruffed for the king.

[A1213] Item di yerde of crimosyn satten.

[A1214] Item di yerde of purpull satten.

[A1215] Item di yerde of white satten.

[A1216] Item di yerde of grene satten.

[A1217] Item di yerde of blake satten

[A1218] Item di yerde of Russet satten.

[A1219] Item di yerde of yelowe satten.

[A1213–19] RM: delyuerd to Hylton for stomagers for the kinges grace.

[A1220] Item delyuerd to Hilton iij quarters of blake saten for ij nyght bonettes for ye king.

[A1221] Item delyuerd to Hilton iij yerdes of crimosyn saten for an armyng doblet for ye king.

[A1221–24] LM: anno ix^{mo} xij^{mo} die Julii.[290]

[A1222] Item delyuerd to Hilton vj yerdes di of purpull satten for the lynyng of half a Cote of white cloth of tissewe & purpull veluete pirled for ye king.

[A1223] Item delyured to Hilton vj yerdes <di> yerdes of white satten for the lynyng of half a Coote of white cloth of tissewe & purpull velwet pyrled.

[A1224] Item delyuerd by the kinges commaundement to James James[291] Worsley v yerdes di of blake satten for half a Cote.

Henry R

[A1225] Item delyuerd to Hilton by the kinges commaundement iiij yerdes of grene satten for the garding of ij Cotes of grene velwete for the king.

[A1225] LM: anno ix^{mo} xviij° die Julii.[292]

Henry R

iiij^{C} iiij^{xx} xv yerdes di

f. 41r

Sattens of dyuerse collors

[A1226] Item delyuerd to mortymer by the kinges commaundement a quarter yerde of crimosyn satten for Roses for iiij Ridyng Cotes for ij yomen of the garde.

[A1226–31] LM: anno ix^{mo} xxv^{to} die Octobris.[293]

[A1227] Item delyuerd to William hosyer by the kinges commaundement ij yerdes di of Russet saten for ye stockes for the stockes[294] of ij payr of hose for the kinges grace.

[A1228] Item delyuerd to Hilton by the kinges commaundement iij quarters of Russet saten for ij nyght bonettes of the king.

[A1229] Item delyuerd to Hilton by the kinges commaundement viij yerdes quarter of Russet satten for ij doblets with bases for the kinges grace.

[A1230] Item delyuerd to the quenes grace by the kinges commaundement iij yerdes of tawnye satten for a kyrtelle for my lady princes.

[A1231] Item delyuerd to the quenes grace by the kinges commaundement di yerde of crimosyn satten for a stomager.

[A1232] Item delyuerd to Hilton by the kinges commaundement iij quarters of blacke satten for ij Ridyng Cappes for the kinges grace.

[A1232–33] LM: anno ix^{mo} iiij^{to} die Nouembris.[295]

[A1233] Item delyuerd by the kinges commaundement to Hilton iij quarters of crimosyn satten for ij stomagers for the kinges grace.

[A1234] Item delyuerd to Hilton by the kinges commaundement xv yerdes of purpull tylsent for a mantelle for the kinges grace.

[A1234–43] LM: anno ix^{mo} iiij^{to} die decembris.[296]

[A1234–43] LM: Tilsenttes of dyuerse collors whiche shulde be enterd.

[A1235] Item delyuerd to Hilton xv yerdes di of blacke tylsent by the kinges commaundement for a Jaquet and ij doblets for the king.

[A1236] Item delyuerd to William Hosier by the kinges commaundement ij yerdes di of blacke tylsent for the stocking of ij pair of hose for the king.

[A1237] Item delyuerd to Hilton by the kinges commaundement xiij yerdes of blake tylsent for a Coote for the kinges grace.

[A1238] Item delyuerd to Richard Justice by the kinges commaundement vij yerdes of purpull Tilsent for the quenes grace.

[A1239] Item delyuerd to Richard Justice by the kinges commaundement vij yerdes blake tylsent for the quenes grace.

[A1240] Item delyuerd to Richard Justice by the kinges commaundement vij yerdes of blewe tylsent for the quenes grace.

[A1241] Item delyuerd to Richard Justice by the kinges commaundement vij yerdes of crimosyn <Saten rawed> tylsent for the quenes grace.

[A1242] Item delyuerd by the kinges commaundement to Hilton iiij yerdes di of blacke tylsent for an almayn doblet enbrauderd with damaske gold for ye king.

[A1242–45] LM: anno ix^{mo} iij^{to} die Januarii.[297]

[A1243] Item delyuerd to Willliam Hosier by the kinges commaundement a yerde quarter of blacke tylsent for stocking of a paire of hose to the same doblet.

[A1244] Item delyuerd to Hilton by the kinges commaundement vj yerdes of Russet satten for ij doblettes for the kinges grace.

[A1245] Item delyuerd to William Hilton by the kinges commaundement di yerd of crimosyn saten for a brest of a doblet.

t — lxxij yerdes iij quarters

Henry R

xxiij yerdes quarter

f. 41v

Sattens of diuerse collors

[A1246] Item delyuerd by the kinges commaundement to Willian Hosier ij yerdes di of Russet satten for ij payr of Russet hose.

[A1246–50] LM: anno ix^{mo} vj^{to} die Februarii.[298]

[A1247] Item delyuerd by the kinges commaundement to Hilton vj yerdes crimosyn satten for ij doblets for the kinges grace.

[A1248] Item delyuerd by the kinges commaundment to Hilton ij yerdes di of crimosyn satten for the stocking of a pair of hose to ye same doblet.

[A1249] Item delyuerd by the kinges commaundement to Hilton iij yerdes quarter of crimosyn saten for a longe doblet for the kinges grace.

[A1250] Item delyuerd by the kinges commaundement to the said Hilton di yerde of crimosyn satten for a placard for the king.

[A1251] Item delyuerd by the kinges commaundement to Hilton ij yerdes di of blac satten ij yerdes di of Russet satten and ij yerdes di of crimosyn satten for making iij doblets for lytell master Carre.

[A1251–52] LM: anno ix^{mo} xxvj^{to} die marcii.[299]

[A1252] Item delyuerd to mr Wyse at Richemond ij yerdes of crimosyn satten for the kinges graces vse.

Henry R

[A1253] Item delyuerd to Hilton by the kinges commaundement iiij yerdes of grene satten for a doblet with Ruff slyves for the kinges grace.

[A1253–59] LM: anno x^{mo} xij^{mo} die aprilis.[300]

[A1254] Item delyuerd to William Hosyer by the kinges commaundement a yerde quarter of grene satten for stockes for hoses to the same doblet.

[A1255] Item delyuerd to Hilton by the kinges commaundement vij yerdes of grene satten for Jaquet for the kinges grace.

[A1256] Item delyuerd to Hilton by the kinges commaundement xv yerdes of Crimosyn satten for ij Jaquettes for the kinges grace.

[A1257] Item delyuerd to Hilton by the kinges commaundement vj yerdes ~~vj yerdes~~ of crimosyn satten for ij doblettes for the kinges grace.

[A1258] Item delyuerd to William Hosier by the kinges commaundement ij yerdes di of crimosyn satten for stockes for hoses to the same doblettes.

[A1259] Item delyuerd to William Hosier by the kinges commaundement ij yerdes di of blacke satten for stockes for ij payre of hoses.

[A1260] Item delyerd to Hilton by the kinges commaundement iij yerdes of grene satten for a doblet for the kinges grace.

[A1260–63] LM: anno x^{mo} xv^{mo} die Maii.[301]

[A1261] Item delyuerd by the kinges commaundement a yerde di of grene satten for a partelet for the kinges grace.

[A1262] Item delyuerd to Hilton by the kinges commaundement a yerde di of blacke satten for a partelet for the kinge grace.

[A1263] Item delyuerd to Hilton by the kinges commaundement <iiij yerdes> iij quarters di quarter of white satten for a stalkyng Cote & a bonet for the kinges grace.

Henry R

lxxiij yerdes quarter di

f. 42r

Sattens of diuerse collors

[A1264] Item delyuerd to Syr Rauf Egerton knight by the kinges commaundement iij yerdes of blacke sattyn for a doblet.

[A1264–71] LM: anno x^{mo} primo die Junii.[302]

[A1265] Item delyuerd by the kinges commaundement to mr Knolles gentylman vssher iij yerdes of blacke satten for a doblet.

[A1266] Item delyuerd to Hilton by the kinges commaundement of [a] demy yerde of crimosyn saten / di yerde of blacke saten / di yerde of white saten / di yerde of yelow saten / di yerde of Russet satten / di yerde of blewe saten / di yerde of grene satten / di yerde of crimosyn saten and di yerde of grene satten for stomagers for ye king.

[A1267] Item delyuerd to William Hosyer a yerde quarter of crimosyn satten delyuerd by the kinges commaundement for stockes of a payre of scarlet hoses.

[A1268] Item delyuerd to William Hosier by the kinges commaundement iij yerdes iij quarters of crimosyn satten for stockes of iij payre of hose for the king.

[A1269] Item delyuerd to Hilton by the kinges commaundment ix yerdes of crimosyn satten for to couer ij doblettes with Russet slyves.

[A1270] Item delyuerd to Hilton ij yerdes di of crimosyn satten by the kinges commaundement for to couer the stockes of hoses.

[A1271] Item delyuerd to Hilton by the kinges commaundement di yerde of blewe satten to lyne a boke coueryng for the kinge.

[A1272] Item delyuerd to Hilton by the kinges commaundement xiiij yerdes of grene satten to lyne a gowne of grene velwete.

[A1272–74] LM: anno x^{mo} xiij^{o} die Junii.[303]

[A1273] Item delyuerd to Hilton by the kinges commaundement xiiij yerdes of blac saten for lynyng of a gowne of blacke velwete for the king.

[A1274] Item delyuerd to Babam sergeaunt of the Confessonary by the kinges commaundement iij yerdes of blacke satten for a doblet.

Henry R

[A1275] Item delyuerd by the kinges commaundemente di yerde of grene saten di yerde of russet saten di yerde of crimosyn saten and di yerde of purpull saten — For stomagers for the quenes grace.

[A1275] LM: iiij^{to} die augusti anno x^{mo}.[304]

[A1276] Item delyuerd by the kinges commaundement to Hilton xvij yerdes of purpull saten for lynyng of a glaudkyn of purpull cloth of gold dammaske.

[A1276–78] LM: xvij^{mo} die augusti a x^{mo}.[305]

[A1277] Item delyuerd to the said Hilton xiij yerdes quarter of crimosyn saten for lynyng of a glaudkyn of white cloth of siluer with wyde slyves cut & pointed opon cloth of gold with a border Richely enbrauderd for the kinges grace.

[A1278] Item delyuerd to William Hilton xxvij yerdes of crimosyn saten for a longe gowne with wyde slyves lyned with riche cloth of gold tissewe for the kinge.

Henry R

Cxxv yerdes iij quarters

f. 42v

Satens of diuerse collors

[A1279] Item delyuerd by the kinges commaundement to Hilton xiij yerdes di of purpull saten to couer a doblet & a Jaquet of purpull cloth of gold tissewe for the kinges grace — xiij yerdes di.

[A1279–81] LM: xvij^{mo} die augusti anno x^{mo}.[306]

[A1280] Item delyuerd to William hosier a yerde quarter of purpull saten to couer the stockes of a payre of hose of purpull cloth of gold tissewe for the king.

[A1281] Item delyuerd to William hosyer ij yerde di of crimosyn saten for ye stockes of ij payr of hose for the kinges grace.

[A1282] Item delyuerd by the kinges commaundement to Richard Gibson for vj lades garmentes to euery garment xv yerdes of blewe saten for the kinges disguysyng ayenst the komyng of thembassadors of Fraunce — iiij^{xx} x yerdes.

[A1282–83] LM: xvij^{mo} die augustii anno x^{mo}.[307]

[A1283] Item delyuerd by the kinges commaundement to the same Richard Gibson for vj garmentes for vj lordes to every garment vj yerdes of blewe saten for the said disguysing ayenst the comyng of the said enbassadors — xxxvj yerdes.

Henry R

[A1284] Item delyuerd by the kinges commaundement to Richard Gibson towardes the kinges Riche mumrye in blew satten at iij diuerse tymes the somme of CCCvij yerdes iij quarters di.

[A1284] LM: xix^{o} die Septembris anno x^{mo}.[308]

[A1285] Item delyuerd by the kinges commaundement to Richard Gibson towardes the kinges riche memrye in white saten amountyng vnto the somme of lxvij yerdes iij quarters.

[A1286] Item delyuerd by the kinges commaundement to Syr Edwarde Guylforde towardes a base & a trapper in blacke saten in all xv yerdes.

[A1287] Item delyuerd to Hilton xiiij yerdes of blacke satten for a chammer with iij borders of blacke velwete furred with sabulles for the king.

[A1287–88] LM: primo die Octobris anno x^{mo}.[309]

[A1288] Item delyuerd to Hilton a yerde di of crimosyn saten to performe a cape of a gowne of crimosyn saten latesed furred with sabulles.

Henry R

[A1289] Item delyuerd to John Copynger by the kinges commaundement a Remnaunte [of] ij yerdes di & nayle of crimosyn saten.

[A1289–91] LM: xxij^{do} die Octobris anno x^{mo}.[310]

[A1290] Item delyuerd to Hilton by the kinges commaundement x yerdes of russet satten for a Jaquet & a partelet for the kinges grace.

[A1291] Item delyuerd to Hilton by the kinges commaundement xiiij yerdes of blacke saten for [a] Chammer for the kinges grace.[311]

Henry R

v^{C} lxxv yerdes iij quarters di.

f. 43r

Satens of diuerse collors

[A1292] Item delyuerd to Hilton by the kinges commaundement vj yerdes of white satten for ij doblettes for the kinges grace.

[A1292–300] LM: primo die Nouembris anno x^{o}.[312]

[A1293] Item delyuerd to William Hosyer by the kinges commaundement ij yerdes di of white saten to stock ij payre of hose for the king.

[A1294] Item delyuerd to William Hilton by the kinges commaundement iij quarters di of blacke saten for ij closse Cappes for the king.

[A1295] Item delyuerd by the kinges commaundement to Hilton iij yerdes of crymosyn saten for a doblet for the king.

[A1296] Item delyuerd to Hilton by the kinges commaundement iij yerdes of blac saten for a doblet for the king.

[A1297] Item delyuerd to William Hosyer by the kinges commaundement a yerde quarter of crimosyn saten for stockes to a payre of hose for the king.

[A1298] Item delyuerd to Mortymer by the kinges commaundement ij yerdes iij quarters of blewe saten for thenbrauderyng of Carres his Cote.

[A1299] Item delyuerd to mastres Jenyns by the kinges commaundement a quarter di of crimosyn saten for to make two purses for the king.

[A1300] Item delyuerd to mastres Jenyns by the kinges commaundement a quarter di of blacke sattyn to make ij porses for the king.

[A1301] Item delyuerd by the kinges commaundement to Hilton iij yerdes of crimosyn satten for to make a doblet for the king.

[A1301–02] LM: iiij^{to} die Februarii anno x^{mo}.[313]

[A1302] Item delyuerd by the kinges commaundement to the said Hilton iij quarters of blake saten for ij close Cappes for the kinges grace.

Henry R

[A1303] Item delyuerd to Hilton by the kinges commaundement xv yerdes iij quarters of blacke saten for a gowne for the king.

[A1303–07] LM: anno x^{mo} primo die marcii.[314]

[A1304] Item delyuerd by the kinges commaundement to Hilton iij yerdes of crimosyn saten for a doblet for the king.

[A1305] Item delyuerd to Hilton by the kinges commaundement iij yerdes of blac saten for a doblet for the king.

[A1306] Item delyuerd to William Hosyer a yerde quarter of crimosyn saten for a payre of stalkyng hose for the king.

[A1307] Item delyuerd to William Hosyer a yerde quarter of blake saten for stocking of a payre of hose for the king.

[A1308] Item delyuerd to Hilton iij yerdes of crimosyn saten for a doblet for Carre.

[A1308–09] LM: anno x^{mo} iij^{o} die aprilis.[315]

[A1309] Item delyuerd by the kinges commaundement to massy Viliart Babam sergeaunt of the confessionary Syr xofer[316] Grenishe James Vaughan mr Knolles & mr Palmer euery of theim iij yerdes of blacke satten for euery of theim a doblet — xviij yerdes of blake saten.

Henry R

lxix yerdes di quarter

f. 43v

Sattens of diuerse collors

[A1310] Item delyuerd by the kinges commaundement to Hilton vj yerdes of crimosyn saten for ij doblettes for the kinges grace.

[A1310–15] LM: anno xj^{mo} xvj^{o} die maii.[317]

[A1311] Item delyuerd to Hilton xv yerdes di of purpull saten for lynyng of a gowne of purpull tylsent for the king.

[A1312] Item delyuerd to Hilton by the kinges commaundement xv yerdes di of crimosyn saten for a gowne for the king.

[A1313] Item delyuerd to Hilton xv yerdes di of purpull saten for lynyng of a mantelle of purpull tylsent of the spanysshe facion for the king.

[A1314] Item delyuerd to Hilton xij yerdes of grene saten to couer and to be cut opon a ~~doblet~~ <frocke> of grene tylsent for the king.

[A1315] Item delyuerd to Hilton xv yerdes di of blacke saten for lynyng of a gowne of blake tylsent for the king.

[A1316] Item delyuerd to William Hilton xviij yerdes of grene saten for lynyng of a gowne of grene tissewe y^{t} was furred with Ermyns with greate wyde slyues.

[A1316] LM: anno xj^{mo} xxij^{do} die maii.[318]

Henry R

[A1317] Item delyuerd by the kinges commaundement to Hilton xv yerdes di of blake saten for lynyng of a gowne of blake veluete for ye king.

[A1317–22] LM: anno xj^{mo} xxvj^{o} die maii.[319]

[A1318] Item delyuerd by the kinges commaundement to Hilton xv yerdes di of blake saten for lynyng of a mantelle of blake veluete for the king.

[A1319] Item delyuerd by the kinges commaundement to Hilton iij yerdes of grene saten to couer a doblet of grene tylsent for the king.

[A1320] Item delyuerd to Hilton by the kinges commaundement xj yerdes di of crimosyn saten to couer a cote of cloth of gold for the king.

[A1321] Item delyuerd to Hilton by the kinges commaundement xij yerdes of grene saten for a frocke for the king.

[A1322] Item delyuerd to William Hosyer a yerde quarter of grene saten to couer the stockes of grene tylsent of a payre of hose for the king.

[A1323] Item delyuerd by the kinges commaundement to Hilton vj yerdes of white satten for ij doblettes for the kinges grace.

[A1323–28] LM: anno xj^{o} xxiij^{o} die Junii.[320]

[A1324] Item delyuerd to William Hosyer iij yerdes iij quarters of white saten for stockyng of iij payres of white hose for the king.

[A1325] Item delyuerd to William Hilton by the kinges commaundement iij yerdes of crimosyn saten for a doblet for the king.

[A1326] Item delyuerd to Hilton by the kinges commaundement vj yerdes of whit saten for ij doblettes for the kinges grace.

[A1327] Item delyuerd by the kinges commaundement iij yerdes of grene saten for a doblet for the kinges grace.

[A1328] Item delyuerd to William Hosyer by the kinges commaundement a yerde quarter of white saten for stockyng of a payre of hose for the king.[321]

Henry R

Clxxix yerdes iij quarters

f. 44r

Satens of diuerse collors

[A1329] Item delyuerd to William Hilton by the kinges commaundement iij yerdes of crimosyn saten for a doblet for the kinges grace.

[A1329–32] LM: anno xj^{mo} xvj^{mo} die Julii.[322]

[A1330] Item delyuerd to Hilton by the kinges commaundement xvj yerdes grene saten for a Ridyng Coote and a di Cote for the king.

[A1331] Item delyuerd to Hilton xv yerdes of blake saten by the kinges commaundement for a frocke and a doblet for the king.

[A1332] Item delyuerd to William Hosyer ij yerdes di of blake saten by the kinges commaundement for stockes for ij payre of hose for the king.

[A1333] Item delyuerd by the kinges commaundement to Fraunces Bryan & lytell Carre a pece of <blacke> Saten conteignyng xlij yerdes parted betwixt theim for their own vse.

[A1333–34] LM: anno xj^{mo} xiij^{mo} die Octobris.[323]

[A1334] Item delyuerd by the kinges commaundement to mastres Carewe a pece of tawny saten conteignyng xxxvij yerdes for hir owne vse.

[A1335] Item delyuerd by the kinges commaundement to John de Parris taillor vij yerdes di of white saten for lynyng of a Jaquet of white siluer tissewe for the king.

[A1335–37] LM: anno xj^{mo} xiij^{o} die Octobris.[324]

[A1336] Item delyuerd to William Hosyer a yerde quarter of white siluer reysed after tissewe for stockes of a payre of hoses for the king.

[A1337] Item delyuerd by the kinges commaundement to John de Parres iij yerdes of white saten for a doblet for the kinges grace.

[A1338] Item delyuerd to John de Parris by the kinges commaundement xvij yerdes of blake saten for a Frocke & a doblet for the kinges grace.

[A1338] LM: anno xj^{mo} xxiiij^{o} die Octobris.[325]

[A1339] Item delyuerd to John de Paris xvij yerdes of crimosyn saten for a Frocke & a doblet for the kinges grace.

[A1339–40] LM: anno xj^{mo} ij^{do} die Nouembris.[326]

[A1340] Item delyuerd by the kinges commaundement to William Hosyer a yerd quarter of crimosyn saten for a payre of hose for the kinges grace.

Henry R

[A1341] Item delyuerd to John de paris by the kinges commaundement xvij yerdes of crimosyn saten for a frocke & a doblet for the king.

[A1341–44] LM: anno xj^{mo} v^{o} die Nouembris.[327]

[A1342] Item delyuerd to William Hosyer by the kinges commaundement ij yerdes di of blacke saten for stocking of ij payre of hoses for the king.

[A1343] Item delyuerd to the same William ij yerdes di of crimosyn saten for stocking of ij payre of hoses for the king.

[A1344] Item delyuerd to mastres Worshoppe by the kinges commaundemente iij quarters of blacke saten for ij pursses for the king.

[A1345] Item delyuerd to John deparis a yerde di quarter of purpull saten for new making of a false quarters & ouer bodies of a Jaquet & a doblet of purpull saten.

[A1345–47] LM: anno xj^{mo} vij^{mo} die Nouembris.[328]

[A1346] Item delyuerd to ye same John a yerde di di quarter of purpull saten for new making & mending of a Jaquet & a doblet of purpull saten enbrauderd.

[A1347] Item delyuerd to the said John di yerde of Russet saten for mendyng of a doblet of russet saten for the kinges grace.

Henry R

Summa totalis — M^{l} ix^{C} viij yerdes di quarter
Ciiij^{xx} iiij yerdes

f. 44v

Memorandum delyuerd by the kinges commaundement sithen ye viewe taken vltimo die Nouembris anno xj^{mo} by the duck of Suffolk & other the kinges commissioners thies parcelles ensuyng parcell of the clere Remayn of the said viewe[329]

[A1348] Furste delyuerd by the kinges commaundement xvij yerdes quarter of crimosyn saten for a gowne weltid with iij weltes of the same saten for ye king.

[A1348–56] LM: anno xj^mo vltimo die Nouembris.[330]

[A1349] Item delyuerd to John deparis ix yerdes of white saten for lynyng of a Jaquet of riche tissewe pyrled with damaske siluer for the king.

[A1350] Item delyuerd by the kinges commaundement to Syr Rauf Ellercar iij yerdes of russet saten for a doblet.

[A1351] Item delyuerd to mr Palmer iij yerdes of russet saten for a doblet.

[A1352] Item delyuerd to mr Knolles iij yerdes of blac saten for a doblet.

[A1353] Item delyuerd to mr Vaughan iij yerdes of russet saten for a doblet.

[A1354] Item delyuerd to Cutbert iij yerdes of russet saten for a doblet.

[A1355] Item delyuerd by the kinges commaundement to William Hosyer iij yerdes iij quarters of white saten for stockyng of iij payre of hoses for the king.

[A1356] Item delyuerd by the kinges commaundement to William Hosyer a yerde quarter of blacke saten for stocking of a payre of hose for the king.

Certan peces & Remnauntes of Satens of diuerse collors delyuerd by the kinges commaundement by Jamys Worsley yoman of his Robes to Syr Andrewe Wyndesore knight master of the kinges greate warderobe for ye kinges vse anno xj^o

Yelowe satens

[A1357] a pece conteignyng xxj yerdes.

[A1357–69] LM: delyuerd to Syr Andrewe Wyndesore knight for the king his vse xxvj^o die marcii anno ~~x~~xj^mo H viij^ui.[331]

[A1358] a Remnaunte conteignyng v yerdes.

[A1359] a Remnaunte conteignyng iiij yerdes.

[A1360] a Remnaunte conteignyng iij yerdes.

[A1361] a Remnaunte conteignyng iij yerdes.

[A1362] a Remnaunte conteignyng ij yerdes iij quarters.

[A1363] a Remnaunte conteignyng iij yerdes di quarter.

[A1364] a Remnaunte conteignyng ij yerdes.

[A1365] a Remnaunte conteignyng iij quarters di.

Saten orenge collor

[A1366] a pece conteignyng xxvij yerdes quarter.

[A1367] a pece conteignyng xxv yerdes di.

[A1368] a Remnaunte conteignyng vj yerdes quarter.

[A1369] a Remnaunte conteignyng ij yerdes di.[332]

Henry R

Summa pagine — Cliij yerdes di

f. 45r

Grene saten

[A1370] a pece conteignyng xxxvij yerdes di.

[A1370–401] LM: delyuerd to Syr Andrewe Wyndesore knight for the kinges vse xxvj^o die marcii anno xj^mo H viij^ui.[333]

[A1371] a pece conteignyng xj yerdes iij quarters.

Blewe saten Figure

[A1372] a pece conteignyng ij yerdes iij quarters.

Tawny saten of bruges pyrled grene

[A1373] a Remnaunte conteignyng iiij yerdes iij quarters.

Blewe saten

[A1374] a pece conteignyng xxxj yerdes.

[A1375] a pece conteignyng xxxix yerdes di.

[A1376] a pece conteignyng xxx yerdes di di quarter.

[A1377] a pece conteignyng xxij yerdes quarter.

[A1378] a pece conteignyng xxviij yerdes quarter.

[A1379] a pece conteignyng xxviij yerdes di.

[A1380] a pece conteignyng xxiij yerdes di.

[A1381] a pece conteignyng xxvj yerdes quarter.

[A1382] a pece conteignyng xxxv yerdes.

[A1383] a pece conteignyng xxxiij yerdes quarter.

[A1384] a pece conteignyng xix yerdes.

[A1385] a pece conteignyng xxv yerdes di.

[A1386] a pece conteignyng xlv yerdes quarter di.

[A1387] a pece conteignyng xxv yerdes quarter.

[A1388] a pece conteignyng xxij yerdes di.

[A1389] a pece conteignyng xxiiij yerdes quarter.

[A1390] a pece conteignyng xxij yerdes iij quarters.

[A1391] a pece conteignyng xxxiij yerdes iij quarters.

[A1392] a pece conteignyng xxv yerdes iij quarters di.

[A1393] a pece conteignyng xxvij yerdes.

[A1394] a pece conteignyng xxiiij yerdes quarter.

[A1395] a pece conteignyng xxj yerdes.

[A1396] a pece conteignyng xix yerdes iij quarters.

[A1397] a pece conteignyng xxv yerdes di.

[A1398] a pece conteignyng xxxv yerdes quarter.

[A1399] a pece conteignyng xxviij yerdes di di quarter.

[A1400] a pece conteignyng xxiiij yerdes di.

[A1401] a pece conteignyng xxiiij yerdes di.

Henry R

Summa pagine — DCCCxxiij yerdes
Figure — ij yerdes iij quarters
Bruges saten — iiij yerdes iij quarters di

f. 45v

Blewe satens

[A1402] a pece conteignyng viij yerdes iij quarters.

[A1402–35] LM: delyuerd to Syr Andrewe Wyndesore knight for for[334] the kinges vse xxvj^o die marcii anno xj^mo H viij^ui.[335]

[A1403] a pece conteignyng iiij yerdes.

[A1404] a pece conteignyng v yerdes di.

[A1405] a pece conteignyng ij yerdes.

White satens

[A1406] a pece conteignyng xxx yerdes quarter di.

[A1407] a pece conteignyng xxxvj yerdes iij quarters.

[A1408] a pece conteignyng xxxix yerdes iij quarters.

[A1409] a pece conteignyng xxvij yerdes quarter.

[A1410] a pece conteignyng xxiiij yerdes iij quarters.

[A1511] Item delyuerd by the kinges commaundement xiiij yerdes of blake dammaske for a Gowne for Fraunces Poynes.

[A1512] Item delyuerd by the kinges commaundement xiiij yerdes of blake dammaske for a gowne for Henry Norres.

[A1513] Item delyuerd by the kinges commaundement xiiij yerdes of blacke dammaske for a gowne for lytell Carre.

Henry R

[A1514] Item delyuerd by the kinges commaundement to John de Paris xij yerdes of Russet Dammaske for a gowne for the kinges grace.

[A1514] LM: anno xj^mo v^to die Nouembris.[356]

Henry R

iiij^C xxiiij yerdes *Damaskes*

f. 48v

Memorandum delyuerd by the kinges commaundement sithen the view taken vltimo die Nouembris by the ducke of Suffolke & other the kinges commissioners anno xj^o thies parcelles ensuyng parcel of the clere Remaigne of the said viewe[357]

[A1515] Furste delyuerd by the kinges commaundement to John de Parres xij yerdes of Russet dammaske for a gowne for the king.

[A1515–16] LM: anno xj^mo vltimo die Nouembris.[358]

[A1516] Item delyuerd by the kinges commaundement to Robert Haselrigge xij yerdes of white dammaske for a gowne for [. . .].

Certan peces & Remnauntes of clothes of gold damaske of diuerse collors delyuerd by the kinges commaundement by James Worsley yoman of the Robes to syr Andrewe Wyndesore knight master of the kinges greate warderobe for the kinges vse anno xj^mo

yelowe damaskes

[A1517] a pece conteignyng xij yerdes.

[A1517–36] LM: delyuerd to Syr Andrewe Wyndesore knight for the kinges vse xxvj^to die marcii anno xj^to.[359]

[A1518] a pece conteignyng xxxij yerdes iij quarters di.

[A1519] a pece conteignyng xxx yerdes quarter.

[A1520] a pece conteignyng viij yerdes di.

[A1521] a pece conteignyng iij yerdes.

Grene damaskes

[A1522] a pece conteignyng xvij yerdes di.

[A1523] a pece conteignyng xxx yerdes iij quarters.

[A1524] a pece conteignyng xij yerdes di.

[A1525] a pece conteignyng xxv yerdes quarter di.

[A1526] a pece conteignyng xvj yerdes di.

[A1527] a pece conteignyng xvij yerdes.

[A1528] a pece conteignyng xix yerdes di quarter.

[A1529] a pece conteignyng xij yerdes di di quarter.

[A1530] a pece conteignyng viij yerdes quarter.

[A1531] a pece conteignyng xx yerdes di quarter.

[A1532] a pece conteignyng xxij yerdes quarter.

Blewe damaskes

[A1533] a pece conteignyng xxiij yerdes di di quarter.

[A1534] a pece conteignyng xij yerdes quarter di quarter.

[A1535] a pece conteignyng xxx yerdes di di quarter.

[A1536] a pece conteignyng xxxj yerdes iij quarters.[360]

Henry R

Summa pagine — CCCCxj yerdes

f. 49r

Blew damaskes

[A1537] a Remnaunte conteignyng iiij yerdes.

[A1537–62] LM: delyuerd to Syr Andrewe Wyndesore knight for the kinges vse xxvj^to die marcii anno xj^to.[361]

[A1538] a Remnaunte conteignyng ij yerdes quarter.

[A1539] a Remnaunte conteignyng v yerdes.

[A1540] a Remnaunte conteignyng v yerdes.

[A1541] a Remnaunte conteignyng vij yerdes iij quarters.

White damaskes

[A1542] a pece conteignyng xxij yerdes.

[A1543] a pece conteignyng xix yerdes.

[A1544] a pece conteignyng xxxv yerdes iij quarters.

[A1545] a pece conteignyng xiiij yerdes iij quarters.

[A1546] a pece conteignyng xxiiij yerdes quarter.

[A1547] a pece conteignyng xxxij yerdes quarter.

[A1548] a pece conteignyng iiij yerdes iij quarters di.

[A1549] a pece conteignyng vij yerdes quarter.

[A1550] a pece conteignyng iij yerdes quarter di.

Blacke damaskes

[A1551] a pece conteignyng xxix yerdes.

[A1552] a pece conteignyng v yerdes di di quarter.

[A1553] a pece conteignyng xix yerdes.

Russet damaskes

[A1554] a pece conteignyng vj yerdes quarter di.

Crimosyn damaskes

[A1555] a pece conteignyng xj yerdes di di quarter.

[A1556] a pece conteignyng v yerdes iij quarters di.

[A1557] a pece conteignyng ij yerdes.

[A1558] a pece conteignyng xiij yerdes.

[A1559] a pece conteignyng ij yerdes quarter.

[A1560] a Remnaunte conteignyng ij yerdes iij quarters.

[A1561] a Remnaunte conteignyng iij yerdes.

[A1562] a Remnaunte conteignyng ij yerdes.

Henry R

Summa pagine — CCiiij^xx vij yerdes di quarter

f. 49v

Delyuerd by the kinges commaundement to Richard Gibson at diuerse tymes from the xix^th day of marche anno xj^mo vnto the iij^de day of may anno xij^mo for certan apparell for diuerse gentelmen & other yeueng their attendunce opon the king at his Justes holdyn at Calais ayenst the comyng of the frenche king[362]

[A1563] Furst in Russet damaske — ix yerdes.

[A1563–65] LM: To Richard Gibson for the kinges wayters.

[A1564] Item in yelowe damaske — iiij^{xx} iij yerdes.

[A1565] Item in white damaske — lxxv yerdes iij quarters.

Henry R

Summa partes — Clxvij yerdes iij quarters

Summa totalis dammaskes of diuerse collors delyuerd at diuerse tymes by the kinges commaundement as herebefore writen particulerly maketh mencion a viij^{ui} die decembris anno xj^{mo} RR H viij^{ui} vsque xxv^{mo} diem Julii anno xij^{mo} euisdem R[363]

— DCCClxv yerdes iij quarters di

[A1566] Item delyuerd by the kinges commaundement to John a Parris xv yerdes of blacke dammaske for a Frocke and a doblet for the king.

[A1567] Item delyuerd to Richard Gibson iiij^{xx} x yerdes of Russet dammaske for masking garmentes made after freres facon.[364]

Henry R

Summa — Cv yerdes

f. 50r[365]

Sarcenettes of dyuerse collors delyuerd by the kinges commaundement at diuerse tymes

[A1568] Item delyuerd by the kinges commaundement to Mortemer ij yerdes of white sarcenet for Roses for vj^{xx} Riche Cotes of rede cloth for the kinges garde.

[A1568–69] LM: anno viij^{o} vij^{mo} die Februarii.[366]

[A1569] Item delyuerd to Richard Gibson xxxvj yerdes di of white sarcenet towardes the lynyng of xv bases & xv trappers of white velwete for xv men of armys at the Justes holden at grenewiche at Whitsontydes anno ix^{o}.

[A1570] Item delyuerd to Richard Gibson ix yerdes di of blewe sarcenet for the lynyng of ij bases and ij trappers for ij men on the kinges side at [the] Justes.

[A1570–75] LM: anno ix^{o} xxviij^{o} die Juni.[367]

[A1571] Item delyuerd to Richard Gibson Cv yerdes di quarter of white sarcenet for the lynyng of bases and trappers & short Cootes for xxviij wayters & for Cootes for xvj Corsermen & other waiters on fote at ye said Justes.

[A1572] Item delyuerd to Richard Gibson vj yerdes quarter of Russet sarcenet for half Cootes for wayters.

[A1573] Item delyuerd to Richard Gibson vj yerdes di quarter of crimosyn sarsenet spent for half Cotes for wayters.

[A1574] Item delyuerd to Richard Gibson vij yerdes <quarter> di of yelowe sarcenet spent for half Cotes for wayters.

[A1575] Item delyuerd to Richard Gibson v yerdes of grene sarcenet for half Cootes for wayters.

Henry R

[A1576] Item delyuerd by the kinges commaundement to Richarde Gibson xxxij yerdes of sarcenet of dyuerse collours.

[A1576] LM: anno ix^{no} xviij^{o} die Julii.[368]

[A1577] Item delyuerd to Hilton iij yerdes of grene sarcenet for lynyng of ij doblettes one of grene velwete ruffte & thoder of grene sarcenet Ruffte for the king.

[A1577–81] LM: anno x^{mo} iiij^{to} die Maii.[369]

[A1578] Item delyuerd to Hilton xx^{ti} yerdes of grene sarcenet for lynyng of two Riding Cotes and ij di Cotes of grene velwete for the king.

[A1579] Item delyuerd to Hilton by the kinges commaundement viij yerdes of grene sarcenet for lynyng of a Riding Coote for the king.

[A1580] Item delyuerd to Hilton by the kinges commaundement v yerdes of grene sarcenet for lynyng of a Jaquet of grene satten for the king.

[A1581] Item delyuerd to Hilton xiij yerdes of grene sarcenet for lynyng of a Riding Coote of kendall with a di Cote & ij doblettes of grene saten for the king.

[A1582] Item delyuerd to Hilton by ye kinges commaundement ix yerdes of crimosyn sarcenet for lynyng of ij Jaquettes of crimosyn satten for the king.

[A1582–83] LM: anno x^{mo} xiiij^{o} die maii.[370]

[A1583] Item delyuerd to Hilton by the kinges commaundement ~~ix~~ <iij> yerdes of crimosyn sarcenet for lynyng of ij doblettes of Crimosyn saten for the kinges grace.

Henry R

ij^{C} lxx yerdes iij quarters di *Sarcenettes*

f. 50v

Sarcenettes of diuerse collors

[A1584] Item delyuerd [to Hilton] by the kinges commaundement a yerde di of blak sarcenet for lynyng of a partelet of blake saten & a Cappe for the king.

[A1584–90] LM: anno x^{mo} primo die Junii.[371]

[A1585] Item delyuerd to Hilton by the kinges commaundement iij yerdes of whit sarcenet for lynyng of a stalkyng Cote & a Cappe for the king.

[A1586] Item delyuerd to Hilton xix yerdes of grene sarcenet for the lynyng of ij Cootes thone of kendalle & thoder of grene cloth cotened for ye king.

[A1587] Item delyuerd to Hilton by the kinges commaundement iij yerdes of crimosyn sarcenet for to lyne ij doblettes for the king.

[A1588] Item delyuerd to Hilton by the kinges commaundement a yerde di of grene sarcenet to lyne a hode and a partelet for the king.

[A1589] Item delyuerd by the kinges commaundement xxij yerdes di of black sarcenet to lyne a gowne for Mr Carewe anoy^{er} for Mr Norres & ye iij^{de} for Poynz.

[A1590] Item delyuerd by the kinges commaundement vij yerdes of blake sarcenet for to lyne a gowne of blacke damaske for lytelle Carrewe.

Henry R

[A1591] Item delyuerd by the kinges commaundement to Richard Gibson in Redde sarcenet for lynyng xij garmentes for the kinges disguysyng made ayenste the comyng of thembassadors of Fraunce the somme of iiij^{xx} yerdes.

[A1591] LM: xvij^{mo} die augusti anno x^{mo}.[372]

Henry R

[A1592] Item delyuerd by the kinges commaundement to Richard Gibson lx & xvj yerdes di of blewe sarcenet for the kinges riche mumrye.

[A1592–94] LM: ix^{o} die Octobris anno x^{mo}.[373]

[A1593] Item delyuerd by the kinges commaundement to Richard Gibson lvij yerdes di of Crimosyn sarcenet for the kinges forsaid mumrye.

[A1594] Item delyuerd by the kinges commaundement to Richard Gibson lx yerdes di of blewe sarcenet for the kinges forsaid mumrye.

Henry R

[A1595] Item delyuerd by the kinges commaundement to Richard Gibson xliiij yerdes of yelowe sarcenet for the mumrye.

[A1595–98] LM: anno x^{mo} primo die Nouembris.[374]

[A1596] Item delyuerd by the kinges commaundement to Richard Gibson lxj yerdes iij quarters of blewe sarcenet for the kinges mumrye.

[A1597] Item delyuerd to Richard Gibson by the kinges commaundement xxv yerdes iij quarters of grene sarcenet for the said mumrye.

[A1598] Item delyuerd to Richard Gibson by the kinges commaundement xj yerdes iij quarters of white sarcenet for the said mumrye.[375]

Henry R

iiij^{C} lxxiiij yerdes iij quarters

f. 51r

Taffata and sarcenettes

[A1599] Item delyuerd by the kinges commaundement to Richard Gibson iiij^{xx} viij yerdes of fyne brode <sarcenet> taffeta aswell for the kinges Justes as also for his Revelles of maskelyn holden at grenewyche after the manner of Italye.

[A1599–602] LM: anno x^{mo} viij^{o} die marcii.[376]

[A1600] Item delyuerd by the kinges commaundement to Richard Gibson vj yerdes of white sarcenet spent aboutes the forsaid busynes.

[A1601] Item delyuerd by the kinges commaundement to Richard Gibson iiij^{xx} vj yerdes of blake sarcenet spent aboutes the forsaid busynes of Justes & maskelyn at grenewyche the said tyme.

[A1602] Item delyuerd by the kinges commaundement to the forsaid Richard Gibson xlvij yerdes of yelowe sarcenet spent aboutes the kinges Justes & maskelyn & other busynes at grenewyche as may appere by Gibsons boke of declaracion of all the promisses.

Henry R

Certan peces & Remnauntes of Sarcenettes Tartrons & Chamlettes of diuerse collers delyuerd by the kinges commaundement by Jamys Worsley yoman of the kinges Robes to Syr Andrewe Wyndesore knight master of the kinges greate warderobe for his vse anno xj^{mo}

Crimosyn Sarcenettes

[A1603] a pece conteignyng xiij yerdes quarter.

[A1603–14] LM: delyuerd to Syr Andrewe Wyndesore knight for the kinges vse xxvj^{o} die marcii anno xj^{mo}.[377]

[A1604] a pece conteignyng iij yerdes di di quarter.

Russet Sarnettes

[A1605] a pece conteignyng xlv yerdes iij quarters.

[A1606] a pece conteignyng xxxj yerdes.

[A1607] a pece conteignyng xxvij yerdes iij quarters.

Chaungeabill sarcenet

[A1608] a pece of Carnacion — xxix yerdes quarter.

[A1609] a pece of Tawny — xxxviij yerdes quarter.

[A1610] a pece of grene — xxij yerdes di.

Grene sarcenet

[A1611] a pece conteignyng xxxviij yerdes.

[A1612] a pece conteignyng ix yerdes.

yelowe sarcenet

[A1613] a pece conteignyng xxij yerdes.

[A1614] a pece conteignyng xviij yerdes iij quarters.

Henry R

Summa in sarcenetes — CCiiij^{xx} xix yerds di quarter

ix^{C} lxxij yerdes di di quarter

f. 51v

White sarcenet

[A1615] a pece conteignyng xxiiij yerdes quarter.

[A1615–33] LM: delyuerd to Syr Andrewe Wyndesore knight for the kinges vse xxvj^{o} die marcii anno xj^{mo}.[378]

[A1616] a pece conteignyng xxxij yerdes quarter.

[A1617] a Remnaunte conteignyng iij yerdes di.

[A1618] a Remnaunte conteignyng v yerdes di.

Blewe sarcenet

[A1619] a pece conteignyng xxviij yerdes iij quarters.

[A1620] a pece conteignyng xxj yerdes iij quarters.

[A1621] a pece conteignyng iij yerdes iij quarters.

[A1622] a pece conteignyng vij yerdes.

Tartrons of diuerse collors

[A1623] a pece of blew chaungeable — vj yerdes quarter.

[A1624] a pece of crimosyn — viij yerdes iij quarters.

[A1625] a pece of crimosyn — viij yerdes iij quarters.

[A1626] a Remnaunte of carnacion collor — vij yerdes di.

Corse White Chamlettes

[A1627] a pece conteignyng ix yerdes.

[A1628] a pece conteignyng ix yerdes quarter di.

[A1629] a pece conteignyng ix yerdes di.

[A1630] a pece conteignyng viij yerdes iij quarters.

[A1631] a pece conteignyng ix yerdes di.

[A1632] a pece conteignyng ix yerdes di.

Grene Chamlet

[A1633] a pece conteignyng vij yerdes.

Henry R

Summa in sarcenettes — Cxxvj yerdes iij quarters

Summa in ~~sarcenettes~~ Tatrons — xxxj yerdes quarter

Summa in chamlettes — lxij yerdes di di quarter

Summa totalis of sarcenettes of diuerse collors delyuerd to Syr Andrewe Wyndesore knight for the kinges vse a viij^{mo} die decembris anno xj^{o} RR H viij^{ui} vsque xxv^{mo} die Julii anno xij^{mo} euisdem R[379]

— CCCCxxv yerdes iij quarters di

Summa totalis in Tatrons delyuerd ut patet — xxxj yerdes quarter

Summa totalis in Chamlettes delyuerd ut patet — lxij yerdes di di quarter

Henry R

f. 52r

[A1634] Item delyuerd by the kinges commaundement to John aparis v yerdes of blacke sarcenet for lynyng of ij staking Cootes of grene saten for ye king.

[A1634–36] LM: anno xij^{mo} vij^{mo} die Octobris.[380]

[A1635] Item delyuerd to John aparis xvij yerdes of blacke dobille sarcenet for gowne for the king and for lynyng of the same gowne.

[A1636] Item delyuerd to John a Paris viij yerdes of blac sarcenet for lynyng of a Frocke & a doblet of crimosyn saten paned with crimosyn tylsent for ye king.

Henry R[381]

f. 52v [blank][382]

f. 53r[383]

Dyaper & Lynen cloth delyuerd by the kinges commaundement at dyuerse tymes as foloweth

[A1637] Item delyuerd by the kinges commaundement to William Hosier a yerde of lynen cloth for a [payr of] hose for the kinges grace.

[A1637] LM: anno viij^{o} xx^{mo} die Februarii.[384]

Henry R

Certan peces of dyaper and lynen cloth delyuerd by the kinges commaundement to Syr Andrewe Wyndesore knight master of the kinges greate warderobe for the kinges vse by Jamys Worsley yoman of the kinges Robes anno xj^{mo}

Dyaper cloth

[A1638] a pece conteignyng xiiij yerdes di.

[A1639] a pece conteignyng vj yerdes quarter.

[A1640] a pece conteignyng vj yerdes di.

xxvij yerdes quarter

Braband cloth

[A1641] a pece conteignyng xxx elles.

[A1642] a pece conteignyng xviij yerdes.

Holland cloth

[A1643] a pece conteignyng xxiiij elles iij quarters.

iiij^{xx}vj yerdes quarter

Lynen cloth

[A1644] a pece conteignyng xviij yerdes di.

[A1645] a pece conteignyng xj yerdes.

[A1646] a pece conteignyng v yerdes.

[A1647] a pece conteignyng ix yerdes iij quarters.

xliiij yerdes quarter

Corse holand cloth

[A1648] a pece conteignyng xl yerdes.

Clxx yerdes di

Henry R

Dyaper & [. . .]

Summa totalis of diaper delyuerd by the kinges commaundement at diuerse tymes for the kinges vse a viij^{uo} die decembris anno xj^{mo} RR H viij^{uo} vsque xxv diem Julii anno xij^{mo} euisdem R — [. . .]
Summa totalis in lynen cloth delyuerd ut supra — [. . .]
Summa totalis of holand & braband delyuerd ut supra — [. . .]

f. 53v [blank][385]

Notes

1 There is a vellum tab on this folio with the word '*Mantelles*'. Also stuck to the front of this folio, close to the binding edge, is a second tab with the words '*Coronacion Robes*'. While the king's coronation robes were not listed in this document, it is possible that this tab originally belonged to BL Harley 4217.
2 20 December 1516.
3 10 August 1518.
4 24 October 1518.
5 There is a stamp on this folio with the text 'MVSEVM BRITANNICVM'. This folio is followed by four blank folios.
6 There is a vellum tab attached to this folio with the word '*Gownes*'.
7 10 July 1517.
8 20 October 1517.
9 20 February 1518.
10 For *duke*.
11 23 March 1518.
12 10 August 1518
13 10 August 1518.
14 26 September 1518.
15 24 October 1518.
16 20 April 1519.
17 December 1519.
18 The reference to '*sir William S*' may be an uncorrected error.
19 This folio is followed by one blank folio.
20 4 December 1519.
21 21 December 1519.
22 21 December 1519.
23 21 December 1519.
24 21 December 1519.
25 26 December 1519.
26 For *blacke*.
27 This folio is followed by one blank folio.
28 26 December 1519.
29 26 December 1519.
30 14 December 1519.
31 1 January 1520.
32 18 January 1520.
33 March 1520.
34 30 April 1520.
35 4 May 1520.
36 13 May 1520.
37 Entry 126 does not appear to be included within the bracket.
38 Or possibly *Lestne*.
39 23 June 1520.
40 Uncorrected duplication.
41 26 July 1520.
42 6 October 1520.
43 The rest of the date is not given.
44 This folio is followed by one blank folio.
45 There is a vellum tab on this folio with the words '*Cootes Jaquettes Doblettes*'.
46 12 July 1517.
47 20 October 1517.
48 The vellum tab covers some of the text.
49 20 February 1518.
50 There is no heading on this folio.
51 20 March 1518.
52 29 May 1517.
53 10 August 1518.
54 26 September 1518.
55 24 October 1518.
56 18 May 1519.
57 1 December 1519.
58 30 September 1519.
59 1 April 1520.
60 18 November 1519.
61 30 November 1519.
62 27 May 1519.
63 30 April 1520.
64 30 April 1520.
65 4 May 1520.
66 For *syngell*.
67 23 June 1520.
68 This folio is followed by three blank folios.
69 6 October 1520.
70 12 January 1521.
71 January 1521.
72 The rest of the folio is blank.
73 There are three blank folios after this one.
74 There is a vellum tab attached to this folio with the word '*Spourres*'.
75 28 August 1518.
76 2 September 1518.
77 30 November 1519.
78 29 May 1519.
79 29 March 1520.
80 24 April 1520.
81 This folio is followed by one blank folio.
82 There is a vellum tab on this folio with the word '*Gyrdelles*'.
83 17 June 1520.
84 Uncorrected duplication.
85 This folio is followed by six blank folios.
86 There is a vellum tab on this folio with the word '*Coopes*'.
87 1 January 1520.
88 For *length*.
89 This folio is followed by eleven blank folios.
90 20 May 1520.
91 There is a vellum tab on this folio with the words '*Hangynges*'.
92 18 December 1519.
93 24 April 1519.
94 19 May 1520.
95 This folio is followed by eight blank folios.
96 There is no vellum tab on this folio.
97 12 July 1517.
98 1 July 1518.
99 30 December 1516.
100 26 December 1517.

[B25] Item a shamer of cloth of golde of dammaske Reysed with siluer furred with sabullus valet Cxl^{li}.

[B26] Item a gowne of white cloth of gold of dammaske furred with sabullus valet CCCxxxv^{li}.

[B26] RM: the furre taken oute & put into a new gowne of sarsenet anno xij thoutsyde Remaynyng.[15]

[B27] Item a gowne of tawny cloth of golde tissewe Reysed furred with high luzardes valet CCxxxij^{li}.

[B28] Item a gowne of tawny tylsent furred with sabullus — CCCxxx^{li}.

[B29] Item a gowne of white tylsent furred with blacke Jenettes — Cxl^{li}.

[B30] Item a gowne of purpull veluete pyrled furred with sabullus valet — CCCCxxx^{li}.

[B31] Item a shamer of Russet veluete furred with sabullus with xj buttons and xj payre and one aglet of gold — xx^{li} besides the goldsmithswerke.

[B31] LM: Ex to Mr Care anno xiij^{o} xviij^{o} die Octobris.[16]

[B32] Item a gowne of crimosyn saten furred with sabullus sett with viij Roses of diamoundes and x payre of aglettes of golde valet CCC^{li} besidis ye goldsmith werke.

[B33] Item a gowne of Russet dammaske welted with russet weluete[17] furred with blacke conye valet vj^{li}.

[B33] LM: Ex to Rauf Worsley anno xiij^{o} xviij^{o} Octobris.[18]

[B34] Item a shamer of blacke veluete welted with ij weltes of the same furred with sabullus — xx^{li}.

[B34] LM: Ex to Mr Wyse anno xij^{o} viij^{o} die Februarii[19] and ye the furre put into a shamer of blake saten anno xij^{o} xij^{o} die Marcii.[20] Ex to Jamys Worsley anno xiiij^{o} and the sabullus put into a newe gowne of Russet veluete anno xv^{o}.[21]

[B35] Item a night gowne of russet veluete furred with sabullus — xl^{li}.

[B36] Item a gowne of russet veluete furred with luzardes set with x buttons of gold valet l^{li} besides the goldsmiths werke.

[B37] Item a gowne of blacke saten furred with sabullus — CCC^{li}.

[B38] Item a gowne of blacke veluete furred with bugie set with x buttons of gold valet xxvj^{li} vj^{s} viij^{d} besides the goldsmithes werke.

[B38] LM: Ex to Master Compton mensis Nouembris anno xv.[22]

[B39] Item a gowne of blacke veluete furred with bugie — xiij^{li} vj^{s} viij^{d}.

[B39] LM: Ex to Mr Bryan anno xiij^{o} xvj^{o} die Februarii.[23]

Nicholas Vaux
Henry Guldeford

Summa pagine — M^{l} M^{l} M^{l} DCCClxxij^{li} xiij^{s} iiij^{d}

f. 2v

Gownes shamers frockes clokes glaudkyns & mantelles lyned

[B40] Item a Cloke of crimosyn veluete with a border of cloth of gold wrought in the stole lyned with blacke saten — lx^{li}.

[B41] Item a gowne of white cloth of golde tissewe damaske gold lyned with cloth of siluer valet Cl^{li}.

[B42] Item a shorte Frocke of crimosyn cloth of gold of tissewe lyned with sarcenet valet lx^{li}.

[B43] Item a mantell of white tilsent lyned with grene cloth of gold tissewe valet Cxx^{li}.

[B43] LM: Ex to my lorde of Warmonde[24] anno xiiij^{o} xij^{o} die Augustii.[25]

[B44] Item a Frocke of white tylsent lyned with white sarcenet — xxvj^{li} xiij^{s} iiij^{d}.

[B44] LM: Ex to my lorde of devonshire Mensis Nouembris anno xv^{o}.[26]

[B45] Item a gowne of purpull tylsent lyned with purpull saten — l^{li}.

[B45] LM: Ex to Sir Thomas Boleyn anno xiiij^{o} iiij^{o} die Junii.[27]

[B46] Item a gowne of crimosyn veluete lyned with white cloth of golde valet lx^{li}.

[B47] Item a gowne of grene veluete lyned with grene saten — xx^{li}.

[B47] LM: Ex to therle of Kent anno xiij^{o} xiiij^{o} die Marcii.[28]

[B48] Item a glaudkyn of purpull veluete opon veluete pyrled lyned with yelowe cloth of golde of baudkyn — iiij$^{xx\ li}$.

[B49] Item a gowne of purpull veluete pyrled with ruft slyves lyned with white tylsent valet C^{li}.

[B50] Item a mantell of grene veluete lyned with grene saten of the spanisshe faccon valet xx^{li}.

[B50] LM: Ex to Mr Wyse anno xiij^{o} viij^{o} die Februarii.

[B51] Item a Cloke of crimosyn veluete opon veluete edged with cloth of gold lyned with crimosyn saten — xl^{li}.

[B52] Item a gowne of blake veluete lyned with blacke saten — xvij^{li}.

[B52] LM: Ex to Mr Wallop anno xiij^{o} xvj^{o} die Februarii.[29]

[B53] Item a gowne of crimosyn veluete lyned with cloth of siluer — liij^{li}.

[B53] LM: Ex to my lorde chamberlayne anno xiiij^{o} xxv^{o} die Februarii.[30]

[B54] Item a Frocke of blacke veluete enbrauderd with venis gold lyned with blacke sarcenet valet xx^{li}.

[B54] LM: Ex to yonge Bullayn anno xiiij^{o} xxv^{o} die Februarii.[31]

[B55] Item a Frocke of purpull veluete enbrauderd with venys gold lyned with sarcenet valet xxiiij^{li}.

[B55] LM: Ex to Master Care mensis Nouembris anno xv^{o}.[32]

[B56] Item a mantell of blacke veluete lyned with blacke saten — xviij^{li}.

[B56] LM: Ex to Gonston anno xiiij^{o} iiij^{o} die Junii.[33]

[B57] Item a gowne of crimosyn saten lyned with purpull cloth of gold tissewe with rufte slyves valet Clxvj^{li} xiij^{s} iiij^{d}.

[B57] LM: Ex to Therle of Anguysshe mensis Julii anno xvj^{o}.[34]

[B58] Item a gowne of crimosyn saten lyned with cloth of gold of baudkyn valet l^{li}.

[B58] LM: Ex to ~~Edward~~ <Thomas> Bullayn anno xiiij^{o} xxiij^{o} die Julii.[35]

[B59] Item a Frocke of blacke saten enbrauderd lyned with sarcenet valet xvj^{li}.

[B59] LM: Ex to Mr Russell anno xiij^{o} xvj^{o} die Februarii.[36]

[B60] Item a gowne of crimosyn cloth of gold tissewe lyned with cloth of siluer tylsent with dropes valet Cxxvj^{li}.

[B61] Item a gowne of white playne cloth of golde lyned with purpull veluete valet lx^{li}.

[B61] LM: Ex to the greate aneylle anno xij^{o} viij^{o} die Februarii.[37]

[B62] Item a dobyll Clooke of blacke cloth of golde of dammaske lyned with cloth of siluer valet iiij^{xx} xij^{li}.

Nicholas Vaux
Henry Guldeford

Summa pagine — M^{l} CCCiiij^{xx} j^{li} vj^{s} viij^{d}

f. 3r

Gownes shamers frockes clookes glaudkyns and mantelles lyned

[B63] Item a doubill Clooke of blacke tylsent lyned with blacke cloth of gold of dammaske valet iiij$^{xx\ li}$.

[B64] Item a spanishe Cloke of blacke tylsent lyned with cloth of gold valet lx^{li}.

[B64] LM: Ex to Hanyball Themperors seruant mensis Julii anno xv^{o}.[38]

[B65] Item a mantell of blacke cloth of gold after baudkyn lyned with russet tylsent valet iiij$^{xx\ li}$.

[B66] Item a gowne of brode taffata welted with iij weltes of blacke veluete lyne with the same taffata — viij^{li}.

[B66] LM: Ex to Master Tyler mensis Julii anno xv^{o}.[39]

[B67] Item a Frocke of blacke veluete welted with blacke saten lyned with blacke saten set with xix payr of aglettes & one — xiij li vjs viijd besides the goldsmith werke.

[B67] LM: Ex to Mr Carewe anno xiij^{o} xviij^{o} die Octobris with aglettes & all.[40]

[B68] Item a gowne of purpull veluete lyned with white tissewe yeuen to the king by the frenche king anno xij^{mo} — Cx li.

[B68] LM: Ex to my lorde Morles mensis Septembris anno xv^{o}.[41]

[B69] Item a Cloke of tissewe lyned with purpull cloth of gold of damaske yeuen to the king by the frenche king anno xij^{mo} — Cxl^{li}.

[B70] Item a shamer of cloth of tissewe lyned with cloth of gold of dammaske welted with white cloth of tissewe yeuen to the king by the frenche king anno xij^{mo} Regni Regis Henric viij^{ui} — C iiij^{xx} ^{li}.

[B71] Item a Frocke of blacke veluete & cloth of gold tissewe lyned with purpull sarcenet youen to the king by the frenche king set with xxiiij payre of aglettes of gold — xl^{li} besides the goldsmiths werke.

[B71] LM: Ex to Mr Carewe anno xiij^{o} xvj^{o} die Februarii with aglettes & all.[42]

[B72] Item a Frocke of crimosyn veluete tylsent & crimosyn saten paned lyned with blacke sarcenet valet xl^{li}.

[B72] LM: Ex to bastarde Faulconbridge anno xiiij^{o} xxv^{o} die Februarii.[43]

[B73] Item a Frocke of russet veluete lyned with sarcenet valet x^{li}.

[B73] LM: Ex to John Copynger anno xiij^{o} xiiij^{o} die Marcii.[44]

Gownes and shamers syngle

[B74] Item a night gowne of blacke veluete single of P. A.[45] — xx^{li}.

[B75] Item a slyue of a gowne of crimosyn veluete opon veluete.[46]

[B76] Item a gown of blacke saten welted with blacke veluete — Cxiij^{s} iiij^{d}.

[B77] Item a lynyng of blacke saten that was in a gowne.[47]

[B77] RM: Remaynyng in Hiltons handes.

[B78] Item an olde gowne of purpull veluete syngle that was king Henry the vijth.[48]

[B79] Item a gowne of white dammaske paned with white cloth of siluer enbrauderd with goldsmithes werke syngle valet xvj^{li} besides ye goldsmiths werke.

[B79] LM: Ex to Mr Amadas the goldsmythes werke per Indenture anno xvj^{o}.[49]

[B80] Item a night gowne of russet veluete single valet xiij^{li}.

[B81] Item a shamer of crimosyn saten cutt opon cloth of gold lozenge wyse and hemmed with cloth of gold single — xl^{li}.

[B82] Item a shamer of blacke saten cutt opon cloth of gold lozenge wyse valet xxx^{li}.

[B82] LM: Ex to Mr Care anno xiij^{o} xiiij^{o} die Marcii.[50]

Nicholas Vaux
Henry Guldeford

Summa pagine — DCCCiiij^{xx} vj^{li}

f. 3v

Gownes shamers frockes clokes glaudkyns & mantelles lyned

[B83] Item a Frocke of blacke saten furred with sabullus.

[B83] LM: anno xiij^{o} xxiiij^{o} die Augustii.[51]

[B83] LM: Memorandum the Furre putte into a gowne of russet veluete anno xv^{mo} and the Frocke of blake saten Ex to Rauf Worsley anno xv^{o} xiiij^{o} die Decembris.[52]

[B84] Item a Gowne of taffata welted with iij weltes of blacke veluete Furred with sabullus.

[B84–85] LM: anno xiij^{o} xvj^{o} die Februarii.[53]

[B85] Item a Shamer of blacke crimosyn tylsent dammask golde doubyll welted furred with luzardes.

[B86] Item a Gowne of blake veluete with brode borders of the same furred with blake bugie.

[B86–90] LM: anno xiiij^{o} xxvj^{o} die Julii.[54]

[B86] LM: Ex to Mr Russell anno xiiij^{o} xiij^{o} die Augustii.[55]

[B87] Item a Gowne of blake veluete with ij borders lyned with blacke saten.

[B87] LM: Ex to my lorde Leonard anno xiiij^{mo} primo die Januarii.[56]

[B88] Item a Gowne of tawny veluete lyned with tawny saten.

[B88] LM: Ex to Sir William Hussey mensis Septembris anno xv^{o}.[57]

[B89] Item a mantell of cloth of siluer chekerd with borders of the same lyned with cloth of siluer.

[B90] Item a Gowne of white cloth of tissewe lyned with tylsent.

[B91] Item a spanyshe Cloke of blake veluete lyned with blake sarcenet.

[B91–98] LM: anno xiiij^{mo} iij^{o} die Januarii.[58]

[B91] LM: Ex to monsir Sha a spanyerd anno xv^{mo} xiiij^{o} die Decembris.[59]

[B92] Item a Gowne of blake veluete furred with bugie borderd with a brode border of blake saten.

[B92] LM: Ex to Sir Richard Cornwall anno xvj^{o} xiiij^{o} die Decembris.[60]

[B93] Item a Gowne of blake saten furred with luzardes with a border of blake veluete.

[B94] Item a Shamer of blake veluete furred with sabullus borderd with vj borders of blake saten.

[B95] Item a Shamer of blake saten furred with luzardes borderd with vj borders of blake veluete.

[B96] Item a Cloke of sabullus lyned with redde sarcenet & bokeram.

[B96] LM: Memorandum that the fure of sabullus was leyd into ye gowne of purpull veluete purled agenst anno xv^{o} / folio primo.[61]

[B97] Item a frenche Cloke of tawny tylsent lyned with blake veluete.

[B98] Item a dobell mantell of blake veluete borderd full of borders of the same lyned with blake saten.

[B99] Item a Frocke of blacke veluete with ij crestes of the same furred with blake coneys.

[B99–103] LM: anno xv^{mo} xxviij die Maii.[62]

[B100] Item a night gowne of russet veluete furred with sabullus.

[B101] Item a Gowne with blake veluete with a rounde cape lyned with blake saten with ij borgonyon gardes of the same.

[B102] Item a Cloke of frenche blacke lyned with blake saten and crested with iij crestes of blake saten.

[B103] Item a Gowne of blake veluete with a high coller lyned with blake saten with ij burgonyon gardes of blake veluete.

[B103] LM: Ex to master Buttler mensis Julii anno xv^{o}.[63]

[B104] Item a Gowne of taffata crested with iij crestes of blake veluete and lyned with blake veluete.

[B104–10] LM: anno xv^{o} viij^{o} die octobris.[64]

[B105] Item a Gowne of tawny taffata lyned with tawny veluete and crested with iij crestes of tawny veluete.

[B105] LM: Extra the lynyng to Sir Jamys Worseley knight.

[B105] RM: Memorandum newe furred with luzardes Anno xvj^{o} the lynyng Remaynyng.[65]

f. 4r

Gownes shamers frockes clokes glaudkyns & mantelles lyned

[B106] Item a Gowne of russet taffata lyned with russet veluete crested with iij crestes of russet veluete.

[B106–10] LM: die & anno proscripto.

[B107] Item a spanisshe Cloke of blake taffata lyned with blake veluete and crestyd with iij crestes of blake veluete.

[B108] Item a Gowne of blake veluete lyned with blake satten with ij burgonyon gardes of blake veluete.

[B109] Item a mantell of purpull frisado lyned with purpull veluete & borderd with ij borders of purpull veluete.

[B110] Item a nyght Gowne of blake veluete furred with blake conye.

[B110] LM: Ex to mistres Care mensis Octobris anno xv^{mo}.[66]

[B111] Item a Cloke of blake saten with ij borgonyon gards of blake veluete lyned with blake sarcenet & white felte.

[B111–15] LM: anno xvj^{mo} iiij^{to} die maii.[67]

[B112] Item a Cloke of blake saten borderd with ij borders & an egge[68] of blake veluete lyned with blake sarcenet.

[B113] Item a Gowne of blake veluete borderd with ij borders of blake saten furred with blake bugie.

[B114] Item a Gowne of blake dammaske welted with blake veluet furred with blake bugie.

[B115] Item a Gowne of blake saten egged with blake veluete furred with sabullus.

[B116] Item a Gowne of blake dammaske welted with iij weltes of blake veluete furred with blake bugie.

[B116–21] LM: anno xvj^{o} viij^{o} die Februarii.[69]

[B117] Item a Gowne of Russet dammaske welted with iij weltes of Russet veluete furred with blake bugie.

[B118] Item a Gowne of purpull saten borderd with iij borders of purpull veluete furred with luzardes.

[B119] Item a Shamer of white syluer & blake tylsent paned and welted furred with sabullus.

[B120] Item a Gowne of purpull cloth of gold tissue furred with Jenettes.

[B121] Item a Shamer of blake saten borderd with iij borders of blake veluete furred with sabullus.

[B122] Item A gowne of blake dammaske furred with blak Budgy with a high coller weltyd with iij weltys of blak veluet.[70]

[B122] LM: mensis decembris anno xvij^{o}.[71]

[B123] Item a gowne of Tawny Taffata furred with luzardys garded with ij burgonion gardys of tawny veluet with viij Buttons and vj payer of Agglettes of gold.

[B124] Item a froke of blak dammaske furred with blak Budgy garded and welted with blak veluet.

[B125] Item a mantell of blake Frisado garded with Blak veluet the Cape tyed with viij payer of Smalle Agglettes.

[B126] Item a froke of Blak Satten furred with Blak conny garded and weltyd with Blak veluet.

f. 4v[72]

Gownes shamers Frockys Clokis and Mantellis lyned

[B127] Item a froke of Russet Satten furred with blak conny garded and welted with Russet veluet.

[B127] LM: Extra to Sir Edward Darell the xxix die decembris anno xvij^{o}.[73]

[B128] Item a frok of Blake Satten lyned with felte and blak Sarcenet.

[B129] Item a Cloke of Blake Satten weltid with iij weltis of Blak veluet lyned with felt and blake Sarcenet.

[B130] Item a Clooke of Russet Satten welted with iij weltis of Russet veluet lyned with felte and blak Sarcenet.

[B131] Item a Shamer of purple veluet furred with luzardys weltid with the same the vpper slevis and forslevys sett with xlvj Trayfullis of pearlis Sett in gold and oon euery trayfoile v pearlis and xvj other Trayfullis of pearlis Sett in gold and in euery trayfull iij pearlys and on diamounde in the middys of euery trayfull one Pearle lacking byfore they came into the warderobe.

[B132] Item A gowne of purple cloth of golde Tyssue furred with Sabulles the slevis sett with xxvij payer of Agglettes of golde and xxvij small Buttons of gold.

[B133] Item a nyght gowne of blak dammaske furred with blak budge.

[B134] Item a Shamer of purple veluet pirled furred with blake Budge with xx payer of Smalle wrethen Agglettes and xxiiij Smalle Buttons of golde weltid with iij weltys of cloth of Siluer.

[B135] Item a gowne of Blak Taffata Bordered with blak veluet lyned with Taffata.

[B136] Item a gowne of grene Sarcenet lyned with the same weltid with iij Weltis of grene veluet.

[B137] Item a cloke of wolvis Skynnes lyned with blak Satten with twoo Bukkelles and pendauntes of golde geven to the kinges grace by my lorde Sandys.

[B138] Item a cloke of violett frisado garded with purple veluet the cape tyed with vj flatte Agglettes of golde.

[B139] Item a Spaynisshe cloke of Blak Frisado with a Border of Goldesmythis worke geven by the Quenes grace to the king.[74]

f. 5r[75]

Cotes and Jaquettes furred for wynter

[B140] Item a Cote of russet veluete garded with russet saten and furred with Conye valet xiij^{li} vj^{s} viij^{d}.

[B140] LM: Ex to Jamys Worsley anno xiij^{o} xiiij^{o} die Januarii.[76]

[B141] Item a Jaquet of Russet veluete furred with conye — viij^{li} xiij^{s} iiij^{d}.

[B141] LM: Ex to Rauf Worsley anno xiiij^{o} primo die Januarii.[77]

[B142] Item a Jaquet of russet veluete edged with cloth of gold furred with bugie valet viij^{li}.

[B143] Item a di Cote of vlffes[78] skynnes with slyves lyned with blacke saten valet vj^{li} xiij^{s} iiij^{d}.

[B143] LM: Ex to Mr Care anno xv^{o} xiiij^{o} die decembris.[79]

[B144] Item a Jaquet of russet saten furred with conye valet C^{s}.

[B144] LM: Ex to Mr Mevymar anno xiiijo xiiijo Januarii.[80]

Cotes and Jaquettes Lyned for somer

[B145] Item a iiij quarterd Jaquet of crimosyn cloth of gold tissewe lyned with blake valet iiij^{li}.

[B146] Item a litell iiij quarterd Jaquet of purpull cloth of gold of dammaske lyned with blacke saten valet iiij^{li}.

[B147] Item a Cote thone half of cloth of gold and thoder half of blewe veluete Richely garnissed with hawthornes and lettres of plate of gold valet xxij^{li} besides ye goldsmiths werke.

[B147] LM: Ex to Mr Amadas ye goldsmythes werke per Indenture anno xvj^{o}.[81]

[B148] Item a litell shorte iiij quarterd Jaquet of crimosyn veluete opon veluete lyned with blacke sarcenet valet xl^{s}.

[B149] Item a Jaquet of crimosyn veluete opon veluete lyned with saten valet xiij^{li} vj^{s} viij^{d}.

[B150] Item a Base for an armyng Cote with di slyues of veluete cutte with lettres and vndre with cloth of gold — xij^{li}.

[B151] Item a Jaquet of crimosyn veluete cutte opon cloth of gold richely enbrauderd with goldsmyth werke lyned with crimosyn saten valet xxx^{li} besides ye goldsmithes werke.

[B151] LM: Ex to Mr Amadas ye goldsmythes werke per Indenture anno xvj^{o}.[82]

[B152] Item a Cote of russet saten enbrauderd lyned with Russet sarcenet valet xx^{li}.

[B153] Item a lytelle partelet of tawny saten lyned with sarcenet.

[B154] Item a lytelle partelet of crimosyn saten.

[B155] Item a lytelle partelet of tawnye saten.

valet xx^{s} [83]

[B156] Item a lytell Cloke of scarlet lyned with blacke saten borderd with <cloth> of gold valet vj^{li} xiij^{s} iiij^{d}.

[B157] Item a Jaquet of white dammaske garnisshed with goldsmyth werke valet x^{li}.

Nicholas Vaux
Henry Guldeford

Summa pagine — Clxvj^{li}

f. 5v[84]

Cotes and Jaquettes lyned

[B158] Item a Jaquet of purpull cloth of gold tissewe newe couerd with siluer tissewe lyned with purpull saten tyed with [. . . .] aglettes of gold valet iiij^{xx} ^{li} besides ye goldsmithes werke.

[B159] Item a Jaquet of crimosyn cloth of gold tissewe enbrauderd with white cloth of siluer lyned with crimosyn saten — lxxv^{li}.

[B160] Item a Jaquet of cloth of gold of damaske couerd with crimosyn veluete enbrauderd and cutt opon the same lyned with crimosyn saten valet xxvj^{li} xiij^{s} iiij^{d}.

[B161] Item a Jaquet of crimosyn veluete enbrauderd lyned with saten — xxiiij^{li}.

[B161] LM: Ex to Sir Robert Wyngfeld anno xiij^{o} iij die Aprilis.[85]

[B162] Item a Jaquet of crimosyn veluete opon veluete enbrauderd lyned with saten valent[86] xxvij^{li}.

[B162] LM: Ex to Sir Thomas Bullayn anno xiiij^{o} xxiij^{o} die Julii.[87]

[B163] Item a Jaquet of purpull veluete Richely set with perles & goldsmythes werke cut opon cloth of gold lyned with purpull saten valet xxij^{li} besides the perles and goldsmithes werke.

[B164] Item a Jaquet of blacke veluete with di slyves enbrauderd with cloth of gold lyned with blacke saten — xxx^{li}.

[B165] Item a Jaquet of grene veluete & grene tylsent paned — x^{li}.

[B166] Item a Cote of russet veluete enbrauderd with venis golde lyned with russet sarcenet — xvj^{li}.

[B166] LM: Ex to my Lorde Lysle menis anno xv^{o} / in Julii.[88]

[B167] Item a Jaquet of purpull saten enbrauderd lyned with saten — xxx^{li}.

[B167] LM: Ex to the greate anneylle anno xij^{o} viij^{o} die Februarii.[89]

[B168] Item a Riding Cote of crimosyn saten cut opon clothe of golde of baudkyn lyned with crimosyn sarcenet welted with many weltes of cloth of gold — xl^{li}.

[B168] LM: Ex to Mr Carewe anno xiij^{o} iiij^{o} die Aprilis.[90]

[B169] Item a Riding Cote of crimosyn cloth of gold tissewe newe clocked at guysnys with cloth of siluer tissewe lyned with blacke saten valent[91] Cxl^{li}.

[B170] Item a Cote of blacke veluete tissewe lyned with blake saten — iiij^{xx} xvj^{li}.

[B171] Item a Cote of crimosyn tissewe and blake tylsent lyned with blake saten valet lxx^{li}.

[B172] Item a Jaquet of crimosyn tissewe clocked with siluer tilsent with dropes lyned with blacke saten valet iiij^{xxli}.

[B173] Item a Jaquet of blacke cloth of siluer welted with cloth of gold — xxx^{li}.

[B173] LM: Ex to Mr Bryan anno xiij^{o} primo die Junii.[92]

[B174] Item a Cote of white siluer tissewe newe couerd at guisnes with cloth of gold of siluer tissewe lyned with purpull saten — CC^{li}.

[B175] Item a Jaquet of crimosyn tylsent couerd with crimosyn saten lyned with blake saten valet xxvj^{li} xiij^{s} iiij^{d}.

[B175] LM: Ex to Mr Norres anno xiij^{o} iiijt^{o} die Aprilis.[93]

[B176] Item a Jaquet with di slyves of cloth of gold tissewe Reysed with damaske siluer lyned with white saten — Cij^{li}.

[B177] Item a Jaquet of siluer tissewe newe clocked at guysnes with crimosyn cloth of gold tissewe lyned with blacke saten — Cij^{li}.

Nicholas Vaux
Henry Guldeford

Summa pagine — M^{l} CCxxvij^{li} vj^{s} viij^{d}

f. 6r

Cotes and Jaquettes lyned

[B178] Item a Jaquet of purpull veluete with spangelles of gold smythes werke paned with cloth of siluer reysed with dammaske golde lyned with blake saten valet lviij^{li} besides the goldsmithes werke.

[B179] Item a Jaquet of blacke tylsent lyned with blacke saten <the saten woren & new with sarcenet> — xx^{li}.

[B180] Item a Jaquet of blacke damaske cloth of siluer & blacke tylsent paned & doubill welted with the same lyned with blacke saten — xxiiij^{li}.

[B181] Item a Jaquet of crimosyn cloth of gold tissewe lyned with blacke saten valet lxxiiij^{li}.

[B182] Item a Jaquet of tawny cloth of gold tissewe lyned with blacke saten valet l^{li}.

[B183] Item a Jaquet of cloth of siluer tylsent with dropes lyned with blacke saten valet xx^{li}.

[B184] Item a Jaquet of white cloth of siluer tissewe lyned with blacke saten valet lxx^{li}.

[B185] Item a Jaquet of cloth of siluer tissewe lyned with blake saten valet xl^{li}.

[B185] LM: Ex to Laco themperors seruant anno xiiij^{o} x^{o} die Julii.[94]

[B186] Item a riding Cote of russet tylsent and crimosyn cloth of gold lyned with violet saten — xl^{li}.

[B186] LM: Ex to Vise Roye of Naples seruant mensis Julii anno xv^{o}.[95]

[B187] Item a Riding Cote of cloth of gold carnacion collor & clothe of siluer lyned with purpull saten valet xl^{li}.

[B187] LM: Ex to Cezar Master of themperors horse anno xiiij^{o} x^{o} die Julii.[96]

[B188] Item a Cote of blacke veluete lyned with sarcenet — vj^{li} xiij^{s} iiij^{d}.

[B188] LM: Ex to Mr Compton anno xiij^{o} iiij^{o} die Aprilis.[97]

Cotes and Jaquettes syngle

[B189] Item a Jaquet of crimosyn cloth of gold of dammaske syngle valued at vj^{li}.

[B190] Item ij fore quarters and ij slyues of crimosyn cloth of gold of tissewe for a Jaquet — iiij^{li}.

[B191] Item iij Jaquettes of white & grene saten of bruges syngle for the kinges garde valet lx^{s}.

[B192] Item half a Cote of purpull veluete pyrled lyned with saten — x^{li}.

Dobblettes of diuerse makynges

[B193] Item a doublet of crimosyn veluete cut opon clothe of gold richely enbrauderd with goldsmythes werke lyned with crimosyn sarcenet with hose to the same — C^{s} besides the goldsmithes werke.

[B193] LM: Ex to Mr Amadas ye goldsmythes werke per Indenture anno xvj^{o}.[98]

[B194] Item a doublet of cloth of gold of damaske couerd with crimosyn veluete enbrauderd cutt opon ye same lyned with sarcenet with hose to the same — xiij^{li} vj^{s} viij^{d}.

Nicholas Vaux
Henry Guldeford

Summa pagine — CCCCiiij^{xx} [. . .][99]

f. 6v

yet doblettes

[B195] Item a doblet of purpull cloth of gold tissewe lyned with blacke saten couerd with siluer tissewe cut & edged with siluer tissewe with hose to the same — xlix^{li}.

[B196] Item a doblet of crimosyn cloth of gold tissewe enbrauderd with white cloth of siluer lyned with crimosyn sarcenet — xxxvij^{li}.

[B197] Item a doblet of white tylsent lyned with white sarcenet with hose to the same — vj^{li} xiij^{s} iiij^{d}.

[B197] LM: Ex to sir William Kingstone anno xiiij^{o} vj^{o} die Maii.[100]

[B198] Item a doblet of crimosyn veluete enbrauderd lyned with scarlet with hose to the same — xiij^{li} xiij^{s} iiij^{d}.

[B198] LM: Ex to sir Robert Wyngfeld anno xiij^{o} iiij^{o} die aprilis.[101]

[B199] Item a doblet of crimosyn veluete opon veluete enbrauderd lyned with sarcenet with hose to the same — xvij^{li}.

[B199] LM: Ex to sir Thomas Bullayn anno xiiij^{o} xxiij^{o} die Julii.[102]

[B200] Item a doblet of blacke veluete enbrauderd tufte with fyne lynen cloth lyned with blacke saten with hose to the same — vj^{li} xiij^{s} iiij^{d}.

[B200] LM: Ex to yonge Bullayn anno xiiij^{o} xxiij^{o} Julii.[103]

[B201] Item a doblet of blacke veluete enbrauderd lyned with blacke saten and tufte with lynen cloth cut in panes tyed togeders with CC perles set in gold ouer & aboue lij perles delyuerd to the kinges owne handes by Mr Wyse anno xij^{o} — xij^{li} besides the goldsmithes werke & perles.

[B201] LM: delyuerd by Mr Worsley to the kinges owne handes the CC perles set in golde in Januarii anno xij^{o}.[104]

[B202] Item a doblet of blacke veluete enbrauderd lyned with fustian the coller slyves and handes lyned with blacke sarcenet with hose to the same — Cvj^{s} viij^{d}.

[B202] LM: Ex to master Russell anno xij^{o} iiij^{o} die Aprilis.[105]

[B203] Item a doblet of purpull veluete enbrauderd with venis gold tufte with lynen cloth lyned with saten with hose to the same valued at viij^{li}.

[B203] LM: Ex to master Care anno xv^{o} ijd^{o} die decembris.[106]

[B204] Item a doblet of russet veluete enbrauderd with venis gold tufte with lynen cloth lyned with fustyan with hose to the same valued at vj^{li}.

[B204] LM: Ex to my Lorde Lysle mensis July anno xv^{o}.[107]

[B205] Item a doblet of purpull saten enbrauderd lyned with scarlet with hose to the same — xij^{li}.

[B205] LM: Ex to the greate aneyle anno xij^{o} viij^{o} die Februarii.[108]

[B206] Item a doblet of blake saten enbrauderd with venis gold lyned with blake sarcenet with hose to the same — vj^{li}.

[B206] LM: Ex to Mr Guyfford anno xiiij^{o} iiij^{o} die aprilis / & the hose to Rauf Worsely.[109]

[B207] Item a doblet of crimosyn saten enbrauderd lyned with white sarcenet with hose to the same — xij^{li}.

[B208] Item a doblet of russet saten garded with scrole werke with hose to the same — xx^{li}.

[B209] Item a doblet of cloth of gold tissewe reysed with damaske siluer lyned with blacke saten with hose to the same — xliiij^{li}.

[B210] Item a doblet of siluer tissewe couerd with clothe of gold siluer tissewe lyned with blake saten with xv syphirs and iiij payre of aglettes of gold with hose to the same — lx ^{li} besides ye goldsmithes werke.

[B210] LM: delyuerd by James Worsley to the kinges owne hande the xv syphers and iiij payre of aglettes of gold anno xiiij^{o} xiiij^{o} die Januarii.[110]

Nicholas Vaux
Henry Guldeford

Summa pagine — CCCxv^{li} vj^{s} viij^{d}

f. 7r

yet dobblettes

[B211] Item a doblet of crimosyn cloth of gold tissewe paned with tilsent siluer dropes lyned with blake saten with hose to the same valet xxxij^{li}.

[B212] Item a doblet of purpull veluete set with spangelles of goldsmythes werke paned with cloth of siluer reysed with damaske gold lyned with blake saten with hose to the same — xx^{li} besides ye goldsmithes werke.

[B213] Item a doblet of blake tilsent lyned with blake saten set with xlj payre of aglettes and lj buttons of gold with hose & [. . .] — x^{li} besides ye goldsmithes werke.

[B214] Item a doblet of blake damaske cloth of siluer & blacke tylsent lyned with blake saten with hose to the same — x^{li}.

[B215] Item a doblet of blake damaske cloth of siluer lyned with blake saten with [. . . .] small agletts of gold — x^{li}.

[B215] LM: Ex to Mr Bryan anno xiij^{o} primo die Junii / with the aglettes of gold.[111]

[B216] Item a doblet of crimosyn tylsent couerd with crimosyn saten with [. . . .] small aglettes of gold lyned with saten — xij^{li}.

[B216] LM: Ex to Henry Norres anno xiij^{o} iiij^{o} die aprilis ye aglettes Remaynyng with officers.[112]

[B217] Item a doblet of crimosyn cloth of gold tissewe lyned with blake saten with hose to [the] same — xxxvj^{li}.

[B217] LM: Ex to Mr Gifford anno xiiij^{o} primo die Januarii.[113]

[B218] Item a doblet of tawny cloth of gold tissewe lyned with blake saten with hose to the same — xx^{li}.

[B219] Item a doblet of cloth of siluer tylsent with dropes lyned with blake saten with hose to the same — x^{li}.

[B219] LM: Ex to master Cornishe anno xiiij^{o} xxv^{o} die Februarii.[114]

[B220] Item a doblet of cloth of siluer tissewe lyned with blake saten with hose to the same — xx^{li}.

[B221] Item a doblet of white siluer tissewe lyned with blake saten with hose to the same — xvj^{li}.

[B222] Item a doblet of blake tylsent garded lyned with purpull saten & cameryke with hose to ye same of thamayn[115] facion — xij^{li}.

[B222] LM: Ex to Mr Norre xij^{o} die Augustii anno xiiij^{o}.[116]

[B223] Item a doblet of blake cloth of gold after baudkyn garded with the same lyned with Russet saten & camerke — x^{li}.

[B223] LM: Ex to my Lorde of Devon mensis Nouembris anno xv^{o}.[117]

[B224] Item a doblet of cloth of siluer & russet tylsent lyned with russet saten & cameryke with hose to the same of thalmayn faccon — x^{li}.

[B224] LM: Ex to master Care anno xv° ij^{de} die decembris.[118]

[B225] Item a doblet of white tissewe with a high collor welted with cloth of gold tissewe tyed with white paris aglettes yeuen to the king by the frenche king anno xij^{mo} — xv^{li}.

[B225] LM: Ex to Laco themperors seruant anno xiiij° x° die Julii.[119]

[B226] Item a doblet of cloth of gold tissewe & cloth of siluer tissewe paned tyed with white paris aglettes youen to the kinges grace by the frenche king anno xij^{mo} — xxvj^{li} xiij^{s} iiij^{d}.

Nicholas Vaux
Henry Guldeford

Summa pagine — CClxix^{li} xiij^{s} iiij^{d}

f. 7v[120]

yet dobblettes

[B227] Item a doblet of cloth of siluer the placard & foreslyves richely enbrauderd with paris aglettes youen to the king by the frenche king anno xij^{mo} — xx^{li} besides ye aglettes.

[B228] Item a doblet of blake veluete enbrauderd with venis gold drawen with lynen cloth set with Clxxix perles of a sorte of a sorte[121] with hose to the same — x^{li} besides ye perles.

[B228] LM: delyuerd by Mr Worsley Clxxix perles to the kinges owne handes xxiiij° die Januarii anno xij°.[122]

[B229] Item a doblet of cloth of siluer the placard & foreslyues Richely enbrauderd set with pares aglettes youen to the kinges grace by the frenche king anno xij^{mo} — xx ^{li} besides ye aglettes.

[B230] Item a doblet of crimosyn saten welted with crimosyn tylsent with hose to the same — vj^{li}.

[B230] LM: Ex to bastarde Faulconbridge anno xiiij° xxv° die Februarii.[123]

[B231] Item iij doblettes of white tylsent lyned with fustian with hose to the same — xxx^{li}.

[B231] LM: Ex to arthor poulle one & a nother to an Iryssheman anno xiij° iiij° die aprilis[124] and the iij^{de} to my lorde of devon mensis Nouembris anno xv°.[125]

[B232] Item a doblet of blake veluete the placard & foreslyues tuffed with lynen cloth enbrauderd with damaske golde lyned with sarsenet youen to the king anno xij^{mo} — xx^{li}.

[B233] Item a Cote of crimosyn cloth of gold after baudkyn doubill lyned with white saten and blacke saten.

[B233–35] LM: anno xij^{mo} xvj^{mo} die marcii.

[B233] LM: Ex to yonge Bullayn mensis Nouembris anno xvo.[126]

[B234] Item a doblet of cloth of gold after baudkyn lyned with canvas cameryke and blacke saten.

[234] LM: Ex to yonge Bullayn mensis Nouembris anno xv°.[127]

[B235] Item a Jaquet of blacke veluete lyned with blacke sarcenet.

[B235] LM: Ex to William Rolte anno xiij° primo die Junii.[128]

Nicholas Vaux
Henry Guldeford

[B236] Item a Jaquet of blacke veluete lyned with tuke.

[B236–37] LM: anno xiij° xxiiij° die augustii.[129]

[B236–37] LM, RM: Vac hic for ye yoman of ye Robes wilnot be charged with Cote Jaquet nor doblet of veluete nor of saten excepte they be Richely enbrauderd with golde or siluer by y^{is} boke but onely by ye boke of warauntes.

[B237] Item a Jaquet of blacke veluete lyned with blake sarcenet.

[B238] Item a Jaquet of tawny tylsent damaske welted with tawny veluete lyned with coton and ouer with sarcenet.

[B238] LM: Ex to John Darell anno xiij° iiij° die aprilis.[130]

f. 8r

yet doblettes & Jaquetes

[B239] Item a doblet of crimosyn saten welted with crimosyn veluete lyned with canvas cambrike and sarcenet.

[B239–44] LM: anno xiij° xxiiij° die Augustii.[131]

[B239–42] LM: vac hic qz.

[B239–42] RM: The yoman of ye Robes wylnot be charged by this boke with nomaner Cote Jaquet nor doblet of veluete playne nor of saten excepte they be richely enbrauderde but onely by ye boke of warauntes.

[B240] Item a doblet of blacke saten welted with blacke veluete lyned with canvas cambrike and sarcenet.

[B241] Item a doblet of blacke saten lyned with canvas & sarcenet.

[B242] Item a doblet of blacke saten lyned with canvas & sarcenet.

[B243] Item a doblet of tawny tylsent damaske lyned with canvas & sarcenet welted with tawny veluete.

[B243] LM: Ex to John Darell anno xiij° iiij° die Aprilis.[132]

[B244] Item a doblet of tawny tylsent damaske welted with tawny veluete lyned with canvas and sarcenet.

[B244] LM: Ex to Henry Norres anno xiij° xviij° die Julii.[133]

[B245] Item a doubled[134] of blacke tylsent welted with iij weltes of blake veluete lyned with fustian.

[B245–49] LM: anno xiij° xvj° die Februarii.[135]

[B245] LM: Ex to Mr Bryan anno xv° primo die decembris.[136]

[B246] Item a doublet of crimosyn saten enbrauderd lyned with blacke saten.

[B247] Item a doublet of cloth of siluer lyned with blacke saten.

[B248] Item a Riding Cote of blake tylsent couerd with grey cloth all the cote welted with tylsent lyned with sarcenet.

[B249] Item a Coote of blake veluete & blake tylsent full of weltes of the same lyned with sarcenet.

[B249] LM: Ex to master Bryand anno xvo ij^{de} die decembris.[137]

[B250] Item a Riding Cote of blake veluete lyned with sarcenet welted with the same and tufted after thalmayn faccon.

[B250–60] LM: anno xiiij^{mo} xxvj^{to} die Julii.[138]

[B251] Item a Riding Cote with slyves of blake veluete crested & welted with the same.

[B251] LM: Ex to John Copynger anno xiiij^{mo} xij^{mo} die augusti.[139]

[B252] Item a shorte Cote of blake veluete with slyves crested & welted with the same.

[B252] LM: Ex to Rauf Worsley anno xv° xiiij° die decembris.[140]

[B253] Item a Cote panyd with clothe of golde of baudkyn & crimosyn saten lyned with sarcenet.

[B254] Item a Cote of tawny tylsent crested with tawny saten lyned with blake sarcenet.

[B254] LM: Ex to Sir Edwarde Guylford mensis Julii anno xv°.[141]

[B255] Item a Riding Cote of white tissewe & blake tissewe panyd lyned with white cloth of siluer & blake clothe of siluer panyd.

[B256] Item a Riding Cote of grene veluete lyned with grene sarcenet.

[B257] Item a doblet of cloth of tissewe tuffed with lynen cloth.

[B258] Item a doblet of tawny veluete & tawny tylsent panyd lyned with sarcenet tufted with lynen cloth.

[B258] LM: Ex to Mr Carewe anno xiiij° primo die Januarii.[142]

[B259] Item an almayn doblet of tawny tylsent lyned with blake sarcenet tufted with lynen cloth.

[B260] Item an almayn doblet of tylsent with oken Levis lyned with blake sarcenet tufted with fyne lynen cloth.

f. 8v

Cotes Jaquettes and doblettes

[B261] Item a Jaquet panyde with grene tylsent and grene velvete lyned with grene sarcenet.

[B261–66] LM: anno xiiij° iij° die Januarii.[143]

[B262] Item a Cote of blake tylsent & blake saten paned lyned with sarcenet.

[B262] LM: Ex to Mr Norres anno xv° ijdo die decembris.[144]

[B263] Item a Cote with di slyves of cloth of syluer Reysed with freres knottes of gold lyned with sarcenet & bokeram.

[B264] Item a doblet of blake tylsent crested with blake saten.

[B264] LM: Ex to Mr Norres anno xv° ijdo die decembris.[145]

[B265] Item a panyd doblet of cloth of gold & crimosyn saten the saten enbrawderd lyned with crimosyn sarcenet & bokeram.

[B266] Item a doblet of cloth of siluer raysed with freves[146] knottes of gold lyned with sarcenet and bokeram.

[B267] Item a Cote of cloth of siluer with di slyves crested with ij crestes of cloth of siluer lyned with blake sarcenet.

[B267–69] LM: anno xv° xxviij° die maii.[147]

[B268] Item a doblet of frenche blake lyned with cloth of siluer & sarcenet.

[B269] Item a doblet of cloth of siluer lyned with sarcenet.

[B270] Item a Cote of cloth of siluer with di slyves crested with ij crestes of cloth of cloth[148] of siluer lyned with blake sarcenet.

[B270–81] LM: anno xvmo viij° die Octobris.[149]

[B271] Item a Ryding Cote of russet veluete borderd with ij borders of russet saten and lyned with sarcenet.

[B272] Item a shorte Cote of russet veluete borderd with ij borders of russet saten lyned with russet sarcenet.

[B273] Item a Riding Cote of blake saten with ij cutt bordders of blake veluete & ij in the myddes with <a> ruffet partelet of blake veluete lyned with blake sarcenet.

[B274] Item a Cote of blake saten with iiij borders of blake veluet cutte & lyned with blake sarcenet.

[B275] Item a shorte Cote of blake saten with iiij borders of blake veluete cutte with a ruffet partlet of blake veluete lyned with sarcenet.

[B276] Item a doblet of cloth of gold tissewe crested with iij crestes of blake veluete lyned with white sarcenet.

[B277] Item a doblet of tylsent crested with iij crestes of blake veluete lyned with white sarcenet.

[B278] Item a doblet of blake cloth of gold with iij crestes of the same lyned with white sarcenet.

[B278] LM: Ex to John Copynger anno xv° xiiij° die decembris.[150]

[B279] Item a doblet of tynsell crested with iij crestes of the same lyned with white sarcenet.

[B280] Item a doblet of cloth of siluer crested with cloth of siluer lyned with white sarcenet.

[B281] Item a doblet of white saten with foreslyves and placarde of stole werke lyned with white sarcenet.

f. 9r

Cotes Jaquetes & doblettes

[B282] Item a doblet of blake veluete the placard and foreslyves enbrauderd lyned with blake sarcenet.

[B282–89] LM: anno xvjmo iiijto die maii.[151]

[B283] Item a Jaquet of cloth of tissewe crested with ij crestes of blake veluete lyned with cotton and blake saten.

[B284] Item a doblet of cloth of tissewe crested with [. . . .] of blake veluete and lyned with blake saten.

[B285] Item a Jaquet of purpull veluete pyrled and white cloth of tissue paned and crested lyned with blake saten.

[B286] Item a doblet of purpull veluete pyrled & white cloth of tissue paned crested lyned with saten.

[B287] Item a Jaquet of white cloth of siluer & blake tylsent paned and crested with blake saten.

[B288] Item a doblet of cloth of siluer and blake tylsent paned and crested with blake saten.

[B289] Item a doblet of blake saten with placard & foreslyues of blake tensell crested with blake veluete lyned with white sarcenet.

[B289–90] LM: anno xvjmo xviijmo die Julii.[152]

[B290] Item a doblet of white saten with placard & foreslyues of white cloth of siluer and russet tynsell paned & welted with the same lyned with white sarcenet.

[B291] Item a Riding Cote of blake veluete borderd with vj borders of blake saten lyned with blake sarcenet.

[B291–99] LM: anno xvjmo viij° die Februrii.[153]

[B292] Item a Jaquet of Russet veluete lyned with blake sarcenet.

[B293] Item a doblet of Russet tylsent crested with iij crestes of Russet veluete.

[B294] Item a doblet of tawny tylsent crested with ij crestes of tawny veluete.

[B295] Item a Jaquet of tawny veluete crested with ij crestes of tawny tylsent lyned with sarcenet.

[B296] Item a Jaquet of purpull cloth of gold tissue with iij crestes ij of white siluer and one of blake tyslent lyned with blake saten.

[B297] Item a doblet of purpull cloth of tissue with iij crestes ij of white siluer and j of blake tylsent lyned with blake saten.

[B298] Item a Jaquet of white siluer and blake tylsent paned lyned with blake saten.

[B299] Item a doblet of cloth of siluer crested with iij crestes of tylsent lyned with saten.

[B300] Item a doblet of Blak Tilsent with dropis lyned with white Sarcenet with hose to the same.[154]

[B300] LM: anno xvij° xxiiij° die decembris.[155]

f. 9v[156]

Cotes Jaquettes and doblettes

[B301] Item a doblet of purple cloth of golde of dammaske weltyd with purple veluet lyned with blak Sarcenet of my lorde ferris gyfte.

[B301–22] LM: Anno xvij° xxiiij° die decembris.[157]

[B302] Item An Armyng doblet of Crymsyn Satten enbrawdered and lyned with white Sarcenet.

[B303] Item a doblet of playne cloth of Siluer weltid with iij weltys of Blak veluet lyned with white Sarcenet with hose to the same.

[B304] Item a doblet of Blak Tylsent lyned with flanon with hose to the same.

[B305] Item a doblet of Tawny Tylsent lyned with fustian with ij weltes of blak veluet.

[B306] Item a doblet of white Tilsent lyned with fustian with hose to the same.

[B307] Item a doblet of Russet Tilsent lyned with flanon with hose to the same.

[B308] Item a doblet of blak siluer Tilsent with oken levis with hose to the same.

[B309] Item a di cote of Russet Satten with a Base of the same furred with conny garded and weltid with Russet veluet.

[B310] Item a di cote with a Base of Russet veluet with iij weltis of Russett Satten lyned with Sarcenet.

[B310] LM: Ex to William Brearton Anno xvij^{o} xxviij^{o} die decembris.[158]

[B311] Item a Jaquet of Russet veluet weltid with iij weltis of Russet satten lyned with cotton and Sarcenet.

[B312] Item a Jaquet of Blak veluet with an edge of the same lyned with cotton and Sarcenet.

[B313] Item a Jaquet of Russet Taffata weltyd with iij weltys of Russett veluet lyned with blak Bokerham.

[B314] Item a Jaquet of Blak Taffata weltid with iij weltys of blak veluet lyned with Bokerham.

[B315] Item a doblet of white cloth of Siluer dammaske weltyd with iij weltys of blak veluet lyned with fustian with hose to the same.

[B316] Item a Jaquet of white cloth of Siluer playne welted with iij weltys of Blak veluet lyned with blak Sarcenet.

[B317] Item a doblet of playne clothe of golde the placard and forslevis enbrawdered lyned with white Sarcenet.

[B318] Item a doblet of Blak Tylsent weltid with blak veluet lyned with fustian.

[B319] Item a Jaquet of Blak Tylsent and purple Tilsent paned drawen with lynen cloth.

[B320] Item a doblet of Blak and purple Tylsent paned drawen with lynen cloth with a payer of hose to the same.

[B321] Item A Jaquet with di slevis of purple blak and white Satten enbrawdered with lettres.

[B322] Item a doblet of purple blak and white Satten enbrawdered with lettres and hose to the same with xij Armyng poyntes with long Agglettes of gold enamylled.[159]

f. 10r[160]

Dyuerse Ryche Furres for the kinges owne vse

[B323] Item a Fure of pure of a Robe with a trayne for a childe.

[B324] Item a <di> Furre of pure of a Taberde.

[B325] Item a Furre of Ermyns of a cappe of maigtanaunce.[161]

[B326] Item ij sabull backes and one lytell pece of sabulles womes.

[B327] Item xiij fyne bugie skynnes. Mistress Jenyns must answer for theim.

[B328] Item a hole furre of Ermyns that was in a gowne of <y^{e}> kinges.

[B329] Item iij lytell peces of estriche skynnes.

[B330] Item a Furre of Ermyns that was in a gowne of purpull cloth of gold tissewe.

[B331] Item a Furre of Ermyns that was in a mantell of purpull tylsent.

[B332] Item a Furre of Ermyns that was in a gowne of blewe veluete.

[B333] Item a Furre of bugie that was in a Riche Jaquet of stole werke.

[B333] LM: Ex to John Porth perisshed with motys.

[B334] Item a Furre of Ermyns that was in a Cote of purpull veluete opon veluete.

Swerdes knyffes & dagers garnisshede with golde & siluer

[B335] Item a Riche swerde that was sent the king from the popes holynes the hafte & shethe of siluer & gilt with a longe gyrdelle of cloth of gold with bokelles pendaunte and studdes of siluer and gilt.

[B336] Item a Cappe of mayntenaunce of russet veluete with the holy goste enbrauderd with perles and a longe gyrdelle of gold of damaske faste to the same.

[B337] Item a berynge swerde with a sheth of crimosyn veluete garnisshed with siluer and gilt.

[B338] Item a swerde with shethe and gyrdelle of crimosyn veluete enbrauderd with gold and of nedelle werke with bokelles pendaunt studdes and chape of golde.

[B339] Item an armyng swerde with a blacke shethe and a chape of golde that was king Henry the vijth.

[B340] Item an armyng swerde with a shethe of clothe of golde tissewe with a chape of siluer and gilt.

[B341] Item a beryng swerde with a shethe of clothe of gold.

[B342] Item a holmes with a blake shethe garnisshed with siluer & gilt.

[B343] Item a longe Tocke iij square the hafte of siluer and the shethe garnisshed with siluer & gilt.

[B344] Item a gilt swerde with a shethe enbrauderd and a chape of golde valued at [. . . .]

Nicholas Vaux
Henry Guldeford

f. 10v[162]

Swerdes garnisshed

[B345] Item a spanishe swerde ye hafte of siluer enameld with a chape of siluer.

[B346] Item a twohande swerde with a sheth of crimosyn veluete enbrauderd.

[B347] Item a spanishe dager with a girdelle to ye same garnisshed with coper & gilt.

[B348] Item a proper holmes the sheth and hafte garnisshed with plate of golde with a gyrdelle the bokelles and pendaunt of siluer & gilt.

[B349] Item an armyng swerde the shethe garnisshed with plate of gold with gyrdell the bokelles and pendauntes of siluer & gilt.

Nicholas Vaux
Henry Guldeford[163]

f. 11r[164]

Diuerse smalle percelles

[B350] Item a bordor of stole werke y^{t} was opon a Riding gowne of russet veluete.

[B351] Item a bordor of stole werke of a womans gowne of crimosyn saten.

[B352] Item a bordor & cuffes of stole werke of a womans gowne of tawny veluete.

[B353] Item a bordor of stole werke that was opon a Jornet of crimosyn veluete.

[B354] Item ij other bordors of stole werke y^{t} was opon ij other Jornettes of crimosyn veluete.

[B355] Item a payr of Irisshe spores garnisshed with siluer & gilt & enameld.

[B356] Item ij gyrdelles of leder enbrauderd garnisshed with siluer & gilt.

[B357] Item xv olde banners of diuerse sortes and makinges.

[B358] Item v banners of blewe and &[165] crimosyn sarcenet with the kinges armes.

[B359] Item xxxvj baners of white sarcenet with the crosse of sainte george.

[B360] Item a baner for a trumpet with a lace & tasselles of silke.

[B361] Item xij speuselles of sarcenet of diuerse collors.

[B362] Item a stremer of blewe & crimosyn sarcenet with Roses & flourdeluces.

[B363] Item xviij Hattes thromyd with silke of diuerse collors.

[B364] Item a goodly bagge of stole werke.

[B365] Item a proper lytell powche well wrought with a girdelle with tasselles of silke & gold.

[B366] Item a pair of brigandyns couerd with grene tylsent ye collor wrought with siluer & gilt.

[B367] Item a payre of tables of euerye[166] garnisshed with siluer di gilt with tabelles men.

[B368] Item a payre of tables of bone with tabilles men & chesmen.

[B369] Item a Crucifix enbrauderd in a case of woode — C^{s}.

[B370] Item a proper Image of sainte kateryne enbrauderd with gold of venis — x^{s}.

[B371] Item a Coueryng of grene cloth of gold tissewe for a boke — x^{s}.

[B372] Item iij englisshe bokes valent [. . .]

[B373] Item a surnappe cloth of launde enbrauderd with golde at both endes and fringed at endes with golde — lx^{s}.

[B374] Item a longe towell of fyne lynen with an edge of rede aboute — x^{s}.

[B375] Item a thine boke of philosophy couerd with purpull veluete.

[B376] Item a boke of troy couerd with grene dammaske with claspes of siluer & gilt.

[B377] Item iiij paynted clothes of corse blacke bokeram.

[B378] Item a stayned cloth that was sent oute of the lande of galico.

[B379] Item ij bondelles of Carlyll leyses.

[B380] Item viij shorte narowe peces of blake saten enbrauderd with neylde werke and lettres of gold of venis.

[B381] Item a Pece of Frenge of damaske golde in a boxe.

[B382] Item iij scochyns enbrauderd with tharmys of spaigne & portingale.

[B383] Item ij Crownes & a flourdeluce enbrauderd opon crimosyn veluete.

[B384] Item an olde shorte quisshon of tawny veluete in a Cheyre.

Nicholas Vaux
Henry Guldeford

Summa pagine — ix^{li} x^{s}.

f. 11v

diuerse smalle percelles

[B385] Item ij longe greate Carpettes wherof one opon thone borde in thone house and thoder opon the borde in thoder house.

[B386] Item ij targettes thone of stile & thoder couered with blake veluete & cloth of gold.

[B387] Item a greate tuske of a bore in a case of crimosyn veluete.

[B388] Item a Roobuckes hed in a case of crimosyn veluete.

[B389] Item iij haukes Cappes of stole werke in a box.

[B390] Item a proper lytell painted coffer.

[B391] Item ij greyhonde collers wrought in the stole garnisshed with tharmys of england of siluer and gilt.

[B392] Item iiij greyhounde collers of stole werke vngarnisshed.

[B393] Item ij gloves enbrauderd with neylde werke.

[B394] Item a payre of spanisshe buskyns enbrauderd with Roses & portcules.

Nicholas Vaux
Henry Guldeford[167]

f. 12r[168]

Russet cloth of gold tissewe the grounde damaske golde

[B395] t — Item a pece conteignyng xx yerdes quarter at viij^{li} the yerde Summa Clxij^{li}.

Crimosyn cloth of gold tissewe the grounde damaske golde

[B396] t — A Remnaunte conteignyng ij yerdes at vij^{li} the yerde in all xiiij^{li}.

Tawny cloth of gold tissewe the grounde damaske golde

[B397] t — A Remnaunte conteignyng j yerde quarter at v^{li} the yerde in all vj^{li} v^{s}.

Siluer tissewe Reised with gold

[B398] t — A pece of white cloth of siluer Reised with gold tissewe conteignyng iij yerdes di yeuen to the king by the frenche quene — xxiij^{li} vj^{s} viij^{d}.

[B399] t — A Remnaunte of siluer tissewe conteignyng iij yerdes at C^{s} the yerde — xv^{li}.

[B400] t — A Remnaunte of siluer tissewe conteignyng j yerde di at iiij^{li} the yerde — vj^{li}.

Crimosyn cloth of damaske

[B401] g — A pece conteignyng xxiij yerdes iij quarters at xlvj^{s} viij^{d} the yerde — lv^{li} viij^{s} iiij^{d}.

White cloth of dammaske

[B402] g — A pece conteignyng xxij yerdes iij quarters at xlvj^{s} viij^{d} the yerde — liij^{li} xx^{d}.

Russet cloth of gold

[B403] g — A Remnaunte conteignyng ij yerdes quarter at xlvj^{s} viij^{d} the yerde — Cv^{s}.

Crimosyn cloth of gold of baudkyn

[B404] g — A Remnaunte conteignyng vj yerdes iij quarters at xlvj^{s} viij^{d} le yerde — xv^{li} xv^{s}.

Blewe cloth of gold after chamlet

[B405] g — A Remnaunte conteignyng xj yerdes quarter di at xl^{s} the yerde — xxij^{li} xv^{s}.

Nicholas Vaux
Henry Guldeford

t — xxxj yerdes di
g — lxvj yerdes iij quarters di
Summa pagine — CCClxxviij^{li} xiiij^{s}

f. 12v

Grene cloth of golde after chamlet

[B406] g — a Remnaunte conteignyng ij yerdes iij quarters at xl^{s} the yerde — Cx^{s}.

Yelowe cloth of golde

[B407] g — Item ij Remnauntes conteignyng ij yerdes di quarter at xl^{s} the yerde — iiij^{li} v^{s}.

Crimosyn cloth of golde of dammaske

[B408] g — A pece youen to ye king by ye duc of Suffolk conteignyng x yerdes — xxx^{li}.

Crimosyn cloth of gold

[B409] g — A Remnaunte conteignyng di yerde at xl^{s} the yerde in all — xx^{s}.

White baudken with floures of gold

[B410] g — A pece sowen togeders conteignyng xviij yerdes at xxxiij^{s} iiij^{d} — xxx^{li}.

Cloth of gold tissewe

[B411] Item ij shorte quarters of cloth of gold tissewe.

Nicholas Vaux
Henry Guldeford

[B412] t — Furst to Peter Fraunces debarde for a pece of white tissewe chekerd conteignyng iij yerdes at iij^{li} the yerde Summa ix^{li}.

[B412–14] LM: anno xij^{o} xviij^{o} die Februarii.[169]

[B413] t — Item for a pece of white tissewe with dropes conteignyng iij yerdes at iij^{li} the yerde Summa ix^{li}.

[B414] g — Item to the said Peter for a pece of cloth of siluer of dammaske conteignyng xxij yerdes at xl^{s} the yerde — xliiij^{li}.

[B415] g — Item to Nicolas Venasses for a Remnaunte of cloth of siluer damaske siluer conteignyng iiij yerdes di at xxxvj^{s} viij^{d} le yerde — viij^{li} v^{s}.

[B415] LM: anno xiiij^{o} xxiij^{o} die maii.[170]

[B416] t — Item to Peter Fraunces debarde for a pece of cloth of golde tissewe damaske golde reysed with dammaske siluer conteignyng Cix^{li} xx^{d}.

[B416–19] LM: anno xiiij^{o} xxiij^{o} die maii.[171]

[B417] g — Item for a pece of blake cloth of siluer of dammaske with chekerwerke conteignyng xix yerdes quarter at xl^{s} the yerdes Summa xxxviij^{li} x^{s}.

[B418] g — Item a Remnaunte of white cloth of siluer dammask of xiiij yerdes at xl^{s} — xxviij^{li}.

[B419] t — Item to William Corsye for a pece of blake cloth of tissewe of dammask siluer reysed with venis siluer [conteignyng] xv yerdes at vij^{li} ye yerde — Cv^{li}.

t — xxxv yerdes iij quarter di
g — iiij^{xx} yerdes di quarter
Summa partes — lxx^{li} x^{s}

f. 13r

Cloth of golde of diuerse makinges & collors

[B420] t — Item to William Corsye for a pece of cloth of siluer of dammaske reysed with venis gold conteignyng xv yerdes at iiij^{li} xiij^{s} iiij^{d} le yerde — lxx^{li}.

[B420–21] LM: anno xiiij^{o} xxiij^{o} die maii.[172]

[B421] g — Item to Peter Fraunces debarde for a pece of cloth of siluer dammaske conteignyng xij yerdes at xl^{s} the yerde Summa xxiiij^{li}.

[B422] t — Item Receyued of Mr Compton at newehall a pece of blacke cloth of golde tissewe dammaske golde conteignyng xix yerdes quarter.

[B422–23] LM: anno xiiij^{mo} xxviij^{o} die augustii.[173]

[B423] t — Item Receyued of Mr Compton a pece of white cloth of tissewe braunched with freres knottes conteignyng xxj yerdes quarter.

[B424] g — Item to Fraunces debarde for a pece of cloth of siluer dammaske conteignyng xix yerdes at xl^{s} the yerde — xxxviij^{li}.

[B424–25] LM: anno xv^{o} xviij^{o} die maii.[174]

[B425] g — Item to Nicolas Pendolphyn for a pece of cloth of siluer of dammaske conteignyng xviij yerdes quarter at xl^{s} the yerde — xxxvj^{li} xv^{s}.

[B426] g — Item to Nicholas Venasses for a pece of cloth of siluer of damask conteignyng xxiiij yerdes at xl^{s} the yerdes. Summa xlviij^{li}.

[B426–27] LM: anno xv^{o} viij^{o} die Octobris.[175]

[B427] g — Item to the same Nicholas for a Remnaunte of blake cloth of gold dammaske conteignyng iiij yerdes di at xl^{s} the yerde — ix^{li}.

[B428] g — Item to Antony Cassidony for a pece of cloth of siluer conteignyng xl yerdes ij quaters at xliij^{s} iiij^{d} the yerde. Summa iiij^{xx}viij^{li} v^{s} x^{d}.

[B428–29] LM: anno xv^{o} xviij^{mo} die Januarii.[176]

[B429] g — Item for a pece of purpull tilsent dammaske gold on thone syde & white cloth of siluer of dammaske on thoder side conteignyng xxj yerdes di at iiij^{li} the yerde. Summa iiijxxvj^{li}.

[B430] g — Item Receyued of master Compton at newe Hall a pece of cloth of golde of dammaske on thoone[177] side and white cloth of siluer on thoder syde conteingyng xvij yerdes di.

[B430] LM: anno xiiij^{mo} xxviiij^{o} die augusti.[178]

[B431] t — Item to Peter Fraunces for a pece of blake cloth of golde tissewe conteignyng xxij yerdes iij quarter at v^{li} the yerde. Summa Cxiij^{li} xv^{s}.

[B431] LM: anno xvj^{mo} xxiiij^{o} die Septembris.[179]

[B432] g — Item to William Buttry for a Remnaunte of cloth of siluer conteignyng ij yerdes quarter di at xl^{s} the yerde. Summa iiij^{li} xv^{s}.

[B432–36] LM: anno xvj^{mo} iiij^{to} die Januarii.

[B433] g — Item to Peter Fraunces for a pece of cloth of siluer conteignyng xxj yerdes quarter at xl^{s} the yerde. Summa xlij^{li} x^{s}.

[B434] g — Item for a pece of cloth of siluer conteingyng xxij yerdes quarter at xls the yerde. Summa xliiij^{li} x^{s}.

[B435] g — Item to the said peter for a pece of cloth of siluer conteignyng xxj yerdes di at xl^{s} the yerde. Summa xliij^{li}.

[B436] t — Item to Mistress Fermar for a pece of purpull cloth of gold tissue conteignyng xxj yerdes di at iiij^{li} xiij^{s} iiij^{d} the yerde — C^{li} vj^{s} viij^{d}.

t — iiij^{xx} xix yerdes iij quarters
g — CCxxv yerdes

f. 13v[180]

Cloth of golde & siluer of diuerse makinges

[B437] t — Item a pece of purpull cloth of gold tissue conteignyng xx yerdes quarter di yeuen to the kinges newyeres yeft.

[B437–38] LM: anno xvj^{mo} primo die Januarii.[181]

[B438] t — Item a doublet cloth of purpull cloth of golde tissue dammaske gold and for stockes for a payre of hose of the same cloth of gold yeuen to the kinges new yeres yeft anno xvj^{o}.

t — xx yerdes quarter di

[B439] Item Receyuid by thandes of maister Compton a pece of purple Tyssue contaynyng xix yerdes iij quarters di.[182]

[B439–45] LM: anno xvij^{o} xx^{o} die Januarii.[183]

[B440] Item Receyuid of the same maister Compton a pece of white tyssue contaynyng xx^{ti} yerdes iij quarters.

[B441] Item Receyuid of Nicholas Venassis a pece of white tyssue contaynyng xviij yerdes iij quarters at iiij^{li} xv^{s} le yerd. Summa iiij^{xx}iiij^{li} vij^{s} vj^{d}.

[B442] Item of the same Nicholas a pece of cloth of siluer contaynyng xxxiij yerdys at xxxvj^{s} viij^{d} le yerd. Summa lx^{li} x^{s}.

[B443] Item to peter Frauncys for a pece of clothe of gold dammaske contaynyng xxviij^{ti} yerdes quarter at xl^{s} le yerd. Summa lvj^{li} x^{s}.

[B444] Item Receyuid of maister Carewe a pece of purple tyssue conteignyng xxij yerdes.

[B445] Item Receyuid by the handys of maister Compton iij pecys of Tyssue conteignyng lxiij yerdes.[184]

f. 14r[185]

Purpull Tilsent

[B446] Item a Remnaunte conteignyng vij yerdes at xl^{s} the yerde in all xiiij^{li}.

Crimosyn Tilsent

[B447] A Remnaunte conteignyng ij yerdes at xl^{s} the yerde in all iiij^{li}.

Russet Tilsent

[B448] A Remnaunte conteignyng iij yerdes at xl^{s} the yerde in all vij^{li}.

Blacke Tylsent

[B449] A Remnaunte conteignyng ij yerdes di.

[B450] A Remnaunte conteignyng ij yerdes di.

[B451] A Remnaunte conteignyng iij yerdes.

at xl^{s} the yerde — xviij^{li}

Tawny Tylsent

[B452] A Remnaunte conteignyng ij yerdes at xl^{s} the yerde in all vj^{li}.

Grene Tylsent

[B453] A Remnaunte conteignyng ij yerdes di quarter at xl^{s} the yerde — iiij^{li} v^{s}.

Yelowe Tylsent

[B454] A Remnaunte conteingyng iij yerdes at xl^{s} the yerde in all — vj^{li}.

Tawny Dornix

[B455] A Remnaunte conteignyng ij yerdes di quarter at xl^{s} the yerde — iiij^{li} v^{s}.

Grene saten Rawed

[B456] A Remnaunte conteignyng ij yerdes iij quarters at xiij^{s} iiij^{d} le yerde — xxxvj^{s} viij^{d}.

Nicholas Vaux
Henry Guldeford

[B457] Furst to Peter Fraunces debarde for a pece of blake tylsente with dropes conteignyng xxxj yerdes iij quarters at xl^{s} the yerde — lxiij^{li} x^{s}.

[B457–59] LM: anno xij^{o} xviij^{o} die Februarii.[186]

[B458] Item to the same Peter for a pece of blake siluer tylsent conteignyng xxxij yerdes quarter at xl^{s} the yerde. Summa lxiiij^{li} x^{s}.

[B459] Item to Peter Corse for a pece of tawny tylsent conteignyng xxvj yerdes iij quarters at xl^{s} the yerde. Summa liij^{li} x^{s}.

Summa in yerdes — Cxxiij yerdes iij quarters
Summa partes — lxiiij^{li} vj^{s} viij^{d}

f. 14v[187]

Tilsenttes of diuerse colloures

[B460] Item to Fraunces de barde for a pece of tawny tylsent dammaske gold conteignyng xxij yerdes quarter di at xliij^{s} iiij^{d} le yerde — xlviij^{li} x^{s} vij^{d}.

[B460–62] LM: anno xiij^{o} xiiij^{o} die augusti.[188]

[B461] Item to the same Fraunces for a pece of tawny tylsent dammaske golde conteignyng xx yerdes iij quarters at xliij^{s} iiij^{d} — xliiij ^{li} xix^{s} ij^{d}.

[B462] Item to the same Fraunces for a pece of blake tylsent venis gold conteignyng xxvij yerdes quarter at xxxvj^{s} viij^{d} le yerde — xlix^{li} xix^{s} ij^{d}.

[B463] Item to Peter Fraunces for a pece of blake tylsent dammaske gold conteignyng xxiiij yerdes di at xl^{s} the yerde. Summa xlix^{li}.

[B463–67] LM: anno xiiij^{mo} xxiiij^{o} die ~~d~~ maii.[189]

[B464] Item to the same Peter for a pece of blake tylsent conteignyng xxxviij yerdes at xl^{s} the yerde. Summa lxxvj^{li}.

[B465] Item to the same Peter for a pece of blake tylsent conteignyng xxxv yerdes iij quarters at xl^{s} the yerde. Summa lxxj^{li} x^{s}.

[B466] Item to the same Peter for a pece of russet tylsent of golde of damaske conteignyng xxxij yerdes di at xl^{s} the yerde. Summa lxv^{li}.

[B467] Item to the same Peter for a pece of tawny tylsent of gold of dammaske contignyng xvij yerdes at xl^{s} the yerde. Summa xxxiiij^{li}.

[B468] Item to William Buttry for iiij yerdes quarter of grene tylsent at xl^{s} the yerde. Summa viij^{li} x^{s}.

[B468] LM: anno xiiij^{mo} xxiiij^{o} die augusti.[190]

[B469] Item to Nicolas Pendolphen for a pece of white tylsent conteignyng xvij yerdes iij quarters xxxvj^{s} viij^{d} le yerde — xxxij^{li} x^{s} x^{d}.

[B469–70] LM: anno xv^{mo} xviij^{mo} die maii.[191]

[B470] Item to Peter Fraunces for a pece of white tylsent conteignyng xxiiij yerdes iij quarters at xxxvj^{s} viij^{d} the yerde — xlv^{li} vij^{s} vj^{d}.

[B471] Item to Peter Fraunces for a pece of blewe tilsent conteignyng xxj yerdes at xxxvj^{s} vij^{d} the yerde. Summa xxxviij^{li} x^{s}.

[B471–72] LM: anno xvj^{mo} iiij^{to} die Januarii.[192]

[B472] Item for a pece of purpull tylsent conteignyng xxv yerdes iij quarters at xxxvj^{s} viij^{d} the yerde. Summa xlvij^{li} iiij^{s} ij^{d}.[193]

Summa in yerdes — CCCxj yerdes di di quarter

f. 15r[194]

Purpull Veluete opon Veluete perled

[B473] Item a pece conteignyng viij yerdes quarter.

[B474] A pece conteignyng iij yerdes di di quarter.

[B475] A pece conteignyng ij yerdes di quarter.

at xl^{s} le yerde in all xxiiij^{li}

Purpull Veluete perled

[B476] A pece conteignyng v yerdes di.

[B477] A pece conteignyng iiij yerdes di.

[B478] A pece conteignyng iiij yerdes quarter di.

at xxxiij^{s} iiij^{d} le yerde — xxv^{li} iiij^{s} ij^{d}

Purpull Veluete opon Veluete

[B479] A pece conteignyng xx yerdes iij quarters.

[B480] A pece conteignyng xx yerdes.

at xxxiij^{s} iiij^{d} le yerdes — lxviij^{li} xviij^{s} iiij^{d}

Crimosyn veluete opon veluete perled

[B481] A pece conteignyng xxj yerdes iij quarters at xxxiij^{s} iiij^{d}.

[B482] A pece conteignyng j yerdes di at xxxiij^{s} iiij^{d}.

xxxviij^{li} xv^{s}.

Crimosyn veluete perled

[B483] A pece conteignyng xv yerdes at xxxiij^{s} iiij^{d} the yerde — xxv^{li}.

Crimosyn veluete

[B484] A pece conteignyng xj yerdes di at xxvj^{s} viij^{d} the yerde — xvj^{li} vj^{s} viiij^{d}.

Crimosyn veluete

[B485] A pece conteignyng iiij yerdes iij quarters di.

[B486] A pece conteignyng iij yerdes di.

[B487] A pece conteignyng iiij yerdes iij quarters.

[B488] A pece conteignyng iij yerdes di quarter.

at xxvj^{s} viij^{d} the yerde — xxj^{li} xiij^{s}

Russette veluete opon veluete perled

[B489] A pece conteignyng xvij yerdes di at xl^{s} the yerde — xxxv^{li}.

Russet veluete perled

[B490] A Remnaunte conteignyng iiij yerdes quarter at xxxiij^{s} iiij^{d} the yerde — vij^{li} xv^{s}.

Nicholas Vaux
Henry Guldeford

Summa in yerdes — Clvj yerdes iij quarters
Summa pagine — CCxlvij^{li} viij^{s} vj^{d}

f. 15v

Russet Veluete

[B491] Item a Remnaunte conteignyng ij yerdes.

Glossary

The glossary has been compiled using Ashelford, *Visual History*; Cunnington, *Handbook*; Hayward, *1542 Inventory*; Monnas, 'Tissues'; Monnas, *Merchants*; Scott, *Visual History*; Starkey, *Inventory*; June Swann, personal communication; Veale, *Fur Trade*. In the entries, (m) refers to an item of male dress and (f) refers to an item of female dress.

AGLET ornamental metal tags that could be attached to points or used in pairs with no visible tie ends; they could be used as a fastening or as a decorative trimming

ALB a long-sleeved linen vestment worn over the cassock and under the chasuble, tunicle, dalmatic or cope and worn as a suit with an amice, apparel and girdle

ALMAIN COAT or JACKET a short, close-fitting coat or jacket with long hanging sleeves, open on the front seam and short flared skirts, in the German or 'Almain' style

ALMAIN HOSE paned hose with the lining pulled out in puffs, in the German or 'Almain' style

AMICE a panel of white linen worn as a neck cloth

APPAREL a decorative embroidered panel applied to the alb and amice

ARMING DOUBLET a padded doublet worn under armour

BAG a girdle pouch; this term can also mean a pocket

BAG-RINGS the rings which stiffened the bag's opening

BASE-COAT a jacket or jerkin with a pleated skirt, often with short sleeves; the half-base coat or demi-base coat was for military use

BASES the pleated skirt of a jacket or jerkin; sometimes a separate item worn with armour

BAUDEKIN a rich figured silk, imported from the thirteenth century; from the fifteenth century, baudekins were lampas silks that could be plain or figured, monochrome or polychrome, and with metal threads

BEARING CLOTH the outer wrapping for a baby; a sumptuous blanket used at christenings

BED the cloth in which a swaddled child was wrapped; it was held in place with bands and enclosed the feet

BIB a piece of cloth worn below the chin of an infant or young child to keep other clothing clean

BIGGIN a child's plain, close-fitting cap or coif

BILIMENT/HABILIMENT the decorative border worn with a French hood; the 'nether' biliment was worn at the front of the bonnet and the 'upper' biliment was worn on the crown

BLACKWORK embroidery in black silk on linen

BLANKET a baby's outdoor wrapping, often of woollen cloth; undyed cloth or a thick, white cloth of average quality

BODY the bodice of a gown or kirtle; the front of the bodice was sometimes known as the 'fore-body'

BODYES a woman's bodice was referred to as a 'pair of bodyes', as it was made in two sections joined together at the sides

BONNET a small head covering

BOOT HOSE stockings worn inside boots to protect the netherstocks; usually of coarser material than the netherstocks

BOOTS footwear extending over the ankles and often to the knee; 'single' boots were often unlined, while fur-lined boots were worn during the winter; they could pull on or be fastened with laces or buckles

BORDERS decorative bands of fabric or goldsmith's work that could be applied to the front and hem of gowns, sleeves, etc, similar to guards; another names for biliments

BOTEWS another name for buskins

BRIGANDINE textile or leather doublet lined from small riveted plates

BROAD CLOTH a fine quality woollen cloth; its width was set at 63 in. (160 cm) by Edward VI

BROCADE a textile usually made from silk; the pattern is usually formed by the introduction of one or more supplementary wefts; the brocading wefts are confined to the patterned areas and so do not run from selvedge to selvedge

BUCKRAM a union cloth, probably linen and cotton

BUDGE imported lambskin

BUSKINS knee-high, pull-on boots with a turned down top, often with lacing for fastening, made from both leather and silk

CADDIS a worsted tape

CAFFA a rich silk cloth; a coarse type of taffeta

CALABRE squirrel skins

CAMBRIC a fine, light-weight linen cloth

CAMLET a warp faced tabby cloth with a pronounced weft rib, made of silk, wool, mohair or camel hair; it could incorporate metal thread, it could be figured, watered or waved

CANVAS a coarse, plain weave linen

CAP a small, close-fitting head covering, often made of soft material

CARCAN/CARCANET bands of jewels worn as necklaces

CARNATION red

CASSOCK a long, loose coat, often buttoned down the front, sometimes with a cape collar; the cassock got shorter as the century progressed; also a term for the coat with a closed or open front worn by young children

CAUL an openwork coif or skull cap, often made from silk or metal threads

CHAMMER a rich gown, open at the front

CHAPE a metal plate on the point of a scabbard

CHASUBLE the vestment worn by the priest while celebrating mass; it was cut away at the sides to allow the priest to raise his arms as he elevated the host

CHEMISE female undergarment, usually linen, knee length and with short sleeves

CLOTH a woollen cloth

CLOTH OF GOLD/SILVER a term used to cover silk fabrics produced in a range of weaves with a high percentage of metal thread. The additional wefts could be of gold or silver-gilt metal wire or thread (either a flat metal strip or a metal strip wound round a silk or linen core); it was produced in a variety of colours

CLOUT, DOUBLE CLOUT, TAIL CLOUT double pieces of linen cloth used as a nappy

COAT a sleeveless or short sleeved jacket or jerkin, worn over the doublet; full-length, front-fastening garment worn by young boys

CODPIECE a pouch-like appendage, attached to the hose by points to conceal the front opening

COIF a close-fitting linen cap, often covering the ears

COLLET a band of metal encircling a stone and holding it in place

CONEY rabbit fur
CORKS shoes with a heel and sole of cork
CORPORAL CASE (burse) a case to protect the corporal cloth
COTTON a woollen cloth with a raised nap
CRESPIN a hair her or fine liner caul, often embroidered with silk or metal thread
CREST CLOTH a linen cloth often used for linings
CREWEL see Sipers
CUTWORK patterns created by cutting out sections of fabric; the term is also used to describe appliqué
CYPRUS a fine lawn
DALMATIC a sleeved, T-shaped, calf-length tunic worn by deacons assisting the priest at mass
DAMASK a monochrome figured cloth with a reversible pattern created by using contrasting faces of the weave, usually a satin; the ground was usually of satin (warp-faced) and the pattern in sateen (weft-faced); it could be made from silk, linen or wool; the defining features were the warp and weft count, the composition of the warp, the evenness of the surface and whether the handle of the fabric was soft or firm
DEMI-GOWN a short gown, often worn for riding
DEMI-SLEEVE a wide sleeve ending at the elbow
DICKER ten; the traditional unit of exchange of hides or skins
DOUBLE lined
DOUBLET the main garment for the upper body for men and boys once they were breeched, could be made with or without sleeves
DRAWN WORK weft threads were pulled out and the remaining warp and weft threads were whipped stitched and then linked with blanket stitch; used to decorate shirts, smocks
ENGLISH HOOD/GABLE or PEDIMENT HEADDRESS a hood, with a wire under-structure, that formed a pointed arch above the forehead; from *c.* 1500–25 the hood hung in folds to the shoulders, with the face bordered by lappets, it was worn with an under-cap but the hair was still visible; after *c.* 1525 the front lappets were shortened and often pinned up on top of the head and folds at the back were replaced with two pendant sections; the hair was no longer visible
FARTHINGALE a framework with hoops of wood or whalebone worn under women's skirts to extend it
FITCH fur of the polecat
FLANNEL a woollen cloth with an open texture made of slightly twisted yarns
FLOWER a jewel, not necessarily flower shaped
FOINES, FOYNES fur of the stone marten
FOREPART a triangular piece of cloth that filled in the central section of the skirt
FORE-SLEEVES the fore-sleeves were often made of richer material than the upper sleeves which were not seen as they were covered by over sleeves; they could be separate items
FOX POOTS a fur made up of fox paws
FRENCH CLOAK circular or semicircular, long cloak, often with a collar and a shoulder cape
FRENCH HOOD a small bonnet, worn on the back of the head, with a decorative front band or border stretching from ear to ear, behind this and over the crown was the biliment
FRENCH SLEEVES a style of sleeve that was often pinked or paned
FRIEZE a woollen cloth with a nap
FRISADO, FRIZADO a heavy worsted cloth
FROCK a loose jerkin or jacket, intended to be comfortable; a long garment worn by boys before breeching
FRONTLET a decorative band worn by women across the forehead with a bonnet, coif or caul
FUSTIAN a coarse twill union cloth of linen and cotton, although it sometimes included worsted thread
GABERDINE a long coat with wide sleeves which could be worn loose or with a girdle; fashionable 1510–60
GENETTE, JENNET fur of the civet cat
GIRDLE a cord or band placed around the hips or waist, used to contain loose garments and to hang objects from
GLAUDEKIN a long, full gown
GOWN (m) a long, loose outer garment, usually with long wide sleeves; (f) a woman's dress
GRAIN the red dye derived from the kermes beetle
GUARDS decorative bands of material, applied as borders or along seems; they could be embroidered, slashed or plain
HALF-GOWN another term for demi-gown
HANGING SLEEVE a false, decorative sleeve that usually matched the doublet if worn by a man and the bodice if worn by a woman
HAT a head covering with a crown and brim
HAT BAND a decorative band of silk or ribbon placed around the base of a hat's crown
HOLLAND a fine linen cloth
HOOD a loose covering for the head, sometimes extending onto the shoulders; hoods were often worn for formal mourning
HOSE (m) stockings extending to the hip worn by men; (f) stockings worn to the knee
INCARNATE flesh colour
IN GRAIN wool dyed in the yarn or in the wool, usually dyed with kermes to produce a strong red or crimson
IRISH MANTLE a type of cloak
JACKET a short, upper garment usually worn over the doublet, it was often sleeveless, also known as a jerkin
JERKIN a short upper garment usually worn over the doublet, often sleeveless but could have long sleeves, also known as a jacket
KENDAL a coarse woollen cloth, often in green
KERCHIEF a covering for the head or the neck
KERMES this term can denote the dye-stuff and the colour made from it. It produced the best quality bright red and it was made from the dried bodies of the female kermes beetle
KERSEY a coarse woollen cloth, a double twill
KIRTLE initially a sleeved, long garment, worn under a gown; a full kirtle was the bodice and skirt, a half-kirtle was just the skirt; from the 1540s the kirtle usually consisted of just the skirt
LACE a braid; to lace
LAWN a semi-transparent, very fine linen cloth
LETTICE fur of the snow weasel, more expensive than miniver and less expensive than ermine
LETTICE CAP or BONNET a bonnet made of lettice covering the ears
LIBERD, LEOPARD fur of the leopard, popular in the sixteenth century
MANTLE a long gown with a train for ceremonial wear, a long, wrapping outer garment, usually without sleeves; worn for mourning
MARBLE parti-coloured
MEDLEY a woollen cloth, where the warp and weft are different colours
MILAN BONNET a soft, beret-shaped cap with a turned-up brim, often slit at the sides
MINIVER furs made from the bellies of squirrel skins, white with a little grey
MINIVER GROS white belly skins with all the grey hairs left on
MINIVER PURE white belly skins with all of the grey hairs trimmed off
MINK pale fur of a small stoat-like animal
MOTLEY a worsted of mixed colours
MUCKMINDER a slang term for a napkin or handkerchief
MUFFLER a length of cloth worn round the neck and over the chin
MULES soled shoes with no quarters; either an indoor shoe or slipper or an overshoe worn over other footwear outdoors
MURREY purple red
NETHERSTOCKS the hose, covering the legs
NIGHTGOWN a loose, lined gown worn by men and women either indoors for warmth or outdoors as an over-garment; usually lined with fur
OES spangles, often of silver or silver gilt

ORPHREY a band of woven or embroidered textile used to decorate vestments
PAMPILION lamb skins from Pampeluna, capital of Navarre
PANES decorative effect created by long stripes of material joined at the top at bottom. Through the gaps the shirt or lining would be visible and possibly pulled through. Found on sleeves and hose
PARTLET (m) a sleeveless jacket or a decorative covering for the upper chest and neck; (f) an in-fill for a low neckline, made with a high collar from the 1530s
PASSEMENTERIE ornamental braids or trimmings
PATTENS overshoes with wooden soles which were worn with boots or shoes and secured using leather straps
PETTICOAT (m) an under doublet worn for warmth and so often padded, unusual after 1520; (f) an undergarment
PINK to split, especially of ermine before adding powderings
PINKING decorative technique consisting of small slits or holes made in a garment to form a pattern, especially after 1545
PINSON an indoor shoe, sometimes furred, which could be worn with an overshoe
PIRLED VELVET a velvet enriched with patterns worked in uncut loops of metal thread
PLACKARD (m) a stomacher or covering to infill the front of a low-cut doublet or jacket; (f) a stomacher or front section of a gown or kirtle
POCKET a small pouch which could be worn separate of the garment or by the 1530s and 1540s was integral in some garments
POINTS ties of silk, ribbon or leather with aglets at the ends to join garments and to create decorative effects
POOTS furs made from the paws of animals
POPINJAY blue green
POWDERINGS ermine skins decorated with ermine tails or with small pieces of black budge used instead of the tails
PUFFS or PULLING OUT quantities of fabric pulled out through panes or slits
PUKE an imported woollen cloth, often black in colour
PURE a term used to describe miniver, meaning trimmed
PURFIL a decorative border or edging; trimming or edging
RUFF a collar pleated or gathered into a band, often starched and goffered; often with matching frills at the wrists
RUSSET a coarse woollen cloth, usually brown or grey
SABLE a dark brown fur from the sable marten from the arctic and sub arctic regions of Europe and Asia
SACKCLOTH a coarse cloth made of hemp
SAD a dark, muted colour
SAFEGUARD overskirt worn by women to protect their skirts while riding
SANGUIN blood red
SARSENET a thin, lightweight, plain silk often used as a lining fabric; either a tabby or a twill
SATIN a fabric with a smooth lustrous surface characterised by long floating threads; these will be warp-floats on one face and weft floats on the reverse face; some of the satins bought by Henry VIII were patterned and striped
SATIN OF BRUGES/BRIDGES OF SATIN a mixed fabric with silk warps and woollen wefts
SAY a fine twill cloth either all silk, all wool or with a silk warp and a wool weft
SCARLET a fine quality woollen cloth and a red colour
SHIRT an undergarment worn next to the skin, with a neck band and small upright collar; one of the first garments worn by new born babies
SHOES generally flat with a range of fastenings including a bar and t-strap; some slip-on shoes were available through the early and mid-Tudor period, as were high-cut ankle shoes
SHORT COATING when an infant was about six months old and started to crawl, it was short coated, i.e. put into clothing that reached the ankles
SINGLE unlined
SIPERS a fine lawn
SLASHING slits of varying length, cut in any part of a garment, but often found on hose or sleeves; at its height between *c.* 1520–35
SLIPPER a light-weight flat, slip-on shoe without fastening; the term can also be used to denote a light indoor shoe
SLOP loose breeches or hose with wide legs; a cloak or nightgown
SMOCK a female undergarment worn next to the skin, often embroidered on the collar
SPANISH CLOAK a short cloak, sometimes with a hood
SQUARE a band of jewels decorating the square neckline of women's gowns
STAMMEL a fine woollen cloth
STAMIN a fine woollen cloth
STARTUPS an ankle or calf length boot
STOCKS the lower part of hose covering the legs, also referred to as netherstocks
STOMACHER (m & f) a V-shaped panel, usually stiffened for women and placed between the robings of the gown or kirtle or in the low neck of the doublet and pinned or laced in place
SURCOTE a female over garment, which could have sleeves or be sleeveless that was only worn for royal mourning by the sixteenth century
SURPLICE worn by all levels of clergy, it was similar to the alb and it was worn for non-Eucharistic worship; also worn by vergers, choristers and servers
SWADDLING BANDS bands of linen or wool to wrap fully or partially the body of a newborn baby
TAFFETA a light-weight, tabby weave silk, often used as a lining
TAWNY orange-brown
THRUMS to decorate with thrums or ends of threads, to create a shaggy pile
TIMBER a quantity of furs; a package containing 40 skins
TINSEL, TILSENT an expensive silk cloth that could be plain or figured and incorporated gold, silver or silver-gilt flat metal strips as brocading wefts; often woven with a satin weave
TIPPET a short shoulder cape worn with a gown or doublet
TISSUE the most expensive form of cloth of gold/silver; woven in the sixteenth century with raised loops of filé metal thread in several heights and thicknesses above a lampas, brocatelle or velvet ground
TRUNK HOSE a style of hose that swelled out from the waistband and then were close-fitting on the thighs
TRUNK SLEEVES a sleeve with a very wide top and a narrow wrist, the swollen shape was achieved by padding
TUKE a type of buckram
TUNICLE a small tunic worn by subdeacons
TURKEY GOWN a long coat with long narrow sleeves; a gown in the Turkish style
UPPERSTOCKS the breeches, worn with the hose or netherstocks
VELVET a silk cloth with a short pile that was formed by placing the supplementary pile warp over rods introduced during the weaving process; the pile could be cut in one height, cut in different heights (velvet upon velvet), left uncut or a combination of these. Velvets could have a solid cut pile or they could have cut pile on a voided satin ground. The latter could be polychrome and could incorporate metal thread
VENT a slit up from the hem on coats and shirts
WAISTCOAT a close-fitting jacket without sleeves, usually buttoning at the front, worn by men and women
WELT a decorative border, similar to a guard
WING a roll of stiffened material that hid the join between the sleeve and the armhole; it could be decorated
WORSTED a cloth made from long staple wool combed out before spinning

Document Index

References prefixed **A** come from BL Harley MS 2284 and references prefixed **B** come from BL Harley MS 4217. Most references refer to the entry numbers; a few relate to folio numbers. The entries from both documents have been grouped under the following headings as follows: cloth to be made up, makers, objects, places, recipients of cloth and clothing and suppliers.

CLOTH DELIVERED TO THE KING'S ARTIFICERS

This section mainly relates to the new items of clothing, accessories and a few items of furniture ordered for the king to be made up by his tailor, hosier, furrier and listed in BL Harley MS 2284. The entries should be cross referenced with the section on the individuals who made them.

PLACES

RECIPIENTS OF CLOTH AND CLOTHING

Index to the Text

This index presents an alphabetical listing of the people, places, objects, materials and decorative techniques mentioned in the main text. In addition there are some group headings: accessories, armour, battles, cleaning, clothing, court, cut and construction, decorative motifs, decorative techniques, embroidery, fastenings, footwear, fur, gemstones, goldsmiths' work, headwear, heralds, horse harness, household, hunting, jewellery, leather, liturgical textiles, liturgical year, livery, London and Westminster, orders of chivalry, packing materials, palaces and royal houses, passementerie, perfumes, places, regalia, robes, shaving stuff, sport, styles of dress, textiles, treaties, wardrobe of the robes and weapons. Some abbreviations have been used:

AB	Anne Boleyn
AC	Anne of Cleves
CA	Catherine of Aragon
CH	Catherine Howard
CP	Catherine Parr
E6	Edward VI
EY	Elizabeth of York
H7	Henry VII
H8	Henry VIII
HF	Henry Fitzroy
JS	Jane Seymour
LMB	Lady Margaret Beaufort